MACROMEDIA®

Dreamweaver® MX 2004

Introductory Concepts and Techniques

Gary B. Shelly
Thomas J. Cashman
Dolores J. Wells

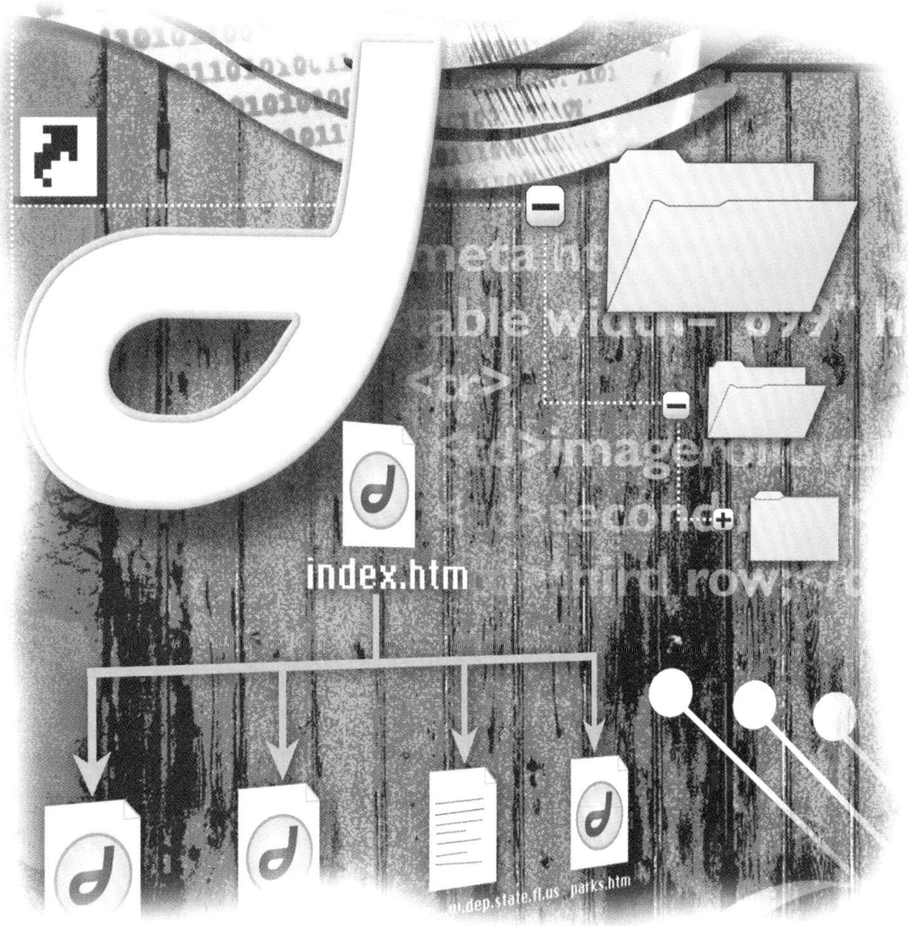

THOMSON COURSE TECHNOLOGY

THOMSON COURSE TECHNOLOGY
25 THOMSON PLACE
BOSTON MA 02210

SHELLY CASHMAN SERIES®

Australia • Canada • Denmark • Japan • Mexico • New Zealand • Philippines • Puerto Rico • Singapore
South Africa • Spain • United Kingdom • United States

THOMSON
COURSE TECHNOLOGY

Macromedia Dreamweaver MX 2004: Introductory Concepts and Techniques

Gary B. Shelly
Thomas J. Cashman
Dolores J. Wells

Managing Editor:
Alexandra Arnold

Senior Acquisitions Editor:
Dana Merk

Senior Product Manager:
Karen Stevens

Product Manager:
Reed Cotter

Associate Product Manager:
Selena Coppock

Print Buyer:
Laura Burns

Production Editor:
Pamela Elizian

Copy Editor:
Lori Silfen

Proofreader:
Nancy Lamm

QA Manuscript Reviewers:
Alex White, John Freitas,
Burt LaFountain, Marianne Snow

Cover Artist:
John Still

Composition:
GEX Publishing Services

Printed in the United States of America

2 3 4 5 6 7 8 9 10
BM 09 08 07 06 05

For more information, contact
Thomson Course Technology
25 Thomson Place
Boston, Massachusetts 02210

Or find us on the World Wide Web at:
www.course.com

ISBN 0-619-25491-2

MACROMEDIA®

Dreamweaver MX 2004

Introductory Concepts and Techniques

Contents

Project Three

Tables and Page Layout

Appendix A

Dreamweaver Help

Appendix B

Dreamweaver and Accessibility

Appendix C

Publishing to a Web Server

Preface

The Shelly Cashman Series® offers the finest textbooks in computer education. We are proud of the fact that our textbook series has been the most widely used books in education. With each new edition of our Dreamweaver books, we have made significant improvements based on the software and comments made by the instructors and students. *Macromedia® Dreamweaver® MX 2004: Introductory Concepts and Techniques* continues with the innovation, quality, and reliability that you have come to expect from the Shelly Cashman Series.

Macromedia Dreamweaver is known as the standard in visual authoring. Macromedia Dreamweaver MX 2004 enhances the work experience for users in the following ways: (1) richer CSS support; (2) dynamic cross-browser validation; (3) built-in graphics editing; (4) secure FTP; (5) seamless integration with external files and code; (6) tighter integration with other Macromedia tools; (7) enhanced coding tools; and (8) an improved user interface.

In this *Macromedia Dreamweaver MX 2004* book, you will find an educationally sound and easy-to-follow pedagogy that combines a step-by-step approach with corresponding screens. All projects and exercises in this book are designed to take full advantage of the Dreamweaver MX 2004 enhancements. The popular Other Ways and More About features offer in-depth knowledge of Dreamweaver MX 2004. The new Q&A feature provides answers to common questions students have about the Web design process. The Learn It Online page presents a wealth of additional exercises to ensure your students have all the reinforcement they need. The project material is developed carefully to ensure that students will see the importance of learning Dreamweaver for future coursework.

Objectives of This Textbook

Macromedia Dreamweaver MX 2004: Introductory Concepts and Techniques is intended for a course that offers an introduction to Dreamweaver MX 2004 and creation of Web sites. No experience with a computer is assumed, and no mathematics beyond the high school freshman level is required. The objectives of this book are:

- To teach the fundamentals of Dreamweaver MX 2004
- To expose students to proper Web site design and management techniques
- To acquaint students with the proper procedures to create Web sites suitable for coursework, professional purposes, and personal use
- To develop an exercise-oriented approach that allows learning by doing
- To introduce students to new input technologies
- To encourage independent study and help those who are working alone

The Shelly Cashman Approach

Features of the Shelly Cashman Series *Macromedia Dreamweaver MX 2004* books include:

- **Project Orientation** Each project in the book presents a practical problem and complete solution using an easy-to-understand approach.
- **Step-by-Step, Screen-by-Screen Instructions** Each of the tasks required to complete a project is identified throughout the project. Full-color screens with call outs accompany the steps.
- **Thoroughly Tested Projects** Unparalleled quality is ensured because every screen in the book is produced by the author only after performing a step, and then each project must pass Thomson Course Technology's award-winning Quality Assurance program.
- **Other Ways Boxes and Quick Reference** The Other Ways boxes displayed at the end of many of the step-by-step sequences specify the other ways to do the task completed in the steps. Thus, the steps and the Other Ways box make a comprehensive reference unit. The Quick Reference at the back of the book provides a quick reference to common keyboard shortcuts.

More About and Q&A Features These marginal annotations provide background information, tips, and answers to common questions that complement the topics covered, adding depth and perspective to the learning process.

- **Integration of the World Wide Web** The World Wide Web is integrated into the Dreamweaver MX 2004 learning experience by (1) More About annotations that send students to Web sites for up-to-date information and alternative approaches to tasks; and (2) the Learn It Online page at the end of each project, which has project reinforcement exercises, learning games, and other types of student activities.

Organization of This Textbook

Macromedia Dreamweaver MX 2004: Introductory Concepts and Techniques provides detailed instruction on how to use Dreamweaver MX 2004. The material is divided into an introduction chapter, three projects, three appendices, and a quick reference summary.

Introduction – Web Site Development and Macromedia Dreamweaver MX 2004 In the Introduction, students are presented with the basics of the Internet and World Wide Web and their associated terms. Topics include differentiating between Web pages and Web sites and types of Web pages; identifying Web browser features; an overview of planning, designing, developing, testing, publishing, and maintaining a Web site; a discussion of HTML; various methods and tools used in Web site creation; and a brief description of the new features in Dreamweaver MX 2004.

Project 1 – Creating a Dreamweaver Web Page and Local Site In Project 1, students are introduced to the Dreamweaver environment. Students create a local site and the home page for the Web site that they develop throughout the projects in the book. Topics include starting and quitting Dreamweaver; an introduction to the Dreamweaver workspace and panel groups; creating a local site; creating a Web page, applying a background image, and formatting Web page properties; inserting line breaks and special characters; inserting a horizontal rule; using the Check Spelling feature; previewing and printing a page in a Web browser; and an overview of Dreamweaver Help.

Project 2 – Adding Web Pages, Links, and Images In Project 2, students learn how to add new pages to an existing Web site and then how to add links and images. Topics include using Dreamweaver's file browser feature; understanding and modifying image file formats; adding page images to a Web page; creating relative, absolute, and e-mail links; changing the color of links and editing and deleting links; using the site map; displaying the page in Code view; using Code view to modify HTML code; and an overview of Dreamweaver's accessibility features.

Project 3 – Tables and Page Layout In Project 3, students are introduced to techniques for using tables in Web site design. Topics include an introduction to page layout using tables in Standard view and Layout view to design a Web page; modifying a table structure; understanding HTML table tags; adding content to a table and formatting the content; formatting the table; and creating head content.

Appendices The book includes three appendices. Appendix A presents an introduction to the Macromedia Dreamweaver Help system. Appendix B discusses Dreamweaver and Accessibility features; and Appendix C illustrates how to define and publish a Web site to a remote server.

Quick Reference In Dreamweaver, you can accomplish a task in a number of ways, such as using the mouse, menu, context menu, and keyboard. The Quick Reference provides a quick reference to common keyboard shortcuts.

End-of-Project Student Activities

A notable strength of the Shelly Cashman Series *Macromedia Dreamweaver MX 2004* books is the extensive student activities at the end of each project. Well-structured student activities can make the difference between students merely participating in a class and students retaining the information they learn. The activities in the Shelly Cashman Series *Macromedia Dreamweaver MX 2004* books include the following:

- What You Should Know A listing of the tasks completed within a project together with the pages on which the step-by-step, screen-by-screen explanations appear.
- Learn It Online Every project features a Learn It Online page comprising ten exercises. These exercises include True/False, Multiple Choice, Short Answer, Flash Cards, Practice Test, Learning Games, Tips and Tricks, Newsgroup usage, Expanding Your Horizons, and Search Sleuth.
- Apply Your Knowledge This exercise usually requires students to open and manipulate a file on the Data Disk. To obtain a copy of the Data Disk, follow the instructions on the inside back cover of this textbook.
- In the Lab Three in-depth assignments per project require students to utilize the project concepts and techniques to solve problems on a computer.
- Cases and Places Five unique real-world case-study situations, including one small-group activity.

Shelly Cashman Series Instructor Resources

The Shelly Cashman Series is dedicated to providing you with all of the tools you need to make your class a success. Information on all supplementary materials is available through your Thomson Course Technology representative or by calling one of the following telephone numbers: Colleges and Universities and Private Career Colleges, 1-800-648-7450; High Schools, 1-800-824-5179; Canada, 1-800-268-2222; Corporations with IT Training Centers, 1-800-648-7450; and Government Agencies, Health-Care Organizations, and Correctional Facilities, 1-800-477-3692.

The Instructor Resources for this textbook include both teaching and testing aids. The contents of each item on the Instructor Resources CD-ROM (ISBN 1-4188-4353-9) are described below.

INSTRUCTOR'S MANUAL The Instructor's Manual is made up of Microsoft Word files, which include detailed lesson plans with page number references, lecture notes, teaching tips, classroom activities, discussion topics, projects to assign, and transparency references. The transparencies are available through the Figure Files described below.

LECTURE SUCCESS SYSTEM The Lecture Success System consists of intermediate files that correspond to certain figures in the book, allowing you to step through the creation of an application in a project during a lecture without entering large amounts of data.

SYLLABUS Sample syllabi, which can be customized easily to a course, are included. The syllabi cover policies, class and lab assignments and exams, and procedural information.

FIGURE FILES Illustrations for every figure in the textbook are available in electronic form. Use this ancillary to present a slide show in lecture or to print transparencies for use in lecture with an overhead projector. If you have a personal computer and LCD device, this ancillary can be an effective tool for presenting lectures.

POWERPOINT PRESENTATIONS PowerPoint Presentations is a multimedia lecture presentation system that provides slides for each project. Presentations are based on project objectives. Use this presentation system to present well-organized lectures that are both interesting and knowledge based. PowerPoint Presentations provides consistent coverage at schools that use multiple lecturers.

SOLUTIONS TO EXERCISES Solutions are included for the end-of-project exercises, as well as the Project Reinforcement exercises.

TEST BANK & TEST ENGINE The ExamView test bank includes 110 questions for every project (25 multiple-choice, 50 true/false, and 35 completion) with page number references, and when appropriate, figure references. A version of the test bank you can print also is included. The test bank comes with a copy of the test engine, ExamView, the ultimate tool for your objective-based testing needs. ExamView is a state-of-the-art test builder that is easy to use. ExamView enables you to create paper-, LAN-, or Web-based tests from test banks designed specifically for your Course Technology textbook. Utilize the ultra-efficient QuickTest Wizard to create tests in less than five minutes by taking advantage of Course Technology's question banks, or customize your own exams from scratch.

DATA FILES FOR STUDENTS All the files that are required by students to complete the exercises are included. You can distribute the files on the Instructor Resources CD-ROM to your students over a network, or you can have them follow the instructions on the inside back cover of this book to obtain a copy of the Data Disk.

ADDITIONAL ACTIVITIES FOR STUDENTS These additional activities consist of Project Reinforcement Exercises, which are true/false, multiple choice, and short answer questions that help students gain confidence in the material learned.

Online Content

Thomson Course Technology offers textbook-based content for Blackboard, WebCT, and MyCourse 2.1.

BLACKBOARD AND WEBCT As the leading provider of IT content for the Blackboard and WebCT platforms, Thomson Course Technology delivers rich content that enhances your textbook to give your students a unique learning experience. Thomson Course Technology has partnered with WebCT and Blackboard to deliver our market-leading content through these state-of-the-art online learning platforms.

MYCOURSE 2.1 MyCourse 2.1 is Thomson Course Technology's powerful online course management and content delivery system. Completely maintained and hosted by Thomson, MyCourse 2.1 delivers an online learning environment that is completely secure and provides superior performance. MyCourse 2.1 allows non-technical users to create, customize, and deliver World Wide Web-based courses; post content and assignments; manage student enrollment; administer exams; track results in the online gradebook; and more.

Macromedia Dreamweaver MX 2004 30-Day Trial Edition

A copy of the Dreamweaver MX 2004 30-Day trial edition can be found on the Macromedia Web site (www.macromedia.com). Point to Downloads in the top navigation bar, click Free Trials, and then follow the on-screen instructions. When you activate the software, you will receive a license that allows you to use the software for 30 days. Thomson Course Technology and Macromedia provide no product support for this trial edition. When the trial period ends, you can purchase a copy of Macromedia Dreamweaver MX 2004, or uninstall the trial edition and reinstall your previous version.

The minimum system requirements for the 30-day trial edition is a 600 MHz Intel Pentium III processor or equivalent; Windows XP, Windows 2000, Windows 98 SE (4.10.2222 A), or Windows Server 2003; 128 MB RAM (256 MB recommended); and 275 MB available disk space.

Macromedia
DREAMWEAVER MX 2004

MACROMEDIA

Dreamweaver MX 2004

MACROMEDIA
Dreamweaver MX 2004

Web Site Development and Macromedia Dreamweaver MX 2004

Objectives

You will have mastered the material in this project when you can:

- Describe the significance of the Internet and its associated terms
- Describe the World Wide Web and its associated terms
- Identify the difference between the Internet and the World Wide Web
- Specify the difference between a Web page and a Web site
- Define Web browsers and identify their main features
- Identify the nine types of Web sites
- Discuss how to plan, design, develop, test, publish, and maintain a Web site
- Identify the various methods and tools used to create a Web page and Web site
- Recognize the basic tags within HTML
- Discuss the advantages of using Web page authoring programs such as Dreamweaver

The Internet

The **Internet**, sometimes simply called the **Net**, is a global network, connecting millions of computers. Within this global network, a user who has permission at any one computer can access and obtain information from any other computer within the network. A **network** is a group of computers and associated devices that are connected by communications facilities. A network can span a global area and involve permanent connections, such as cables, or temporary connections made through telephone or other communications links. Within this global network are local, regional, national, and international networks. Each of these networks provides communications, services, and access to information.

The Internet has had a relatively brief, but explosive, history. This network grew out of an experiment begun in the 1960s by the U.S. Department of Defense (DOD). Today, the Internet is a public, cooperative, and self-sustaining facility that is accessible to hundreds of millions of people worldwide.

The World Wide Web and Web Browsers

The **World Wide Web** (**WWW**), also called the **Web**, is the most popular service on the Internet. The Web consists of a system of global **network servers** that supports specially formatted documents and provides a means for sharing these resources with many people at the same time. A network server is known as the **host computer**, and your computer, from which you access the information, is called the **client**. The protocol that enables the transfer of data from the host computer to the client is the **Hypertext Transfer Protocol** (**HTTP**).

Accessing the Web

Users access Web resources, such as text, graphics, sound, video, and multimedia, through a **Web page**. Every Web page is identified by a unique address, or Uniform Resource Locator (URL). The URL provides the global address of the location of the Web page. URLs are discussed later in this Introduction. Viewing data contained on a Web page requires a Web browser. A **Web browser** is a software program that requests a Web page, interprets the code contained within the page, and then displays the contents of the Web page on your computer display device.

Web Browsers

Web browsers contain special buttons and other features to help you navigate through Web sites. The more popular Web browser software programs are **Microsoft Internet Explorer** and **Netscape Navigator**. This book uses Internet Explorer as the primary browser. When you start Internet Explorer, it opens a Web page that has been set as the start, or home, page (Figure I-1). The home page can be any page on the Web and can be designated by the user through the browser's Tools menu. Important features of Internet Explorer are summarized in Table I-1 on the next page.

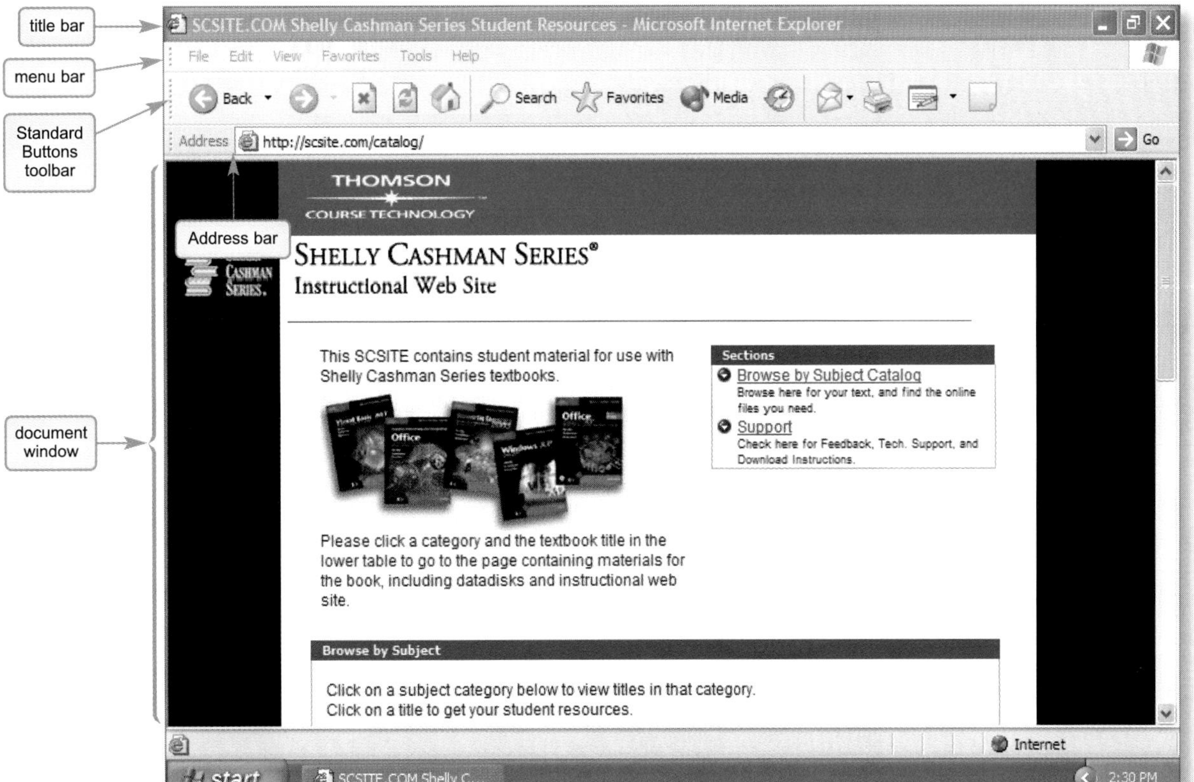

FIGURE I-1

Table I-1 Internet Explorer Features

FEATURE	DEFINITION
Title bar	Displays the name of the program and the name of the Web page you are viewing
Menu bar	Displays the names of the menus; each menu contains a list of commands you can use to perform tasks such as printing, saving, and editing
Standard Buttons toolbar	Contains buttons, boxes, and menus that allow you to perform tasks more quickly than using the menu bar and related menus
Address bar	Displays the Web site address, or URL, of the Web page you are viewing
Document window	Contains the Web page content

Nearly all Web pages have unique characteristics, but almost every Web page contains the same basic elements. Common elements you find on most Web pages are headings or titles, text, pictures or images, background enhancements, and hyperlinks. A **hyperlink**, or **link**, can link to another place in the same Web page or to an entirely different Web page. Normally, you click the hyperlink to follow the link pathway. Figure I-2 contains a variety of link types with the pointer over one of the links. Clicking a link causes the Web page associated with the link to be displayed in a browser window. The linked object might link to another Web page within the same Web site or might link to a Web page at a different Web site in another city or country. In both instances, the linked page might appear in the same browser window or in a separate browser window, depending on the HTML code associated with the link. HTML is discussed later in this Introduction.

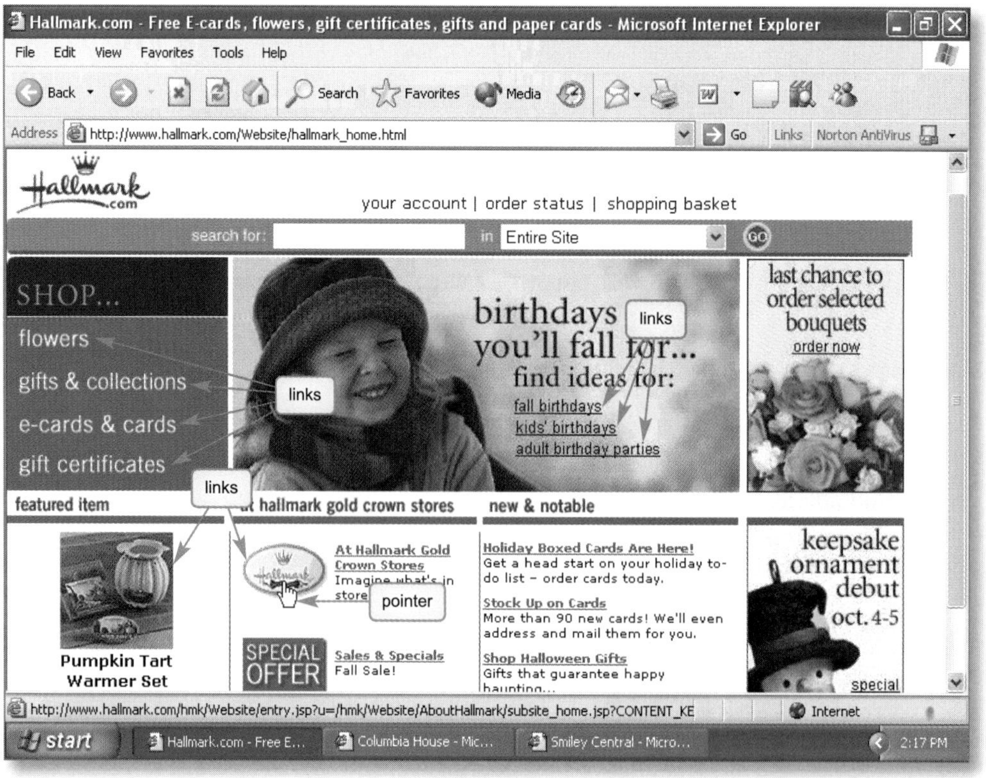

FIGURE I-2

Most Web pages are part of a Web site. A **Web site** is a group of linked Web pages. Most Web sites contains a home page, which generally is the first Web page visitors see when they enter the site. A **home page** (also called an **index page**) typically provides information about the Web site's purpose and content. Most Web sites also contain additional content and pages. An individual, company, or organization owns and manages each Web site.

Accessing the Web requires a connection through a regional or national Internet service provider (ISP), an online service provider (OSP), or a wireless service provider (WSP). Figure I-3 illustrates ways to access the Internet using these service providers. An **Internet service provider** (**ISP**) is a business that has a permanent Internet connection and provides temporary connections to individuals, companies, or other organizations. An **online service provider** (**OSP**) is similar to an ISP, but provides additional member-only services, such as financial data and travel information. America Online is an example of an OSP. A **wireless service provider** (**WSP**) provides Internet access to users with Web-enabled devices or wireless modems. Generally, all of these providers charge a fee for their services.

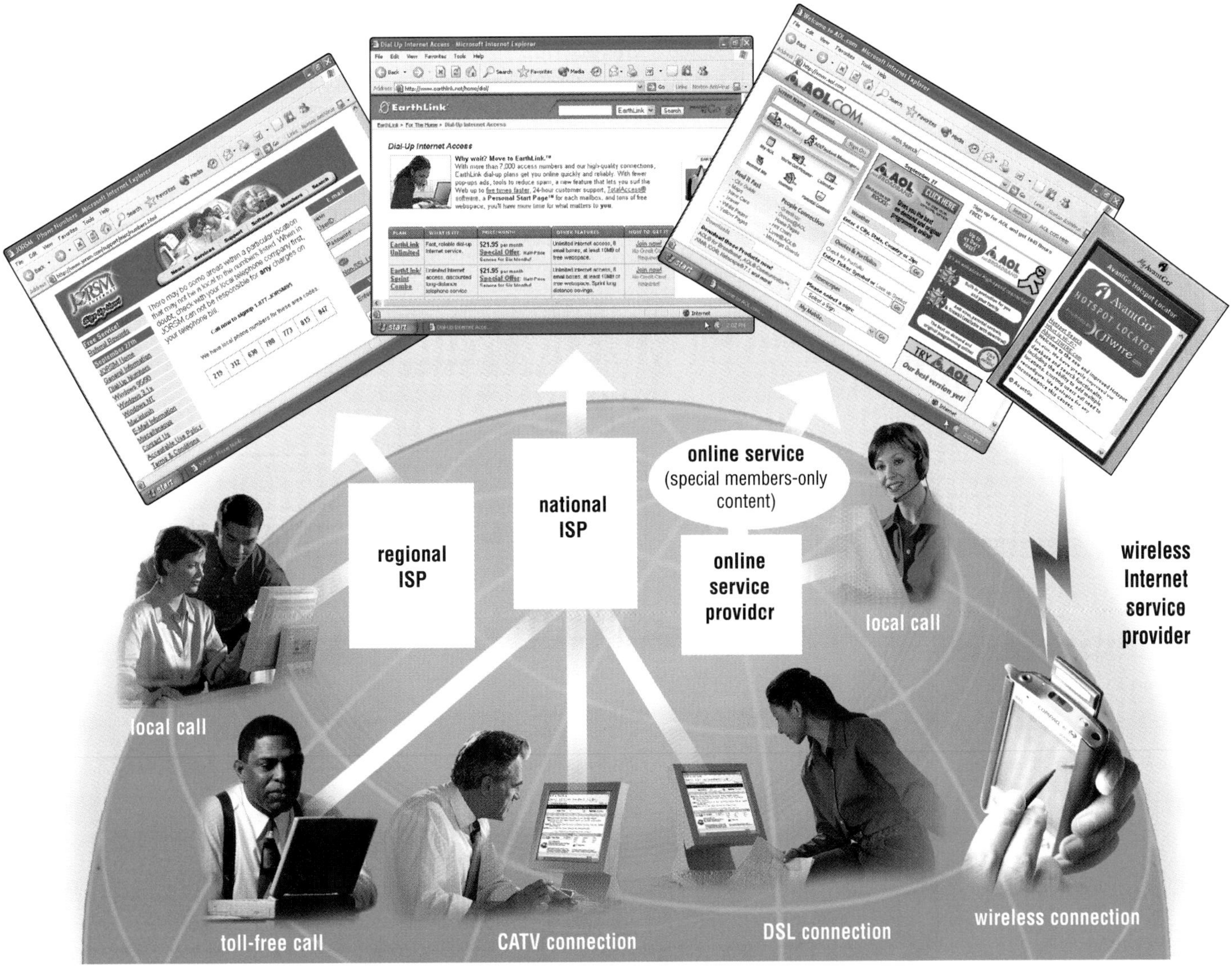

FIGURE I-3

Types of Web Sites

The nine basic types of Web sites are portal, news, informational, business/marketing, educational, entertainment, advocacy, personal, and blog. A **portal Web site** (Figure I-4a) provides a variety of Internet services from a single, convenient location. Most portals offer free services such as search engines; local, national, and worldwide news; sports; weather; reference tools; maps; stock quotes; newsgroups; chat rooms; and calendars. A **news Web site** (Figure I-4b) contains news articles relating to current events. An **informational Web site** (Figure I-4c) contains factual information, such as research and statistics. Governmental agencies and nonprofit organizations are the primary providers of informational Web pages. A **business/marketing Web site** (Figure I-4d) contains content that promotes or sells products or services. An **educational Web site** (Figure I-4e) provides exciting, challenging avenues for formal and informal teaching and learning. An **entertainment Web site** (Figure I-4f) offers an interactive and engaging environment and contains music, video, sports, games, and other similar features. Within an **advocacy Web site** (Figure I-4g), you will find content that describes a cause, opinion, question, or idea. A **personal Web site** (Figure I-4h) is published by an individual or family and generally is not associated with any organization. A **blog** (Figure I-4i), which is short for Web log, is a Web site that uses a regularly updated journal format to reflect the interests, opinions, and personality of the author and sometimes of site visitors. As you progress through this book, you will have an opportunity to learn more about all these types of Web pages.

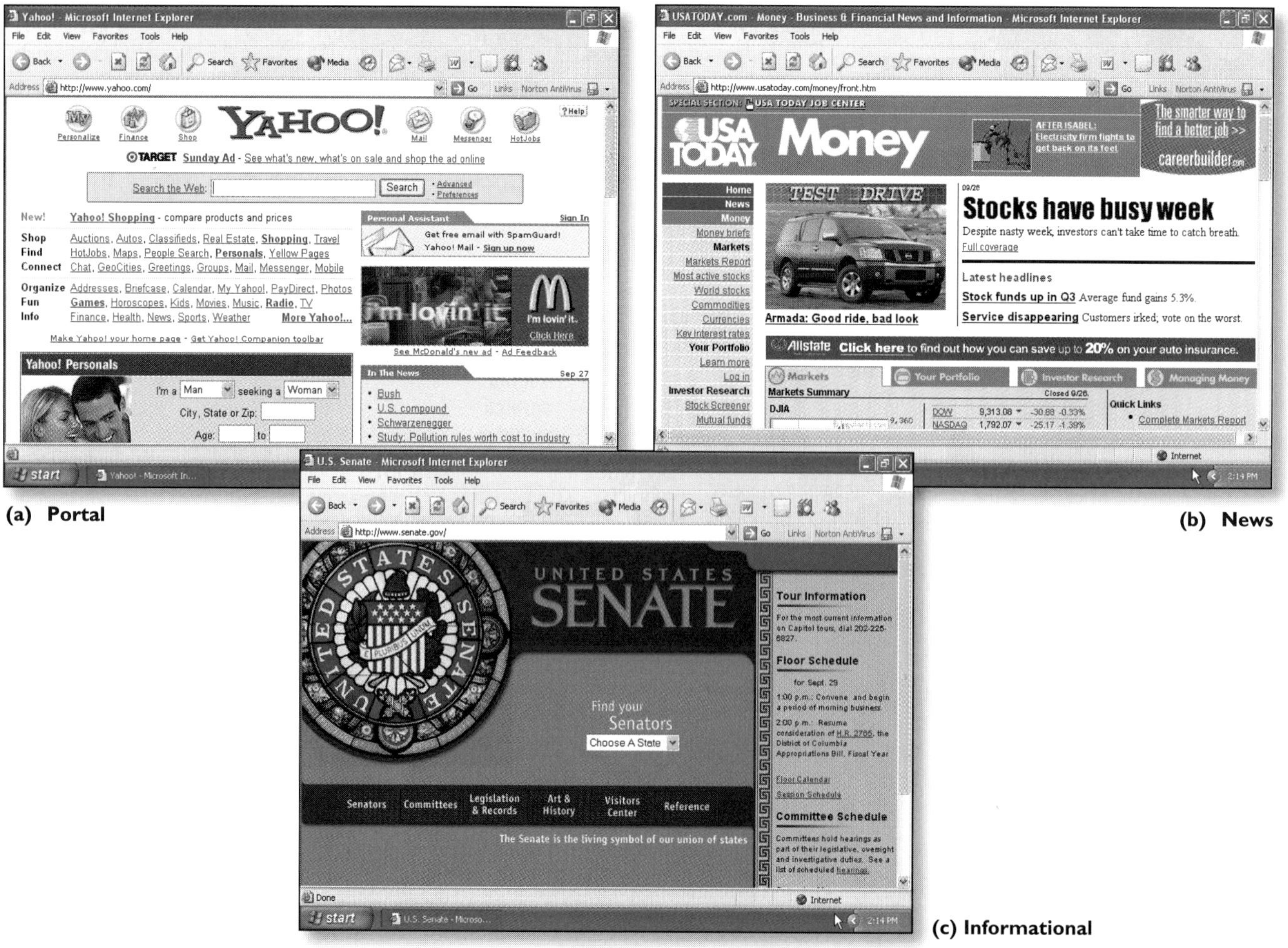

(a) Portal

(b) News

(c) Informational

FIGURE I-4

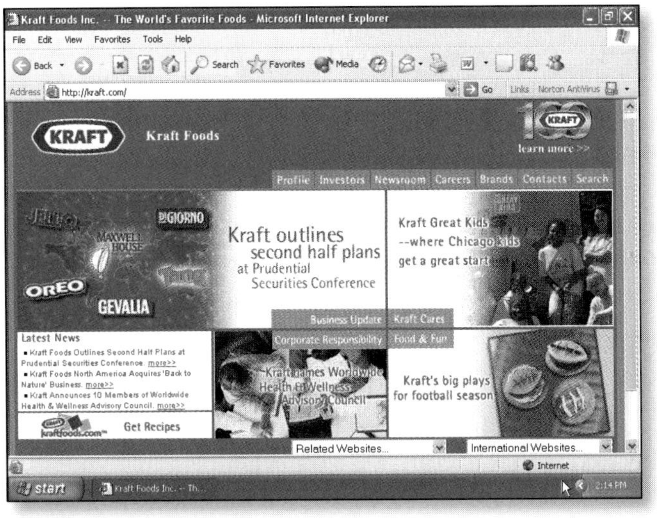

(d) **Business/marketing**

(e) **Educational**

(f) **Entertainment**

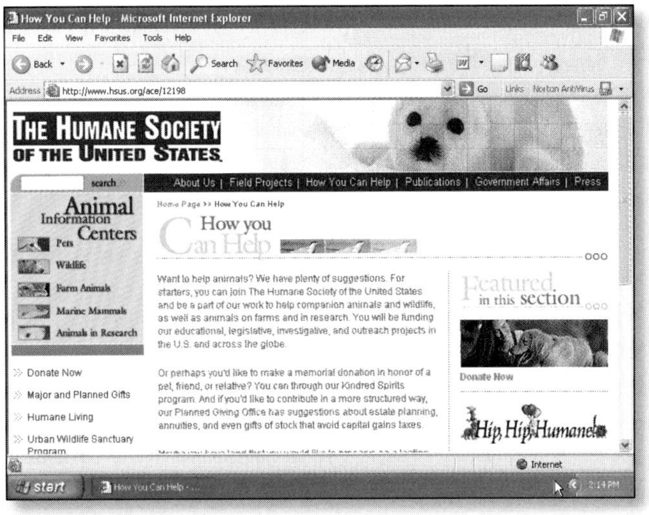

(g) **Advocacy**

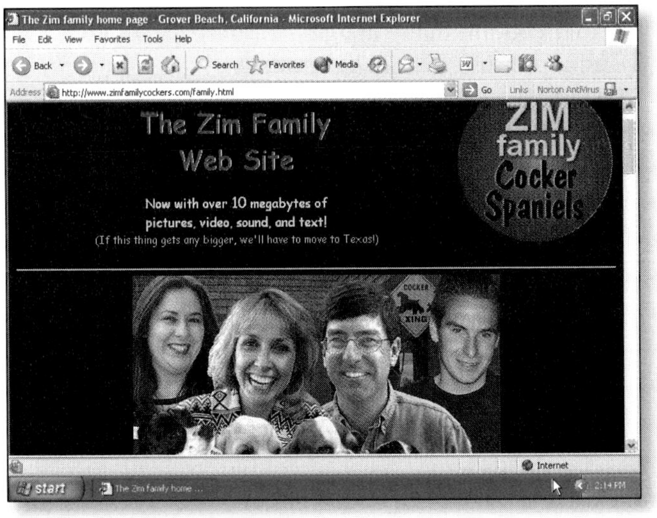

(h) **Personal**

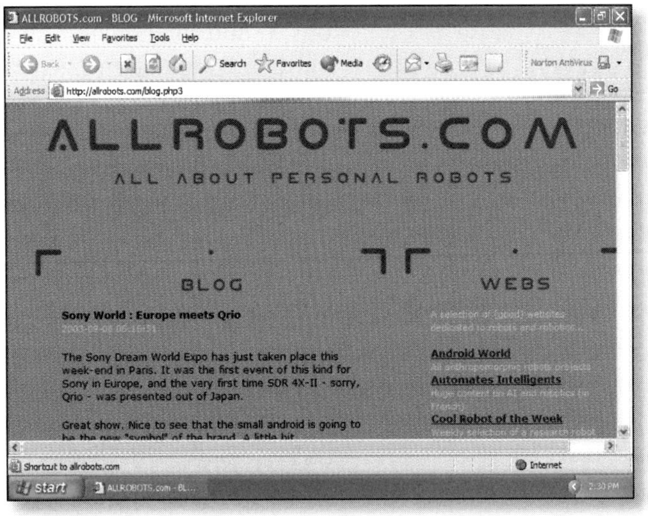

(i) **Blog**

FIGURE I-4 ***(continued)***

Planning a Web Site

Although publishing a Web page and/or a Web site is easy, advanced planning is paramount in ensuring a successful Web site. Publishing a Web site, which makes it available on the Internet, is discussed later in this Introduction. Thousands of individuals create and publish Web pages every day, some using word processing software or markup languages to create their pages. Others use professional design and management editors such as Dreamweaver.

Planning Basics — Purpose

Those who rush into the publishing process without the proper planning tend to design Web sites that are unorganized and difficult to navigate. Visitors to this type of Web site will lose interest quickly and will not return. As you begin planning your Web site, consider the following guidelines to ensure you set and attain realistic goals.

PURPOSE AND GOAL Determine the purpose and goal of your Web site. Create a focus by developing a **purpose statement**, which communicates the intention of the Web site. Consider the nine basic types of Web sites mentioned previously. Will your Web site consist of just one basic type or a combination of two or more types?

TARGET AUDIENCE Identify your audience. The people who visit your Web site will determine whether your Web site is a success. Although you welcome all visitors, you need to know as much as possible about your target audience. To learn more about the visitors to your Web site, determine whether you want to attract people with similar interests, and consider the gender, education, age range, income, profession/job field, and computer proficiency of your target audience.

NEW WEB TECHNOLOGIES Evaluate whether your potential visitors have access to high-speed broadband media or to baseband media, and use this information to determine what elements to include within your Web site. **Broadband** transmits multiple signals simultaneously and includes media and hardware such as **T1 lines**, **DSL** (**digital subscriber lines**), **ISDN** (**Integrated Services Digital Network**), **fiber optics**, and **cable modems. Baseband** transmits one signal at a time and includes media and hardware such as 28K to 56K modems. Baseband works well with a Web site composed mostly of text and small images. Web sites that contain many images or **multimedia**, such as video and animations, generally require that the visitors have a broadband connection.

WEB SITE COMPARISON Visit other Web sites that are similar to your proposed site. What do you like about these sites? What do you dislike? Look for inspirational ideas. How can you make your Web site better?

Planning Basics — Content

An informative, well-planned Web site is not difficult to create. To ensure a successful Web experience for your visitors, consider the following guidelines to provide appropriate content and other valuable Web page elements.

VALUE-ADDED CONTENT Consider the different types of content to include within your Web site. Use the following questions as guidelines:

- What topics do you want to cover?
- How much information will you present about each topic?
- What will attract your target audience to your Web site?

- What methods will you use to keep your audience returning to your site?
- What changes will you have to make to keep your site updated?

TEXT Because text is the primary component of most Web pages, be brief and incorporate lists whenever possible. Use common words and simple language, and check your spelling and grammar. Create your textual content to accomplish your goals effectively.

IMAGES After text, images are the most commonly included content. Ask yourself these questions with respect to your use of images:

- Will you have a common logo and/or theme on all Web pages?
- Are these images readily available?
- What images will you have to locate?
- What images will you have to create?
- How many images per page will you have?

COLOR PALETTE The color palette you select for your Web site can enhance or detract from your message or goal. Do not think in terms of your favorite colors. Instead, consider how color can support your goal. Ask yourself the following questions:

- Do your selected colors work well with your goal?
- Are the colors part of the universal 216 browser-safe color palette?
- Did you limit the number of colors to a selected few?

MULTIMEDIA Multimedia adds interactivity and action to your Web pages. Animation, audio, and video are types of multimedia. If you plan to add multimedia, determine whether the visitor will require plug-ins. A **plug-in** extends the capability of a Web browser. Some of the more commonly used plug-ins are Shockwave Player, Macromedia Flash, and Windows Media Player. Most plug-ins are free and can be downloaded from the Web.

Web Site Navigation

It is not possible to predict how a visitor will access a Web site or at what point the visitor will enter within the Web site structure. Visitors can arrive at any page within a Web site by a variety of ways: a hyperlink, a search engine, a directory, typing a Web address directly, and so on. On every page of your Web site, you must provide clear answers to the three basic questions your visitors will ask: Where am I? Where do I go from here? How do I get to the home page? A well-organized Web site provides the answers to these questions. Once the visitor is at a Web site, **navigation**, which is the pathway through your site, must be obvious and intuitive. Individual Web pages cannot be isolated from the rest of the site if the site is to be successful. At all times and on all pages in your site, you must give the visitor a sense of place, of context within the site. Most Web designers use a navigation map to visualize the navigation pathway.

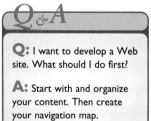

> **Q&A**
>
> **Q:** I want to develop a Web site. What should I do first?
>
> **A:** Start with and organize your content. Then create your navigation map.

Design Basics — Navigation Map

A **navigation map** outlines the structure of the entire Web site, showing all of the pages within the site and the connections from one page to others. The navigation map provides the structure, or road map, through the Web site, but does not provide detail as to the content of the individual pages. Web site navigation should be consistent from page to page, so your visitors do not have to guess where they are within the site each time they encounter a new page. All pages in the site should contain a link to the home page. Consider the following for site navigation.

STRUCTURE The goal and the type of a Web site is a major determinant in the type of structure selected for a specific Web site. The navigation map serves as a blueprint for your navigational structure. Consider the following navigational structure types and determine which one best meets your needs:

- In a **linear structure** (Figure I-5a), the user navigates sequentially, moving from one page to the next. This is the simplest way to organize a Web site. Information that flows as a narrative, as a timeline, or in logical order is ideal for sequential treatment. Simple sequential organization, however, usually works only for smaller sites. Many online tutorials use a linear structure.
- A **hierarchical structure** (Figure I-5b) is one of the better ways to organize complex bodies of information. This type of structure is well-suited for Web sites because most visitors are familiar with hierarchical charts. For a hierarchical structure to be effective requires thorough organization of the content.
- A **Web structure** (Figure I-5c), which also is called a **random structure**, places few restrictions on organizational patterns. This type of structure is associated with the free flow of ideas and can be confusing to a user. A random structure is better suited for experienced users looking for further education or enrichment and is not recommended if your goal is to provide a basic understanding of a particular topic. If a Web site is relatively small, however, a random structure could work well.
- If a Web site consists of a number of topics of equal importance, a **grid structure** (Figure I-5d) could be the best navigational choice. Procedural manuals, events, and item lists are examples of content well-suited for this type of structure.
- Large Web sites frequently use a **hybrid structure**, which is a combination of the previous listed structures, to organize information (Figure I-6 on the next page).

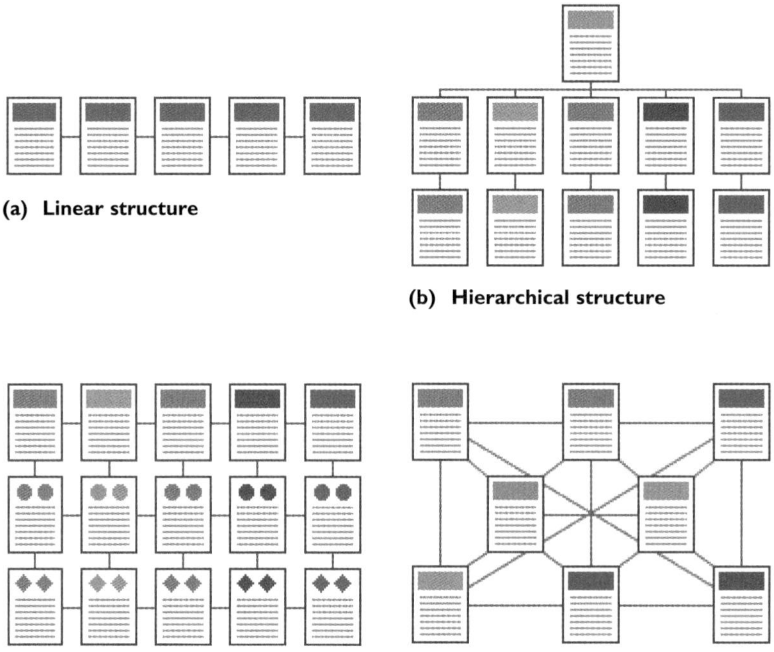

(a) Linear structure

(b) Hierarchical structure

(c) Web structure

(d) Grid structure

FIGURE I-5

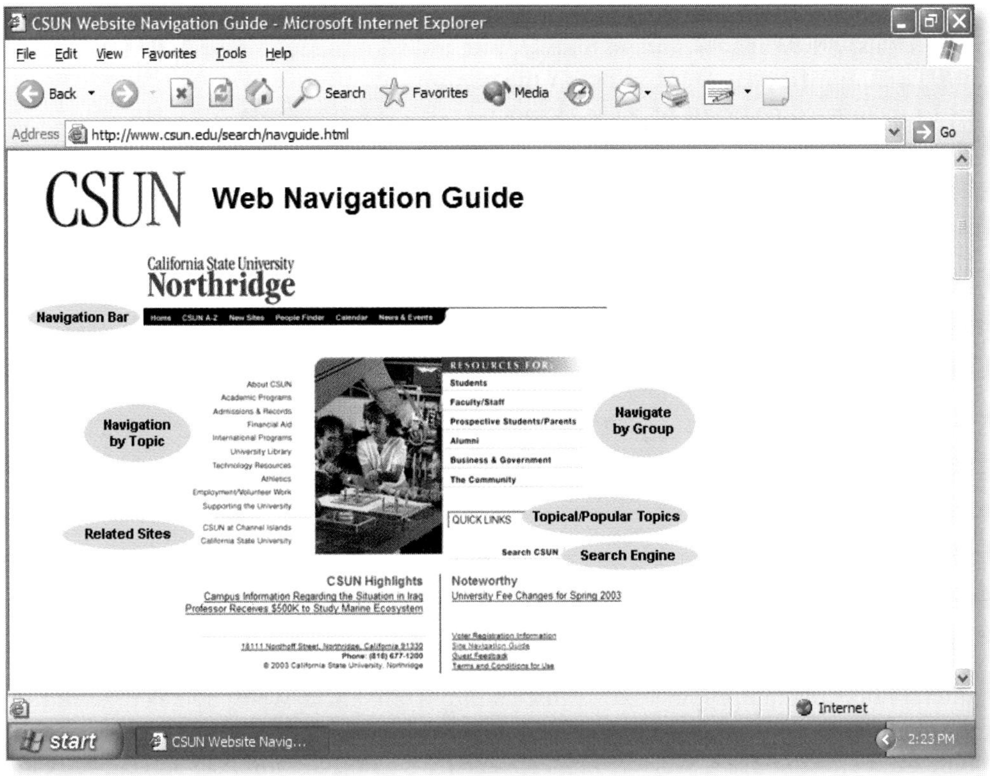

FIGURE I-6

TOOLS Determine the tool to be used to create the navigation map. If your Web site is small, the organizational chart included in the Microsoft Office applications, as shown in Figure I-7 using PowerPoint, is an easy-to-use tool. For larger, more diverse Web sites, Visio Professional, Flow Charting PDQ, FlowCharter Professional, and OrgPlus are some of the programs you can use to chart and organize your Web site. Dreamweaver provides a site map feature. The Dreamweaver site map shows the site structure two levels deep, starting from the home page and is an ideal tool for laying out a site structure.

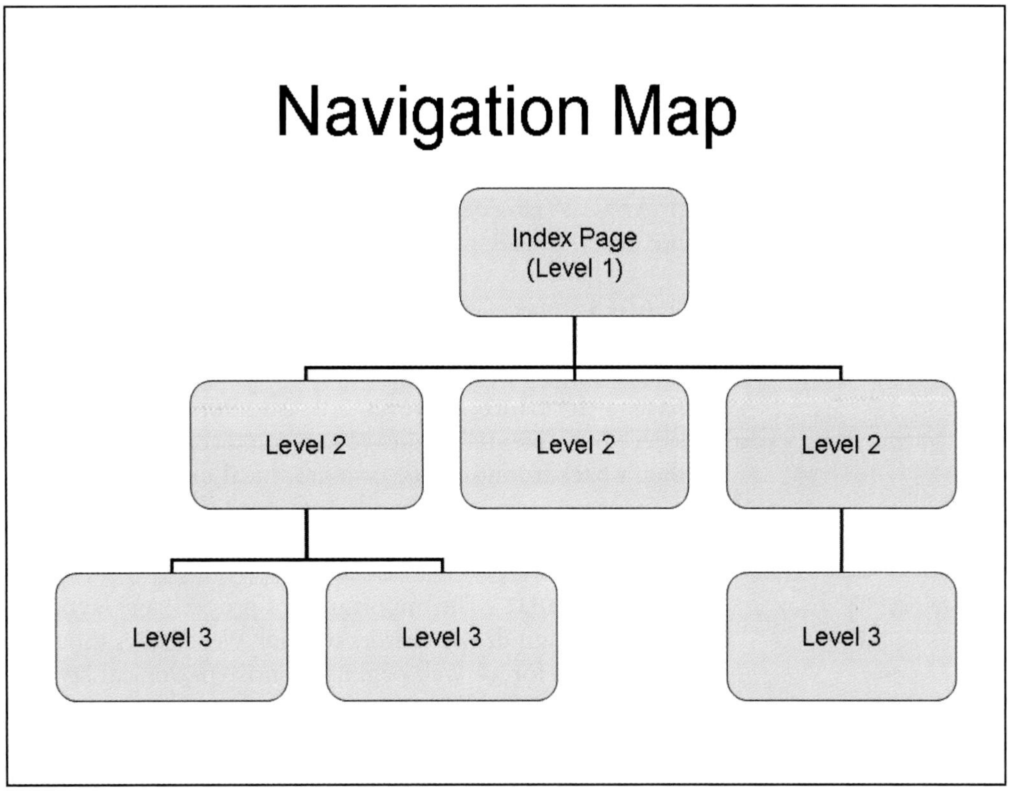

FIGURE I-7

NAVIGATION ELEMENTS The more common types of navigation elements include text, buttons, other images, image maps, a site index, a menu, a search feature, navigation bars, and frames. Depending on the complexity of your Web site, you may want to include some or all of these elements.

Developing a Web Site

Once the structure is complete, the next step is to develop the Web site. Because text and images are a Web site's more common elements, make them your main focus. Then consider page layout and color.

Development Basics — Typography, Images, Page Layout, and Color

The combination of typography, images, page layout, and color comprise the elements of your finished Web site. Correct use of these elements plays an important part in the development process. Consider the following guidelines.

TYPOGRAPHY Good **typography**, which is the appearance and arrangement of the characters that make up your text, is just as important for a Web page as it is for any other medium. A **font** consists of all the characters available in a particular style and weight for a specific design. Selecting fonts for display on a computer screen, however, is different from selecting fonts for a magazine, a book, or another printed medium. That the text displays on a computer screen and not on a piece of paper is immaterial; it still should be easy to read. As a viewer of a Web page, you may never consciously notice the **typeface**, which is the design of the text characters, but the typeface subconsciously affects your reaction to the page.

When selecting a font, determine its purpose on your Web page. Is it to be used for a title? For onscreen reading? Is it likely to be printed? Will the font fit in with the theme of the Web site? Is it a Web-safe font, such as Times New Roman, Courier, or Arial? **Web-safe fonts** are the more popular fonts and the ones that most visitors are likely to have installed on their computers.

Q&A

Q: Many pages on the Web contain multiple elements and are very "busy." Is this a good practice?

A: Not necessarily. Simple pages download faster and make an immediate impression on the reader.

IMAGES Images can enhance almost any Web page if used appropriately. Without the visual impact of shape, color, and contrast, Web pages can be uninteresting graphically and will not motivate the visitor to investigate their contents. Images and page performance, however, are issues for many visitors. When adding images, consider your potential audience and the technology they have available. Also remember that a background image or a graphical menu increases visitor download time. You may lose visitors who do not have broadband access if your Web page contains an excessive number of graphical items.

PAGE LAYOUT The importance of proper page layout cannot be overemphasized. A suitable design draws visitors to your Web site. Although no single design system is appropriate for all Web pages, a consistent, logical layout allows you to add text and images easily. The Web page layouts shown in Figure I-8 on the next page illustrate two different layouts. The layout on the left (Figure I-8a on the next page) illustrates a plain page with a heading and text. The page layout on the right (Figure I-8b on the next page) presents strong visual contrast by using a variety of layout elements.

Maintaining consistency and updating changes throughout a site are two of the biggest challenges faced by Web designers. A **template** is a special type of HTML document that can help with these challenges. Dreamweaver provides several page layout templates that can be modified easily. In laying out your Web pages, consider the following guidelines to ensure visitors have the best viewing experience:

- Include only one topic per page
- Control the vertical and horizontal size of the page
- Start text on the left to accommodate the majority of individuals, who read from left to right
- Use concise statements and bulleted points to get your point across; studies indicate most people scan the text

COLOR When creating a Web page, use color to add interest and vitality to your site. Color can be used in tables, as backgrounds, and with fonts. Use the right combination of colors to decorate the layout and tie the Web site pages together.

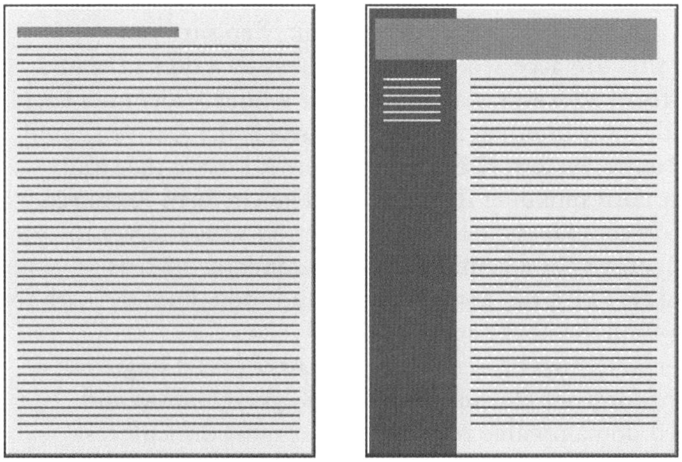

(a) (b)

FIGURE I-8

Reviewing and Testing a Web Site

Some Web site developers argue that reviewing and testing should take place throughout the developmental process. While this may be true, it also is important to review and test the final product. This ongoing process ensures that you identify and correct any problems before publishing to the Web. When reviewing and testing your Web site, ask the following questions:

- Is the Web site free of spelling and/or grammatical errors?
- Is the page layout consistent, and does it generate a sense of balance and order?
- Are any links broken?
- Do multimedia interactivity and forms function correctly?
- Does the Web site display properly in the more widely used browsers?
- Does the Web site function properly in different browsers, including older browser versions?
- Have you initiated a **group test**, in which you have asked other individuals to test your Web site and provide feedback?

Publishing a Web Site

After your Web site has been tested thoroughly, it can be published. **Publishing** a Web site is the process of making it available to your visitors. This step involves the actual uploading of the Web site to a server. After the uploading process is completed, all pages within the Web site should be tested again.

Publishing Basics — Domain Name, Server Space, and Uploading

With your Web site thoroughly tested and any problems corrected, you must make the site available to your audience by obtaining a domain name, acquiring server space, and uploading the site. Consider the following to ensure site availability.

OBTAIN A DOMAIN NAME To allow visitors to access your Web site, you must obtain a domain name. Web sites are accessed by an IP address or a domain name. An **IP address** (**Internet Protocol address**) is a number that uniquely identifies each computer or device connected to the Internet. A **domain name** is the text version of an IP address. The **Domain Name System** (**DNS**) is an Internet service that translates domain names into their corresponding IP addresses. The **Uniform Resource Locator** (**URL**), also called a **Web address**, tells the browser on which server to locate the Web page. A URL consists of a communications standard, such as **Hypertext Transfer Protocol (HTTP)**, the domain name, and sometimes the path to a specific Web page (Figure I-9 on the next page).

More About

Selecting a Domain Name

When selecting a domain name, keep it simple. If possible, avoid hyphens. To learn more about domain name selection, visit the Dreamweaver MX 2004 More About Web page (scsite.com/dreamweavermx04/more.htm) and then click Domain Name Selection.

Domain names are unique and must be registered. The **Accredited Registrar Directory** provides a listing of **Internet Corporation for Assigned Names and Numbers** (**ICANN**) accredited domain name registrars. Your most difficult task likely will be to find a name that is not already registered. You can locate a name by using a specialized search engine at one of the many accredited domain name registrars listed on the ICANN Web site (icann.org/registrars/accredited-list.html). In addition to registering your business name as a domain name, you may want to register the names of your products, services, and/or other related names. Expect to pay approximately $15 to $35 per year for a domain name.

Consider the following guidelines when selecting a domain name:

- Select a name that is easy to pronounce, spell, and remember.
- Select a name that relates to the Web site content and suggests the nature of your product or service.
- If the Web site is a business, use the business name.
- Select a name that is free and clear of trademark issues.
- Purchase variations and the .org and .net versions of your domain name.
- Some ISPs will obtain a domain name for you if you use their service to host your Web site.

ACQUIRE SERVER SPACE Locate an ISP that will host your Web site. Recall that an ISP is a business that has a permanent Internet connection. ISPs offer temporary connections to individuals and companies free or for a fee.

If you select an ISP that provides free server space, most likely your visitors will be subjected to advertisements and pop-up windows. Other options to explore for free server space include the provider from which you obtain your Internet connection; **online communities**, such as Yahoo!GeoCities (geocities.yahoo.com), Tripod (tripod.lycos.com), and MSN Web Communities (communities.msn.com); and your educational institution's Web server.

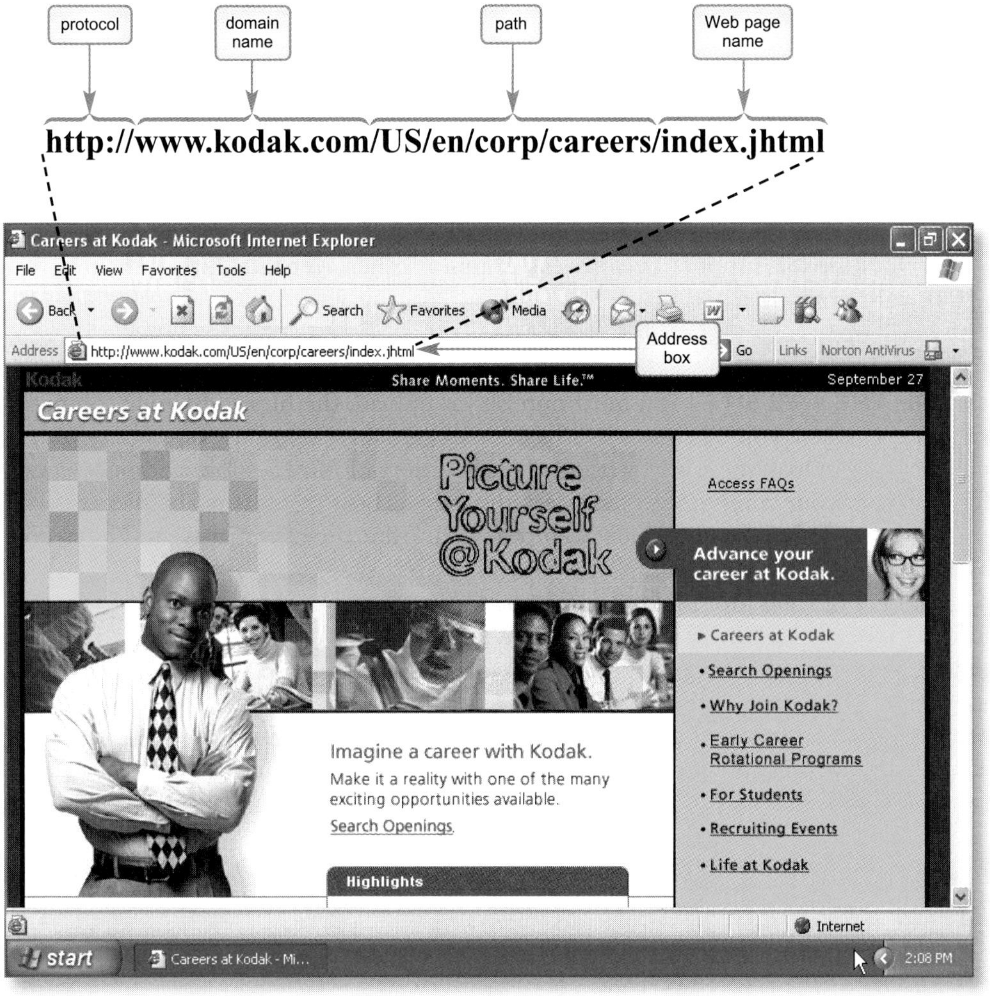

FIGURE I-9

If the purpose of your Web site is to sell a product or service or to promote a professional organization, you should consider a fee-based ISP. Use a search engine such as Google (google.com) and search for Web site hosting, or visit Hosting Repository (hostingrepository.com), where you will find thousands of Web hosting plans, as well as reviews and ratings of Web hosting providers. Selecting a reliable provider requires investigation on your part. Many providers provide multiple hosting plans. When selecting an ISP, consider the following questions and how they apply to your particular situation and Web site:

1. What is the monthly fee? Is a discount available if you sign up for a year? Are setup fees charged?
2. How much server space is provided for the monthly fee? Can you purchase additional space? If so, how much does it cost?
3. What is the average server uptime on a monthly basis? What is the average server downtime?
4. What are the server specifications? Can the server handle many users? Does it have battery backup power?
5. Are **server logs**, which keep track of the number of accesses, available?
6. What is the ISP's form of connectivity — that is, how does it connect to the Internet: OC3, T1, T3, or some other way?
7. Is a money-back guarantee offered?

8. What technical support does the ISP provide and when is it available? Does it have an online knowledge base?
9. Does the server on which the Web site will reside have CGI capabilities and Active Server Page (ASP) support?
10. Does the server on which the Web site will reside support e-commerce, multimedia, and **Secure Sockets Layer** (**SSL**) for encrypting confidential data such as credit card numbers? Are additional fees required for these capabilities?
11. Does the ISP support Dreamweaver and/or other Web site development software programs?
12. Are mailboxes included in the package? If so, how many?

PUBLISH THE WEB SITE You must publish, or upload, the files from your computer to the server where your Web site will be accessible to anyone on the Internet. Publishing, or **uploading**, is the process of transmitting all the files that comprise your Web site from your computer to the selected server or host computer. The files that make up your Web site can include Web pages, PDF documents, images, audio, video, animation, and others.

A variety of tools and methods exist to manage the upload task. Some of the more popular of these are FTP programs, Windows Web Publishing Wizard, Web Folders, and Web authoring programs such as Dreamweaver. These tools allow you to link to a remote server, enter a password, and then upload your files. Dreamweaver contains a built-in function similar to independent FTP programs. The Dreamweaver FTP function to upload your Web site is covered in Project 3 and in Appendix C.

Maintaining a Web Site

Most Web sites require maintenance and updating. Some types of ongoing Web maintenance include the following:

- Changing content, either by adding new text and images or by deleting obsolete ones
- Checking for broken links and adding new links
- Documenting the last change date (even when no revisions have been made)

Use the information from the server logs provided by your ISP to determine what needs to be updated or changed. Statistics contained within these logs generally include the number of visitors trying to access your site at one time, what resources they request, how long they stay at the site, at what point they enter the site, what pages they view, and what errors they encounter. Learning to use and apply the information contained within the server log will help you to make your Web site successful.

After you make updates and/or changes to the site, notify your viewers with a What's New announcement.

Methods and Tools Used to Create Web Pages

Web developers have several options for creating Web pages: a text editor, an HTML editor, software applications, or a WYSIWYG text editor (discussed in detail on page DW 19). Microsoft Notepad and WordPad are examples of a **text editor**. These simple, easy-to-use programs allow the user to enter, edit, save, and print text. An **HTML editor** is a more sophisticated version of a text editor. In addition to basic text-editing functions, more advanced features, such as syntax highlighting, color-coding, and spell checking, are available. **Software applications**, such as Microsoft Word, Excel, and

Publisher, provide a Save as Web Page command on the File menu. This feature converts the application document into an HTML file. Examples of a **WYSIWYG text editor** are programs such as Microsoft FrontPage and Macromedia Dreamweaver. These programs provide an integrated text editor with a graphical user interface that allows the user to view both the code and the document as it is being created.

A Web developer can use any of these options to create Web pages. Regardless of the option selected, however, it still is important to understand the specifics of HTML.

HTML

Web pages are written in plain text and saved in the American Standard Code for Information Interchange format. The **American Standard Code for Information Interchange**, or **ASCII** (pronounced ASK-ee), format is the most widely used coding system to represent data. Using the ASCII format makes Web pages universally readable by different Web browsers regardless of the computer platform on which they reside.

Hypertext Markup Language (**HTML**) is an authoring language that defines the structure and layout of a document so that it displays as a Web page in a Web browser such as Microsoft Internet Explorer or Netscape Navigator. A Web page has two components: source code and document content. The **source code**, which contains tags, is program instructions. The **tags** within the source code control the appearance of the document content. The **document content** is the text and images that the browser displays. The browser interprets the tags contained within the code, and the code instructs the browser how to display the Web page. For instance, if you define a line of text on your Web page as a heading, the browser knows to display this line as a heading.

All HTML tag formats are the same. They start with a left angle bracket (< or less than symbol), followed by the name of the tag, and end with a right angle bracket (> or greater than symbol). Most tags have a start and an end tag and are called **two-sided tags**. The end tags are the same as the start tags except they are preceded by a forward slash (/). Some HTML tags, such as the one used to indicate a line break <br>, do not have an end tag. These are known as **one-sided tags**. Other tags, such as the one to indicate a new paragraph <p>, have an end tag, but the end tag can be omitted. For consistency, it is better with this type of tag to include both the start and end tags.

Some tags can contain an **attribute**, or **property**, which is additional information placed within the angle brackets. Attributes are not repeated or contained in the end tag. Some attributes are used individually, while other attributes can include a value modifier. A **value modifier** specifies conditions within the tag. For example, you can use a value modifier to specify the font type or size or the placement of text on the page. To create and display a centered heading, for instance, you would use the following code:

```
<h1 align=center>This is the largest header tag and the text will be centered</h1>
```

In this example, h1 is the HTML tag, align is the attribute, and center is the value modifier. Notice that the attribute does not appear as part of the end tag, </h1>.

You can use Microsoft Notepad or WordPad (which are text editors) to create HTML documents. Place each tag in a pair around the text or section that you want to define (**mark up**) with that tag. HTML tags are not case-sensitive; therefore, you can enter HTML tags in uppercase or lowercase or a combination of both. To be consistent, however, you should adopt a standard practice when typing tags. The examples in this book use lowercase.

More About

HTML

The World Wide Web Consortium (W3C) develops and updates Web protocols. To learn more about the most recent changes to HTML, visit the Dreamweaver MX 2004 More About Web page (scsite.com/dreamweavermx04/more.htm) and then click W3C.

Q&A

Q: Should I test my Web page in more than one browser?

A: Yes—at a minimum you should test a Web page in the most recent versions of Internet Explorer and Netscape Navigator.

HTML tags also are used to format the hyperlinks that connect information on the World Wide Web. HTML tags number in the hundreds, but some are used more than others. All documents, however, require four basic tags. Figure I-10 illustrates the basic tags required for all HTML documents. Table I-2 summarizes the more commonly used HTML tags.

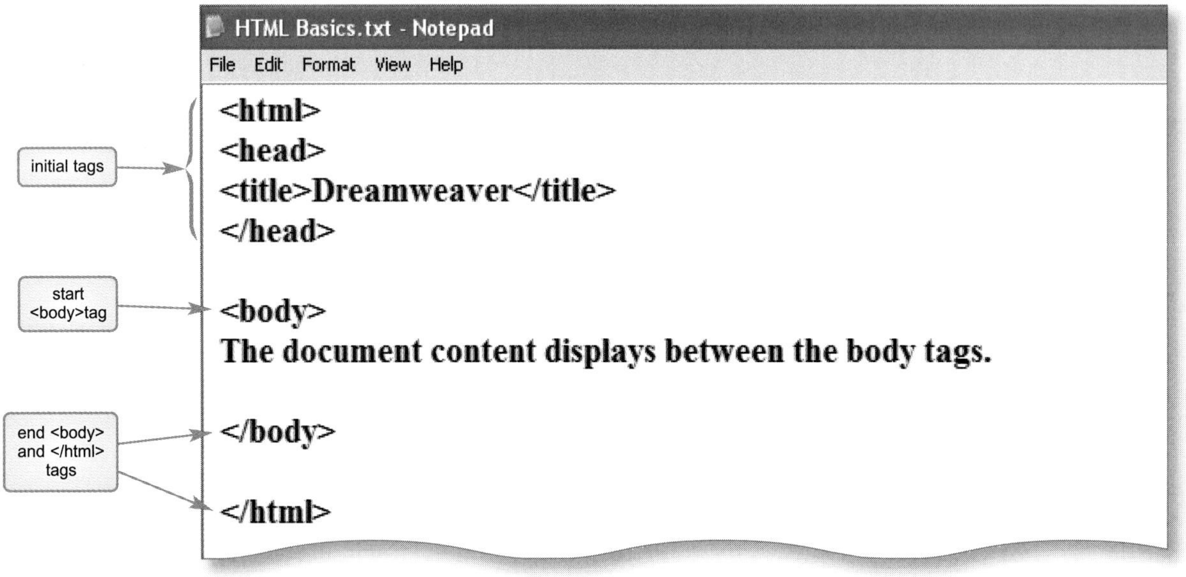

FIGURE I-10

Table I-2 Commonly Used HTML Tags

TAG	STRUCTURE
<html>...</html>	Encloses the entire HTML document
<head>...</head>	Encloses the head of the HTML document
<body>...</body>	Encloses the body of the HTML document
TAG	**TITLE AND HEADINGS**
<title>...</title>	Indicates the title of the document
<h1>...</h1>	Heading level 1
<h2>...</h2>	Heading level 2
<h3>...</h3>	Heading level 3
<h4>...</h4>	Heading level 4
<h5>...</h5>	Heading level 5
<h6>...</h6>	Heading level 6
TAG	**PARAGRAPHS, BREAKS, AND SEPARATORS**
<p>...</p>	Plain paragraph; end tag optional
 	Line break
<hr>	Horizontal rule line
<ol>...</ol>	Ordered, numbered list
<ul>...</ul>	Unordered, bulleted list
<menu>...</menu>	Menu list of items

Table I-2 Commonly Used HTML Tags (continued)

TAG	PARAGRAPHS, BREAKS, AND SEPARATORS
<dir>...</dir>	Directory listing
<li>...</li>	List item, used with <ol>, <ul>, <menu>, and <dir>
<dl>...</dl>	Definition of glossary list
<dt>...</dt>	Definition term; part of a definition list
<dd>...</dd>	Definition corresponding to a definition term
TAG	CHARACTER FORMATTING
<b>...</b>	Bold text
<u>...</u>	Underlined text
<i>...</i>	Italic text
TAG	LINKS
<a>...</a>	Combined with the HREF attribute, creates a link to another document or anchor
<a>...</a>	Combined with the NAME attribute, creates an anchor which can be linked to
TAG	IMAGE
<img>...</img>	Inserts an image into the document

Web Page Authoring Programs

Many of today's Web page authoring programs, including Dreamweaver, are What You See Is What You Get (WYSIWYG) HTML text editors. A WYSIWYG text editor allows a user to view a document as it will appear in the final product and to edit the text, images, or other elements directly within that view. Before programs such as Dreamweaver existed, Web page designers were required to type, or hand-code, Web pages. Educators and Web designers still debate the issue surrounding the necessity of knowing HTML. You do not need to know HTML to create Web pages in Dreamweaver, but an understanding of HTML will help you if you need to alter Dreamweaver-generated code. If you know HTML, then you can make changes to code and Dreamweaver will accept the changes.

Macromedia Dreamweaver MX 2004

Dreamweaver is the standard in visual authoring. Macromedia Dreamweaver MX 2004 is part of the MX 2004 product family, which includes Macromedia Flash MX 2004, ColdFusion MX 2004, and Fireworks MX 2004. Dreamweaver provides features that access these separate products. Some of the new features of Dreamweaver MX 2004 include the following:

- Cross-browser validation for compatibility across all the leading browsers
- More powerful CSS support
- Built-in graphics editing with Macromedia Fireworks
- Secure FTP

- Increased support for a platform-independent development environment
- Better integration with external files and code from such programs as Microsoft Word and Excel
- Enhanced coding and editing tools
- Tighter integration with other Macromedia tools

Dreamweaver makes it easy to get started and provides you with helpful tools to enhance your Web design and development experience. Working in a single environment, you create, build, and manage Web sites and Internet applications. The workspace environment is customizable to fit your particular needs.

Coding tools and features that are included within Dreamweaver are references for HTML, CSS, and JavaScript and code editors that allow you to edit the code directly. **Macromedia Roundtrip HTML technology** imports HTML documents without reformatting the code. Downloadable extensions from the Macromedia Web site make it easy to add functionality to any Web site. Examples of some of these extensions include shopping carts and online payment features.

Instead of writing individual HTML files for every page, use a database to store content and then retrieve the content dynamically in response to a user's request. Implementing and using this feature, you can update the information once, in one place, instead of manually editing many pages.

Dreamweaver provides the tools that help you author accessible content. These accessible pages comply with government guidelines and Section 508 of the Federal Rehabilitation Act. Another key feature is Cascading Style Sheets styles (CSS styles). CSS styles are collections of formatting definitions that affect the appearance of Web page elements. You can use CSS styles to format text, images, headings, tables, and so forth. Implementing and applying this feature, you can update the formatting one time across many Web pages.

Dreamweaver allows you to publish Web sites with relative ease to a local area network, which connects computers in a limited geographical area, or to the Web, for anyone with Internet access to see. The concepts and techniques presented in this book provide the tools you need to plan, develop, and publish professional Web sites, such as the Web sites shown in Figure I-11 and I-12 on the following page.

Summary

The Introduction to Web Site Development and Macromedia Dreamweaver MX 2004 provided an overview of the Internet and the World Wide Web and the key terms associated with those technologies. An overview of the nine basic types of Web pages also was presented. The Introduction furnished information on developing a Web site, including planning basics. The process of designing a Web site and each phase within this process were discussed. Information about testing, publishing, and maintaining a Web site also was presented, including an overview of obtaining a domain name, acquiring server space, and uploading a Web site. Methods and tools used to create Web pages were introduced. A short overview of HTML and some of the more commonly used HTML tags were presented. Finally, the advantages of using Dreamweaver in Web development were discussed. These advantages include a WYSIWYG text editor; a visual, customizable development environment; accessibility compliance; downloadable extensions; database access capabilities; and Cascading Style Sheets.

For an updated list of links, visit the Dreamweaver companion site at http://scsite.com/dreamweavermx04.

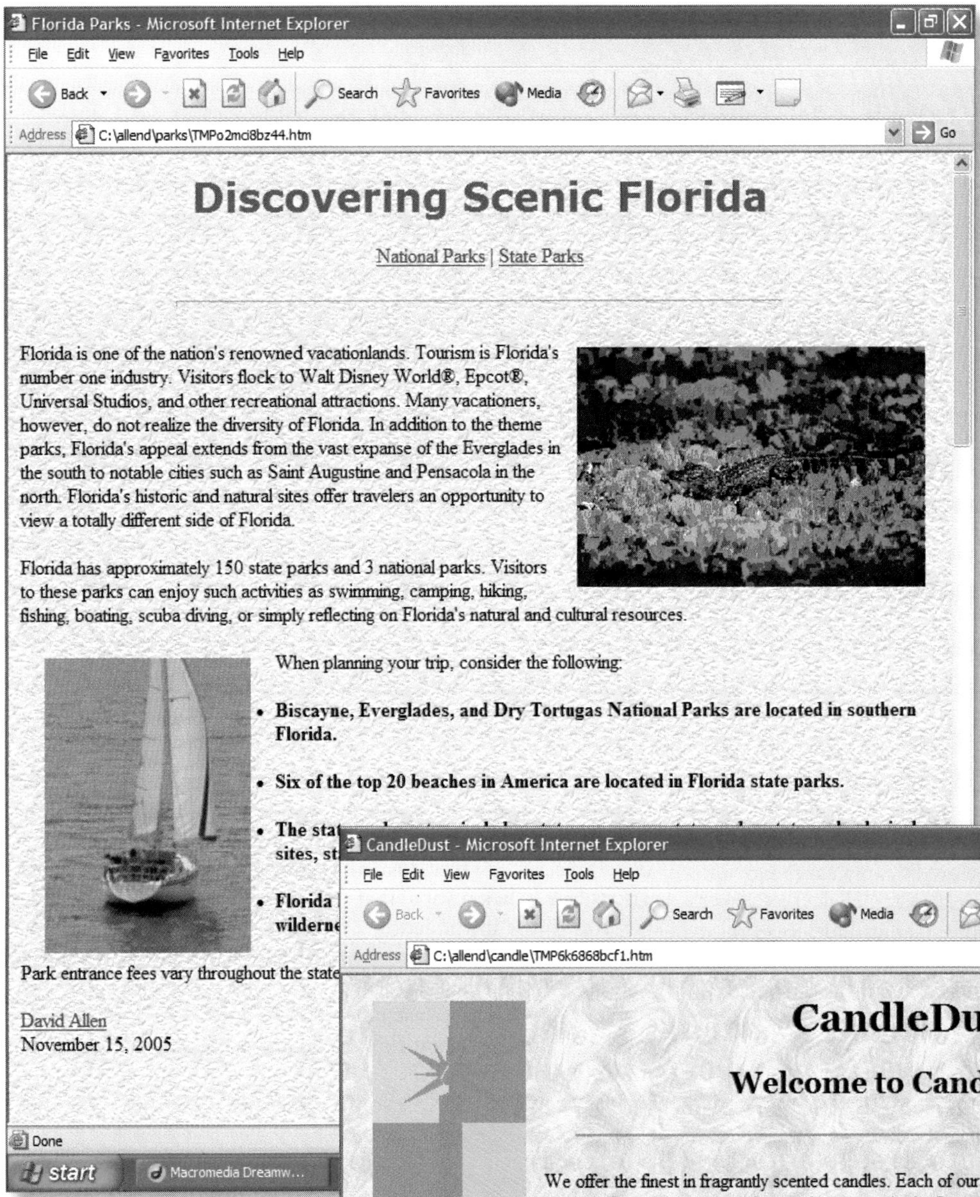

FIGURE I-11

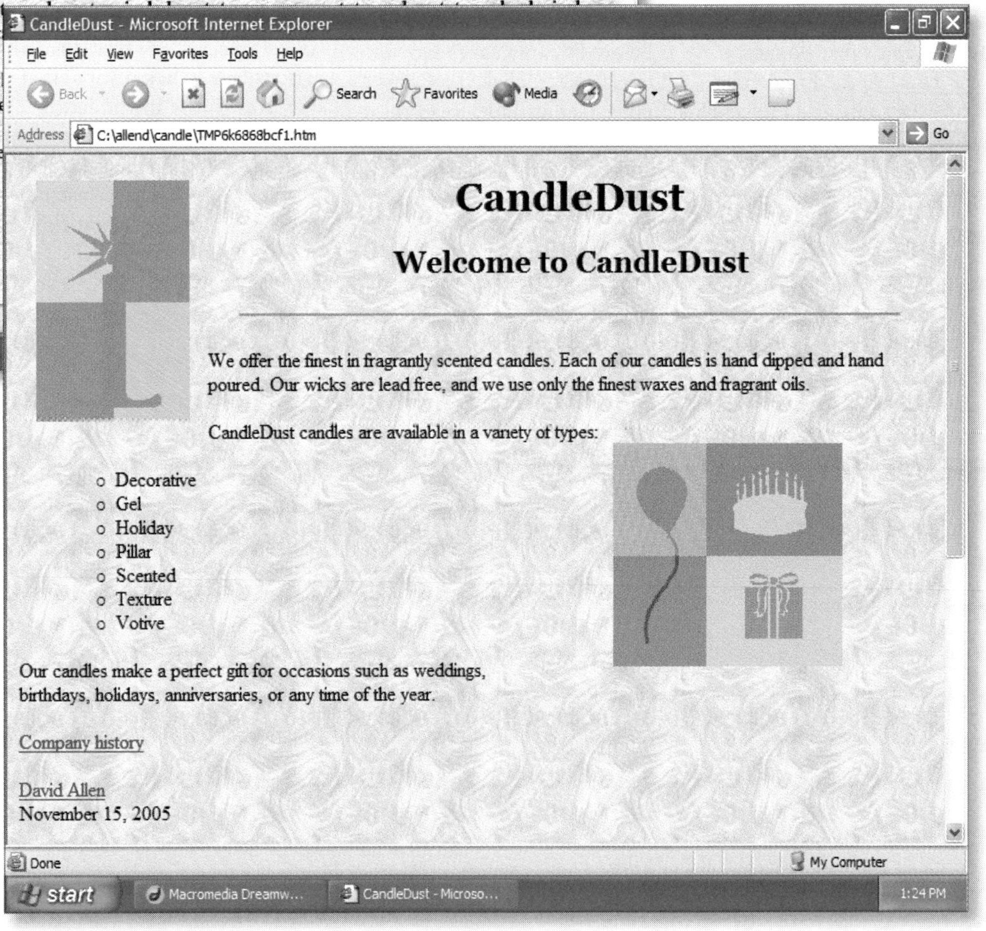

FIGURE I-12

Learn It Online

Instructions: To complete the Learn It Online exercises, start your browser, click the Address bar, and then enter the Web address `scsite.com/dreamweavermx2004/learn`. When the Dreamweaver MX 2004 Learn It Online page is displayed, follow the instructions in the exercises below. Each exercise has instructions for printing your results, either for your own records or for submission to your instructor.

1 Project Reinforcement TF, MC, and SA

Below Dreamweaver Introduction Project, click the Project Reinforcement link. Print the quiz by clicking Print on the File menu for each page. Answer each question.

2 Flash Cards

Below Dreamweaver Introduction Project, click the Flash Cards link and read the instructions. Type 20 (or a number specified by your instructor) in the Number of playing cards text box, type your name in the Enter your Name text box, and then click the Flip Card button. When the flash card is displayed, read the question and then click the ANSWER box arrow to select an answer. Flip through Flash Cards. If your score is 15 (75%) correct or greater, click Print on the File menu to print your results. If your score is less than 15 (75%) correct, then redo this exercise by clicking the Replay button.

3 Practice Test

Below Dreamweaver Introduction Project, click the Practice Test link. Answer each question, enter your first and last name at the bottom of the page, and then click the Grade Test button. When the graded practice test is displayed on your screen, click Print on the File menu to print a hard copy. Continue to take practice tests until you score 80% or better.

4 Who Wants To Be a Computer Genius?

Below Dreamweaver Introduction Project, click the Computer Genius link. Read the instructions, enter your first and last name at the bottom of the page, and then click the PLAY button. When your score is displayed, click the PRINT RESULTS link to print a hard copy.

5 Wheel of Terms

Below Dreamweaver Introduction Project, click the Wheel of Terms link. Read the instructions, and then enter your first and last name and your school name. Click the PLAY button. When your score is displayed, right-click the score and then click Print on the shortcut menu to print a hard copy.

6 Crossword Puzzle Challenge

Below Dreamweaver Introduction Project, click the Crossword Puzzle Challenge link. Read the instructions, and then enter your first and last name. Click the SUBMIT button. Work the crossword puzzle. When you are finished, click the Submit button. When the crossword puzzle is redisplayed, click the Print Puzzle button to print a hard copy.

7 Tips and Tricks

Below Dreamweaver Introduction Project, click the Tips and Tricks link. Click a topic that pertains to the Introduction Project. Right-click the information and then click Print on the shortcut menu. Construct a brief example of what the information relates to in Dreamweaver to confirm you understand how to use the tip or trick.

8 Newsgroups

Below Dreamweaver Introduction Project, click the Newsgroups link. Click a topic that pertains to the Introduction Project. Print three comments.

9 Expanding Your Horizons

Below Dreamweaver Introduction Project, click the Expanding Your Horizons link. Click a topic that pertains to the Introduction Project. Print the information. Construct a brief example of what the information relates to in Dreamweaver to confirm you understand the contents of the article.

10 Search Sleuth

Below Dreamweaver Introduction Project, click the Search Sleuth link. To search for a term that pertains to this project, select a term below the Introduction Project title and then use the Google search engine at google.com (or any major search engine) to display and print two Web pages that present information on the term.

Apply Your Knowledge

1 Web Site Creation

Instructions: As discussed in this project, creating a Web site involves planning, designing, developing, reviewing and testing, publishing, and maintaining the site. Open the Apply I-1 Web Site Creation file on the Dreamweaver Data Disk. See the inside back cover of this book for instructions for downloading the Data Disk or see your instructor for information on accessing the files required for this book. As shown in Table I-3, the Apply I-1 Web Site Creation file contains information about the Web site creation process. Use the information contained in this table to develop a plan for creating a Web site.

Table I-3 Creating a Web Site

PLANNING	
Web site name:	What is your Web site name?
Web site type:	What is the Web site type: portal, news, informational, business/marketing, educational, entertainment, advocacy, personal, or blog?
Web site purpose:	What is the purpose of your Web site?
Target audience:	How can you identify your target audience?
Web technologies to be used:	Will you design for broadband or baseband? Explain your selection.
Content:	What topics will you cover? How much information will you present on each topic? How will you attract your audience? What will you do to entice your audience to return to your Web site? How will you keep the Web site updated?
Text, images, and multimedia:	Will your site contain text only? What type of images will you include? Where will you obtain your images? Will you have a common logo? Will plug-ins be required?
DESIGNING	
Navigation map:	What type of structure will you use? What tools will you use to design your navigation map?
Navigational elements:	What navigational elements will you include?
DEVELOPING	
Typography:	What font will you use? How many different fonts will you use on your site?
Images:	How will you use images to enhance your site? Will you use a background image?
Page layout:	What type of layout will you use? How many topics per page? How will text be presented: bulleted or paragraph style? Will the audience need to scroll the page?
Color:	What color combinations will you use for your site? To what elements will you apply the color(s) — fonts, background, tables, other elements?

(continued)

Apply Your Knowledge

Web Site Creation *(continued)*

Table I-3 Creating a Web Site *(continued)*

REVIEWING AND TESTING	
Review:	What elements will you review? Will you use a group review?
Testing:	What elements will you test? Will you use self-testing? Will you use group testing?
PUBLISHING	
Domain name:	What is your domain name? Have you registered your domain name? What ISP will host your Web site? What criteria did you use to select the ISP?
MAINTAINING	
Ongoing maintenance:	How often will you update your Web site? What elements will you update? Will you add additional features? Does your ISP provide server logs? Will you use the server logs for maintenance purposes?

Perform the following steps using your word processing program and browser.

1. With the Apply I-1 Web Site Creation file open in your word processing program, select a name for your Web site.
2. Use a specialized search engine at one of the many accredited domain name registrars to verify that your selected Web site name is available.
3. Answer each question in the table. Use complete sentences to answer the questions. Type your answers in column 3.
4. Save the document with the file name, Apply I-1 My Web Site Creation.doc. Submit a copy to your instructor.

In the Lab

1 Using Internet Explorer

Problem: Microsoft's Internet Explorer (IE) has many new features that can make your work on the Internet more efficient. Using the Media feature, for example, you can play music, video, or multimedia files; listen to your favorite Internet radio station; and enhance your browsing experience. You can customize the image toolbar that displays when you point to an image on a Web page. IE also includes other enhancements. Visit the Microsoft Internet Explorer How-to-Articles Web page (Figure I-13) and select three articles concerning topics with which you are not familiar. Read the articles and then create a word processing document detailing what you learned.

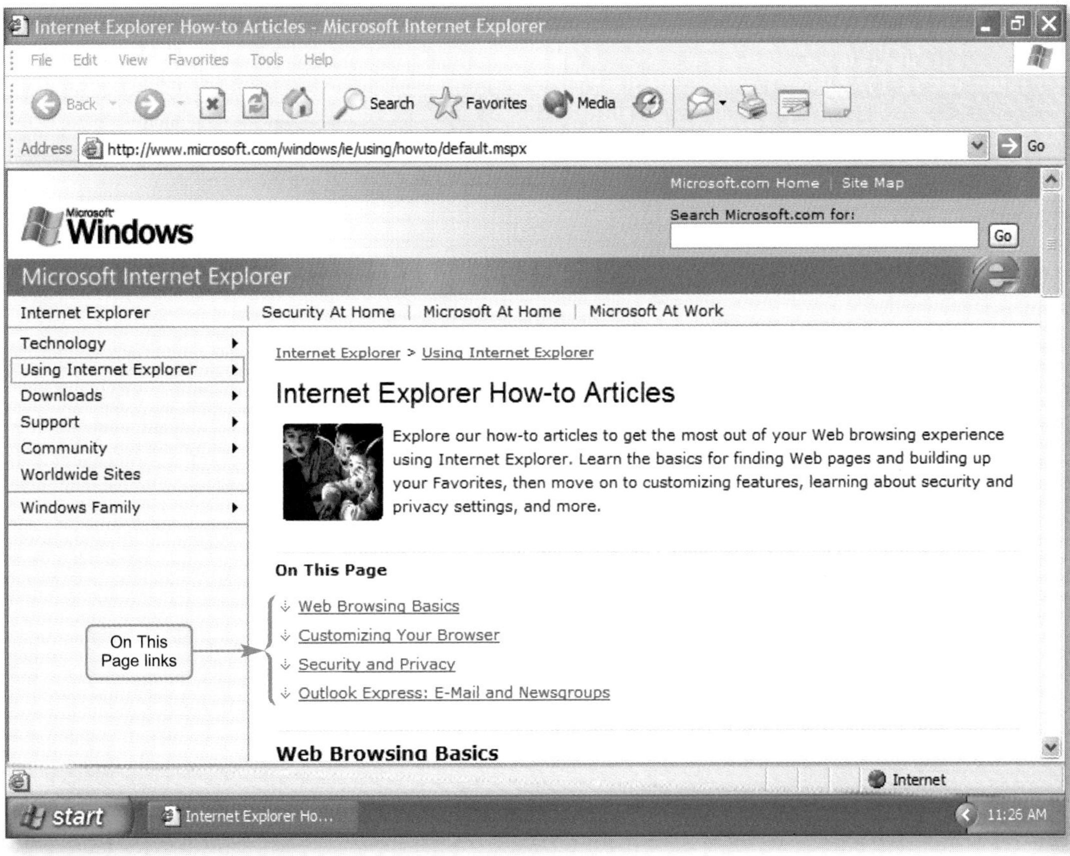

FIGURE I-13

Instructions: Perform the following tasks.

1. Start your browser. Open the Microsoft Internet Explorer How-to Articles Web page (microsoft.com/windows/ie/using/howto/default.mspx).
2. Click one of the On This Page links.
3. Select three articles that contain information with which you are not familiar.
4. Click the link for each article and read the article.
5. Start your word processing program.
6. List three important points that you learned from this Web site.
7. Write a summary of what you learned from each article. Include within your summary your opinion of the article and if you will apply what you learned or use it with your Web browser.
8. Save the document with the file name, Lab I-1 How-to.doc. Print a copy of the document.

In the Lab

2 Types of Web Pages

Problem: A Web designer is familiar with different types of Web pages and the sort of information displayed on these types of Web pages. The Introduction describes nine types of Web pages. Search the Internet and locate at least one example of each type of Web page.

Instructions: Perform the following tasks.

1. Start your browser. Open the Google (google.com) search engine Web page (Figure I-14) and search for an example of each of the following types of Web pages: portal, news, informational, business/marketing, educational, entertainment, advocacy, personal, and blog.

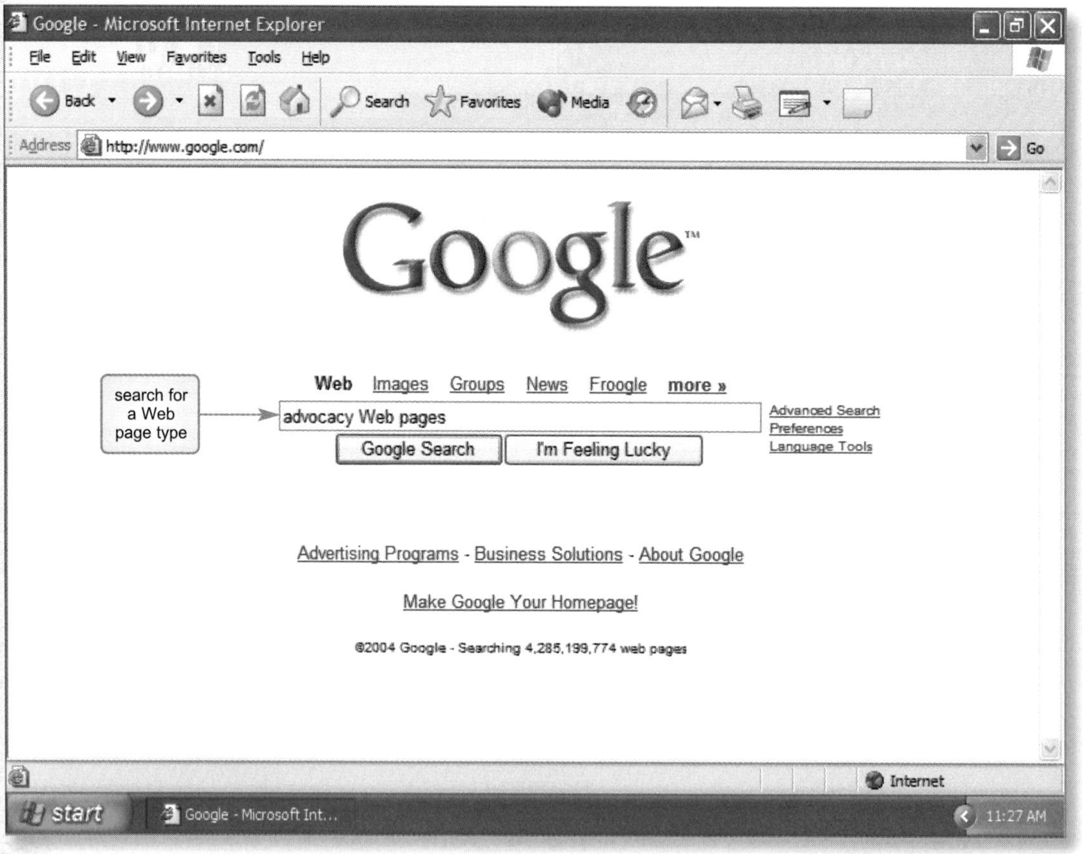

FIGURE I-14

2. Start your word processing program.
3. Copy and paste the link from each of these Web page types into your word processing document.
4. Identify the type of Web page for each link.
5. Explain why you selected this Web page and how it fits the definition of the specific type.
6. Save the document with the file name, Lab I-2 Web Page types.doc. Print a copy of the document if instructed to do so.
7. Submit the assignment to your instructor.

In the Lab

3 Web Site Hosting

Problem: Selecting the correct host or ISP for your Web site can be a confusing process. Many Web sites offer this service, but determining which one is best for your particular needs can be somewhat complicated. Assume your Web site will sell a product. Compare several ISPs and select the one that will best meet your needs.

Instructions: Perform the following tasks.

1. Review the information and questions on pages DW 15–16 discussing the guidelines for acquiring active server space to host your Web site.
2. Start your browser. Open the Hosting Repository Web page shown in Figure I-15 (hostingrepository.com).

FIGURE I-15

3. Click the Ecommerce link.
4. Click one of the host server links and review the information relating to the services offered by your selected ISP.
5. Start your word processing program.
6. Read and answer the questions on pages DW 15–16. Use the information provided in the list of services offered by your selected ISP.
7. Write a short summary explaining why you would or would not select this ISP to host your Web site.
8. Save the document with the file name, Lab I-3 Web Site Hosting.doc. If instructed to do so, print a copy of the document and hand it in or e-mail it to your instructor.

Cases and Places

The difficulty of these case studies varies:
■ are the least difficult and ■■ are more difficult. The last exercise is a group exercise.

1 ■ Use a search engine such as Google (google.com) and research information about planning a Web site. Use your word processing program and write a two-page summary of what you learned. Save the document as caseI-1.doc. Print a copy and hand it in or e-mail a copy to your instructor.

2 ■ Your goal is to create a personal Web site navigation map that contains three pages — the home page, a page about your favorite hobbies, and a page about places you like to visit. On a piece of paper, draw a navigation map for your proposed Web site. Write a sentence or two describing the type of structure you used and why you selected that structure.

3 ■■ Plug-ins are used on many Web sites. Start your browser and search for plug-ins. Prepare a list of the plug-ins you found. Create a summary statement describing how and why you could use each plug-in in a Web site. Include the link where you can download each of the plug-ins.

4 ■■ Typography within a Web page is one of its more important elements. Start your browser and search for examples of Web sites that include what you consider appropriate typography and Web sites with inappropriate typography. Write a short summary of why you consider these to be appropriate and inappropriate. Copy and paste the Web site addresses into your document.

5 ■■ **Working Together** Each team member is to search the Internet for Web sites illustrating each of these structures. Each team member then will use word processing software to write a minimum of 100 words describing the Web sites and explaining why they think this is an appropriate or inappropriate structure for that particular Web site. The team then will coordinate its research to complete a final document.

MACROMEDIA Dreamweaver MX 2004

Creating a Dreamweaver Web Page and Local Site

PROJECT 1

CASE PERSPECTIVE

Florida native David Allen worked with you last summer at a state environmental agency. Your job at the agency included Internet communications. Because you both love the outdoors, particularly Florida's state and national parks, you became good friends. David visits several parks every year. During each visit, he discovers something new and exciting. David wants to share his knowledge and to provide a way to make Florida residents and visitors aware of the uniqueness, beauty, and wildlife of the parks.

David knows the far-reaching capabilities of the Internet. He wants to use the Web to communicate to the public about Florida's parks, but he has limited knowledge about Web design and development. David knows that your interest and experience with the Internet could assist him in this endeavor, and he asks for your help. You like the idea and tell him that you can create a Web site using Dreamweaver. You get together to define the Web site and to plan the index page. When you are finished creating the Discovering Scenic Florida Web page, you will show it to David for his feedback.

As you read through this project, you will learn how to use Dreamweaver MX 2004 to define a local site and create a Web page and how to display the Web page in a browser.

MACROMEDIA
Dreamweaver MX 2004

Creating a Dreamweaver Web Page and Local Site

PROJECT 1

Objectives

You will have mastered the material in this project when you can:

- Describe Dreamweaver and identify its key features
- Start Dreamweaver
- Describe the Dreamweaver window and workspace
- Define a local site
- Add a background image
- Create and save a Web page
- Open and close panels
- Display and describe the Property inspector
- Format and modify text elements on a Web page
- Define and insert a line break and special characters
- Add a horizontal rule
- Change a Web page title
- Check spelling
- Preview a Web page in a Web browser
- Print a Web page
- Define Dreamweaver Help
- Quit Dreamweaver
- Open a new Web page

What Is Macromedia Dreamweaver MX 2004?

Macromedia Dreamweaver MX 2004 is a powerful Web page authoring and Web site management software program and HTML editor used to design, code, and create professional-looking Web pages, Web sites, and Web applications. The visual editing features of Dreamweaver allow you to create pages without writing a line of code. Dreamweaver provides many tools and features, including the following:

- **Automatic Web Page Creation** — Dreamweaver provides tools you can use to develop your Web pages without having to spend hours writing HTML code. Dreamweaver automatically generates the HTML code necessary to publish your Web pages.
- **Web Site Management** — Dreamweaver enables you to view a site, including all local and remote files associated with the selected site. Using Dreamweaver, you can perform standard maintenance operations such as viewing, opening, and moving files; transferring files between local and remote sites; and designing your site navigation with the Site Map.
- **Standard Macromedia Web Authoring Tools** — Dreamweaver includes a user interface that is consistent across all Macromedia authoring tools. This consistency enables easy integration with other Macromedia Web-related programs, such as Macromedia Flash, Director, Shockwave, and ColdFusion.

Other key features include the integrated user interface, the integrated file explorer, panel management, database integration, and standards and accessibility support. Dreamweaver MX 2004 is customizable and can run in operating systems such as Windows XP, Windows 2000, Windows NT, and Mac OS X.

Project One — Florida Parks

To create documents similar to those you will encounter on the Web and in academic, business, and personal environments, you can use Dreamweaver to produce Web pages such as the Discovering Scenic Florida Web page shown in Figure 1-1. The Web page shown in Figure 1-1 is the index page for the Florida Parks Web site. This informational page provides interesting facts about Florida's state and national parks. The page begins with a centered main heading, followed by a horizontal rule. Following the rule are two short informational paragraphs. The first paragraph contains two occurrences of the registered trademark symbol. Following the second paragraph is an introductory sentence for a bulleted list. The list contains four bulleted items. A concluding sentence, the author's name, and current date end the page. A background image is applied to the page.

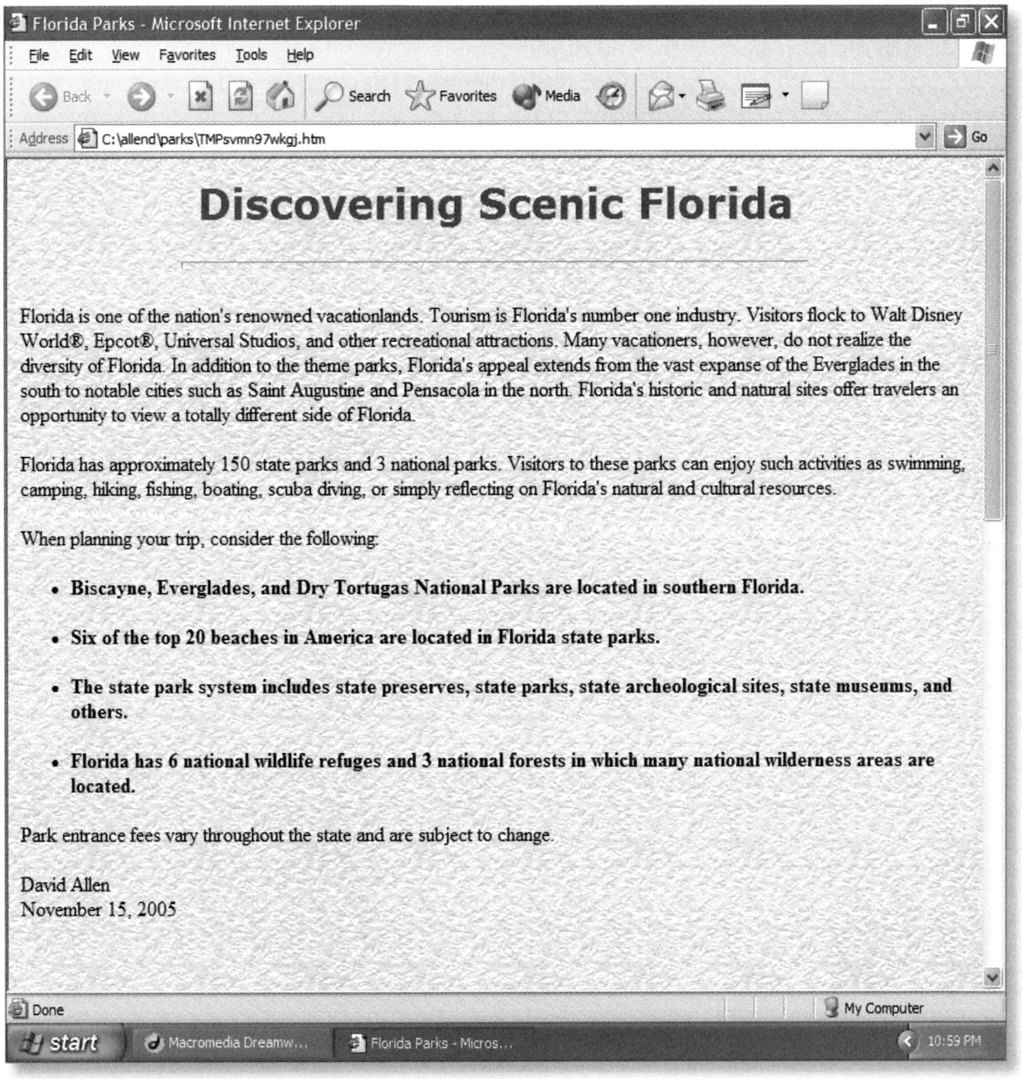

FIGURE 1-1

More About

Dreamweaver Features

For more information about Dreamweaver MX 2004 features, visit the Dreamweaver MX 2004 More About Web page (scsite.com/dreamweavermx04/more.htm) and then click Dreamweaver MX 2004 Features.

Starting Dreamweaver

If you are stepping through this project on a computer and you want your screen to agree with the Dreamweaver figures in this book, then you should change your screen's resolution to 800 × 600. The browser used to display the Web page figures is Internet Explorer. The browser text size is set to Medium.

Getting started in Dreamweaver is as easy as opening an existing HTML document or creating a new document. The Dreamweaver environment consists of toolbars, windows, objects, panels, inspectors, and tools you use to create your Web pages and to manage your Web site, which is a collection of Web pages. It is important to understand the basic concepts behind the Dreamweaver workspace and how to choose options, use inspectors and panels, and set preferences that best fit your work style.

The first time Dreamweaver MX 2004 is launched after the initial installation, a Workspace Setup dialog box is displayed with two options: Designer or Coder. This Workspace Setup choice is a one-time event. Programmers who work primarily with HTML and other languages generally select the Coder workspace. The Designer workspace contains a visual integrated workspace and is ideal for beginners and non-programmers. For the exercises in this book, select the Designer workspace.

Following the Workspace Setup choice, the Dreamweaver MX 2004 program starts. The settings on your computer determine what displays. By default, the Start page is displayed each time you start Dreamweaver. The Start page's visual representation is a good tool for beginners, but more proficient Dreamweaver users generally disable this feature. You disable the Start page at the end of this project. If you are opening Dreamweaver from a computer at your school, most likely the program is set up and ready to use.

To start Dreamweaver, Windows must be running. The following steps show how to start Dreamweaver or ask your instructor how to start Dreamweaver.

To Start Dreamweaver

1

- **Click the Start button on the Windows taskbar, point to All Programs on the Start menu, point to Macromedia on the All Programs submenu, and then point to Macromedia Dreamweaver MX 2004 on the Macromedia submenu.**

The Start menu, All Programs submenu, and Macromedia submenu are displayed (Figure 1-2). Your Start menu will display different programs than those in Figure 1-2.

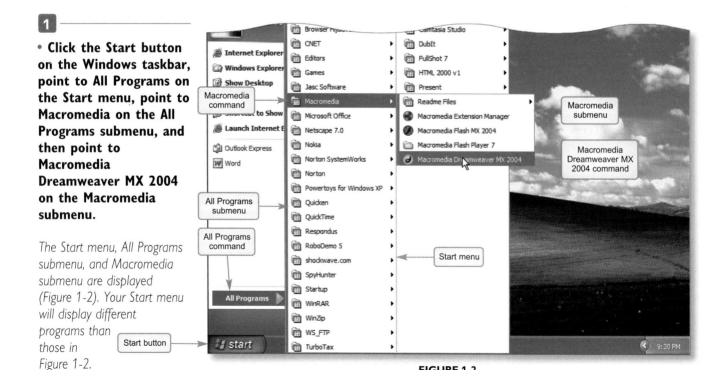

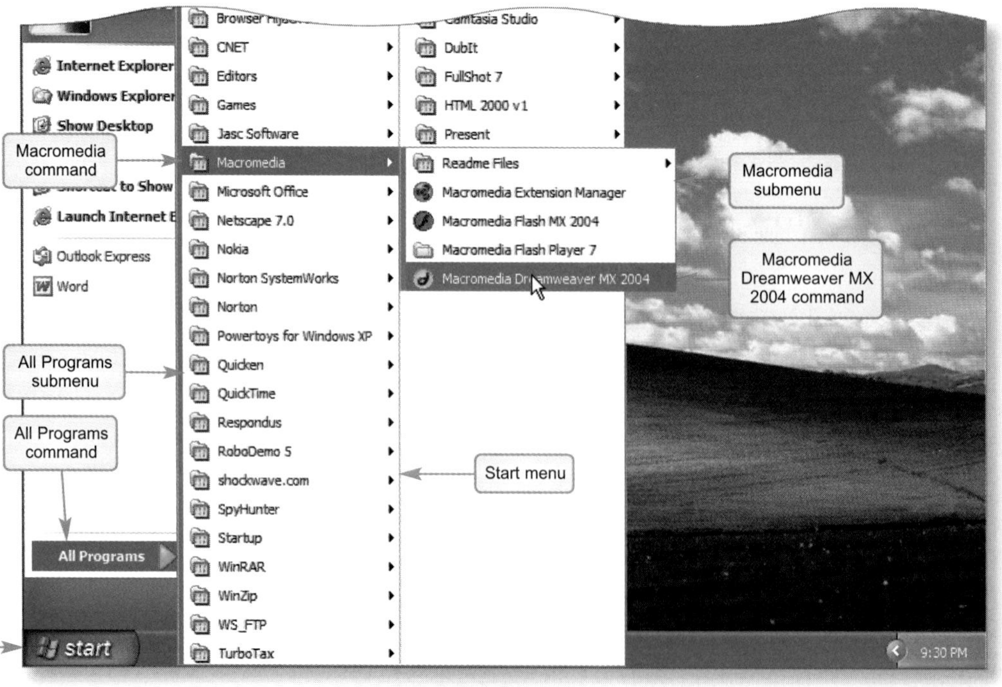

FIGURE 1-2

2

• Click Macromedia Dreamweaver MX 2004.

The Start page appears (Figure 1-3). A portion of the Start page is hidden by Dreamweaver panels. You disable the Start page at the end of this project.

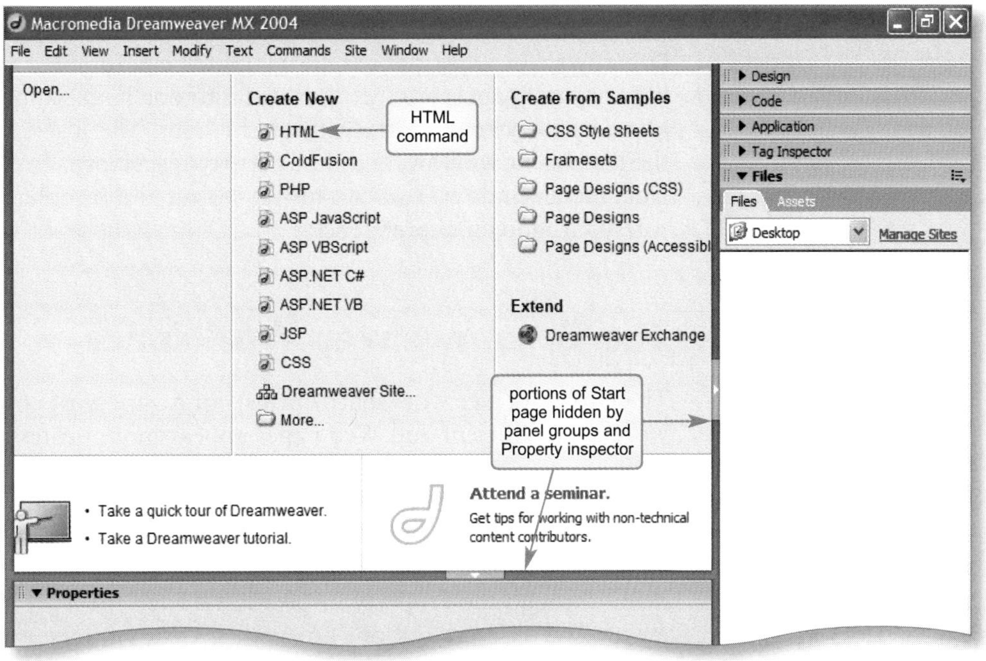

FIGURE 1-3

3

• Click HTML in the Create New column. If necessary, maximize the Dreamweaver window and the Document window by clicking the Maximize button in the upper-right corner of the windows.

• If necessary, click Window on the menu bar and then click Insert.

The Start page closes, and the Dreamweaver workspace is displayed (Figure 1-4). The Dreamweaver workspace contains menu names, toolbars, and panel groups. The Windows taskbar displays the Macromedia Dreamweaver MX 2004 button, indicating Dreamweaver is running.

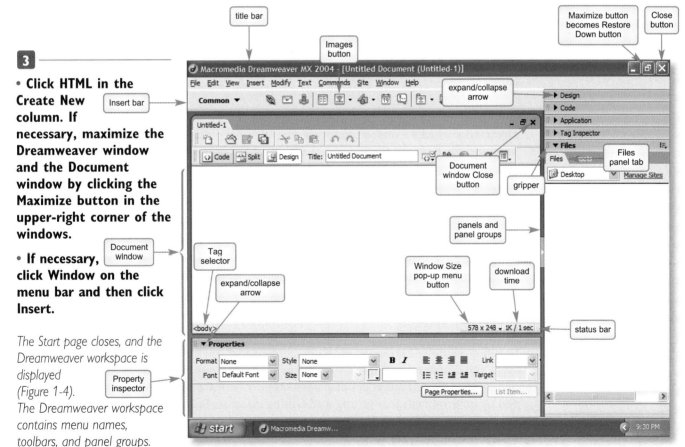

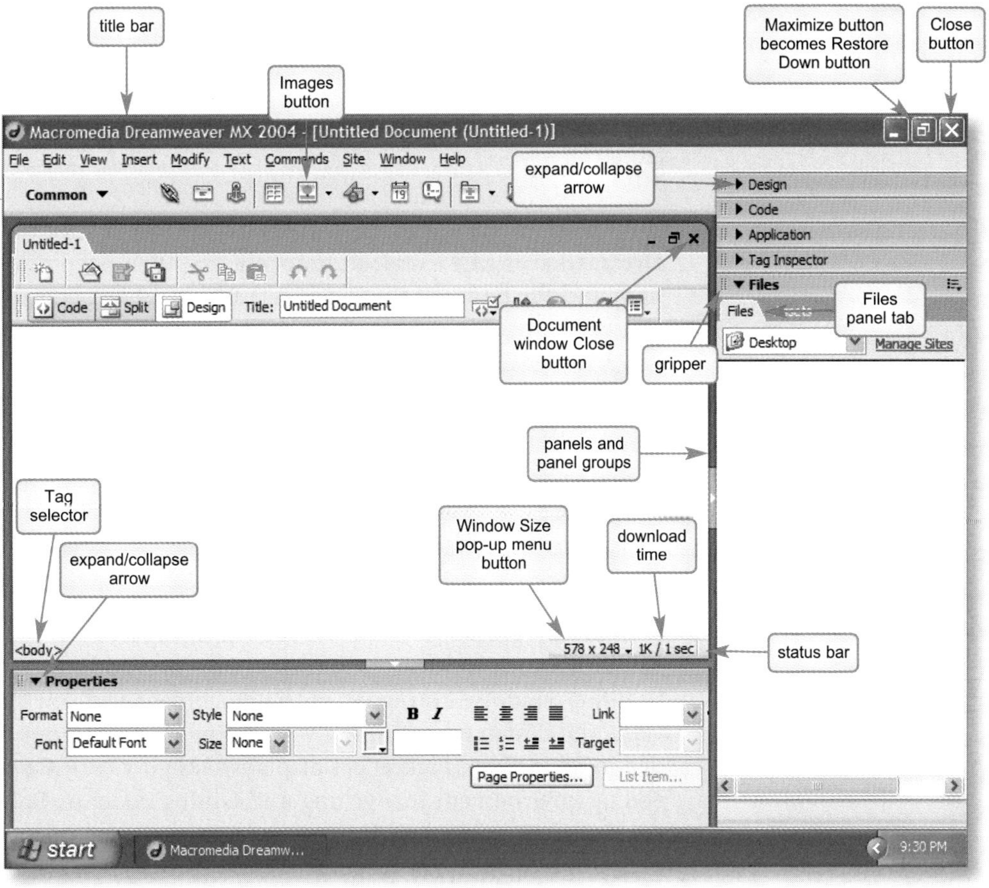

FIGURE 1-4

Other Ways

1. Double-click Dreamweaver icon on desktop

The screen in Figure 1-4 on the previous page shows a typical Dreamweaver workspace, with some of the more commonly used components displayed. The **Dreamweaver workspace** is an integrated environment in which the Document window and panels are incorporated into one larger application window. The panel groups are docked, or attached, on the right. The Insert bar is located at the top of the Document window, and the Property inspector is located at the bottom of the Document window. You can move, resize, and/or collapse the panels to accommodate your individual preferences.

The Dreamweaver Workspace

The Dreamweaver workspace consists of a variety of components to make your work more efficient and Web pages appear more professional. This section discusses the following components of the Dreamweaver workspace: title bar, Document window, panels and panel groups, status bar, menu bar, and toolbars.

As you learn to use each of these tools, you will discover some redundancy among these elements. To apply a Font tag, for instance, you can access the command through the Property inspector, through the Text menu, or through the context menu. The different options are available for various user preferences. The projects in this book present the more commonly used methods. The Other Ways boxes at the end of many of the step-by-step sequences give other ways to accomplish a task when they are available. As you become proficient working in the Dreamweaver environment, you will develop a technique for using the tools that best suits your personal preferences.

Title Bar

The **title bar** (Figure 1-4) displays the application name, Macromedia Dreamweaver MX 2004; in brackets, the Web page title; and, in parentheses, the file path and file name of the displayed Web page. In Figure 1-4, the title bar displays [Untitled Document (Untitled-1)]. Untitled Document represents the Web page title, and Untitled-1 represents the file path and file name. Following the file name, Dreamweaver displays an asterisk if you have made changes that have not yet been saved. After you give a Web page a title and save the document, the title bar reflects these changes by displaying the path and title and removing the asterisk.

Document Window

The **Document window** displays the current document, or Web page, including text, tables, graphics, and other items. In Figure 1-4, the Document window is blank. The Document window is similar in appearance to the Internet Explorer or Netscape browser window. You work in the Document window in one of three views: **Design view**, the design environment where you assemble your Web page elements and design your page (Figure 1-4 displays Design view); **Code view**, which is a hand-coding environment for writing and editing code; or **Split view**, which allows you to see both Code view and Design view for the same document in a single window. When you open a new document in Dreamweaver, the default view is Design view. These views are discussed in detail in Project 2.

Panels and Panel Groups

Panel groups are sets of related panels docked together below one heading. Panels provide control over a wide range of Dreamweaver commands and functions. Each panel group can be expanded or collapsed, and can be docked or undocked with other panel groups. Panel groups also can be docked to the integrated Document window. This makes it easy to access the panels you need without cluttering your workspace. Panels within a panel group are displayed as tabs.

Some panels, such as the Property inspector and the Insert bar, are stand-alone panels. The **Insert bar** allows quick access to objects and behaviors. It contains buttons for creating various types of objects, such as images, tables, layers, frames, and tags, and inserting them into a document. Each object is a piece of HTML code that allows you to set various attributes as you insert it. For example, you can insert a table by clicking the Table button on the Insert bar Common category and then set the table attributes through the Property inspector. The buttons on the Insert bar are organized into several categories, which you can switch through a pop-up menu on the left side of the Insert bar. Some categories also have buttons with pop-up menus. When you select an option from a pop-up menu, it becomes the default action for the button. The default position for the Insert bar is at the top of the Document window (Figure 1-4 on page DW 33). When you start Dreamweaver, the category in which you were last working is displayed.

The **Property inspector** (Figure 1-4) displays settings for the selected element's properties or attributes. This panel is context-sensitive, meaning it changes based on the selected element, which can include text, tables, images, and other elements. When Dreamweaver starts, the Property inspector is positioned at the bottom of the Document window and displays text properties if a Document window is open. Otherwise, the Property inspector is blank.

To expand or collapse a panel group, click the expand/collapse arrow to the left of the group's name; to undock and move a panel group, drag the gripper at the left edge of the group's title bar (Figure 1-4). To open panels, use the Window menu. Each panel is explained in detail as it is used in the projects throughout the book.

More About

Panel Groups

To drag a floating (undocked) panel group without docking it, drag the panel group by the bar above its title bar. The panel group does not dock as long as it is not dragged by its gripper.

Status Bar

The **status bar** at the bottom of the Document window (Figure 1-4) provides additional information about the document you are creating. The status bar presents the following information:

- **Tag selector:** Displays the hierarchy of tags surrounding the current selection. Click any tag in the hierarchy to select that tag and all its contents.
- **Window Size pop-up menu button:** Displays the Window Size pop-up menu, which includes the window's current dimensions (in pixels).
- **Estimated document size and download time:** Displays the size and estimated download time of the current page. Dreamweaver MX 2004 calculates the size based on the entire contents of the page, including all linked objects such as images and plug-ins.

Vertical Bar

A vertical bar separates the panel groups, and a horizontal bar separates the Property inspector from the Document window. Both bars contain an expand/collapse arrow. Clicking this arrow hides/displays the panel groups and the Property inspector (Figure 1-5 on the next page). If your screen resolution is set to 800 × 600, a portion of the Property inspector does not display when the panel groups are expanded.

Menu Bar

The **menu bar** displays the Dreamweaver menu names (Figure 1-5). Each menu contains a list of commands you can use to perform tasks such as opening, saving, modifying, previewing, and inserting data into your Web page. When you point to a menu name on the menu bar, the area of the menu bar containing the name is highlighted.

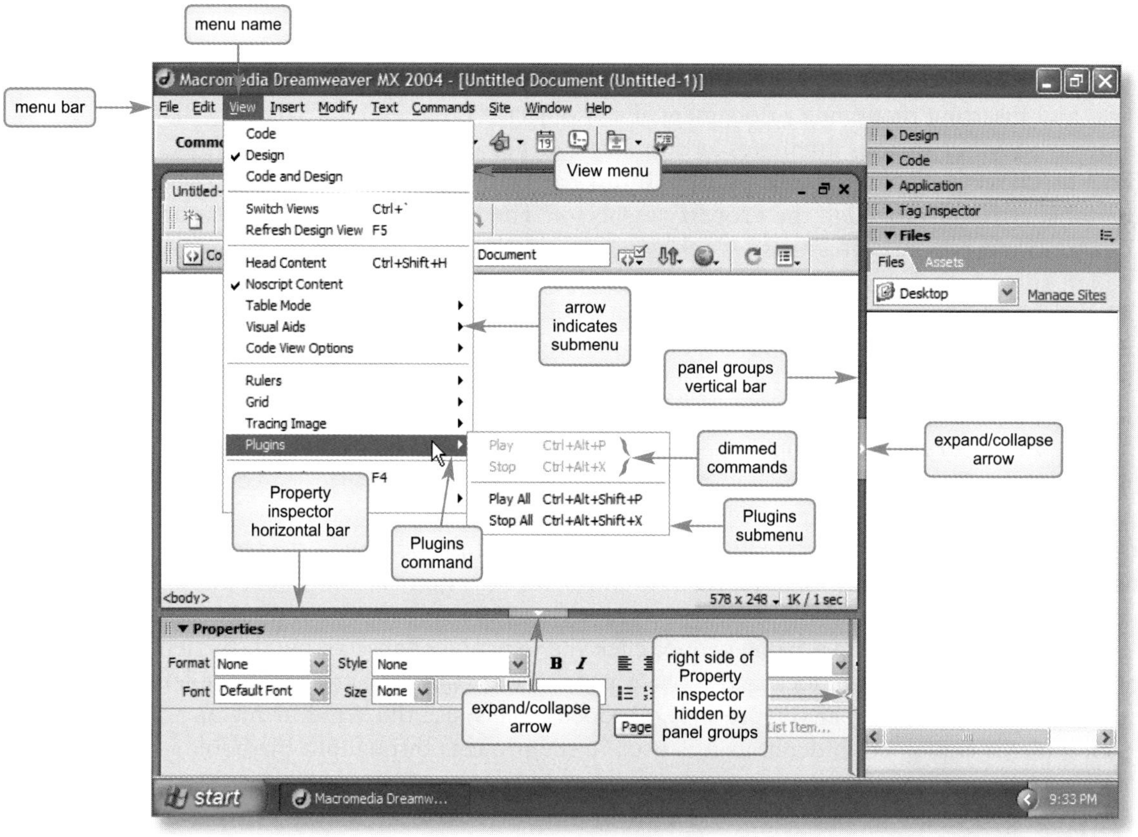

FIGURE 1-5

To display a menu, such as the View menu (Figure 1-5), click the menu name on the menu bar. If you point to a menu command that has an arrow at its right edge, a submenu displays another list of commands. Many menus display some commands that appear gray, or dimmed, instead of black, which indicates they are not available for the current selection.

Toolbars

Dreamweaver contains two toolbars: the Document toolbar and the Standard toolbar. You can choose to display or hide the toolbars by clicking View on the menu bar and then clicking Toolbars. If a toolbar name has a check mark next to it, it is displayed in the window. To hide the toolbar, click the name of the toolbar with the check mark, and it no longer displays.

The **Document toolbar** (Figure 1-6 on the next page) is the default toolbar that displays in the Document window. It contains buttons that provide different views of the Document window (e.g., Code, Split, and Design) and some common operations, such as No Browser Check Errors, File Management, Preview/Debug in Browser, Check Cross-Browser Compatibility, Web Page Title, Refresh Design View, and View Options. All View option commands also are available through the View menu.

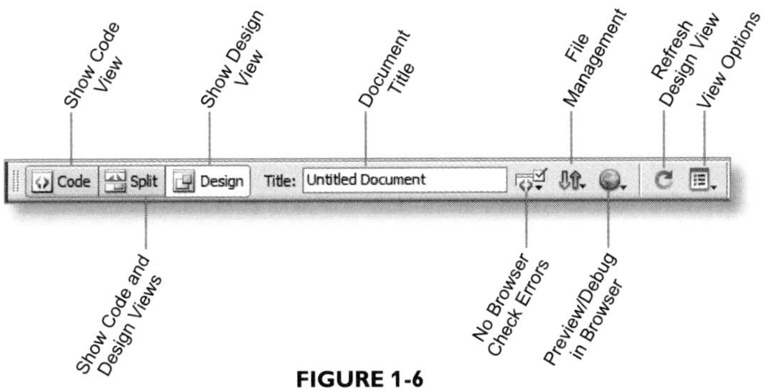

FIGURE 1-6

The **Standard toolbar** (Figure 1-7) contains buttons for common operations from the File and Edit menus: New, Open, Save, Save All, Cut, Copy, Paste, Undo, and Redo. The Standard toolbar does not display by default in the Dreamweaver Document window when you first start Dreamweaver. You can display the Standard toolbar through the Toolbars command on the View menu, or by right-clicking a toolbar anywhere but on a button and then clicking Standard on the context menu. Similar to other toolbars and panels, you can dock/undock and move the Standard toolbar, so it may be displayed in a different location on your screen.

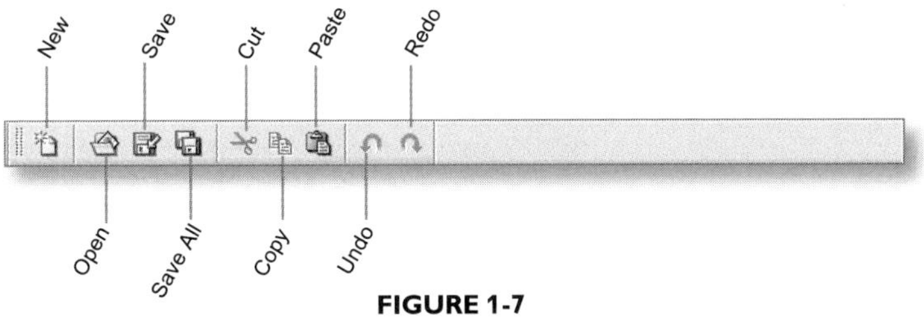

FIGURE 1-7

Opening and Closing Panels

The Dreamweaver workspace accommodates different styles of working and levels of expertise. Through the workspace, you can open and close the panel groups and display/hide other Dreamweaver features as needed. To open a panel group, select and then click the name of a panel on the Window menu. Closing unused panels provides uncluttered workspace in the Document window. To close an individual panel group, click Close panel group on the Options pop-up menu accessed through the panel group's title bar (Figure 1-8 on the next page). To expand/collapse a panel, click the panel's expand/collapse arrow at the left of the group's name.

Opening and closing each panel individually is a time-consuming task. Dreamweaver provides a shortcut to accomplish this job quickly. The F4 key is a toggle key that opens and/or closes all panels and inspectors at one time. The step on the next page illustrates how to close all open panels.

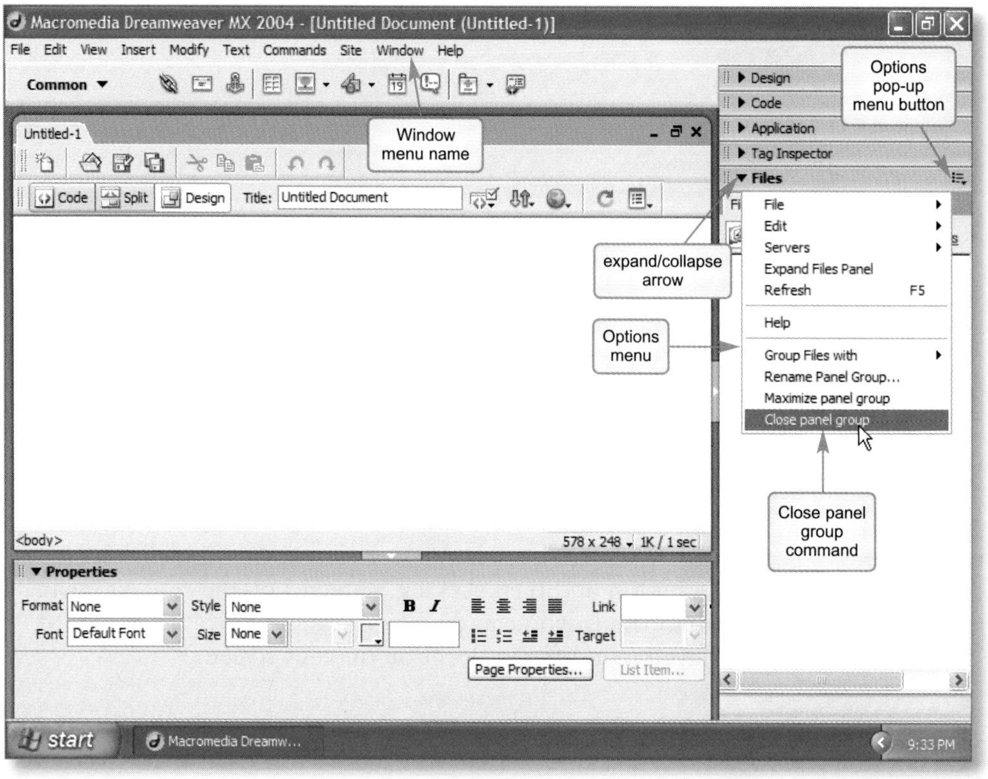

FIGURE 1-8

To Close and Open Panels

1

- **Press the F4 key.**

All the open panels and inspectors close, and the maximum workspace is available in the Document window (Figure 1-9).

2

- **Press the F4 key again to redisplay the panels.**

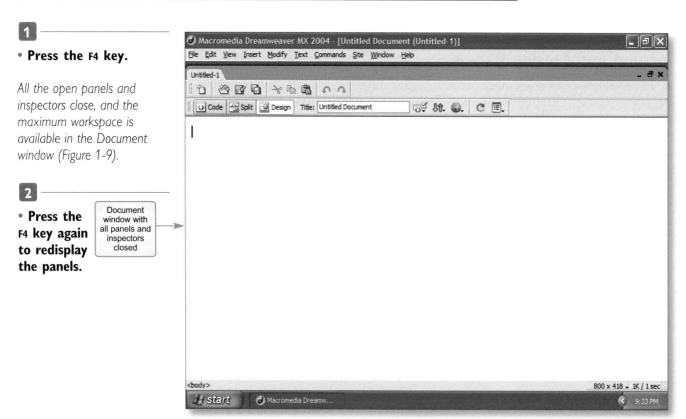

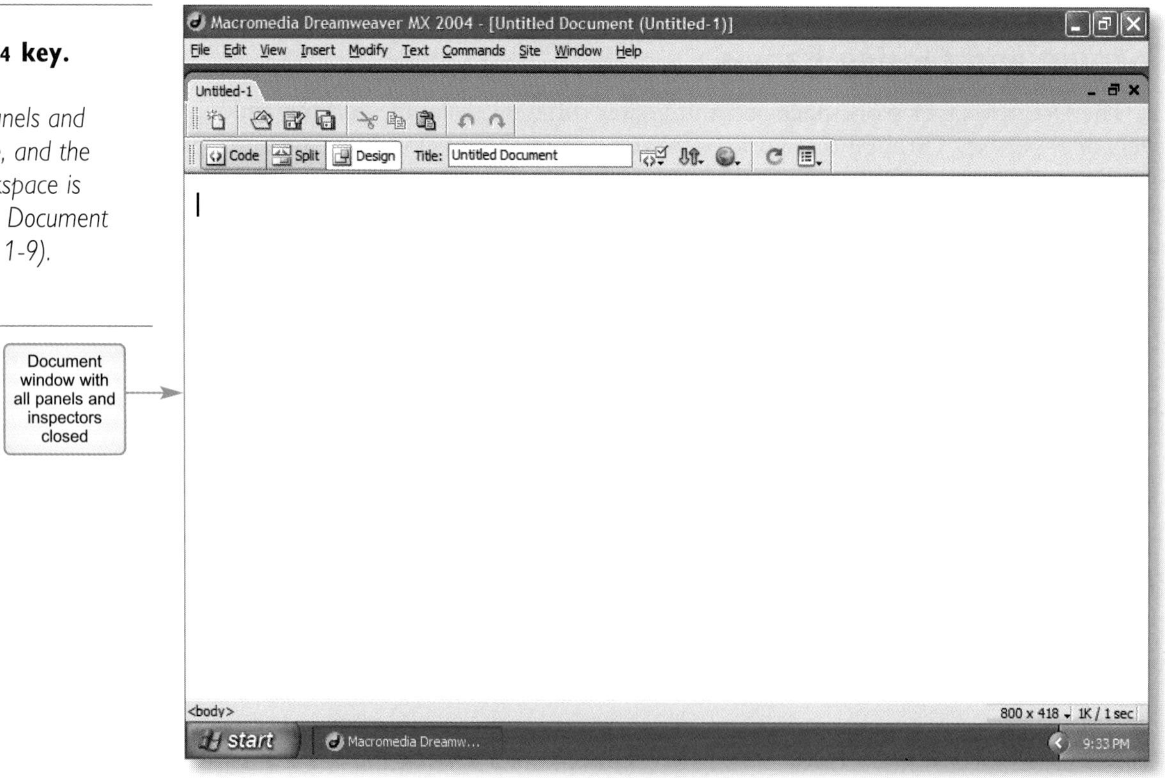

FIGURE 1-9

Defining a Local Site

Web design and Web site management are two important skills that a builder of Web sites must understand and apply. Dreamweaver MX 2004 is a site creation and management tool. To use Dreamweaver efficiently, you first must define the local site. After defining the local site, you then publish to a remote site. Publishing to a remote site is discussed in Project 3 and Appendix C.

The general definition of a **site**, or Web site, is a set of linked documents with shared attributes, such as related topics, a similar design, or a shared purpose. In Dreamweaver, however, site can refer to any of the following:

- A **Web site**, which is a set of pages on a server that are viewed through a Web browser by a visitor to the site.
- A **remote site**, which are files on the server that make up a Web site, from the author's point of view rather than a visitor's point of view.
- A **local site**, which are files on your local disk that correspond to the files on the remote site. You edit the files on your local disk, and then upload them to the remote site.
- A **Dreamweaver site definition**, which is a set of defining characteristics for a local site, plus information on how the local site corresponds to a remote site.

All Dreamweaver Web sites begin with a local root folder. As you become familiar with Dreamweaver and complete the projects in this book, you will find references to a **local root folder**, a **root folder**, and **root**. These terms are interchangeable. This folder is no different from any other folder on your computer's hard drive or other storage media, except for the way in which Dreamweaver views it. When Dreamweaver looks for Web pages, links, images, and other files, the program defaults to the designated root folder. Any media within the Web site that are outside of the root folder will not display when the Web site is previewed in a Web browser. Within the root folder, you can create additional folders or subfolders to organize images and other elements. A **subfolder** (also called a **nested folder**) is a folder inside another folder.

Dreamweaver provides two options to define a site and create the hierarchy: create the root folder and any subfolders, or create the pages and then create the folders when saving the files. In this book, you create the root folder and subfolders and then create the Web pages.

One of Dreamweaver's more prominent organizational tools is its Files panel. Use the **Files panel** for standard file maintenance operations, such as the following:

- Creating files
- Viewing, opening, and moving files
- Creating folders
- Deleting items
- Managing a site

The Files panel enables you to view a site, including local, remote, and testing server files associated with a selected site. In this project, you view only the local site.

Creating the Local Root Folder and Subfolders

Several options are available to create and manage your local root folder and subfolders: Dreamweaver's Files panel, Dreamweaver's Site Definition feature, or Windows file management. In this book, you use Dreamweaver's Site Definition feature to create the local root folder and subfolders, Dreamweaver's Files panel to manage and edit your files and folders, and Windows file management to download the data files.

To organize and create a Web site and understand how you access Web documents, it is important to understand paths and folders. The term, path, sometimes is confusing for new users of the Web. It is, however, a simple concept: A **path** is the succession of folders that must be navigated to get from one folder to another. In the DOS world, folders are referred to as **directories**. These two terms often are used interchangeably.

A typical path structure has a **master folder**, usually called the root and designated by the symbol "\". This root folder contains within it all of the other subfolders or nested folders. Further, each subfolder may contain additional subfolders or nested folders. These folders contain the Web site files. One of the more commonly used subfolders contains the site's images.

Because many files are required for a Dreamweaver Web site, it is advisable to create the projects using another type of media rather than the floppy drive (A:). Steps in this project instruct you to create the local site on the C:\ drive, on the computer's hard drive. It is suggested, however, that you check with your instructor to verify the location and path you will use to create and save your local Web site. Other options may include a Zip drive, USB flash drive, or a network drive.

For this book, you first create a local root folder using your last name and first initial. Examples in this book use David Allen as the Web site author. Thus, David's local root folder is allend. Next, you create a subfolder and name it parks. Finally, you create another subfolder within parks and name it images. All Florida Parks related files and subfolders are stored within the parks folder. When you navigate through this folder hierarchy, you are navigating along the path. The path and folder within the Florida Parks Web site are C:\allend\parks\. The path to the images folder is C:\allend\parks\images\. When you create your folders, you will use your last name and first initial for the root folder. In all references to allend, substitute your last name and first initial.

Using Site Definition to Create a Local Site

You create a site definition using Dreamweaver's Site Definition dialog box. Two options are available: Basic or Advanced. The Basic method, or **Site Definition Wizard**, guides you through site setup step by step and takes you through a series of six screens. In the Advanced method, all options are contained on one screen. The Advanced method is a more efficient method. Using this view, you set all the same basic information that the Site Wizard collects, plus additional options such as the following:

- **Refresh local file list:** Updates the site list whenever a new file is added to the site folder; checked by default
- **Enable cache**: Allocates memory to store frequently used site data; checked by default
- **Default images folder:** An option feature to specify the location of images in the site
- **HTTP address**: Used to define the URL of a Web site and to verify absolute links

The two main categories in a site definition are **Local Info** (Local Information) and **Remote Info** (Remote Information). In this project, you create the local site definition using the Advanced method. The site definition is stored in the Windows registry and is not part of the site. If you use removable media to store your files and move to another computer, you must recreate the site definition on that computer. Remote site definition is discussed in Project 3.

After you have completed the Site definition, the hierarchy structure displays in Dreamweaver's Files panel. This hierarchy structure is similar to the Windows XP file organization. The Files panel provides a view of the devices and folders on your computer and shows how these devices and folders are organized. A small device icon or folder icon is displayed next to each object in the list. The device icon represents a device such as the Desktop or a disk drive, and the folder icon represents a folder. Many of these icons have a plus or minus sign next to them, which indicates whether the device or folder contains additional folders. The plus and minus signs are controls that you can click to expand or collapse the view of the file hierarchy. In the Files panel, the site folders and files appear in a different color than non-site folders and files so that you easily can distinguish between the two.

You define a local site by telling Dreamweaver where you plan to store local files. Use the Site Definition Advanced approach and the following steps to show how to create a local Web site.

To Use Site Definition to Create a Local Web Site

1

- **Click Site on the menu bar and then point to Manage Sites.**

The Site menu is displayed, and the Manage Sites command is selected (Figure 1-10).

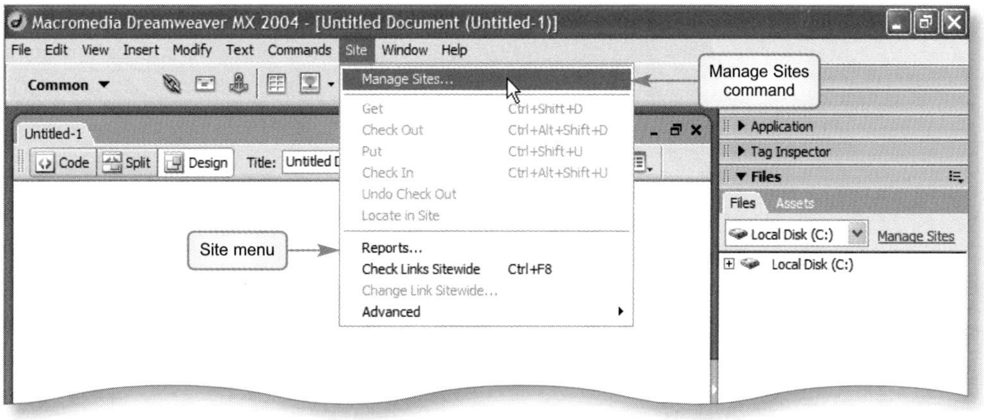

FIGURE 1-10

2

- **Click Manage Sites.**

The Manage Sites dialog box is displayed (Figure 1-11).

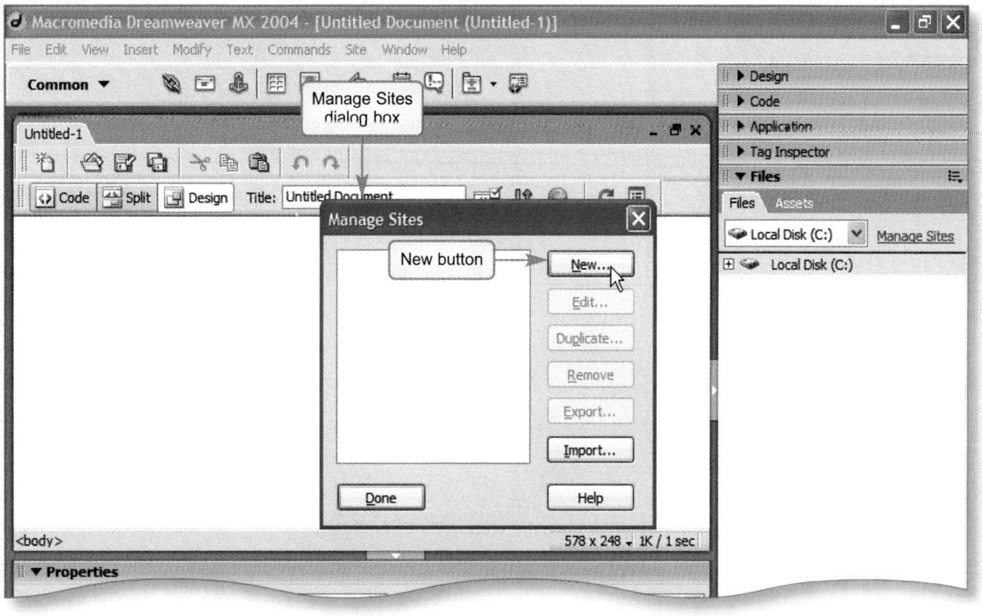

FIGURE 1-11

3

- **Click the New button.**

A pop-up menu is displayed (Figure 1-12).

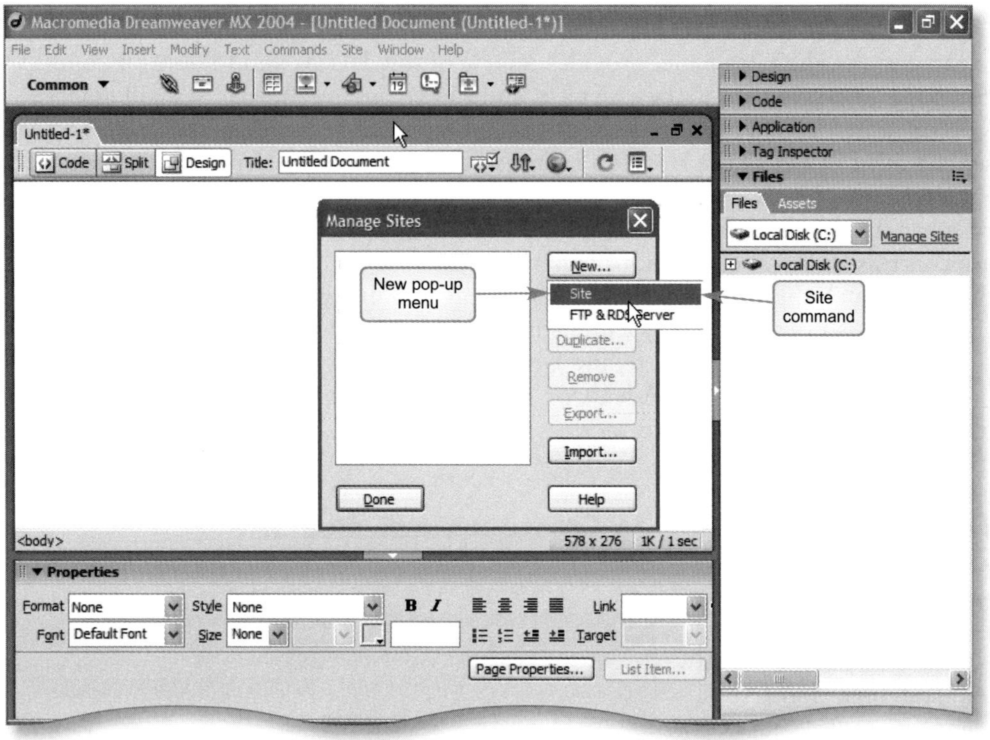

FIGURE 1-12

4

- **Click Site on the pop-up menu.**
- **If necessary, click the Advanced tab. Verify that Local Info is selected in the Category column.**

The Site Definition window is displayed, and the Advanced tab is selected. Unnamed Site 1 is highlighted in the Site name text box (Figure 1-13).

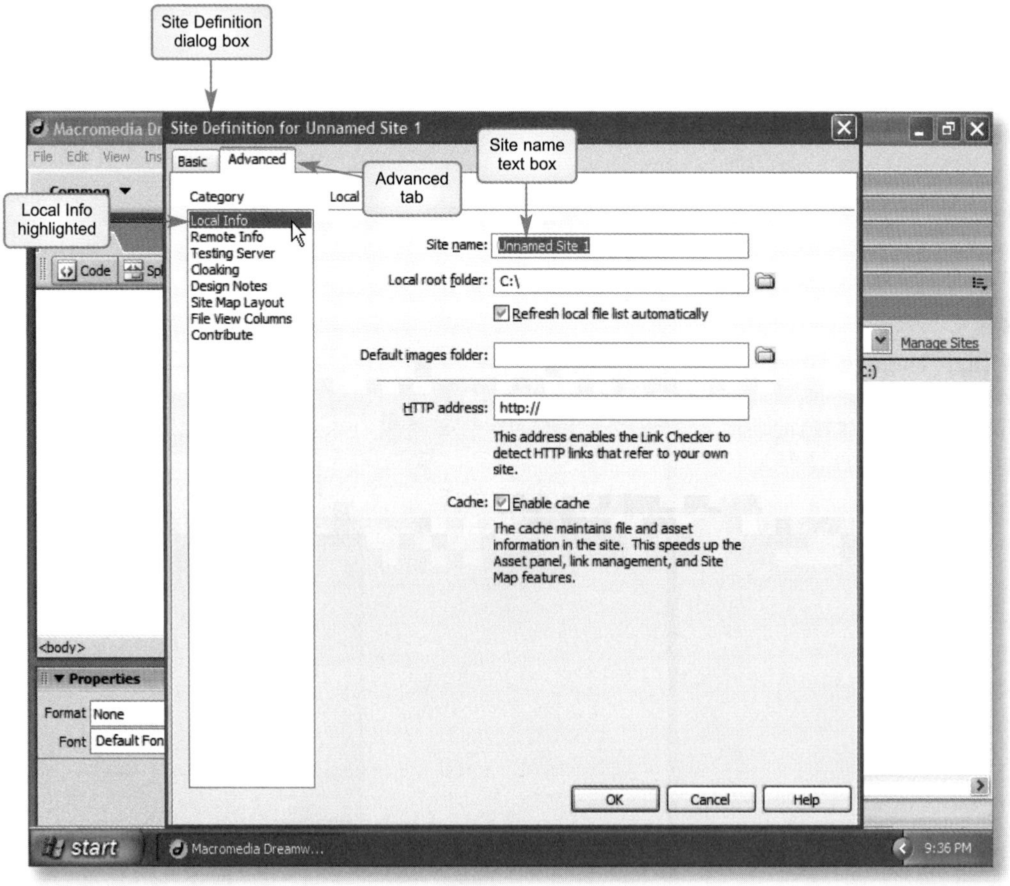

FIGURE 1-13

5

• **Type** `Florida Parks` **as the site name.**

This name is for your reference only. It is not part of the path and is not visible to viewers of your site (Figure 1-14).

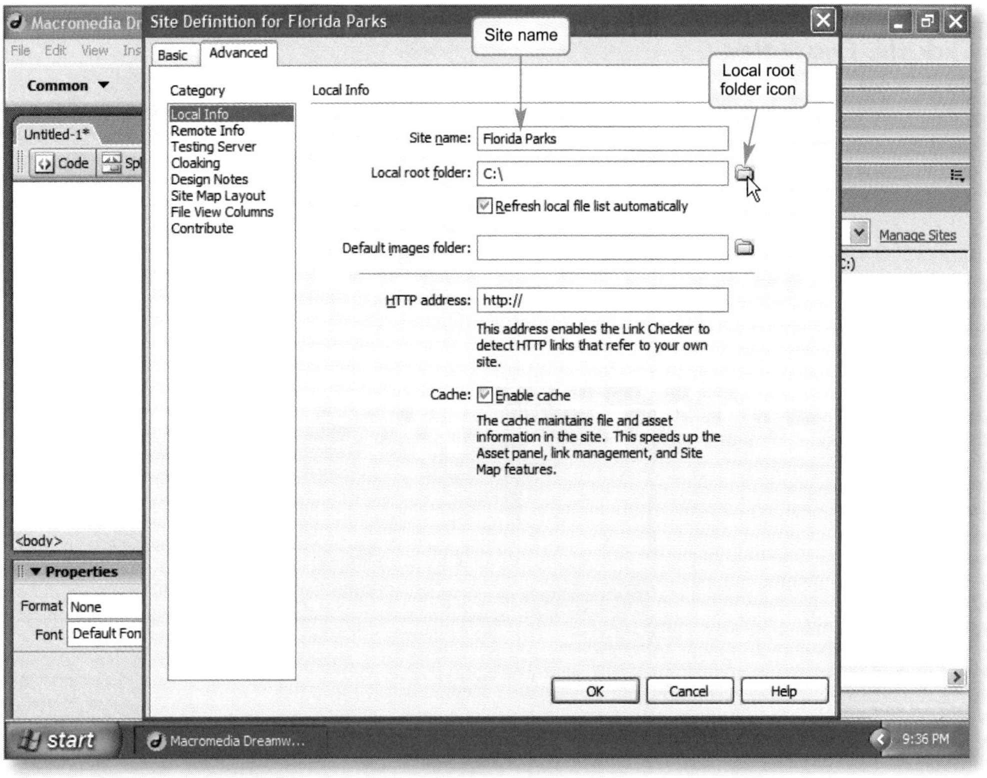

FIGURE 1-14

6

• **Click the folder icon to the right of the Local root folder text box.**

• **If you are creating and saving your sites at another location or on other media, navigate to that location and substitute the location for Local Disk (C):.**

The Choose local root folder for site dialog box is displayed. Local Disk (C): appears in the Select text box (Figure 1-15).

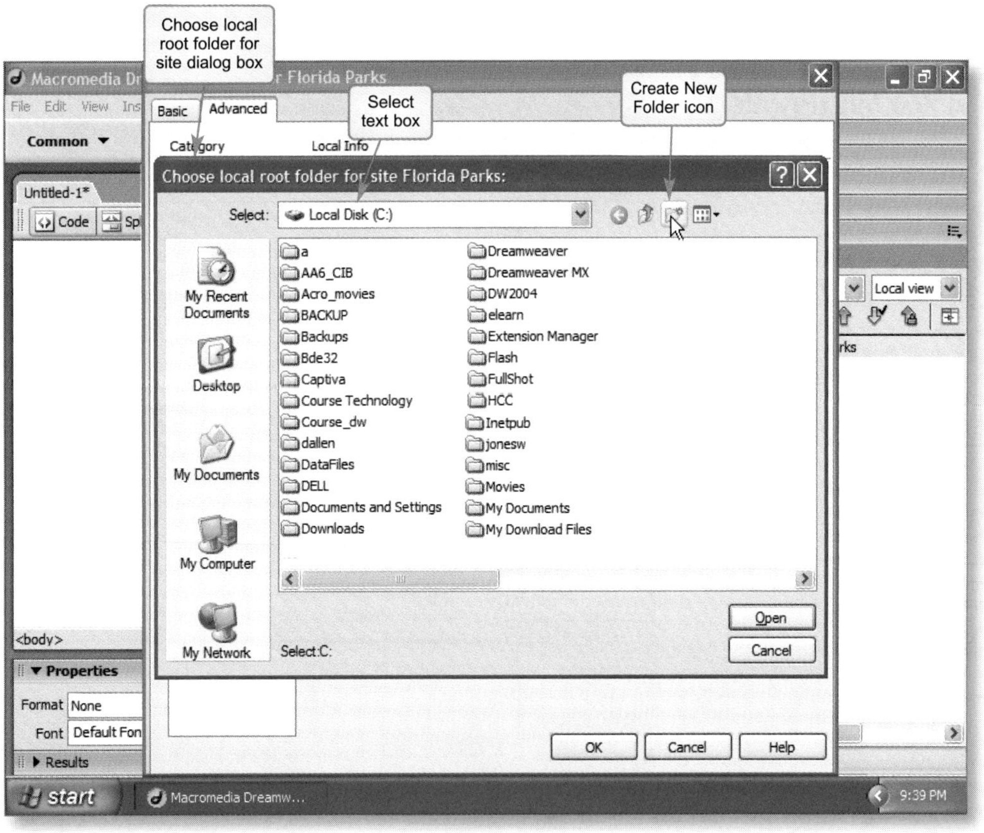

FIGURE 1-15

7

• **Click the Create New Folder icon.**

The New Folder (1) text box is displayed (Figure 1-16). New Folder(1) is highlighted. The folder number on your computer may be different or absent.

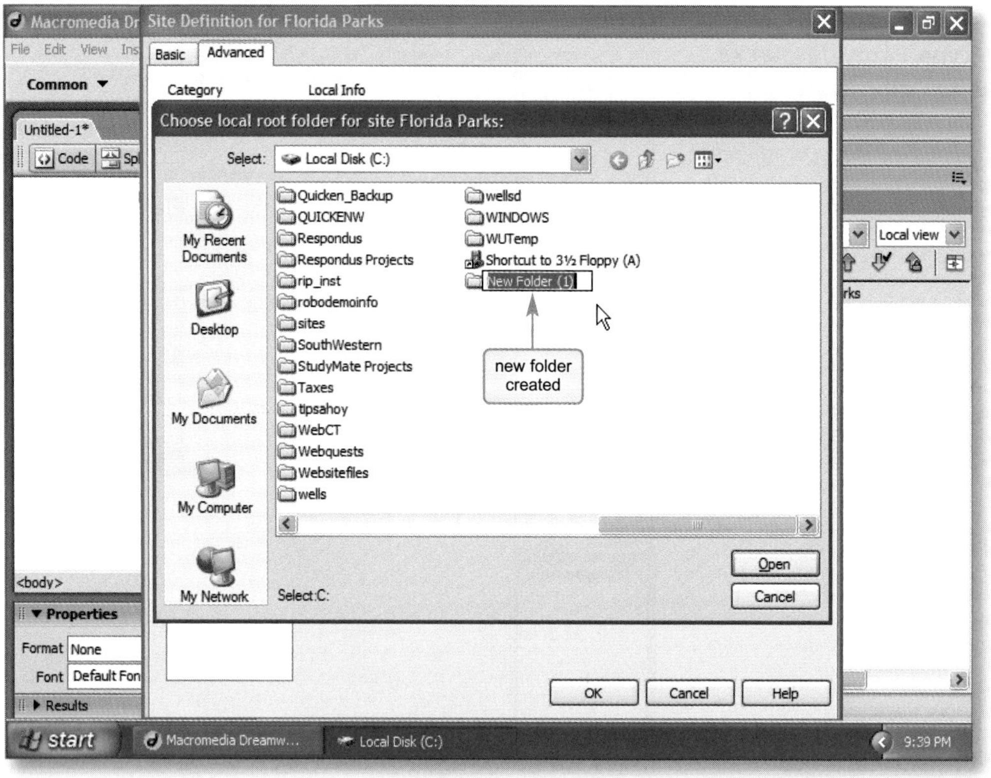

FIGURE 1-16

8

• **Type your last name and first initial (with no spaces between your last name and initial) in the folder text box.**

• **Press the ENTER key to select the folder.**

Your last name and first initial are displayed in the folder's text box (Figure 1-17).

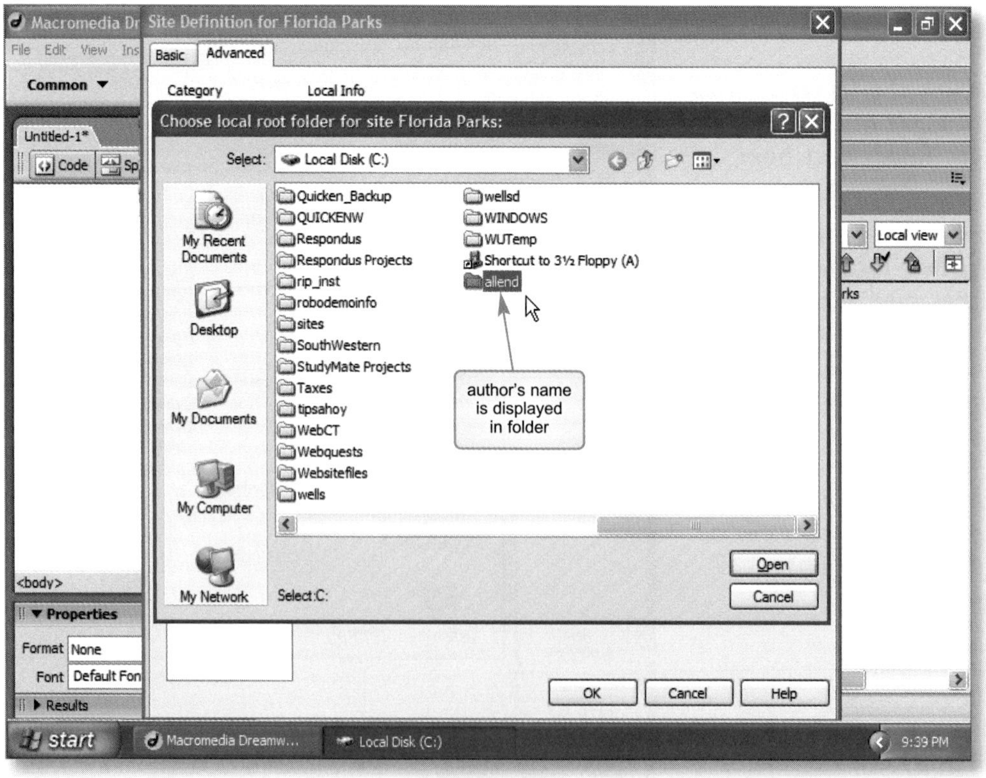

FIGURE 1-17

9

• **Double-click the your name folder.**

The author's folder name is displayed in the Select text box (Figure 1-18).

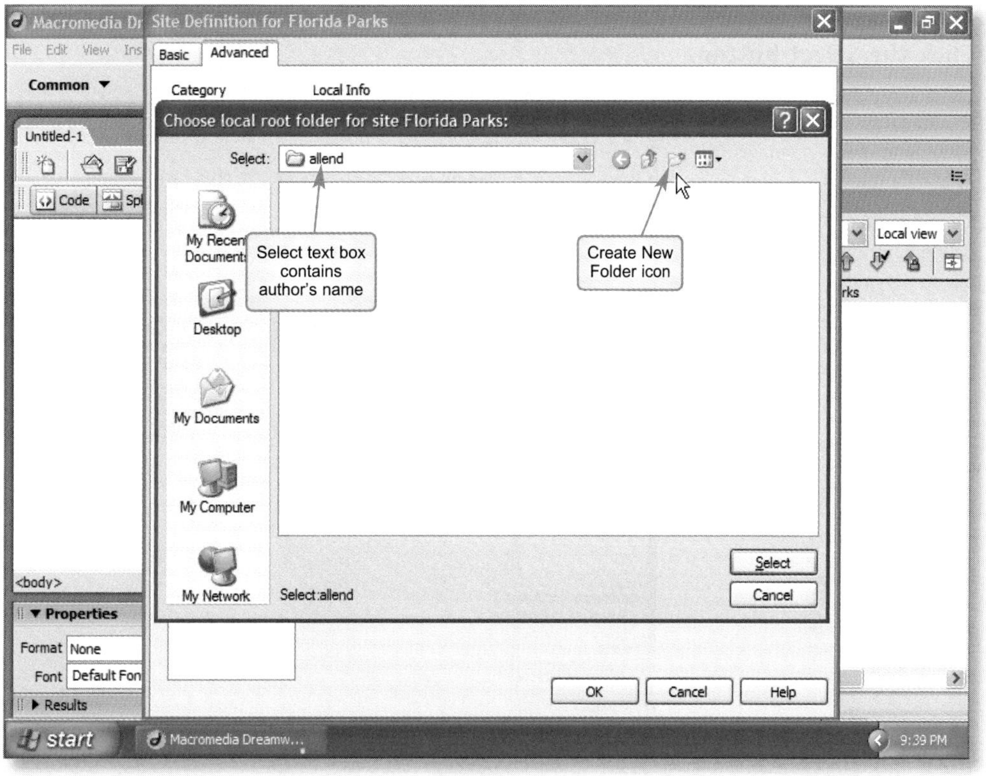

FIGURE 1-18

10

• **Click the Create New Folder icon.**

• **Type** `parks` **as the name of the new folder and then press the ENTER key.**

• **Double-click the parks folder name.**

The parks subfolder is created, and the folder name is displayed in the Select text box (Figure 1-19).

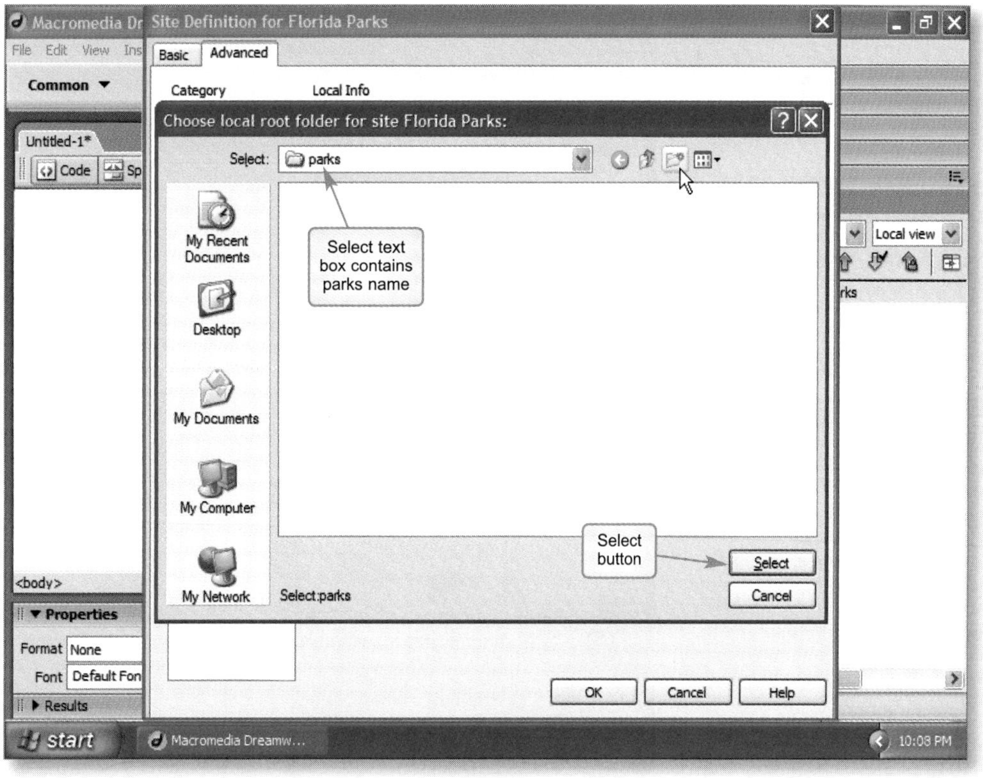

FIGURE 1-19

11

• **Click the Select button.**

The Site Definition dialog box is displayed, the Advanced tab is selected, and the Local root folder text box contains the C:\allend\parks\ path (Figure 1-20).

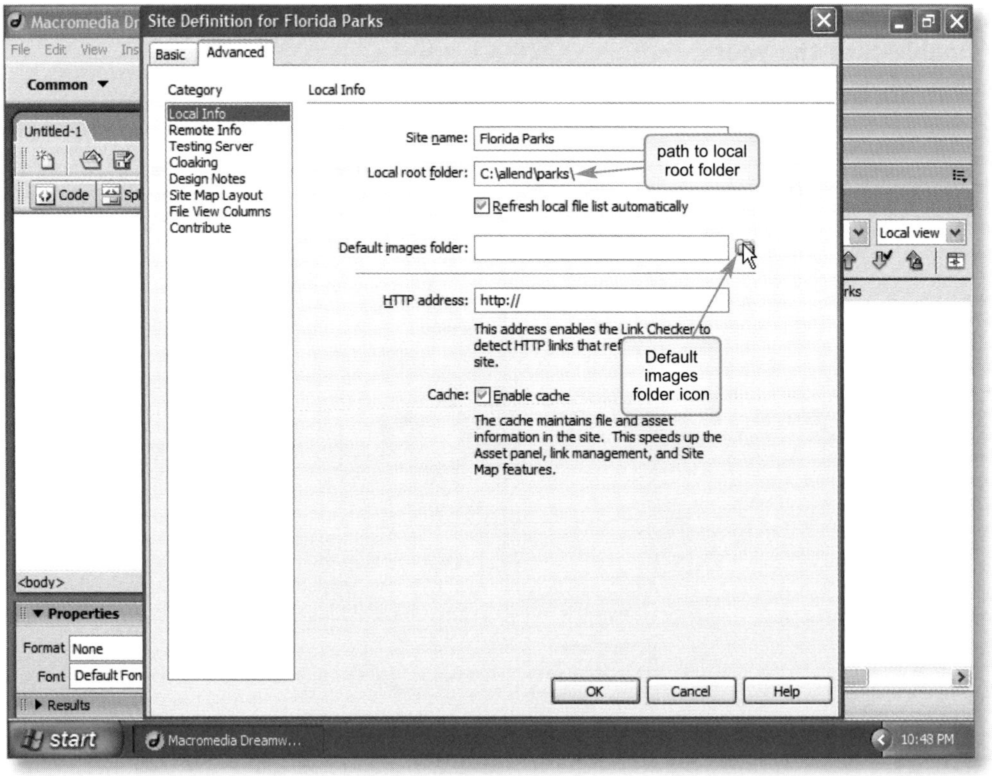

FIGURE 1-20

12

• **Click the folder icon to the right of the Default images folder text box.**

• **Navigate to the your name\parks folder.**

• **Click the Create New Folder icon.**

• **Type** `images` **as the name of the new folder and then press the ENTER key. Double-click the images folder name.**

An images subfolder is created, and the folder name is displayed in the Select text box (Figure 1-21).

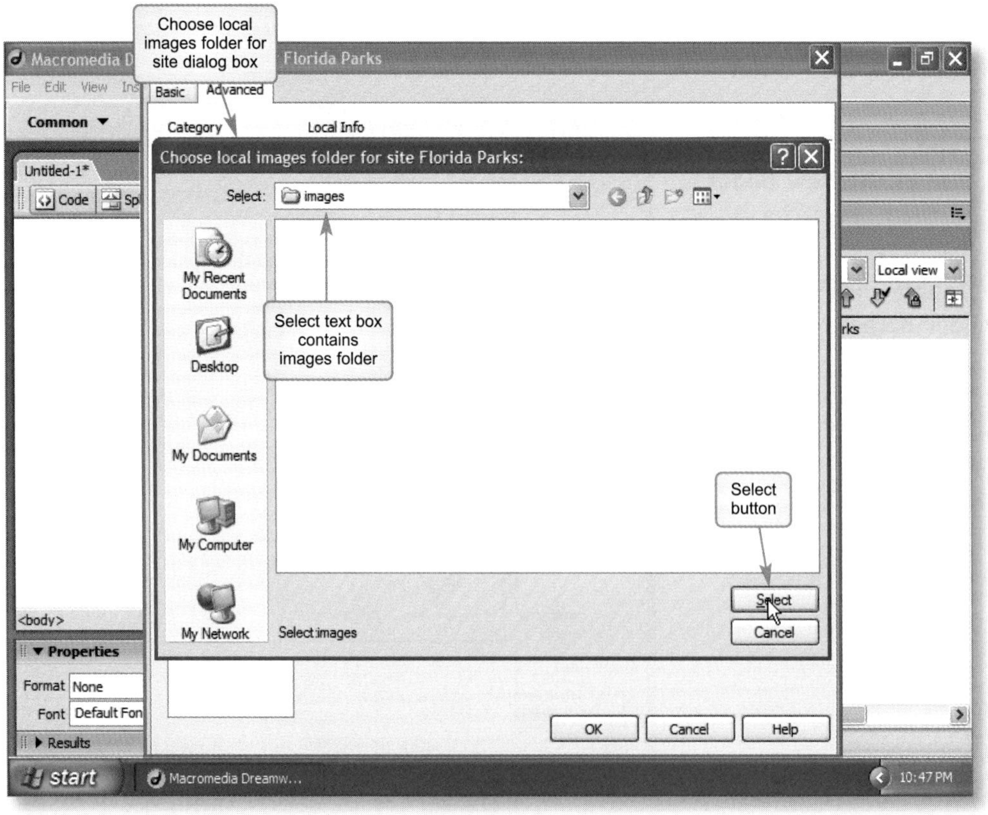

FIGURE 1-21

13

- **Click the Select button.**
- **Verify that the Refresh local file list automatically and the Enable cache check boxes are selected in the Site Definition dialog box.**
- **Point to the OK button.**

The Site Definition dialog box is displayed, and the path for the default images folder is displayed in the Default images folder text box (Figure 1-22).

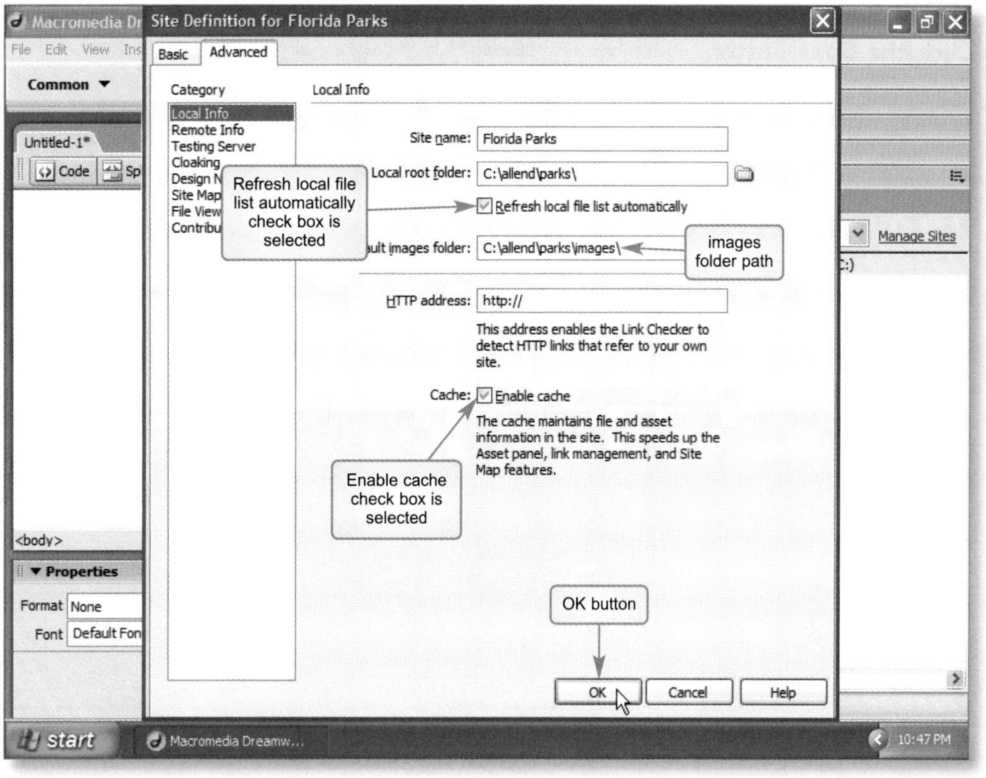

FIGURE 1-22

14

- **Click the OK button.**

The Manage Sites dialog box is displayed, and the Florida Parks site is added to the dialog box (Figure 1-23).

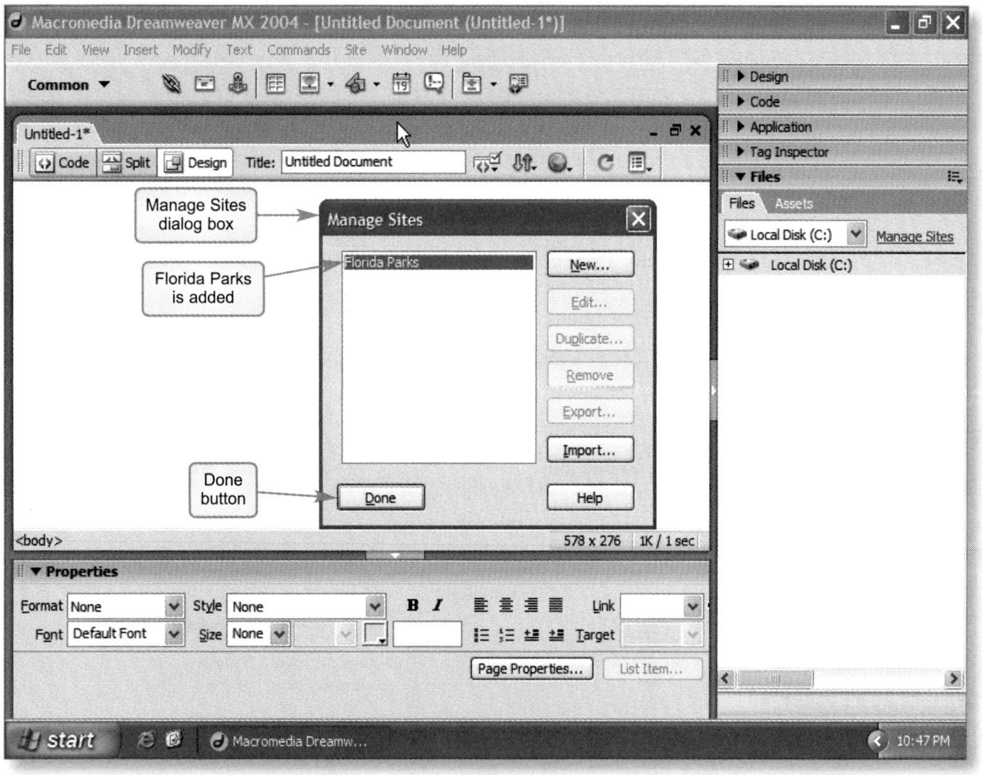

FIGURE 1-23

15

• **Click the Done button.**

The Dreamweaver workspace is displayed. The Florida Parks Web site hierarchy is displayed in the File panels (Figure 1-24).

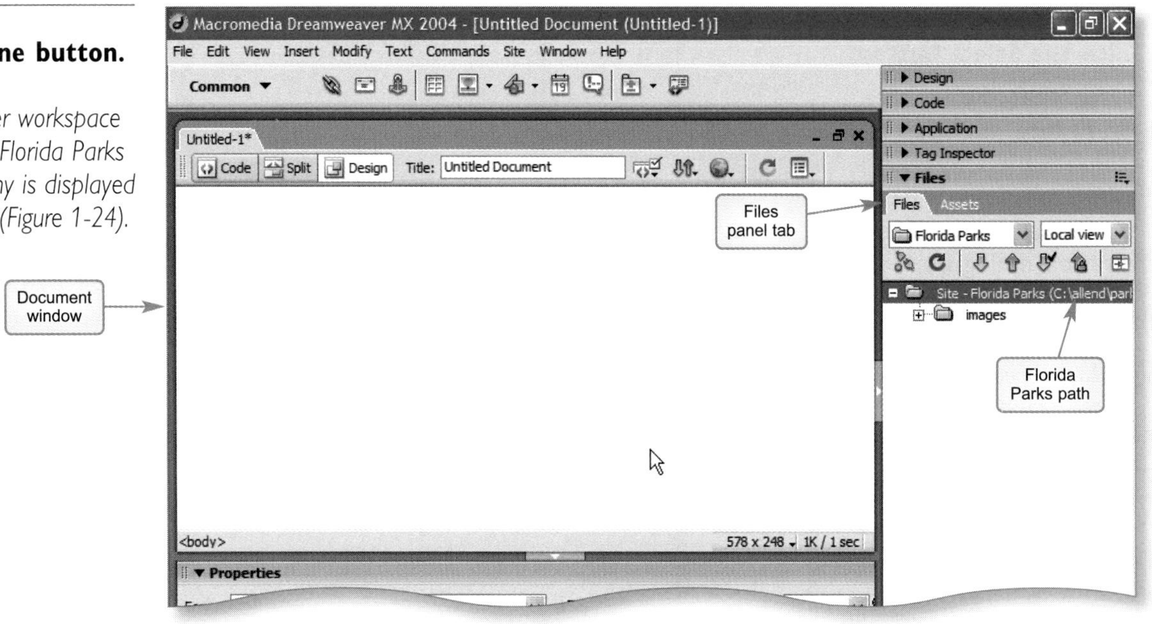

FIGURE 1-24

Other Ways

1. Click Site menu, click New Site, click Basic tab

Copying Data Files to the Florida Parks Folder

Your data disk contains background images for Project 1. You can copy data files one by one through the Dreamweaver Files panel as you progress through this project. Alternatively, using the Windows My Computer option, you can establish the basic framework for the parks Web site by copying all the files and images at one time. Windows provides several ways through the View menu for you to arrange and identify your files when viewing them: Show in Groups, Thumbnails, Tiles, Filmstrip, Icons, List, and Details. The figures in this book use the List view when using the Windows My Computer option to copy the data files. Your computer may use a different view to display the files. The following steps illustrate how to copy data files to the local Web site.

To Copy Data Files to the Local Web Site

1

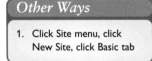

• **Click the Start button on the Windows taskbar and then click My Computer.**

The My Computer window is displayed (Figure 1-25).

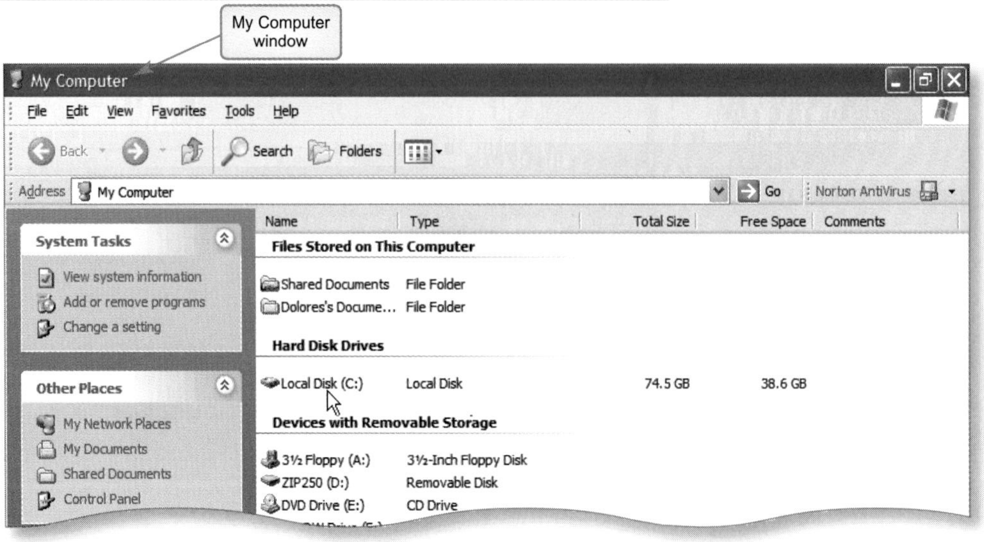

FIGURE 1-25

2

• **Double-click Local Disk (C:) and then navigate to the location of the data files for Project 1.**

If necessary, check with your instructor to verify the location of the data files. In Figure 1-26, the data files are located on Drive C:\.

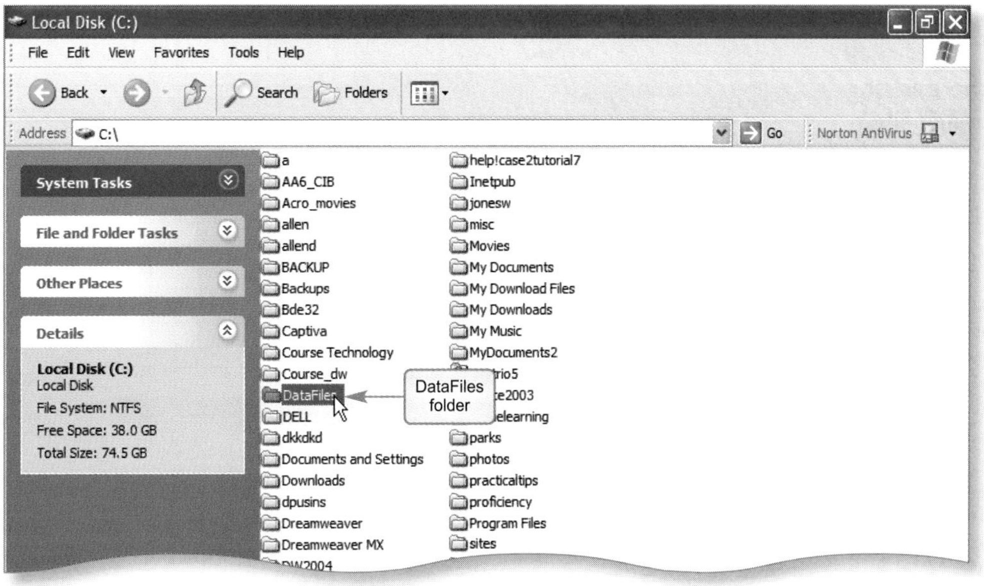

FIGURE 1-26

3

• **Double-click the DataFiles folder and then double-click the Proj01 folder.**

The Proj01 folder is selected, and the path to Proj01 is displayed in the Address text box (Figure 1-27).

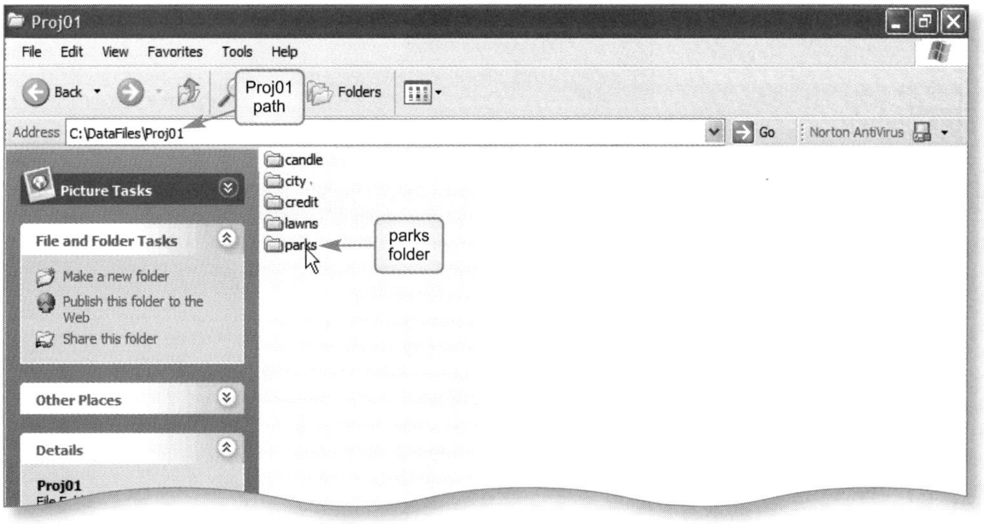

FIGURE 1-27

4

• **Double-click the parks folder and then double-click the images folder.**

The images folder is selected, and the path to the images folder is displayed in the Address text box (Figure 1-28).

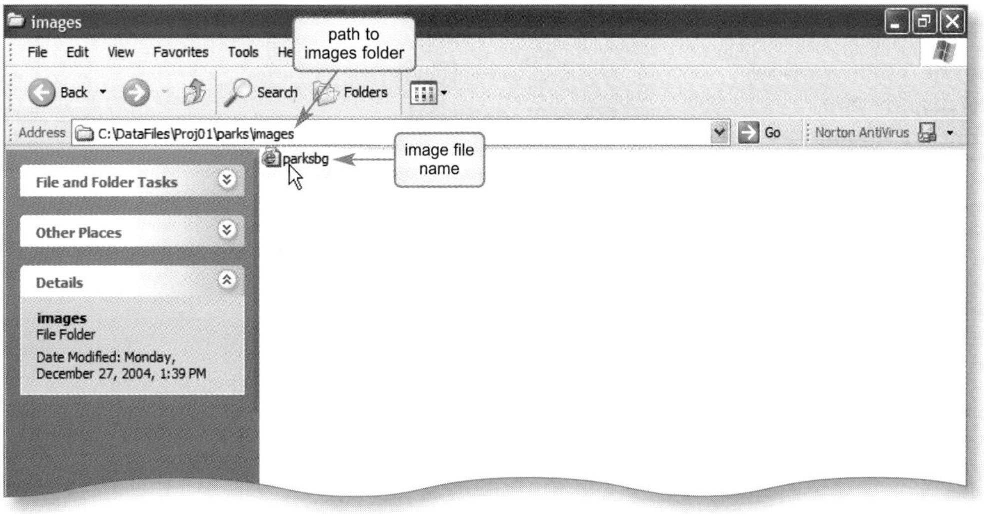

FIGURE 1-28

5

- **Right-click the parksbg image file.**

The context menu is displayed (Figure 1-29).

- **Point to the Copy command.**

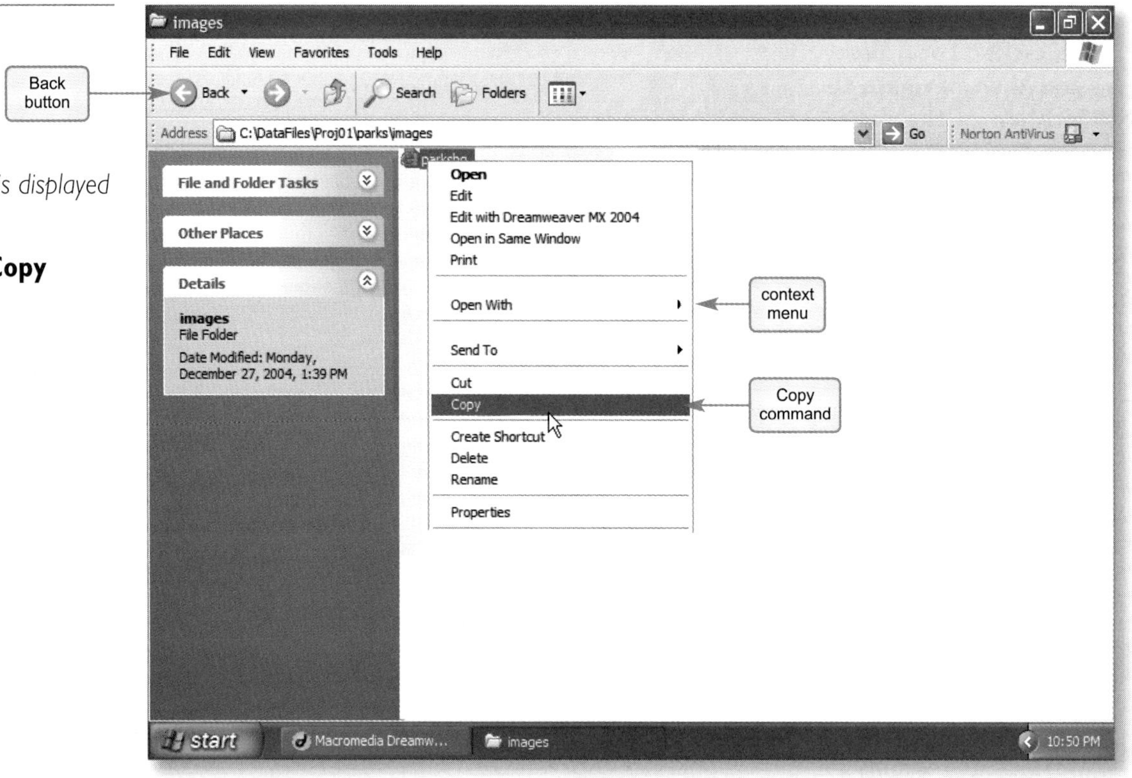

FIGURE 1-29

6

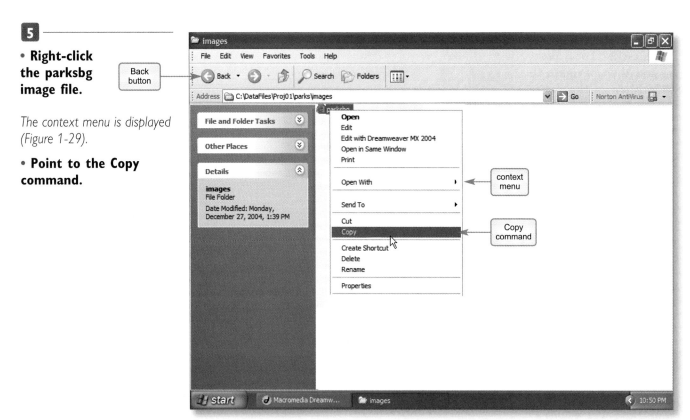

- **Click Copy and then click the My Computer Back button the number of times necessary to navigate to the your name folder.**
- **Double-click the your name folder, double-click the parks folder, and then double-click the images folder.**
- **Right-click anywhere in the open window to display the context menu.**
- **Point to the Paste command.**

The context menu is displayed and Paste is highlighted (Figure 1-30).

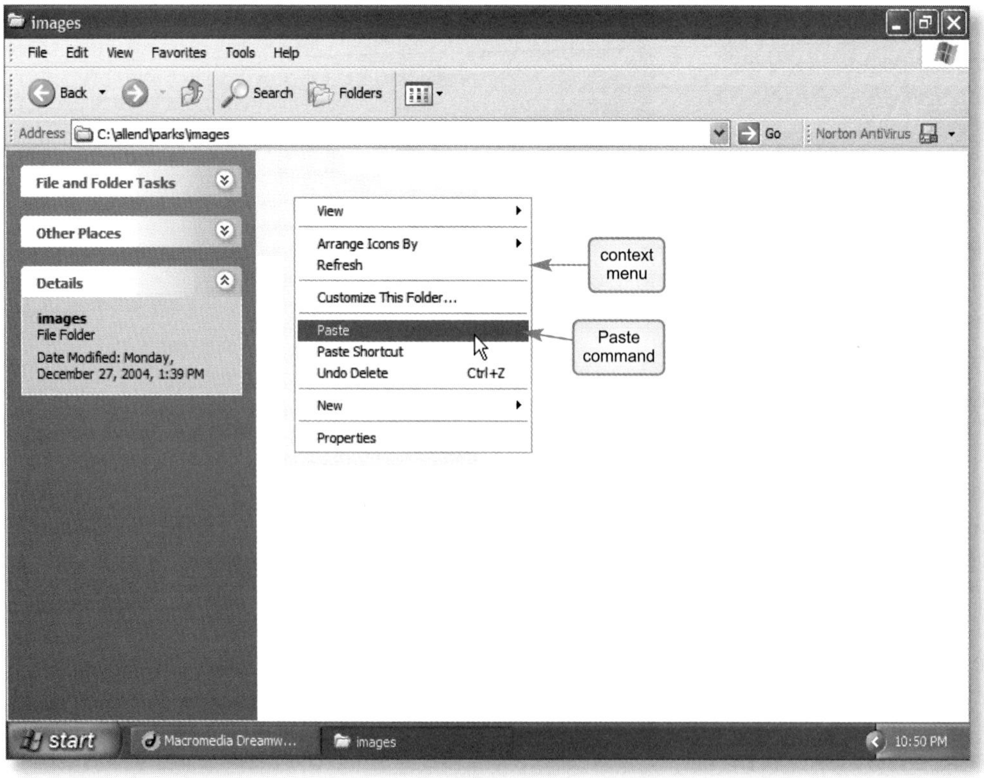

FIGURE 1-30

7

• **Click the Paste command.**

The parksbg image is pasted into the Florida Parks Web site images folder (Figure 1-31).

8

• **Click the images window Close button.**

The image window closes and Dreamweaver appears. The images folder is displayed in Dreamweaver's Files panel.

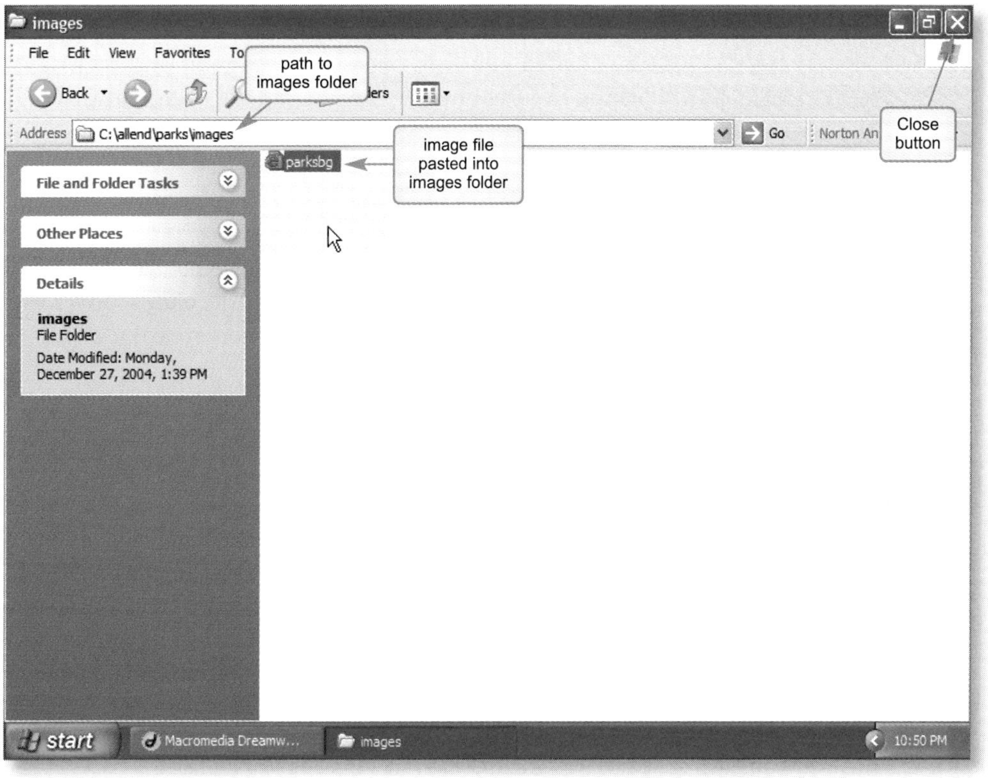

FIGURE 1-31

Your site definition and file hierarchy structure is complete, and your data files are copied into the images folder.

Removing or Editing a Web Site

On occasion, you may need to remove or edit a Web site. To remove or edit a Web site, click Site on the menu bar and then click the Manage Sites command. This displays the Manage Sites dialog box. Select the site name and then click the Remove button to remove the site. Dreamweaver displays a Dreamweaver MX 2004 caution box providing you with an opportunity to cancel. Click the No button to cancel. Otherwise, click the Yes button, and Dreamweaver removes the site. To edit a site, click the site name and then click the Edit button. Dreamweaver displays the Site Definition dialog box, and from there, you can change any of the options you selected when you first created the site. Removing a site in Dreamweaver removes the settings for the site. The files and folders remain and must be deleted separately.

Saving a Web Page

With the Florida Parks site defined and the data files copied to the site, the next step is to save the untitled Dreamweaver document. When you defined the site, you designated C:\allend\parks\ as the local root folder. You can copy and paste files into this folder using Windows XP or use Dreamweaver's file management tools to copy and paste. You also can save a Dreamweaver document into this folder. Dreamweaver treats any item placed in the folder as part of the site.

When a document is saved as a Web page, the Web page also remains in the computer's memory and is displayed in the Document window. It is a good practice to save when you first open the document and then save regularly while you are working in Dreamweaver. By doing so, you protect yourself from losing all the work you have done since the last time you saved.

The Standard Toolbar

The Standard toolbar contains buttons for common operations from the File and Edit menus: New, Open, Save, Save All, Cut, Copy, Paste, Undo, and Redo. It is useful to have this toolbar displayed when creating and saving Web pages.

The Index Page

The **home page** is the starting point for the rest of your Web site. For most Web sites, the home page is named index. This name has special significance because most Web servers recognize index.htm (or index.html) as the default home page. When you save your document, Dreamweaver automatically appends the extension .htm to the file name. Documents with the .htm extension display in Web browsers. The home page for your Florida Parks Web site is named index. The following steps show how to display the Standard toolbar and to save the untitled document as index.htm in the parks local root folder.

To Display the Standard Toolbar and Save a Document as a Web Page

1

• **Click View on the menu bar, point to Toolbars, and then point to Standard on the Toolbars submenu.**

Dreamweaver displays the View menu and the Toolbars submenu (Figure 1-32).

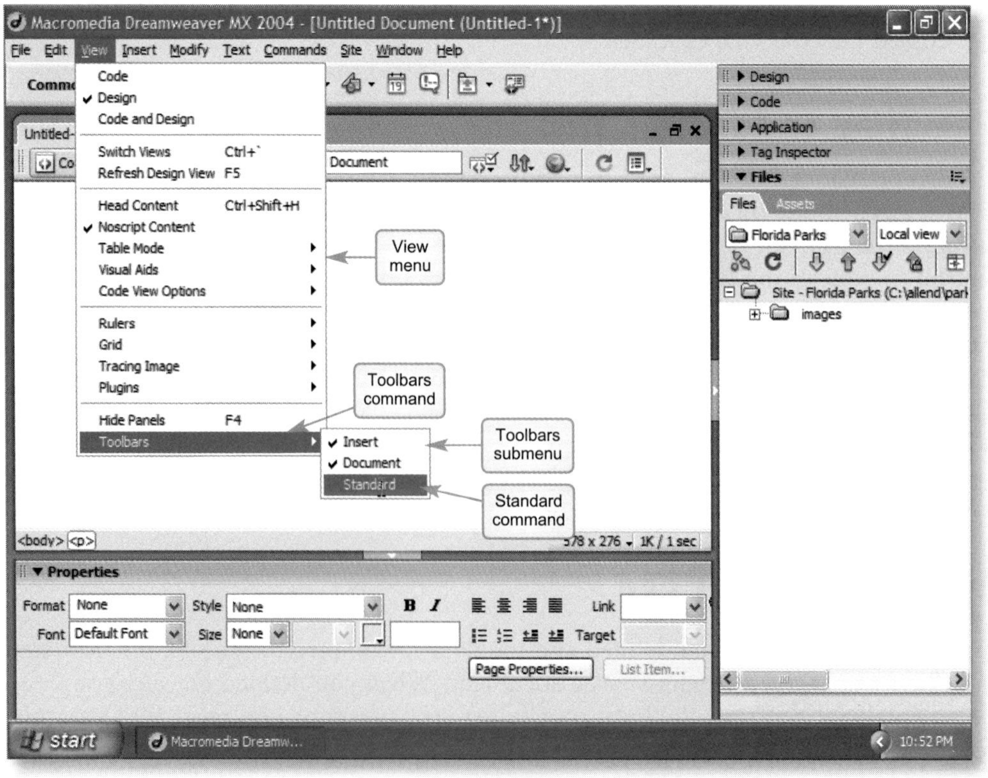

FIGURE 1-32

2

- **Click Standard.**

The Standard toolbar is displayed in the Dreamweaver workspace (Figure 1-33). Previous settings determine the location of the Standard toolbar. The Standard toolbar on your computer may be displayed below the Document toolbar or in another location.

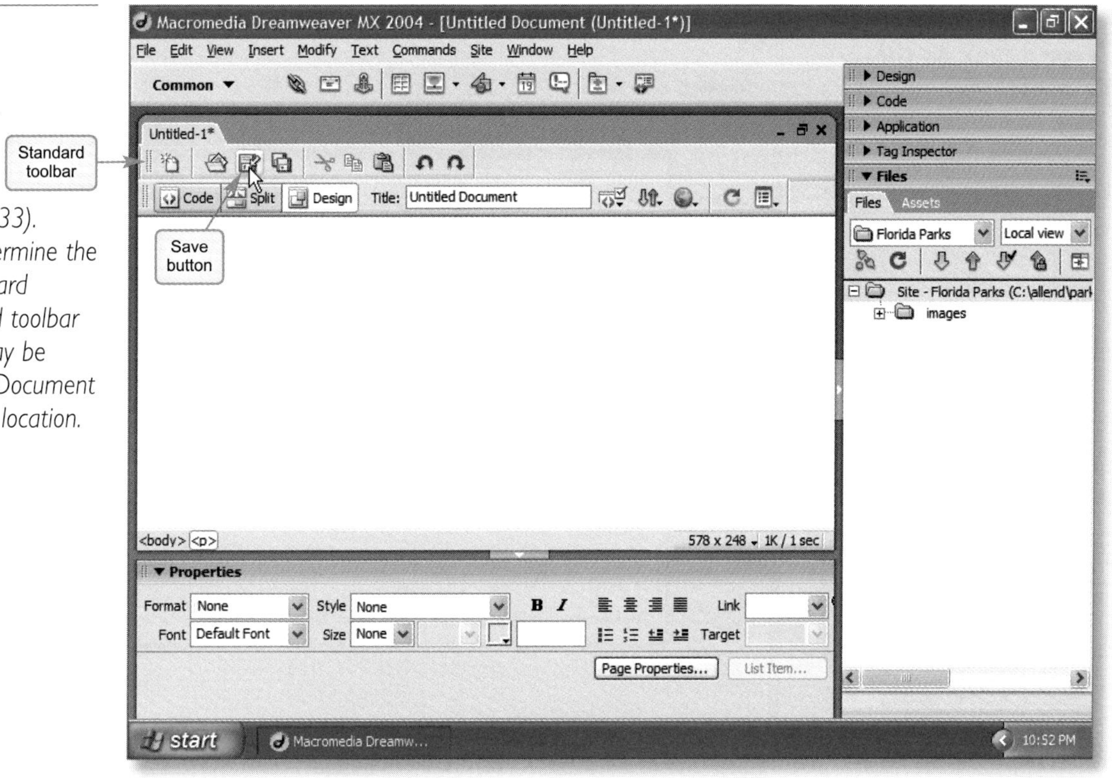

FIGURE 1-33

3

- **Click the Save button on the Standard toolbar.**

The Save As dialog box is displayed (Figure 1-34). The parks folder name is displayed in the Save in text box. The default file name, Untitled-1, is highlighted in the File name text box.

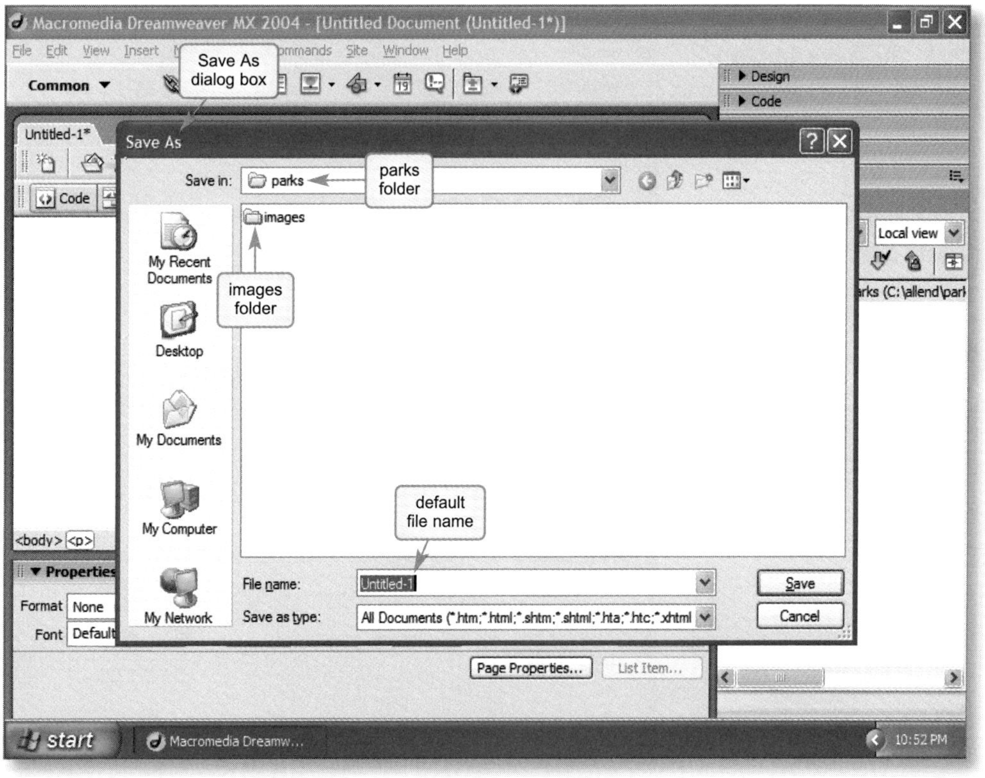

FIGURE 1-34

4

• **Type** `index` **as the file name.**

The index file name is displayed in the File name text box (Figure 1-35).

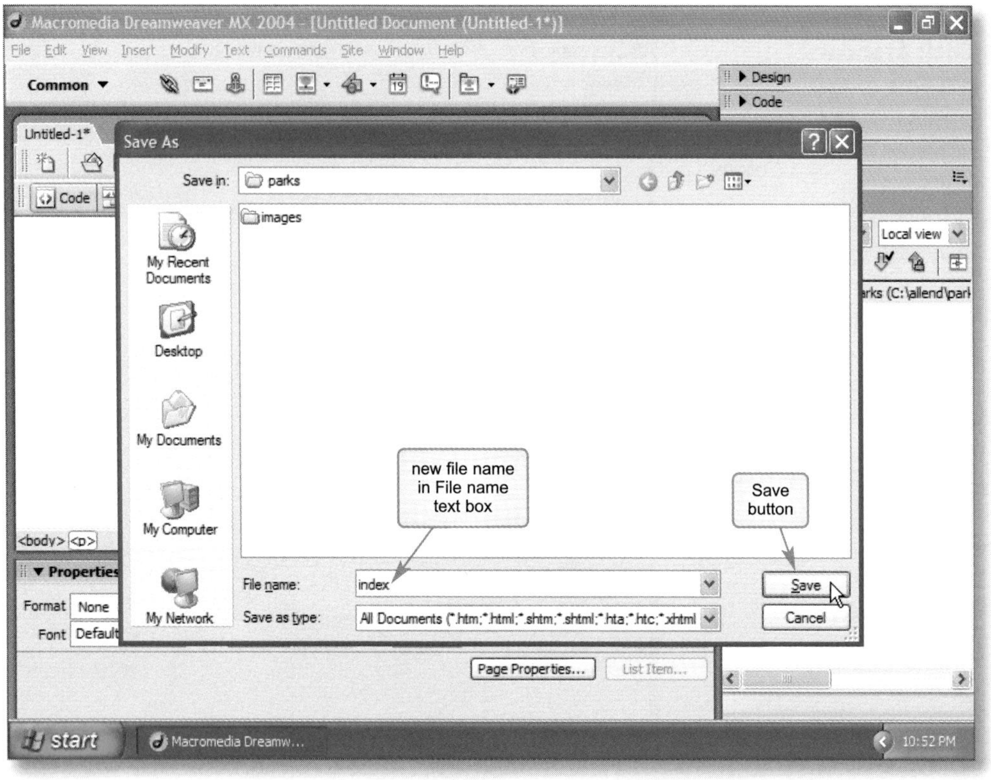

FIGURE 1-35

5

• **Click the Save button.**

The parks index page is saved in the parks local folder and is displayed in the Files panel (Figure 1-36). The path and file name (parks/index.htm) are displayed on the Dreamweaver title bar.

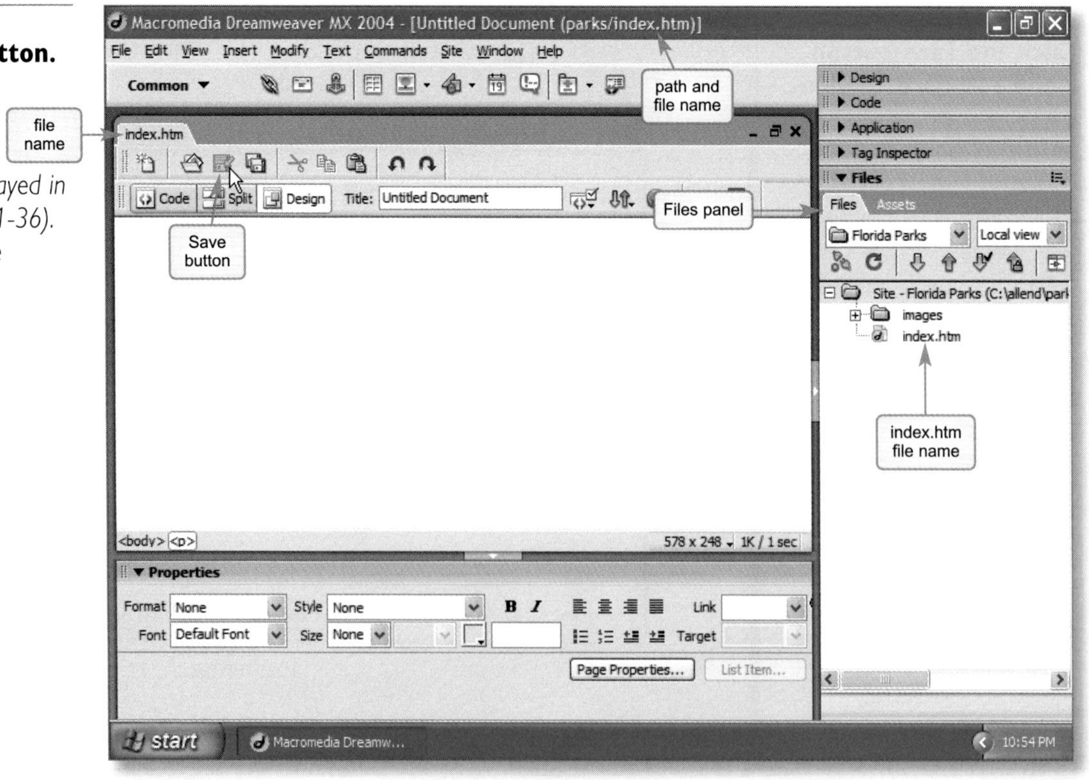

FIGURE 1-36

Web Page Backgrounds

Each new Web page you create displays with a default white or gray background and other default properties. You can modify these default properties using the **Page Properties** dialog box. The Page Properties dialog box lets you specify appearance, links, and many other aspects of page design. You can assign new page properties for each new page you create, and modify those for existing pages. The page properties you select apply only to the active document.

You can change the default and enhance your Web page, for example, by adding a background image and/or background color. If you use both a background image and a background color, the color appears while the image downloads, and then the image covers the color. Additionally, Dreamweaver provides a series of Web-safe color schemes, accessed through the Commands menu. In this project, you add a background image to the Web page.

Adding a Background Image

When you copied the data file earlier in this project, you copied an image file that is the background for the Florida Parks Web site. You use background images to add texture and interesting color to a Web page. Use background images cautiously, however. Web page images displayed on top of a busy background image may not mix well, and text may be difficult to read. Images and image formats are discussed in more detail in Project 2.

The following steps illustrate how to use the Page Properties dialog box to add a background image to the home page.

To Add a Background Image to the Index Page

1

- **Click Modify on the menu bar and then point to Page Properties (Figure 1-37).**

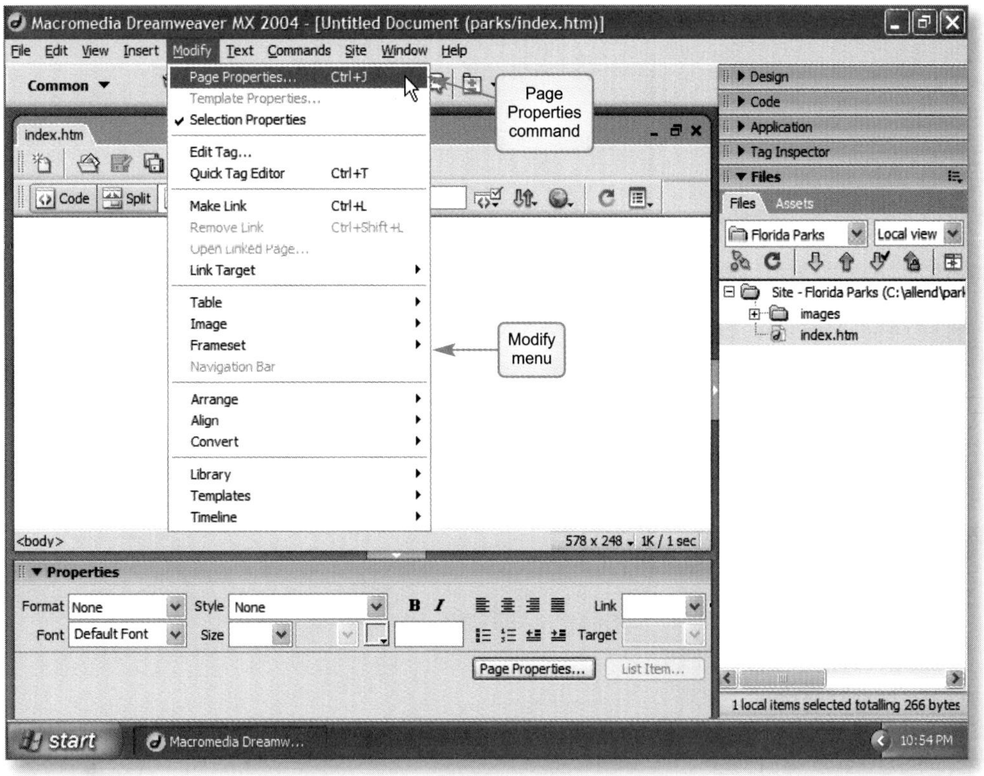

FIGURE 1-37

2

- **Click Page Properties.**
- **Verify that the Appearance category is selected.**

The Page Properties dialog box is displayed, and the Appearance category is highlighted (Figure 1-38).

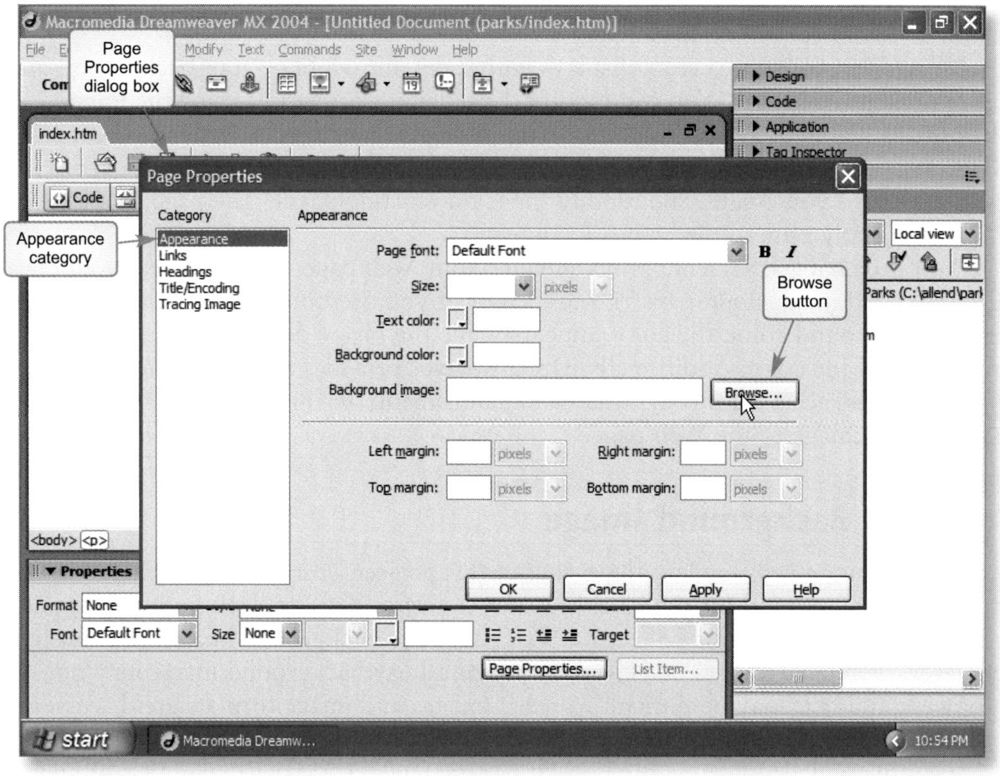

FIGURE 1-38

3

- **Click the Browse button and then click the images folder.**

Dreamweaver displays the Select Image Source dialog box (Figure 1-39). The parks folder name is displayed in the Look in text box, and the images folder is highlighted.

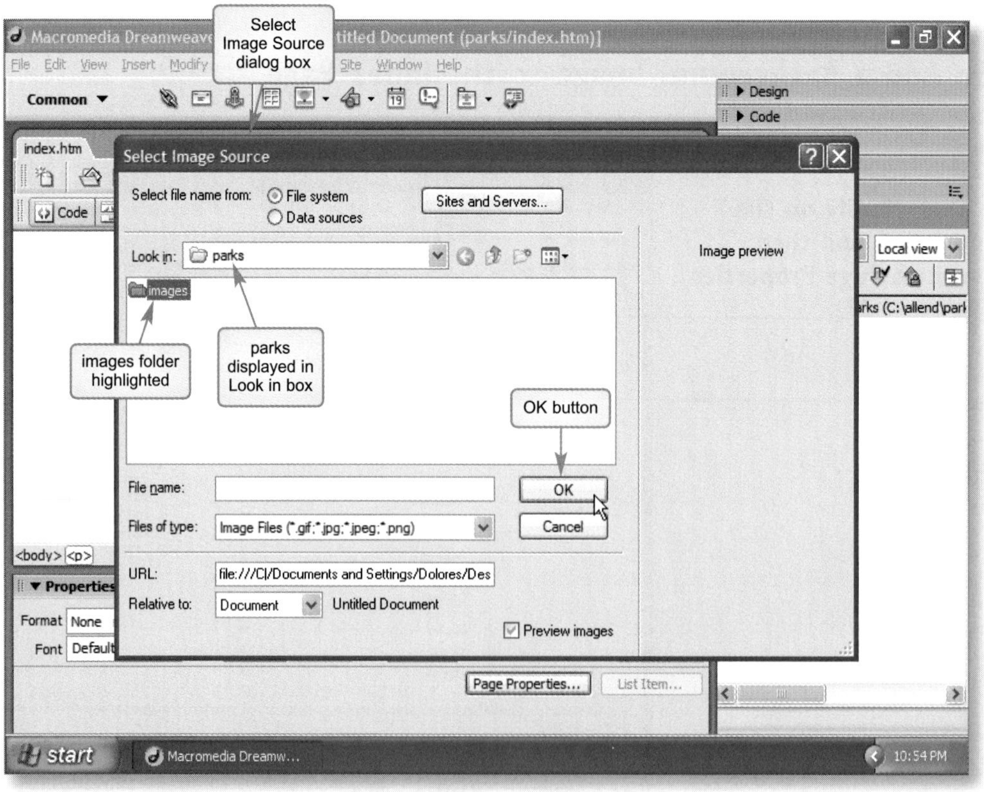

FIGURE 1-39

4

- **Click the OK button.**
- **Click the parksbg file.**
- **If necessary, click the Preview images check box to select it.**

The images folder is opened and displayed in the Look in text box. The file name, parksbg is displayed in the File name text box. A preview of the image is displayed in the Image preview area. The dimensions of the image, type of image, file size, and download time are listed below the image (Figure 1-40).

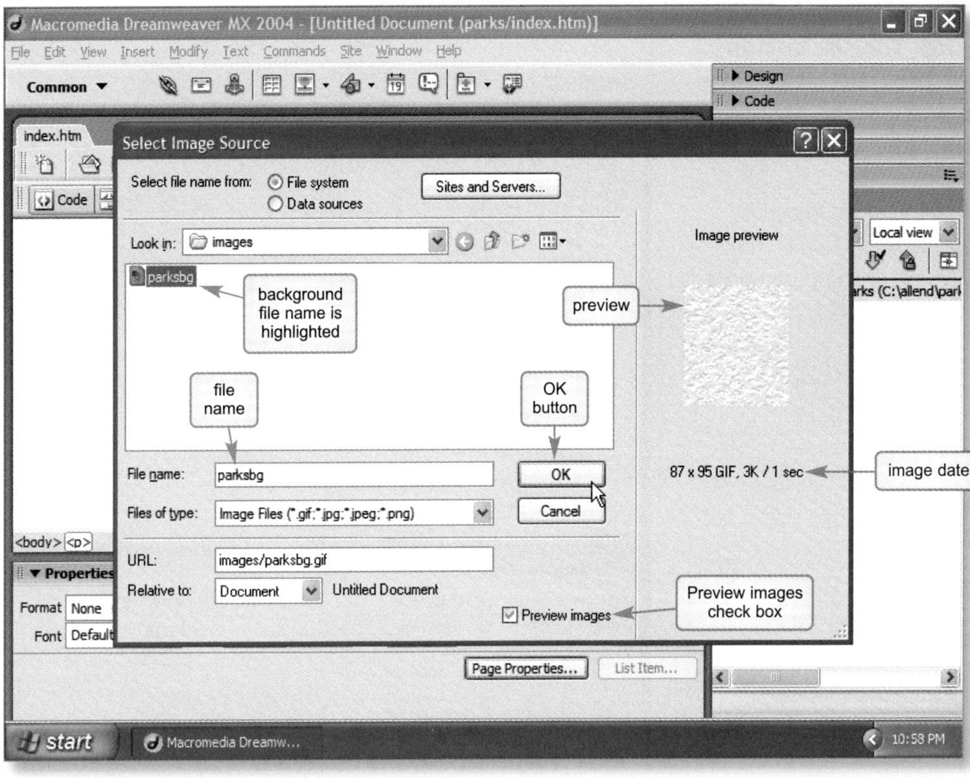

FIGURE 1-40

5

- **Click the OK button in the Select Image Source dialog box and then point to the OK button in the Page Properties dialog box.**

The Page Properties dialog box is displayed with the folder and file name in the Background image text box (Figure 1-41).

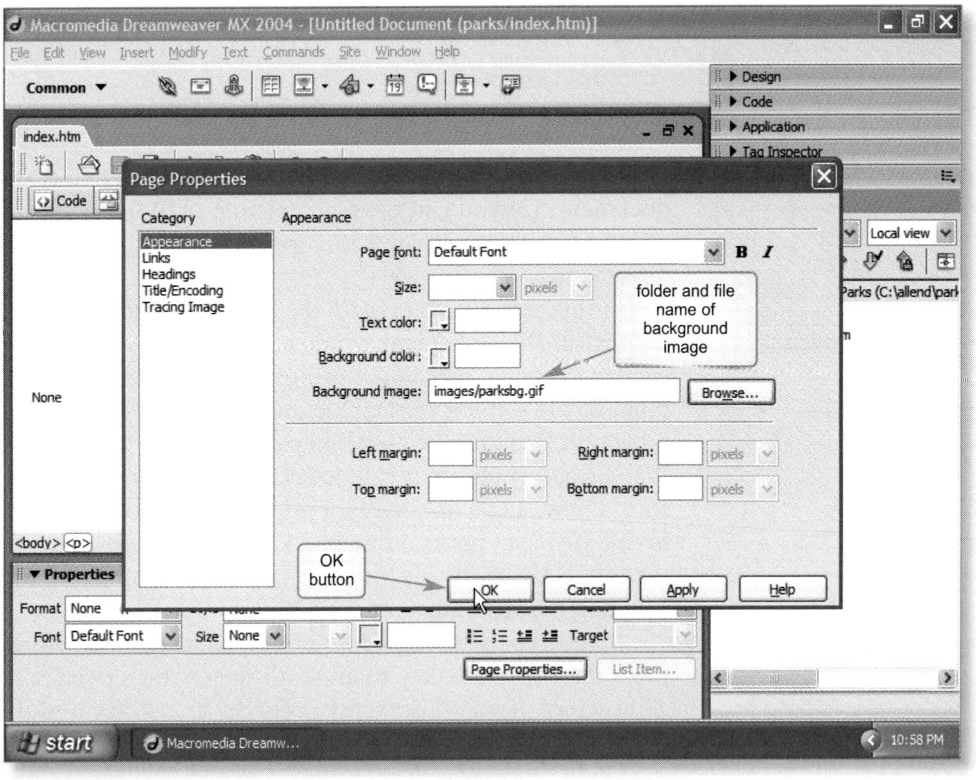

FIGURE 1-41

6

• Click the OK button and then click the Save button on the Standard toolbar.

The background image is applied to the Florida Parks page, and the updated page is saved (Figure 1-42).

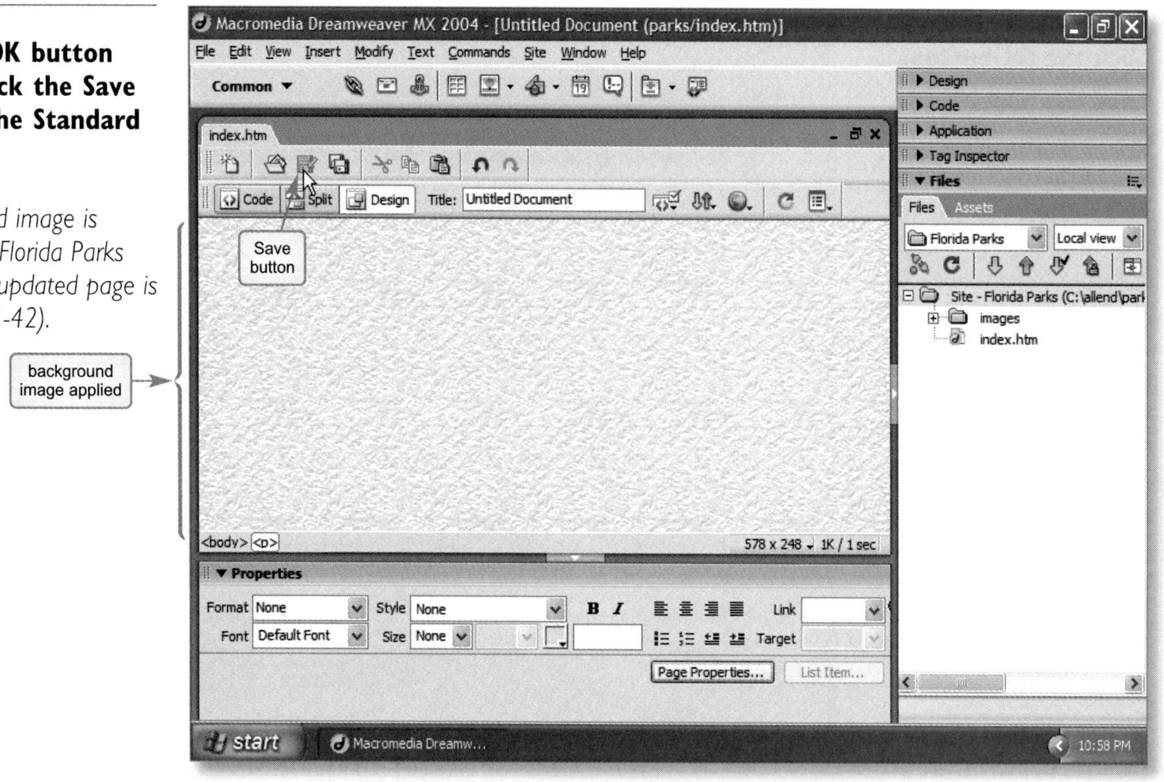

FIGURE 1-42

Other Ways

1. Right-click Document window, click Page Properties on shortcut menu
2. Click Modify on menu bar, click Page Properties

Adding Text to a Web Page

In Dreamweaver, you can create a Web page in several ways: (1) you can type a new document; (2) you can open an existing HTML document, even if it was not created in Dreamweaver; (3) you can copy and paste text; and (4) you can import a Word document.

In this project, you create the index page for Florida Parks Web page by typing the text in the Document window. Entering text into a Dreamweaver document is similar to typing text in a word processing document. You can position the insertion point at the top left of the Document window or within another element, such as a table cell. Pressing the ENTER key creates a new paragraph and inserts a blank line. Web browsers automatically insert a blank line of space between paragraphs. To start a new single line without a blank line between lines of text requires a **line break**. You can insert a line break by holding down the SHIFT key and then pressing the ENTER key or by clicking the Line Break command on the Insert HTML Special Characters submenu.

If you type a wrong letter and notice the error before pressing the ENTER key, press the BACKSPACE key to erase all the characters back to and including the one that is incorrect. If you mistakenly press the ENTER key and then discover the error, simply press the BACKSPACE key to return the insertion point to the previous line. Clicking the **Undo** button on the Standard toolbar reverses the most recent actions. The **Redo** button reverses the last undo action. The Undo and Redo commands also are accessible on the Edit menu.

Organizing Your Workspace

To organize your workspace, you hide the panel groups and collapse the lower portion of the Property inspector. This gives you additional workspace in the Dreamweaver Document window. The following steps show how to organize your workspace by hiding the panel groups.

To Hide the Panel Groups

1

- **Click the expand/collapse arrow on the panel groups vertical bar.**
- **Click the Property inspector expander arrow.**

The panel group is hidden, and the Property inspector is collapsed (Figure 1-43).

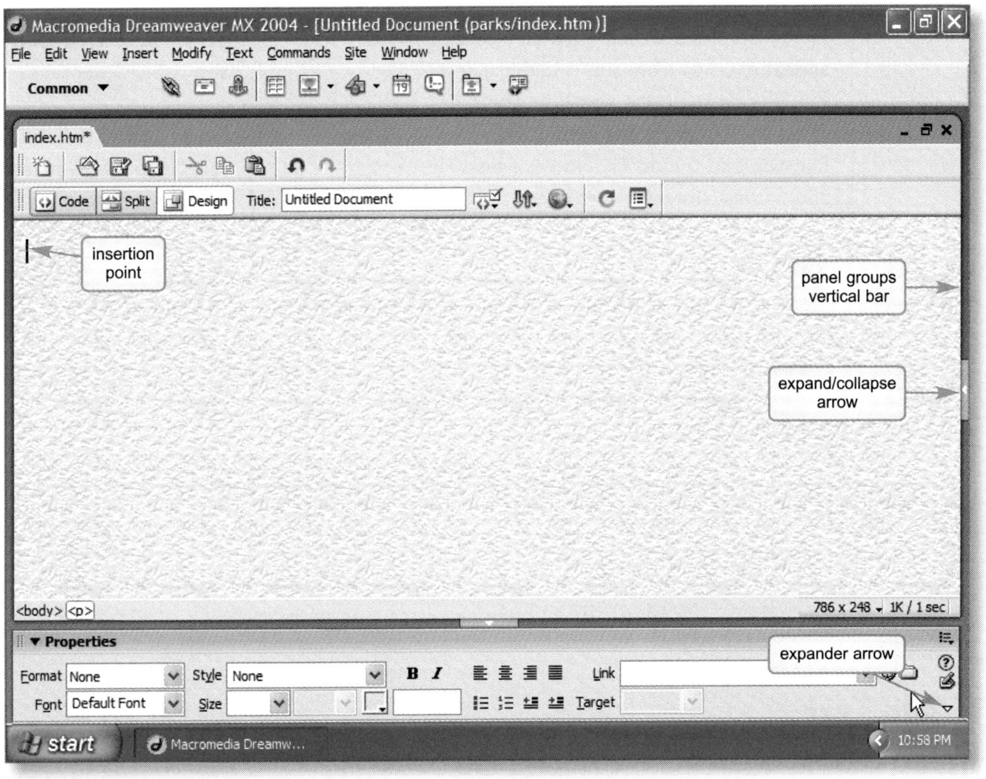

FIGURE 1-43

Adding Text

Table 1-1 includes the text for the Florida Parks Web page. After typing the sections of the document, you will press the ENTER key to insert a blank line.

Table 1-1 Discovering Scenic Florida Web Page Text

SECTION	HEADING, PART 1, AND PART 2	SECTION	PART 3, ITEMS FOR BULLETED LIST, AND CLOSING
Heading	Discovering Scenic Florida	Part 3	When planning your trip, consider the following:
Part 1	Florida is one of the nation's renowned vacationlands. Tourism is Florida's number one industry. Visitors flock to Walt Disney World, Epcot, Universal Studios, and other recreational attractions. Many vacationers, however, do not realize the diversity of Florida. In addition to the theme parks, Florida's appeal extends from the vast expanse of the Everglades in the south to notable cities such as Saint Augustine and Pensacola in the north. Florida's historic and natural sites offer travelers an opportunity to view a totally different side of Florida.	Items list	Biscayne, Everglades, and Dry Tortugas National Parks are located in southern Florida. <enter> Six of the top 20 beaches in America are located in Florida state parks. <enter> The state park system includes state preserves, state parks, state archeological sites, state museums, and others. <enter> Florida has 6 national wildlife refuges and 3 national forests in which many national wilderness areas are located. <enter>
Part 2	Florida has approximately 150 state parks and 3 national parks. Visitors to these parks can enjoy such activities as swimming, camping, hiking, fishing, boating, scuba diving, or simply reflecting on Florida's natural and cultural resources.	Closing	Park entrance fees vary throughout the state and are subject to change.

The following steps, show how to add text to the Document window and insert blank lines between sections of text.

To Add Text

1

- **Type the heading** `Discovering Scenic Florida` **as shown in Table 1-1, and then press the ENTER key.**

The heading is entered in the Document window (Figure 1-44). Pressing the ENTER key creates a new paragraph.

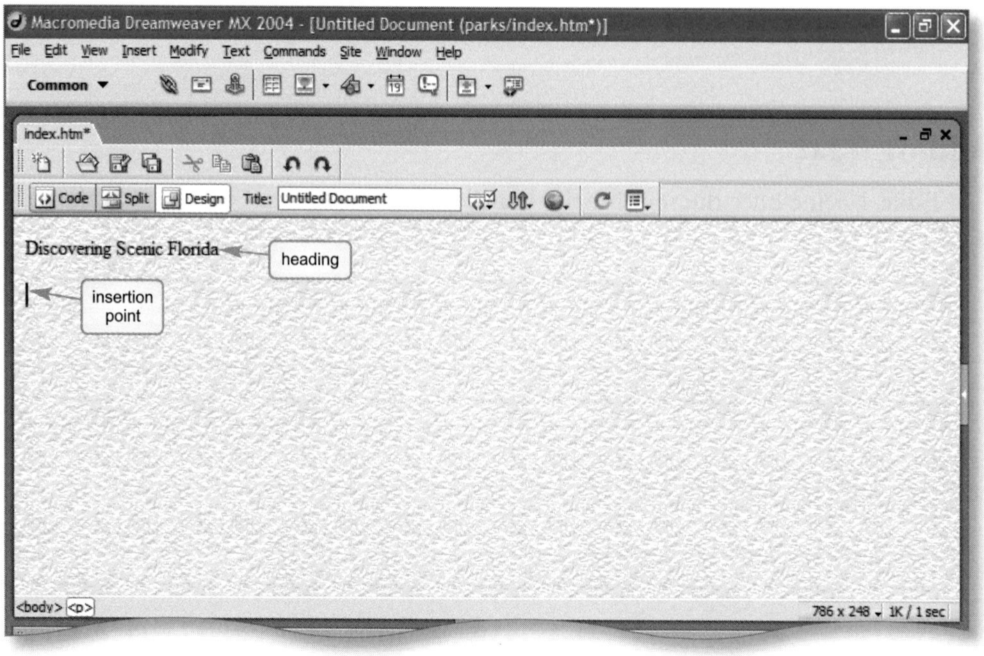

FIGURE 1-44

2

- **Type the text of Part 1 as shown in Table 1-1 on the previous page, and then press the ENTER key.**

The introductory paragraph is entered (Figure 1-45). Pressing the ENTER key creates a new paragraph.

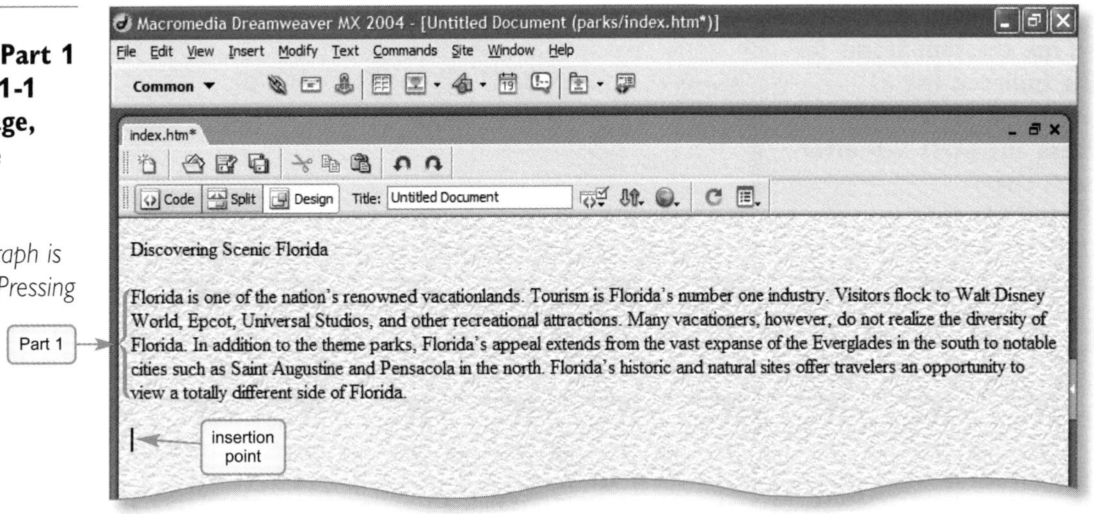

FIGURE 1-45

3

- **Type the text of Part 2 as shown in Table 1-1, and then press the ENTER key.**

The second paragraph is entered (Figure 1-46).

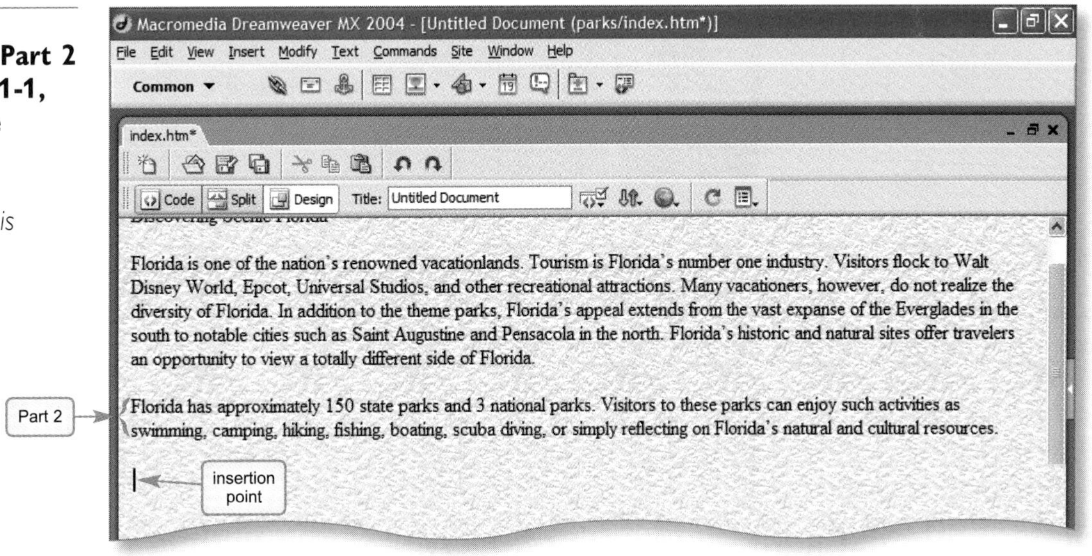

FIGURE 1-46

4

- **Type the text of Part 3 as shown in Table 1-1, and then press the ENTER key.**

The third paragraph is entered (Figure 1-47).

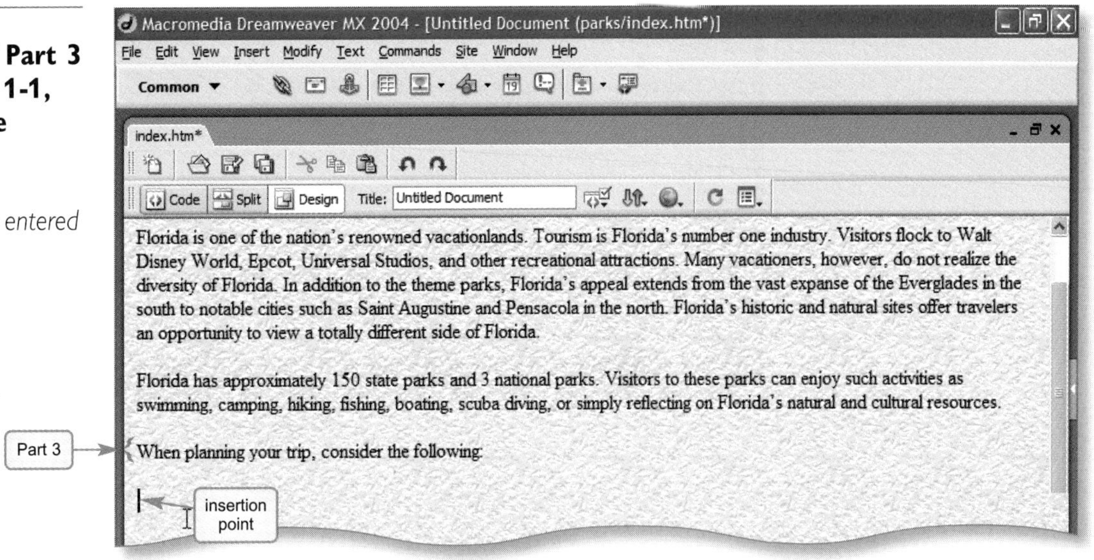

FIGURE 1-47

5

- **Type the four items for the bulleted list as shown in Table 1-1. Press the ENTER key after each entry.**

The items for the bulleted list are entered (Figure 1-48). Later in this project, you will format the list so it becomes a bulleted list.

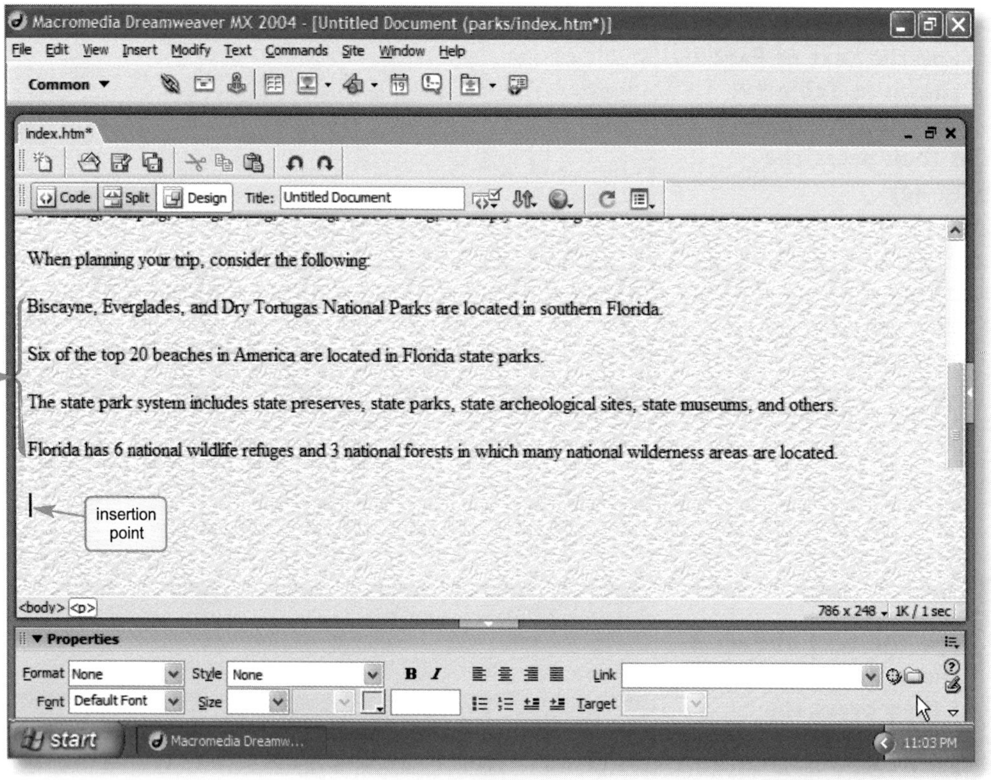

FIGURE 1-48

6

- **Type the closing paragraph shown in Table 1-1 on page DW 60, and then press the ENTER key.**
- **Click the Save button on the Standard toolbar.**

The paragraph is entered (Figure 1-49).

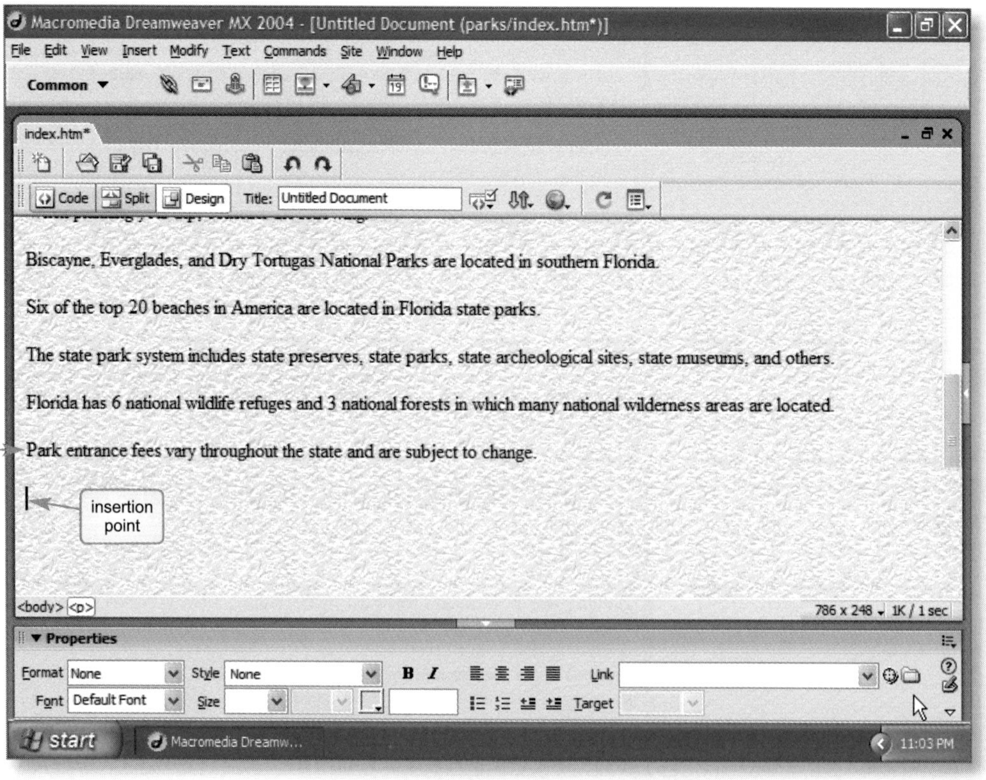

FIGURE 1-49

If you feel you need to start over for any reason, Dreamweaver makes it easy to delete a Web page or other file. Save and close the page, display the panel groups by clicking the vertical bar expand/collapse arrow, click the name of the page you want to delete, right-click to display the context menu, point to Edit, and then point to and click Delete on the Edit submenu. Click the Yes button in the Dreamweaver caution dialog box to delete the page or the No button to cancel the action.

Formatting Text

The next step is to format the text. Dreamweaver provides three options for formatting text: the Text menu, the Insert bar Text category, and the Property inspector. To format the text for the Discovering Scenic Florida Web page, you use the text-related features of the Property inspector. If the panels group is displayed, a portion of the Property inspector is hidden.

The Property inspector is one of the panels you will use most often when creating and formatting Web pages. The Property inspector initially displays the more commonly used attributes, or properties, of the selected object. The object can be a table, text, an image, or some other item. The Property inspector is context-sensitive, so options within the Property inspector change relative to the selected object.

Property Inspector Features

The Property inspector lets you see the current properties of an element and allows you to alter or edit them. The Property inspector is divided into two sections. Clicking the expander arrow in the lower-right corner of the Property inspector collapses the Property inspector to show only the more commonly used properties for the selected element or expands the Property inspector to show more options. Some objects, such as text, do not contain additional properties within the expanded panel (Figure 1-50 on the next page). The question mark icon opens the Help window.

Q&A

Q: When a change is made in the Property inspector, when is the change applied?

A: Most changes are applied immediately. You can confirm that changes are applied, however, by clicking the TAB or ENTER button.

Collapsing/Hiding the Property Inspector

Having panels such as the Property inspector display in the Dreamweaver window requires considerable window space. If you are finished working with this panel, it generally is better to collapse it, hide it, or close it. **Collapsing** it leaves the title bar in the window, which allows you to expand it easily by clicking the expand/collapse arrow instead of using the Properties command on the Window menu. Pressing CTRL+F3 also collapses/expands the Property inspector. **Hiding** it hides the panel and the title bar. To hide the Property inspector and the Property inspector title bar, click the expand/collapse arrow on the horizontal bar. **Closing** it removes it completely from the Document window. To close the Property inspector, display the context menu by right-clicking on the Properties title bar, and then selecting the Close panel group command or click the Options menu and select the Close panel group command from the pop-up menu.

By default, the Property inspector displays the properties for text on a blank document. Most changes you make to properties are applied immediately in the Document window. For some properties, however, changes are not applied until you click outside the property-editing text fields, press the ENTER key, or press the TAB key to switch to another property. The following section describes the text-related features of the Property inspector (Figure 1-50 and Figure 1-51).

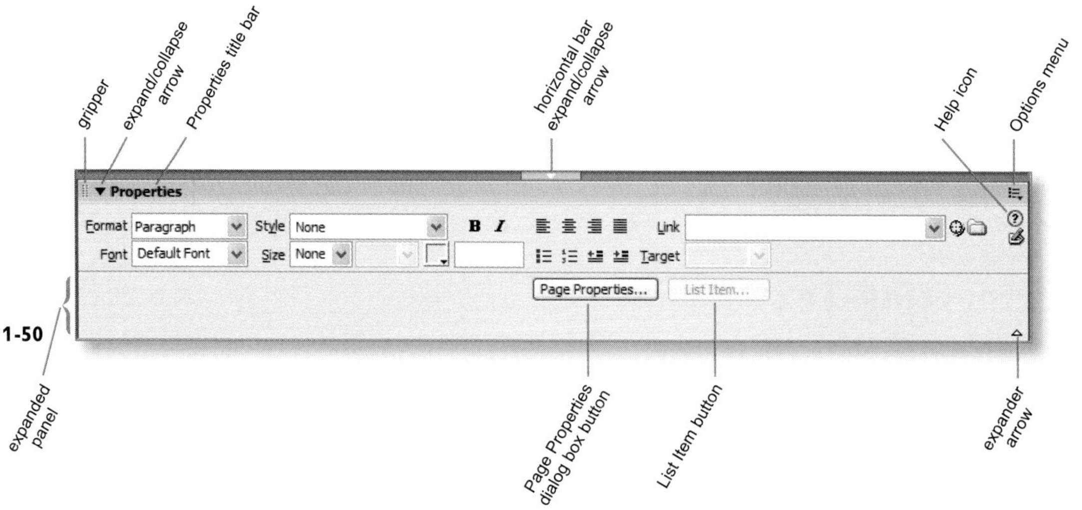

FIGURE 1-50

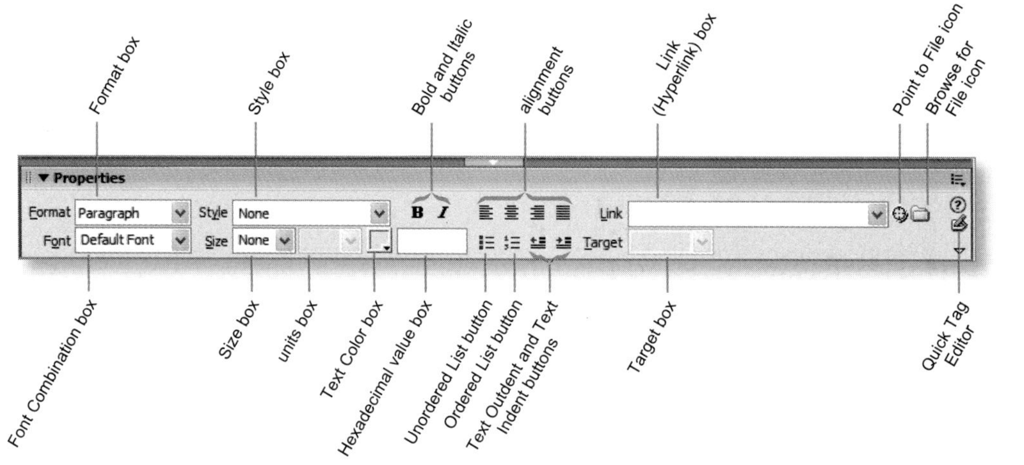

FIGURE 1-51

FORMAT The **Format box** allows you to apply a Paragraph, Heading, or Preformatted style to the text. Clicking the Format box displays a pop-up menu from which you can select a style.

The **Paragraph style** is the normal default style for text on a Web page. **Paragraph formatting** is the process of changing the appearance of text. **Heading styles** are used to create divisions and separate one segment of text from another. The Heading numbers range from 1 through 6 and correspond to the HTML elements H1, H2, and so on. The smaller the number of the heading, the bigger the text displayed when viewed in a Web browser. These formats are displayed based on how different browsers interpret the tags, offering little consistency and control over layout and appearance. When you apply a heading tag to a paragraph, Dreamweaver automatically adds the next line of text as a standard paragraph. Use the **Preformatted style** when you do not want a Web browser to change the line of text in any way.

FONT Font combination applies the selected font combination to the text and determines how a browser displays text on your Web page. The browser uses the first font in the combination that is installed on the user's system. If none of the fonts in the combination are installed, the browser displays the text as specified by the user's browser preferences. Most font faces in common usage on the Web are serif, sans-serif, or monospace fonts. The default font used on most Web pages is Times (also called Times New Roman or New Times), which is a serif font. The most commonly used sans-serif fonts are Arial, Helvetica, Geneva, and Verdana, while the most commonly used monospace font is Courier (also called Courier New). Use the Font combination pop-up menu to apply a font combination.

STYLE By default, Dreamweaver uses Cascading Style Sheets (CSS) styles to format text. **Cascading Style Sheets (CSS)** are a collection of formatting rules that control the appearance of content in a Web page. The styles that you apply to text using the Property inspector or menu commands create CSS rules that are embedded in the head of the current document. To change the default from CSS tags to HTML tags, click the Edit menu and select the Preferences command. Under the General category, Editing options, deselect the Use CSS instead of HTML tags check box. Styles are discussed in Project 5.

SIZE The **Text Size box** provides options that allow you to apply a font size to a single character or to an entire page of text. Font sizes in HTML range from 1 through 7, with size 7 being the largest. The default HTML font size, or **BASEFONT**, is 3, which equates to 12 points in a word processing document.

TEXT COLOR When you create a new document in Dreamweaver, the default text color is black. The **Text Color** box contains palettes of colors you can apply to emphasize, differentiate, and highlight topics. To display the text in a selected Web-safe color, click the Text Color box to access the different methods of selecting preset colors or creating custom ones. Colors also are represented by a hexadecimal value (for example, #FF0000) in the adjacent text field.

BOLD AND ITALIC The **Bold button** and the **Italic button** allow you to format text using these two font styles in the Property inspector. These are the two more commonly used styles. Dreamweaver also supports a variety of other font styles, which are available through the Text menu. To view these other styles, click Text on the menu bar and then point to Style. The Style submenu contains a list of additional styles, such as Underline, Strikethrough, and Teletype.

ALIGN LEFT, ALIGN CENTER, ALIGN RIGHT, AND JUSTIFY In Dreamweaver, the default alignment for text is left alignment. To change the default alignment, select the text you want to align or simply position the mouse pointer at the beginning of the text. Click an alignment button: Align Center, Align Right, or Justify. You can align and center complete blocks of text, but you cannot align or center part of a heading or part of a paragraph.

LINK The **Link (Hyperlink) box** allows you to make selected text or other objects a hyperlink to a specified URL or Web page. To select the URL or Web page, you can click the Point to File or Browse for File icon to the right of the Link box to browse to a page in your Web site and select the file name, type the URL, or drag a file from the Files panel into the Link box. Links are covered in detail in Project 2.

TARGET In the **Target pop-up menu box**, you specify the frame or window in which the linked page should load. If you are using frames, the names of all the frames in the current document are displayed in the list. If the specified frame does not exist when the current document is opened in a browser, the linked page loads in a new window with the name you specified. Once this window exists, other files can be targeted to it.

UNORDERED LIST Web developers often use a list to structure a page. An unordered list turns the selected paragraph or heading into an item in a bulleted list. If no text is selected before the **Unordered List button** is clicked, a new bulleted list is started.

ORDERED LIST An ordered list is similar to an unordered list. This type of list, however, turns the selected paragraph or heading into an item in a numbered list. If no text is selected before the **Ordered List button** is clicked, a new numbered list is started.

INDENT AND OUTDENT To set off a block quote, you can use the Indent feature. The **Text Indent button** will indent a line or a paragraph from both margins. In HTML, this is the blockquote tag. The **Text Outdent button** removes the indentation from the selected text by removing the blockquote tag. In a list, indenting creates a nested list, and removing the indentation unnests the list. A **nested list** is one list inside another list.

PAGE PROPERTIES Clicking the Page Properties button opens the Page Properties dialog box.

LIST ITEM Clicking the List Items button opens the List Properties dialog box. This button is dimmed until an existing list is created and the insertion point is contained within the list.

More About

The Property Inspector

The Property inspector initially displays the most commonly used properties of the selected object. Click the expander arrow in the lower-right corner of the Property inspector to see more of the element's properties.

Applying Property Inspector Text-Related Features

The text for your Web page displays in the Document window. The next step in creating your Web page is to format this text. **Formatting** means to apply different fonts, change heading styles, insert special characters, and insert other such elements that enhance the appearance of the Web page. You use commands from the Property inspector to format the text.

Within Dreamweaver, you can format text before you type, or you can apply new formats after you type. If you have used word processing software, you will find many of the Dreamweaver formatting commands similar to the commands within a word processing program. At this point, your Web page contains only text, so the Property inspector displays attributes related to text.

To set block formatting, such as formatting a heading or an unordered list, position the insertion point in the line or paragraph and then format the text. To set character formatting, such as choosing a font or font size, however, you first must select the character, word, or words.

More About

Text Size

You can set the size of the text in your Web page, but viewers of your Web page also can change the size through their browser. When creating a page, use the font size that looks right for the page you are creating.

Text Headings

Just as in a word processing document, designers use the heading structure in a Web page to set apart document or section titles. The six levels of HTML headings are Heading 1 through Heading 6. **Heading 1 <h1>** produces the largest text and **Heading 6 <h6>** the smallest. By default, browsers will display the six heading levels in the same font, with the point size decreasing as the importance of the heading decreases. The following steps show how to format the heading.

To Format Text with Heading 1

1

- **If necessary, scroll up and then position the insertion point anywhere in the heading text, Discovering Scenic Florida (Figure 1-52).**

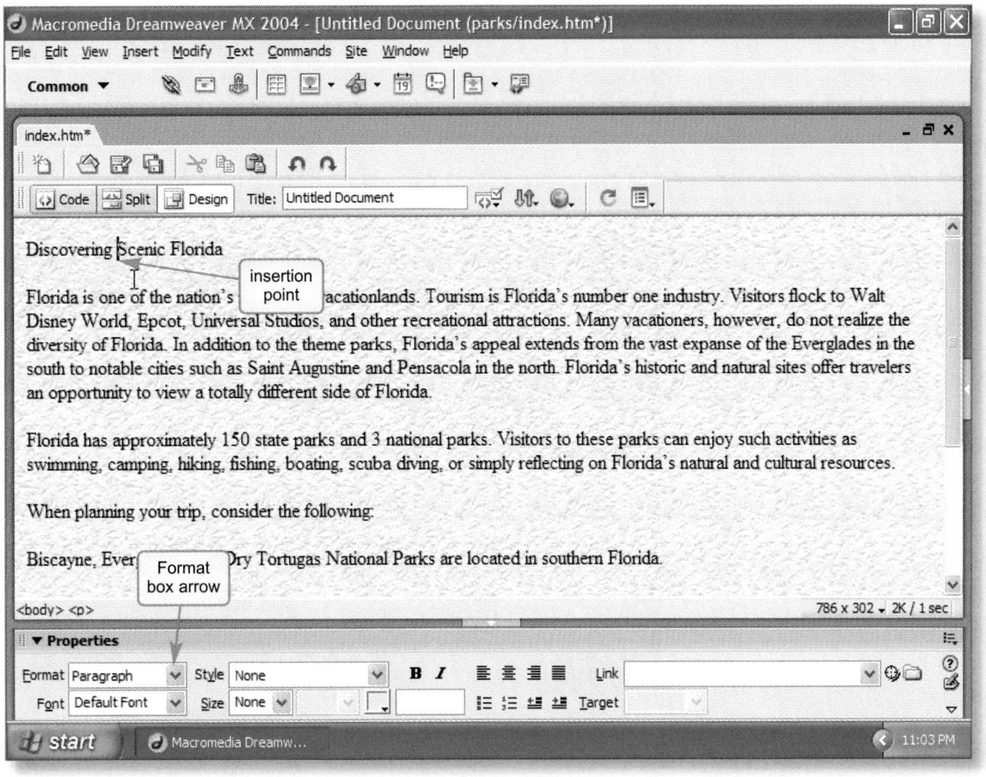

FIGURE 1-52

2

- **Click the Format box arrow in the Property inspector and then point to Heading 1.**

The Format pop-up menu is displayed with a list of formatting styles. Heading 1 is highlighted in the list (Figure 1-53).

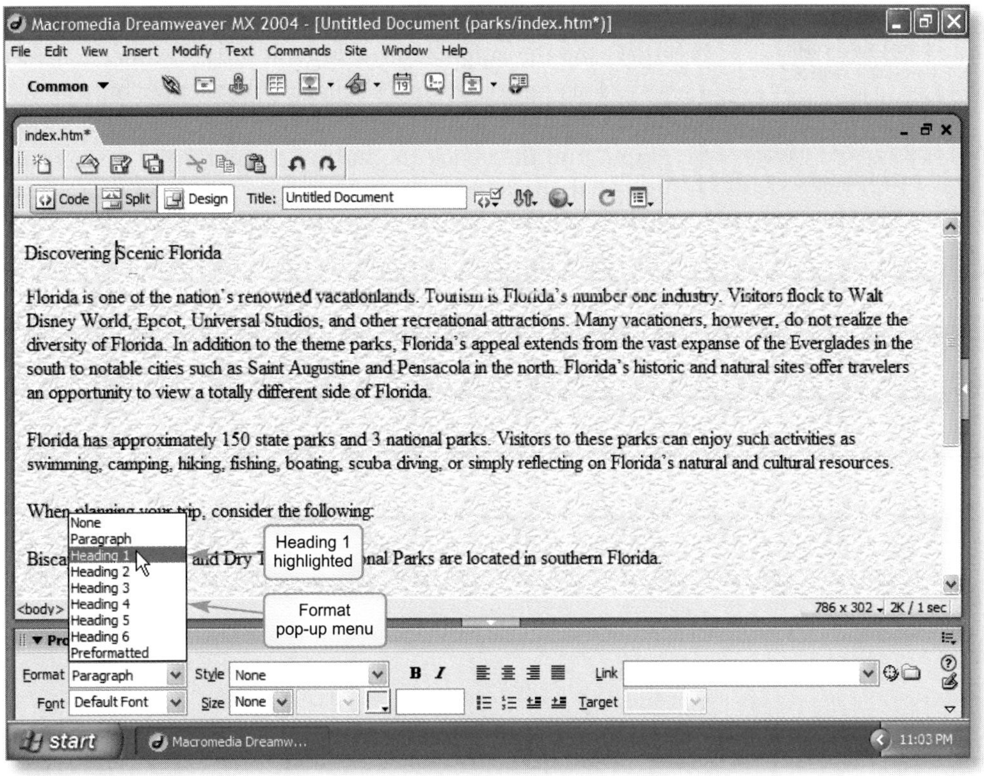

FIGURE 1-53

3

• **Click Heading 1.**

The Heading 1 style is applied to the Discovering Scenic Florida heading (Figure 1-54). The <h1> HTML tag displays in the Tag selector, indicating Heading 1 is selected.

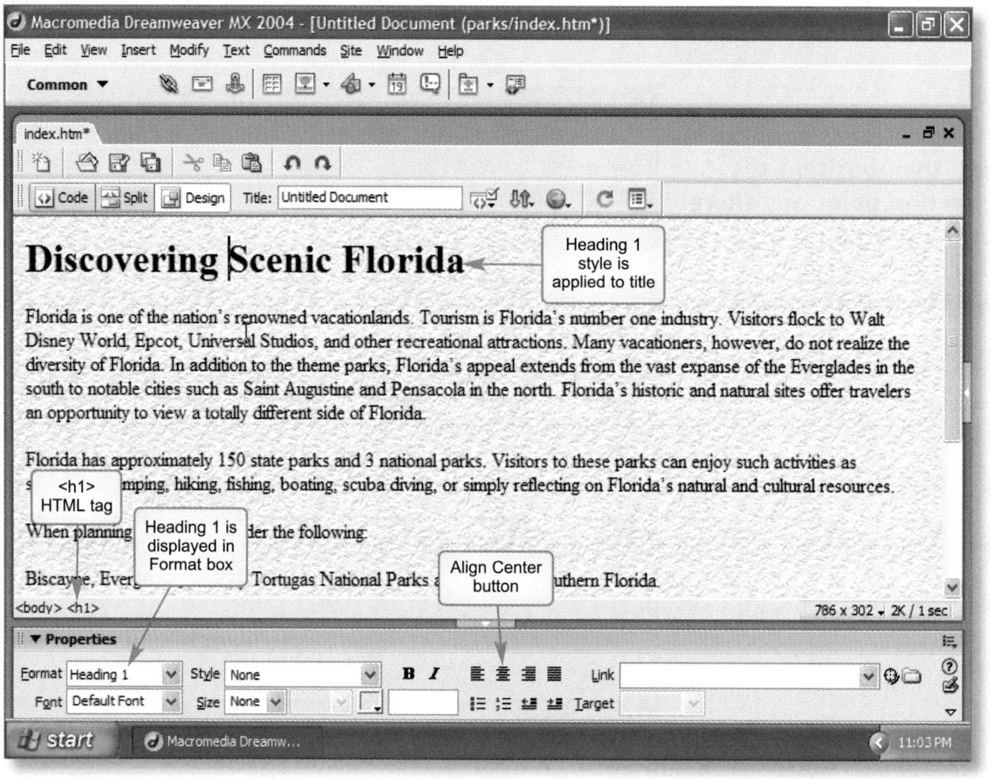

FIGURE 1-54

Other Ways

1. On Text menu point to Paragraph Format, click Heading 1 on Paragraph Format submenu
2. Right-click selected text, point to Paragraph Format on context menu, click Heading 1 on Paragraph Format submenu

Centering Text

Using the **Align Center button** in the Property inspector allows you to center text. This button is very similar to the Center button in a word processing program. To center a single line or a paragraph, position the mouse pointer in the line or paragraph, and then click the button to center the text. You do not need to select a single line or single paragraph to center it. To center more than one paragraph at a time, however, you must select all paragraphs. The following step illustrates how to center the heading.

To Center the Web Page Heading

1

- **If necessary, click anywhere in the heading, Discovering Scenic Florida. Click the Align Center button in the Property inspector.**

The heading, Discovering Scenic Florida, is centered (Figure 1-55).

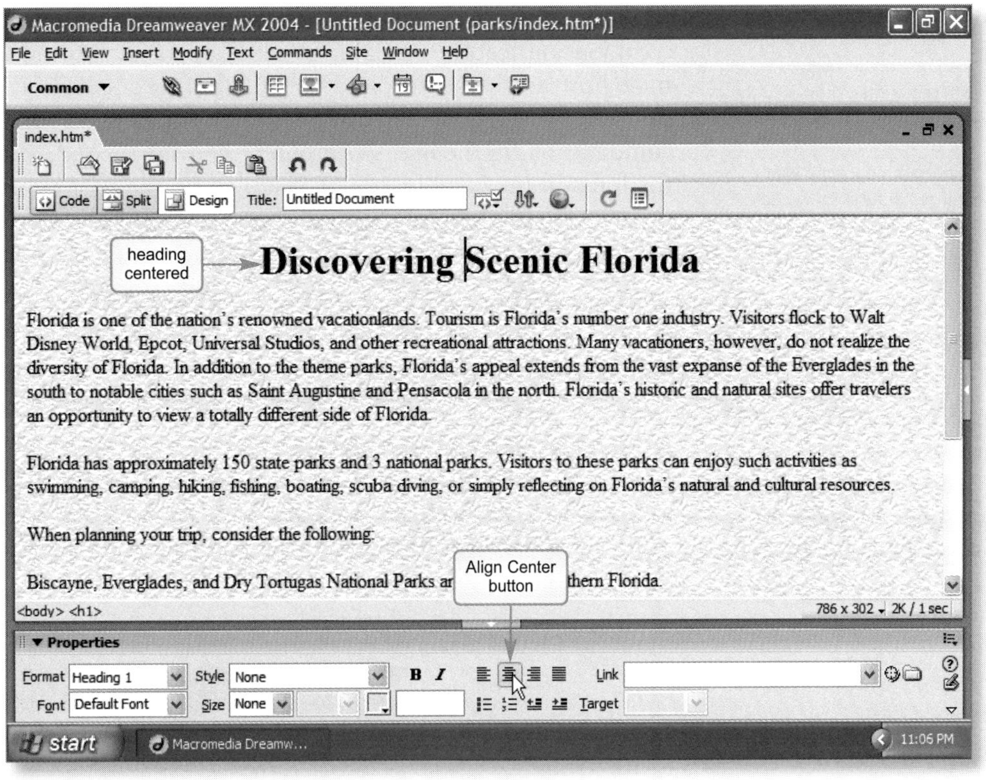

FIGURE 1-55

Other Ways

1. On Text menu click Align, click Center on Align submenu
2. Right-click selected text, point to Align on context menu, click Center on Align submenu
3. Press CTRL+ALT+SHIFT+C

Text is one of the more important elements of most any Web page. How the text displays on a Web page can attract or detract from the overall appearance. Using the appropriate font type can enhance and entice viewers to browse your Web site.

Specifying Font Types

Type is important because it attracts attention, sets the style and tone of a Web page, influences how readers interpret the words, and defines the feeling of the page. The **font type** refers to the basic design of the lettering. Several methods are used to classify fonts. The most common way is to place them in different families based on shared characteristics. The five basic font type families are:

1. Serif, such as Times or Times New Roman
2. Sans-serif, such as Helvetica and Arial
3. Monospace, such as Courier
4. Cursive, such as Brush Script
5. Decorative and fantasy

Two general categories of typefaces are serif and sans-serif. **Sans-serif** typefaces are composed of simple lines, whereas **serif** typefaces use small decorative marks to embellish characters and make them easier to read. Helvetica and Arial are sans-serif types, and Times New Roman is a serif type. A **monospace** font, such as Courier, is

Q&A

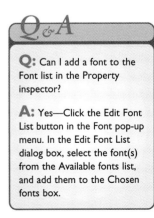

Q: Can I add a font to the Font list in the Property inspector?

A: Yes—Click the Edit Font List button in the Font pop-up menu. In the Edit Font List dialog box, select the font(s) from the Available fonts list, and add them to the Chosen fonts box.

> *More About*
>
> **Formatting Text**
>
> Research shows that people read on-screen text differently than they read the printed word. They are more apt to scan and look for the important concepts. Many changes in formatting could make a site confusing.

one in which every character takes up the same amount of horizontal space. **Cursive** font styles emulate handwritten letterforms. **Decorative and fantasy** is a family for fonts that do not fit any of the other families.

Most Web pages use only the first three families. Dreamweaver provides a font combination feature available in the Property inspector. **Font combinations** determine how a browser displays your Web page's text. In the Property inspector, you can select one of six font combinations. A browser looks for the first font in the combination on the user's computer, then the second, and then the third. If none of the fonts in the combination is installed on the user's computer, the browser displays the text as specified by the user's browser preferences. The following steps show how to change the font type.

To Change the Font Type

1

- **Click to the left of the heading, Discovering Scenic Florida, and then drag through the entire heading.**

The heading is selected (Figure 1-56).

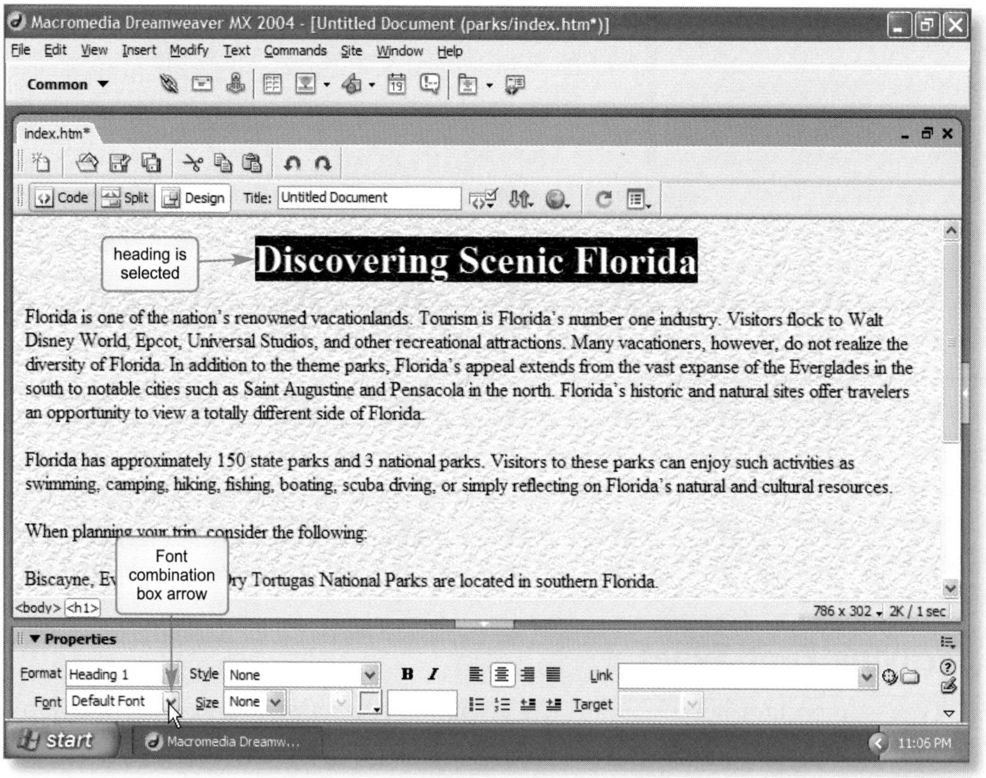

FIGURE 1-56

2

- **Click the Font combination box arrow and then point to Verdana, Arial, Helvetica, sans-serif.**

The Font combination pop-up menu is displayed, and the Verdana, Arial, Helvetica, sans-serif combination is highlighted (Figure 1-57). The menu includes six different font combinations and the default font.

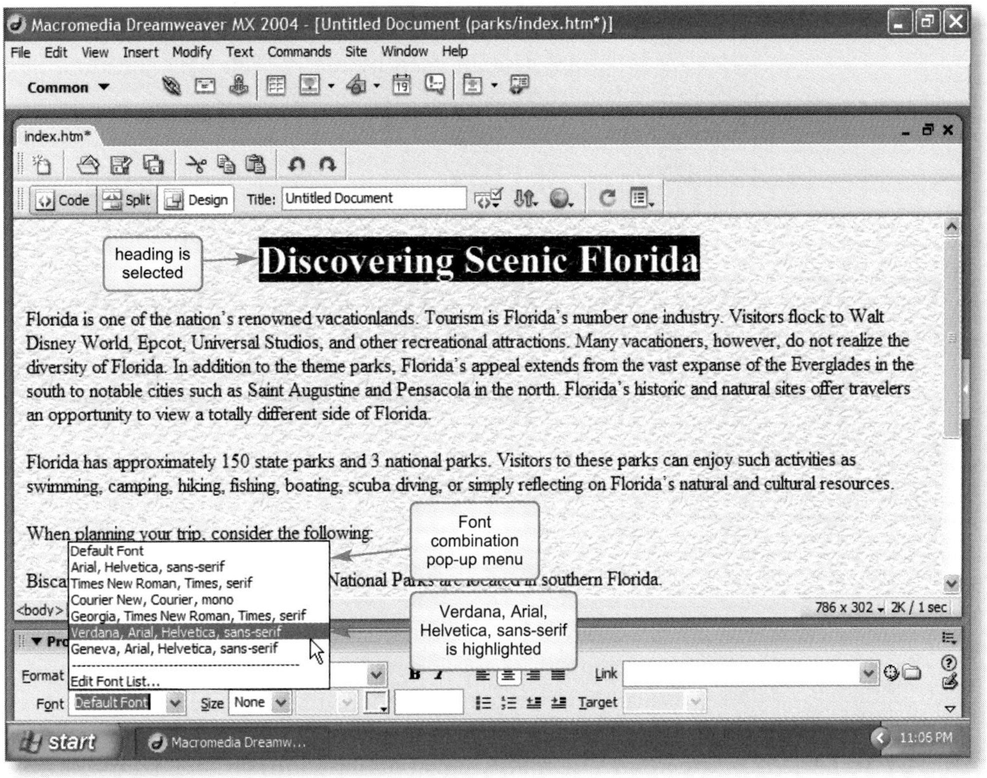

FIGURE 1-57

3

- **Click Verdana, Arial, Helvetica, sans-serif.**

The new font type is applied to the selected heading, and style1 displays in the Style text box (Figure 1-58).

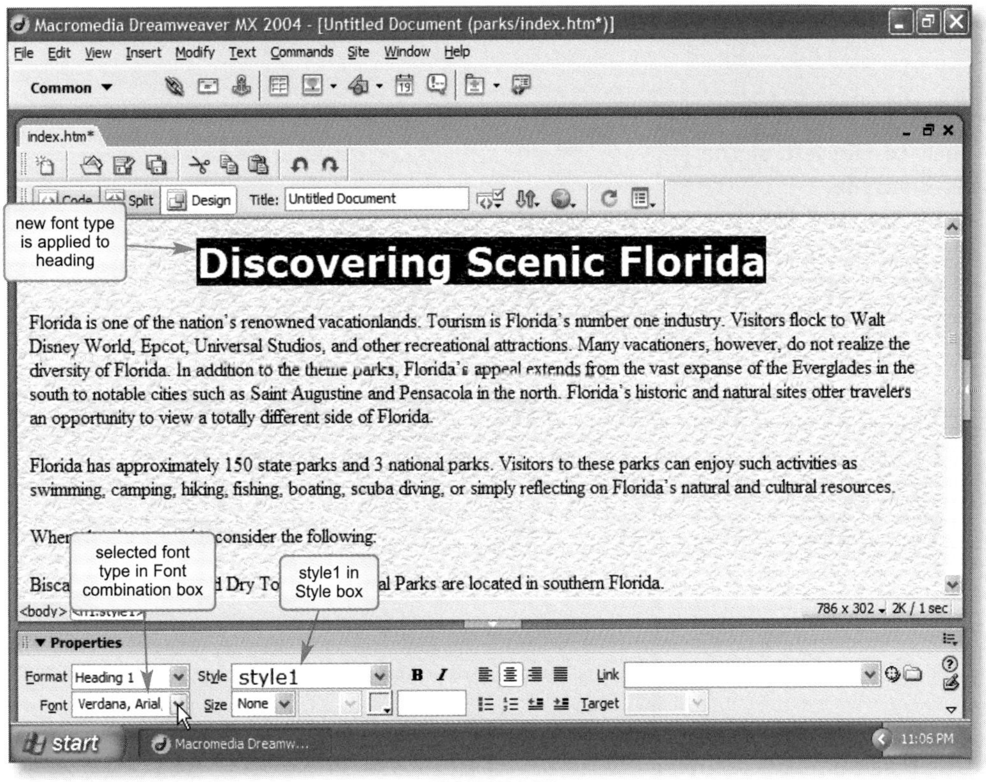

FIGURE 1-58

Other Ways

1. On the Text menu point to Font, click Verdana, Arial, Helvetica, sans-serif
2. Right-click selected text, point to Font on context menu, click Verdana, Arial, Helvetica, sans-serif

In addition to headings and font type attributes, other text design options are available. Presenting information in small chunks, such as bulleted or numbered lists, is a design element used by many Web page authors. Dreamweaver makes it easy to add lists such as these to your Web page.

Types of Lists

One way to group and organize information is by using lists. Web pages can have three types of lists: ordered or numbered, unordered or bulleted, and definition. **Ordered lists** contain text preceded by numbered steps. **Unordered lists** contain text preceded by bullets (dots or other symbols) or image bullets. You use an unordered list if the list items need not be listed in any particular order. **Definition lists** do not use leading characters such as bullet points or numbers. Glossaries and descriptions often use this type of list.

The Unordered List and Ordered List buttons are available in the Property inspector. You access the Definition List command through the Text menu List command submenu. Through the List Properties dialog box, you can set the number style, reset the count, or set the bullet style options for individual list items or for the entire list. To access the List Properties dialog box, click anywhere in the list, and then click the List Item button in the Property inspector.

You can create a new list or you can create a list using existing text. When you select existing text and add bullets, the blank line between the list items is deleted. Later in this project, you add line breaks to reinsert a blank line between each list item. The following steps show how to create an unordered list using existing text.

More About

Lists

You can remove the bullets or numbers from a formatted list just as easily as you added them. Select the formatted list. Click the button in the Properties inspector that you originally used to apply the formatting.

To Create an Unordered List

1

- **Click to the left of the line, Biscayne, Everglades, and Dry Tortugas National Parks are located in southern Florida (Figure 1-59).**

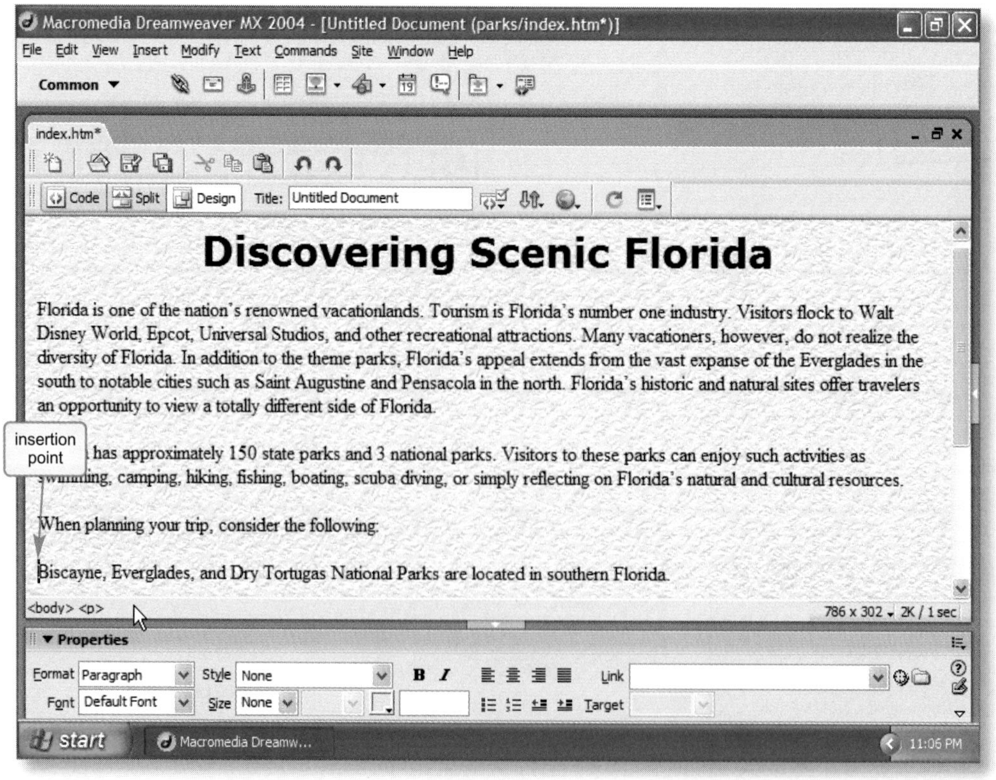

FIGURE 1-59

2

- **Drag to select the text, Biscayne, Everglades, and Dry Tortugas National Parks are located in southern Florida, and the next three lines.**
- **Point to the Unordered List button in the Property inspector.**

The text is selected (Figure 1-60).

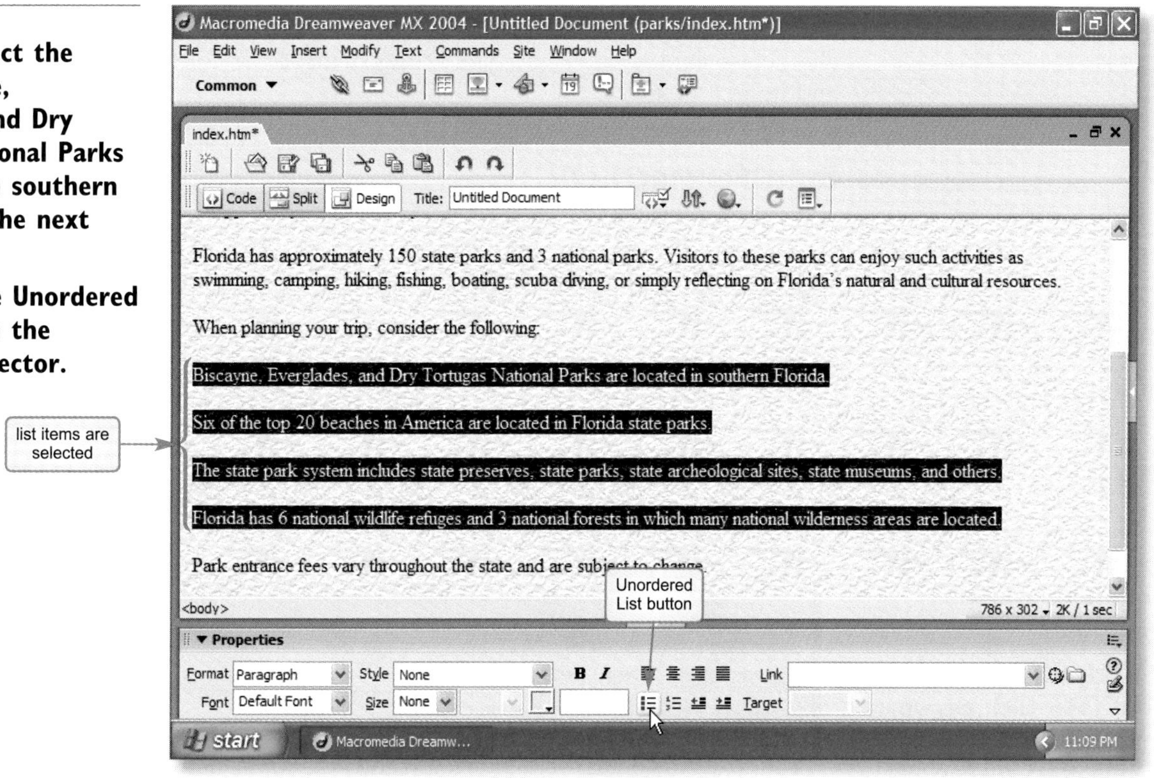

FIGURE 1-60

3

- **Click the Unordered List button.**

A bullet is added to each line, the four lines are indented, and the space between each item is deleted (Figure 1-61).

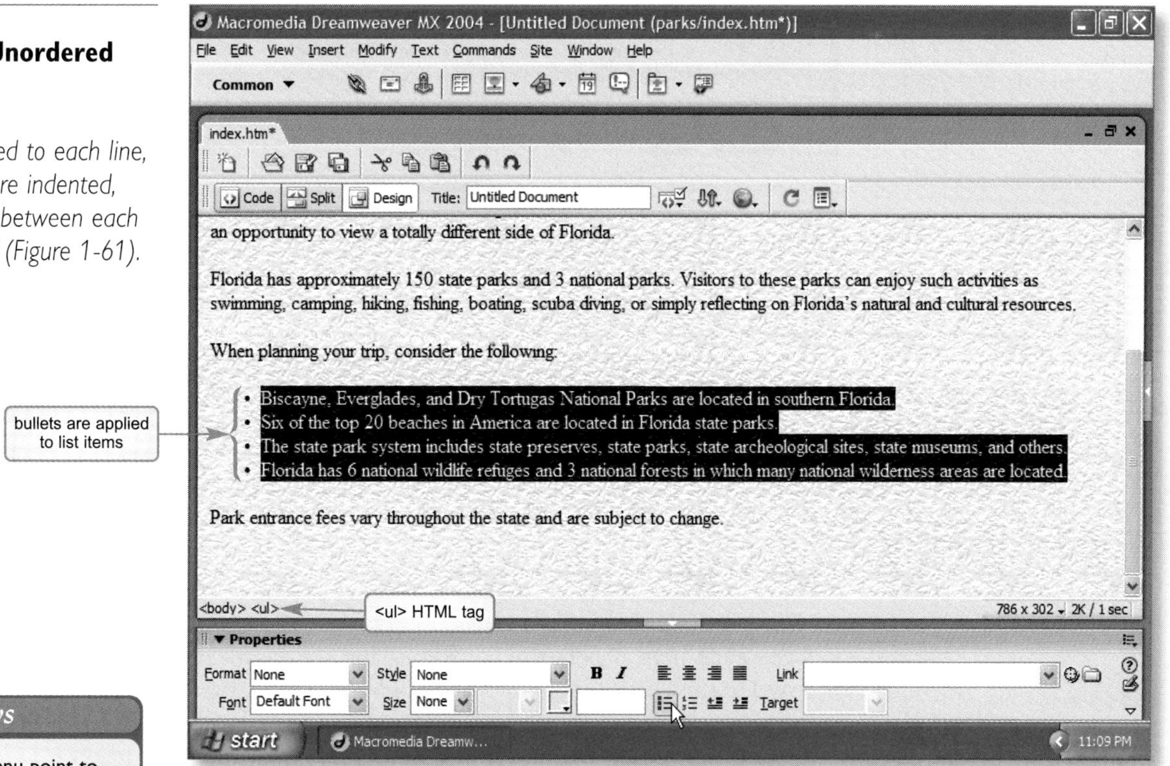

FIGURE 1-61

Other Ways

1. On Text menu point to List, click Unordered List on List submenu
2. Right-click, point to List, click Unordered List on List submenu

Other text formatting options are applying bold or italic styles to text. **Bold** characters display somewhat thicker and darker than those that are not bold. **Italic** characters slant to the right. The Property inspector contains buttons for both bold and italic font styles.

Bold Formatting

To bold text within Dreamweaver is a simple procedure. If you have used word processing software, you are familiar with this process. The next step illustrates how to emphasize the bullet points by applying bold formatting.

To Bold Text

1

- **If necessary, drag through the bulleted points to select all four lines.**
- **Click the Bold button and then click anywhere in the Document window to deselect the text.**

Bold formatting is applied to the unordered list items (Figure 1-62).

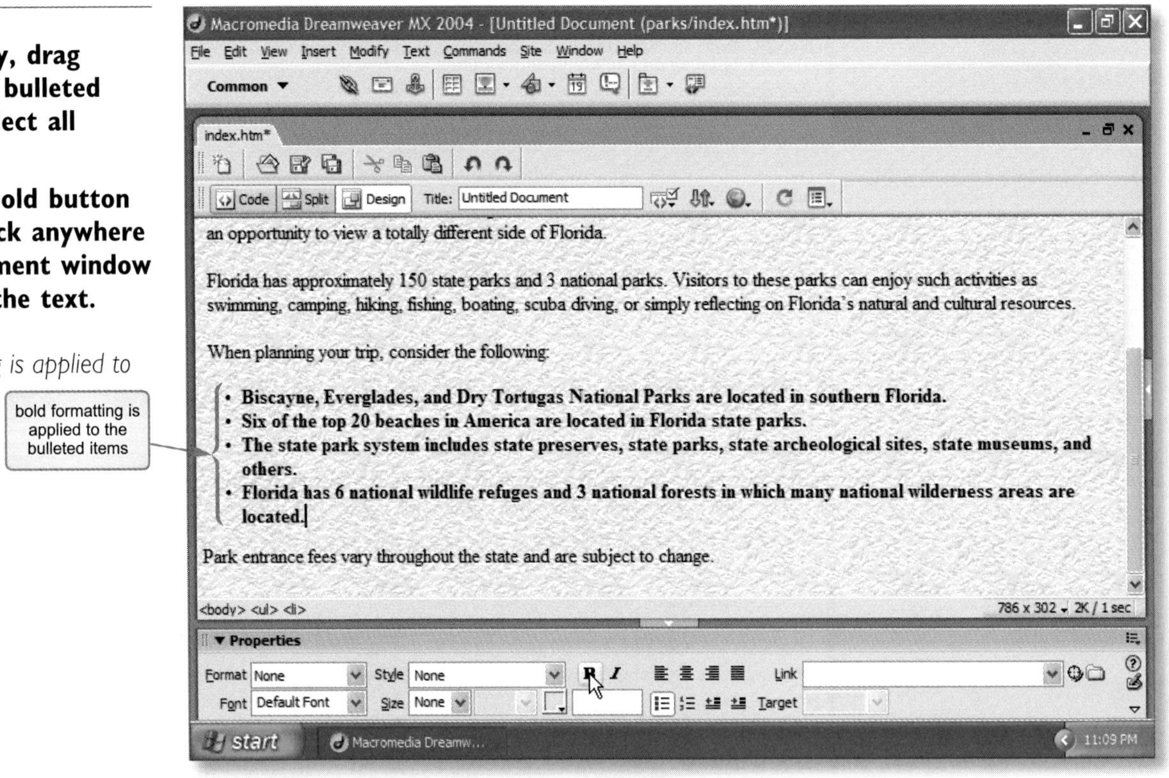

FIGURE 1-62

> ***More About***
>
> **HTML**
>
> For more information about HTML, visit the Dreamweaver MX 2004 More About Web page (scsite.com/dreamweavermx04/more.htm) and then click HTML.

Understanding Line Breaks

When you added bullets to the items list earlier in this project, the blank line between each item was removed. Removing the blank line between items is a result of how Dreamweaver interprets the HTML code. A blank line between the bulleted items, however, will provide better spacing and readability when the Web page is viewed in a browser. You can add blank lines in several ways. You might assume that pressing the ENTER key at the end of each line would be the quickest way to accomplish this. Pressing the ENTER key, however, adds another bullet. The easiest way to accomplish the task of adding blank lines is to insert line breaks. Recall that the line break starts a new single line without inserting a blank line between lines of text. Inserting two line breaks, however, adds a single blank line.

Dreamweaver provides a Line Break command through the Insert HTML Special Characters submenu. It is easier, however, to use the **SHIFT+ENTER** keyboard shortcut. The following steps show how to add a blank line between each of the bulleted items.

To Add a Line Break

1

- **Click at the end of the first bulleted item.**
- **Press SHIFT+ENTER two times.**

Two line breaks are inserted (Figure 1-63). When the Web page is viewed in Dreamweaver, it appears that two blank lines are inserted. When viewed in a browser, however, only one blank line is displayed between each item. You will view your Web page in a browser later in this project.

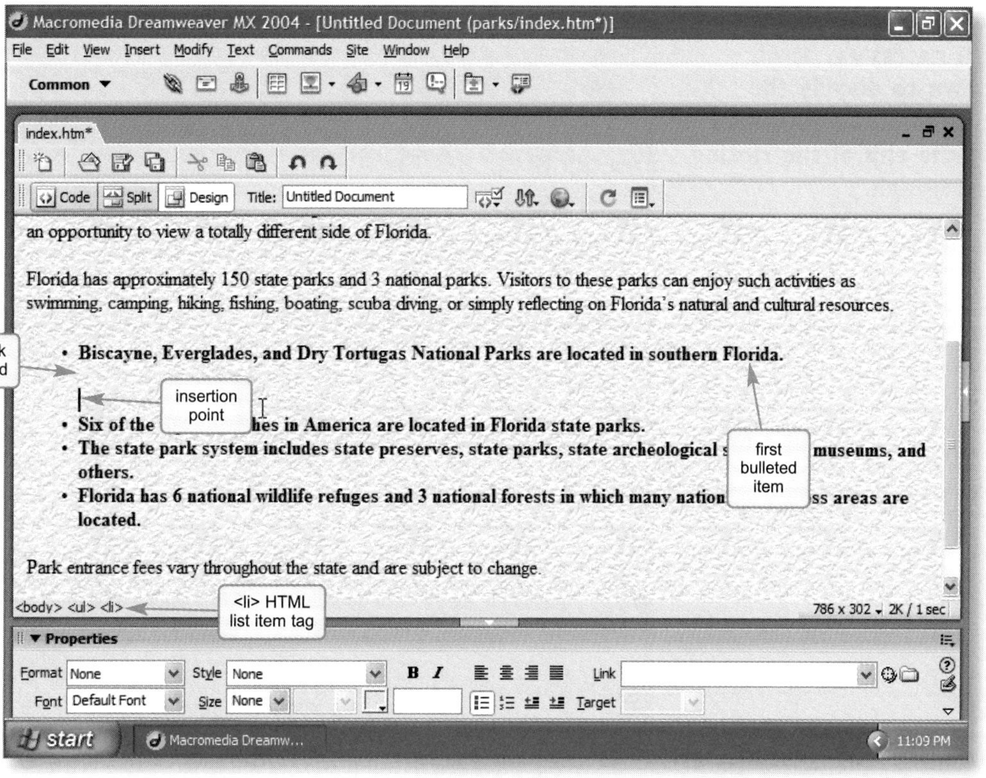

FIGURE 1-63

2

- **Press SHIFT+ENTER two times at the end of the second and third bulleted items to insert blank lines between the second and third and the third and fourth bulleted list items.**

The bulleted items are displayed with blank lines between them in the Document window (Figure 1-64).

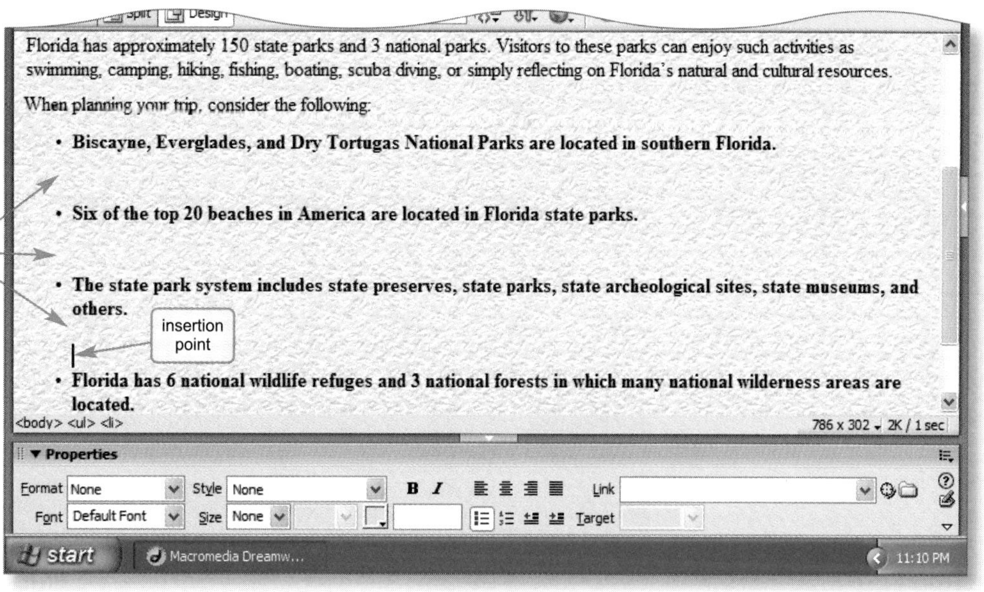

FIGURE 1-64

When creating a Web document, it is a good idea to add your name and date to the document. Insert a single line break between your name and the date. The following steps show how to add this information.

To Add Your Name and Date

1

- **If necessary, scroll down to display the closing paragraph. Click at the end of the closing paragraph.**
- **Press the ENTER key.**

The insertion point moves to the next paragraph (Figure 1-65).

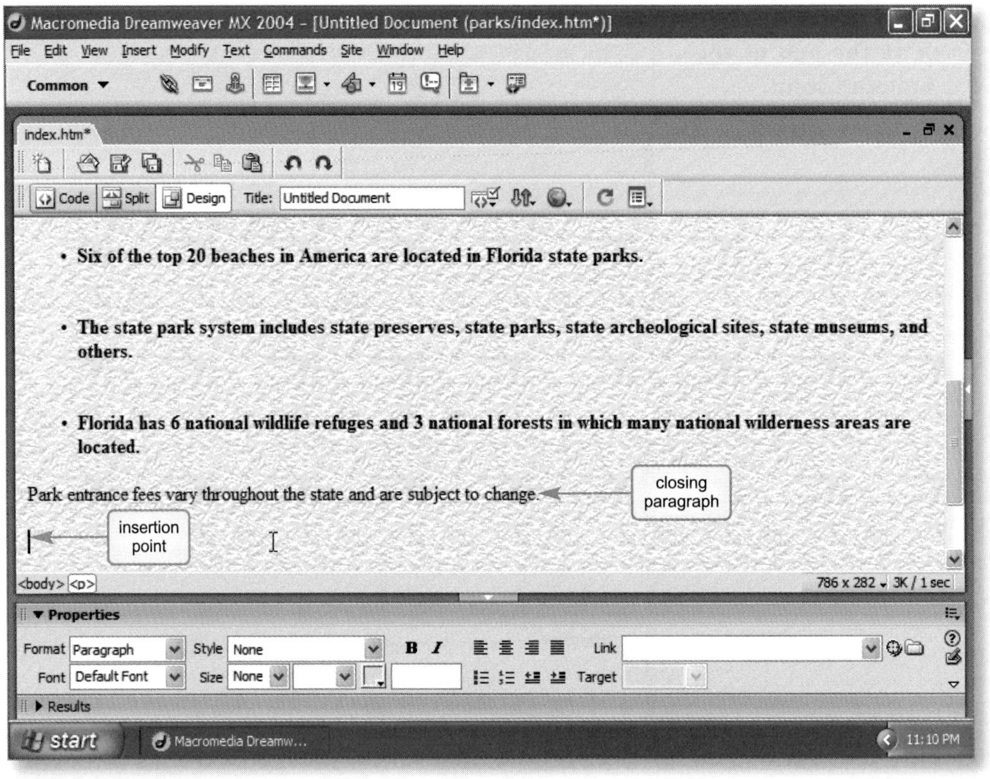

FIGURE 1-65

2

- **Type your name and then press SHIFT+ENTER.**

The insertion point moves to the next line (Figure 1-66). No line space is displayed between the name and the insertion point.

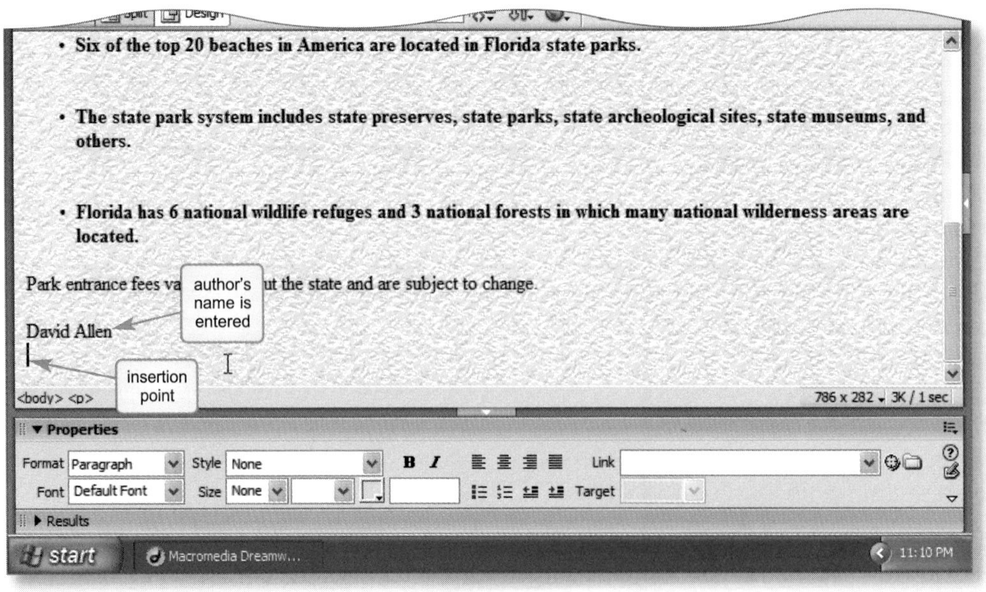

FIGURE 1-66

3

• **Type the current date and then press the ENTER key (Figure 1-67).**

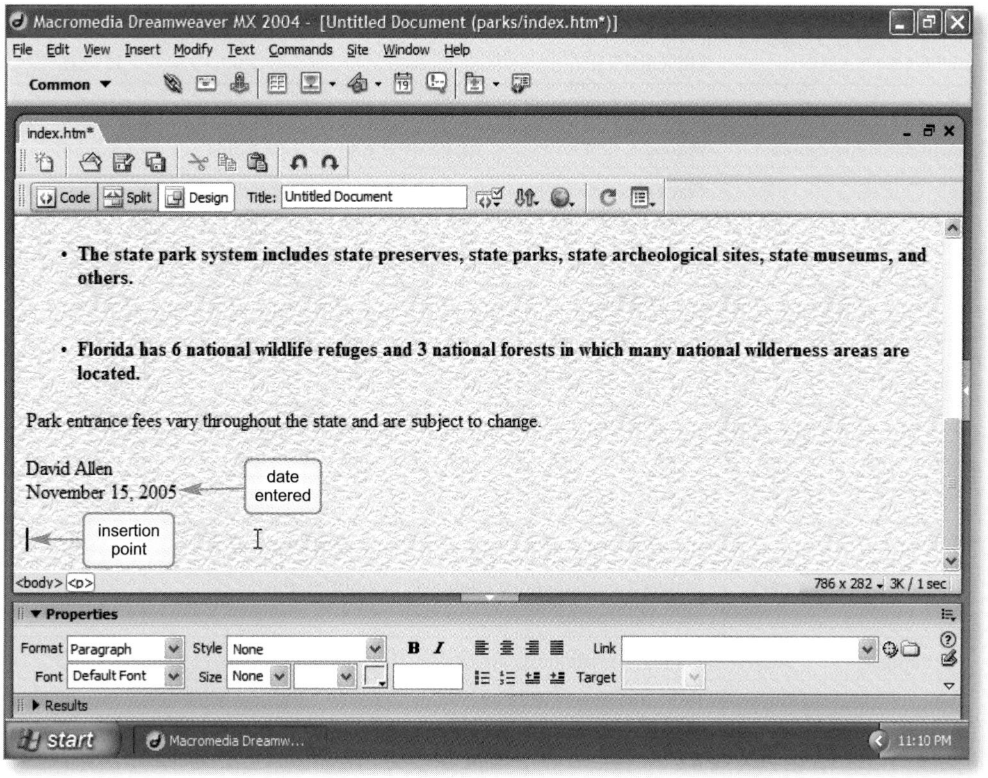

FIGURE 1-67

Special Characters

Sometimes it is necessary to enter non-keyboard characters such as quotes, trademarks, and registrations into a Web page. To have the browser display these special characters requires a character code. Character codes for causing a browser to show special characters generally are called **HTML entities**. HTML represents these codes by a name or a number. HTML includes entity names for characters such as the copyright symbol (©), the ampersand (&), and the registered trademark symbol (®). Each entity has both a name and a numeric equivalent (such as —). Table 1-2 on the next page contains a list of HTML entities supported by Dreamweaver.

Table 1-2 HTML Entities

BUTTON NAME	DESCRIPTION	HTML TAGS AND CHARACTER ENTITIES
Line Break	Places a line break at the insertion point	
Non-Breaking Space	Places a non-breaking space at the insertion point	
Left Quote	Places opening, curved double quotation marks at the insertion point	“
Right Quote	Places closing, curved double quotation marks at the insertion point	”
Em Dash	Places an em dash at the insertion point	—
Pound	Places a pound (currency) symbol at the insertion point	£
Euro	Places a euro (currency) symbol at the insertion point	€
Yen	Places a yen (currency) symbol at the insertion point	¥
Copyright	Places a copyright symbol at the insertion point	©
Registered Trademark	Places a registered trademark symbol at the insertion point	®
Trademark	Places a trademark symbol at the insertion point	™
Other Characters	Provides a set of special characters from which to select	Other ASCII characters

In the Florida Parks Web page, both Walt Disney World® and Epcot® are registered trademarks. The following steps illustrate how to insert the registered trademark symbol next to these names, using the Insert menu and the HTML Special Characters submenu.

To Insert a Registered Trademark Character

1

- **If necessary, scroll up to display the first paragraph in the Web page.**
- **Click to the right of World (in Walt Disney World) and before the comma (Figure 1-68).**

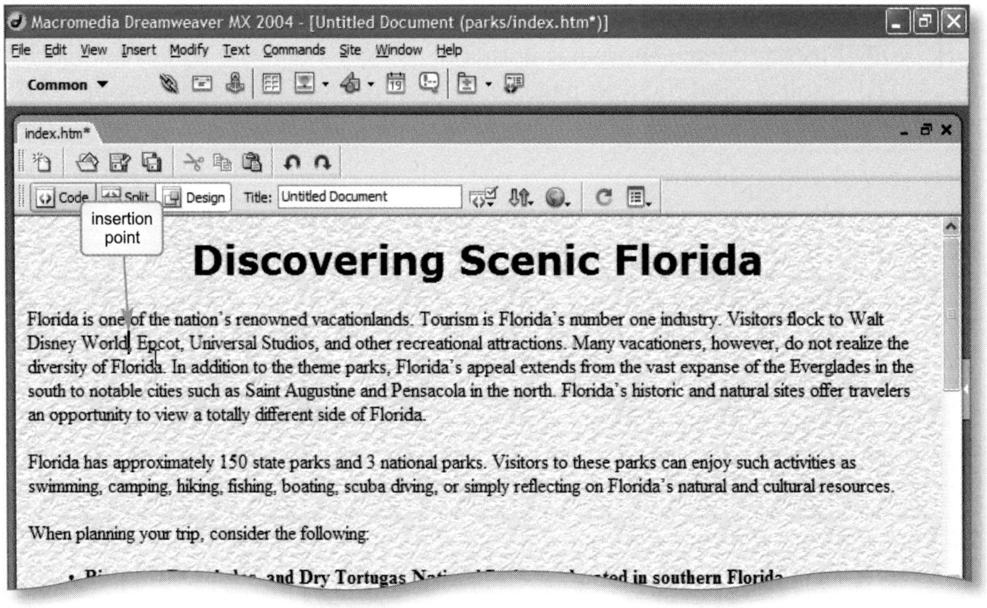

FIGURE 1-68

2

- **Click Insert on the menu bar, point to HTML, point to Special Characters on the HTML submenu, and then point to Registered on the Special Characters submenu.**

Dreamweaver displays the HTML submenu and the Special Characters submenu (Figure 1-69).

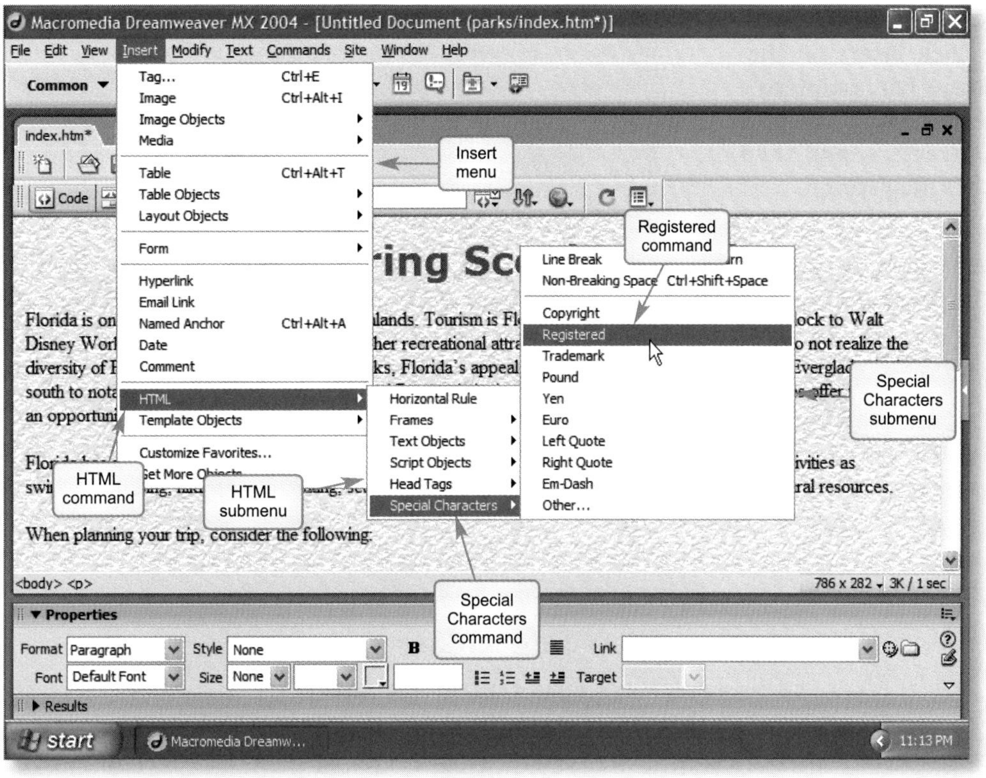

FIGURE 1-69

3

- **Click Registered on the Special Characters submenu.**
- **Click to the right of Epcot and before the comma.**

The registered trademark symbol is inserted into the document and the insertion point is to the right of Epcot (Figure 1-70).

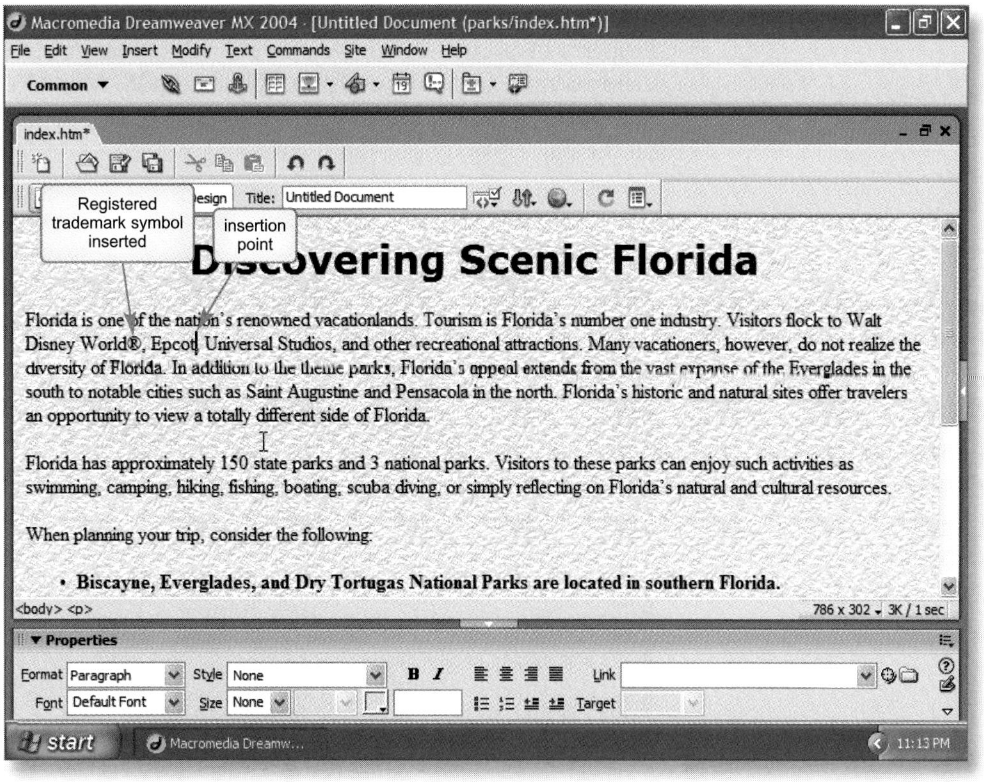

FIGURE 1-70

4

- **Click Insert on the menu bar, point to HTML, point to Special Characters, and then click Registered.**
- **Click anywhere in the document to deselect the symbol.**

The registered trademark symbol is inserted into the document (Figure 1-71).

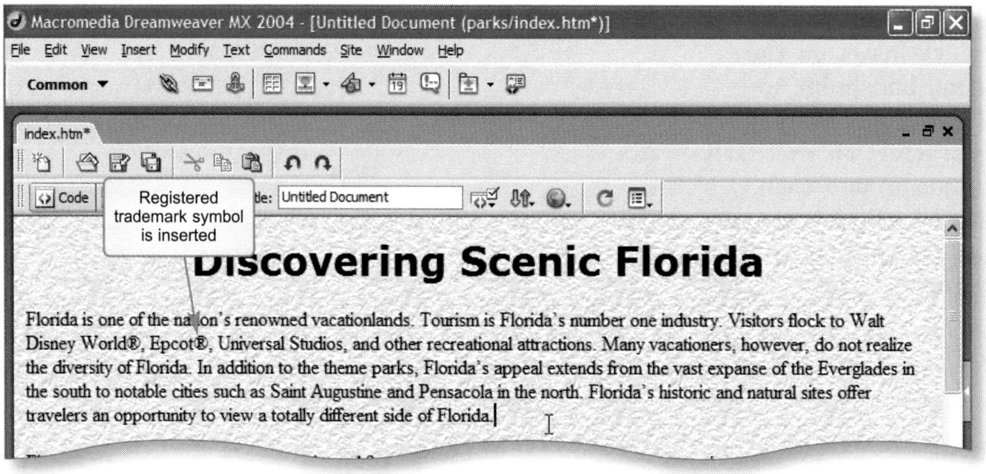

FIGURE 1-71

Web-Safe Colors

Adding color to text can attract attention to important information and emphasize different aspects of a Web page. It is easy to change the color of an individual character, a word, a line, a paragraph, or the text of an entire document. In HTML, colors are expressed either as hexadecimal values (for example, #FF0000) or as color names (such as red).

Use the **color picker** to select the colors for page elements or text. Through the Property inspector, Dreamweaver provides access to five different color palettes: Color Cubes, Continuous Tone, Windows OS, Mac OS, and Grayscale. Color Cubes is the default color palette. Figure 1-72 shows the Color Cubes color palette available on the color palette pop-up menu.

More About

To open the system color picker, click the Color Wheel button.

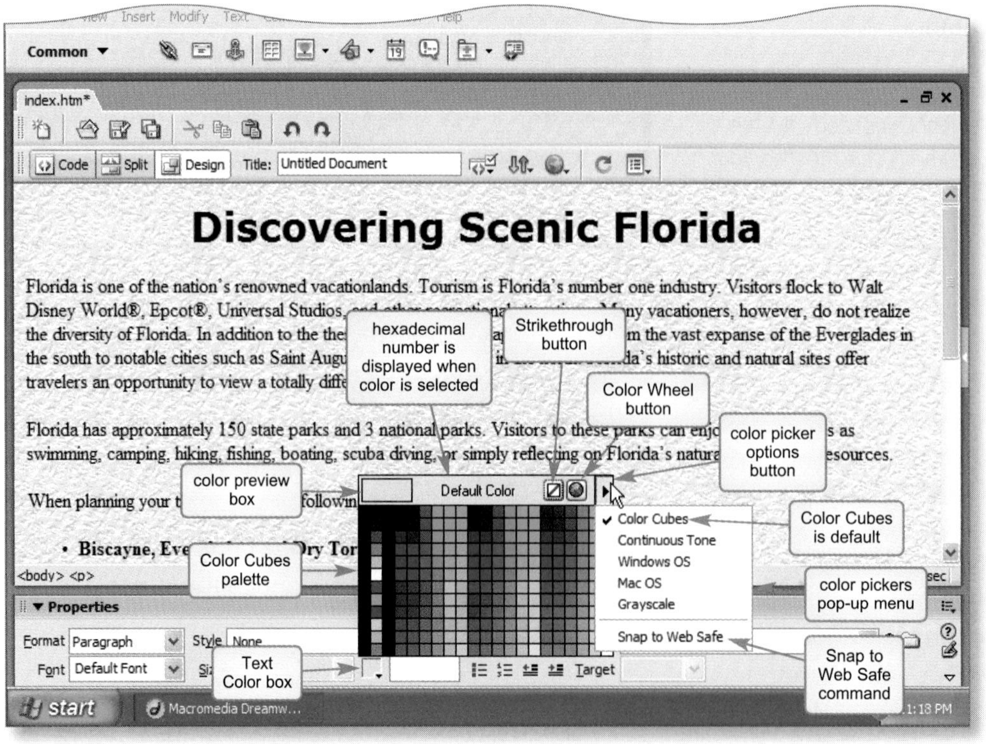

FIGURE 1-72

Two of the color palettes, Color Cubes and Continuous Tone, display Web-safe colors. Web-safe colors are colors that display correctly on the screen when someone is viewing your Web page in a browser. A Web-safe color is one that appears the same in Netscape Navigator and Microsoft Internet Explorer on both Windows and Macintosh systems. Most experts agree that approximately 212 to 216 Web-safe colors exist. Testing by experts, however, suggests that Internet Explorer renders only 212 Web-safe colors. Table 1-3 contains a list of the color picker options.

Q&A

Q: Are there other reasons why I would use Web-safe colors?

A: Another reason to use the Web-safe color palette is if you will be developing for alternative Web devices such as PDA and cell phone displays. Many of these devices offer only black-and-white (1-bit) or 256 color (8-bit) displays.

Table 1-3 Color Picker Options

OPTION	FUNCTION
Color preview box	Provides a preview of the currently selected color or the color picked up by the eyedropper
Hex value area	Displays the hexadecimal value of the current color or the color picked up by the eyedropper
Strikethrough button	Clears the current color and retains the default color
Color Wheel button	Opens the system color pickers via the operating system Color dialog box
Option button	Displays a pop-up menu from which you can select one of five color pickers or the Snap to Web Safe command
Snap to Web Safe command	Automatically changes non-Web-safe colors to the nearest Web-safe values

Dreamweaver has an **eyedropper** feature that lets you select colors and make perfect color matches. When you are working with color palettes, you can use the eyedropper to choose a color from anywhere on the screen, including outside of Dreamweaver, and apply the color to a selected object in the Document window. You place the eyedropper over the color you want to select and then click the mouse button. As soon as you click the mouse button, the color automatically is applied to the selected object. If you move the eyedropper to an object outside of Dreamweaver, the eyedropper changes to the block arrow mouse pointer shape until you move it back into the Dreamweaver window. Clicking the color picker options button and then selecting the Snap to Web Safe command will ensure the selected color is a Web-safe color.

Changing Text Color

The default color for Dreamweaver text is black. The following steps show how to change the text color of the heading to a shade of green.

To Change the Text Color

1

• **Select the heading and then click the Text Color box in the Property inspector.**

The Color Cubes palette is displayed (Figure 1-73). The color palette includes Web-safe colors, the color preview box, and the six-digit hexadecimal number that represents the selected color.

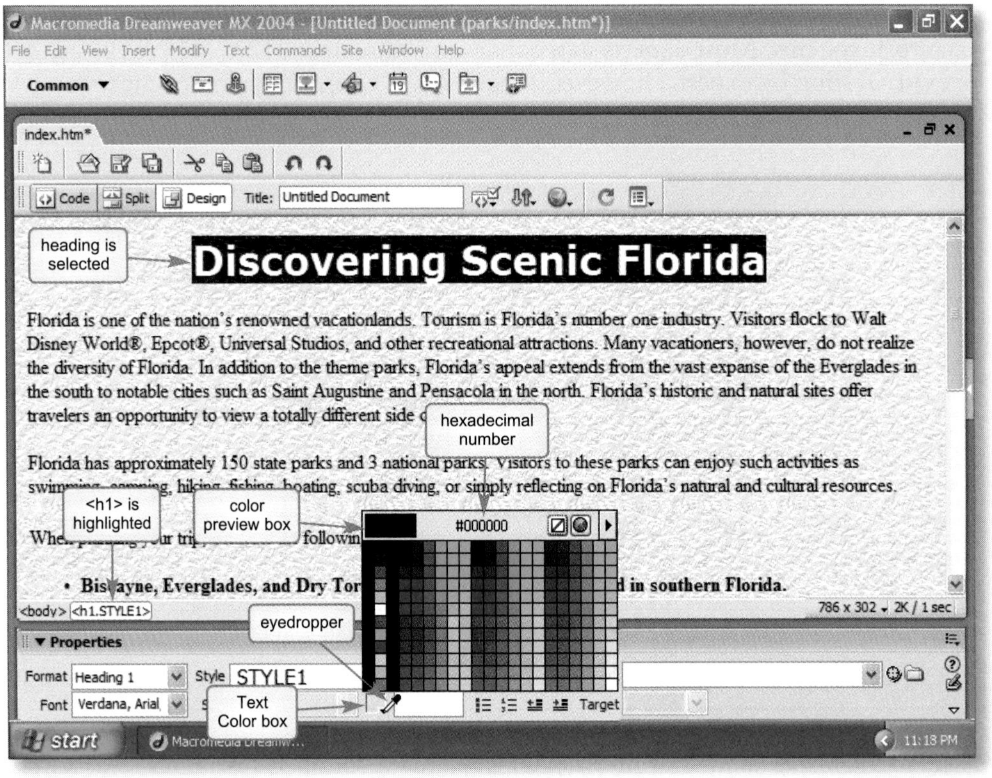

FIGURE 1-73

2

• **Position the eyedropper on the shade of green represented by hexadecimal number #006600 (row 1 and column 6 from the left).**

The selected color is displayed in the color preview box, and the hexadecimal value area displays the number for the color (Figure 1-74).

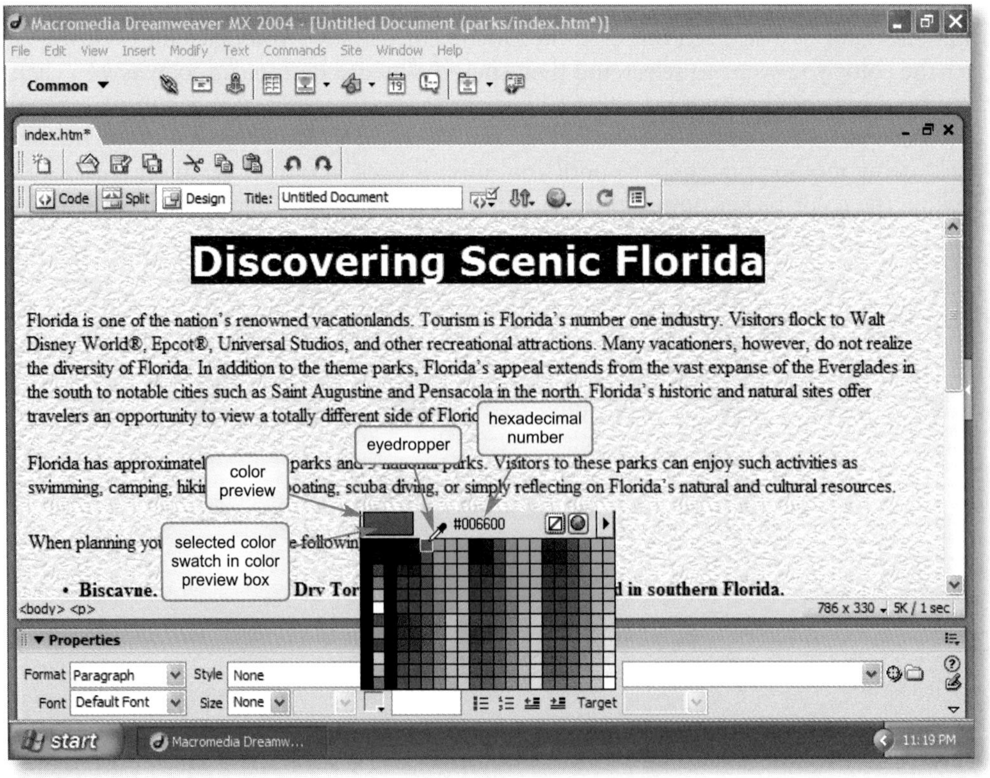

FIGURE 1-74

3

- **Click the eyedropper to apply the color to the selected text.**
- **Click anywhere in the document to deselect the text.**

The color is applied to the text. The heading is displayed in the selected green color (Figure 1-75). Occasionally you may have to press the ESC key to close the picker.

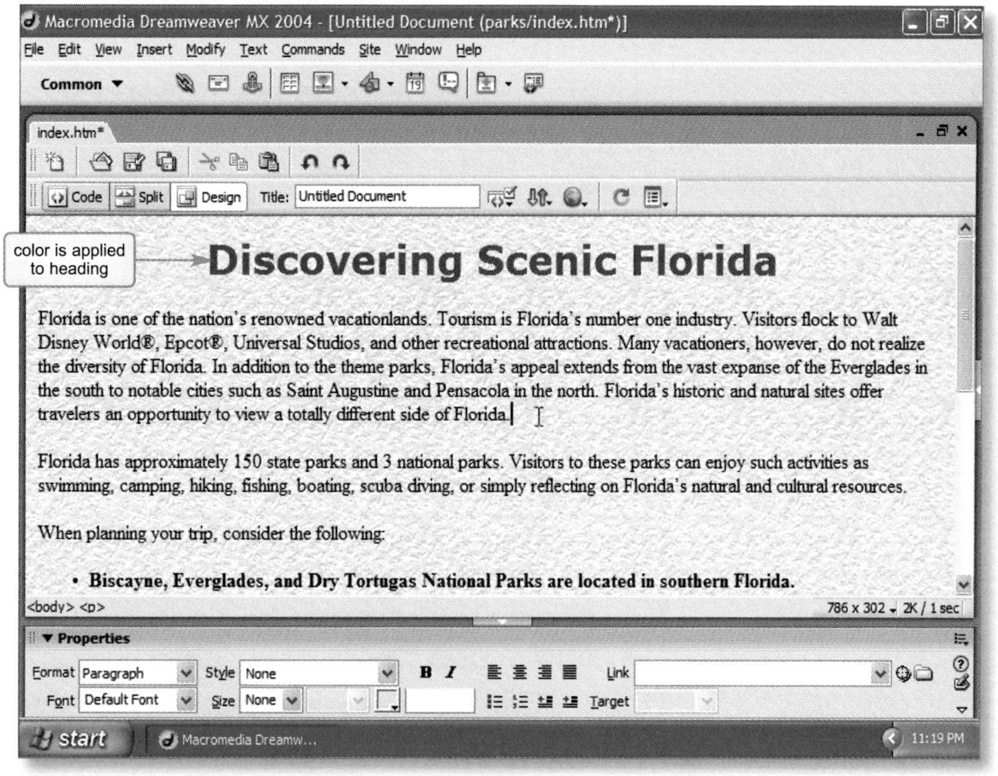

FIGURE 1-75

To add additional details to the Florida Parks Web page, a horizontal rule is inserted below the title. Many Web designers use a horizontal rule to divide a Web page into sections and as a style element.

Horizontal Rules

A horizontal rule (or line) is useful for organizing information and visually separating text and objects. You can specify the width and height of the rule in pixels or as a percentage of the page size. The rule can be aligned to the left, center, or right, and you can add shading or draw the line in a solid color. These attributes are available in the Property inspector. The HTML tag for a horizontal rule is <hr>.

Inserting a Horizontal Rule

On the Discovering Scenic Florida Web page, you insert a horizontal rule between the document heading and text as shown in the following steps. You use the default shaded line, but change the width and the height of the rule and then center the rule.

To Insert a Horizontal Rule

1

- **If necessary, scroll to the top of the page. Click to the right of the heading, Discovering Scenic Florida (Figure 1-76).**

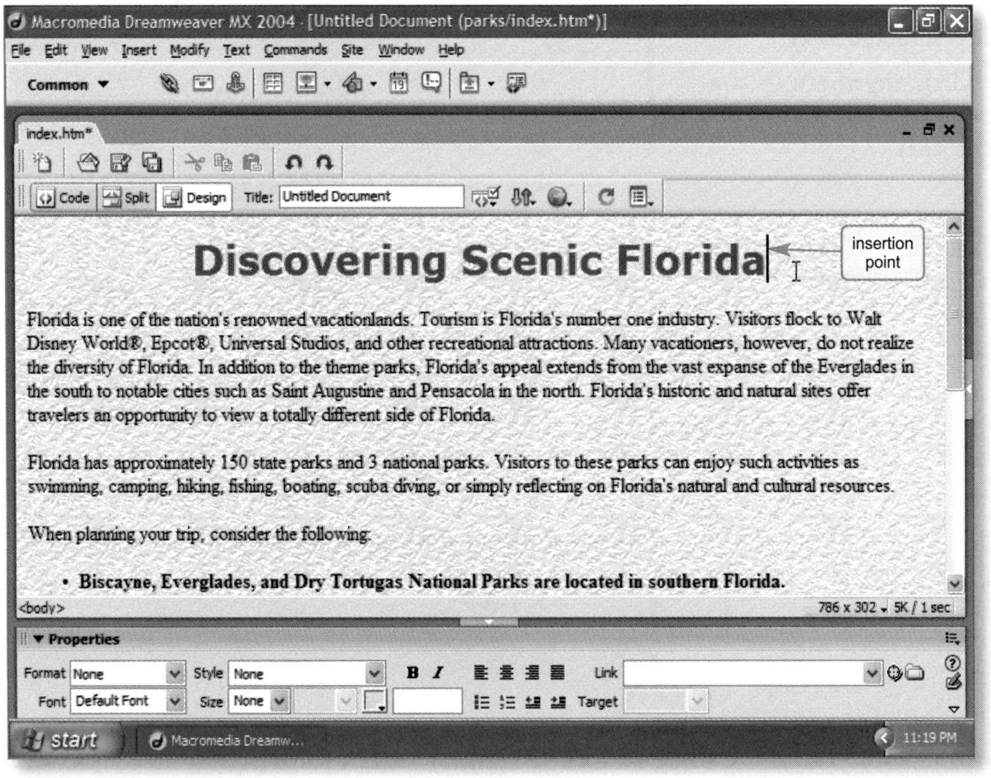

FIGURE 1-76

2

- **Click Insert on the menu bar, point to HTML, and then point to Horizontal Rule (Figure 1-77).**

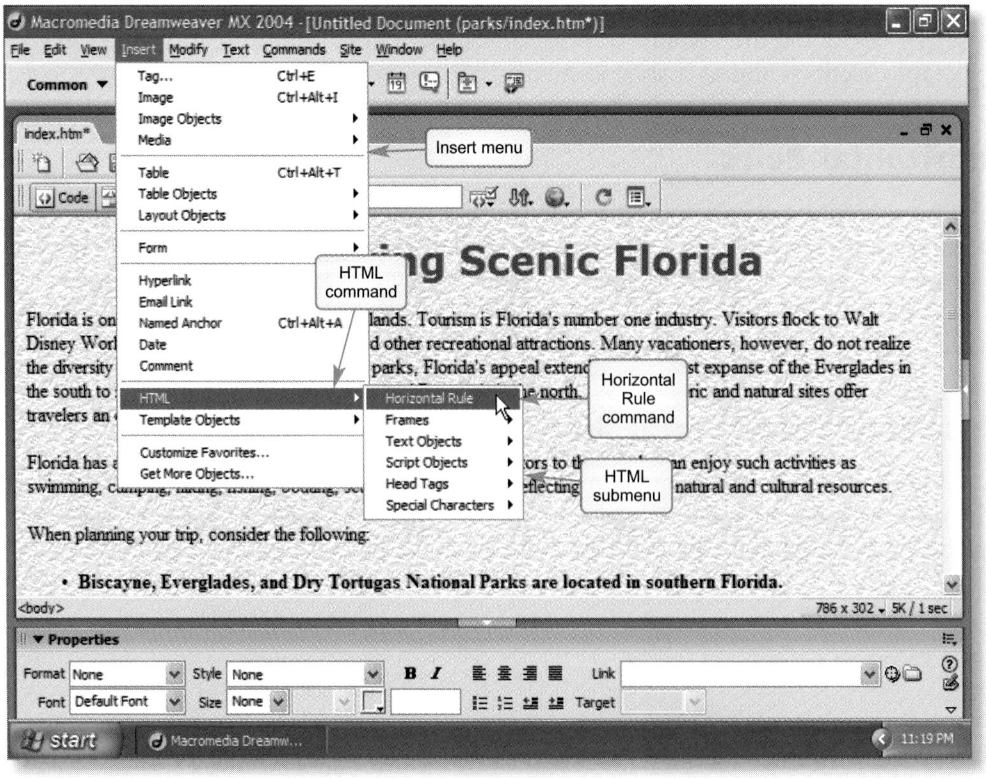

FIGURE 1-77

3

- **Click Horizontal Rule.**

The horizontal rule is inserted below the heading (Figure 1-78). The attributes in the Property inspector change to those for the horizontal rule. The horizontal line on your Web page may display somewhat differently than that shown in the figures.

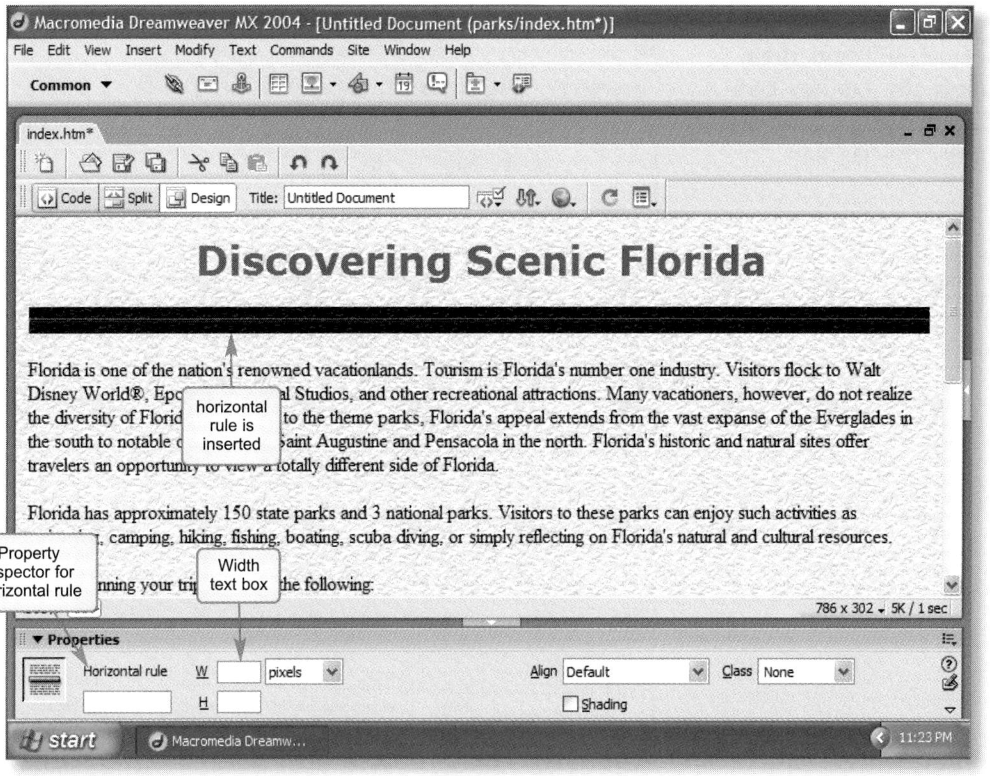

FIGURE 1-78

4

- **Click the Shading check box to select it.**
- **Click the Width text box.**

The attributes in the Property inspector change to those for the horizontal rule. The Shading check box is checked. The insertion point is in the Width text box (Figure 1-79).

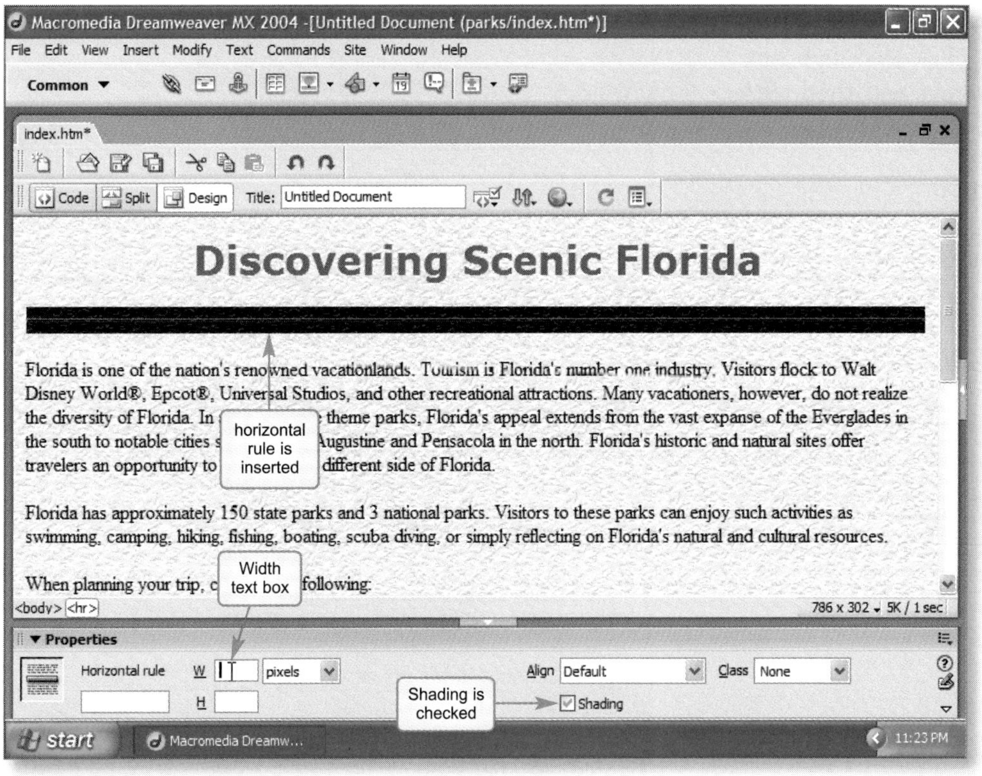

FIGURE 1-79

5

• **Type** 500 **and then press the TAB key two times. Type** 6 **and then press the TAB key.**

The width of the line is decreased, and the height of the line is increased. Default is highlighted in the Align box (Figure 1-80).

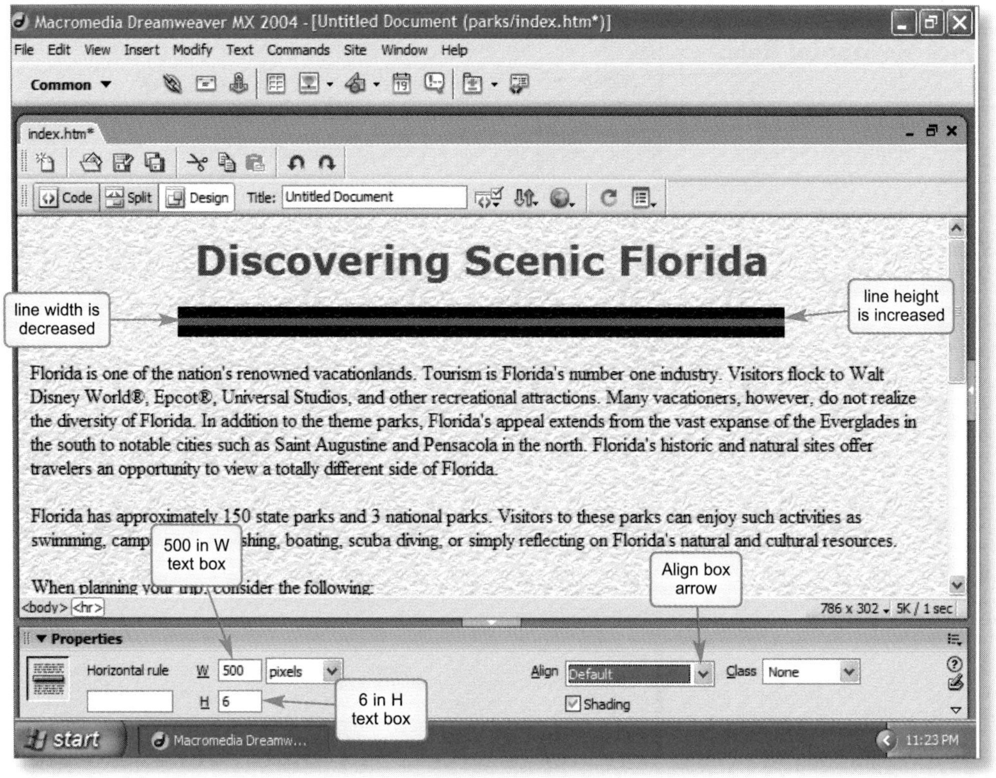

FIGURE 1-80

6

• **Click the Align box arrow and then click Center.**

The rule is centered. Even though the rule appeared centered before applying the Center attribute, it would not necessarily appear centered when viewed in all browsers. Adding the Center attribute assures that it always is centered below the heading.

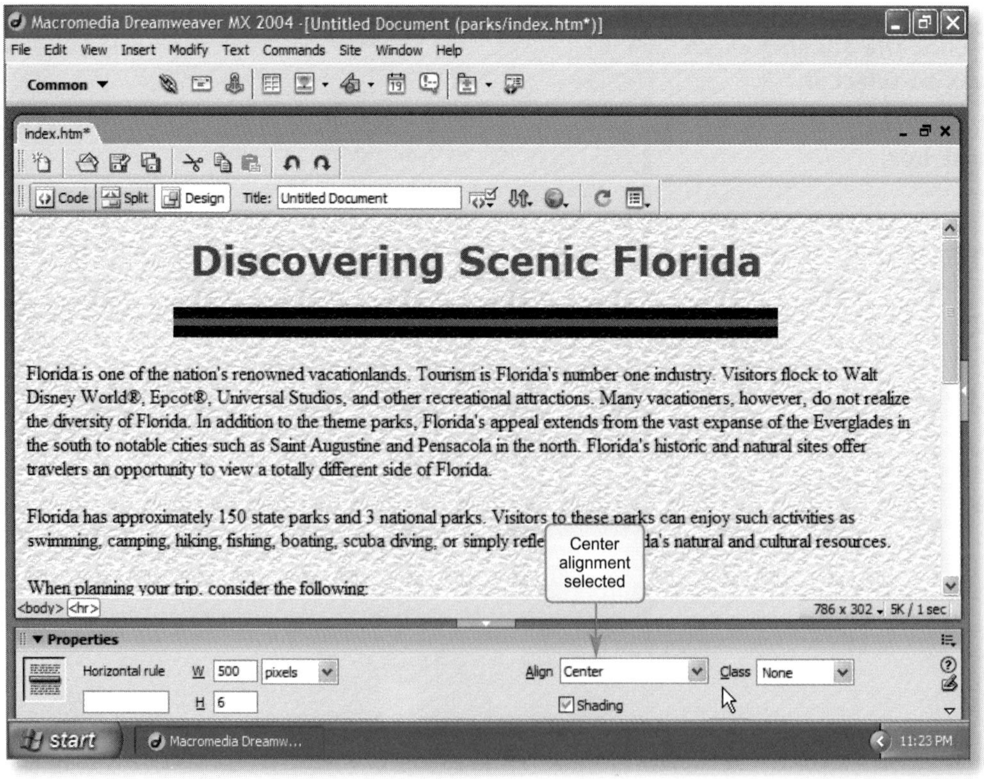

FIGURE 1-81

7

• **Click anywhere in the Document window to deselect the horizontal rule.**

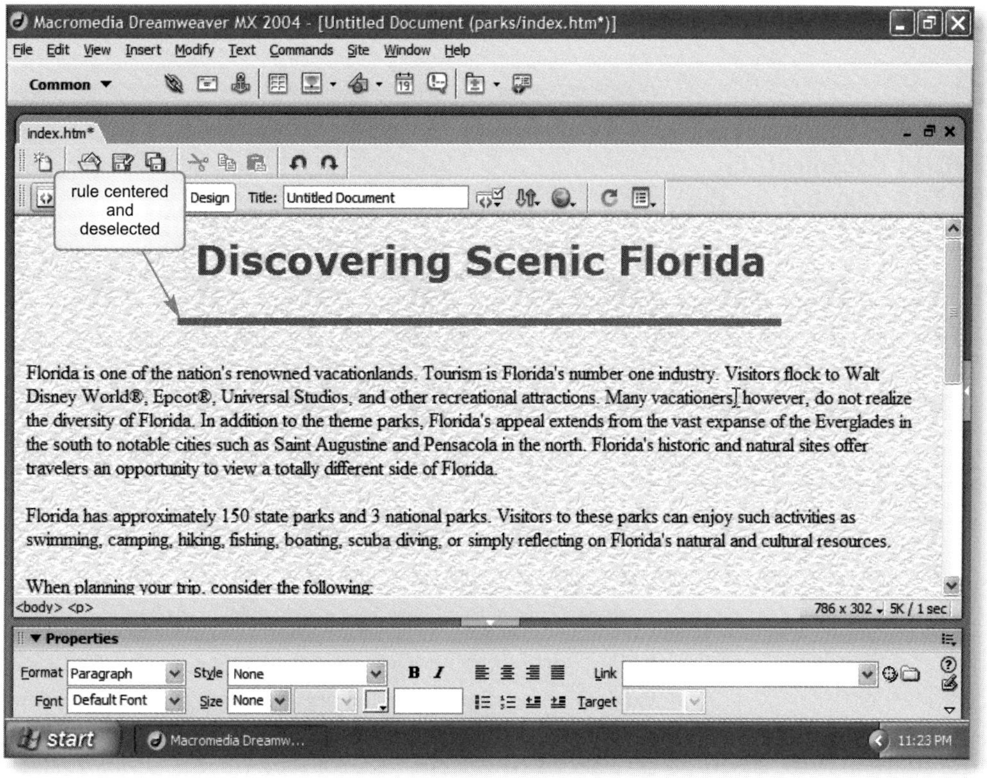

FIGURE 1-82

Web Page Titles

A **Web page title** helps Web site visitors keep track of what they are viewing as they browse. It is important to give your Web page an appropriate title. When visitors to your Web page create bookmarks or add the Web page to their Favorites lists, the title is used for the reference. If you do not title a page, the page will be displayed in the browser window, Favorites lists, and history lists as Untitled Document. Because many search engines use the Web page title, it is important to use a creative and meaningful name. Giving the document a file name by saving it is not the same as giving the page a title.

Changing a Web Page Title

The current title of your Web page is Untitled Document. Unless you change the title of the Web page, this name will be displayed on the browser title bar when the page is opened in a browser window. The following steps show how to change the name of the Web page to Florida Parks.

To Change the Web Page Title

1

• **Drag through the text, Untitled Document, in the Title text box on the Document toolbar.**

The text is highlighted to indicate that it is selected (Figure 1-83).

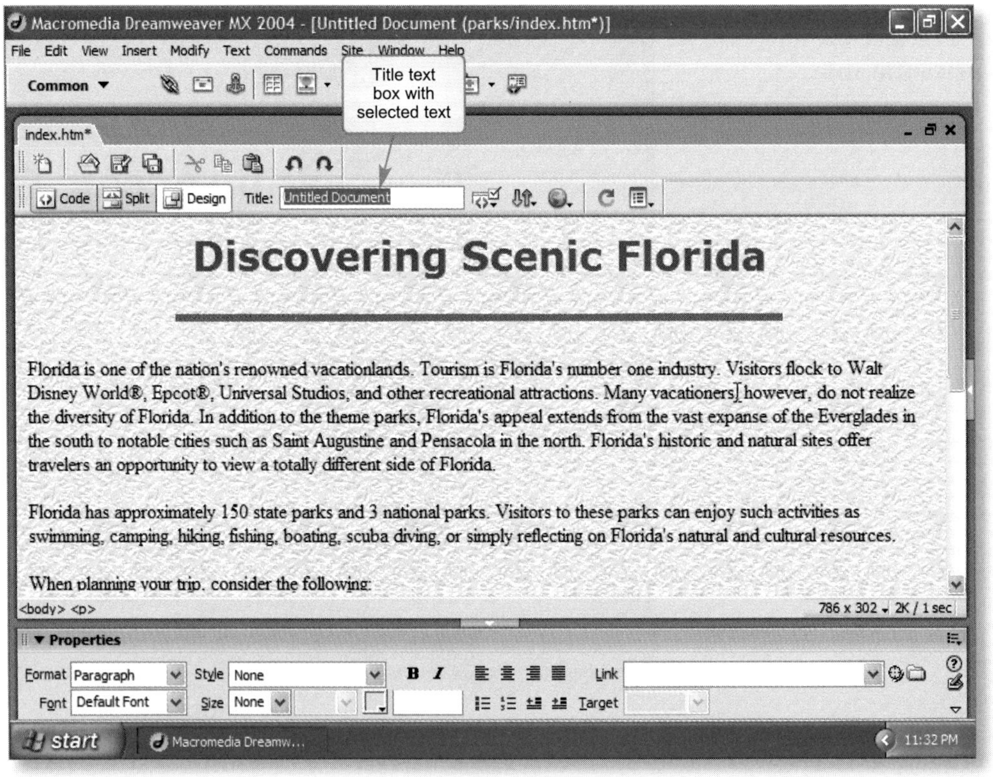

FIGURE 1-83

2

• **Type** `Florida Parks` **in the Title text box and then press the ENTER key.**

The new name, Florida Parks, is displayed in the Title text box and on the Dreamweaver title bar (Figure 1-84).

• **Click the Save button on the Standard toolbar.**

The document changes are saved.

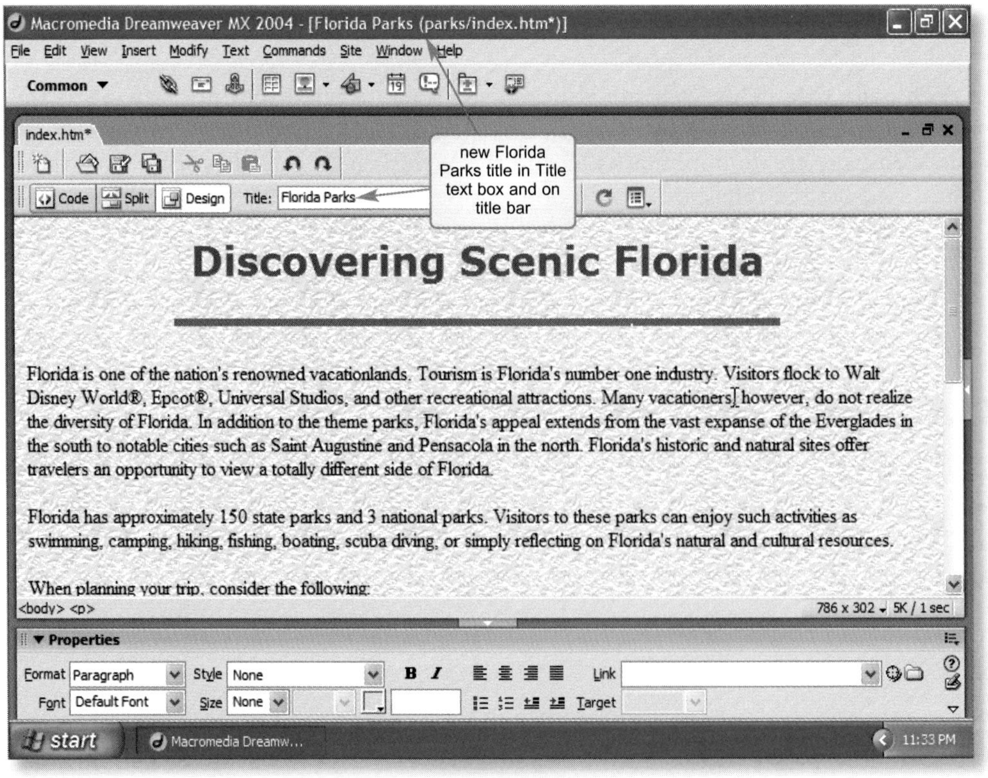

FIGURE 1-84

With all the text of the document entered and formatted, you next check the spelling of the document.

Check Spelling

After you create a Web page, you should check it visually for spelling errors. In addition, you can use Dreamweaver's Check Spelling command to identify possible misspellings. The Check Spelling command ignores HTML tags and attributes. Recall from the Introduction that attributes are additional information contained within an HTML tag.

The following steps show how to start the Check Spelling command and check your entire document. Your Web page may contain different misspelled words depending on the accuracy of your typing.

Q&A

Q: Does Dreamweaver contain a dictionary with American British spelling options?

A: Yes—Dreamweaver contains 14 different spelling option dictionaries, including American British and American Canadian. Access the dictionaries by clicking the Preferences command on the Edit menu, selecting the General category, and then clicking the Spelling dictionary pop-up menu arrow.

To Check Spelling

1

- **Click Text on the menu bar and then point to Check Spelling.**

Dreamweaver displays the Text menu (Figure 1-85).

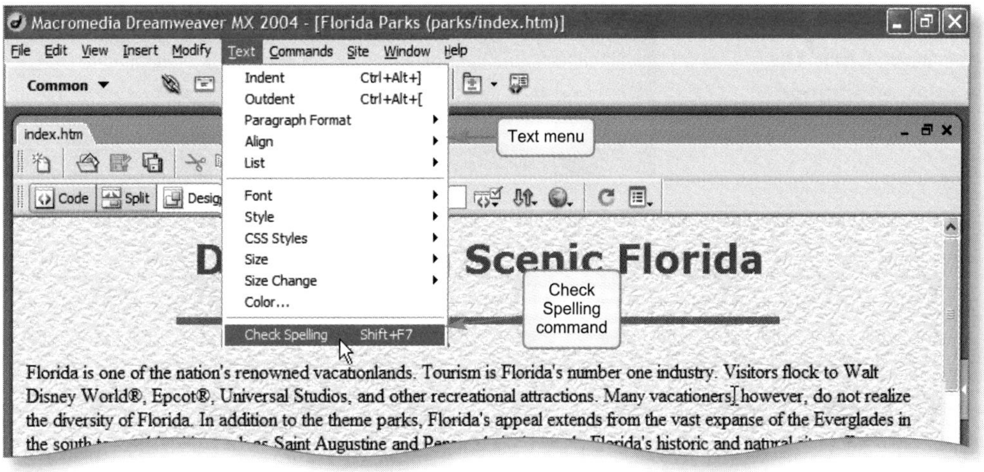

FIGURE 1-85

2

- **Click Check Spelling.**

The Check Spelling dialog box is displayed. The Dreamweaver spelling checker displays the word, Epcot, in the Word not found in dictionary text box. Suggestions for the correct spelling are displayed in the Suggestions list (Figure 1-86).

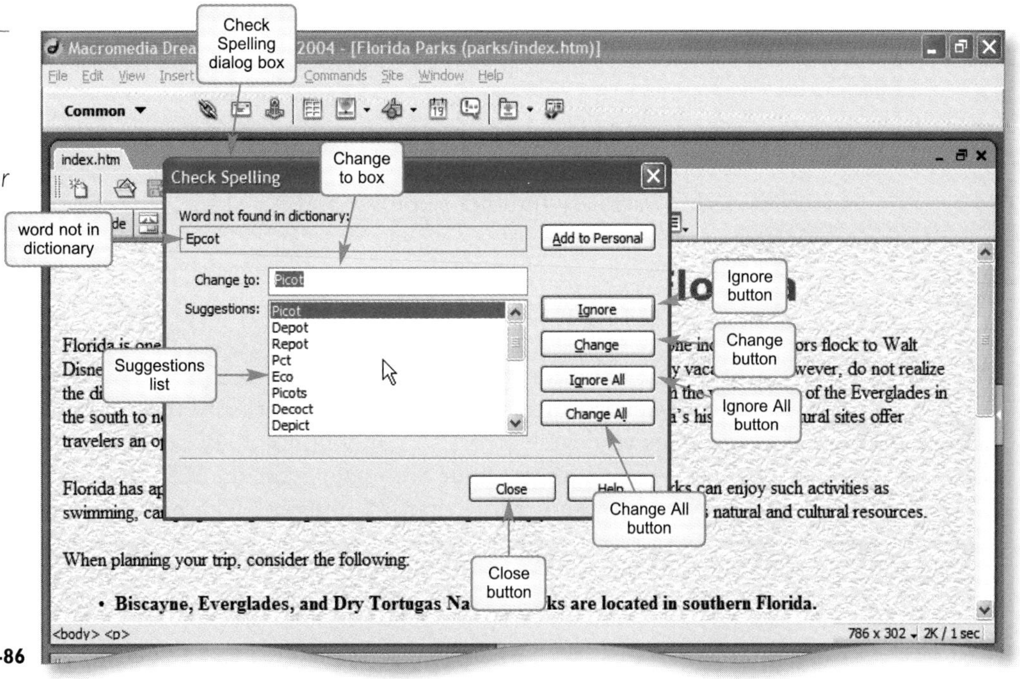

FIGURE 1-86

3

• **Click the Ignore button.**

The spelling checker ignores the word, Epcot, and continues searching for additional misspelled words. If the spelling checker identifies a word that is spelled correctly, clicking the Ignore button skips the word.

4

• **Correct any misspelled word by accepting the suggested replacement or by typing the correct word in the Change to text box. Click the Change or Change All button.**

When Dreamweaver has checked all text for misspellings it displays a Macromedia Dreamweaver MX 2004 dialog box informing you that the spelling check is complete (Figure 1-87).

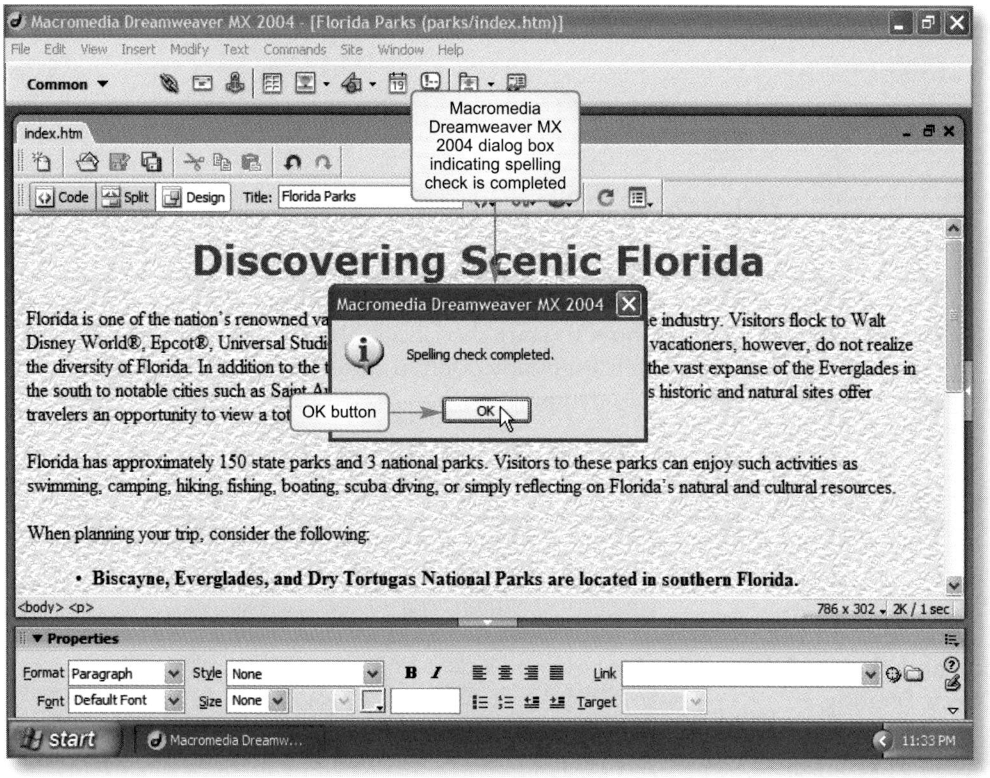

FIGURE 1-87

5

• **Click the OK button and then press CTRL+S to save any changes.**

Dreamweaver closes the Check Spelling dialog box and displays the Document window. The document is saved.

With your Web page ready to share with the world, you next must select browsers to ensure your visitors can view the page properly. The two more popular browsers are Internet Explorer and Netscape.

> *More About*
>
> **Web Page Design**
>
> Web pages reach a global audience. Therefore, to limit access to certain kinds of information, avoid including any confidential data. In particular, do not include your home address, telephone number, or other personal information.

Previewing a Web Page in a Browser

After you have created a Web page, it is a good practice to test your Web pages by previewing them in Web browsers to ensure they display correctly. Using this strategy helps you catch errors so you will not copy or repeat them.

As you create your Web page, you should be aware of the variety of available Web browsers. More than 25 different Web browsers are in use, most of which have been released in more than one version. Most Web developers target recent versions of Netscape Navigator and Microsoft Internet Explorer, which are used by the majority of Web users. You also should know that visitors viewing your Web page might have earlier versions of these browsers. You can define up to 20 browsers for previewing.

> *More About*
>
> **Browsers**
>
> Just as you can specify a primary and secondary browser, you also can remove a browser from your list. Click Edit on the menu bar, click Preferences, and then click the Preview in Browser category. Select the name of the browser you want to remove and then click the minus (–) button.

Selecting a Browser

The browser preferences are selected in the Preferences dialog box. This dialog box provides options to select and define the settings for a primary and a secondary browser. Additionally, a Preview using temporary file option is available. When the check box for this option is checked, you can preview a page without first having to save the page. Although it is a good practice to save before previewing in a browser, occasions will arise when you want to view a page before saving it.

The following steps show how to select your target browsers: Microsoft Internet Explorer and Netscape Navigator. To complete these steps requires that you have both Internet Explorer and Netscape Navigator installed on your computer.

To Select Primary and Secondary Target Browsers

1

- **Click Edit on the menu bar and then point to Preferences.**

Dreamweaver displays the Edit menu and Preferences is highlighted (Figure 1-88).

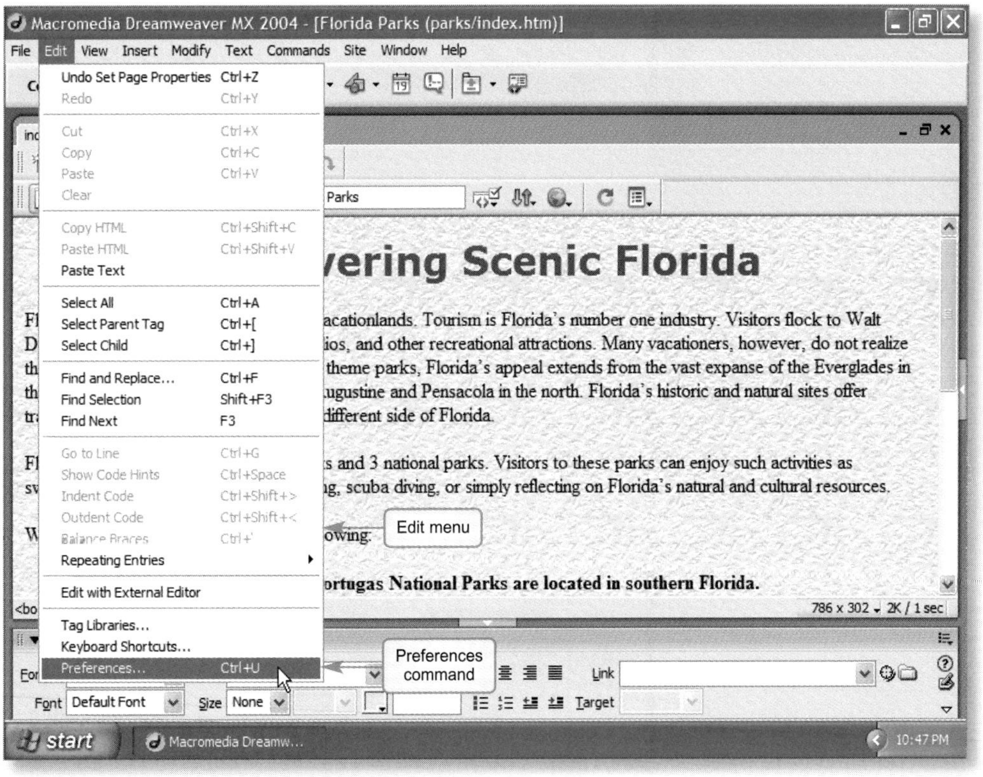

FIGURE 1-88

2

• Click Preferences and then click the Preview in Browser category.

The Preferences dialog box is displayed, and the Preview in Browser category is selected (Figure 1-89). The primary browser was selected when Dreamweaver was installed on your computer. In this book, the primary browser is Internet Explorer. The browser name, iexplore, was selected automatically during the Dreamweaver installation.

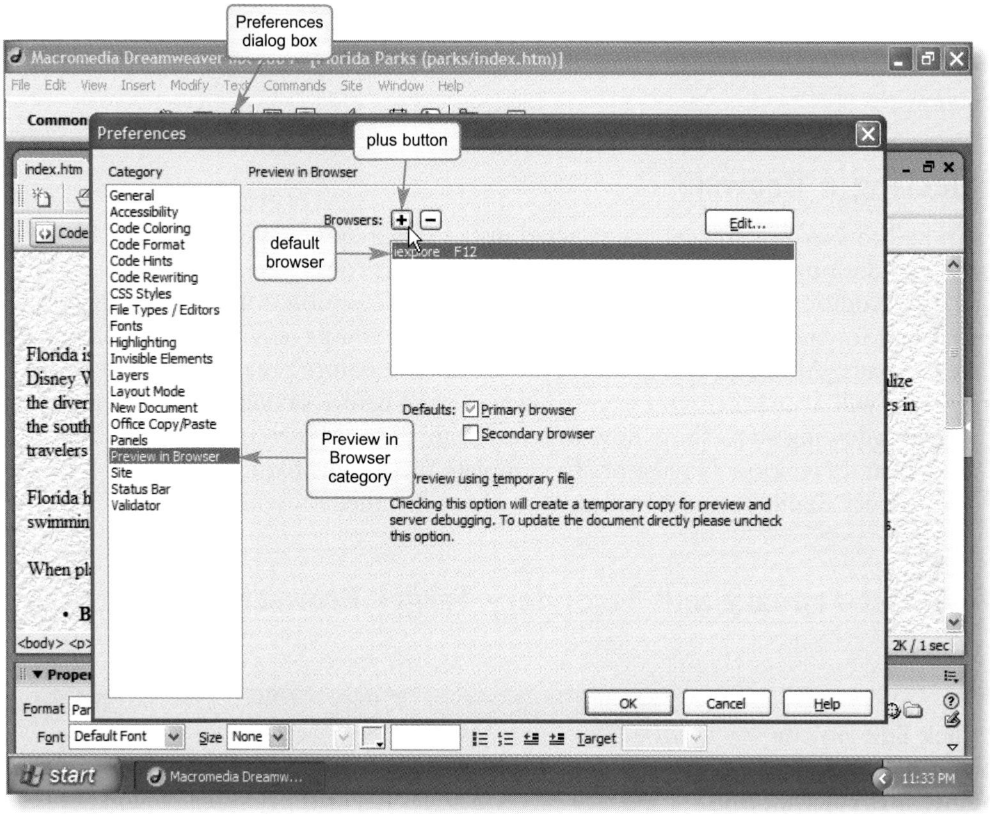

FIGURE 1-89

3

• Click the plus (+) button in the Preview in Browser area.

Dreamweaver displays the Add Browser dialog box (Figure 1-90).

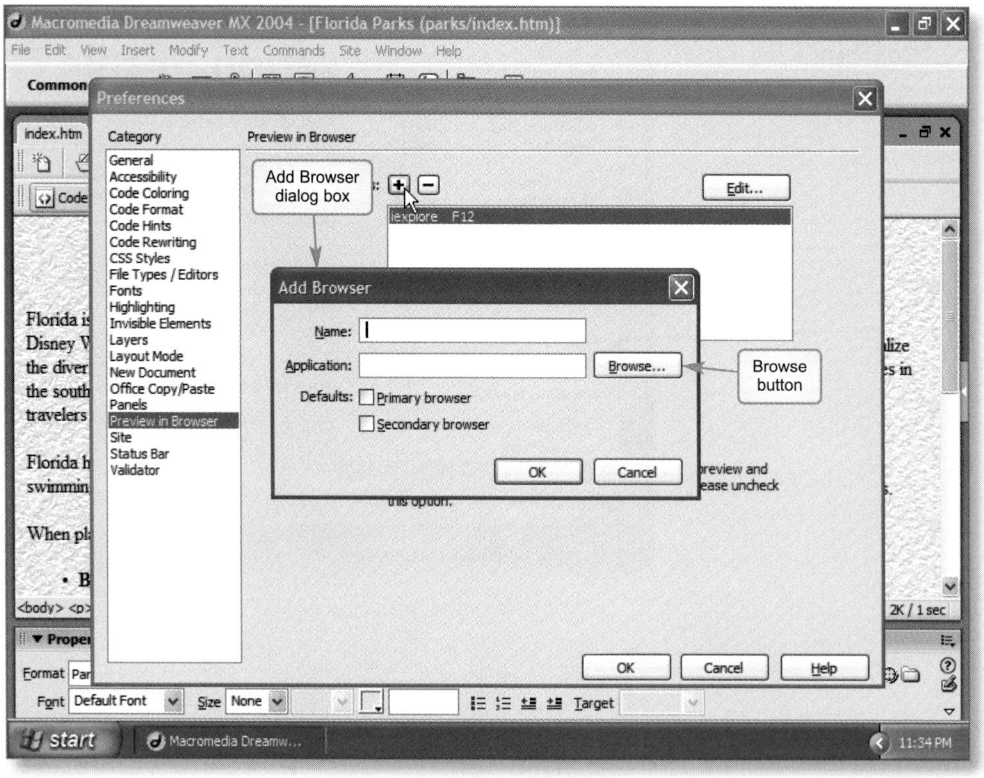

FIGURE 1-90

4

- **Click the Browse button and then locate the Netscp.exe file. Most likely this file is located on Local Drive (C:). Use the following path to locate the file: C:\Program Files\Netscape\Netscape\Netscp.exe, and then click the file name.**

The Select Browser dialog box is displayed (Figure 1-91). The Netscp.exe file is selected. Different versions of Netscape may display a different file name or a different path.

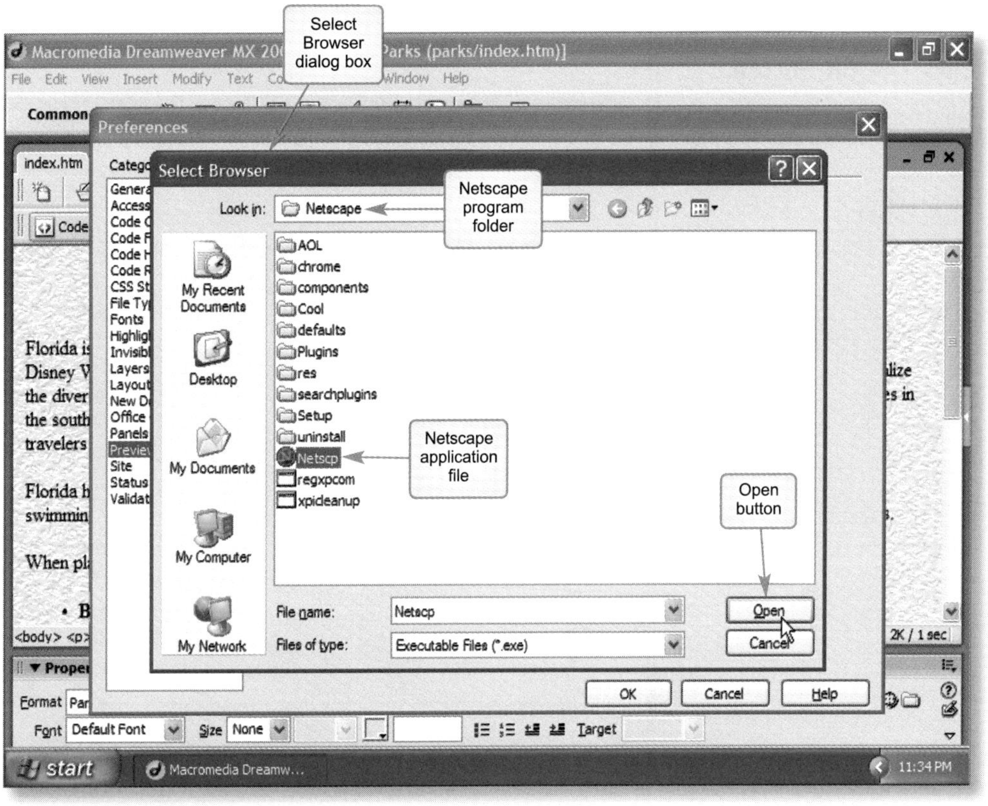

FIGURE 1-91

5

- **Click the Open button.**
- **If necessary, click the Secondary browser check box to select it.**

The Name text box displays Netscp.exe. The Application text box displays the path and file name (Figure 1-92). The path and spelling of Netscape on your computer may be different than those shown.

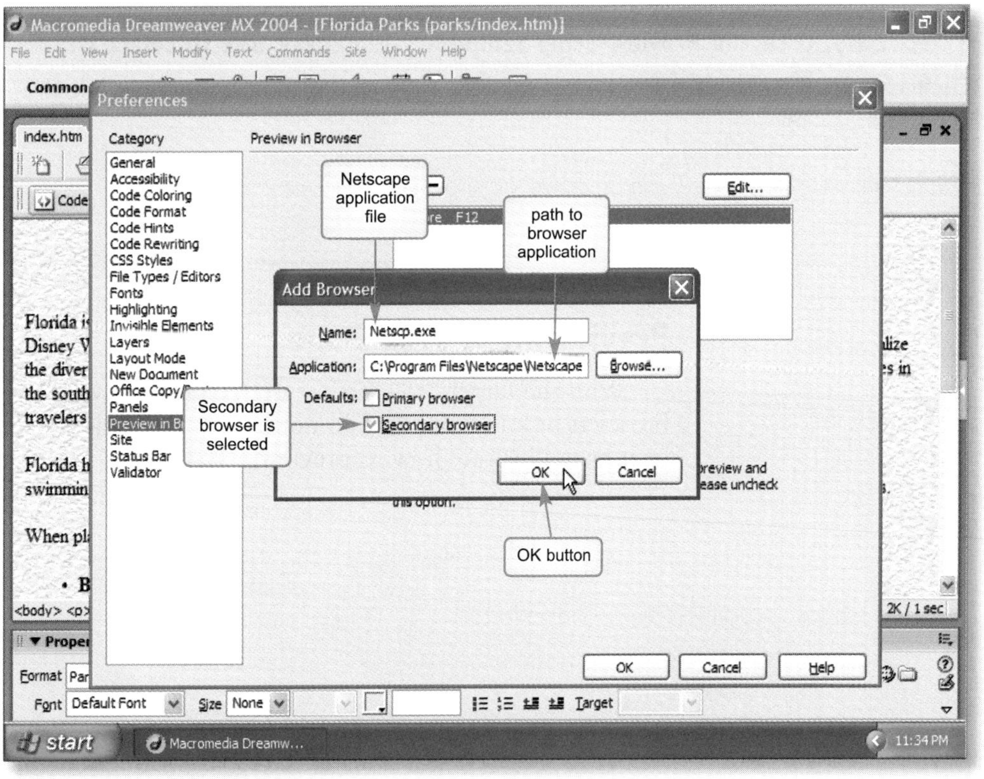

FIGURE 1-92

6

• **Click the OK button.**

Netscape is added as the secondary browser (Figure 1-93).

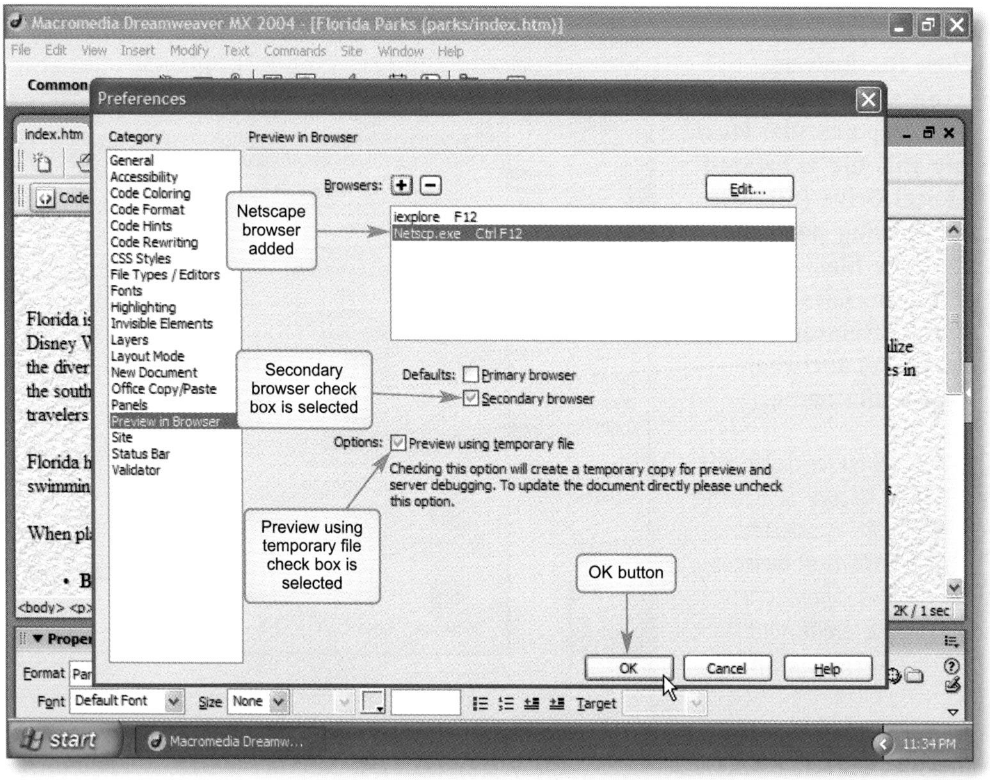

FIGURE 1-93

7

• **If necessary, click the Preview using temporary file check box to select it.**

• **Click the OK button. If a Dreamweaver MX 2004 dialog box appears, click the OK button.**

The target browsers are selected, and Dreamweaver displays the Document window.

Previewing a Web Page

With the target browsers set up, you can preview your Web pages in the browsers at any time. You do not have to save the document first. The steps on the next page illustrate how to preview a Web page.

To Preview the Web Page

1

- **Click File on the menu bar, point to Preview in Browser, and then point to iexplore.**

The File menu and Preview in Browser submenu are displayed (Figure 1-94). The Preview in Browser submenu includes the names of both your primary and secondary browsers and the Edit Browser List command. Clicking the Edit Browser List command displays the Preferences dialog box.

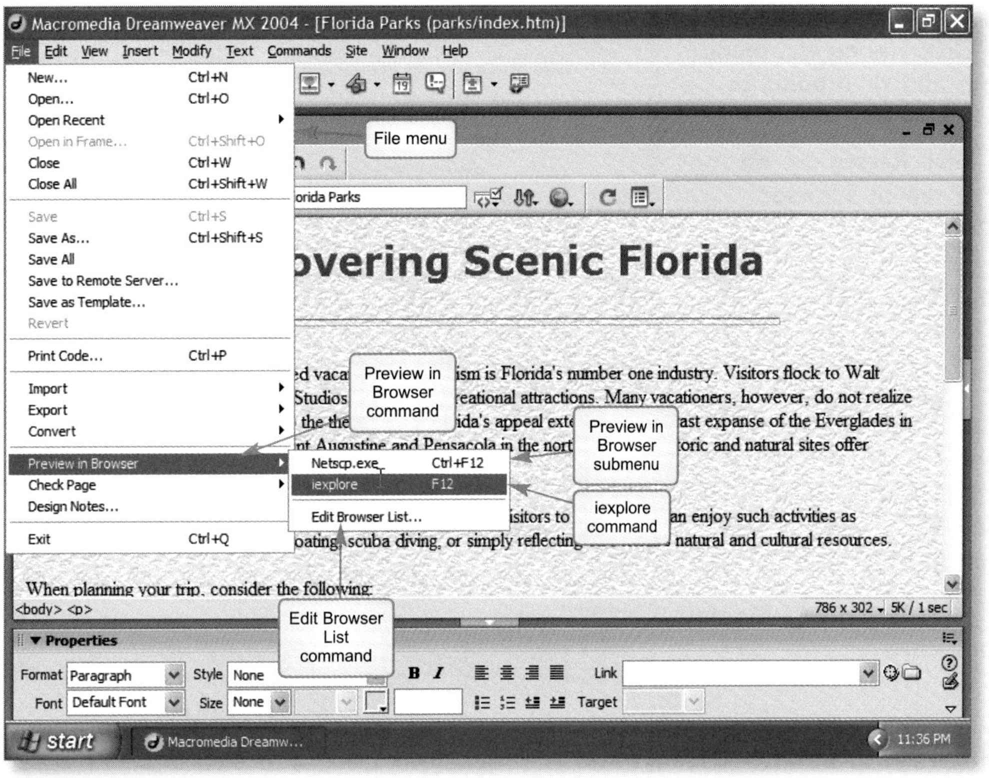

FIGURE 1-94

2

- **Click iexplore (Internet Explorer).**
- **If necessary, maximize your browser window.**

Internet Explorer starts and displays the Web page in a browser window (Figure 1-95). Your browser name may be different. The file name displayed in the Address bar is a temporary name.

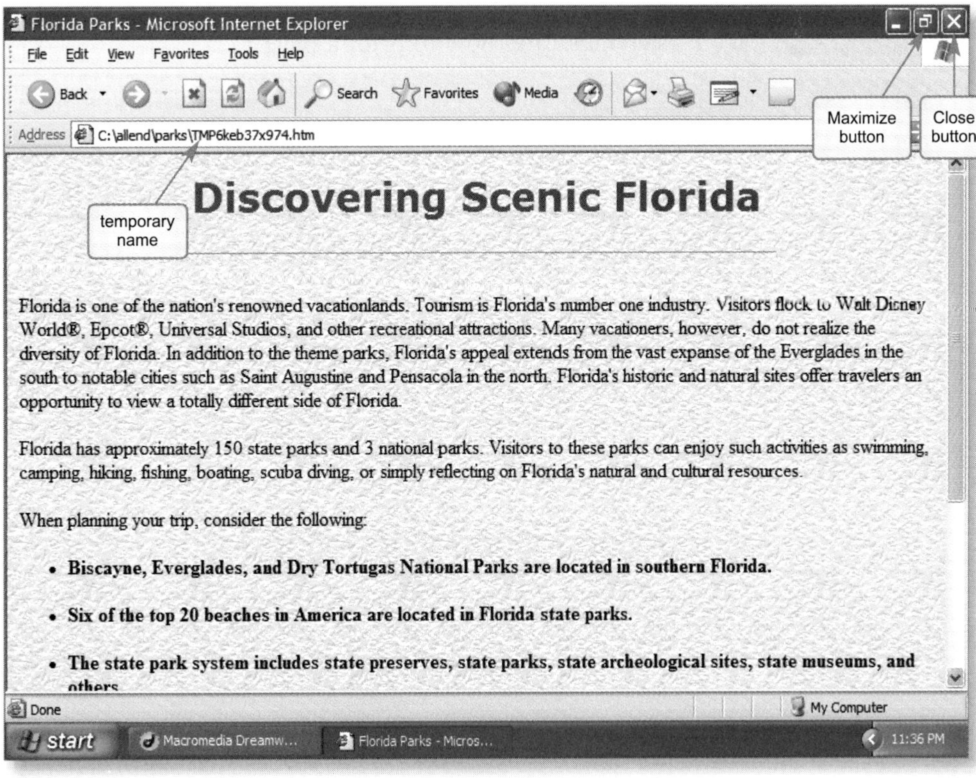

FIGURE 1-95

3

• **Click Internet Explorer's Close button.**

• **Click File on the menu bar and then point to Preview in Browser.**

• **Click Netscp.exe on the Preview in Browser submenu.**

Netscape opens and displays the Web page in a browser window (Figure 1-96). Your browser name may be different. Compare how the files display in the two browsers.

4

• **Click Netscape's Close button.**

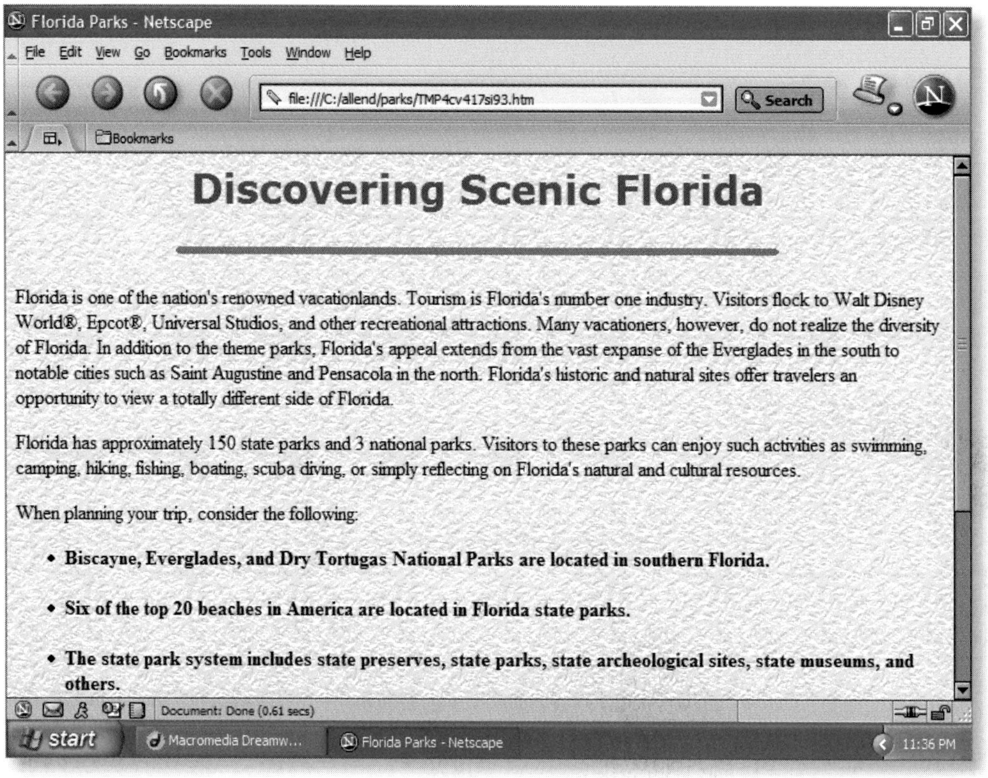

FIGURE 1-96

Other Ways

1. Press F12 to display primary browser
2. Press CTRL + F12 to display secondary browser

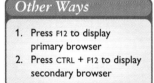

Your instructor may require that you print a copy of your Web page. The next step illustrates how to print a page.

Printing a Web Page

A variety of reasons exists for why you may want to print a Web page. Interestingly, Dreamweaver provides an option to print code, but does not provide a print option to print the Design view. To print a Web page, you first must preview it in a browser. Printing a page from your browser is similar to printing a word processing document. The steps on the next page illustrate how to print the Web page in a browser.

To Print a Web Page

1

- **Press F12.**

The Web page is displayed in Internet Explorer.

2

- **Click File on the menu bar and point to Print (Figure 1-97).**

3

- **Click Print. If necessary, select an appropriate printer.**

Internet Explorer displays the Print dialog box (Figure 1-98). Your selected printer is likely to be different from the one shown in Figure 1-98.

4

- **Click the Print button.**

The Print dialog box closes, and your Web page is sent to the printer.

5

- **Retrieve the printout and then click Internet Explorer's Close button.**

The browser closes, and Dreamweaver displays the Document window.

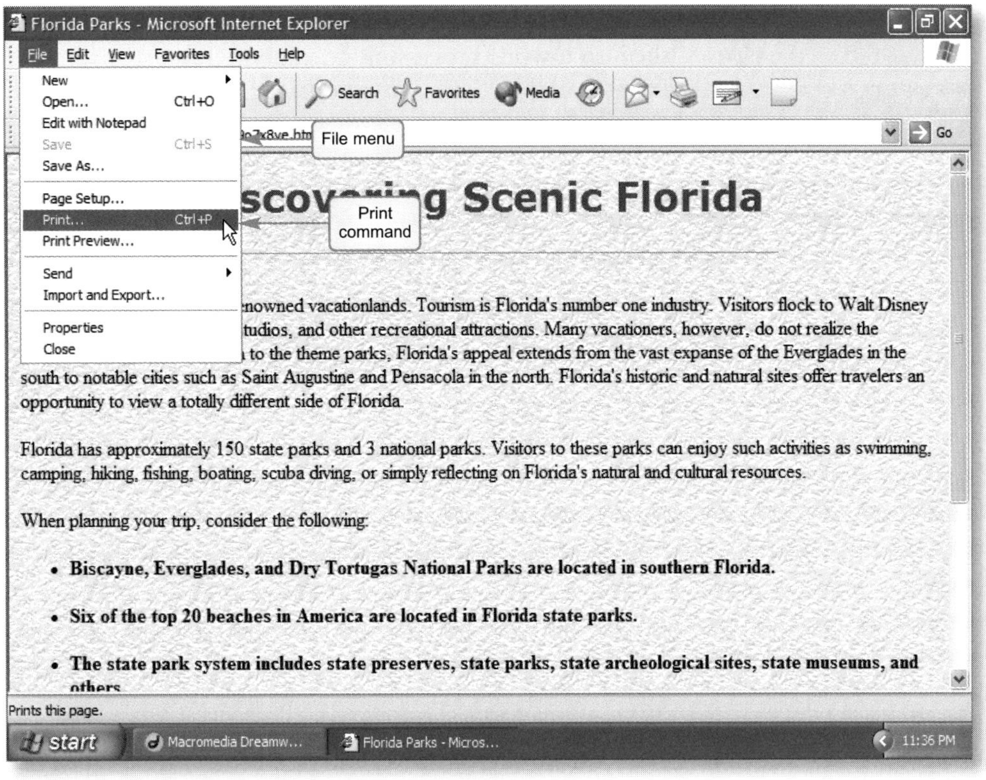

FIGURE 1-97

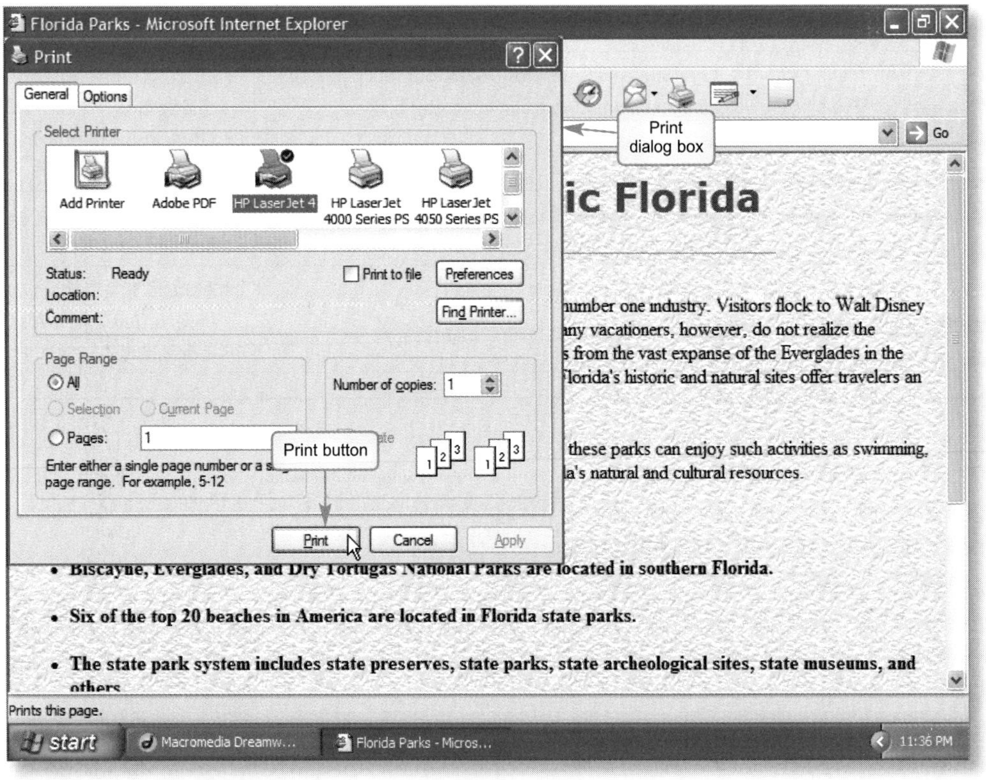

FIGURE 1-98

Dreamweaver Help System

Reference materials and other forms of assistance are available using the Dreamweaver Help system. You can display these documents, print them, or copy them to a word processing document. Table 1-4 summarizes the categories of online Help available. Several methods are available to activate the first four types listed in the table. Appendix A provides detailed instructions on using Dreamweaver Help.

Table 1-4 Dreamweaver Help System

TYPE	DESCRIPTION	HOW TO ACTIVATE
Contents sheet	Use the Contents sheet to view information organized by topic and then by subtopic, as you would in the table of contents of a book.	• Press the F1 key. Click the Contents tab. • Click Help on the menu bar and then click Using Dreamweaver. Click the Contents tab. • Click the options button on the title bar of a panel group and then click Help on the options pop-up menu. Click the Contents tab.
Index sheet	Use the Index sheet to look up specific terms or concepts, as you would in the index of a book.	• Press the F1 key. Click the Index tab. • Click Help on the menu bar and then click Using Dreamweaver. Click the Index tab. • Click the options button on the title bar of a panel group and then click Help on the options pop-up menu. Click the Index tab.
Search sheet	Use the Search sheet to find any character string, anywhere in the text of the Help system.	• Press the F1 key. Click the Search tab. • Click Help on the menu bar and then click Using Dreamweaver. Click the Search tab. • Click the options button on the title bar of a panel group and then click Help on the options pop-up menu. Click the Search tab.
Question Mark button or Help icon	Clicking the Question Mark button provides context-sensitive help in dialog boxes and panels.	• Click a Help button or Question Mark button in a dialog box. • Click the Help icon in an inspector or other kind of window.
Tutorials	Step-by-step lessons that focus on a specific Web design feature or topic.	• Click Help on the menu bar and then click Getting Started and Tutorials.
Dreamweaver online tutorials	Step-by-step online tutorials.	• Access the Dreamweaver tutorial Web site at macromedia.com/desdev/mx/dreamweaver/index.html

Disabling the Start Page and Quitting Dreamweaver

After you create, save, preview, and print the Florida Parks Web page and review how to use Help, Project 1 is complete. The following step shows how to close the Web page, quit Dreamweaver MX 2004, and return control to Windows.

To Disable the Start Page, Close the Web Site, and Quit Dreamweaver

1. **Click Edit on the menu bar and then click Preferences.**
2. **If necessary, click General in the Category column.**
3. **Click the Show start page check box to deselect it, and then click the OK button.**
4. **Click the Close button in the right corner of the Dreamweaver title bar.**

The next time you start Dreamweaver, the Start page will not be displayed. The Document window, the Dreamweaver window, and the Florida Parks Web site all close. If you have unsaved changes, Dreamweaver will prompt you to save the changes. Clicking the Yes button in the Dreamweaver MX 2004 dialog box saves the changes.

Other Ways

1. On File menu click Exit
2. Press CTRL+Q

Starting Dreamweaver and Opening a New Web Page

Opening an existing Web page in Dreamweaver is much the same as opening an existing document in most other software applications: that is, you use the File menu and Open command. In addition to this common method to open a Web page, Dreamweaver provides other options. The Dreamweaver File menu also contains the Open Recent command. Pointing to this command displays the Open Recent submenu, which contains a list of the 10 most recently opened files. Additionally, if you want the page on which you currently are working to display when you next open Dreamweaver, you can select the Reopen Documents on startup command from the Open Recent submenu.

If the page you want to open is part of a Dreamweaver Web site, you can open the file from the Files panel. To open a Web page from the Files panel, you first must select the appropriate Web site. The Files pop-up menu in the Files panel lists sites you have defined. When you open the site, a list of the pages and subfolders within the site displays. To open the page you want, double-click the file name. After opening the page, you can modify text, images, tables, and any other elements.

Earlier in this project, you disabled the Start page. The next time you open Dreamweaver, therefore, the Start page will not display. Instead, a blank window is displayed, requiring that you open an existing document or open a new document. Dreamweaver provides four options to open a new Document window:

- Click File on the menu bar and then click the New command
- Press CTRL+N
- Select the site's root folder, right-click, and then click New File on the context menu
- Click the Files panel Options menu, click File on the pop-up menu, and then click the New File command

The first two options display the New Document dialog box. From this dialog box, you select the Basic page category and HTML Basic page and then click the Create button. When you select either option three or four, a new untitled document is created and is displayed in the Files panel. You then name the document and double-click the name to open the document from the Files panel.

Project Summary

Project 1 introduced you to starting Dreamweaver, defining a Web site, and creating a Web page. You added an image background and used Dreamweaver's Property inspector to format text, change font color, and center text. You also learned how to apply color to text and use an unordered list to organize information. You added line breaks, special characters, and a horizontal rule. Once your Web page was completed, you learned how to save the Web page and preview it in a browser. You also learned how to print using the browser. To enhance your knowledge of Dreamweaver further, you learned basics about the Dreamweaver Help system.

What You Should Know

Having completed this project, you now should be able to perform the tasks below. The tasks are listed in the same order they were presented in the project. For a list of keyboard commands for topics introduced in this project, see the Quick Reference for Windows at the back of this book and refer to the Shortcut column.

1. Start Dreamweaver (DW 32)
2. Close and Open Panels (DW 38)
3. Use Site Definition to Create a Local Web Site (DW 41)
4. Copy Data Files to the Local Web Site (DW 48)
5. Display the Standard Toolbar and Save a Document as a Web Page (DW 52)
6. Add a Background Image to the Index Page (DW 55)
7. Hide the Panel Groups (DW 59)
8. Add Text (DW 60)
9. Format Text with Heading 1 (DW 67)
10. Center the Web Page Heading (DW 69)
11. Change the Font Type (DW 70)
12. Create an Unordered List (DW 72)
13. Bold Text (DW 74)
14. Add a Line Break (DW 75)
15. Add Your Name and Date (DW 76)
16. Insert a Registered Trademark Character (DW 78)
17. Change the Text Color (DW 82)
18. Insert a Horizontal Rule (DW 84)
19. Change the Web Page Title (DW 88)
20. Check Spelling (DW 89)
21. Select Primary and Secondary Target Browsers (DW 91)
22. Preview the Web Page (DW 95)
23. Print a Web Page (DW 97)
24. Disable the Start Page, Close the Web Site, and Quit Dreamweaver (DW 99)

Learn It Online

Instructions: To complete the Learn It Online exercises, start your browser, click the Address bar, and then enter the Web address scsite.com/dreamweavermx2004/learn. When the Dreamweaver MX 2004 Learn It Online page is displayed, follow the instructions in the exercises below. Each exercise has instructions for printing your results, either for your own records or for submission to your instructor.

1 Project Reinforcement TF, MC, and SA

Below Dreamweaver Project 1, click the Project Reinforcement link. Print the quiz by clicking Print on the File menu for each page. Answer each question.

2 Flash Cards

Below Dreamweaver Project 1, click the Flash Cards link and read the instructions. Type 20 (or a number specified by your instructor) in the Number of playing cards text box, type your name in the Enter your Name text box, and then click the Flip Card button. When the flash card is displayed, read the question and then click the ANSWER box arrow to select an answer. Flip through Flash Cards. If your score is 15 (75%) correct or greater, click Print on the File menu to print your results. If your score is less than 15 (75%) correct, then redo this exercise by clicking the Replay button.

3 Practice Test

Below Dreamweaver Project 1, click the Practice Test link. Answer each question, enter your first and last name at the bottom of the page, and then click the Grade Test button. When the graded practice test is displayed on your screen, click Print on the File menu to print a hard copy. Continue to take practice tests until you score 80% or better.

4 Who Wants To Be a Computer Genius?

Below Dreamweaver Project 1, click the Computer Genius link. Read the instructions, enter your first and last name at the bottom of the page, and then click the PLAY button. When your score is displayed, click the PRINT RESULTS link to print a hard copy.

5 Wheel of Terms

Below Dreamweaver Project 1, click the Wheel of Terms link. Read the instructions, and then enter your first and last name and your school name. Click the PLAY button. When your score is displayed, right-click the score and then click Print on the shortcut menu to print a hard copy.

6 Crossword Puzzle Challenge

Below Dreamweaver Project 1, click the Crossword Puzzle Challenge link. Read the instructions, and then enter your first and last name. Click the SUBMIT button. Work the crossword puzzle. When you are finished, click the Submit button. When the crossword puzzle is redisplayed, click the Print Puzzle button to print a hard copy.

7 Tips and Tricks

Below Dreamweaver Project 1, click the Tips and Tricks link. Click a topic that pertains to Project 1. Right-click the information and then click Print on the shortcut menu. Construct a brief example of what the information relates to in Dreamweaver to confirm you understand how to use the tip or trick.

8 Newsgroups

Below Dreamweaver Project 1, click the Newsgroups link. Click a topic that pertains to Project 1. Print three comments.

9 Expanding Your Horizons

Below Dreamweaver Project 1, click the Expanding Your Horizons link. Click a topic that pertains to Project 1. Print the information. Construct a brief example of what the information relates to in Dreamweaver to confirm you understand the contents of the article.

10 Search Sleuth

Below Dreamweaver Project 1, click the Search Sleuth link. To search for a term that pertains to this project, select a term below the Project 1 title and then use the Google search engine at google.com (or any major search engine) to display and print two Web pages that present information on the term.

Apply Your Knowledge

1 B & B Lawn Service Web Site

Instructions: Start Dreamweaver. Perform the following tasks to define a Web site and create and format a Web page for B & B Lawn Service. The Web page as it displays in a browser is shown in Figure 1-99. The text for the Web site is shown in Table 1-5 on the next page.

Software and hardware settings determine how a Web page is displayed in a browser. Your Web pages may display differently in your browser than those in the figures.

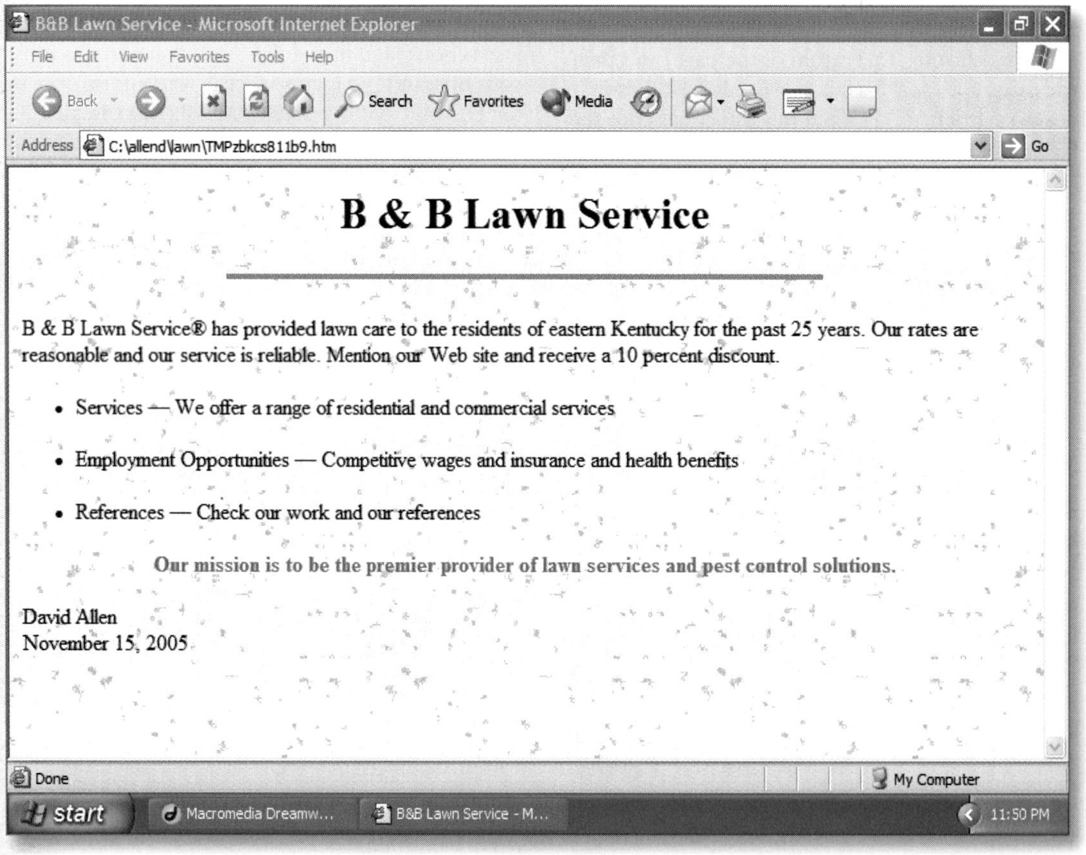

FIGURE 1-99

Apply Your Knowledge

Table 1-5 B & B Lawn Service Web Page

SECTION	WEB PAGE TEXT
Heading	B & B Lawn Service
Introductory Paragraph	B & B Lawn Service® has provided lawn care to the residents of eastern Kentucky for the past 25 years. Our rates are reasonable and our service is reliable. Mention our Web site and receive a 10 percent discount.
List Item 1	Services — We offer a range of residential and commercial services
List Item 2	Employment Opportunities — Competitive wages and insurance and health benefits
List Item 3	References — Check our work and our references
Closing	Our mission is to be the premier provider of lawn services and pest control solutions.

1. Click Site on the menu bar and then click Manage Sites. Use the Site Definition Advanced window option to create a local Web site under the your name folder. In the Site Definition Site name text box, name the site Lawn Service. In the Local root folder text box, create a new subfolder under the your name folder, and name the new subfolder lawn. The path will be C:\yourname\lawn (substitute your name). In the Default images folder text box, create a new subfolder and name the folder images.
2. Click File on the menu bar and then click New. Click Basic Page in the Category column and HTML in the Basic page column in the New Document dialog box and then click Create. If necessary, display the Standard toolbar. Use the Save As command on the File menu to save the page with the name index.
3. Use the Windows My Computer option to copy the data file image to your lawn images folder.
4. Click the Modify menu and then click Page Properties. Apply the background image (located in the images folder) to the index page.
5. Type the Web page text shown in Table 1-5. Press the ENTER key after typing the text in each section and after each one of the list items in the table. The em dash, used in the three list items, is an HTML object. To insert the em dash, click the Insert menu, point to HTML, point to Text Objects, and then click Em.
6. Select the heading text and then apply Heading 1. Click the Align Center button in the Property inspector to center the heading.
7. Select the three list items. Click the Unordered List button in the Property inspector to create a bulleted list with these three items.
8. Select the closing paragraph. Click the Align Center button and then click the Bold button in the Property inspector. Do not deselect the sentence.
9. Click the Text Color box and select hexadecimal color #FF3333. This color swatch is located in the 5th row from bottom and 5th column from the right.

(continued)

Apply Your Knowledge

B & B Lawn Service Web Site *(continued)*

10. Click at the end of the heading and then press the ENTER key. Click Insert on the menu bar, point to HTML, and then click Horizontal Rule. Specify a width of 450 pixels, a height of 4, center alignment, and no shading.
11. Click to the right of B & B Lawn Service in the first paragraph. Click Insert on the menu bar, click HTML, click Special Characters, and then click the Registered command.
12. Click at the end of the first bulleted item. Insert two line breaks between the first and second bulleted items and then insert two line breaks between the second and third bulleted items. (shift + enter)
13. Title the Web page, B&B Lawn Service, using the Title text box on the Document toolbar.
14. Scroll to the bottom of the page. If necessary, click the Align Left button. Type your name, insert a line break. and then type the current date.
15. Click Text on the menu bar and then click Check Spelling. Spell check your document and correct any errors.
16. Click File on the menu bar and then click Save.
17. Press the F12 key to view the Web page in the browser. Print a copy if required and hand it in to your instructor. Click the browser's Close button.
18. Click the Dreamweaver Close button to quit Dreamweaver.

In the Lab

1 CandleDust Web Site

Problem: A friend of yours, Mary Stewart, is starting her own business selling candles. She has asked you to assist her in preparing a Web page to help her advertise her candles (Figure 1-100 on the next page).

Software and hardware settings determine how a Web page is displayed in a browser. Your Web pages may display differently in your browser than those in the figures.

Instructions: Start Dreamweaver. Perform the tasks on the following pages to define a Web site and create and format a Web page for CandleDust. The text for the Web page is shown in Table 1-6 on the next page.

FILE → NEW → BASIC PAGE, HTML → CREATE

(1) SITE on Menu bar

In the Lab

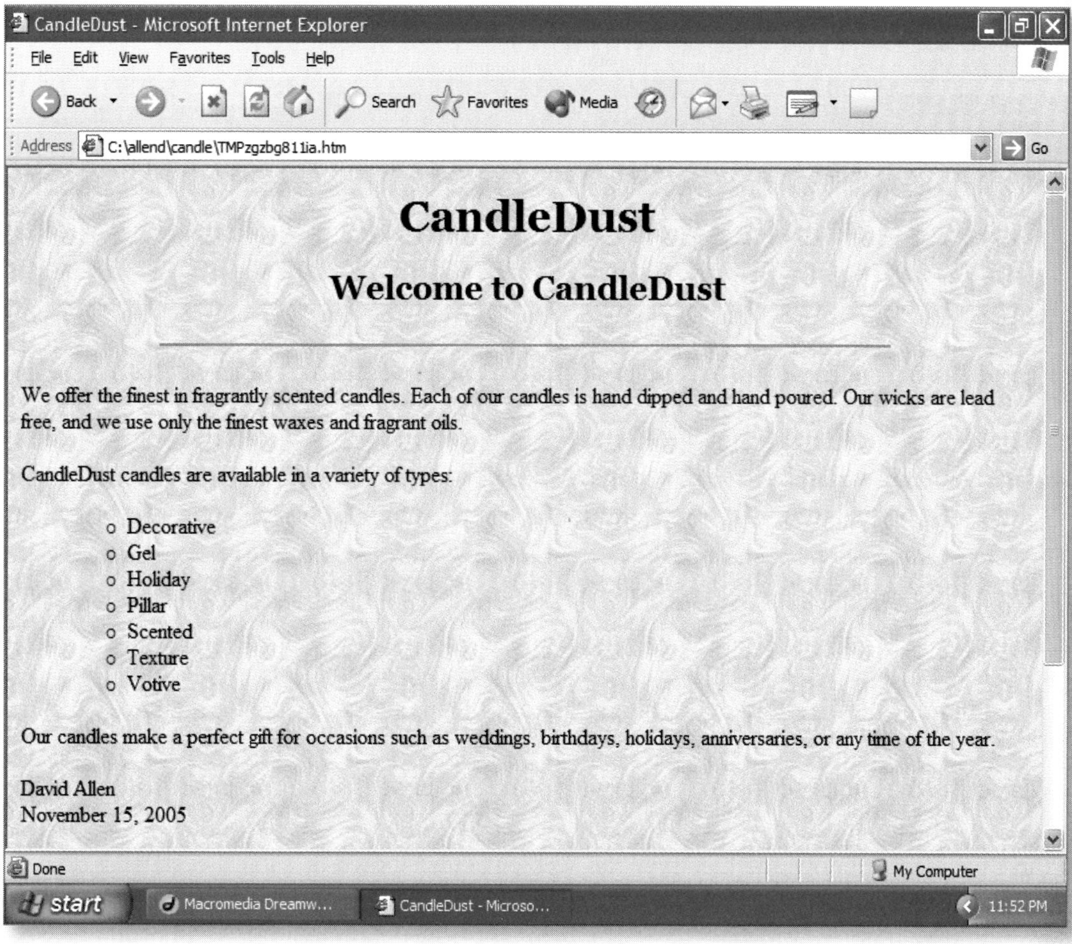

FIGURE 1-100

Table 1-6 CandleDust Web Page

SECTION	WEB PAGE TEXT
Heading	CandleDust
Subheading	Welcome to CandleDust
Introductory Paragraph	We offer the finest in fragrantly scented candles. Each of our candles is hand dipped and handpoured. Our wicks are lead free, and we use only the finest waxes and fragrant oils.
Second Paragraph	CandleDust candles are available in a variety of types:
List Item 1	Decorative
List Item 2	Gel
List Item 3	Holiday
List Item 4	Pillar

(continued)

In the Lab

CandleDust Web Site *(continued)*

Table 1-6 CandleDust Web Page *(continued)*

SECTION	WEB PAGE TEXT
List Item 5	Scented
List Item 6	Texture
List Item 7	Votive
Closing	Our candles make a perfect gift for occasions such as weddings, birthdays, holidays, anniversaries, or any time of the year.

1. Click Site on the menu bar and then click Manage Sites. Use the Site Definition Advanced window option to create a local Web site under the your name folder. In the Site Definition Site name text box, name the site CandleDust. In the Local root folder text box, create a new subfolder under the your name folder, and name the new subfolder candle. The path will be C:\yourname\candle. In the Default images folder text box, create a new subfolder and name the folder images.
2. Click File on the menu bar and then click New. Click Basic Page in the Category column and HTML in the Basic page column in the New Document dialog box and then click Create. Use the Save As command on the File menu to save the page with the name index. If necessary, display the Standard toolbar.
3. Use the Windows My Computer option to copy the data file image to your candle images folder.
4. Click the Modify menu and then click Page Properties. Apply the background image to the index page.
5. Click in the Document window and then type the Web page text shown in Table 1-6 starting on page DW 105. Press the ENTER key after typing each section and after each list item in the table.
6. Select the heading text and apply Heading 1. Select the subheading text and apply Heading 2. Select both headings and then click the Align Center button in the Property inspector to center the titles. Change the font type to Georgia, Times New Roman, Times, serif.
7. Select the list items. Click the Unordered List button in the Property inspector and then click the Text Indent button in the Property inspector.
8. Click at the end of the subheading, Welcome to CandleDust, and then press the ENTER key. Click Insert on the menu bar, point to HTML, and then click Horizontal Rule. Change the width to 550 pixels, and specify no shading and center alignment.
9. Type `CandleDust` as the title in the Title text box.
10. Click at the end of the closing line and then press the ENTER key. Type your name. Insert a line break and then type the current date.
11. Spell check your document and correct any errors.
12. Click the Save button.
13. View the Web page in your browser. Print a copy, if required, and hand it in to your instructor. Close the browser.
14. Quit Dreamweaver.

In the Lab

2 Credit Protection Web Site

Problem: Marcy Cantu is an intern in a small law practice. She recently lost her wallet, which contained all of her credit cards. She called the credit card companies and canceled her credit cards. One of the attorneys suggested she also call the three credit bureaus to make them aware of this problem. Because searching for the names, telephone numbers, and addresses of the three credit bureaus was quite time-consuming, Marcy decided she wants to have this information readily available for herself in the event she ever needs it again and for others who might find themselves in a similar situation. She has asked you to prepare the Web page shown in Figure 1-101.

Software and hardware settings determine how a Web page is displayed in a browser. Your Web pages may display differently in your browser than those in the figures.

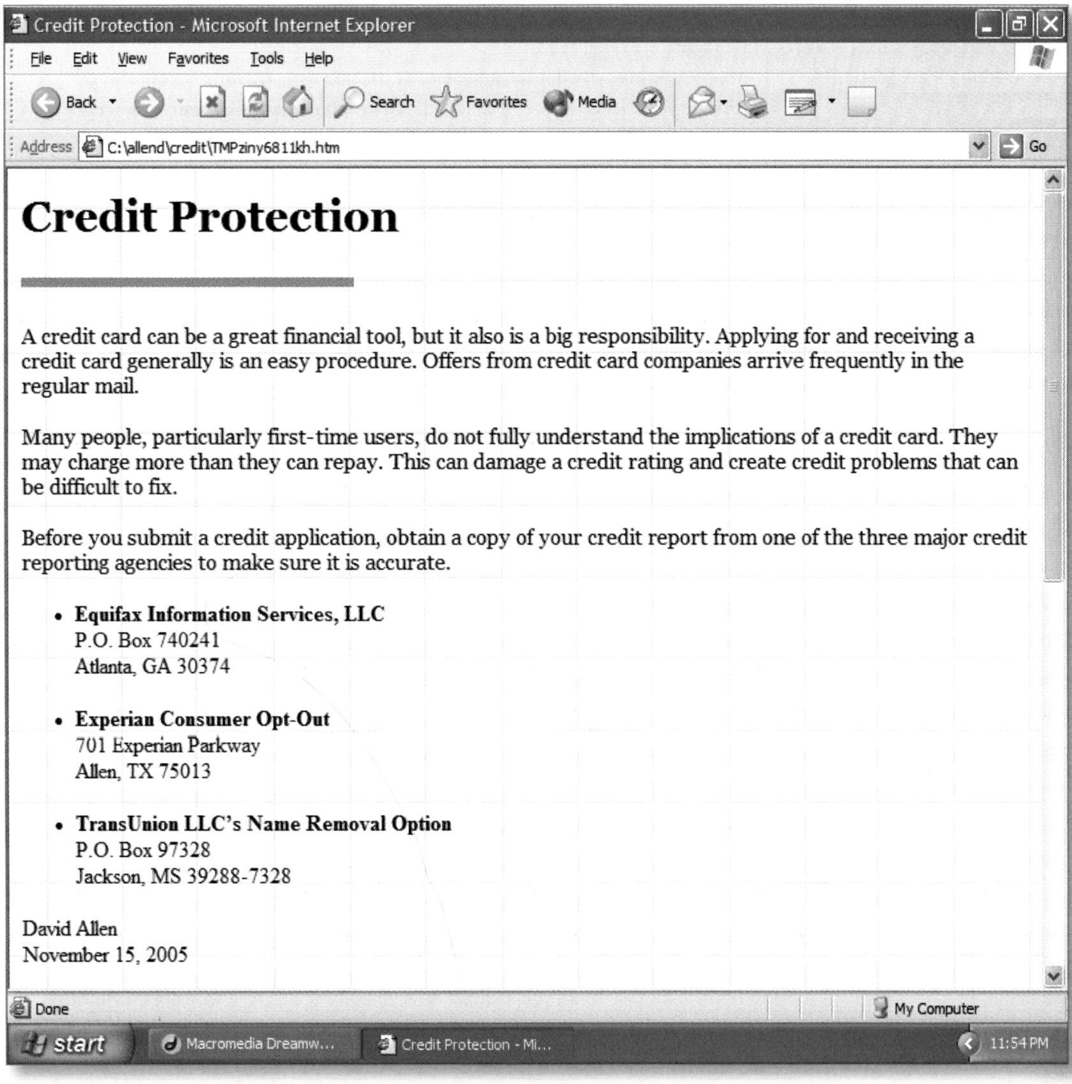

FIGURE 1-101

(continued)

In the Lab

Credit Protection Web Site *(continued)*

Instructions: Start Dreamweaver. Perform the following tasks to define a Web site and create and format an informational Web page on credit protection. The text for the Web page is shown in Table 1-7.

Table 1-7 Credit Protection Web Page

SECTION	WEB PAGE TEXT
Heading	Credit Protection
Introductory Paragraph	A credit card can be a great financial tool, but it also is a big responsibility. Applying for and receiving a credit card generally is an easy procedure. Offers from credit card companies arrive frequently in the regular mail.
Second Paragraph	Many people, particularly first-time users, do not fully understand the implications of a credit card. They may charge more than they can repay. This can damage a credit rating and create credit problems that can be difficult to fix.
Third Paragraph	Before you submit a credit application, obtain a copy of your credit report from one of the three major credit reporting agencies to make sure it is accurate.
List Item 1	Equifax Information Services, LLC P. O. Box 740241 Atlanta, GA 30374
List Item 2	Experian Consumer Opt-Out 701 Experian Parkway Allen, TX 75013
List Item 3	TransUnion LLC's Name Removal Option P.O. Box 97328 Jackson, MS 39288-7328

1. Define a local Web site under the your name folder. Name the site Credit Protection. Create a new subfolder under the your name folder and name the new subfolder credit. Create an images folder and copy the image data file into the images folder.
2. Open a new Document window and use the Save As command to save the page as index. Apply the background image to the index page.
3. Type the heading and first three paragraphs of the Web page text shown in Table 1-7. Press the ENTER key after typing each section of the text in the table.
4. Type list item 1. Insert a line break after the company name and after the address. Press the ENTER key after the city and state. Type list items 2 and 3. Insert a line break after the company name and address and press the ENTER key after the city and state.

In the Lab

5. Select the heading text and apply Heading 1. Align to the left (to ensure the heading is displayed properly in the browser). Insert a horizontal rule following the heading. Align the rule to the left. Use 250 for the width, 7 for the height, and no shading. Deselect the rule.
6. Click Edit on the menu bar and then click Select All. Change the font type to Georgia, Times New Roman, Times, serif for all the text on the Web page.
7. Select the three list items (companies and addresses) and create an unordered (bulleted) list. Insert two line breaks between item 1 and item 2 and between item 2 and item 3.
8. Select the name of the company in the first bulleted list item (Equifax Information Services, LLC) and bold the company name. Apply the bold attribute to the names of the other two companies.
9. Select Untitled Document in the Title text box on the Document toolbar and type `Credit Protection` as the title of the Web page.
10. Click at the end of the last line of text and then press the ENTER key. If a bullet displays, click the Unordered List button in the Property inspector to remove the bullet. Type your name, add a line break, and then type the current date.
11. Spell check your document, correct any errors, and then save the page.
12. View the Web page in your browser. Print a copy, if required, and hand it in to your instructor. Close the browser and then quit Dreamweaver.

3 Plant City Web Site

Problem: Juan Benito recently moved to Plant City, Florida. He discovered that Plant City has a colorful history and that many consider the city to be the Strawberry Capital of the United States. He has asked you to help prepare a Web page (Figure 1-102 on the next page) so he can share information with friends, relatives, and visitors to Florida about the city's historical facts.

Software and hardware settings determine how a Web page is displayed in a browser. Your Web pages may display differently in your browser than those in the figures.

(continued)

In the Lab

Plant City Web Site *(continued)*

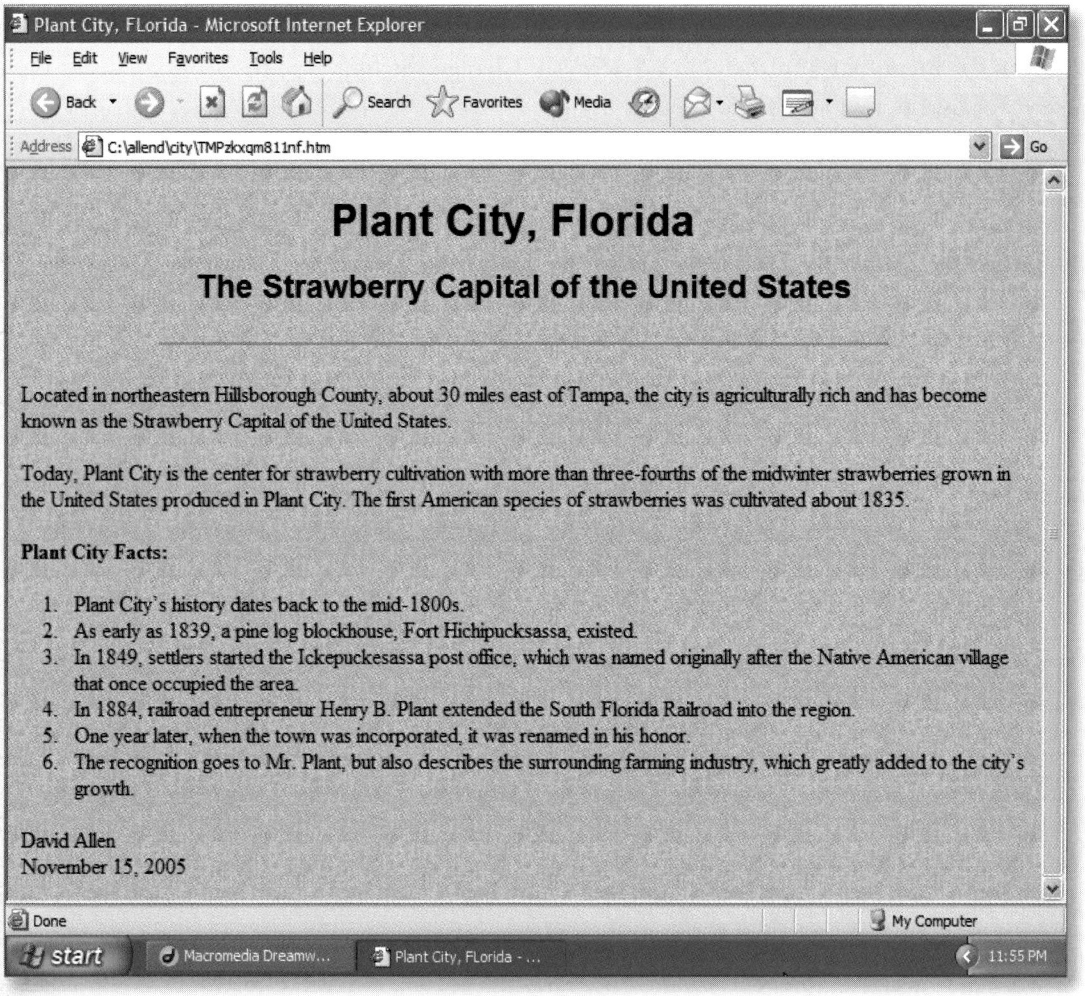

FIGURE 1-102

Instructions: Start Dreamweaver. Perform the tasks on the next page to define a Web site and create and format an informational Web page on Plant City, Florida. The text of the Web page is shown in Table 1-8 on the next page.

In the Lab

Table 1-8 Plant City, Florida Web Site

SECTION	WEB PAGE TEXT
Heading	Plant City, Florida
Subheading	The Strawberry Capital of the United States
Introductory Paragraph	Located in northeastern Hillsborough County, about 30 miles east of Tampa, the city is agriculturally rich and has become known as the Strawberry Capital of the United States.
Second Paragraph	Today, Plant City is the center for strawberry cultivation with more than three-fourths of the midwinter strawberries grown in the United States produced in Plant City. The first American species of strawberries was cultivated about 1835.
Third Paragraph	Plant City Facts:
List Item 1	Plant City's history dates back to the mid-1800s.
List Item 2	As early as 1839, a pine log blockhouse, Fort Hichipucksassa, existed.
List Item 3	In 1849, settlers started the Ickepuckesassa post office, which was named originally after the Native American village that once occupied the area.
List Item 4	In 1884, railroad entrepreneur Henry B. Plant extended the South Florida Railroad into the region.
List Item 5	One year later, when the town was incorporated, it was renamed in his honor.
List Item 6	The recognition goes to Mr. Plant, but also describes the surrounding farming industry, which greatly added to the city's growth.

1. Define a local Web site under the your name folder. Name the site Plant City. Create a subfolder and name it city. Create an images subfolder and copy the image data files into the folder.
2. Open a new Document window and use the Save As command to save the page as index. Apply the background image to the index page.
3. Click in the Document window and then type the Web page text shown in Table 1-8. Press the ENTER key after typing the text in each section in the table.
4. Select the heading text and apply Heading 1. Select the subheading text and apply Heading 2. Center both headings. Change the heading font type to Arial, Helvetica, sans-serif.
5. Insert a centered horizontal line, 550 pixels in width, with no shading, below the subtitle.
6. Select the third paragraph, Plant City Facts:, and then apply bold formatting to the text.
7. Select list items 1 through 6 and apply an ordered list format.
8. Change the Web page title to Plant City, Florida.
9. Insert your name and the current date at the bottom of the Web page.
10. Spell check your document and correct any errors. Save the Web page.
11. View the Web page in the browser. Print a copy, if required, and hand it in to your instructor. Close the browser. Quit Dreamweaver.

Cases and Places

The difficulty of these case studies varies:
■ are the least difficult and ■■ are the most difficult. The last exercise is a group exercise.

1 ■ Define a Web site named Favorite Sports with a subfolder named sports. Prepare a Web page listing your favorite sports and favorite teams. Include a title for your Web page. Bold and center the title, and then apply the Heading 1 style. Include a sentence or two explaining why you like the sport and why you like the teams. Bold and italicize the names of the teams and the sports. Give the Web page a meaningful title. Apply a background image to your Web page. Spell check the document. Use the concepts and techniques presented in the project to format the text. Save the file in the sports folder. For a selection of images and backgrounds, visit the Dreamweaver MX 2004 Media Web page (scsite.com/dreamweavermx04/media).

2 ■ Your instructor has asked you to create a Web page about one of your hobbies. Define the Web site using Hobbies for the site name and hobby for the subfolder name. Italicize and center the title, and then apply the Heading 2 style. Type a paragraph of three or four sentences explaining why you selected the subject. Select and center the paragraph. Add a list of three items and create an ordered list from the three items. Include line breaks between each numbered item. Title the Web page the name of the hobby you selected. Spell check your document. Use the concepts and techniques presented in the project to format the text. For a selection of images and backgrounds, visit the Dreamweaver MX 2004 Media Web page (scsite.com/dreamweavermx04/media).

3 ■■ Define a Web site and create a Web page that gives a description and information about your favorite type of music. Name the Web site Favorite Music and the subfolder music. Apply a background image to the Web page. Include a left-aligned heading formatted with the Heading 1 style. Include a subheading formatted with Heading 2. Insert a horizontal rule following the subheading. List four facts about why you selected this type of music. Include the names of three of your favorite songs and the names of the artists. Bold and italicize the name of the songs and artists and apply a font color of your choice. Create an ordered list from the four facts. Title the Web page Favorite Music. Save the file as index in the music folder. Use the concepts and techniques presented in the project to format the text. For a selection of images and backgrounds, visit the Dreamweaver MX 2004 Media Web page (scsite.com/dreamweavermx04/media).

Cases and Places

4 ■■ Assume you are running for office in your city's local government. Define a Web site using the name of the city in which you live and a subfolder named government. Include the following information in your Web page: your name, centered, with Heading 1 and a font color of your choice; the name of the office for which you are running, bold and italicized; and a paragraph about the duties of the office in Courier font. Create a bulleted list within your Web page. Change the title of the Web page from Untitled Document to your name. Use the concepts and techniques presented in the project to format the text. For a selection of images and backgrounds, visit the Dreamweaver MX 2004 Media Web page (scsite.com/dreamweavermx04/media).

5 ■■ **Working Together** Your school has a budget for student trips. Your assignment and that of your teammates is to put together a Web site and Web page, that list locations and trips from which the student body can select. Apply an appropriate background image. Include a title, formatted with Heading 1, and a subtitle, formatted with Heading 2. Insert a shaded horizontal line following the subtitle. List three locations. Bold and apply a font color to each location name. Add a bullet to each location name. Include information about each location. Title the page Student Government. Use the concepts and techniques presented in the project to format the text. For a selection of images and backgrounds, visit the Dreamweaver MX 2004 Media Web page (scsite.com/dreamweavermx04/media).

MACROMEDIA
Dreamweaver MX 2004

Adding Web Pages, Links, and Images

PROJECT 2

CASE PERSPECTIVE

A coworker at the state environmental agency, Joan Komisky, who also is interested in Florida's parks, viewed the Web page that you and David created. She has offered some suggestions and asked to help with the design. Both you and David agreed, and the three of you have become a team.

Joan suggests adding images to the home page. David proposes that the Web site include a page for Florida's three national parks and another page with information about his three favorite state parks located in northwest Florida. You explain to David and Joan that the addition of each new page will require hyperlinks from the home page and links from each page back to the home page. You assure them that Dreamweaver includes all the tools they need to add these and other types of links, including e-mail links, to related Web sites. You create a navigation map to illustrate how the links will work among the three pages. All team members agree that these two new pages should be added and that the pages will include images and links. With the addition of these two pages, the Web page you created in Project 1 will become a Web site.

As you read through this project, you will learn how to add pages to a Web site, how to add images to a Web page, and how to insert absolute, relative, and e-mail links.

MACROMEDIA
Dreamweaver MX 2004

Adding Web Pages, Links, and Images

PROJECT

2

Objectives

You will have mastered the material in this project when you can:

- Define and set a home page
- Add pages to a Web site
- Describe Dreamweaver's image accessibility features
- Describe image file formats
- Insert, resize, and align images within a Web page
- Describe the different types of links
- Create a relative, absolute, and e-mail link
- Describe how to change the color of links
- Edit and delete links
- Describe and display the Site Map
- Describe Code view, Split view, and Design view
- View Code view

Introduction

Project 2 introduces the addition of Web pages to the local site created in Project 1 and the integration of links and graphics into the Web pages that make up the site. Recall from Project 1 that a site or a Web site is a set of linked documents with shared attributes, such as related topics, a similar design, or a shared purpose.

The Dreamweaver site structure feature provides a way to maintain and organize your files. A Web page essentially is a text document and a collection of HTML code. The HTML (Hypertext Markup Language) code defines the structure and layout of a Web document and is generated automatically by Dreamweaver. Images and other media content are separate files. For example, a page that displays text and three images consists of four separate files — one for the text document and one for each of the three images.

Most Web site builders include images on their Web pages. It is important that you take the time to learn about images, image properties, and the types of images best suited for a particular situation. Image properties, such as alternative text for accessibility issues, alignment, and size adjustment, help you to understand the effects of using images on Web pages.

When a file or image is referenced within the HTML document, a link (or hyperlink) exists within the HTML code to the external file or image. A link (hyperlink) is a Web page element that, when clicked, accesses another Web page, or a different place within the existing Web page. A Web page can contain different types of links: internal, or relative; absolute; e-mail; and named anchors, which are links to a specific place within a document. This project discusses how to create these links.

Project Two — Two New Pages, Links, and Images

In this project, you continue with the creation of the Florida Parks Web site. You add two additional Web pages, add image backgrounds to the two new pages, add images to all three pages, add links to and from the index page, and add absolute links to three state parks (Figures 2-1a, 2-1b, and 2-1c on the next page).

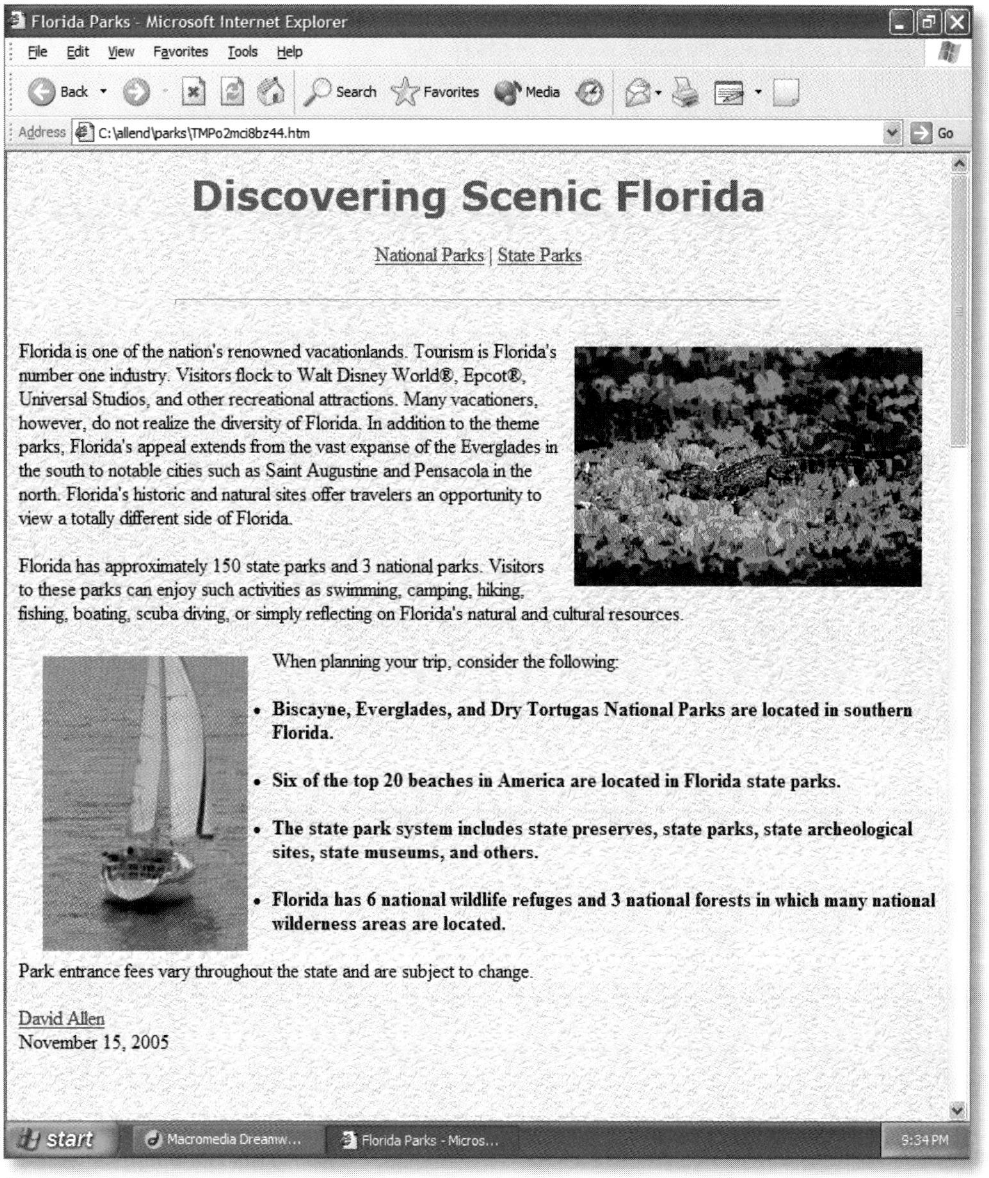

(a) Florida Parks Index (Home) Page

FIGURE 2-1 (*continued*)

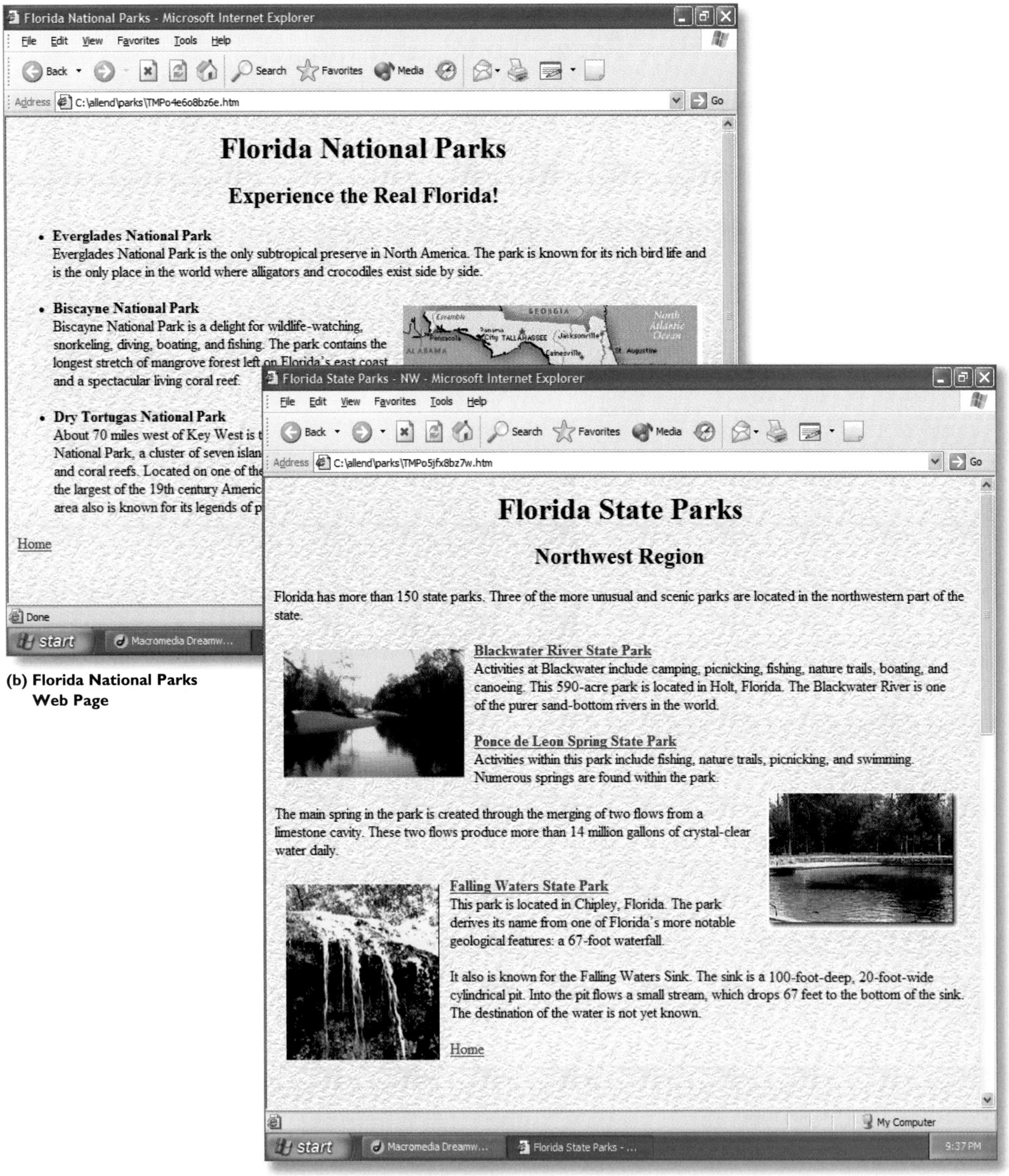

(b) Florida National Parks Web Page

(c) Florida State Parks Web Page

FIGURE 2-1 (*continued*)

In the Introduction project, four types of Web structures were illustrated: linear, hierarchical, web (or random), and grid. This project uses a hierarchical structure (Figure 2-2). The index page is the home page, or entrance to the Web site. From this page, the visitor to this site can link to a page about Florida national parks or to a page about Florida state parks.

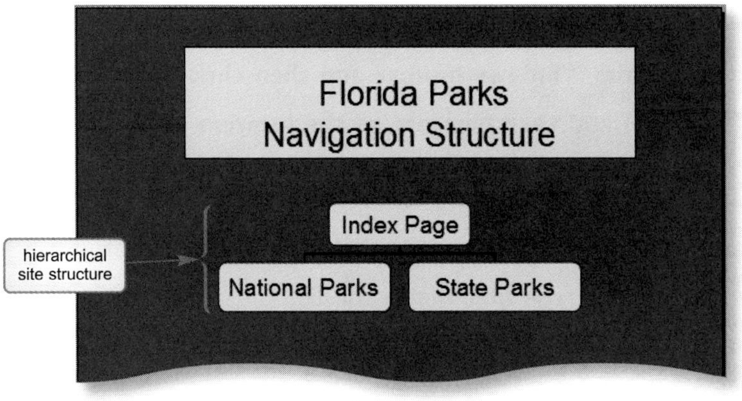

FIGURE 2-2

Managing a Web Site

Organization is a key element of Web design. Dreamweaver works best with entire sites rather than individual Web pages and has many built-in tools to make site creation easy, such as checking links and organizing files. You defined the parks Web site in Project 1 and created the index page. You can add pages to your site by creating a new page and saving it as part of the site or by opening an existing page from another source and saving it as part of the site. In this project, you will create two new pages.

Almost all Web sites have a home page. Compare the home page to your front door. Generally, the front door is the first thing guests see when they visit you. The same applies to a Web site's home page. When someone visits a Web site, he or she usually enters through the home page.

The home page normally is named **index.htm** or **index.html**. This file name has special significance. Most Web servers recognize index.htm (or index.html) as the default home page and automatically display this page without requiring that the user type the full Uniform Resource Locator (URL), or Web address. For example, if you type `http://www.tipsahoy.com` into a Web browser address box and access the Web site, what you see is http://www.tipsahoy.com/index.htm, even though you did not type it that way.

Organizing your Web site and using Dreamweaver's site management features can assure you that the media within your Web page will display correctly. Bringing all of these elements together will start you on your way to becoming a successful Web site developer.

Before you start enhancing your Web site, you copy the data files into the site's folder hierarchy.

Copying Data Files to the Local Web Site

Your Data Disk contains images for Project 2. These images are in an images folder. You use the Windows My Computer option to copy the Project 2 images to your parks images folder. See the inside back cover for instructions for downloading the Data Disk or see your instructor for information about accessing the files required for this book.

The Data Files folder for this project is stored on Local Disk (C:). The location on your computer may be different. If necessary, verify the location of the Data Files folder with your instructor. The following steps show how to copy the files to the parks local root folder.

To Copy Data Files to the Parks Web Site

1. **Click the Start button on the Windows taskbar and then click My Computer.**
2. **Double-click Local Disk (C:) and then navigate to the location of the data files for Project 2.**
3. **Double-click the DataFiles folder and then double-click the Proj02 folder.**
4. **Double-click the parks folder and then double-click the images folder.**
5. **Click the alligator image file or the first file in the list.**
6. **Hold down the SHIFT key and then click the poncedeleon image file, or the last file in the list.**
7. **Right-click the selected files to display the context menu.**
8. **Click the Copy command and then click the My Computer Back button the number of times necessary to navigate to the your name folder.**
9. **Double-click the your name folder, double-click the parks folder, and then double-click the images folder.**
10. **Right-click anywhere in the open window to display the context menu.**
11. **Click the Paste command (Figure 2-3).**
12. **Click the images window Close button.**

The six images are pasted into the Florida Parks Web site images folder, and the folder now contains seven images, including the parksbg image file (Figure 2-3).

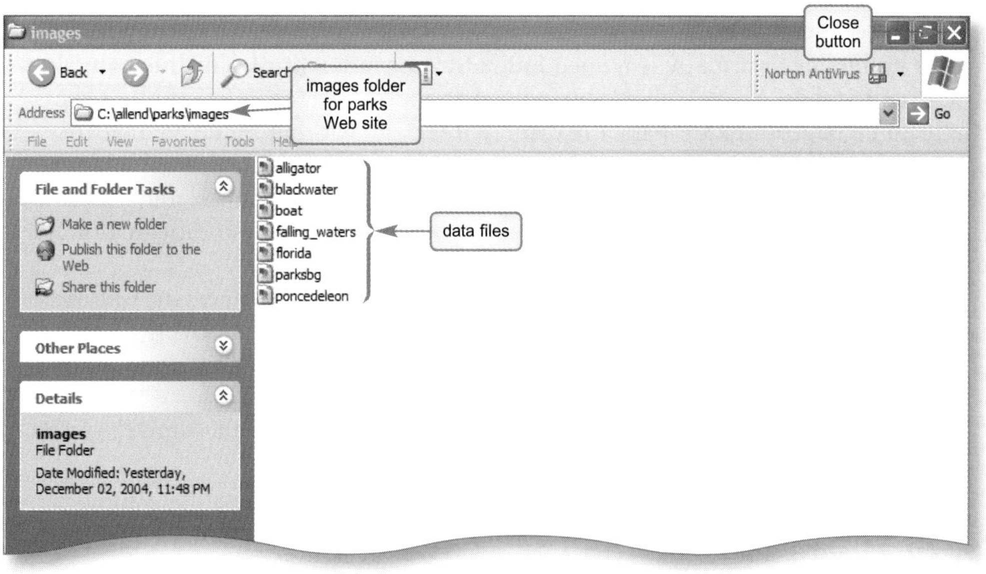

FIGURE 2-3

The data files are copied to the parks Web site file hierarchy. The next step is to start Dreamweaver.

Starting Dreamweaver and Opening a Web Site

Each time you start Dreamweaver, it opens to the last site displayed when you closed the program. It therefore may be necessary for you to open the parks Web site. The **Files pop-up menu** in the Files panel lists sites you have defined. When you open the site, a list of pages and subfolders within the site displays. The following steps illustrate how to start Dreamweaver and open the Florida Parks Web site.

To Start Dreamweaver and Open the Parks Web Site

1

- **Click the Start button on the Windows taskbar. Point to All Programs on the Start menu, point to Macromedia on the All Programs submenu, and then click Macromedia Dreamweaver MX 2004 on the Macromedia submenu. If necessary, display the panel groups.**

Dreamweaver opens and displays panel groups and an empty Document window. If the Start page displays, click Open in the Open a Recent Item column and then select the parks index.htm file.

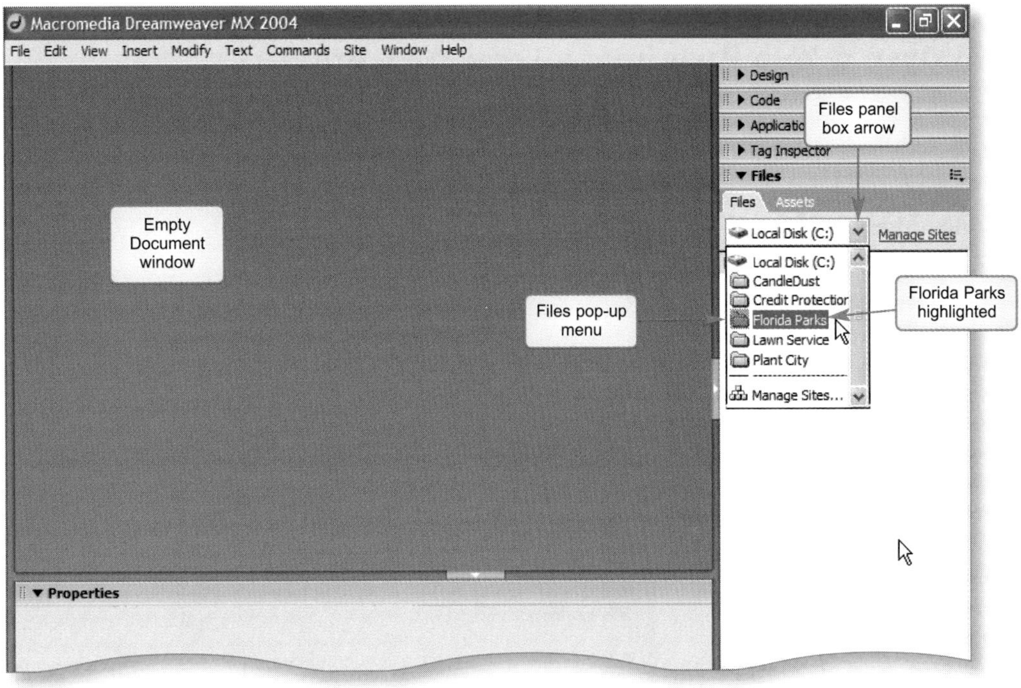

FIGURE 2-4

2

- **Click the Files panel box arrow and point to Florida Parks on the Files pop-up menu (Figure 2-4).**

3

- **Click Florida Parks.**

The Florida Parks Web site hierarchy displays in the Files panel (Figure 2-5).

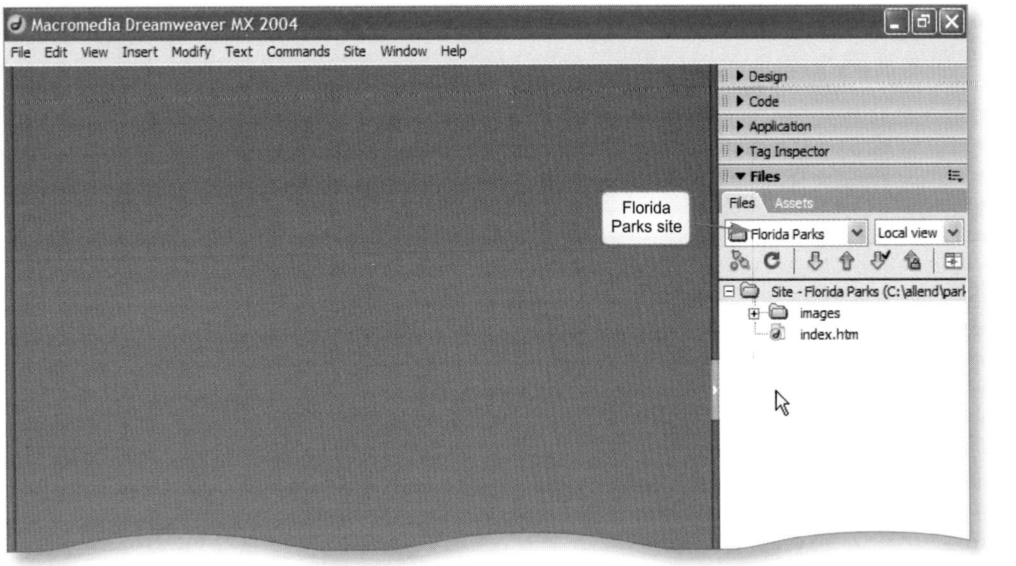

FIGURE 2-5

Opening a Web Page

Once you have created and saved a Web page or copied a Web page to a Web site, you often will have reason to retrieve it from disk. Opening an existing Web page in Dreamweaver is much the same as opening an existing document in most other software applications; that is, you use the File menu and Open command or you can use Dreamweaver's unique File and Open Recent command. If, however, the page is part of a Dreamweaver Web site, you also can open the file from the Files panel.

After opening the page, you can modify text, images, tables, and any other elements. The following step illustrates how to open a Web page from a local site in the Files panel.

To Open a Web Page from a Local Web Site

1

- **Double-click index.htm in the Files panel.**
- **If necessary, click View on the menu bar, point to Toolbars, and then click Standard.**

The Florida Parks index page displays in the Document window, and the name of the page displays on the tab at the top of the window. The Standard toolbar displays (Figure 2-6).

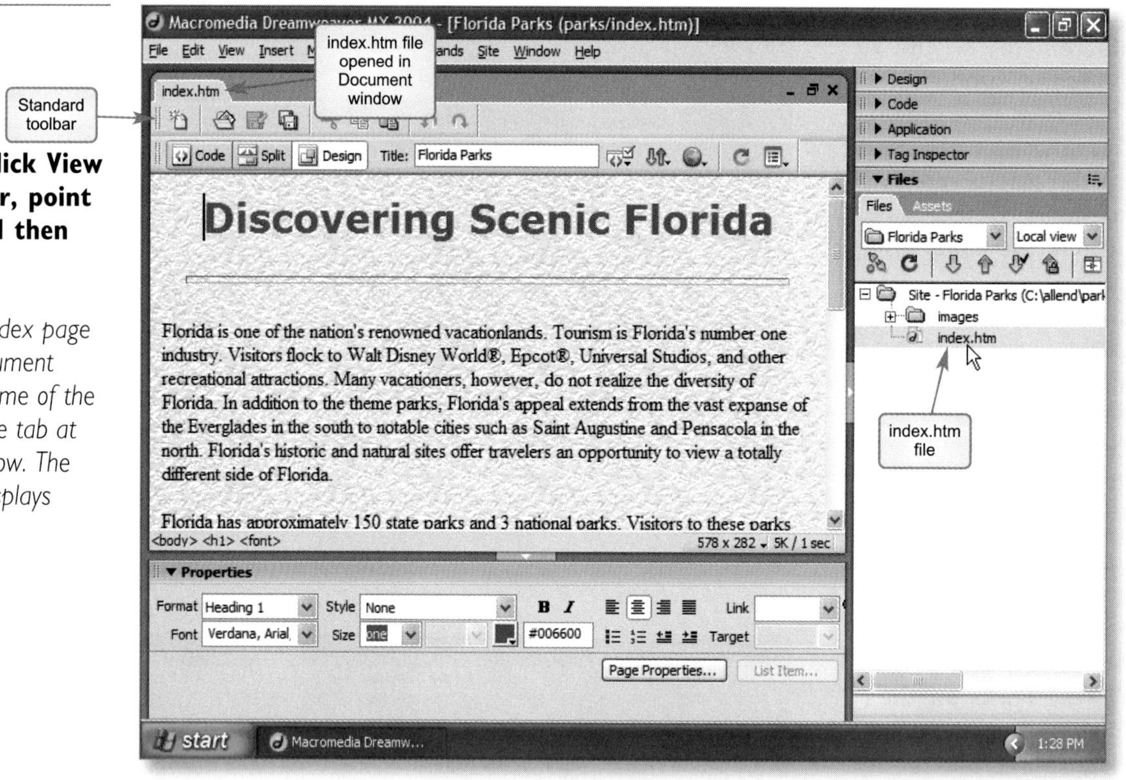

FIGURE 2-6

Other Ways

1. On File menu, click Open

The Files Panel

Organization is one of the keys to a successful Web site. Creating documents without considering where in the folder hierarchy they should go generally creates a difficult-to-manage Web site. The Dreamweaver **Files panel** provides a view of the devices and folders on your computer and shows how these devices and folders are organized. You can create new folders and files for your site through the Files panel, which is similar to the Windows XP file organization method. You also can use the Files panel to drag or copy and paste files to your Web site.

The main directory of a disk is called the **root directory** or the **top-level directory**. A small device icon or folder icon is displayed next to each object in the list. The **device icon** represents a device such as the Desktop or a disk drive, and the **folder icon** represents a folder. Many of these icons have a plus or minus sign next to them, which indicates whether the device or folder contains additional folders or files. Windows XP arranges all of these objects — root directory, folders, subfolders, and files — in a hierarchy. The plus and minus signs are controls that you can click to expand or collapse the view of the file hierarchy. In the Files panel, Dreamweaver uses the same hierarchy arrangement, but site folders appear in a different color than non-site folders so that you easily can distinguish between the two.

More About

Refreshing the Files Panel

To refresh the Files panel, click the Refresh button on the Files panel toolbar or press the F5 key.

The Home Page and the Site Map

Most Web sites have a starting point, called a home page. In a personal home page within a Web site, for example, you probably would list your name, your e-mail address, some personal information, and links to other information on your Web site. The index page you created in Project 1 is the home page for the parks Web site.

Although you cannot tell which page in a Web site is the home page by viewing the site files, Dreamweaver provides a graphical option to view the home page — the Site Map. You access the Site Map through the Files panel. To create a Site Map requires that you designate one page in the Web site as a home page. You will use the Site Map to view the Web site later in this project. The next section sets the home page.

Setting a Home Page

Each Web site you create within Dreamweaver should have a home page. A **home page** is similar to a table of contents or an index in a book. The home page generally contains links to all the other pages within the Web site. Most home pages are named index.htm or index.html. The steps on the next page show how to define the home page through the Files panel.

To Set a Home Page

1

- **Right-click the index.htm file name in the Files panel.**
- **Point to Set as Home Page.**

The context menu displays (Figure 2-7).

2

- **Click Set as Home Page on the context menu.**

The index.htm file is set as the home page for the parks Web site. In the files list, however, no changes are evident.

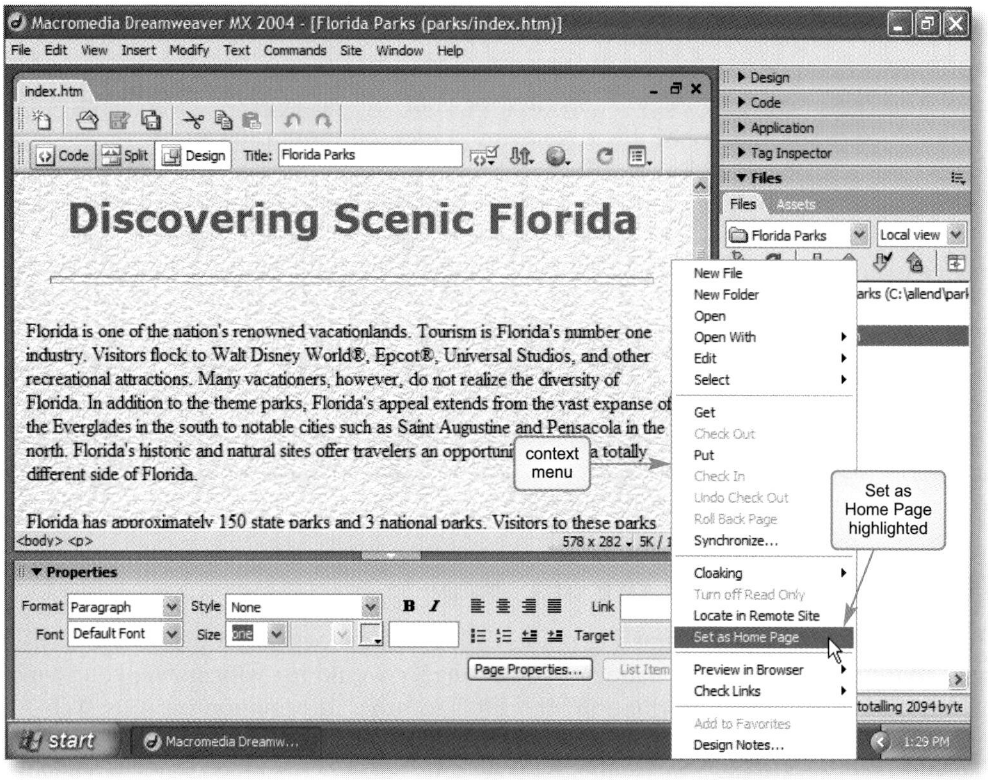

FIGURE 2-7

Other Ways

1. Click Files Option button, click Site, click Set as Home Page

Q&A

Q: Is it necessary to create a folder for images within the Web site?

A: Critical to Web development is the hierarchy of folders and files in a Web site. Even for the very simplest of sites, you should create a separate folder for the images. The folder name can be any name you choose, but it is best to use a descriptive, meaningful name.

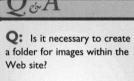

Adding Pages to a Web Site

You copied the files necessary to begin creating your Web site to the parks local root folder in the Files panel, and you set the home page. It is time to start building and enhancing your site. You will add two additional pages to the Web site: Florida National Parks and Florida State Parks. You will add links and page images to the index page and links, a background image, and page images to the two new pages.

Opening a New Document Window

The next step is to open a new Document window. This will become the Florida National Parks page. The following steps illustrate how to open a new document window and save the page as national.htm.

To Open a New Document Window

1

- **Click File on the menu bar and then point to New.**

The File menu is displayed (Figure 2-8).

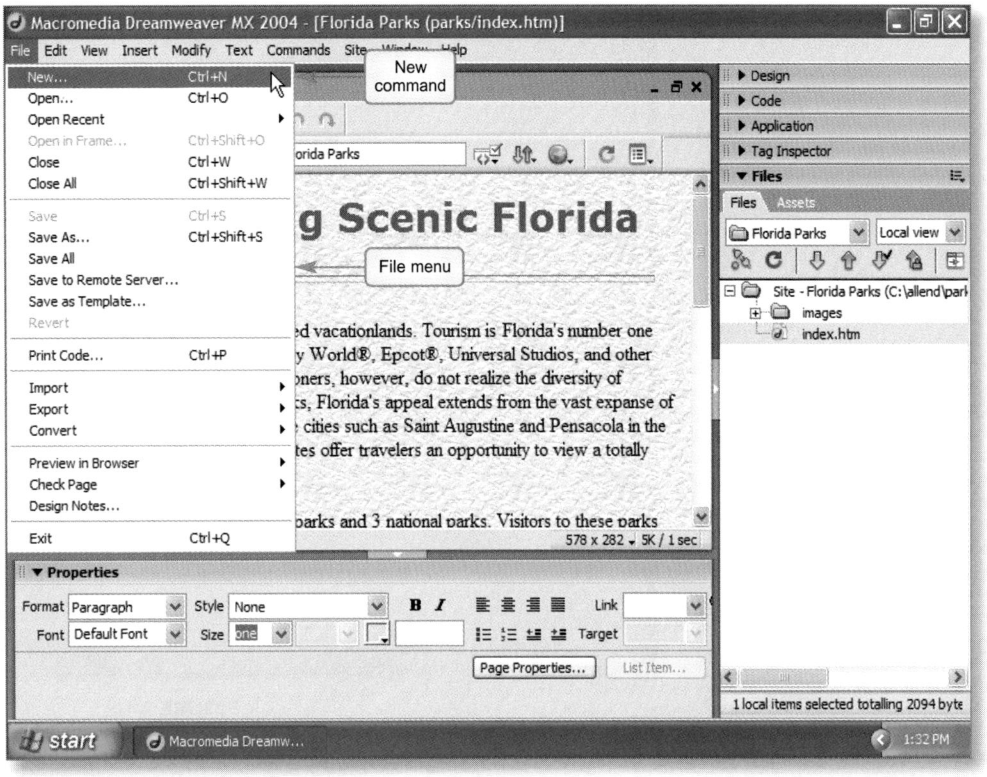

FIGURE 2-8

2

- **Click New. If necessary, click the General tab and then click Basic page in the Category list.**
- **If necessary, click HTML in the Basic page list.**

The New Document dialog box displays. Basic page is highlighted in the Category list. HTML is the default in the Basic page list (Figure 2-9).

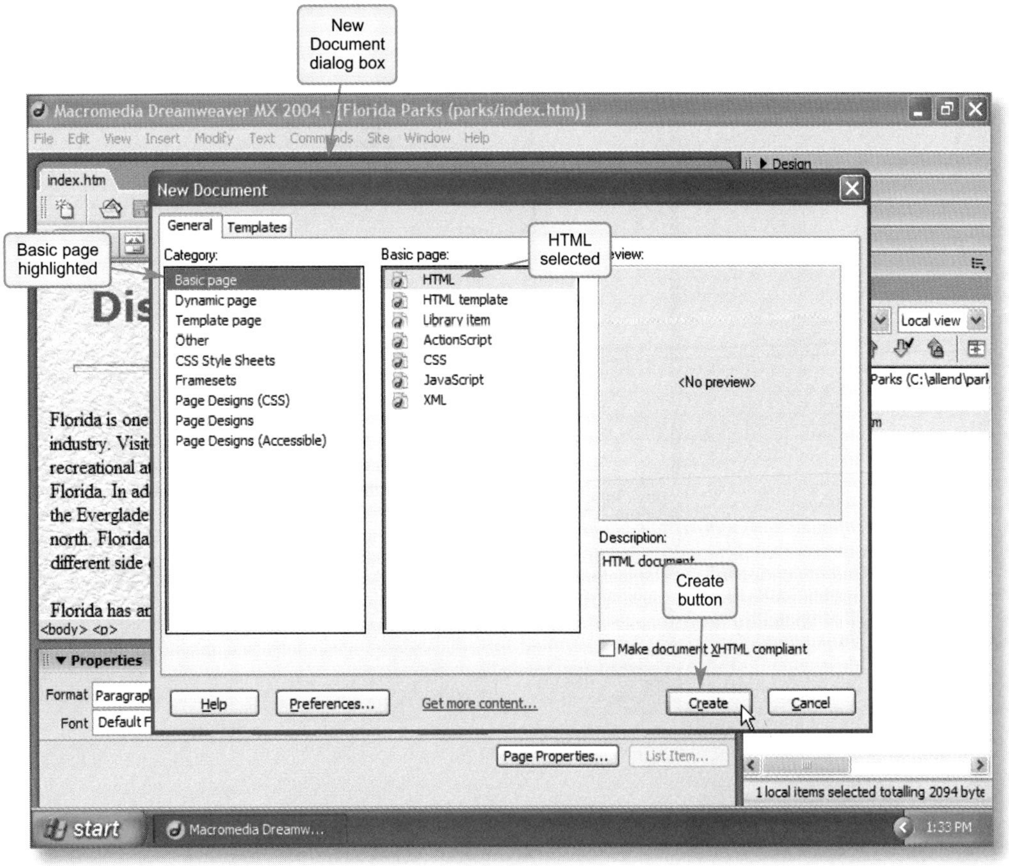

FIGURE 2-9

3

• **Click the Create button.**

A new Untitled-2 Document window displays (Figure 2-10). The number following Untitled increases each time you open a new Document window. Your computer may display a different number.

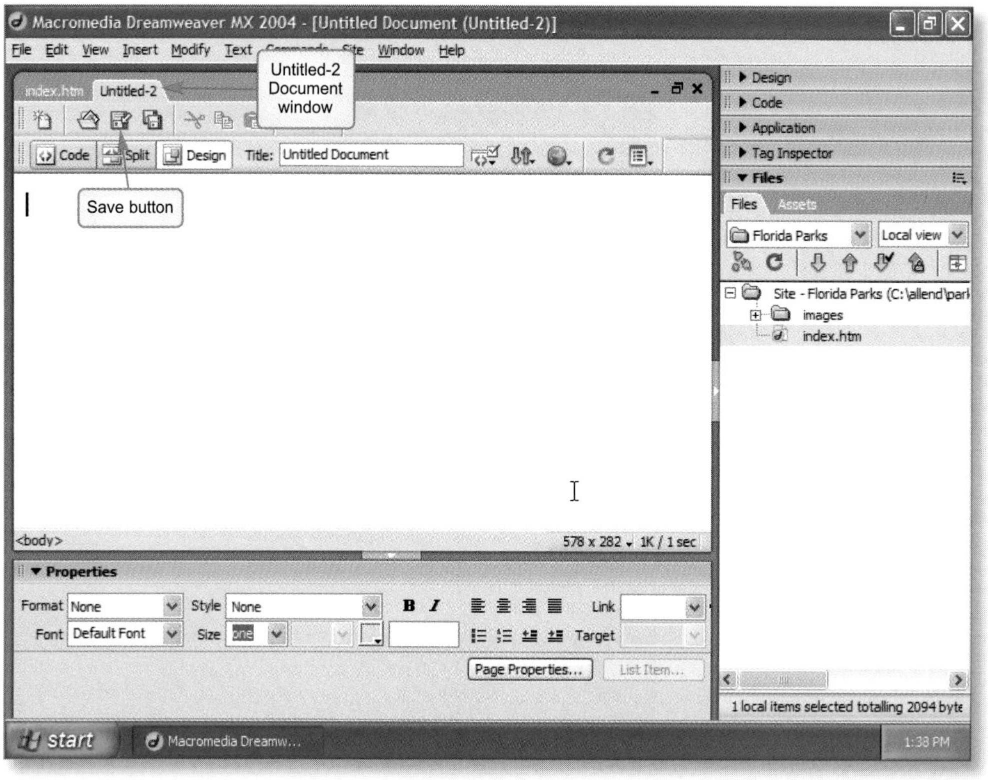

FIGURE 2-10

4

• **Click the Save button on the Standard toolbar.**

The Save As dialog box displays and Untitled-2 is highlighted in the File name text box (Figure 2-11).

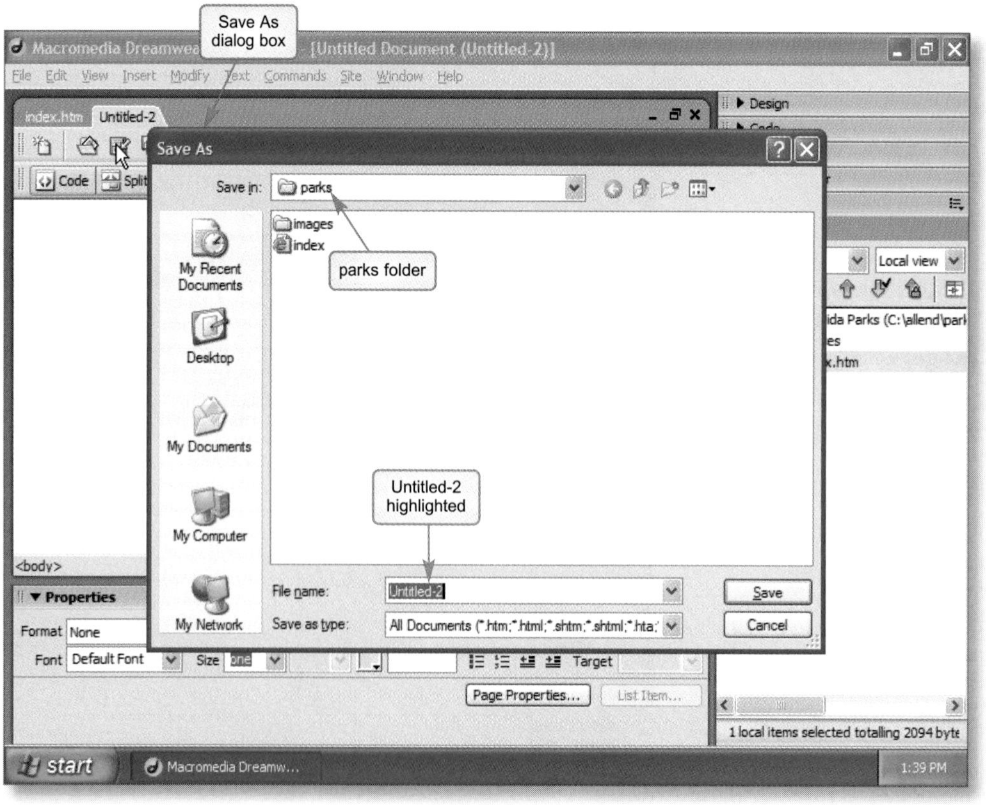

FIGURE 2-11

5

• **Type** `national` **for the file name.**

The national file name displays in the File name text box (Figure 2-12).

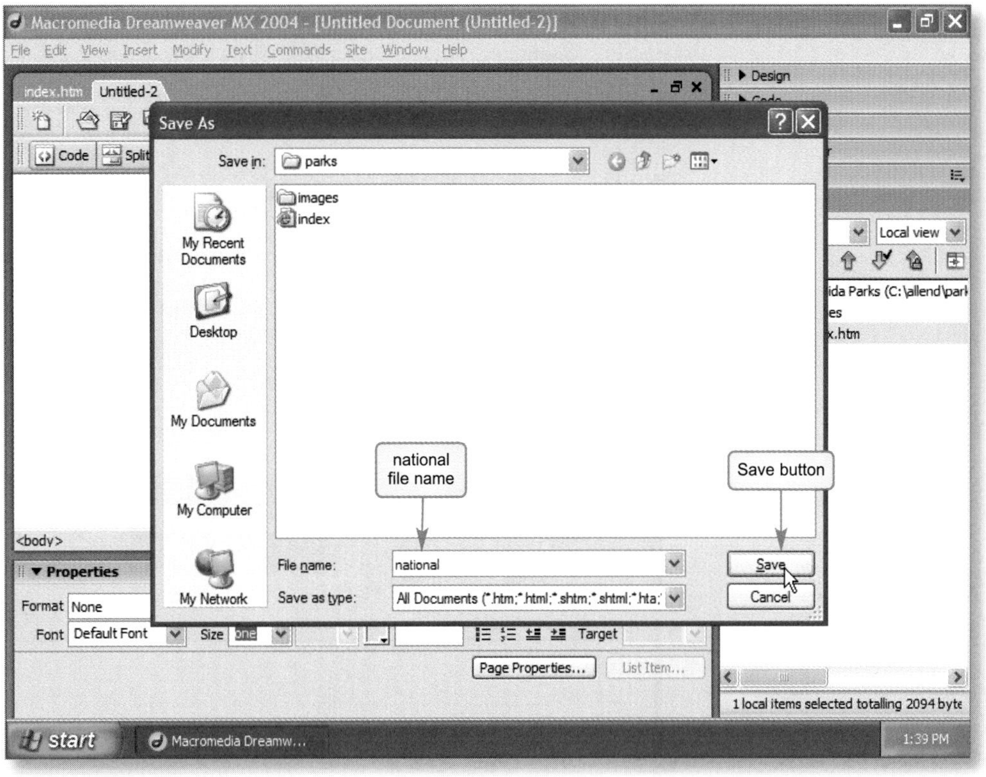

FIGURE 2-12

6

• **Click the Save button.**

The national.htm page is saved in the parks local folder and displays in Dreamweaver's Files panel. The .htm extension is added automatically by Dreamweaver. The path and file name (parks/national.htm) appear on the Dreamweaver title bar (Figure 2-13).

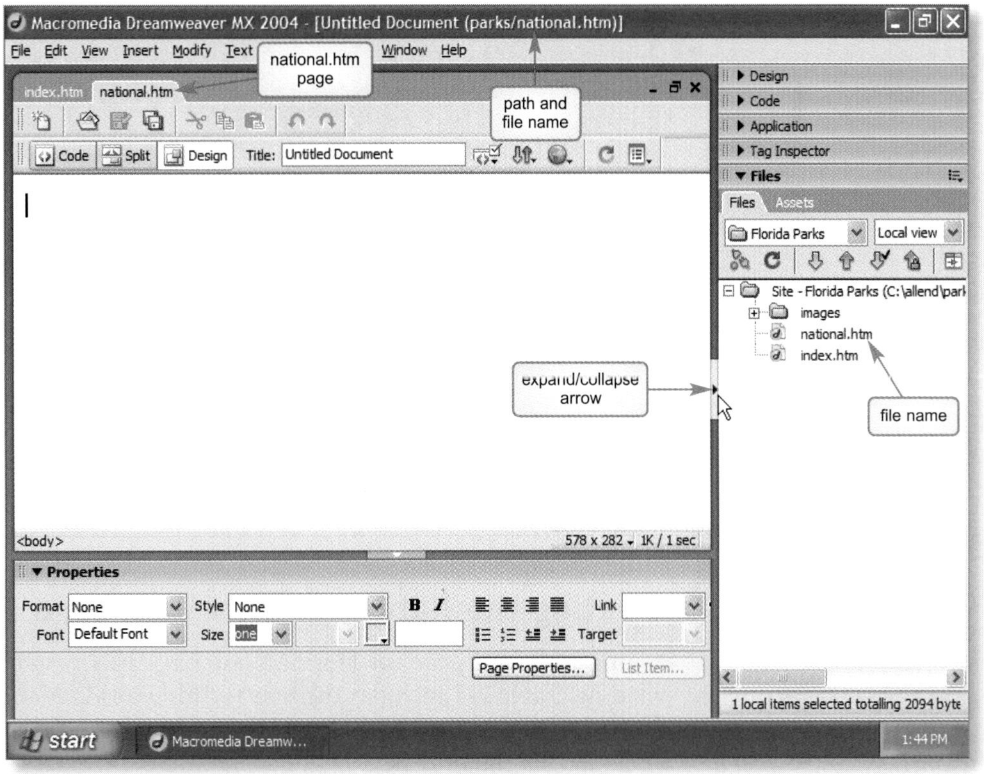

FIGURE 2-13

To organize your workspace, you hide the panel groups and collapse the lower portion of the Property inspector. This gives you additional window space in the Dreamweaver Document window. The following steps show how to organize your workspace by hiding the panel groups.

To Prepare the Workspace

1. **Click the expand/collapse arrow on the panel groups vertical bar.**
2. **Click the Property inspector expander arrow.**

The national.htm Document window displays, the Property inspector is collapsed, and the panel groups are hidden (Figure 2-14).

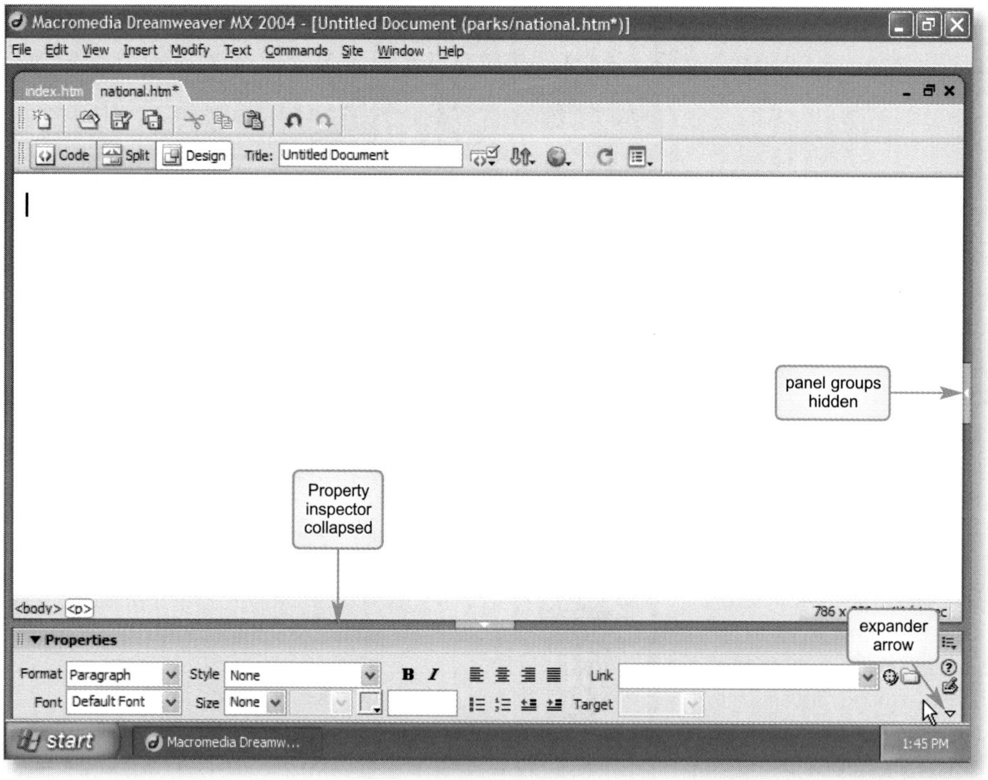

FIGURE 2-14

With the workspace prepared and the Document window displayed, you can begin creating the Web page for Florida National Parks.

> *More About*
>
> **Using the Keyboard Shortcut Editor**
>
> For more information about using keyboard shortcuts, visit the Dreamweaver MX 2004 More About Web page (scsite.com/dreamweavermx04/more) and then click Dreamweaver MX 2004 Shortcut Editor.

Creating the National Parks Web Page

To create the page for Florida National Parks, you type the text in the Document window. Table 2-1 includes the text for the Florida National Parks Web page. Press the ENTER key or insert a line break, or <br>, as indicated in the instructions in Table 2-1 on the next page.

Table 2-1 Florida National Parks Web Page Text

SECTION	WEB PAGE TEXT
Heading	Florida National Parks<ENTER>
Subheading	Experience the Real Florida!<ENTER>
Part 1	Everglades National Park Everglades National Park is the only subtropical preserve in North America. The park is known for its rich bird life and is the only place in the world where alligators and crocodiles exist side by side.<ENTER>
Part 2	Biscayne National Park Biscayne National Park is a delight for wildlife-watching, snorkeling, diving, boating, and fishing. The park contains the longest stretch of mangrove forest left on Florida's east coast and a spectacular living coral reef.<ENTER>
Part 3	Dry Tortugas National Park About 70 miles west of Key West is the Dry Tortugas National Park, a cluster of seven islands, composed of sand and coral reefs. Located on one of the islands is Ft. Jefferson, the largest of the 19th century American coastal forts. The area also is known for its legends of pirates and sunken ships.<ENTER>
Closing	Home<ENTER>

The following steps show how to create the Web page and insert blank lines and line breaks between sections of text as necessary.

To Create the National Parks Web Page

1

• **Type the heading** `Florida National Parks` **as shown in Table 2-1. Press the ENTER key.**

The heading is entered in the Document window (Figure 2-15). Pressing the ENTER key creates a new paragraph.

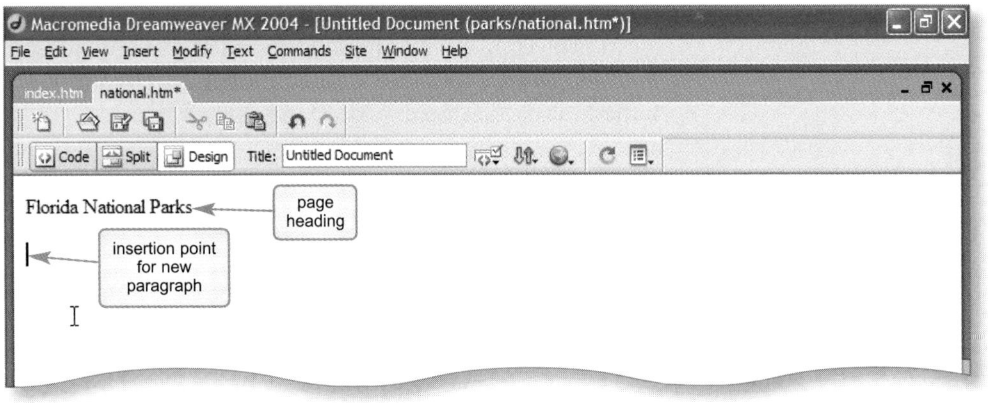

FIGURE 2-15

2

• **Type the subheading** `Experience the Real Florida!` **as shown in Table 2-1, and then press the ENTER key.**

The subheading is entered in the Document window (Figure 2-16).

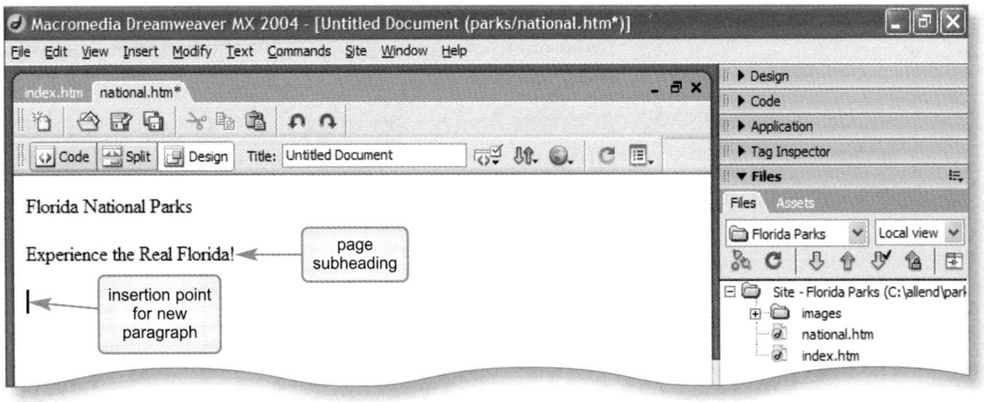

FIGURE 2-16

3

• **Type the rest of the text as shown in Table 2-1. Press the ENTER key and insert line breaks as indicated in the instructions.**

The text for the Florida National Parks is entered (Figure 2-17).

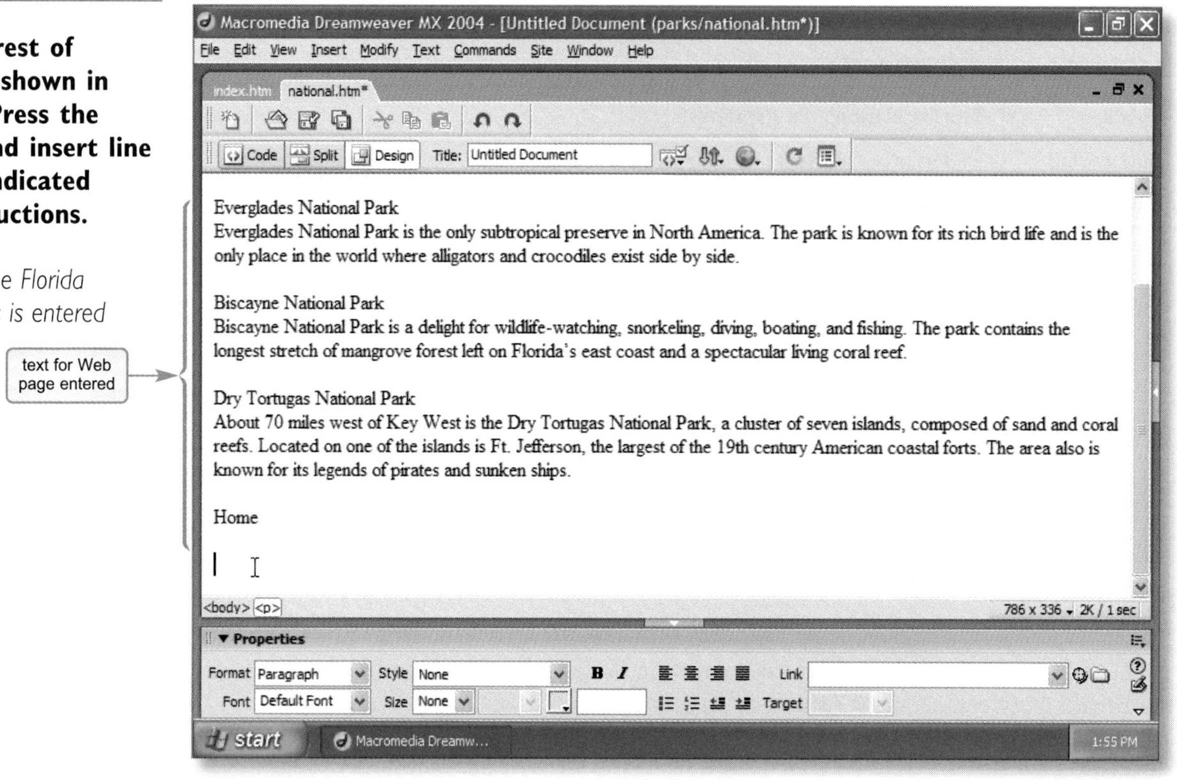

FIGURE 2-17

In Project 1, you formatted the index page by adding headings and bullets, centering, and bolding text. The following steps show how to apply similar formatting to the Florida National Parks page. Recall that SHIFT + ENTER inserts a line break.

To Format the Florida National Parks Page

1. **If necessary, expand the Property inspector, scroll up to the top of the Web page, and then apply Heading 1 to the heading text.**
2. **Apply Heading 2 to the subheading text.**
3. **Center the heading and subheading.**
4. **Add bullets to the following three lines: Everglades National Park, Biscayne National Park, and Dry Tortugas National Park.**
5. **Bold each of these three lines: Everglades National Park, Biscayne National Park, and Dry Tortugas National Park.**
6. **Add two line breaks after the text describing the Everglades National Park and two line breaks after the text describing the Biscayne National Park.**
7. **Type** `Florida National Parks` **as the Web page title.**
8. **Save the national.htm Web page.**
9. **Press F12 to view the page in the browser and to verify that the line spacing is correct, as shown in Figure 2-18. Close the browser.**

The Florida National Parks Web page text is entered, formatted, and saved.

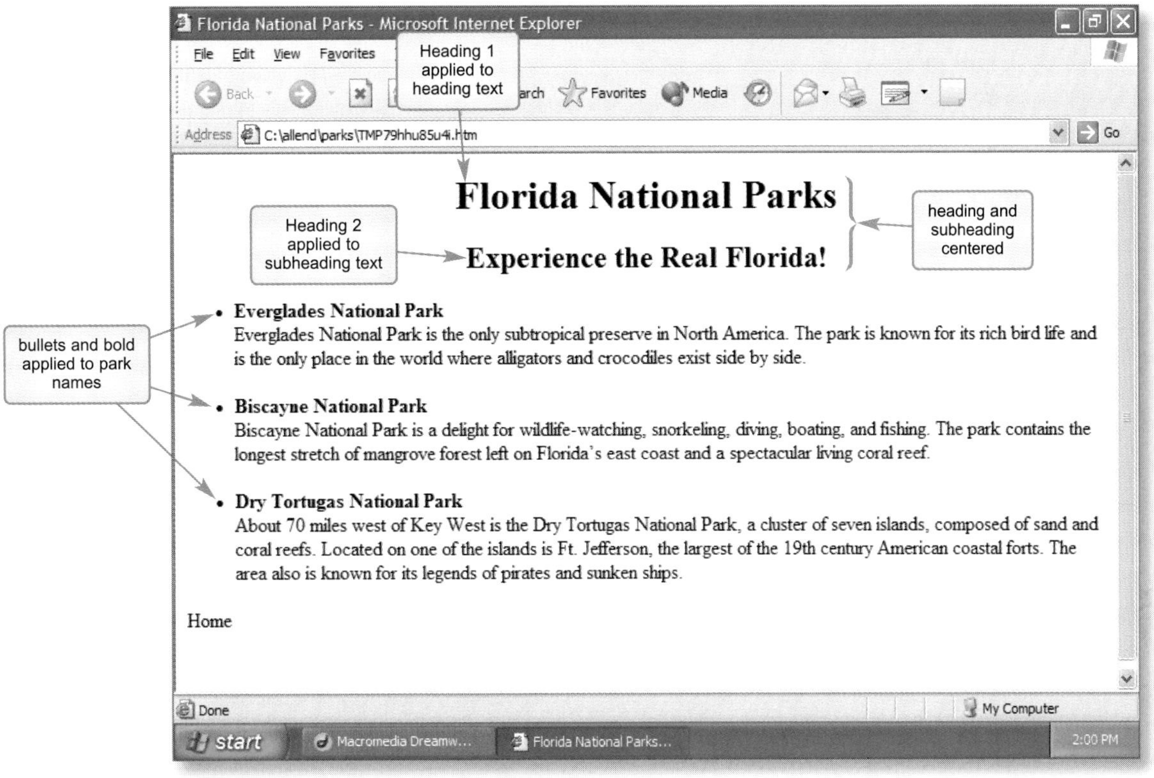

FIGURE 2-18

Creating the State Parks Web Page

You will enter the text for the Florida State Parks Page the same way you entered the text for the Florida National Parks page. Table 2-2 includes all the text for the Florida State Parks Web page.

To Open a New Document Window

1. **Click File on the menu bar and then point to New.**
2. **Click New. If necessary, click the General tab and then click Basic page in the Category list.**
3. **If necessary, click HTML in the Basic page list.**
4. **Click the Create button.**
5. **Save the Web page as state_parks.htm in the parks folder.**

A new Document window displays, and the name of the saved page is displayed on the title bar (Figure 2-19).

Type the text for the State Parks Web page using Table 2-2 on the following page and the following step. Press the ENTER key or insert a line break, or <br>, as indicated in the table.

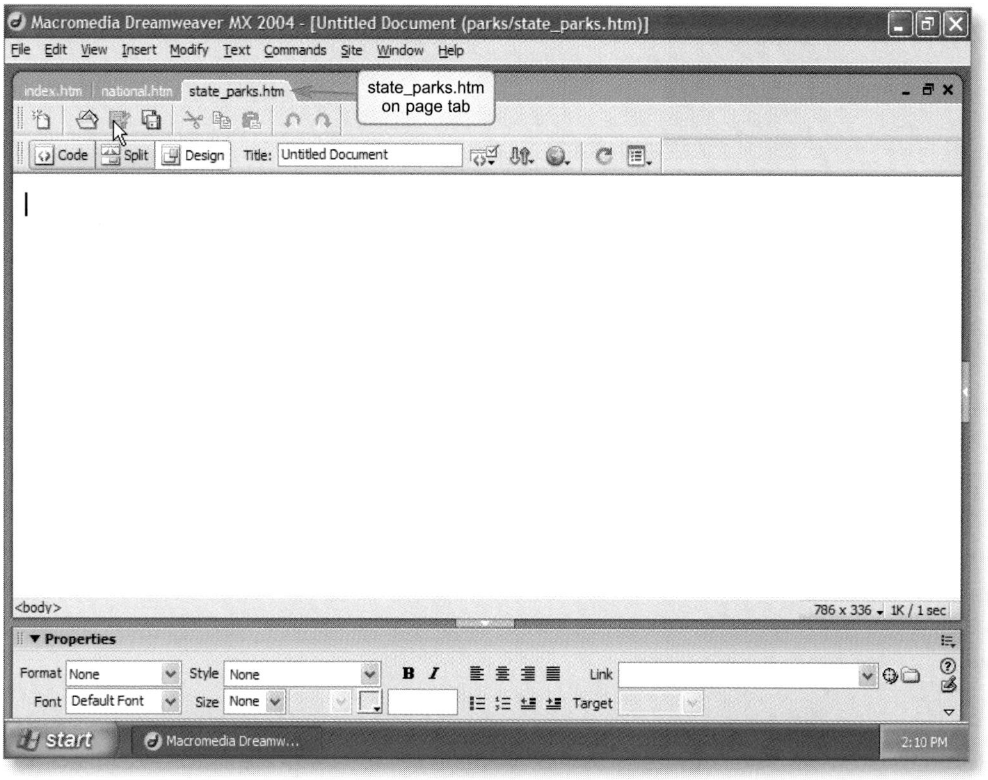

FIGURE 2-19

Table 2-2 Florida State Parks Web Page Text

SECTION	WEB PAGE TEXT
Heading	Florida State Parks<ENTER>
Subheading	Northwest Region<ENTER>
Part 1	Florida has more than 150 state parks. Three of the more unusual and scenic parks are located in the northwestern part of the state.<ENTER>
Part 2	Blackwater River State Park Activities at Blackwater include camping, picnicking, fishing, nature trails, boating, and canoeing. This 590-acre park is located in Holt, Florida. The Blackwater River has one of the purer sand-bottom rivers in the world.<ENTER>
Part 3	Ponce de Leon Spring State Park Activities within this park include fishing, nature trails, picnicking, and swimming. Numerous springs are found within the park.<ENTER>The main spring in the park is created through the merging of two flows from a limestone cavity. These two flows produce more than 14 million gallons of crystal-clear water daily.<ENTER>
Part 4	Falling Waters State Park This park is located in Chipley, Florida. The park derives its name from one of Florida's more notable geological features: a 67-foot waterfall.<ENTER>It also is known for the Falling Waters Sink. The sink is a 100-foot-deep, 20-foot-wide cylindrical pit. Into the pit flows a small stream, which drops 67 feet to the bottom of the sink. The destination of the water is not yet known.<ENTER>
Closing	Home<ENTER>

To Create the State Parks Web Page

1 Type the text of the Web page as shown in Table 2-2.

The text for the Florida State Parks Web page is entered (Figure 2-20).

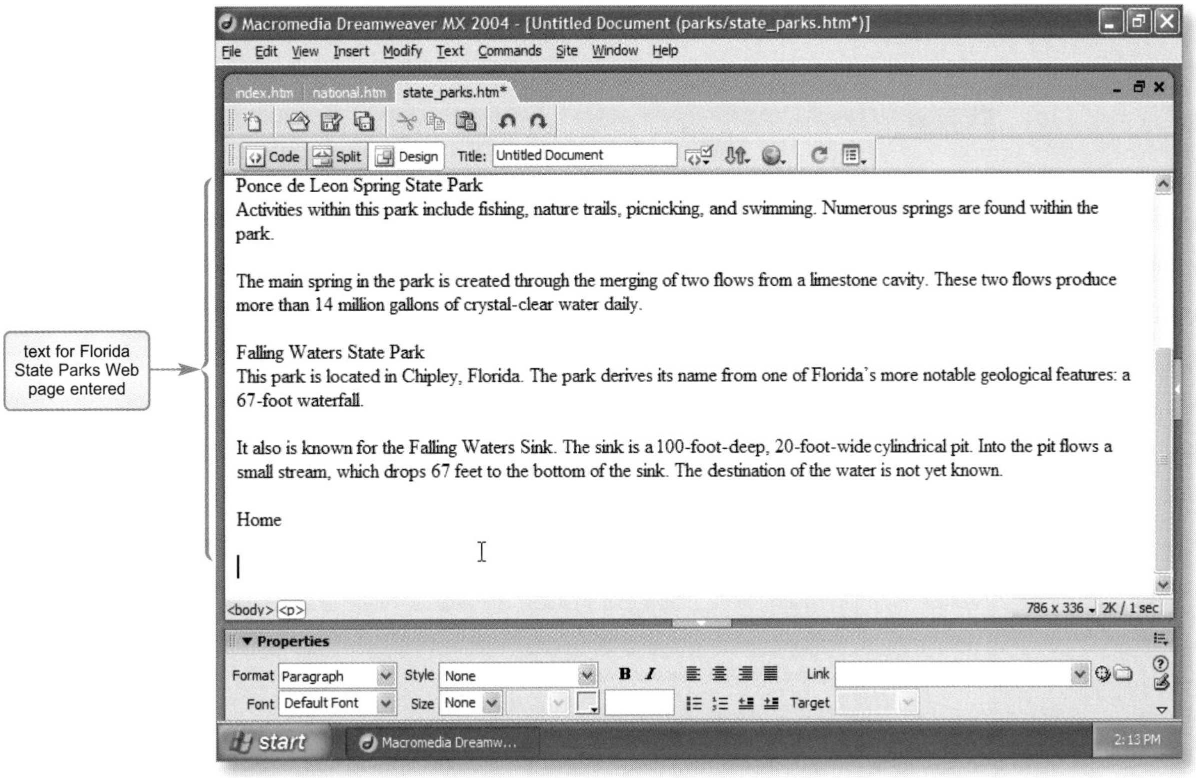

FIGURE 2-20

To Format the Florida State Parks Page

1. **If necessary, scroll to the top of the Web page and then apply Heading 1 to the heading.**
2. **Apply Heading 2 to the subheading.**
3. **Center the heading and subheading.**
4. **Bold the names of each of the three parks where they are used as subtitles.**
5. **Type** `Florida State Parks - NW` **as the Web page title.**
6. **Click the Save button on the Standard toolbar.**
7. **Press F12 to view the page in the browser and to verify that the line spacing is correct, as shown in Figure 2-21 on the next page.**
8. **Close the browser.**

The text for the Florida State Parks page is entered, formatted, and saved.

You have completed entering and formatting the text for the two new pages and copied the images to the parks local root folder in the Files panel. It is time to add additional enhancements to your site. In Project 1, you added a background image to the index page. In this project, you learn more about images. You will add the same background image to the two new pages, and then add page images and links to all three pages.

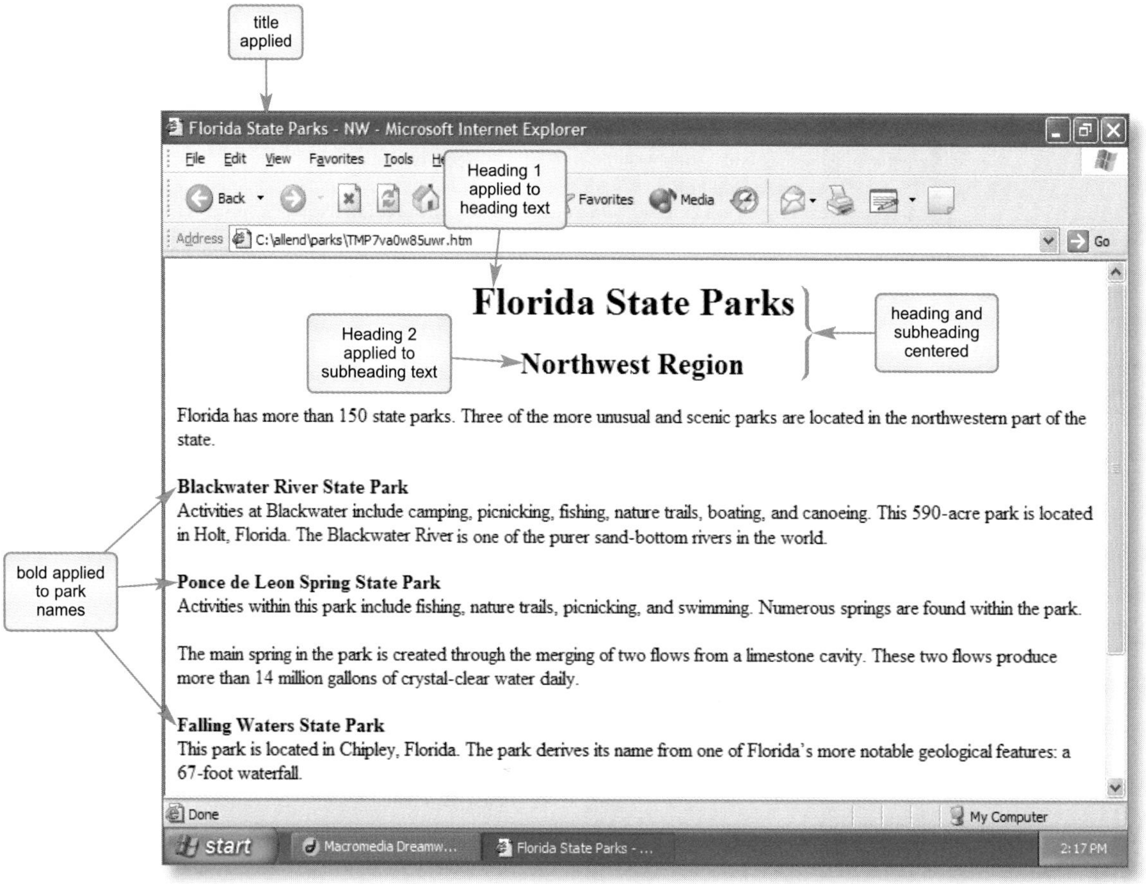

FIGURE 2-21

Images

If used correctly and with an understanding of the Web site audience, images add excitement and interest to a Web page. When you are selecting images for a Web site, it is important to understand that the size and type of image or images used within a Web page affect how fast the Web page downloads and displays in the viewer's Web browser. A Web page that downloads too slowly will turn away visitors.

Image File Formats

Graphical images used on the Web are in one of two broad categories: vector and bitmap. **Vector** images are composed of key points and paths, which define shapes and coloring instructions, such as line and fill colors. The vector file contains a description of the image expressed mathematically. The file describes the image to the computer, and the computer draws it. This type of image generally is associated with Macromedia's Flash or Adobe's LiveMotion animation programs. One of the benefits of vector images is file size, particularly relative to the file size of bitmap images.

Bitmap images are the more common type of image file. A bitmap file maps out or plots an image on a pixel-by-pixel basis. A **pixel**, or **picture element**, is the smallest point in a graphical image. Graphic monitors display images by dividing the display screen into thousands (or millions) of pixels, arranged in a **grid** of rows and columns. The pixels appear connected because they are so close together. This grid of pixels is a **bitmap**. The **bit-resolution** of an image is described by the number of bits used to represent each pixel. An 8-bit image supports up to 256 colors, and a 24- or 32-bit image supports up to 16.7 million colors.

Web browsers currently support three bitmap image file types: GIF, JPEG, and PNG.

GIF **GIF** (.gif) is an acronym for **Graphics Interchange Format**. The GIF format uses 8-bit resolution, supports up to a maximum of 256 colors, and uses combinations of these 256 colors to simulate colors beyond that range. The GIF format is best for displaying images such as logos, icons, buttons, and other images with even colors and tones. GIF images come in two different versions: GIF87 format and GIF89a format. The GIF89a format contains three features not available in the GIF87 or JPEG formats: transparency, interlacing, and animation. The **transparency** feature allows the user to specify a transparency color, which allows the background color or image to display. The **interlacing** feature lets the browser begin to build a low-resolution version of the full-sized GIF picture on the screen while the file is still downloading. Using an animated GIF editor, GIF89a images can be **animated**. Animated GIF images are simply a number of GIF images saved into a single file and looped, or repeated over and over. A number of shareware GIF editors are available to create animated GIFs. If you do not want to create your own animations, you can find thousands of free animated GIFs on the Internet available for downloading.

JPEG **JPEG** (.jpg) is an acronym for **Joint Photographic Experts Group**. JPEG files are the best format for photographic images because JPEG files can contain up to 16.7 million colors. **Progressive JPEG** is a new variation of the JPEG image format. This image format supports a gradually built display such as the interlaced GIFs. Older browsers do not support progressive JPEG files.

PNG **PNG** stands for **Portable Network Graphics.** PNG is the native file format of Macromedia Fireworks. PNG files retain all the original layer, vector, color, and effect information (such as a drop shadow), and all elements are fully editable at all times. Many browsers do not support this format without a special plug-in. Generally, it is better to use GIF or JPEG images in your Web pages.

When developing a Web site that consists of many pages, you should maintain a consistent, professional layout and design throughout all of the pages. The pages in a single site, for example, should use similar features such as background colors or images, margins, and headings.

Background Colors and Background Images

Most Web pages display with a default white or gray background. Generally, the browser used to display the Web page determines the default background. You can enhance your Web page by adding a background image and/or background color or adding one of Dreamweaver's Web-safe color schemes.

If you use a background color, the same cautions apply to background color as they do to text color. You want to use Web-safe colors, such as those in the Dreamweaver color schemes. This means the colors will display correctly on the computer screen when someone is viewing your Web page. To insert an image or color for the page background, you use the Page Properties dialog box.

Background images add texture and interesting color to a Web page and set the overall appearance of the document. Most browsers support background images. A background image can be a large image, but more frequently it is a smaller image. The image tiles to fill the screen in the Dreamweaver Document window and in the browser window. In Project 1, you added a background image to the index page. Now you add the same image to the National Parks Web page and the State Parks page. The following steps illustrate how to add a background image to these two pages.

Q&A

Q: Is it necessary to add a background image to a Web page?

A: No, you do not need to add a background image. If you do add a background image to your Web page, however, select an image that does not clash with the text and other content. The background image should not overwhelm the Web page.

To Add a Background Image to the National Parks Web Page

1. **Click the national.htm tab.**
2. **Click Modify on the menu bar and then click Page Properties.**
3. **Click the Browse button to the right of the Background image box.**
4. **If necessary, navigate to the images folder.**
5. **Click parksbg.gif and then click the OK button in the Select Image Source dialog box.**
6. **Click the OK button in the Page Properties dialog box.**
7. **Click the Save button on the Standard toolbar.**

The background image is applied to the National Parks page (Figure 2-22).

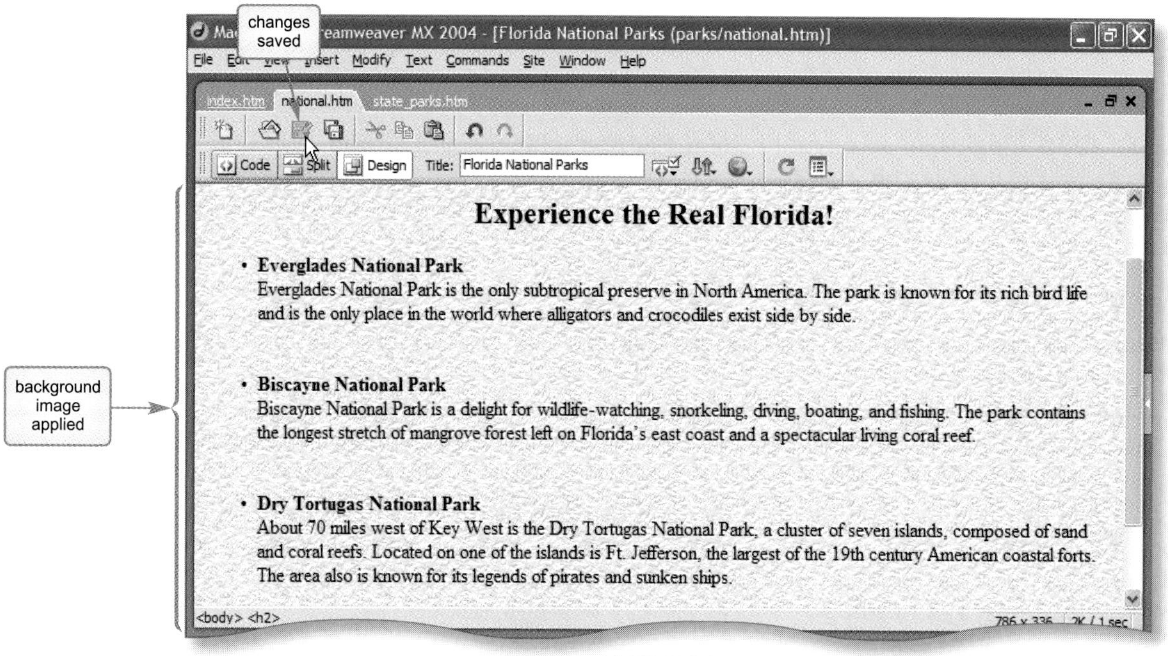

FIGURE 2-22

Other Ways

1. Right-click Document window, click Page Properties on context menu
2. Expand the Property inspector, click Page Properties button

To Add a Background Image to the State Parks Web Page

1. **Click the state_parks.htm tab.**
2. **Click Modify on the menu bar and then click Page Properties.**
3. **Click the Browse button to the right of the Background image box.**
4. **Click parksbg.gif and then click the OK button in the Select Image Source dialog box.**
5. **Click the OK button in the Page Properties dialog box.**
6. **Click the Save button on the Standard toolbar.**

The background image is applied to the State Parks page (Figure 2-23 on the next page).

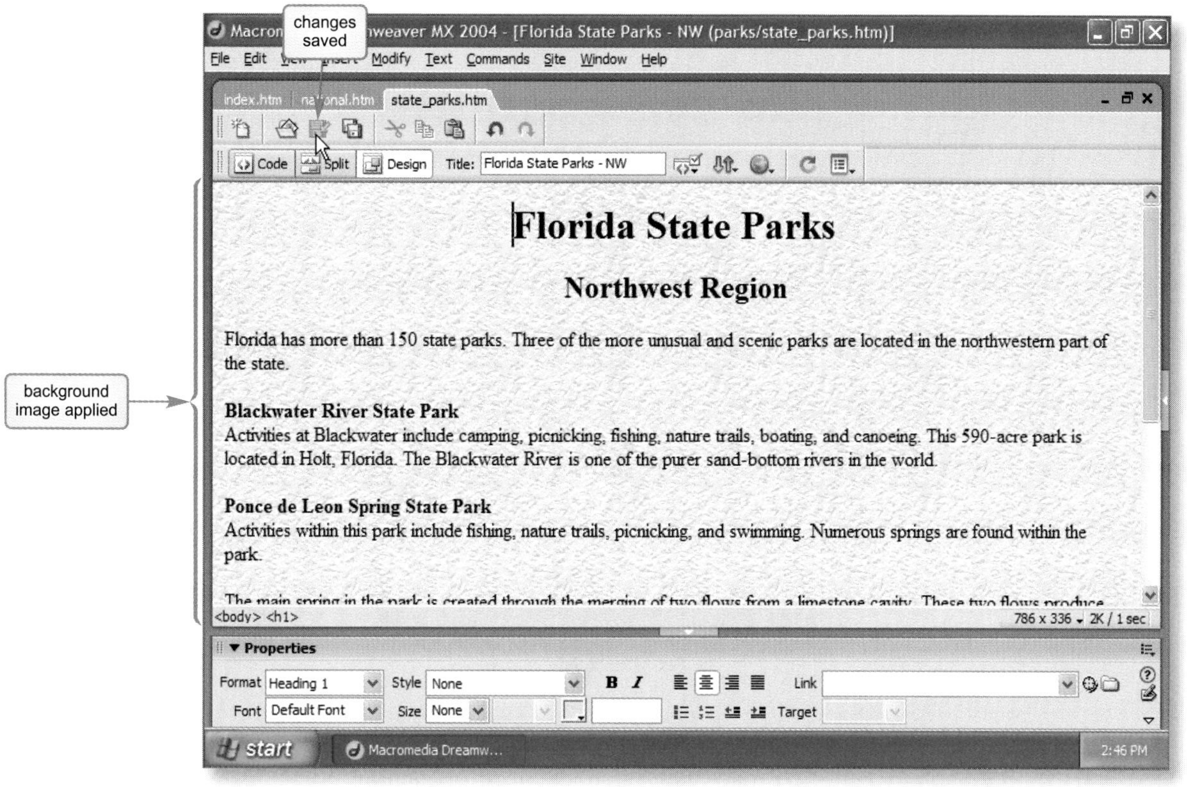

FIGURE 2-23

To enhance your index Web page further, you will add two images. One of the images will display at the top right of the document, and the second image will display at the bottom to the left of the bulleted list. Dreamweaver's Assets panel provides visual cues, and the invisible element feature provides placement control for these images.

Assets Panel

Assets are elements, such as images or Flash files, that you use in building a page or a site. The **Assets panel**, which is grouped with the Files panel, helps you manage and organize your Web site's assets (Figure 2-24 on the next page). This panel contains a list of all the asset types (images, colors, URLs, Flash and Shockwave files, movies, scripts, templates, and library items) within the selected local root folder. The Site list shows all of the assets in your site. The Favorites list shows only the assets you have selected and added to the list. To add an asset to the Favorites list, select the item in the Site list and then click the Add to Favorites button. Remove an item from the list by selecting the item and then clicking the Remove from Favorites button. The Assets panel in Figure 2-24 is resized to show all options. You resize the panels by moving the mouse pointer over the vertical bar until it displays as a two-headed arrow. Then you hold down the mouse button and drag.

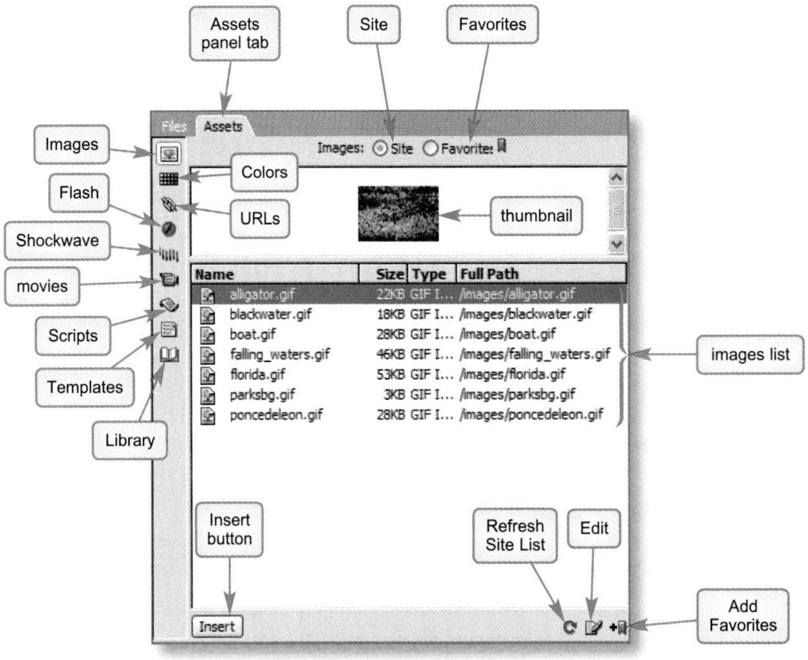

FIGURE 2-24

You can insert most asset types into a document by dragging them into the Document window or by using the Insert button at the bottom of the Assets panel. You also either can insert colors and URLs or apply them to selected text in Design view. Additionally, you can apply URLs to other elements in Design view, such as images. When an image file name is highlighted, a thumbnail of the image displays at the top of the Assets panel. You use the Assets panel to insert the images into the Florida Parks Web pages.

Invisible Elements

Dreamweaver's Document window displays what you would see in a Web browser window. It sometimes is helpful, however, when designing a Web page to see the placement of certain elements. For example, viewing the Line Break code <br> provides a visual cue regarding the layout. Dreamweaver enables you to control the visibility of 13 different codes, including those for image placement, through the Preferences dialog box.

When you insert and align an image into a Document window, Dreamweaver displays an **invisible element marker** that shows the location of the inserted image within the HTML code. This visual aid displays as a small yellow icon. When the icon is selected, it displays as blue and can be used to cut and paste or drag and drop the image. Other aligned elements include tables, ActiveX objects, plug-ins, and applets. To hide all invisible elements temporarily, deselect Visual Aids through the View menu.

The steps on the next page illustrate how to display the invisible element marker for aligned elements such as images and turn on Invisible Elements through the Visual Aids submenu command.

To Set Invisible Element Preferences and Turn on Visual Aids

1

- **Click Edit on the menu bar and then click Preferences.**
- **Click Invisible Elements in the Category list.**

The Preferences dialog box displays, and Invisible Elements is highlighted in the Category list (Figure 2-25).

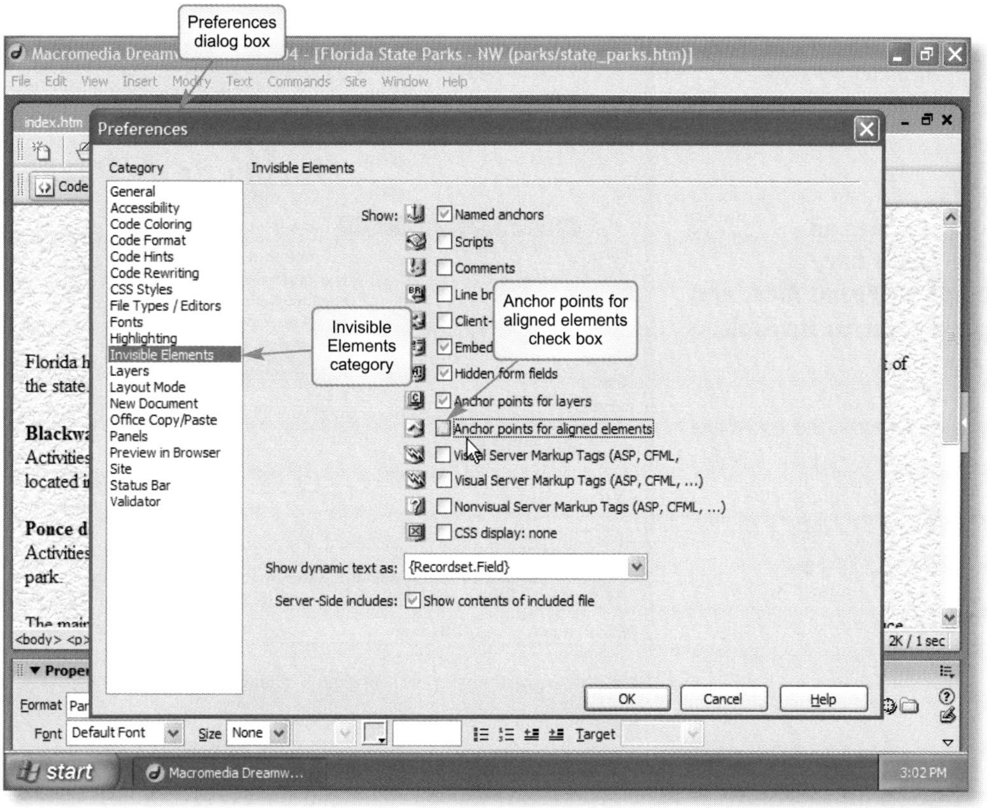

FIGURE 2-25

2

- **Click the Anchor points for aligned elements check box (Figure 2-26).**

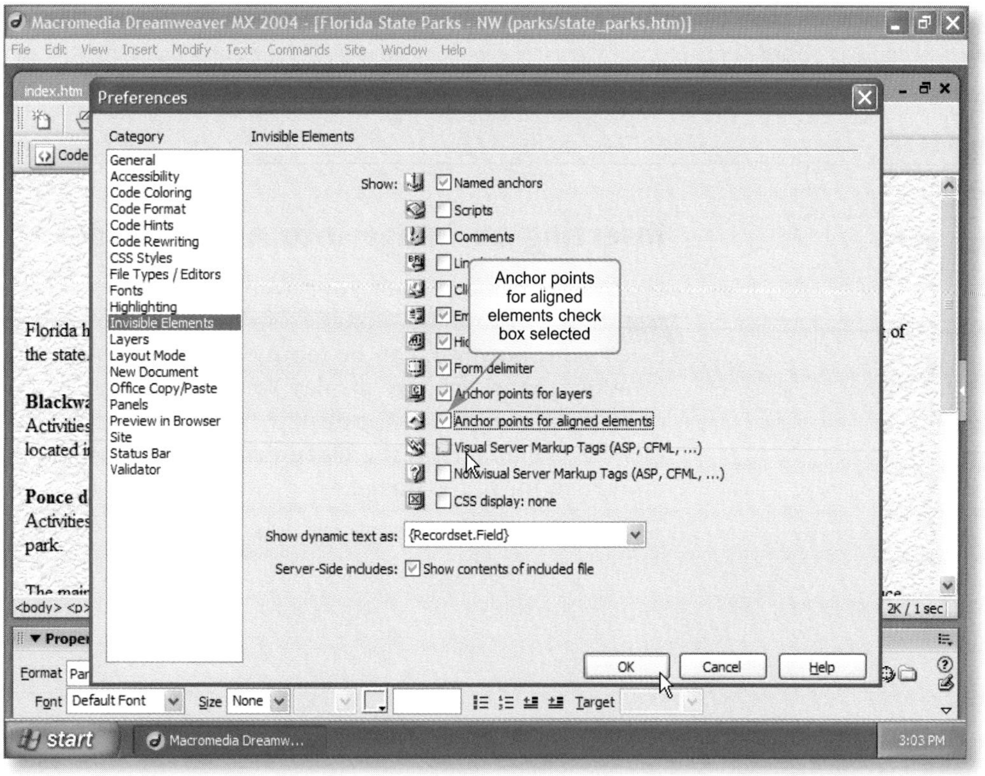

FIGURE 2-26

3

• **Click the OK button.**

The Document window displays with no visible change.

4

• **Click View on the menu bar, point to Visual Aids, and then point to Invisible Elements.**

The View menu and the Visual Aids submenu display. Invisible Elements is highlighted (Figure 2-27). Note: If a check mark already is displayed to the left of the Invisible Elements command, do not complete the next step.

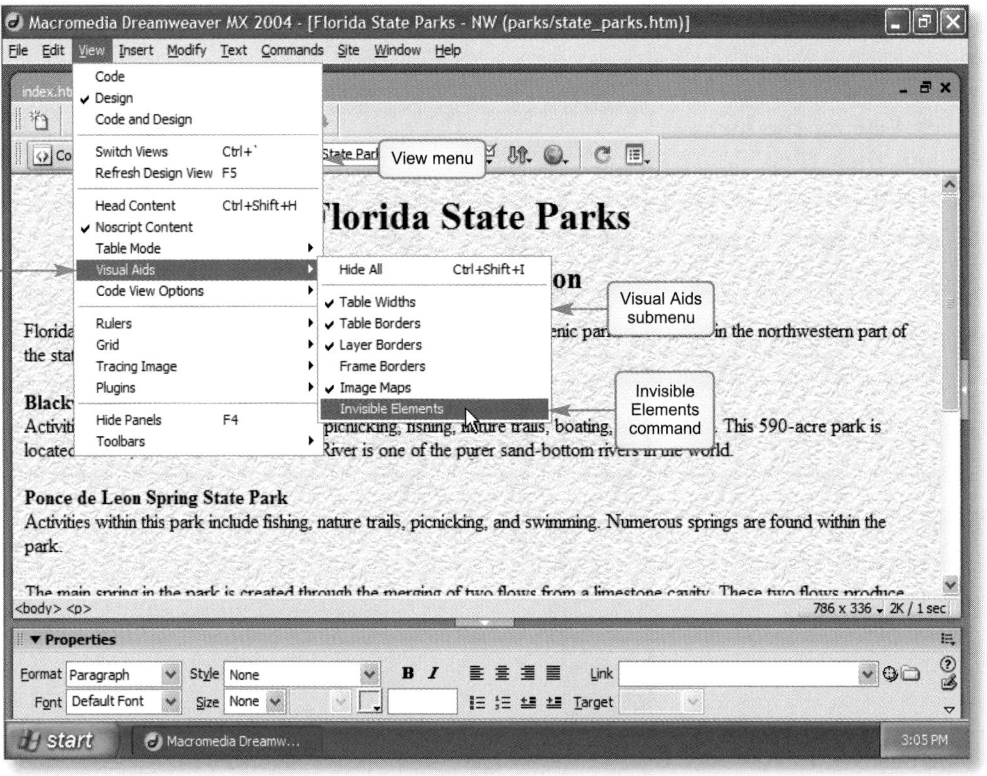

FIGURE 2-27

5

• **Click Invisible Elements.**

A check mark is added to the Invisible Elements command, and the Document window displays with no visible changes.

Inserting an Image into a Web Page

Inserting images into your Web page is easy and quick with Dreamweaver — just drag and drop the image from the Files panel or the Assets panel. Image placement, however, can be more complex. When the Web page is viewed in a browser, the image may display somewhat differently than in the Document window. If the images do not display correctly, you can select and modify the placement of the images in the Document window by dragging the invisible element marker to move the image.

To Insert an Image into the Index Page

1

- **Click the index.htm page tab. If necessary, scroll to the top of the page.**
- **Click the vertical bar expand/collapse arrow to display the panel groups.**
- **If necessary, click the Assets panel tab. Verify that the Images icon is selected.**
- **Click alligator.gif in the Assets panel.**

The index page displays and the Assets panel is selected. The file, alligator.gif is highlighted (Figure 2-28).

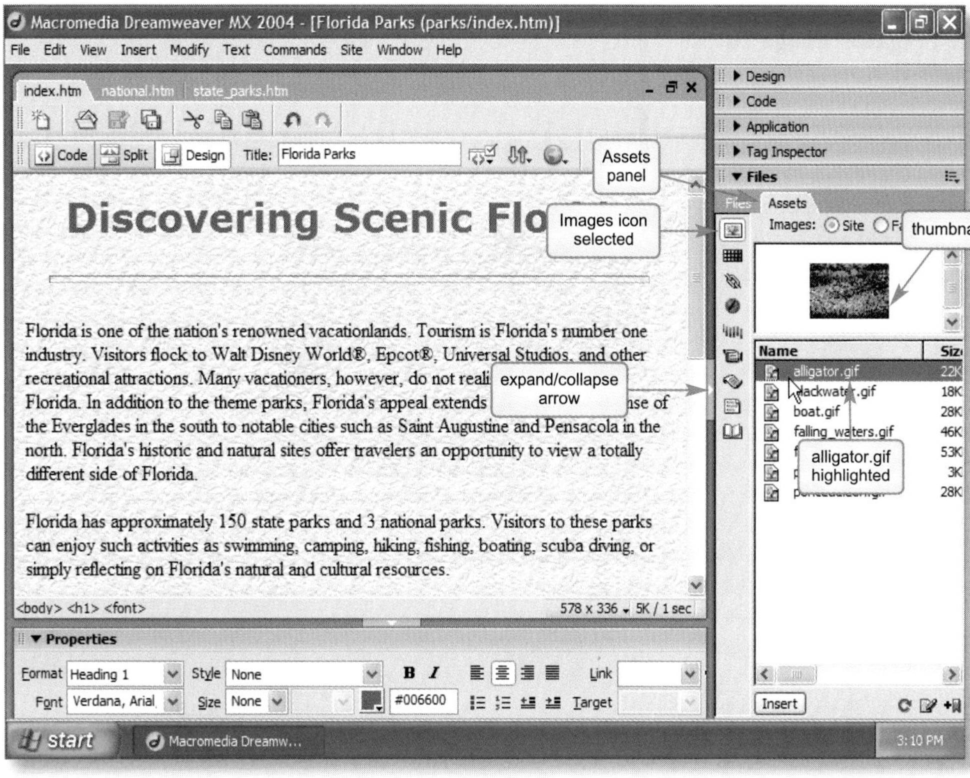

FIGURE 2-28

2

- **If necessary, scroll to the top of the page in the index Document window.**
- **Drag alligator.gif from the Assets panel to the left of the first line of the first paragraph. Do not release the mouse button.**

When you start to drag, a page icon displays next to the mouse pointer (Figure 2-29), indicating the image is being dragged.

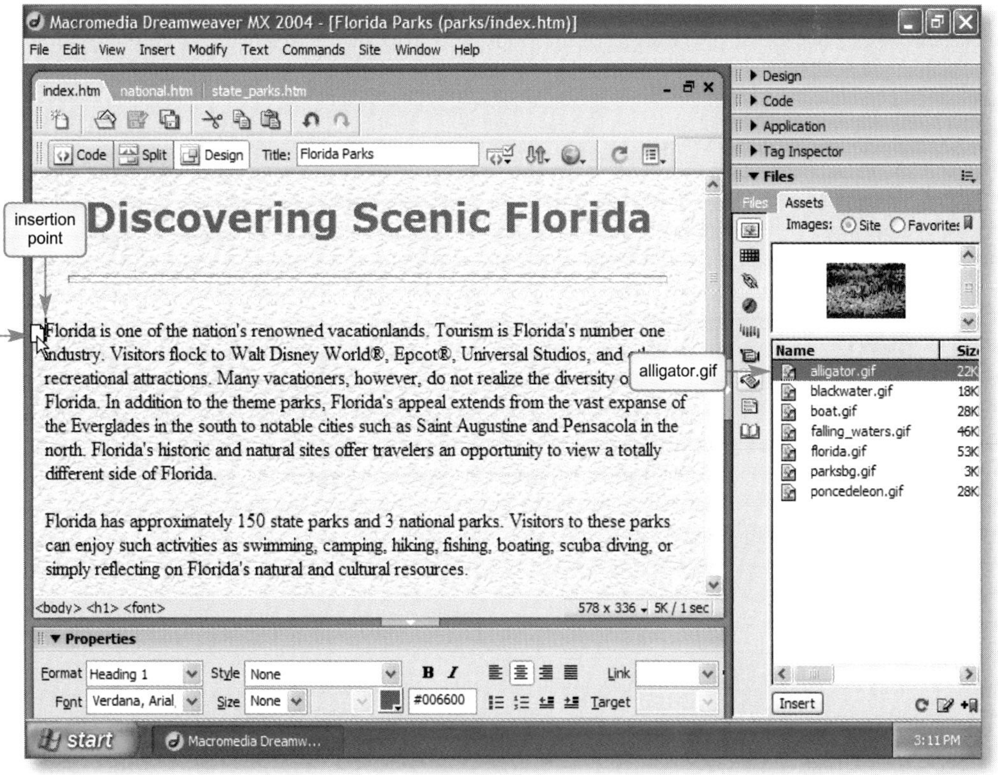

FIGURE 2-29

3

• **Release the mouse button and then click the alligator image to select it if necessary.**

The border and handles around the image indicate it is selected. The attributes change in the Property inspector to reflect the selected object (Figure 2-30).

FIGURE 2-30

In addition to the visual aid feature, you use the Property inspector to help with image placement and add other attributes. When you select an image within the Document window, the Property inspector displays properties specific to that image.

Property Inspector Image Features

The Property inspector lets you see the current properties of the selected element. The Property inspector is divided into two sections. Clicking the expander arrow in the lower-right corner of the Property inspector collapses the Property inspector to show only the most commonly used properties for the selected element or expands the Property inspector to show more options. The Property inspector for images contains several image-related features in the top and lower sections.

The following section describes the image-related features of the Property inspector (Figure 2-31 on the next page). The panel groups are hidden to display a full view of the Property inspector.

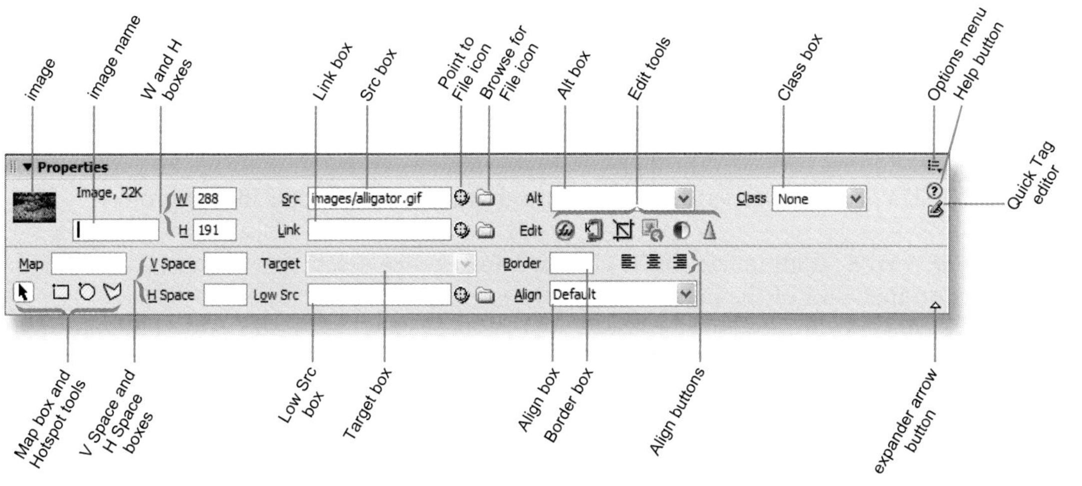

FIGURE 2-31

W AND H The **W** and **H** boxes indicate the width and height of the image, in pixels. Dreamweaver automatically displays the dimensions when an image is inserted into a page. You can specify the image size in the following units: pc (picas), pt (points), in (inches), mm (millimeters), cm (centimeters), and combinations, such as 2in+5mm. Dreamweaver converts the values to pixels in the HTML source code.

LINK The **Link** box allows you to make the selected image a hyperlink to a specified URL or Web page. To create a link, you can click the Point to File or Browse for File icon to the right of the Link box to browse to a page in your Web site, or drag a file from the site window into the Link box. For an external link, you can type the URL directly into the Link box or use copy and paste.

ALIGN **Align** sets the alignment of an image in relation to other elements in the same paragraph, table, or line. Align is discussed in more detail later in this project.

ALT **Alt** specifies alternative text that appears in place of the image for text-only browsers or for browsers that have been set to download images manually. For visually impaired users who use speech synthesizers with text-only browsers, the text is spoken aloud. In some browsers, this text also appears when the pointer is over the image.

MAP AND HOTSPOT TOOLS Use the **Map** box and the **Hotspot tools** to label and create an image map.

V SPACE AND H SPACE V Space and H Space add space, in pixels, along the sides of the image. **V Space** adds space along the top and bottom of an image. **H Space** adds space along the left and right of an image.

TARGET **Target** specifies the frame or window in which the linked page should load. This option is not available when the image is linked to another file.

LOW SRC **Low Src** specifies the image that should load before the main image. Many designers use a small black-and-white version of the main image because it loads quickly and gives visitors an idea of what they will see.

BORDER **Border** is the width, in pixels, of the image's border. The default is no border.

EDIT **Edit** provides five different editing option tools: (a) **Optimize in Fireworks**, which opens the Macromedia Fireworks image-editing application; (b) **Crop**, which lets you edit images by reducing the area of the image; (c) **Image resampling**, which adds or subtracts pixels from a resized JPEG or GIF image file to match the appearance of the original image as closely as possible; (d) **Brightness/Contrast**, which modifies the contrast or brightness of pixels in an image; and (e) **Sharpening**, which adjusts the focus of an image by increasing the contrast of edges found within the image. Editing tools (b) through (e) do not require an external image-editing application. These editing functions are discussed in more detail later in this project.

RESET SIZE If an image size is changed, **Reset Size** resets the W and H values to the original size of the image.

LEFT, CENTER, AND RIGHT In Dreamweaver, the default alignment for an image is left alignment. To change the default alignment, select the image you want to align. Click an alignment button: Align Center, Align Right, or Justify.

SRC **Src** specifies the source file for the image.

After you insert the image into the Web page and then select it, the Property inspector displays features specific to images. As discussed earlier, alignment is one of these features. **Alignment** determines where on the page the image displays and if and how text wraps around the image.

Aligning an Image

When you insert an image into a Web page, by default, the text around the image aligns to the bottom of the image. The image alignment options on the Align pop-up menu in the Property inspector let you set the alignment for the image in relation to other page content. Dreamweaver provides 10 alignment options for images. Table 2-3 describes these image alignment options.

Table 2-3 Image Alignment Options

ALIGNMENT OPTION	DESCRIPTION
Default	Aligns the image with the baseline of the text in most browser default settings
Baseline	Aligns the image with the baseline of the text regardless of the browser setting
Top	Aligns the image with the top of the item; item can be text or another object
Middle	Aligns the image with the baseline of the text or object at the vertical middle of the image
Bottom	Aligns the image with the baseline of the text or the bottom of another image regardless of the browser setting
Text Top	Aligns the image with the top of the tallest character in a line of text
Absolute Middle	Aligns the image with the middle of the current line of text
Absolute Bottom	Aligns the image with the bottom of the current line of text or another object
Left	Aligns the image at the left margin
Right	Aligns the image at the right margin

As indicated in Table 2-3, the Align pop-up menu contains 10 alignment options. The more widely used options are left, right, and center. The steps on the next page show how to align the alligator image to the right and create text wrapping to the left of the image.

To Align an Image

1

- **If necessary, click the alligator image to select it and then click the Align box arrow in the Property inspector. Point to Right on the pop-up menu.**

The Align pop-up menu is displayed, and Right is highlighted (Figure 2-32).

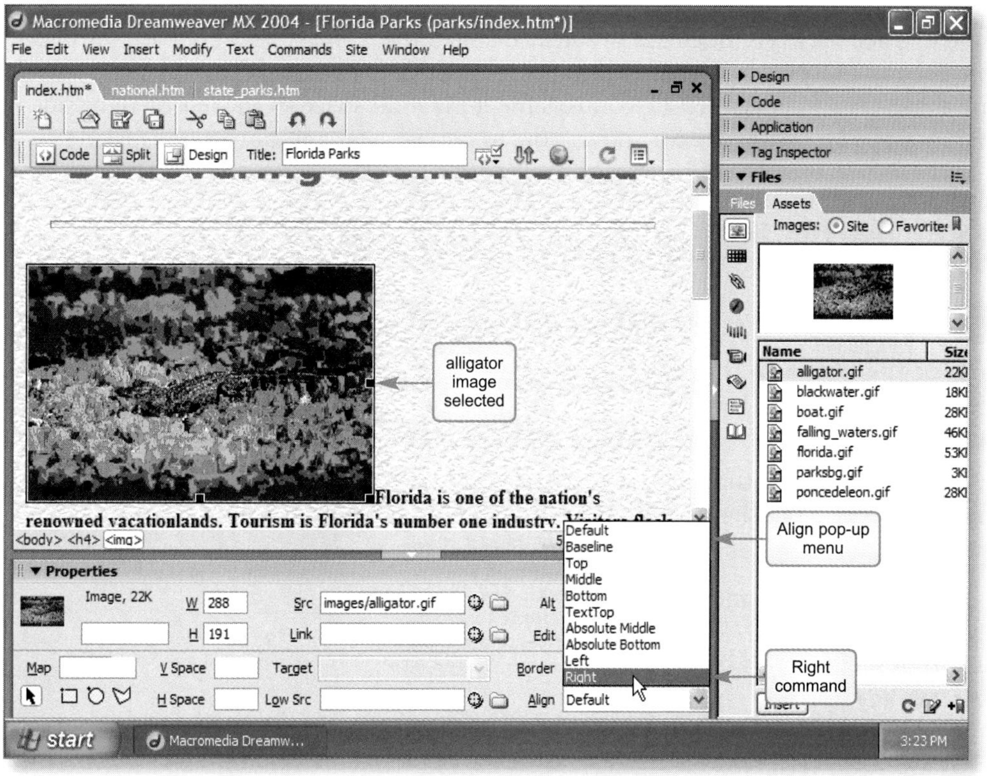

FIGURE 2-32

2

- **Click Right.**

The image moves to the right side of the window and is highlighted (Figure 2-33). An element marker displays to indicate the location of the insertion point. The element marker is highlighted because the image is selected.

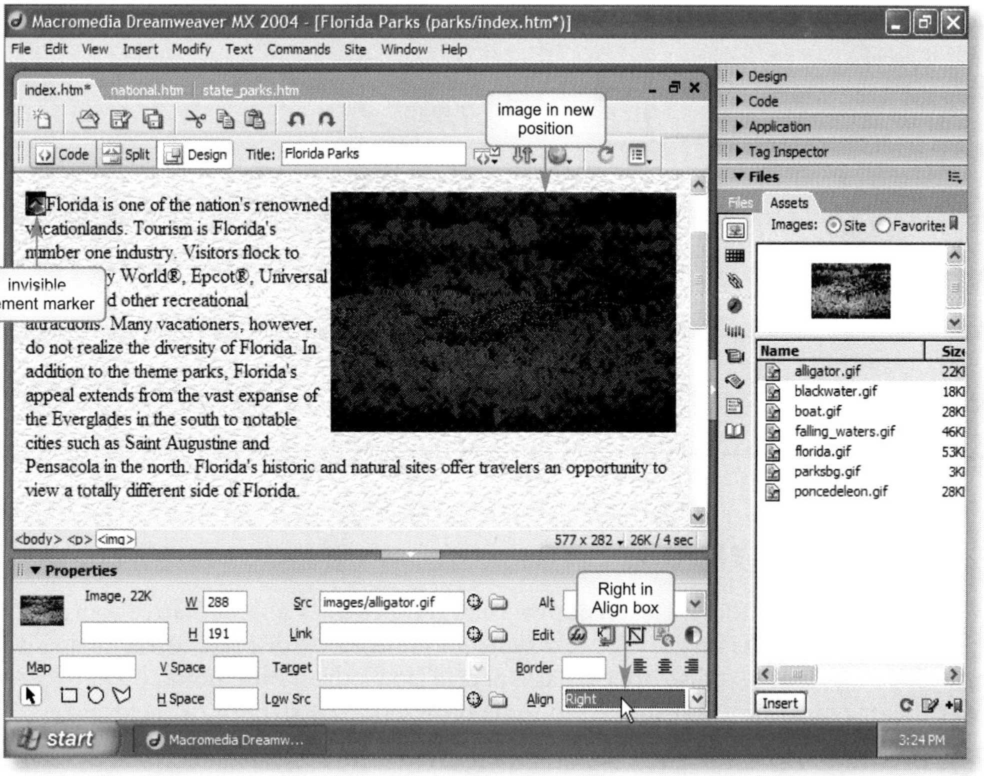

FIGURE 2-33

Adjusting Space around Images

When aligning an image, by default, only about three pixels of space are inserted between the image and adjacent text. You can adjust the amount of vertical and horizontal space between the image and text through the V Space and H Space settings in the Property inspector. The V Space setting controls the vertical space above or below an image. The H Space setting controls the horizontal space to the left or right side of the image. The following step shows how to add vertical and horizontal spacing.

To Adjust the Horizontal and Vertical Space

1

- **Click the image to remove the highlighting.**
- **Click the V Space text box and type** 6 **as the vertical space.**
- **Press the TAB key and type** 12 **as the horizontal space. Press the TAB key.**

Dreamweaver adds additional horizontal and vertical space between the image and the text (Figure 2-34).

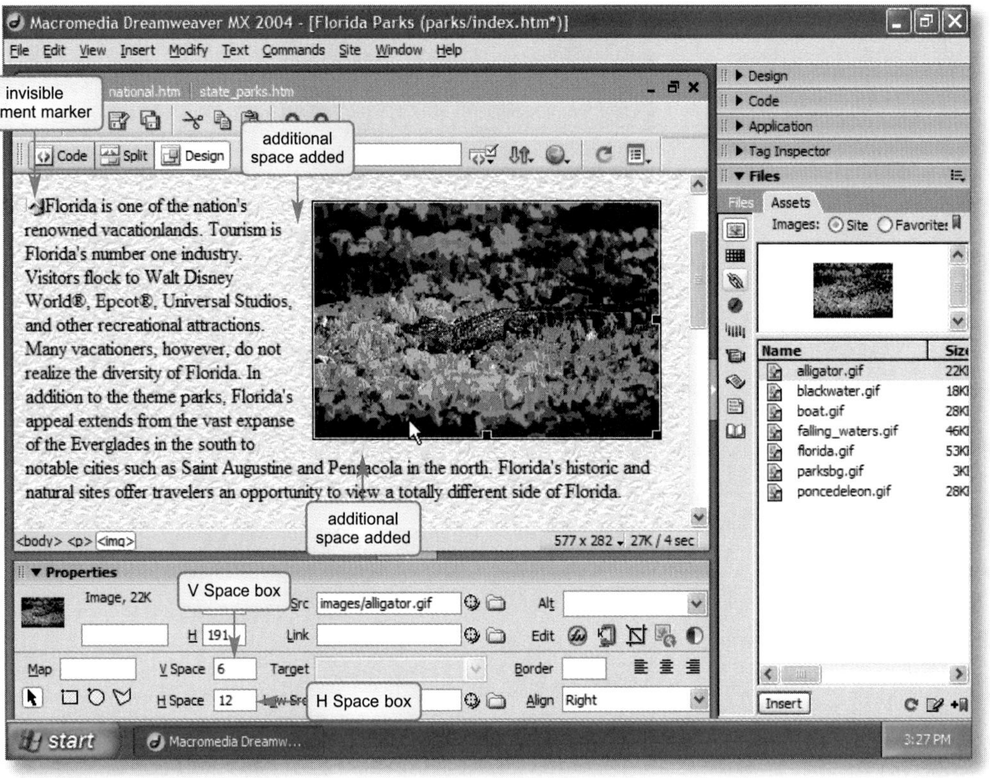

FIGURE 2-34

Another feature within the Property inspector is Alt text. For individuals who are visually impaired, the Alt text can be interpreted by their screen readers. Dreamweaver supports two screen readers — JAWS and Window-Eyes.

Specifying the Alt Text

The **Alt** text is short for **Alternative Text** and provides an alternative source of information about the image. The text typed in the Alt box displays as the image is downloading. This text also appears as a ScreenTip as the mouse pointer is moved over the image when it is displayed in some browsers. The step on the next page illustrates how to add Alt text to the alligator image.

More About

Accessibility Issues

For more information about authoring for accessibility, visit the Dreamweaver MX 2004 More About Web page (scsite.com/dreamweavermx04/more) and then click Dreamweaver MX Accessibility Issues.

To Add Alt Text

1

- **If necessary, click the alligator image to select it. Click the Alt box and then type** `Florida alligator` **as the alternate text.**
- **Press the TAB key.**

The Alt text is entered in the Alt text box (Figure 2-35).

- **If necessary, click the image to deselect the highlighting.**

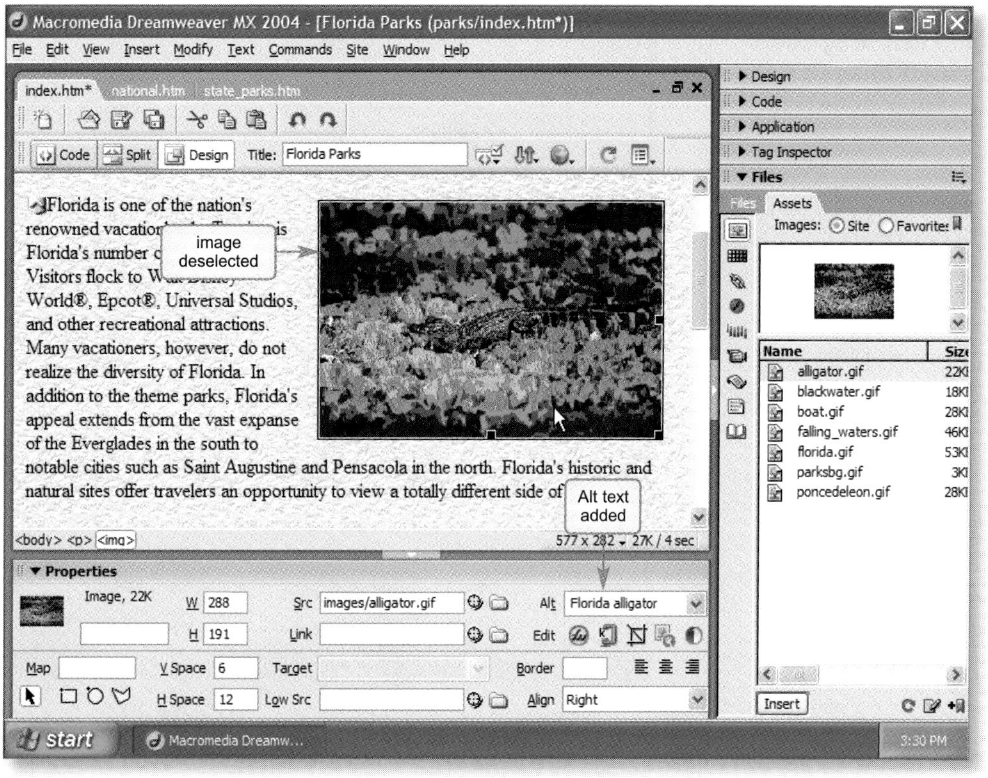

FIGURE 2-35

To enhance your Web page further, you will add a sailboat image. This image is displayed on the left side of the page, to the left of the bulleted items. The following steps show how to insert an image of a sailboat in the Web page.

To Insert the Sailboat Image

1

- **Scroll down and position the insertion point so it is to the left of the sentence introducing the bulleted list (Figure 2-36).**

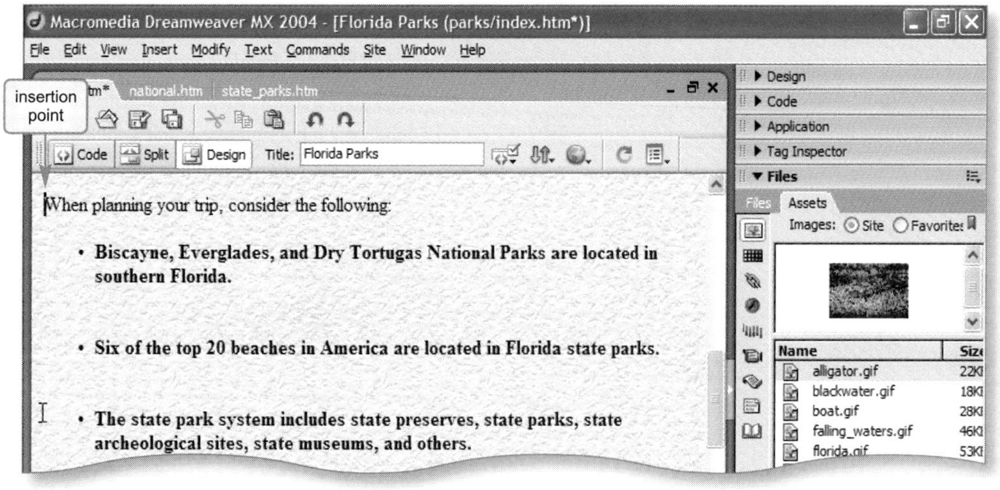

FIGURE 2-36

2

• Click the boat image in the Assets panel and then drag the boat.gif image to the insertion point.

The boat image is displayed (Figure 2-37). The border and handles around the image indicate it is selected.

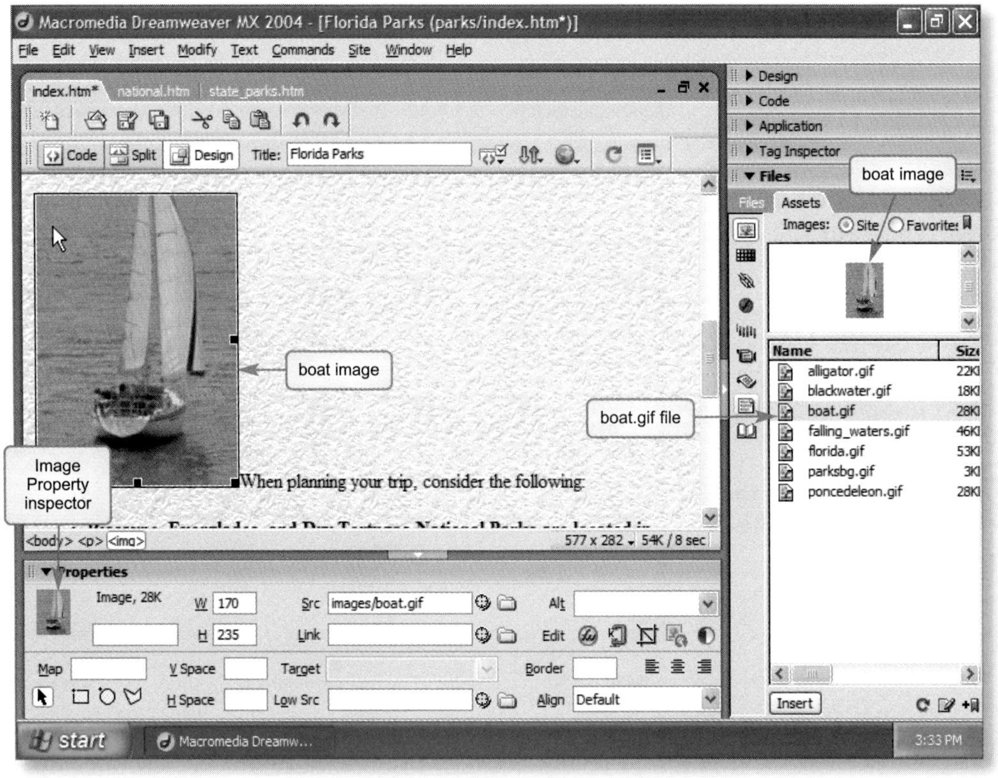

FIGURE 2-37

3

• Click the Align box arrow and then click Left in the Align pop-up menu.

The image moves to the left side of the window, and the text adjusts to the right (Figure 2-38). The bullets do not display, and some of the text is hidden by the image. Adjusting the spacing will display the bullets and text.

FIGURE 2-38

4

- **Click the V Space box and type 6 as the vertical space.**
- **Click the H Space box and type 20 as the horizontal space.**
- **Press the TAB key.**
- **Click anywhere in the Document window to deselect the image.**

Additional horizontal and vertical space is added between the image and the text, and the bullets are displayed (Figure 2-39).

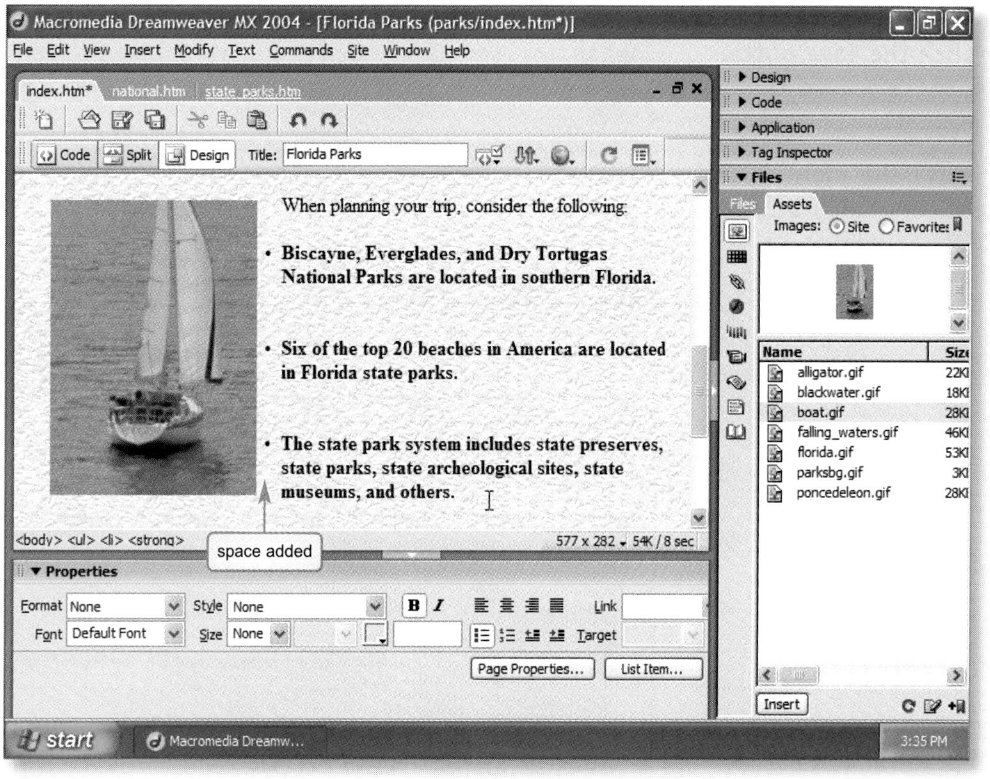

FIGURE 2-39

5

- **Click the image to select it.**
- **Click the Alt box and type Sailboat as the alternate text.**
- **Press the ENTER key.**

The Alt text is applied (Figure 2-40).

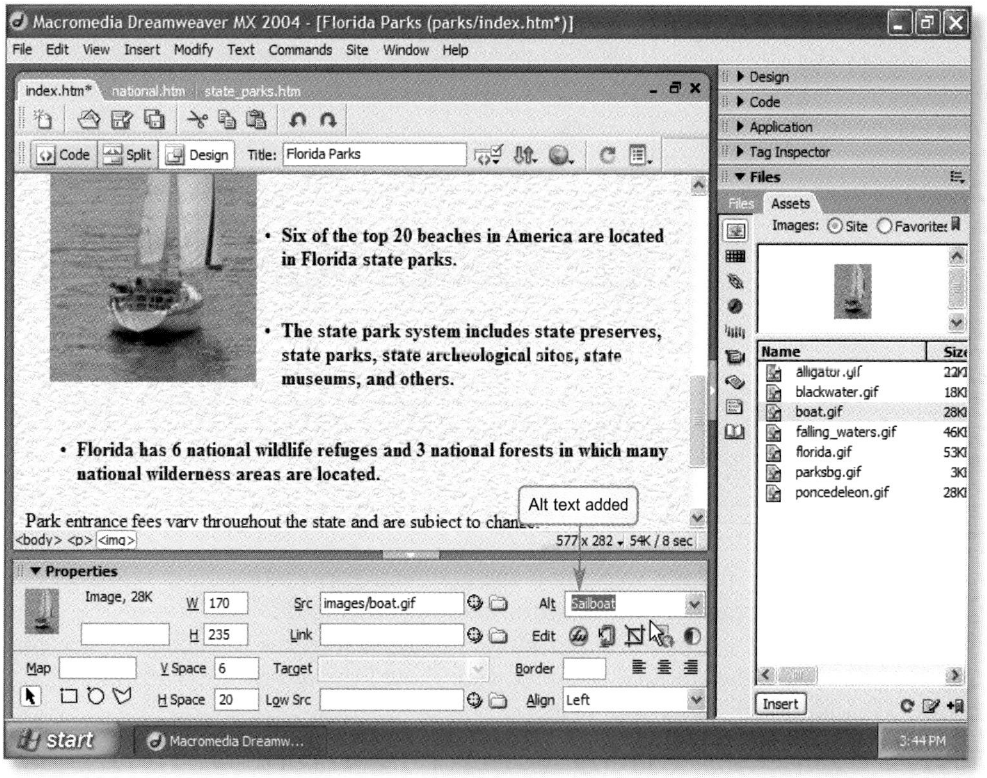

FIGURE 2-40

6

- **Click the Save button on the Standard toolbar.**
- **Press the F12 key.**
- **Move the mouse point over the alligator and sailboat images to display the Alt text.**

The index page displays in your browser and all changes to the index page are saved (Figure 2-41). Web pages may display differently in your browser. The browser and selected text size affect how a Web page displays. In Figure 2-41, the text size is set to Medium.

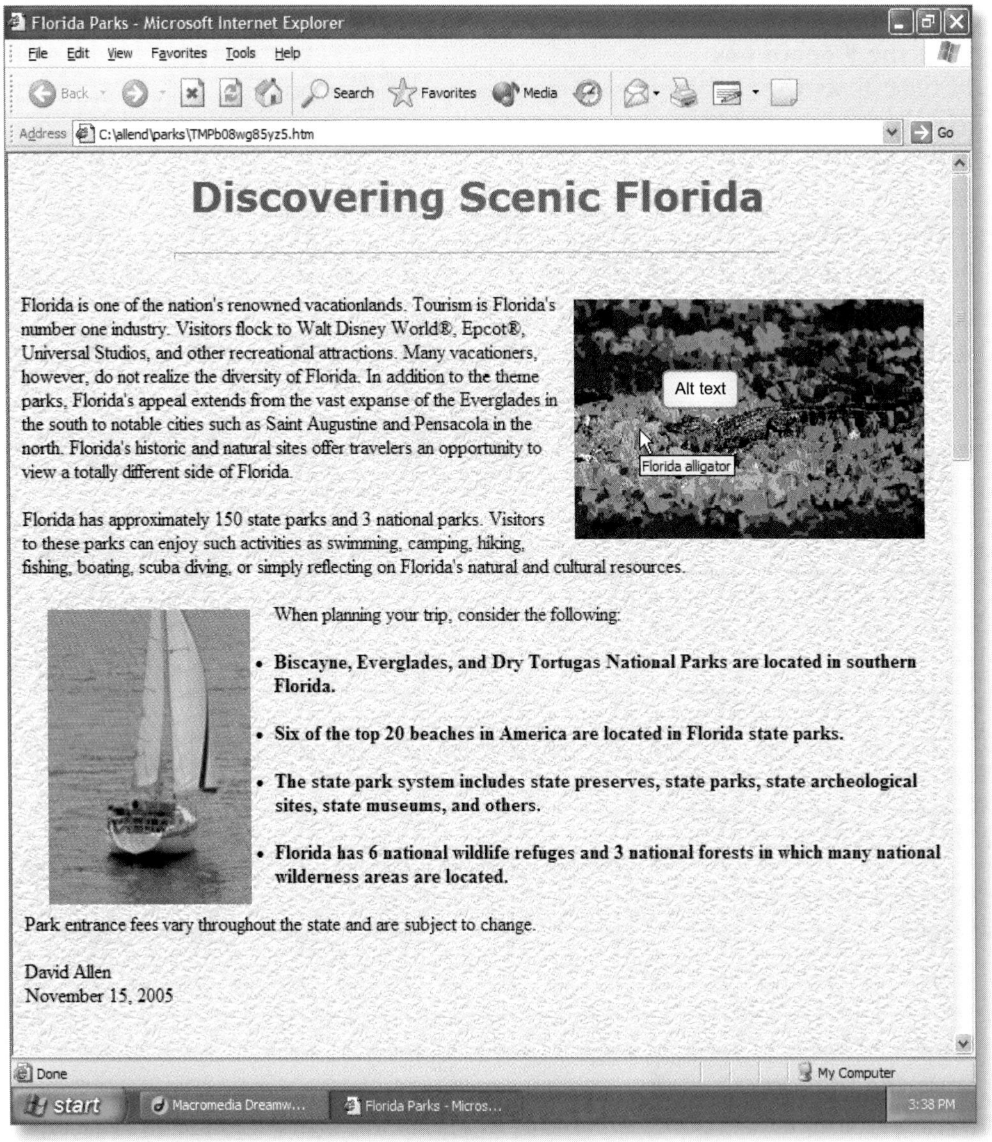

FIGURE 2-41

7

- **Close the browser to return to Dreamweaver.**

The second page in your Web site is the National Parks page. To develop the National Parks page further and add information showing the locations of the three Florida national parks, you will add a Florida map. References to each park are contained on the map. The steps on the next page show how to add the Florida map image to the National Parks Web page.

To Insert and Align an Image in the National Parks Web Page

1

- **Click the national.htm Web page tab.**
- **If necessary, scroll to the top of the page. Position the insertion point between the bullet and the text heading of the second bulleted item (Biscayne National Park).**

The insertion point is positioned to the left of Biscayne National Park and to the right of the bullet (Figure 2-42).

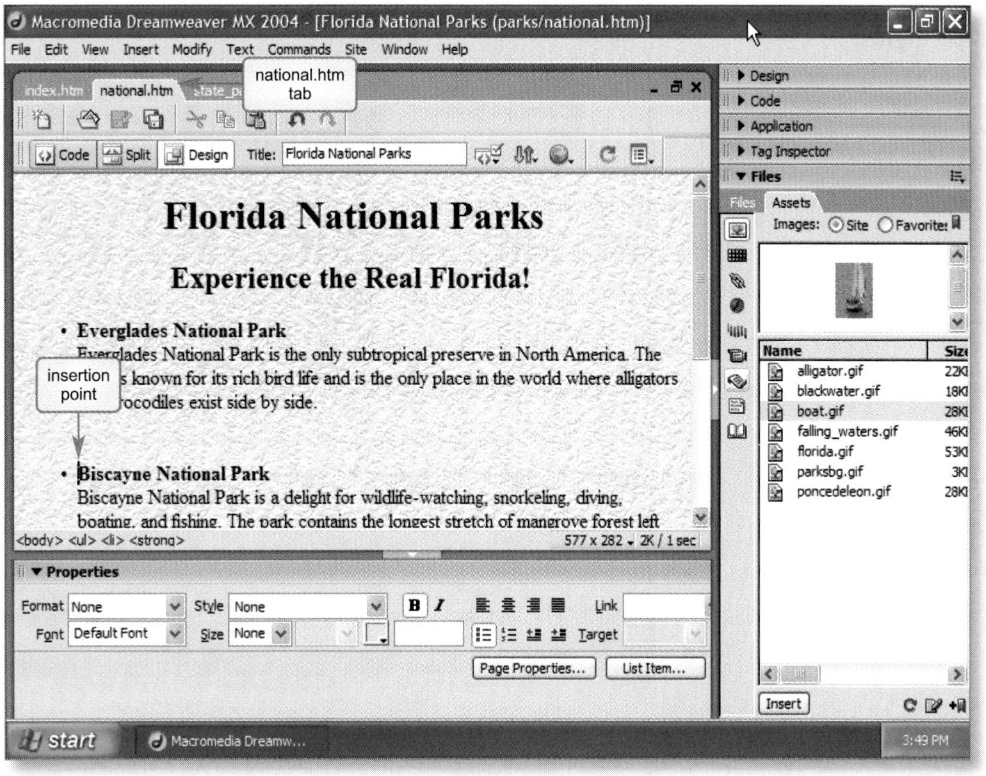

FIGURE 2-42

2

- **Drag the florida.gif file from the Assets panel to the insertion point and then, if necessary, click the image to select it.**

The border and handles around the image indicate it is selected (Figure 2-43). The attributes change in the Property inspector to reflect the selected object.

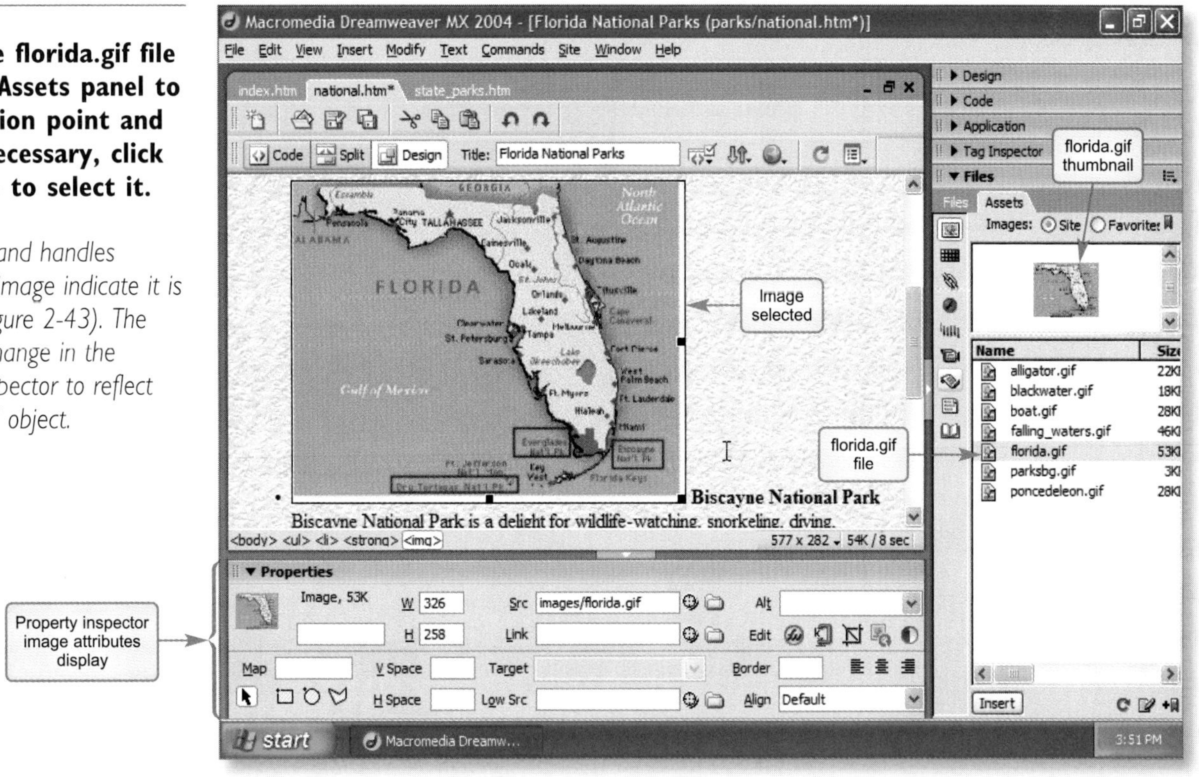

FIGURE 2-43

3

- **Click the Align box arrow and then click Right.**

The image is aligned to the right in the Document window (Figure 2-44).

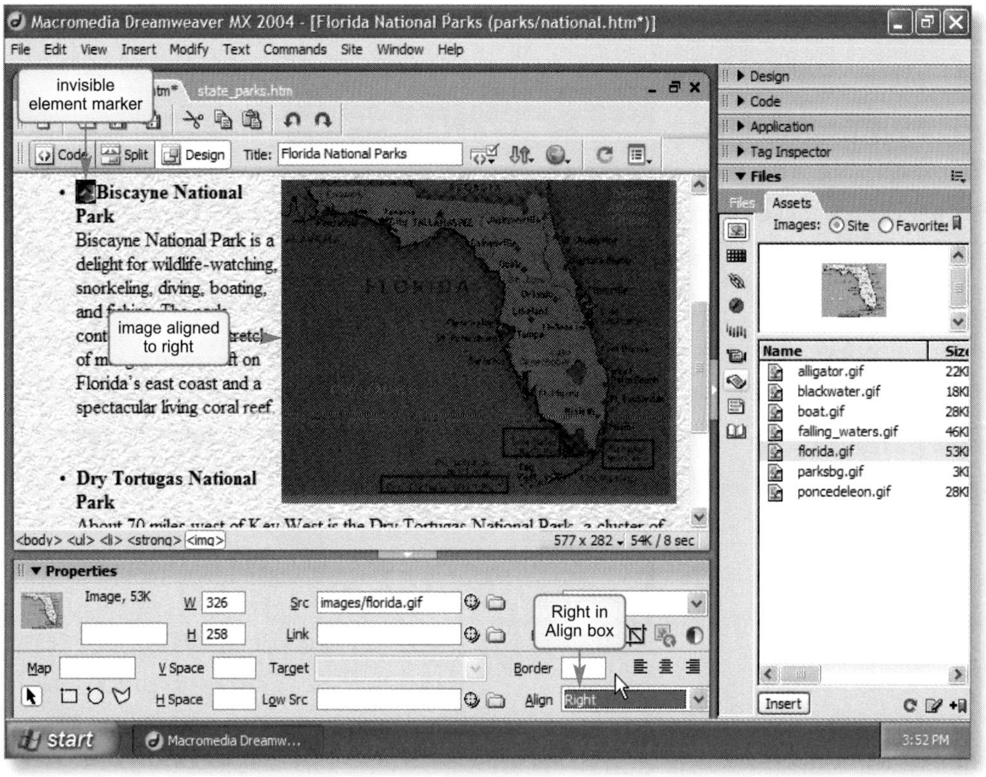

FIGURE 2-44

4

- **Click the V Space box and type** `8` **as the vertical space.**
- **Click the H Space box and type** `10` **as the horizontal space.**
- **Click the Alt box and type** `Florida Map` **as the alternate text.**
- **Press the ENTER key (Figure 2-45).**

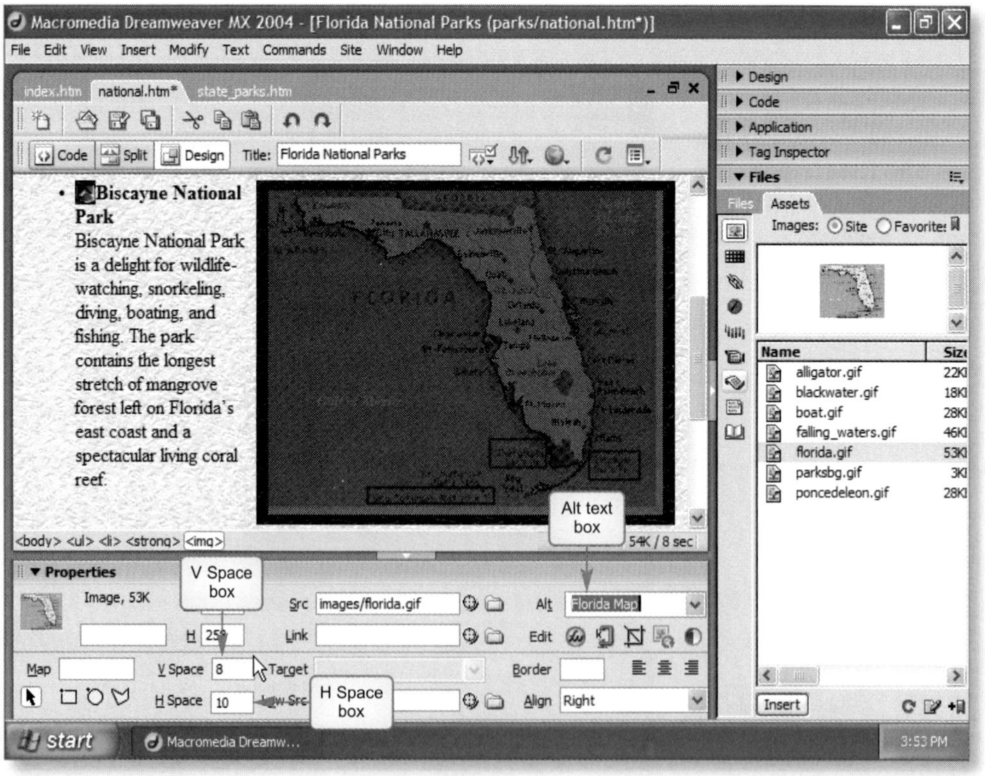

FIGURE 2-45

5

• **Click the Save button on the Standard toolbar.**

The Florida National Parks Web page is saved.

• **Press the F12 key.**

The Florida National Parks Web page is displayed in the browser (Figure 2-46).

6

• **Close the browser to return to Dreamweaver.**

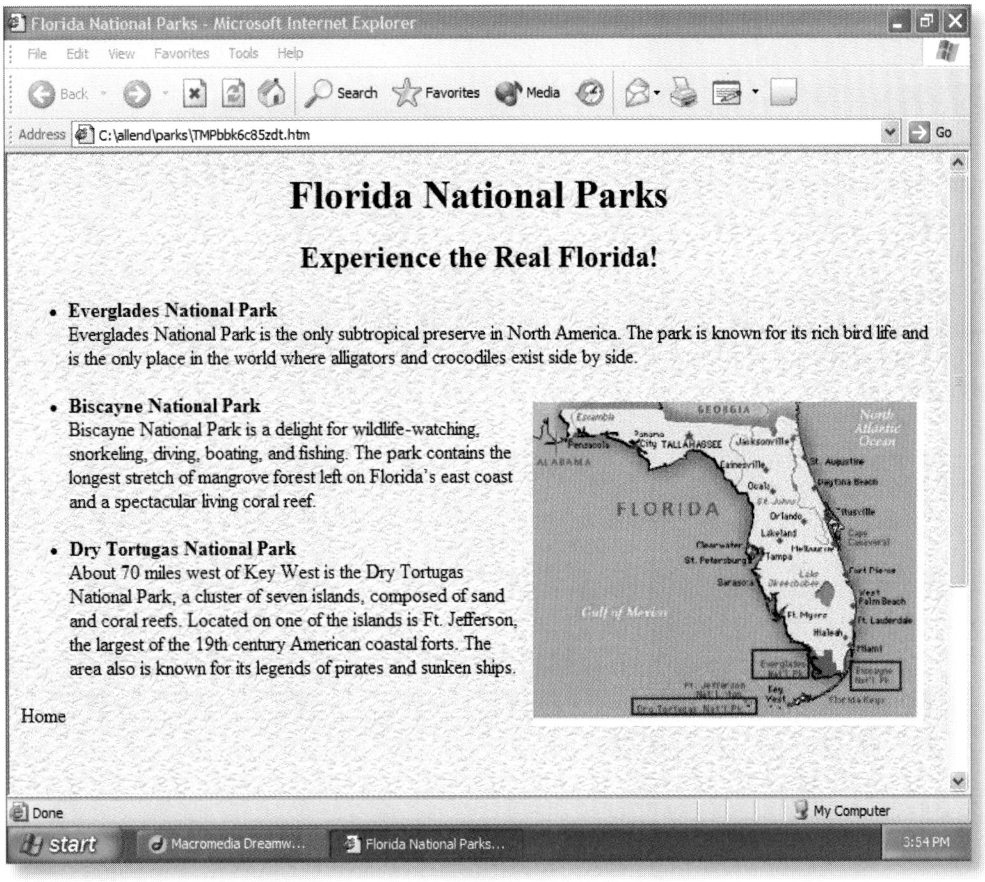

FIGURE 2-46

The third page in your Web site is the Florida State Parks page. To add interest to this page, you will add three images. You will align two of the images to the left and one to the right. The steps on the next page illustrate how to add the images to the Florida State Parks Web page.

To Insert and Align Images in the State Parks Web Page

1

- **Click the state_parks.htm Web page tab.**
- **If necessary, scroll to the top of the document. Position the insertion point to the left of Blackwater River State Park.**

The insertion point is to the left of Blackwater River State Park (Figure 2-47).

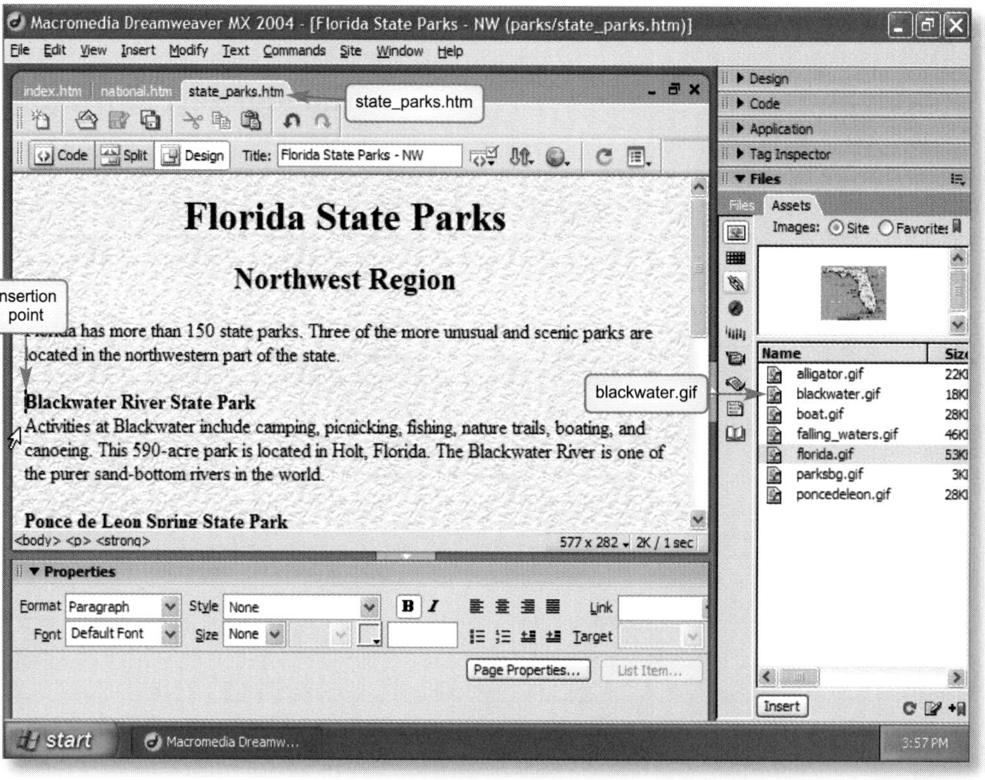

FIGURE 2-47

2

- **Drag the blackwater.gif file from the Assets panel to the insertion point.**
- **If necessary, click the image to select it and then click the Align box arrow in the Property inspector.**
- **Click Left on the Align pop-up menu.**

The image aligns to the left (Figure 2-48).

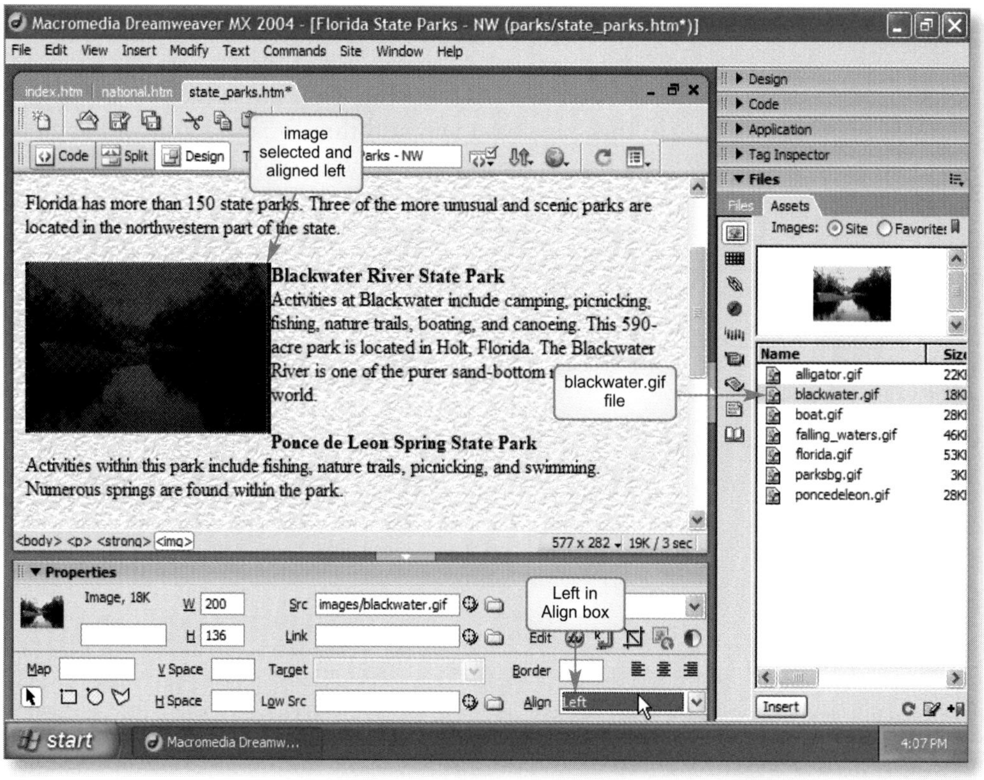

FIGURE 2-48

3

- **Click the V Space box and then type** `8` **as the vertical space.**
- **Click the H Space box and then type** `10` **as the horizontal space.**
- **Click the Alt box, type** `Blackwater River State Park` **as the alternate text, and then press the ENTER key.**

The image is highlighted. The Alt text, V Space, and H Space attributes are added for the Blackwater image (Figure 2-49).

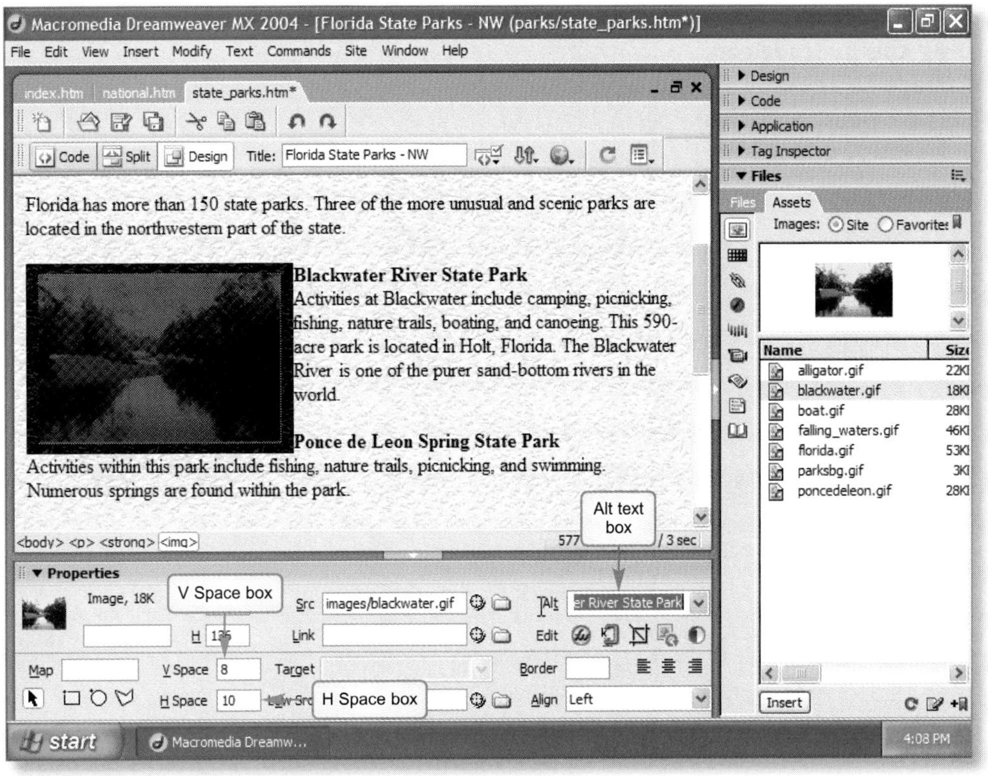

FIGURE 2-49

4

- **If necessary, scroll down and then position the insertion point to the right of the word, park, in the last line in the Ponce de Leon Spring State Park paragraph.**

The insertion point is to the right of the last sentence in the third paragraph (Figure 2-50).

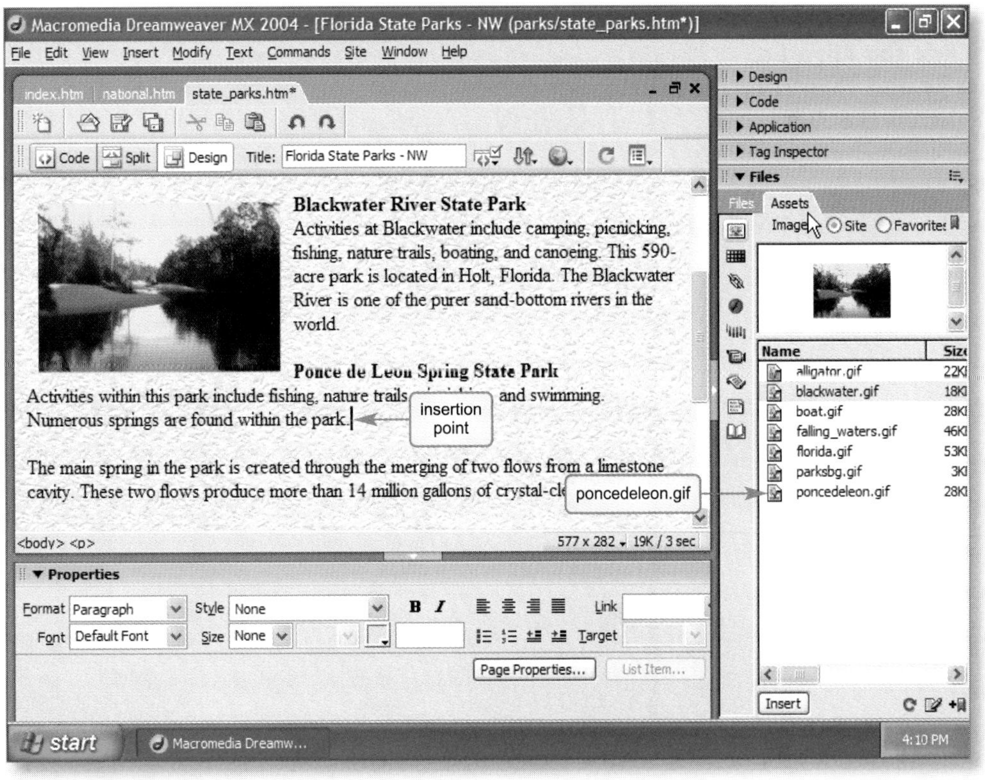

FIGURE 2-50

5

• **Drag the poncedeleon.gif image to the insertion point and then, if necessary, select the image.**

The image is selected (Figure 2-51).

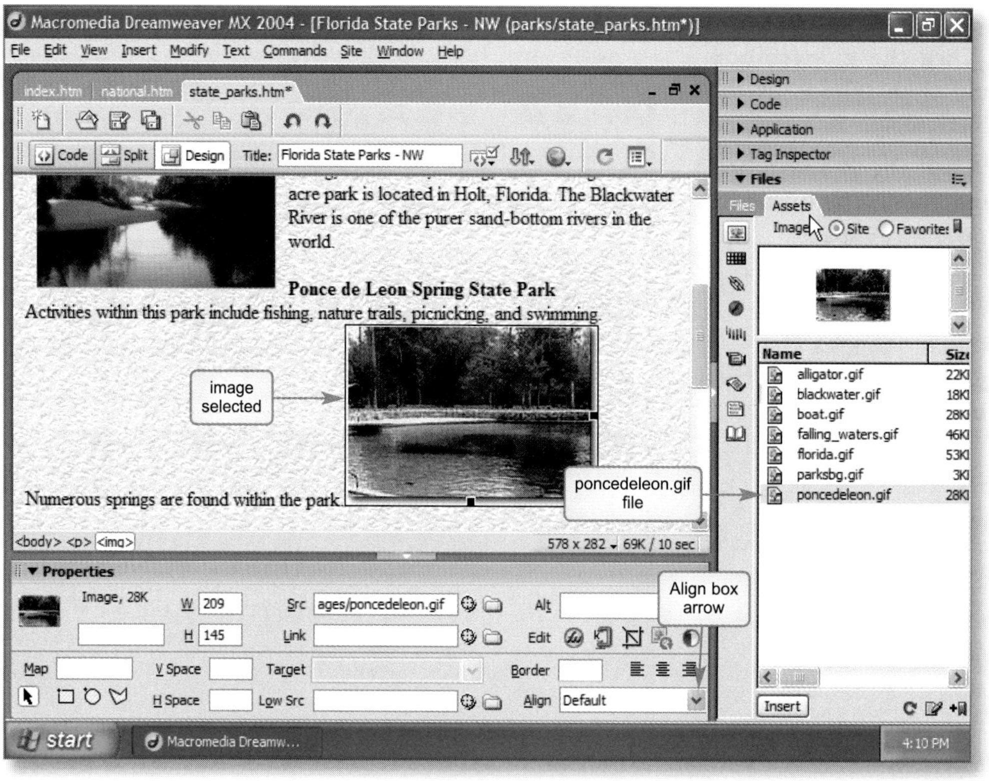

FIGURE 2-51

6

• **Click the Align box arrow and then click Right on the Align pop-up menu.**

The poncedeleon.gif image moves to the right side of the window (Figure 2-52).

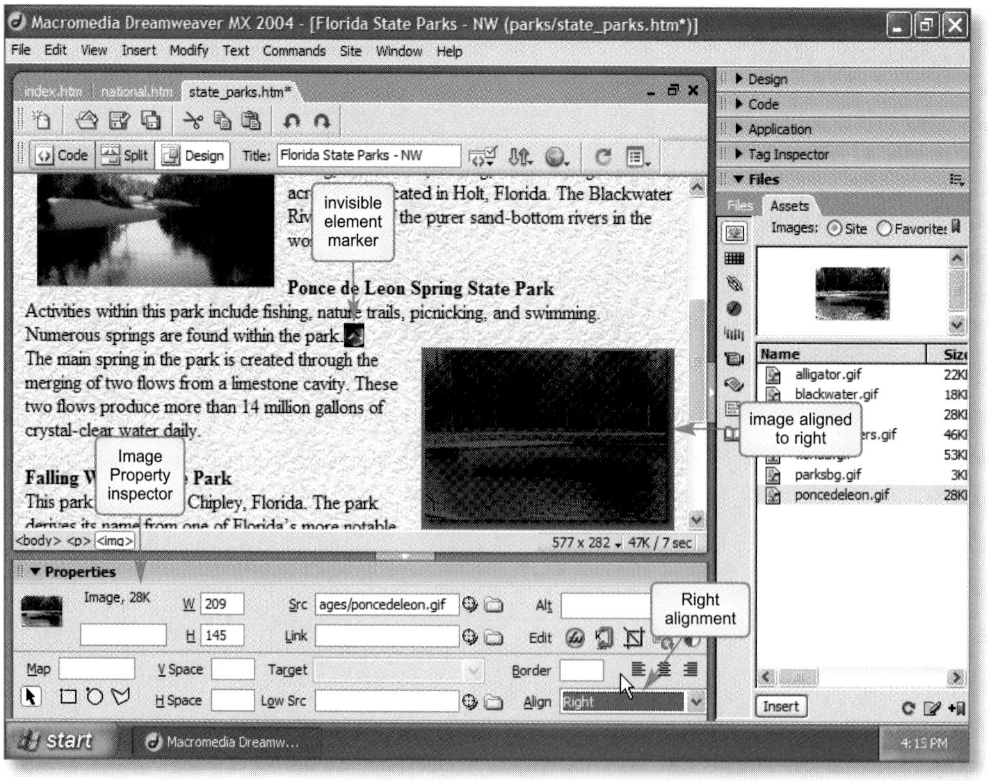

FIGURE 2-52

7

- **Click the V Space box and then type** 6 **as the vertical space.**
- **Click the H Space box and then type** 12 **as the horizontal space.**
- **Click the Alt box, type** Ponce de Leon Spring State Park **as the alternate text, and then press the ENTER key.**

The image is positioned on the page (Figure 2-53).

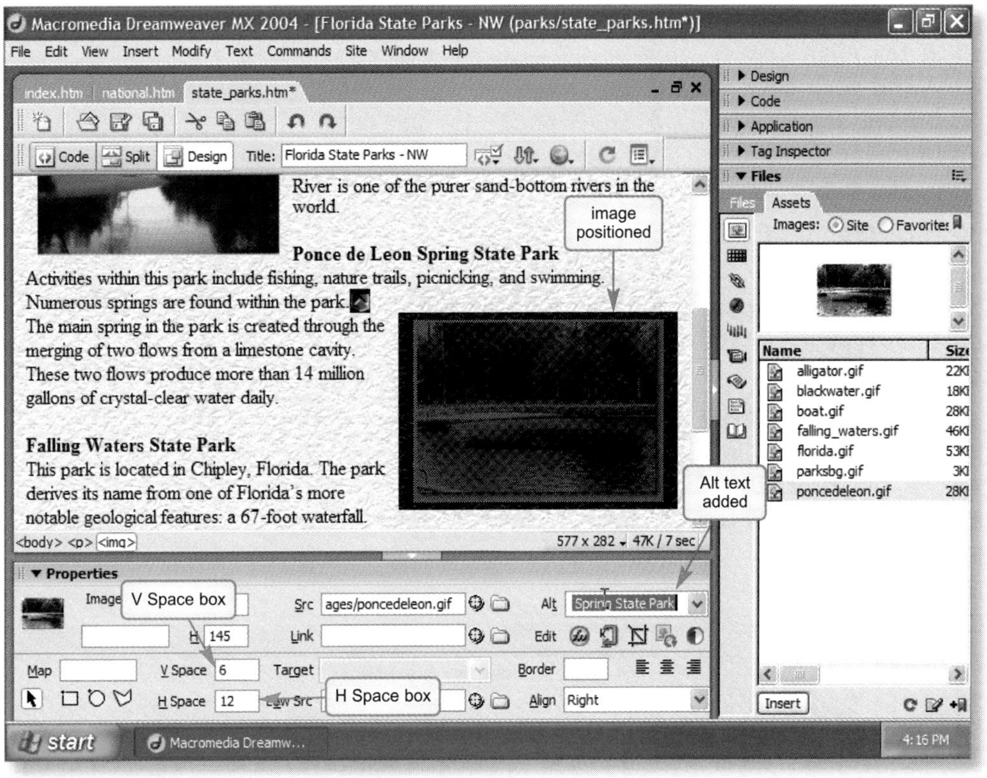

FIGURE 2-53

8

- **Position the insertion point to the left of the words, Falling Waters State Park.**
- **Drag the falling_waters.gif image from the Assets panel to the insertion point and then, if necessary, select the image.**

The Falling Waters image is inserted on the page (Figure 2-54).

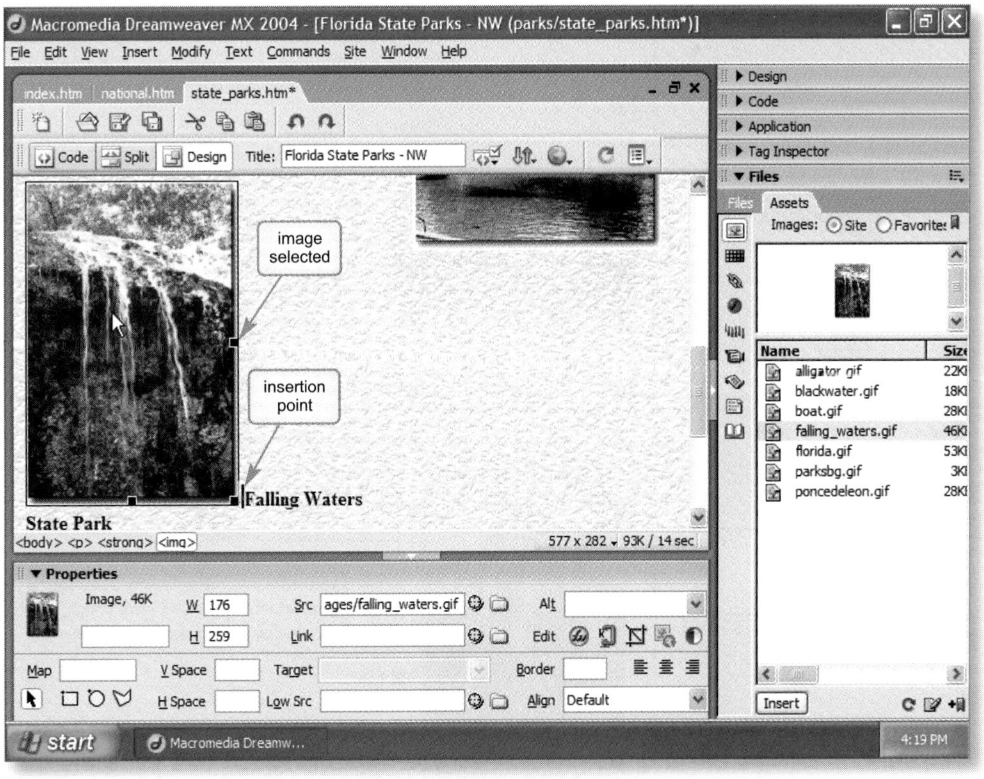

FIGURE 2-54

9

- **Click the Align box arrow and then click Left on the Align pop-up menu.**
- **Click the V Space box and then type** `8` **as the vertical space.**
- **Click the H Space box and then type** `12` **as the horizontal space.**
- **Click the Alt box, type** `Falling Waters State Park` **as the alternate text, and then press the ENTER key.**
- **Click anywhere on the page to deselect the image.**
- **Click the Save button on the Standard toolbar.**

The image is positioned on the page and the Web page is saved (Figure 2-55).

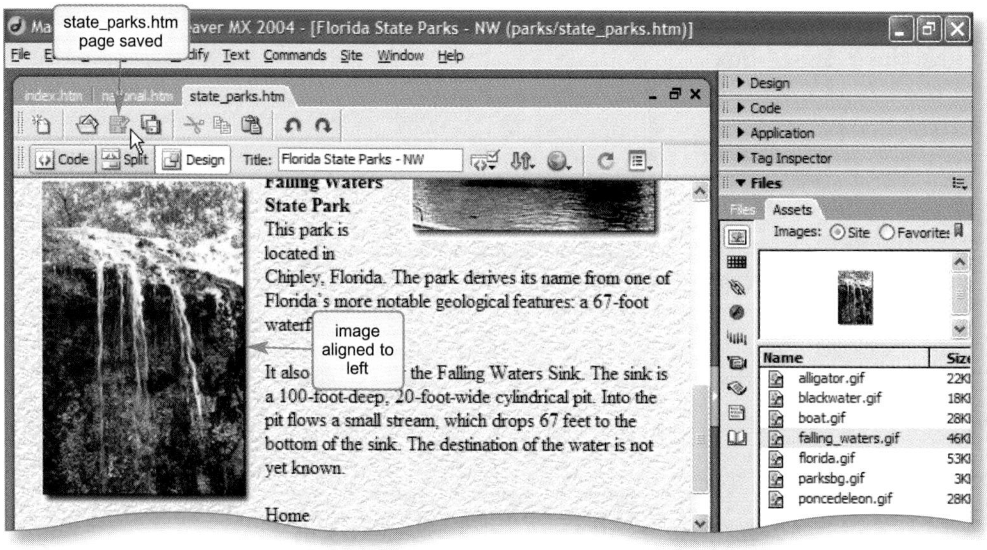

FIGURE 2-55

10

- **Press the F12 key.**

The State Parks page is displayed in the browser (Figure 2-56).

11

- **Close the browser.**

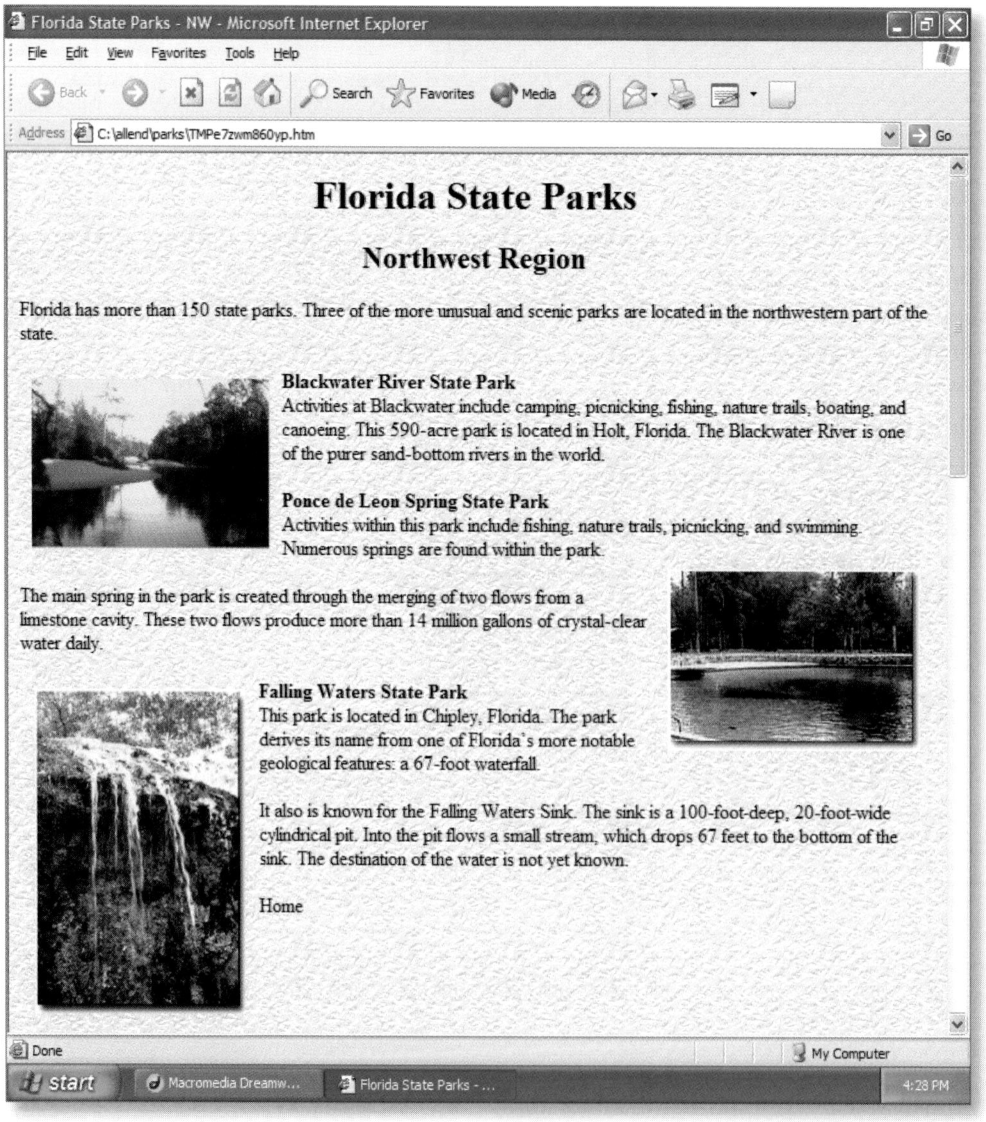

FIGURE 2-56

Image Editing Tools

Dreamweaver makes available several basic image editing tools to modify and enhance an image. You access these functions through the Property inspector.

- Use an external image editor: Macromedia's Fireworks is the default image editor, but you can specify which external editor should start for a specified file type. To select an external editor, click Edit on the menu bar and display the Preferences dialog box. Select File Types/Editors from the Category list to display the Preferences File Types/Editors dialog box. Select the image extension and then browse for the External Code Editor executable file.
- Crop an image: **Cropping** lets you edit an image by reducing the area of the image and allows you to eliminate unwanted or distracting portions of the image. Cropping can be very effective for improving the appearance of a photo by highlighting the main point of interest in an image. When you crop an image and then save the page, the source image file is changed on the disk. To return the image to its original size, click the Undo button on the Standard toolbar. Prior to saving, you may want to keep a backup copy of the image file in the event you need to revert to the original image.
- Brightness/Contrast: The **Brightness/Contrast** tool modifies the contrast or brightness of the pixels in an image. Recall that a pixel is the smallest point in a graphical image. Brightness makes the image lighter or darker overall, while Contrast either emphasizes or de-emphasizes the difference between lighter and darker regions. This affects the highlights, shadows, and midtones of an image. The values for the brightness and contrast settings range from -100 to 100.
- Resampling: The process of **resampling** adds or subtracts pixels from a resized JPEG or GIF image file to match the appearance of the original image as closely as possible. Resampling an image also reduces an image's file size, resulting in improved download performance. When you resize an image in Dreamweaver, you can resample it to accommodate its new dimensions. To resample a resized image, resize the image as previously described and then click the Resample button in the Property inspector.
- Sharpening: **Sharpening** adjusts the focus of an image by increasing the contrast of edges found within the image. The Sharpening icon is hidden when the Panel groups are displayed.

The Falling Waters image in the Florida State Parks page extends somewhat below the last line of the text. Cropping the image and emphasizing the waterfall in the image would enhance the page. The following steps show how to crop the image, and then modify the brightness/contrast.

To Crop and Modify Brightness/Contrast of an Image

1

• If necessary, select the falling waters image.

• Click the Crop Tool icon in the Property inspector. If a Dreamweaver MX 2004 caution dialog box displays, click the OK button.

A bounding box with crop handles appears around the selected image (Figure 2-57).

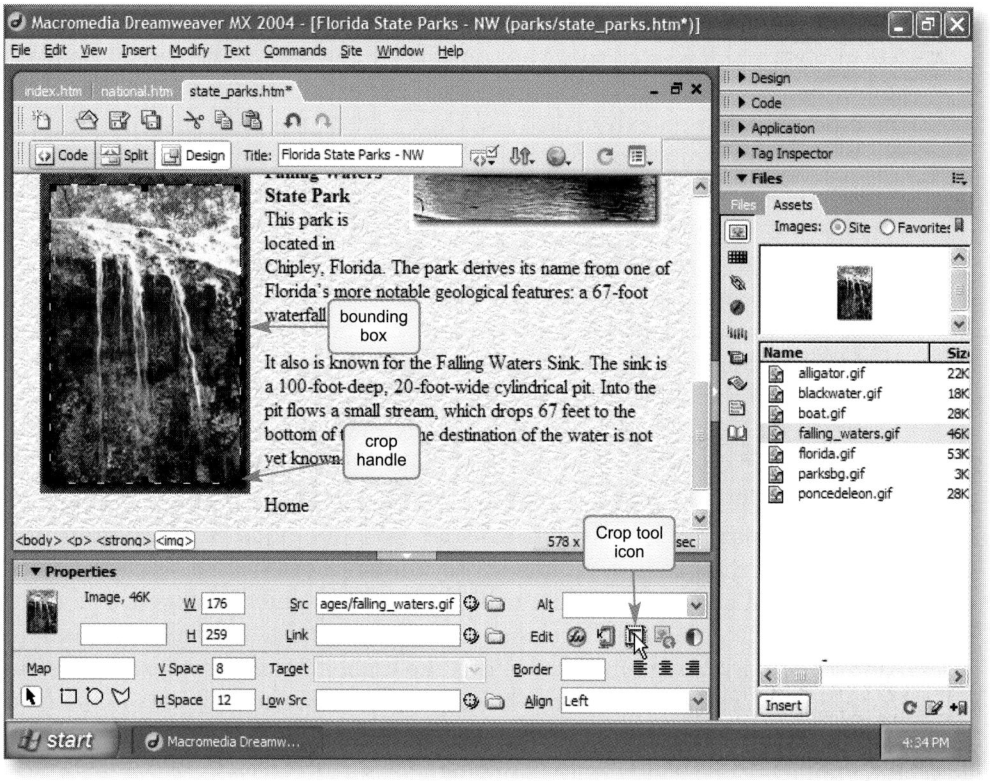

FIGURE 2-57

2

• Click the crop handle in the lower-right corner and adjust the handles until the bounding box surrounds the area of the image similar to that shown in Figure 2-58.

The area of the image to retain is selected (Figure 2-58).

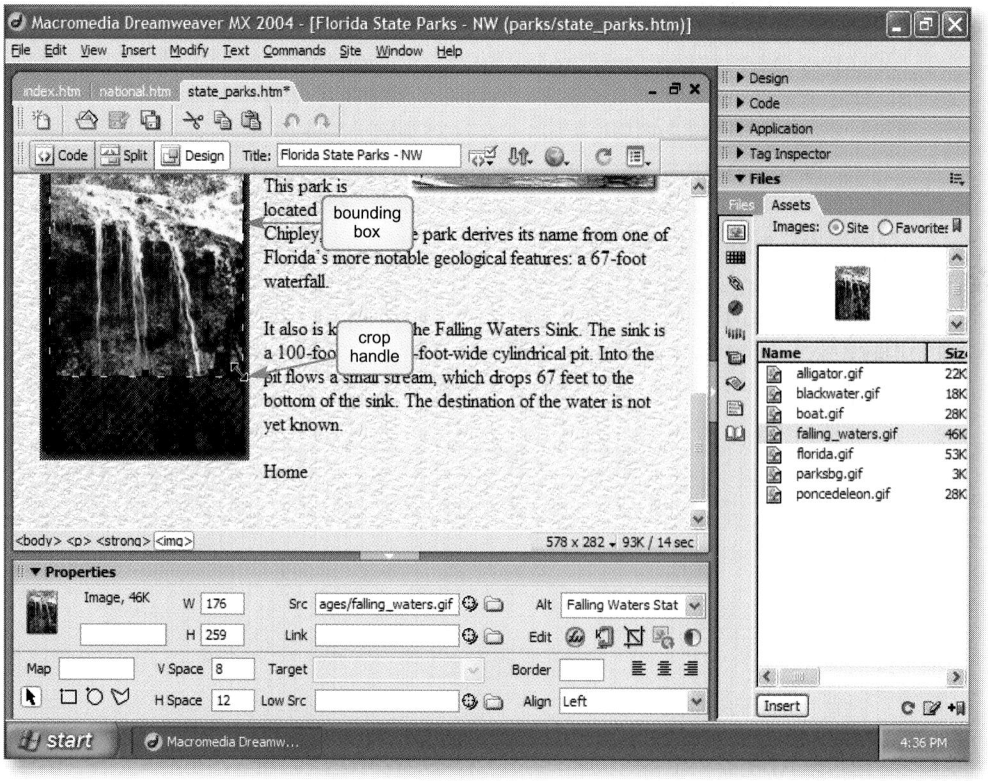

FIGURE 2-58

3

- **Double-click inside the bounding box.**
- **Click the image.**

The image is cropped and selected (Figure 2-59). If you need to make changes, click the Undo button on the Standard toolbar and repeat steps 1 and 2.

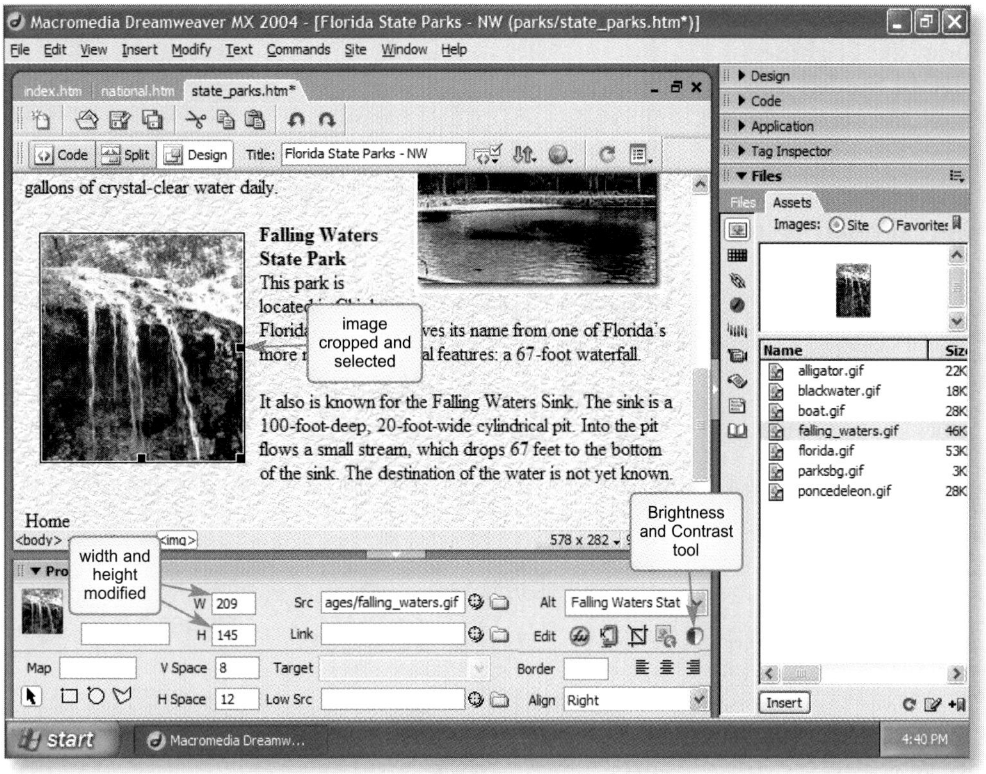

FIGURE 2-59

4

- **Click the Brightness and Contrast tool. If a Dreamweaver MX 2004 caution dialog box displays, click the OK button.**

The Brightness/Contrast dialog box displays (Figure 2-60).

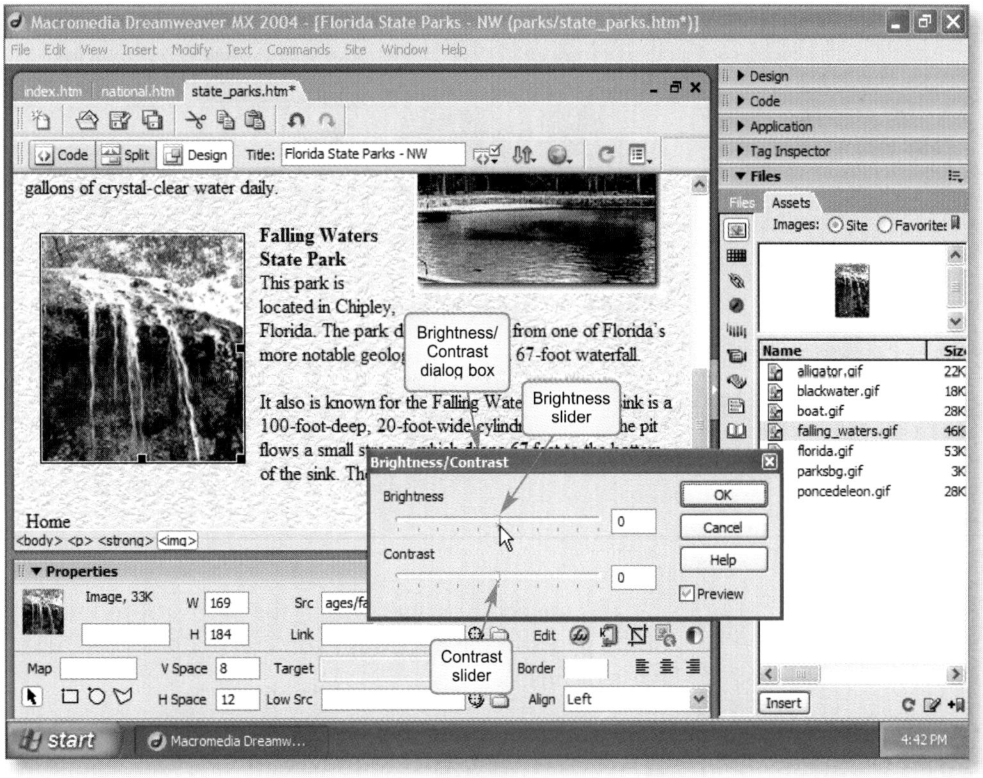

FIGURE 2-60

5

• **Drag the Brightness slider to the left and adjust the setting to -10.**

• **Drag the Contrast slider to the right and adjust the setting to 20.**

The brightness and contrast are changed in the image (Figure 2-61).

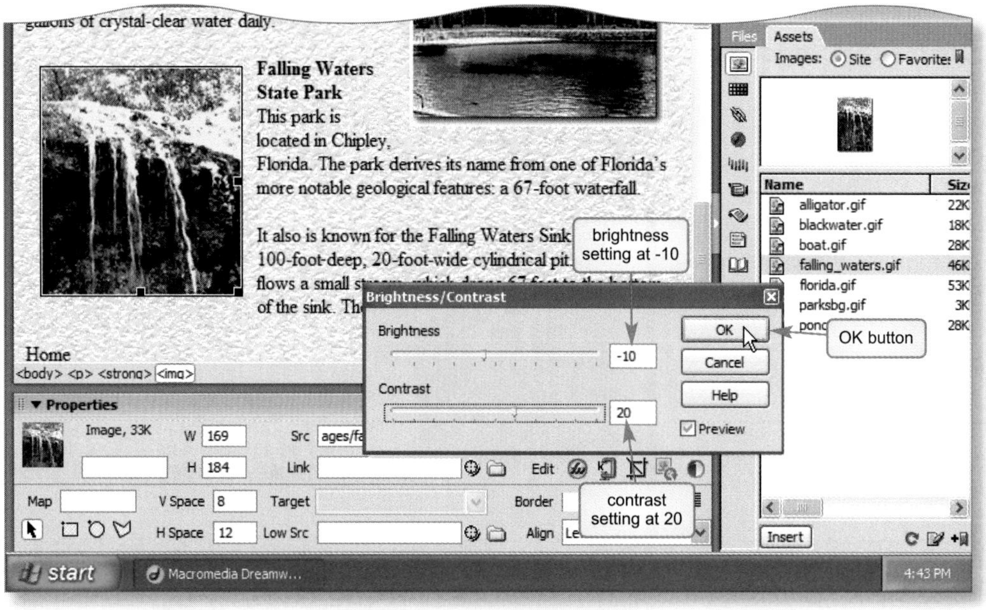

FIGURE 2-61

6

• **Click the OK button.**

• **Click the Save button on the Standard toolbar.**

The State Parks page is saved.

• **Press the F12 key to view the cropped image in your browser.**

The Florida State Parks page is displayed in your browser (Figure 2-62).

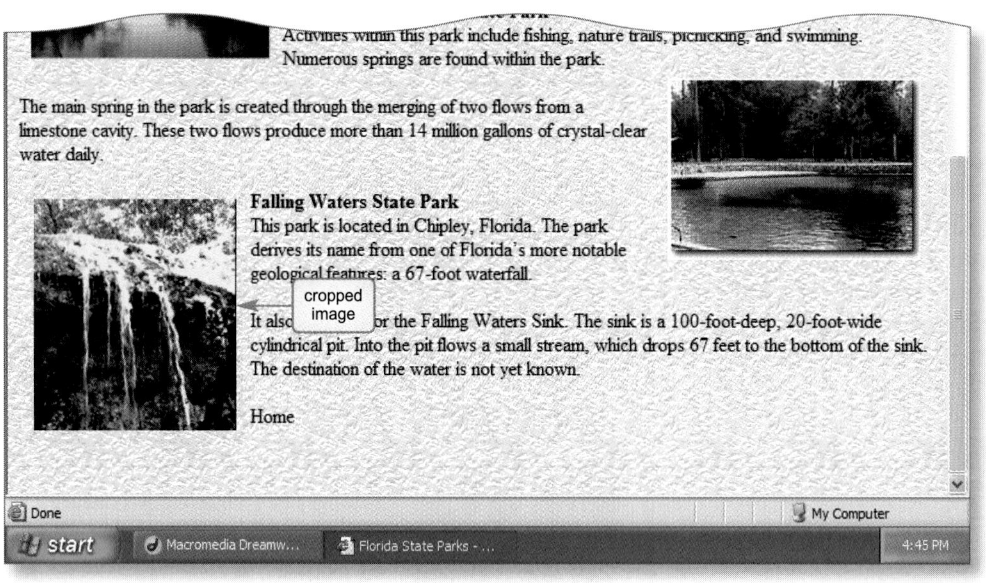

FIGURE 2-62

7

• **Close the browser to return to the Dreamweaver window.**

To connect the pages within the Web site and to display the navigation structure of the pages in the Site Map, you create links. The next section discusses the different types of links.

Understanding Different Types of Links

Links are the distinguishing feature of the World Wide Web. A link, also referred to as a hyperlink, is the path to another document, to another part of the same document, or to other media such as an image or a movie. Most links display as colored and/or underlined text, although you also can link from an image or other object. Clicking a link accesses the corresponding document, other media, or another place within the same document. If you place the mouse pointer over the link, the Web address of the link, or path, usually appears at the bottom of the window, on the status bar.

Three types of link paths are available: absolute, relative, and root-relative. An **absolute link** provides the complete URL of the document. This type of link also is referred to as an **external link**. Absolute links generally contain a protocol (such as http://) and primarily are used to link to documents on other servers.

You use **relative links** for local links. This type of link also is referred to as a **document-relative link**, or an **internal link**. If the linked documents are in the same folder, such as those in your parks folder, this is the best type of link to use. You also can use a relative link to link to a document in another folder, such as the images folder. All the files you see in the Files panel Local View are internal files and are referenced as relative links. You accomplish this by specifying the path through the folder hierarchy from the current document to the linked document. Consider the following examples.

- To link to another file in the same folder, specify the file name. Example: everglades.htm.
- To link to a file in a subfolder of the current Web site folder (such as the images folder), the link path would consist of the name of the subfolder, a forward slash (/), and then the file name. Example: images/gator.jpg.

You use the **root-relative link** primarily when working with a large Web site that requires several servers. Web developers generally use this type of link when they must move HTML files from one folder or server to another folder or server. Root-relative links are beyond the scope of this book.

Two other types of links are named anchor and e-mail links. A **named anchor** lets the user link to a specific location within a document. To create a named anchor, click the Named Anchor command on the Insert menu. An **e-mail link** creates a blank e-mail message containing the recipient's address. Another type of link is a **null**, or **script, link**. This type of link provides for attaching behaviors to an object or executes JavaScript code.

> *More About*
>
> **Undo Cropping**
>
> You can undo the effect of the Crop command and revert to the original image file up until the time that you quit Dreamweaver or edit the file in an external image-editing application. To undo the effects, click Edit on the menu bar and then click the Undo Crop command.

Named Anchor

To create a named anchor, place the insertion point where you want the named anchor. Then click the Named Anchor command on the Insert menu. Type a name for the anchor in the Named Anchor text box.

Relative Links

Another Dreamweaver feature is the variety of ways in which to create a relative link. Three of the more commonly used methods are point to file, drag-and-drop, and browse for file. The point to file and drag-and-drop methods require that the Property inspector and the Files or Assets panels be open. To use the **point to file method**, you drag the Point to File icon to the image in the Files or Assets panel. In the **drag-and-drop method**, you drag the file from the Files or Assets panel to the Link text box in the Property inspector. The **browse for file method** is accomplished through the Select File dialog box. A fourth method is to use the context menu. Select the text for the link, right-click to display the context menu, and then select the Link command.

The next step is to add the text to create the relative links from the home page to the National and State Parks pages. You use the drag-and-drop method to create a relative link from the text to a specific Web page.

Adding Text for the Relative Links

To create relative links from the index page, you add text to the index page and use the text to create the links to the other two Web pages in your Web site. You will center the text directly below the Discovering Scenic Florida heading. The following steps show how to add the text for the links.

To Add Text for Relative Links

1

- **Click the Files panel tab.**
- **Click the index.htm tab in the Document window. If necessary, scroll to the top of the page and then position the insertion point at the end of the title, Discovering Scenic Florida.**
- **Press the ENTER key.**
- **If necessary, click the Text Color hexadecimal box, select the hexadecimal number, press the DELETE key, and then press the ENTER key.**

The insertion point is centered below the title, and the text color is returned to the default. The Files panel displays (Figure 2-63).

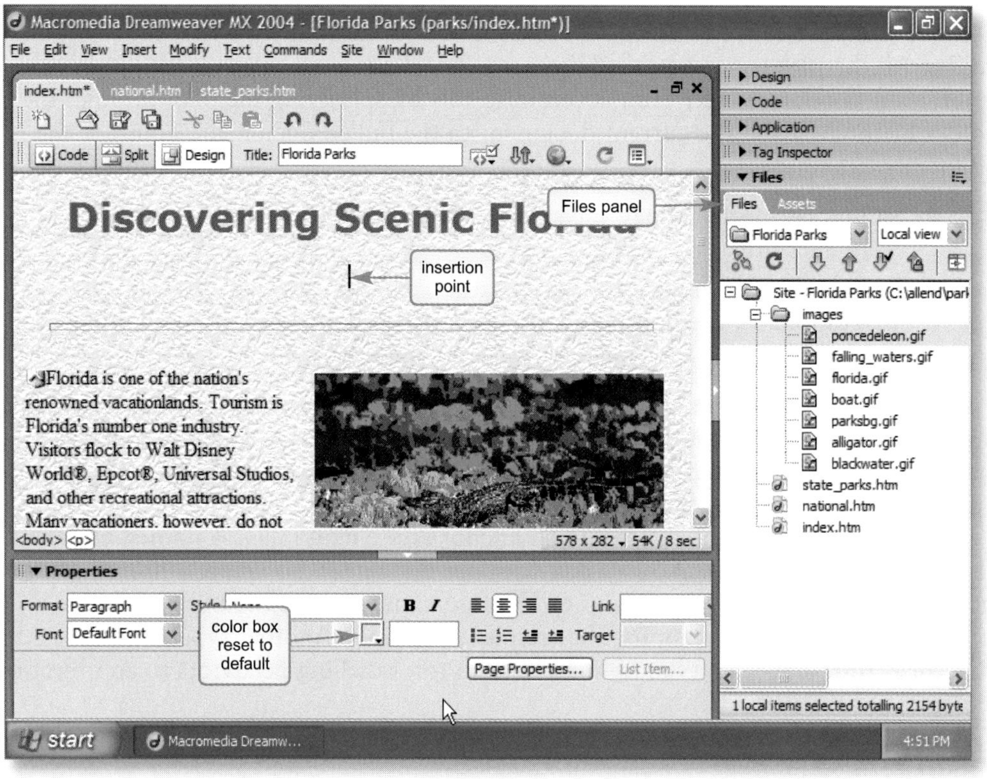

FIGURE 2-63

2

- **Type** `National Parks` **and then press the SPACEBAR.**

The text for the first link, National Parks, is displayed in the Document window (Figure 2-64).

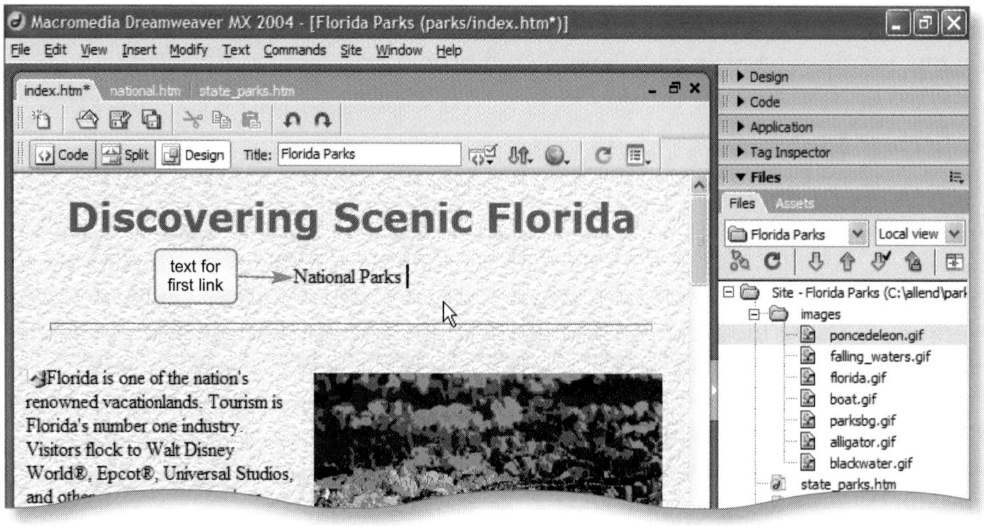

FIGURE 2-64

3

- **Hold down the SHIFT key and then press the vertical line key (|). Press the SPACEBAR and then type `State Parks` as the second link.**

The text for both links is displayed in the Document window (Figure 2-65).

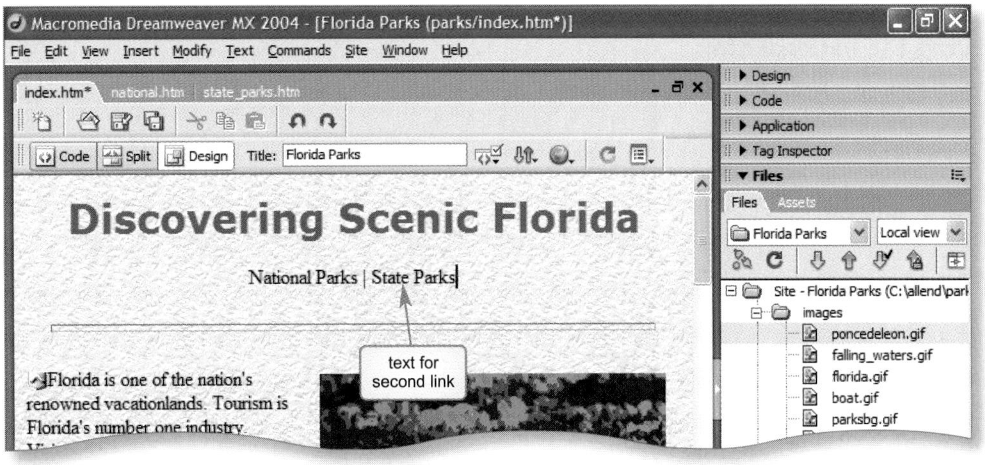

FIGURE 2-65

You will use the text, National Parks, to create a link to the National Parks Web page and the text, State Parks, to create a link to the State Parks page.

Creating a Relative Link Using Drag-and-Drop

A relative link is used to create links between local files or files within one Web site. The drag-and-drop method requires that the Property inspector be displayed and that the site files display in the Files or Assets panel. When you view Dreamweaver with an 800 × 600 resolution, the panel groups hide a portion of the Property inspector. You still can use the drag-and-drop method, however, because the Link text box remains visible in the Property inspector.

The following steps illustrate how to use the drag-and-drop method to create a relative link from the Florida Parks home page to the National Parks Web page.

To Create a Relative Link Using Drag-and-Drop

1

- **Drag to select the text, National Parks.**

The National Parks text is highlighted (Figure 2-66).

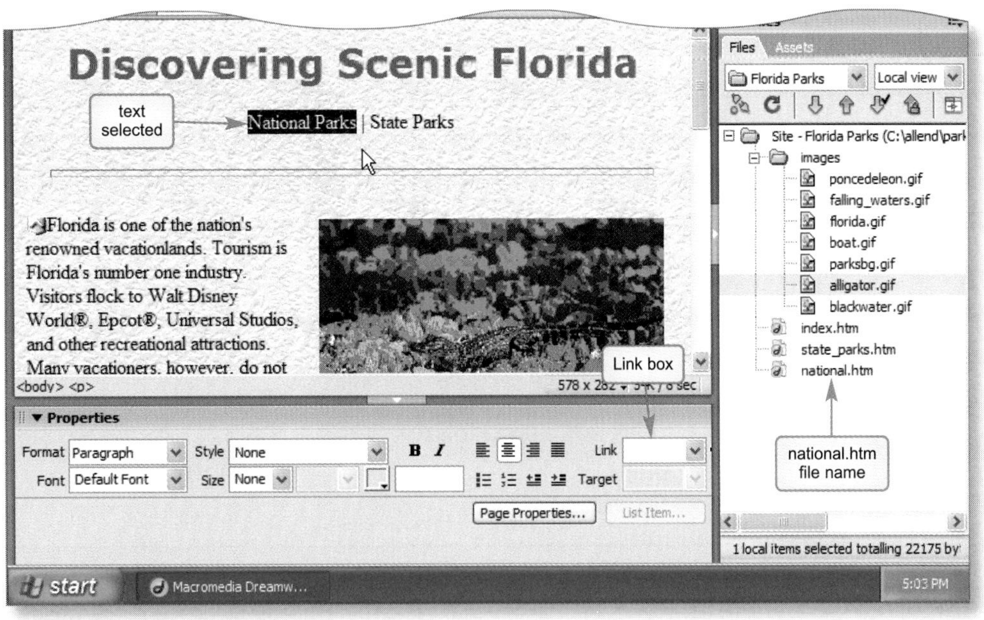

FIGURE 2-66

2

• **Drag the national.htm file from the Files panel to the Link box in the Property inspector. Do not release the mouse button.**

When you start to drag, a circle icon with a diagonal line through it displays next to the mouse pointer (Figure 2-67).

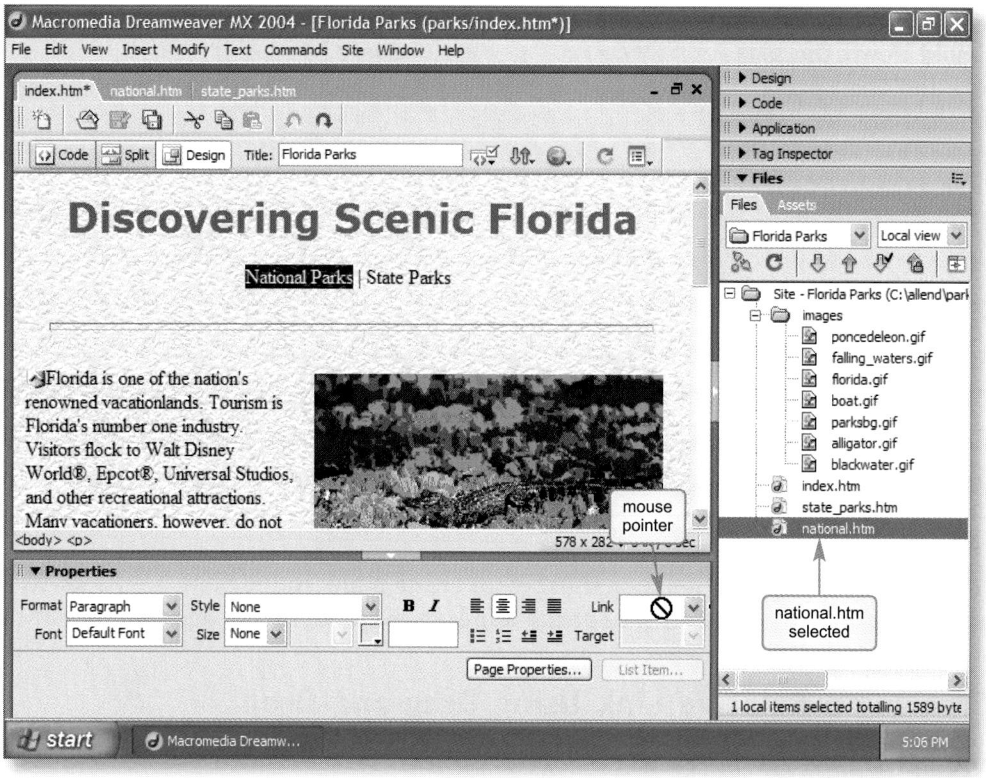

FIGURE 2-67

3

• **Release the mouse button. Click National Parks to display the linked text.**

The linked text displays underlined and in a different color in the Document window, and the link text displays in the Link box (Figure 2-68). If you click anywhere else in the document, the linked document name does not display in the Link box.

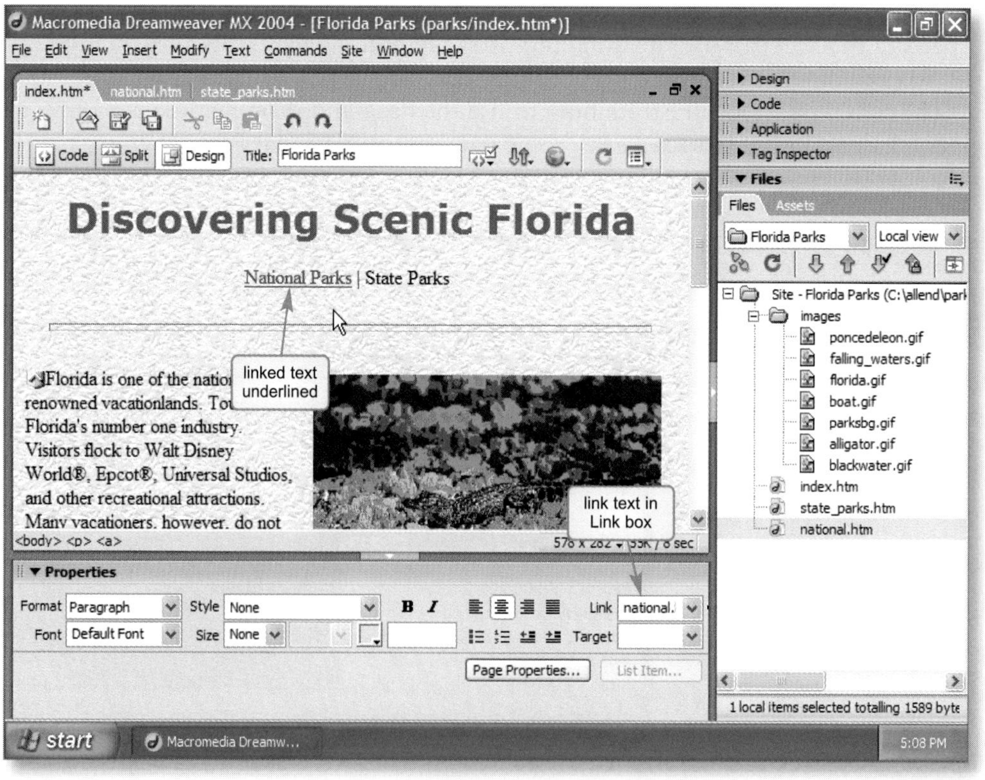

FIGURE 2-68

Creating a Relative Link Using the Context Menu

The context menu is a second way to create a link. Using this method, you select the file name in the Select File dialog box. The following steps illustrate how to use the context menu to create a link to the State Parks page.

> *More About*
>
> **Images as Links**
>
> It is easy to create a link from an image. Just select the image and then type or drag the file name into the Property inspector Link box.

To Create a Relative Link Using the Context Menu

1

- **Drag to select the text, State Parks, and right-click to display the context menu. Point to Make Link.**

The text, State Parks, is highlighted, and the context menu is displayed. The Make Link command is highlighted (Figure 2-69).

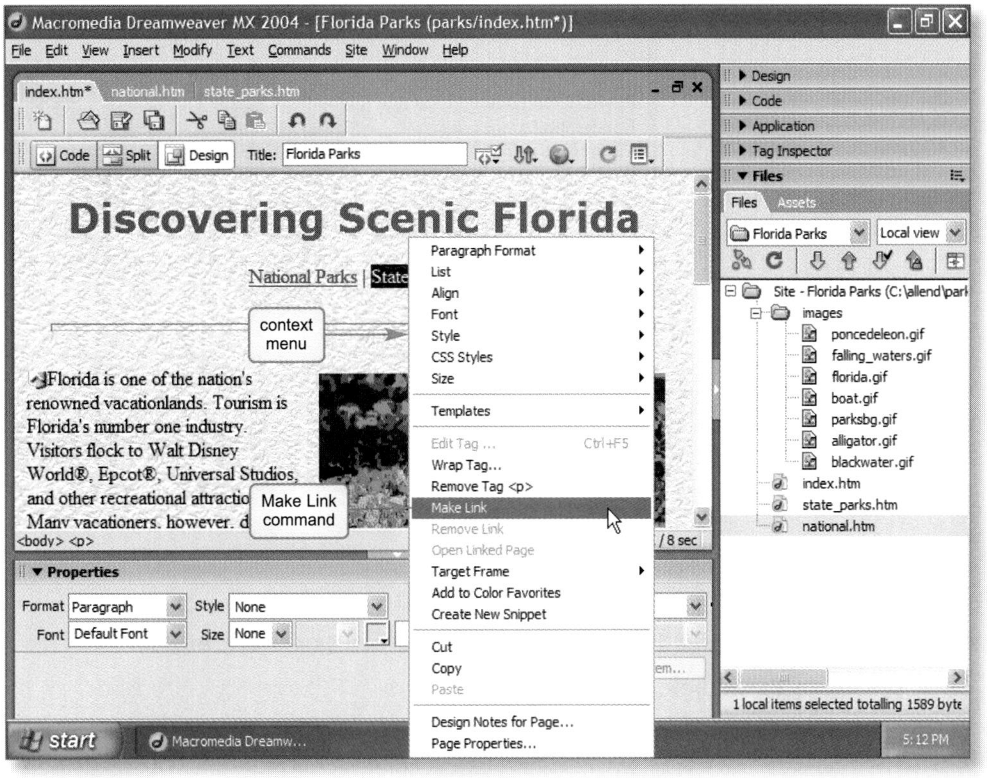

FIGURE 2-69

2

- **Click the Make Link command and click state_parks.**

The Select File dialog box is displayed and state_parks is highlighted (Figure 2-70).

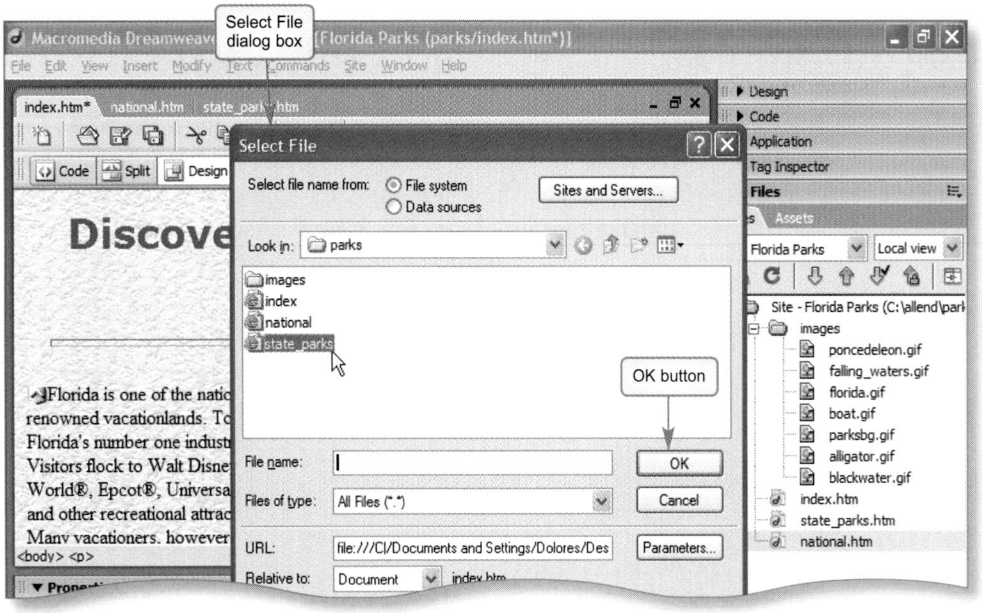

FIGURE 2-70

3

- **Click the OK button and then click the selected text, State Parks, to display the link.**
- **Click the Save button on the Standard toolbar.**

The linked text displays underlined and in a different color in the Document window, and the link text displays in the Link box (Figure 2-71). If you click anywhere else in the document, the linked document name does not display in the Link box.

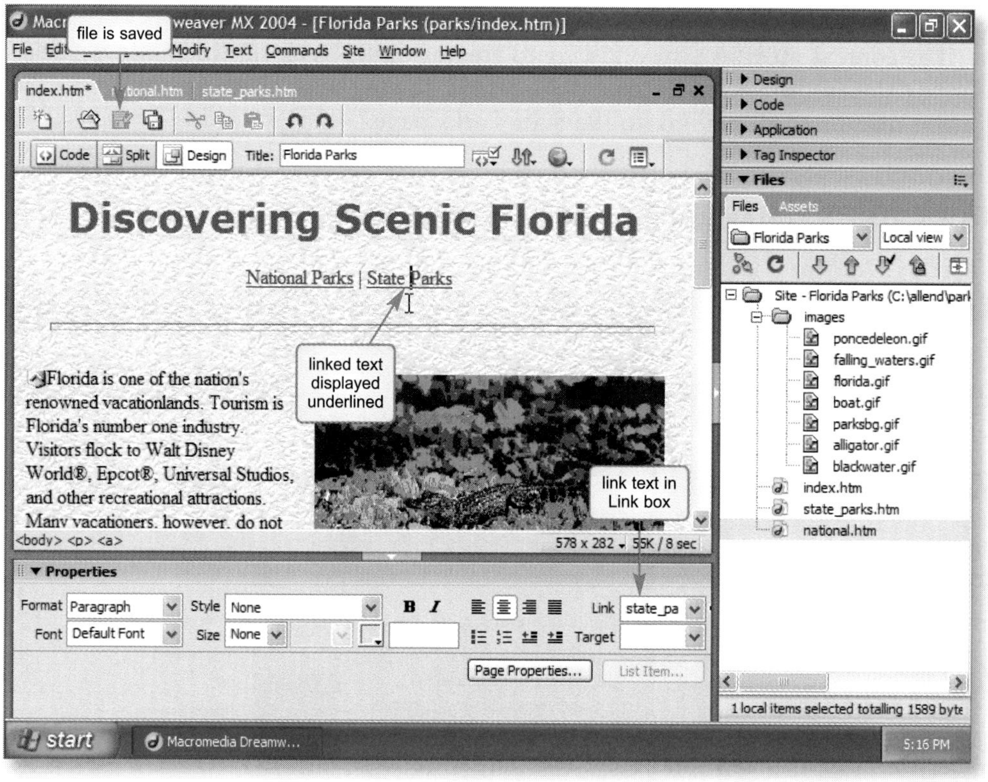

FIGURE 2-71

4

- **Press the F12 key to view the index page in your browser.**
- **Click the National Parks link and then click the browser Back button.**
- **Click the State Parks link.**
- **Close the browser.**

Other Ways

1. Click Link box, type file name
2. Click Point to File icon in Property inspector, drag to file name

Creating a Relative Link to the Home Page

Visitors can enter a Web site at any point, so it is important always to include a link from each page within the site back to the home page. You, therefore, create a relative link to the home page from the National Parks page and from the State Parks page. The following steps show how to create a link from the National Parks page and a link from the State Parks page to the home page.

To Create a Relative Link to the Home Page

1

- **Click the national.htm tab and then scroll to the bottom of the page. Drag to select Home.**

The text, Home, is highlighted (Figure 2-72). This text will become a link.

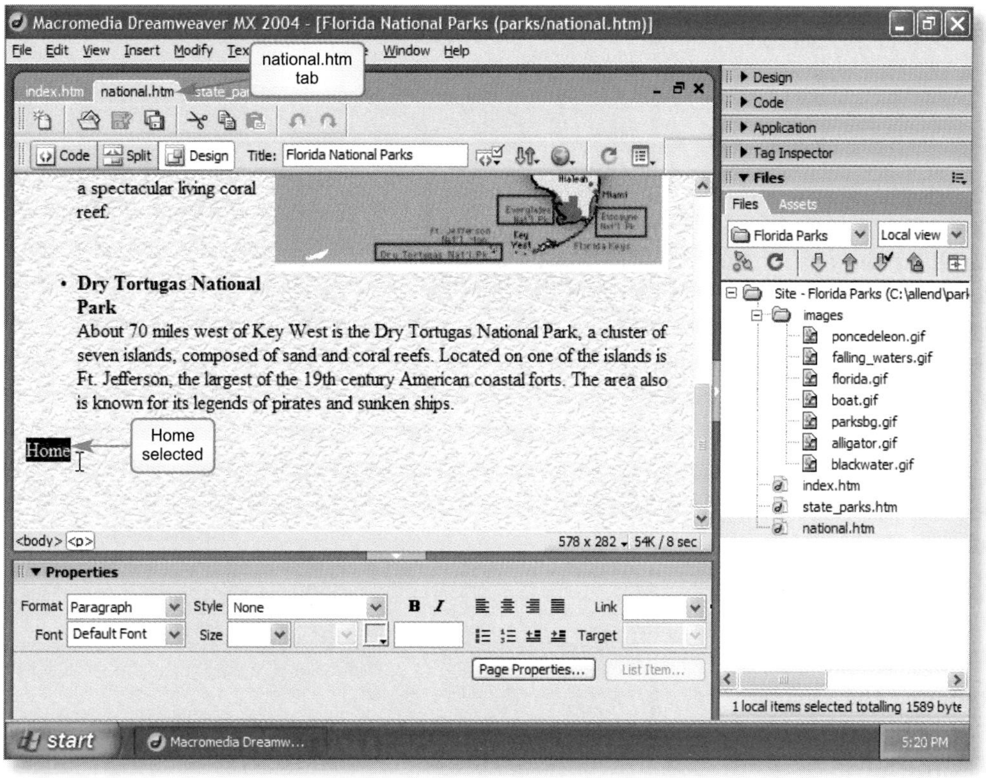

FIGURE 2-72

2

- **Drag the index.htm file name from the Files panel to the Link box.**
- **Click the text, Home, to display the link.**
- **Click the Save button on the Standard toolbar.**

The link is created (Figure 2-73). The National Parks page is saved.

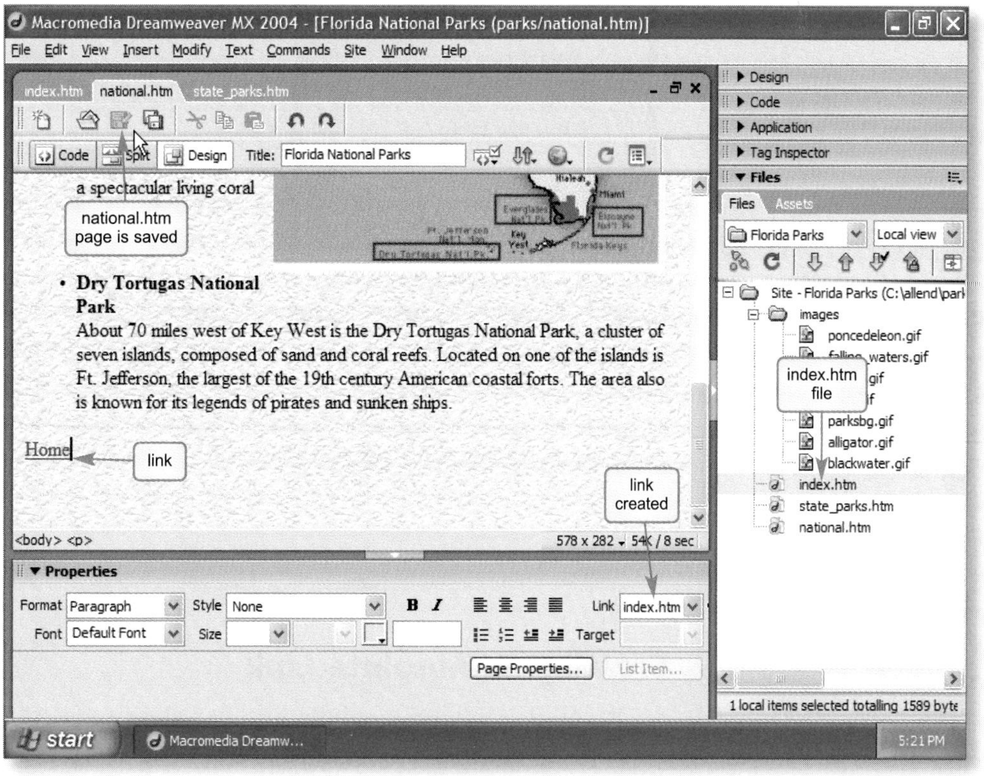

FIGURE 2-73

3

- **Press the F12 key to view the National Parks page in your browser.**
- **Click the Home link.**

The index page displays in the browser.

4

- **Close the browser.**

The browser is closed, and Dreamweaver displays.

5

- **Click the state_parks.htm tab. If necessary, scroll to the end of the document and then drag to select the text, Home (Figure 2-74).**

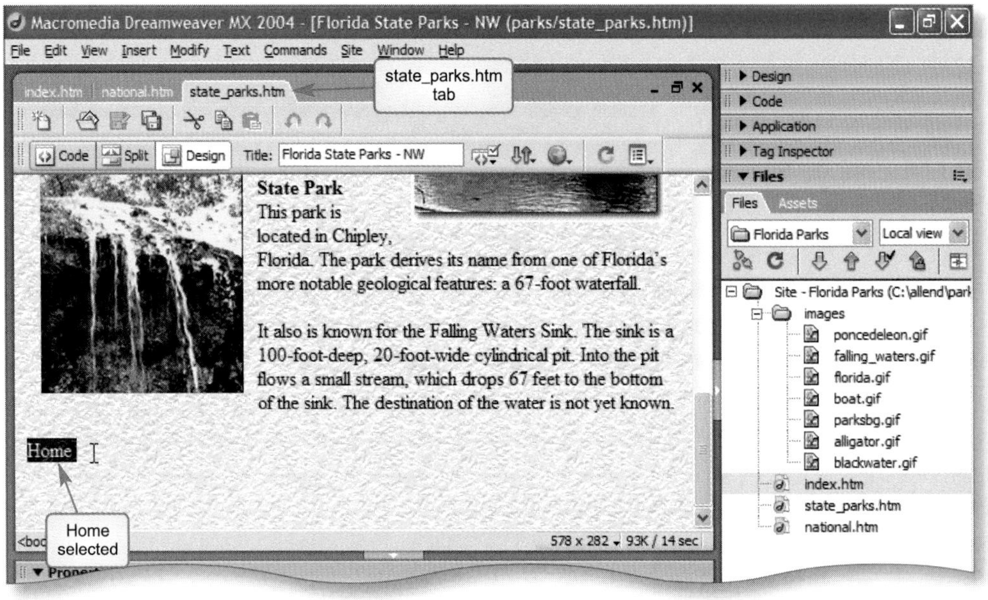

FIGURE 2-74

6

- **Drag the index.htm file name from the Files panel to the Link box.**
- **Click the text, Home, to display the link.**
- **Click the Save button on the Standard toolbar.**

The link is created, and index.htm displays in the Link box (Figure 2-75). The State Parks page is saved.

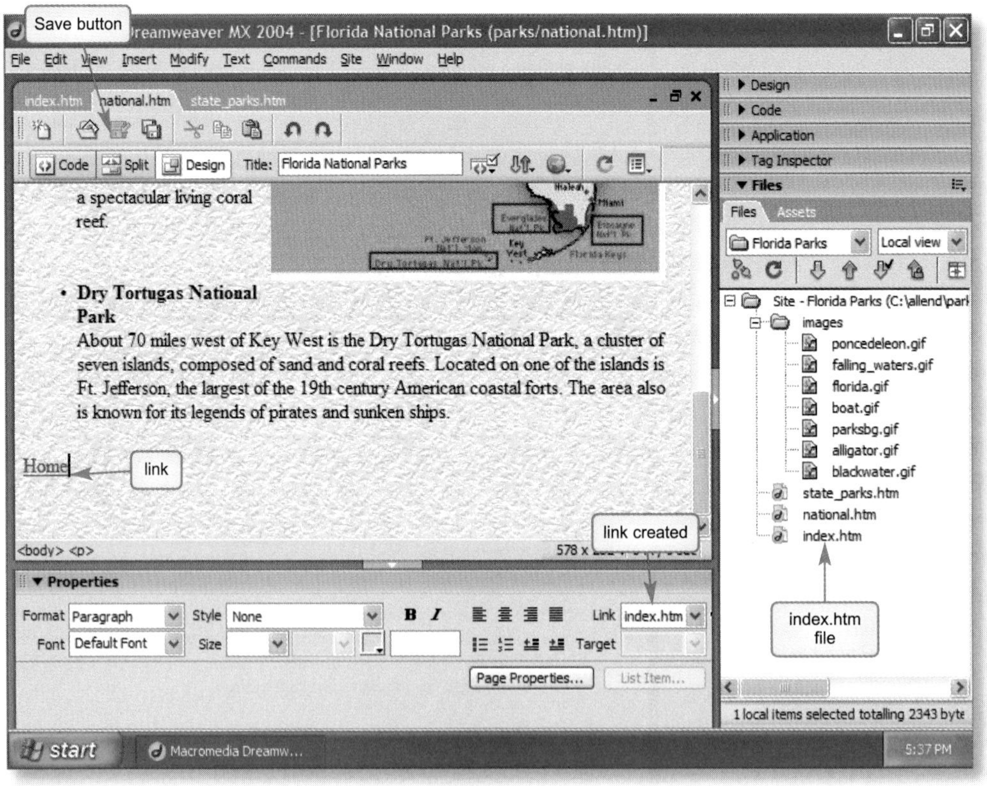

FIGURE 2-75

7

- **Press the F12 key to view the State Parks page in your browser.**
- **Click the Home link to verify that it works.**
- **Close the browser.**

Other Ways

1. Click Link box, type file name

Creating an Absolute Link

Recall that an absolute link (also called an external link) contains the complete Web site address of a document. You create absolute links the same way you create relative links — select the text and drag or type the Web site address. You now will create three absolute links in the State Parks page. These links are from the name of each of the three parks to a Web page about the selected park. The following steps show how to create the three absolute links. Keep in mind that Web site addresses change. If the absolute links do not work, check the Dreamweaver MX 2004 companion site at http://www.scsite.com/dreamweavermx04/ for updates.

To Create an Absolute Link

1. **If necessary, scroll to the top of the page. Drag to select the text, Blackwater River State Park.**
2. **Click the Link box and then type** `http://www.floridastateparks.org/blackwaterriver/` **as the link.**
3. **Drag to select the text, Ponce de Leon Spring State Park. Click the Link box and then type** `http://www.floridastateparks.org/poncedeleonsprings/` **as the link.**
4. **If necessary, scroll down and then drag to select the text, Falling Waters State Park. Click the Link box and then type** `http://www.floridastateparks.org/fallingwaters/` **as the link.**
5. **Click the Save button on the Standard toolbar.**
6. **Press the F12 key and then click each link to verify that they work. Click the browser Back button after clicking each link.**

The three absolute links to the respective state parks pages are added (Figure 2-76), and the Web page is saved.

7. **Close the browser.**

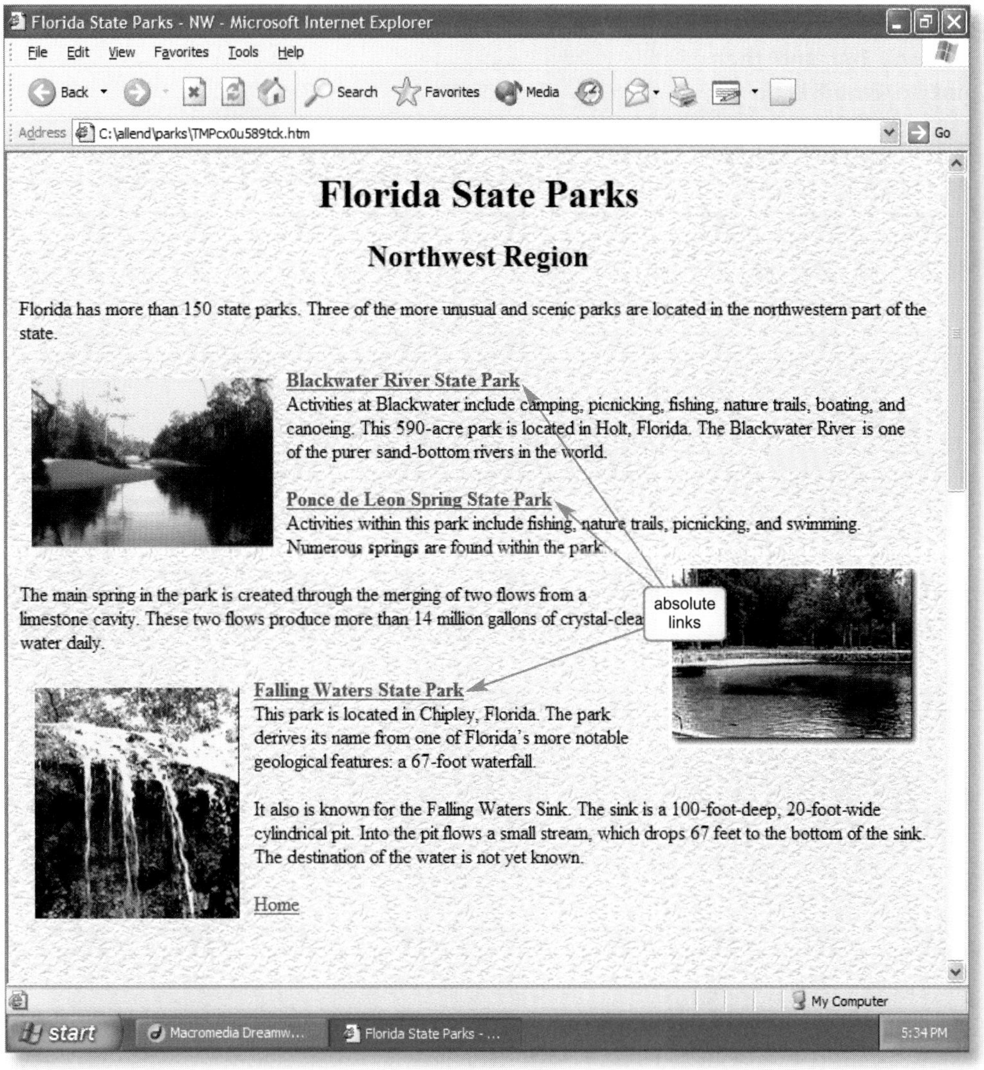

FIGURE 2-76

Other Ways

1. Start browser, open Web page, select URL, copy URL, close browser, paste in Link box

E-Mail Links

An **e-mail link** is one of the foundation elements of any successful Web site. It is important for visitors to be able to contact you for additional information or to comment on the Web page or Web site. When visitors click an e-mail link, their default e-mail program opens to a new e-mail message. The e-mail address you specify is inserted automatically in the To box.

Creating an E-Mail Link

The following steps show how to create an e-mail link for your home page using your name as the linked text. You do this through the Insert menu.

To Add an E-Mail Link

1

- **Click the index.htm tab, scroll down, and then drag to select your name. Click Insert on the menu bar and then point to Email Link.**

In this figure, David Allen is highlighted, and the Insert menu is displayed (Figure 2-77). Your name should be highlighted on your screen.

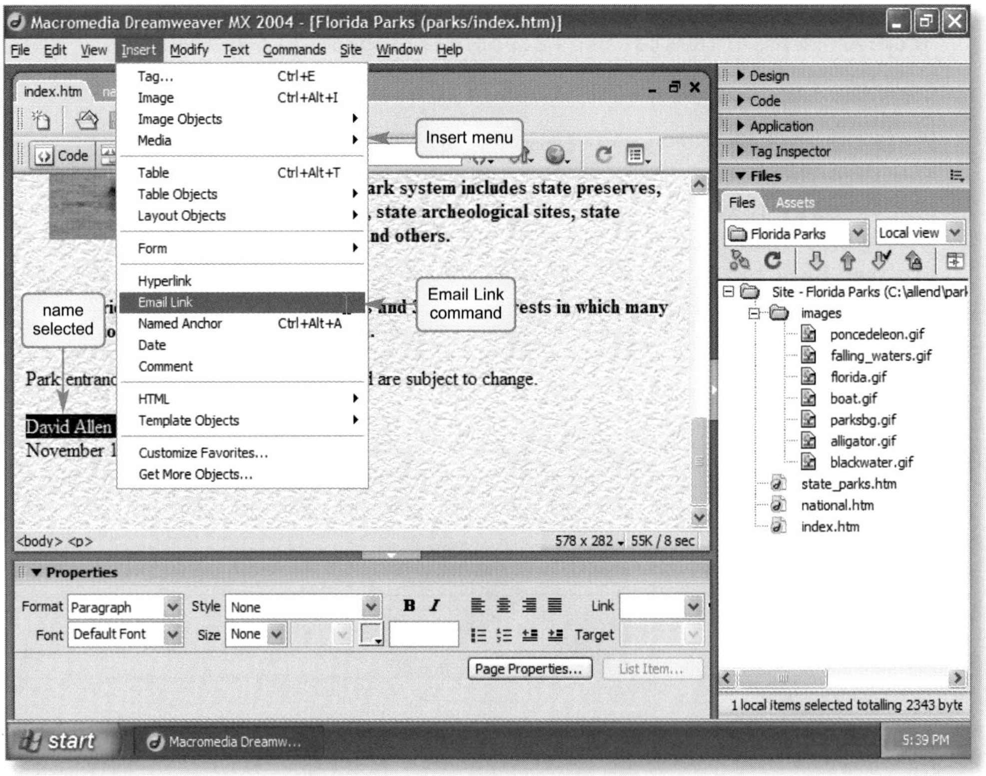

FIGURE 2-77

2

• **Click Email Link.**

The Email Link dialog box is displayed. In this figure, David Allen is highlighted in the Text text box (Figure 2-78). On your computer, your name is displayed in the Text text box.

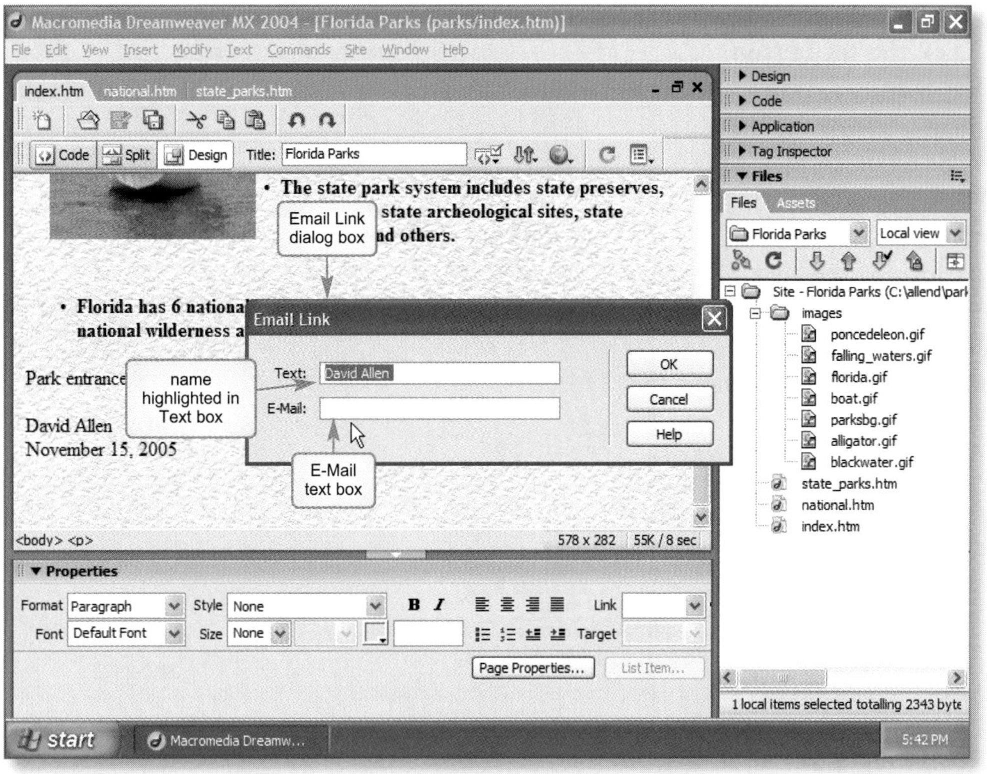

FIGURE 2-78

3

• **Click the E-Mail text box and then type your e-mail address.**

In this figure, the e-mail address for David Allen is displayed in the E-Mail text box (Figure 2-79). On your computer, Dreamweaver displays your e-mail address.

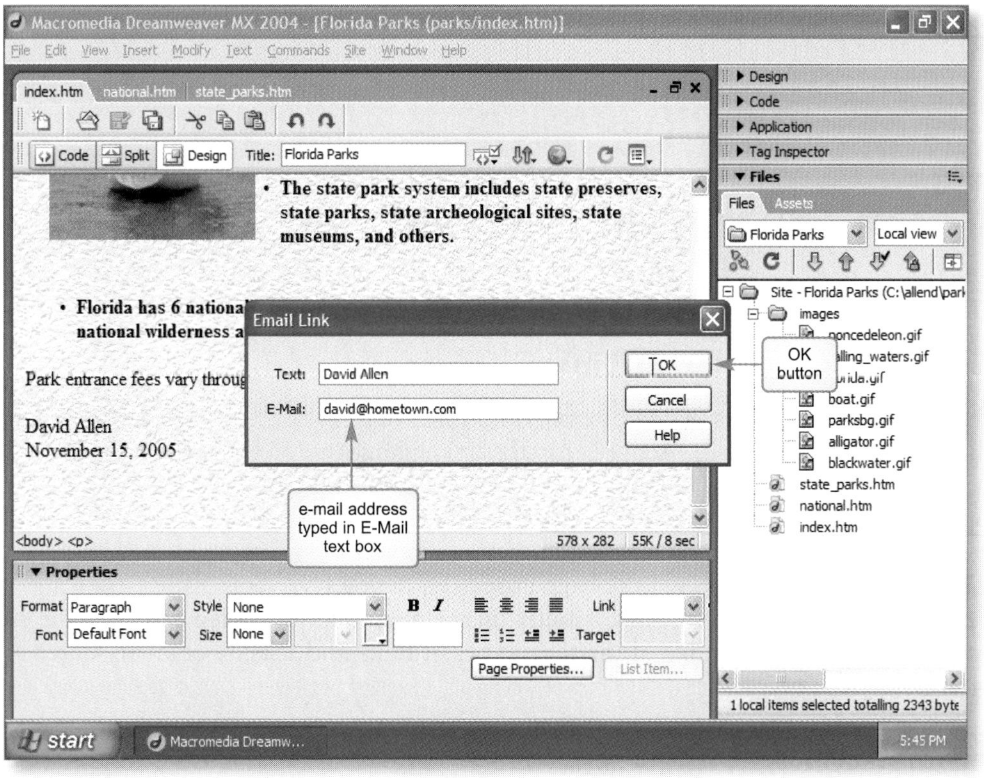

FIGURE 2-79

4

- **Click the OK button.**
- **Click the expand/collapse arrow on the vertical bar to hide the panel groups.**
- **Click anywhere in the highlighted text your name.**
- **Click the Save button on the Standard toolbar.**

The selected text for the e-mail link, David Allen, is displayed as linked text and the index page is saved. The Link box displays the e-mail address (Figure 2-80). On your computer, Dreamweaver displays your name as the linked text.

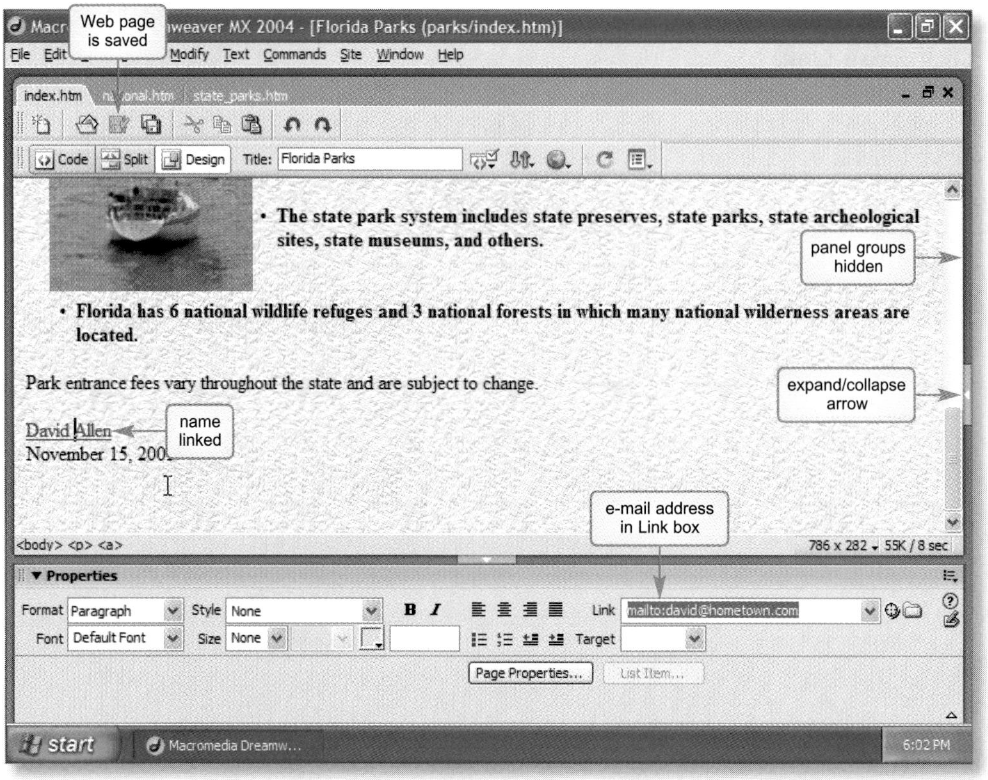

FIGURE 2-80

5

- **Press the F12 key to view the page in your browser. Click your name.**

Your e-mail program opens with your e-mail address in the To text box.

6

- **Close your e-mail program and then close the browser.**

Changing the Color of Links

The Page Properties dialog box provides three options for link colors: Link (the link has not been clicked), Active Link (the link changes color when the user clicks it), and Visited Link (the link has been visited). The default color for the three options is black. It is easy to make changes to these default settings and select colors that complement the background and other colors you are using on your Web pages. This is accomplished through the Page Properties dialog box. You display the Page Properties dialog box by clicking Modify on the menu bar. You then can click the box that corresponds to one of the three types of links and select a color to match your color scheme.

Editing and Deleting Links

Web development is a never-ending process. At some point, it will be necessary to edit or delete a link. For instance, an e-mail address may change, a URL to an external link may change, or an existing link may contain an error.

Dreamweaver makes it easy to edit or delete a link. First, select the link or click within the link you want to change. The linked document name displays in the Link box in the Property inspector. To delete the link without deleting the text on the Web page, delete the text from the Link box in the Property inspector. To edit the link, make the change in the Link box.

A second method to edit or delete a link is to use the context menu. Right-click within the link you want to change and then click Remove Link on the context menu to eliminate the link; click Change Link on the context menu to edit the link. Clicking the URLs icon in the Assets panel displays a list of all absolute and e-mail links within the Web site.

More About

Targeting Links

By default, when you click a link, the linked Web page will open in the current browser window. You can specify, however, that a linked Web page open in a new browser window. First, select the item and create the link. Then, in the Property inspector, click the Target box arrow and click _blank on the Target pop-up menu. When you view the page in a browser and click the link, it will display in a new window.

The Site Map

Earlier in this project, you set the index page as the home page. Dreamweaver provides a visual site map for viewing the relationships among files. The **Site Map** is a graphical representation of the structure of a Web site. You visually can design and modify the Web site structure through the Site Map. The home page displays at the top level of the map, and linked pages display at the lower levels. The Site Map view allows you to create, change, display, save, and print a Web site's structure and navigation. As previously discussed, a Web site's structure is the relationships among the pages in the Web site.

Viewing the Site Map

The home page now contains links to other pages in the site, and each page in the site contains links back to the home page. The State Parks page contains a link to three external Web sites, which are outside of the local site and located on a different server.

You created links from the home page to the two other pages in the Web site (National Parks and State Parks) and links from these two pages back to the home page. You can use the Site Map to view a graphical image of these links. In addition to allowing you to view the Site Map, Dreamweaver also has an option that lets you view your file list and Site Map simultaneously.

Displaying the Site Map and Local Files

The Site Map shows the pages as icons and displays links in the order in which they are encountered in the HTML source code. Starting from the home page, the Site Map default displays the site structure two levels deep. The relative links have a plus sign to their left. If you click the plus (+) sign, pages below the second level display. Some pages have a minus sign to their left. If you click the minus (–) sign, pages linked below the second level are hidden. Text displayed in blue and marked with a globe icon indicates a file on another site or a special link such as an e-mail link. Text displayed in red indicates a broken link. You access the Site Map through the Files panel. The following steps show how to display the site map with the newly created links among the pages in the Florida Parks Web site.

To Display the Site Map and Local Files List

1

- **If necessary, click the index.htm tab.**
- **Click the expand/collapse arrow on the panel groups vertical bar to display the Files panel.**
- **Click the View box arrow and then point to Map view in the View pop-up menu (Figure 2-81).**

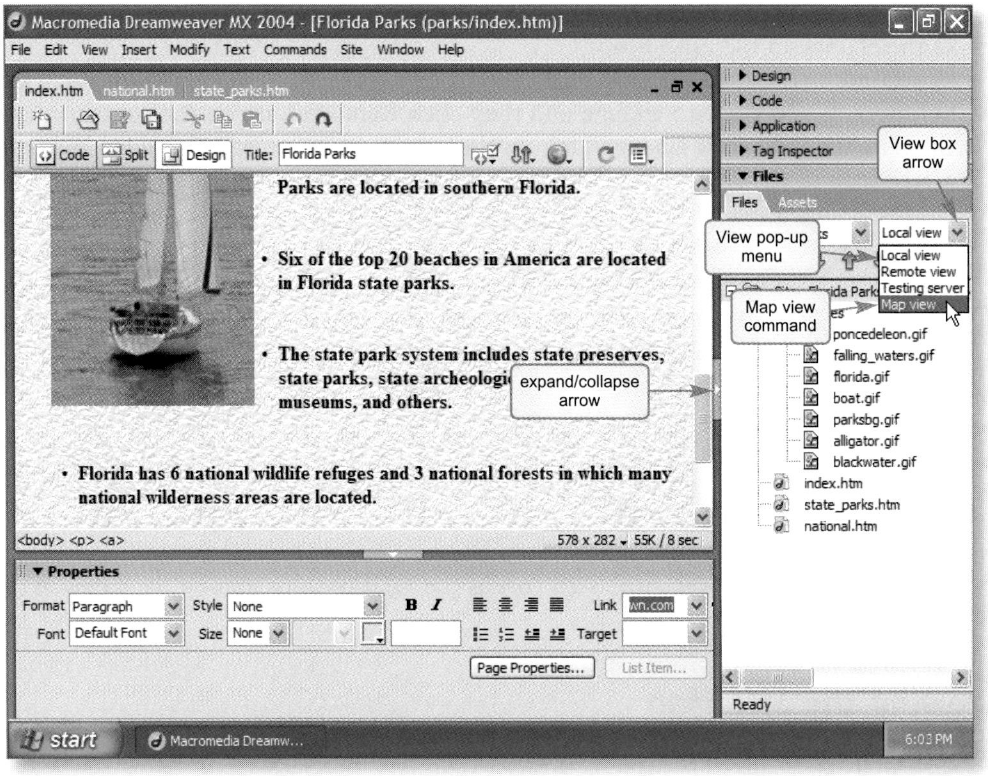

FIGURE 2-81

2

- **Click Map view and then point to the Expand/Collapse button on the Files panel toolbar.**

Dreamweaver displays a graphical view of the Web site in the Files panel, including all links from the index page (Figure 2-82).

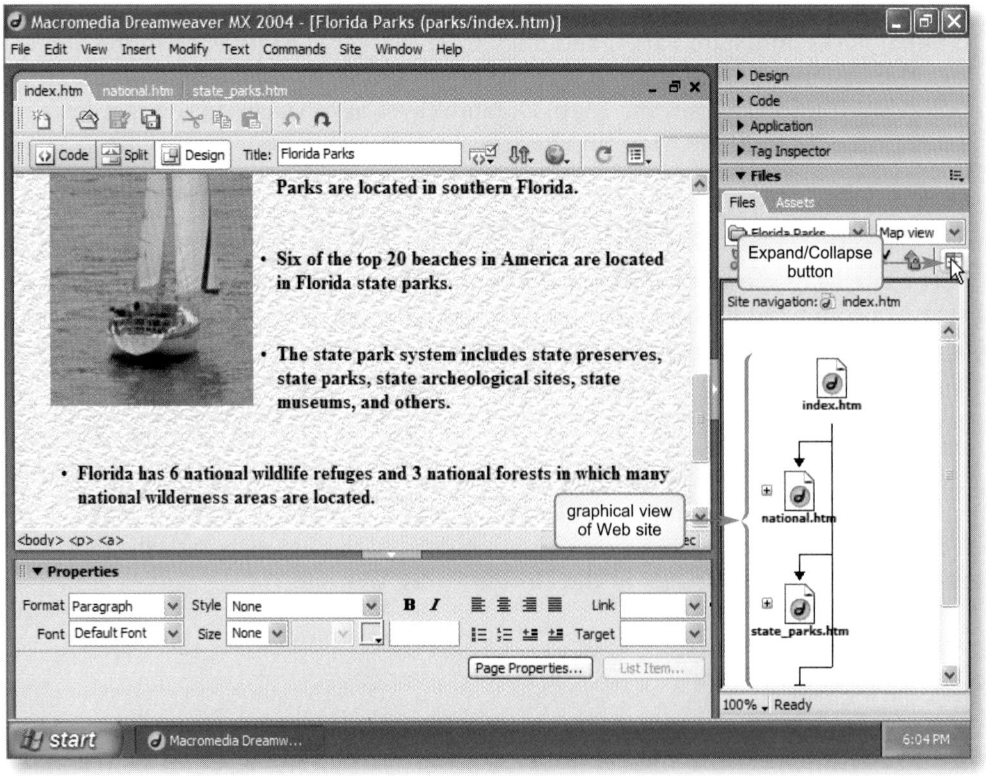

FIGURE 2-82

3

• Click the Expand/Collapse button. Point to the plus sign to the left of the national.htm icon.

The Site Map expands and displays a graphical structure of the links between the index page and the other two pages and external links (Figure 2-83). The plus signs to the left of the national.htm and state_parks.htm pages indicate that additional files or links are below these pages.

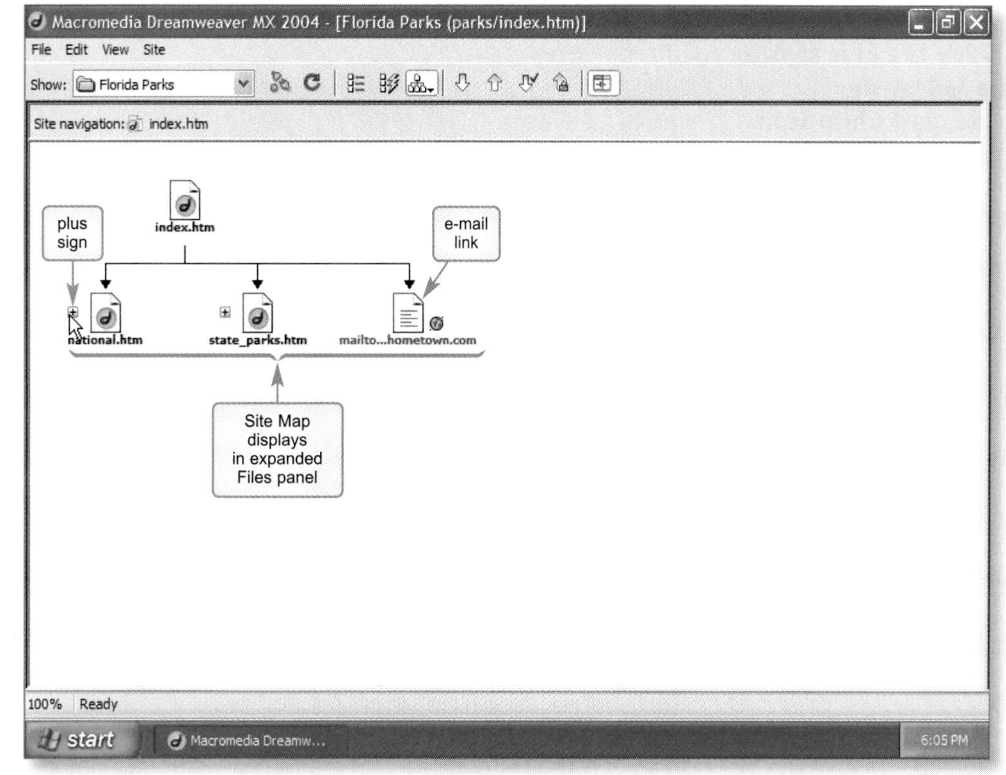

FIGURE 2-83

4

• Click the plus sign to the left of the national.htm icon.

The structure further expands and displays the relative link to the index page from the national.htm page (Figure 2-84).

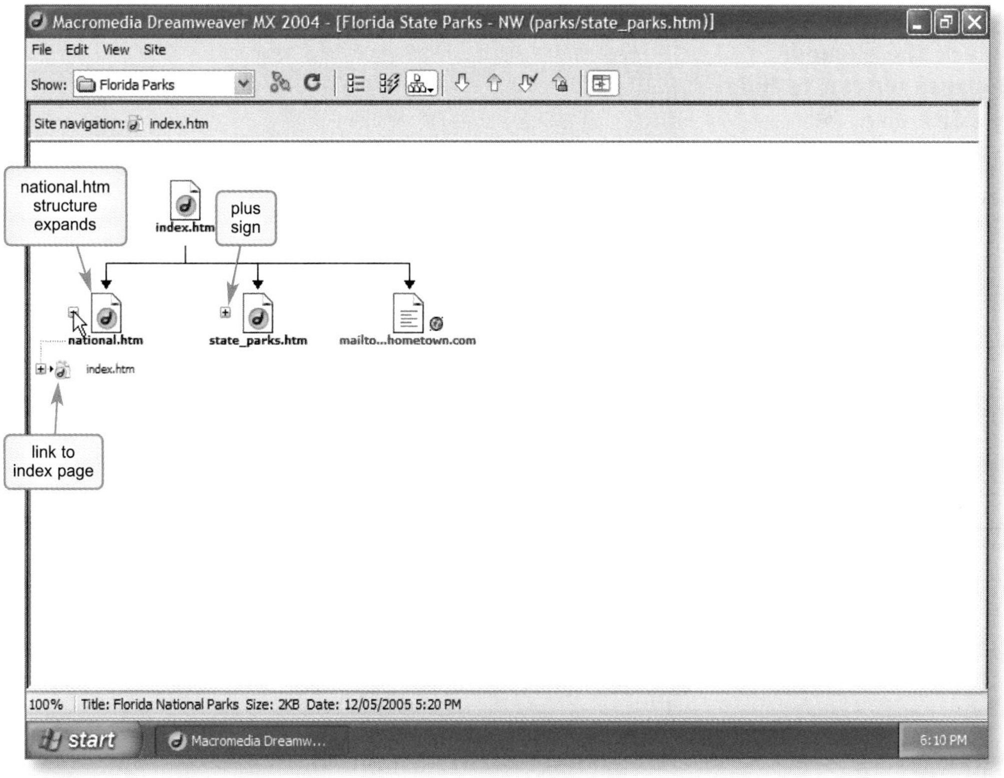

FIGURE 2-84

5

- **Click the plus sign to the left of the state_parks.htm icon.**

The structure further expands and displays the relative link to the index page from the State Parks page and the absolute (external) links to the three state parks (Figure 2-85).

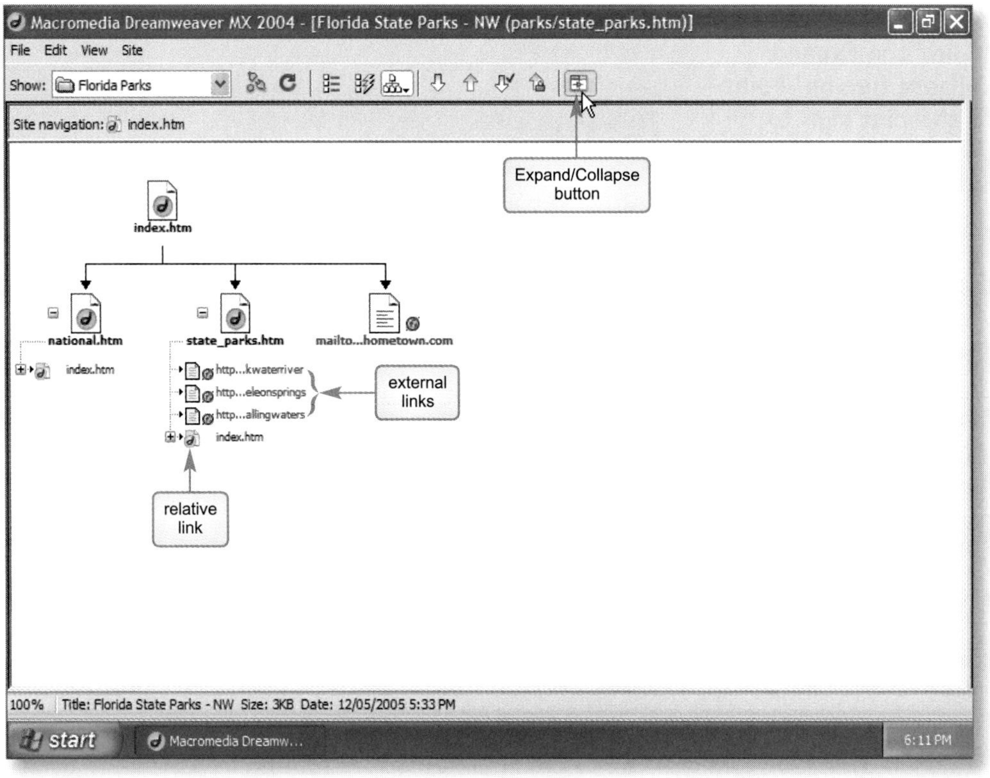

FIGURE 2-85

6

- **Click the Expand/ Collapse button to hide the Site Map.**
- **Click the View box arrow and then point to Local view in the View pop-up menu (Figure 2-86).**

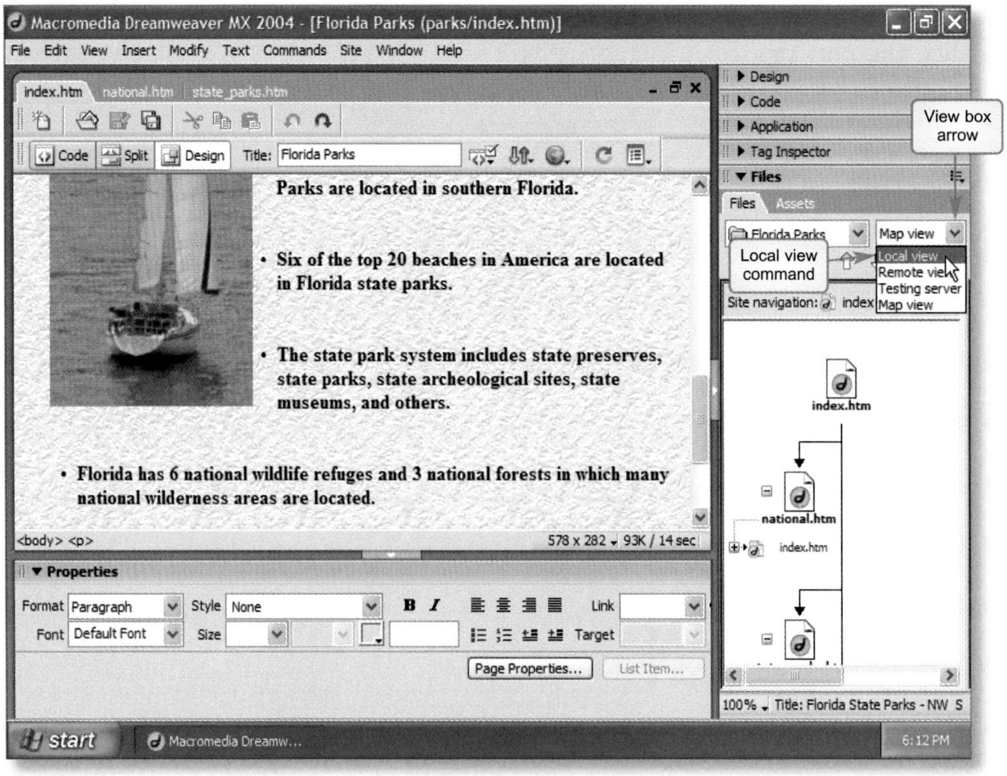

FIGURE 2-86

7

- **Click Local view.**

The Site - Florida Parks file hierarchy displays (Figure 2-87).

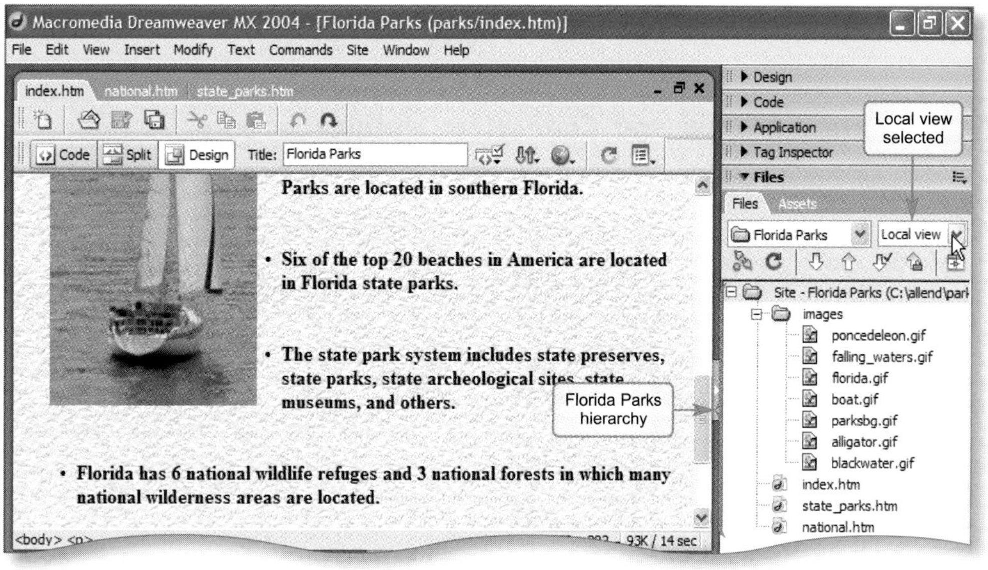

FIGURE 2-87

HTML Code View

Dreamweaver provides two views, or ways, to look at a document: **Design view** and **Code view.** Thus far, you have been working in Design view. As you create and work with documents, Dreamweaver automatically generates the underlying HTML code. Recall that the HTML code defines the structure and layout of a Web document by using a variety of tags and attributes. Even though Dreamweaver generates the code, occasions occur that necessitate the tweaking or modifying of code.

Dreamweaver provides several options for viewing and working with HTML code. You can split the Document window so that it displays both the Code view and the Design view. You can display only the Code view in the Document window, or you can open the Code inspector. The **Code inspector** opens in a separate window, so you can keep the whole Document window reserved for Design view.

Using Code View and Design View

In Split view, you work in a split-screen environment. You can see the design and the code at the same time. Splitting the Document window to view the code makes it easier to view the visual design while you make changes in the HTML code. When you make a change in Design view, the HTML code also is changed but is not visible in the Document window. You can set word wrapping, display line numbers for the code, highlight invalid HTML code, set syntax coloring for code elements, and set indenting through the View menu's Code View Options submenu. Viewing the code at this early stage may not seem important, but the more code you learn, the more productive you will become.

Within the HTML code, tags can be entered in uppercase, lowercase, or a combination of upper- and lowercase. The case of the tags has no effect on how the browser displays the output. When you view the code in Code view in Dreamweaver, some HTML tags display in lowercase letters and some attributes in uppercase letters. This is the Dreamweaver default.

In this book, when describing HTML tags, we use lowercase letters for tags and attributes to make it easier to differentiate them from the other text.

The following steps show how to use the Code View and Design View option to look at the code for the
 (line break) and <p> (paragraph) tags. The paragraph

More About

Using the Quick Tag Editor

For more information about using the Quick Tag Editor to review and edit HTML tags, visit the Dreamweaver MX 2004 More About Web page (scsite.com/dreamweavermx04/more) and then click Dreamweaver MX Quick Tag Editor.

tag has an opening tag, <p>, and a closing tag, </p>. The
 (line break) tag does not have a closing tag.

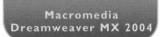

To View Design View and Code View Simultaneously

1

- **Click the state_parks.htm tab.**
- **Hide the Files panel and collapse the Property inspector.**
- **Position the insertion point to the left of the heading, Florida State Parks. Point to the Split button on the Document toolbar (Figure 2-88).**

FIGURE 2-88

2

- **Click the Split button. If necessary, click the View menu, point to Code View Options, and then click Line Numbers.**

The window splits. The upper window displays Code view and the lower window displays Design view (Figure 2-89). The insertion point is displayed in Code view in the same location as in Design view (to the left of the heading). The lines are numbered in Code view. The HTML code is displayed in color and in lowercase surrounded by < (less than) and > (greater than) symbols. Your window may display Design view in the upper window and Code view in the lower window.

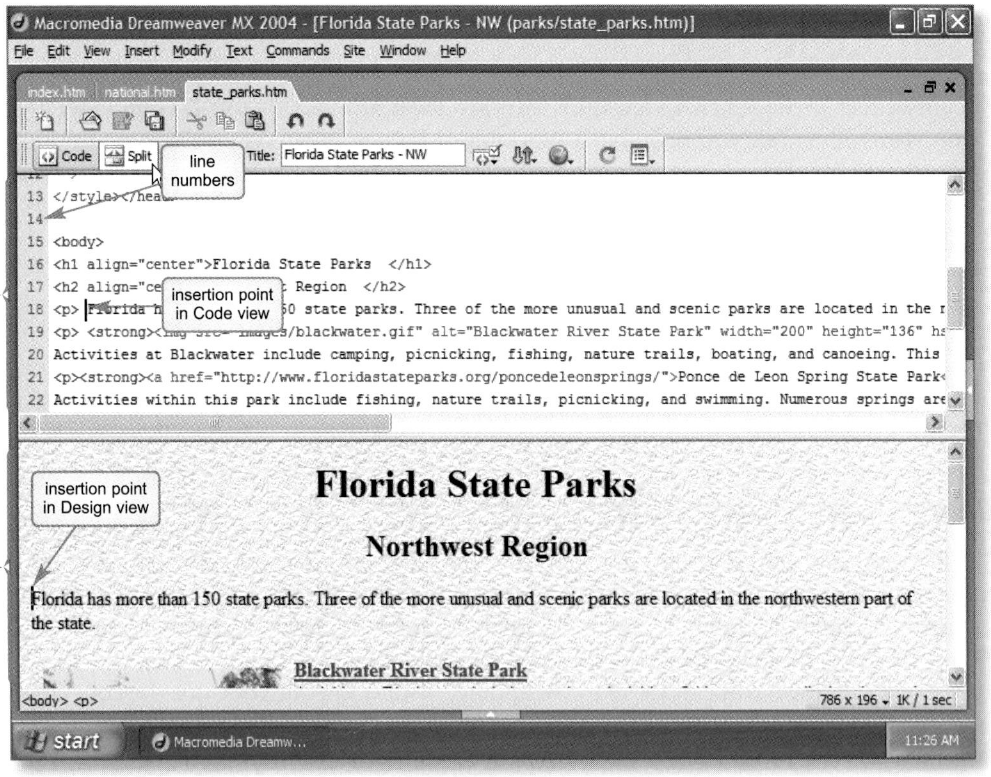

FIGURE 2-89

3

- **Click the Design button.**

The Design view displays.

Modifying HTML Code

One of the more common problems within Dreamweaver and the HTML code relates to line breaks and paragraphs. Occasionally, you inadvertently press the ENTER key or insert a line break and need to remove the tag. Or, you may copy and paste or open a text file that contains unneeded paragraphs or line breaks.

Pressing the BACKSPACE key or DELETE key may return you to the previous line, but does not always delete the line break or paragraph tag within the HTML code. The deletion of these tags is determined by the position of the insertion point when you press the BACKSPACE or DELETE keys. If the insertion point is still inside the HTML code, pressing the BACKSPACE key will not delete these tags and your page will not display correctly. When this occurs, the best solution is to delete the tag through Code view.

Quitting Dreamweaver

After you add pages to your Web site, including images and links, and then verify links using the Site Map, Project 2 is complete. The next step shows how to close the Web site, quit Dreamweaver MX 2004, and return control to Windows.

To Close the Web Site and Quit Dreamweaver

1 Click the Close button on the right corner of the Dreamweaver title bar.

The Dreamweaver window, the Document window, and the Florida Parks Web site all close. If you have unsaved changes, Dreamweaver will prompt you to save the changes. Clicking the Yes button in the Dreamweaver MX 2004 dialog box saves the changes.

Project Summary

Project 2 introduced you to images, links, the Site Map, and how to view HTML code. You began the project by using the Windows My Computer option to copy data files to the local site. You added two new pages, one for Florida national parks and one for Florida state parks, to the Web site you created in Project 1. Next, you added page images to the index page. Following that, you added a background image and page images to the National and State Parks pages. Then, you added relative links to all three pages. You added an e-mail link to the home page and absolute links to the State Parks page. You also learned to use the Site Map. Finally, you learned how to view HTML code.

What You Should Know

Having completed this project, you should be able to perform the tasks below. The tasks are listed in the same order they were presented in this project. For a list of keyboard commands for topics introduced in this project, see the Quick Reference for Windows at the back of this book and refer to the Shortcut column.

1. Copy Data Files to the Parks Web Site (DW 120)
2. Start Dreamweaver and Open the Parks Web Site (DW 121)
3. Open a Web Page from a Local Web Site (DW 122)
4. Set a Home Page (DW 124)
5. Open a New Document Window (DW 125)
6. Prepare the Workspace (DW 128)
7. Create the National Parks Web Page (DW 129)
8. Format the Florida National Parks Page (DW 130)
9. Open a New Document Window (DW 131)
10. Create the State Parks Web Page (DW 132)

Learn It Online

Instructions: To complete the Learn It Online exercises, start your browser, click the Address bar, and then enter the Web address `scsite.com/dreamweavermx2004/learn`. When the Dreamweaver MX 2004 Learn It Online page is displayed, follow the instructions in the exercises below. Each exercise has instructions for printing your results, either for your own records or for submission to your instructor.

1 Project Reinforcement TF, MC, and SA

Below Dreamweaver Project 2, click the Project Reinforcement link. Print the quiz by clicking Print on the File menu for each page. Answer each question.

2 Flash Cards

Below Dreamweaver Project 2, click the Flash Cards link and read the instructions. Type 20 (or a number specified by your instructor) in the Number of playing cards text box, type your name in the Enter your Name text box, and then click the Flip Card button. When the flash card is displayed, read the question and then click the ANSWER box arrow to select an answer. Flip through Flash Cards. If your score is 15 (75%) correct or greater, click Print on the File menu to print your results. If your score is less than 15 (75%) correct, then redo this exercise by clicking the Replay button.

3 Practice Test

Below Dreamweaver Project 2, click the Practice Test link. Answer each question, enter your first and last name at the bottom of the page, and then click the Grade Test button. When the graded practice test is displayed on your screen, click Print on the File menu to print a hard copy. Continue to take practice tests until you score 80% or better.

4 Who Wants To Be a Computer Genius?

Below Dreamweaver Project 2, click the Computer Genius link. Read the instructions, enter your first and last name at the bottom of the page, and then click the PLAY button. When your score is displayed, click the PRINT RESULTS link to print a hard copy.

5 Wheel of Terms

Below Dreamweaver Project 2, click the Wheel of Terms link. Read the instructions, and then enter your first and last name and your school name. Click the PLAY button. When your score is displayed, right-click the score and then click Print on the shortcut menu to print a hard copy.

6 Crossword Puzzle Challenge

Below Dreamweaver Project 2, click the Crossword Puzzle Challenge link. Read the instructions, and then enter your first and last name. Click the SUBMIT button. Work the crossword puzzle. When you are finished, click the Submit button. When the crossword puzzle is redisplayed, click the Print Puzzle button to print a hard copy.

7 Tips and Tricks

Below Dreamweaver Project 2, click the Tips and Tricks link. Click a topic that pertains to Project 2. Right-click the information and then click Print on the shortcut menu. Construct a brief example of what the information relates to in Dreamweaver to confirm you understand how to use the tip or trick.

8 Newsgroups

Below Dreamweaver Project 2, click the Newsgroups link. Click a topic that pertains to Project 2. Print three comments.

9 Expanding Your Horizons

Below Dreamweaver Project 2, click the Expanding Your Horizons link. Click a topic that pertains to Project 2. Print the information. Construct a brief example of what the information relates to in Dreamweaver to confirm you understand the contents of the article.

10 Search Sleuth

Below Dreamweaver Project 2, click the Search Sleuth link. To search for a term that pertains to this project, select a term below the Project 2 title and then use the Google search engine at google.com (or any major search engine) to display and print two Web pages that present information on the term.

Apply Your Knowledge

1 Modifying the B & B Lawn Service Web Site

Instructions: Start Dreamweaver. Data and image files for the B & B Lawn Service Web site are included on the Data Disk. See the inside back cover of this book for instructions for downloading the Data Disk or see your instructor for information on accessing the files in this book.

You add three new pages to the B & B Lawn Service Web site: a services page, an employment page, and a references page. In this exercise, you add relative and absolute links to each page. You also add a background image to the new pages. Next, you insert images on all pages and use the settings in Table 2-4 on page DW 186 to align the images and enter the Alt text. You then add an e-mail link to the home page and relative links from the three new pages to the home page. The pages for the Web site are shown in Figures 2-90a through 2-90d on pages DW 184 through DW 186.

Software and hardware settings determine how a Web page is displayed in a browser. Your Web pages may display differently in your browser than those in the figures do.

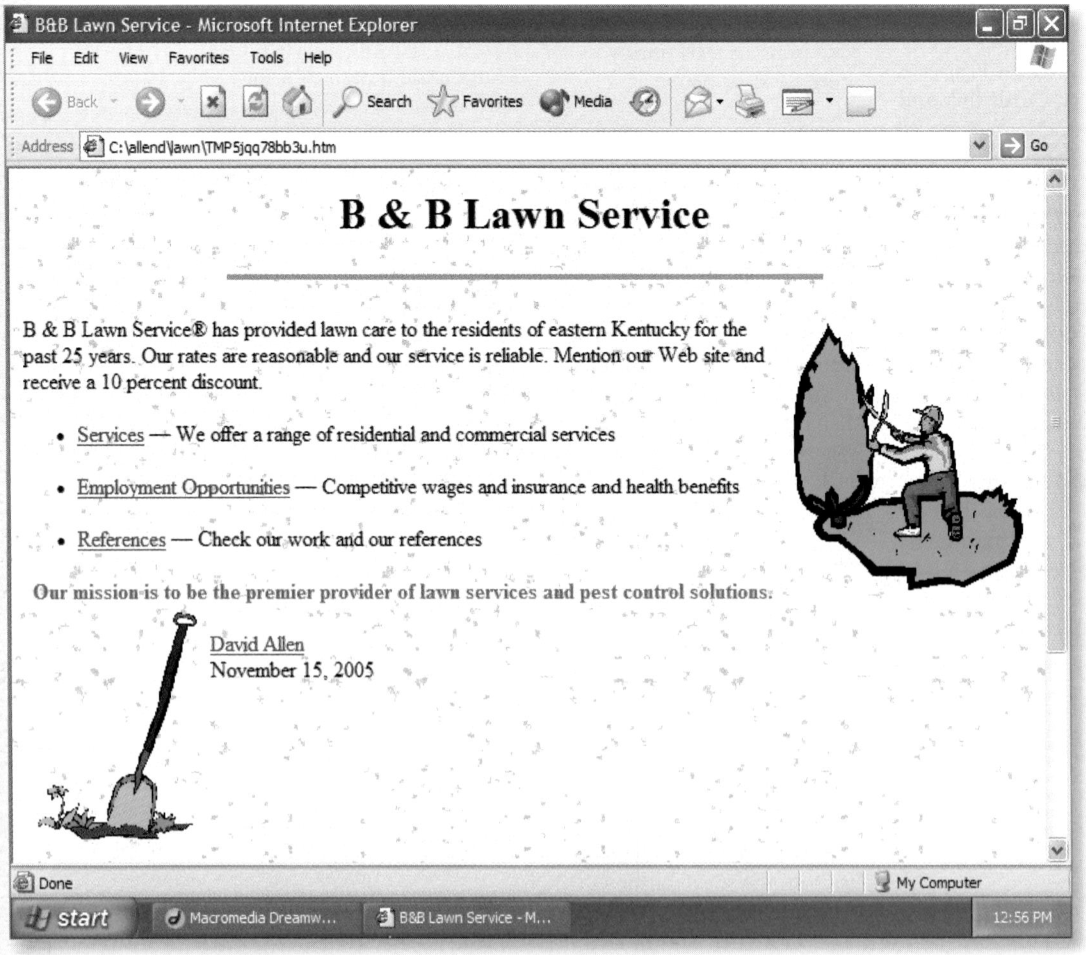

(a) Lawn Services Index (Home) Page

FIGURE 2-90 (*continued*)

Apply Your Knowledge

(b) Lawn Services – Services Page

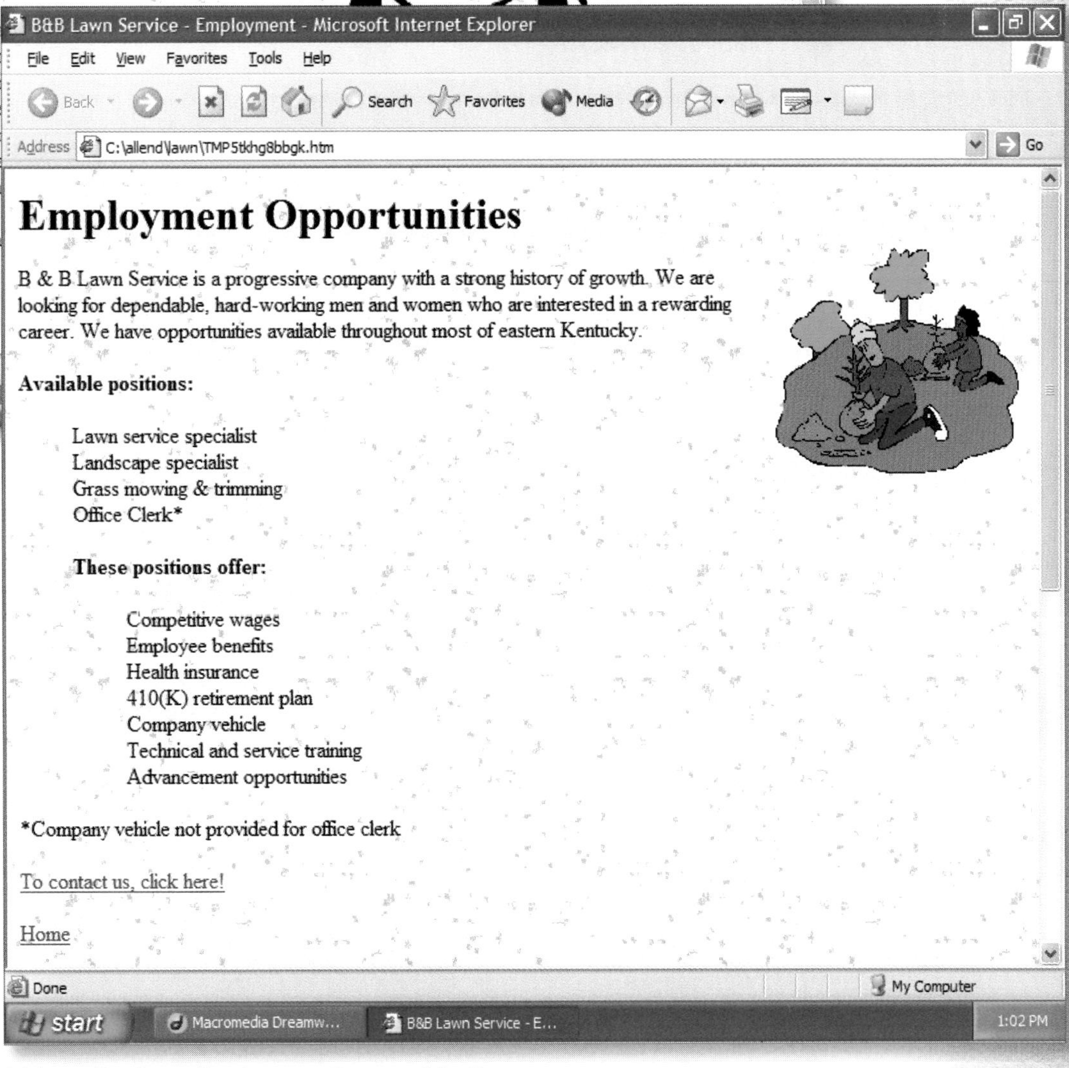

(c) Lawn Services – Employment Opportunities Pages

FIGURE 2-90 (*continued*)

(continued)

Apply Your Knowledge

Modifying the B & B Lawn Service Web Site *(continued)*

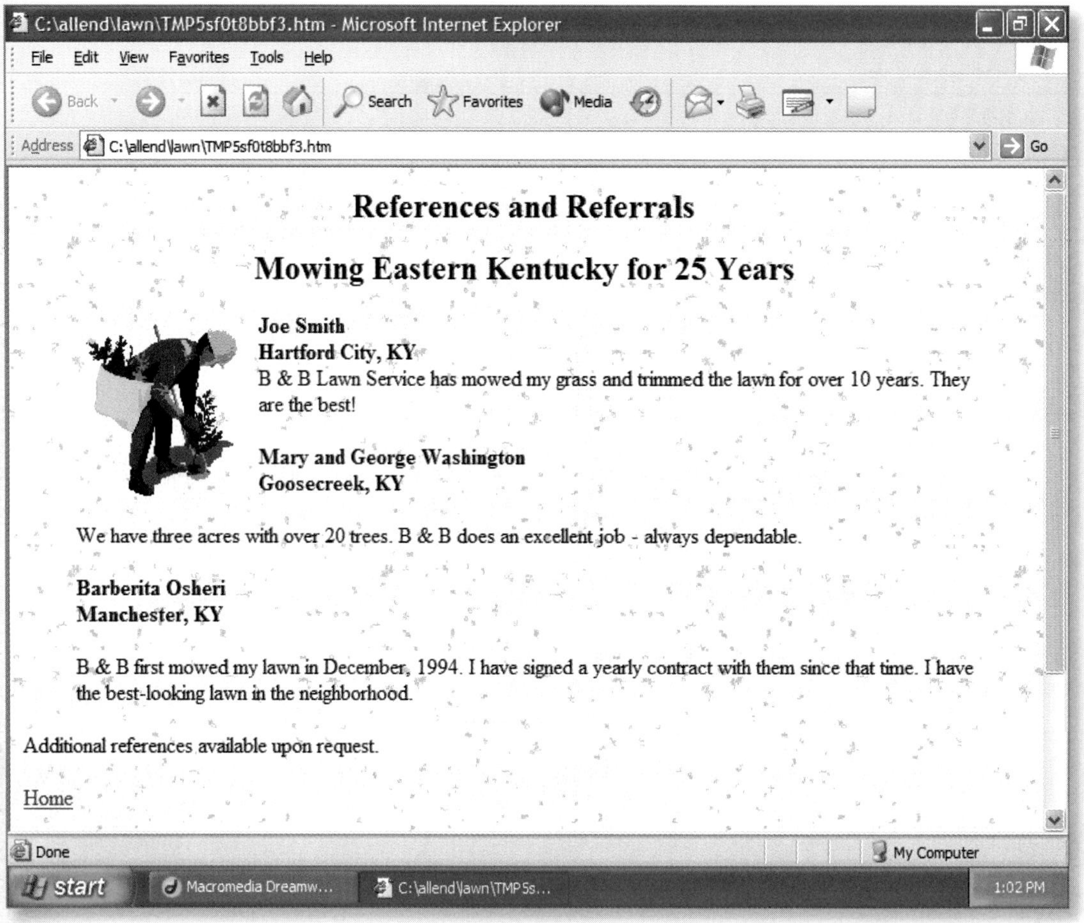

(d) References and Referrals Page

FIGURE 2-90 (*continued*)

Table 2-4 Image Property Settings for the B & B Lawn Service Web Site

IMAGE NAME	W	H	V SPACE	H SPACE	ALIGN	ALT
trimming2.gif	174	193	6	6	Right	Tree trimming
shovel.gif	124	166	6	8	Left	Shovel
mowing.gif	120	135	None	20	Left	Grass mowing
shakehands.gif	200	170	None	150	Right	Shaking hands
planting.gif	186	165	6	None	Right	Tree planting
planting2.gif	122	125	8	8	Left	Tree planting

Apply Your Knowledge

Perform the following tasks:

1. Use the Windows My Computer option to copy the data files and images to your lawn folder.
2. If necessary, display the panel groups. Select Lawn Service on the Files pop-up menu in the Files panel. Double-click the index.htm file in the Files panel. If necessary, click the expander arrow to expand the Property inspector. If necessary, display the Standard toolbar.
3. Click index.htm in the Files panel to select it. Right-click index.htm and then click Set as Home Page on the context menu.
4. Position the insertion point to the left of the first line of the first paragraph. Drag the trimming2.gif image to the insertion point and then select the image. Apply the settings in Table 2-4 on the previous page to align the image and enter the Alt text. If necessary, scroll down. Position the insertion point to the left of the last sentence on the Web page. Drag the shovel.gif image to the insertion point and then select the image. Apply the settings in Table 2-4.
5. If necessary, scroll up. Select Services (the first bulleted item heading). Use the drag-and-drop file method to create a link to the Services page. Repeat this process to add links from Employment Opportunities and References (the second and third bulleted item headings) to their respective Web pages. Select your name. Use the Insert menu to create an e-mail link using your name. Save the index page (Figure 2-90a on page DW 184).
6. Open services.htm. Click Modify on the menu bar and click Page Properties. Click the Background image Browse button to add the background image (lawnbg.gif) to the services.htm page.
7. Position the insertion point to the left of the page heading, drag the mowing.gif image to the insertion point, and then select the image. Apply the settings in Table 2-4 and then click the Resample button. Position the insertion point to the right of the first bulleted item and then drag the shakehands.gif image to the insertion point. Select the image. Apply the settings in Table 2-4.
8. If necessary, scroll down. Select Home and then create a relative link to the index page. Title the page B&B Lawn Service - Services. Save the Services page (Figure 2-90b on page DW 185).
9. Open employment.htm. Add the background image to the employment.htm page as you did in Step 6 to the services.htm page.
10. Position the insertion point to the right of the heading and then drag the planting.gif image to the insertion point. Select the image. Apply the settings in Table 2-4.
11. Scroll to the bottom of the page. Select the words —To contact us, click here!. Use the Insert menu to create an e-mail link using your e-mail address. Select Home at the bottom of the page and then drag index.htm to the Link box in the Property inspector to create a relative link to the index.htm file. Title the page B&B Lawn Service - Employment. Save the Employment page (Figure 2-90c on page DW 185).
12. Open references.htm. Apply the same background image you applied to the other pages in this Web site.
13. Create a link from Home to the index page.
14. Position the insertion point to the left of the text, Joe Smith. Drag the planting2.gif image to the insertion point. Select the image. Apply the settings in Table 2-4. Title the page B & B Lawn Service - References. Save the References page (Figure 2-90d on the previous page).
15. View the Web site in your browser. Check each link to verify that it works. Print a copy of each page if required and hand the copies in to your instructor. Close the browser. Quit Dreamweaver.

In the Lab

1 Modifying the CandleDust Web Site

Problem: Mary Stewart, for whom you created the CandleDust Web site and Web page, is very pleased with the response she has received. She has asked you to create a second page with links and images added to the index page. Mary wants the new page to include information about her company's history. The revised Web site is shown in Figures 2-91a and 2-91b. Table 2-5 on the next page includes the settings and Alt text for the images. Software and hardware settings determine how a Web page displays in a browser. Your Web pages may display differently in your browser than those in the figures do.

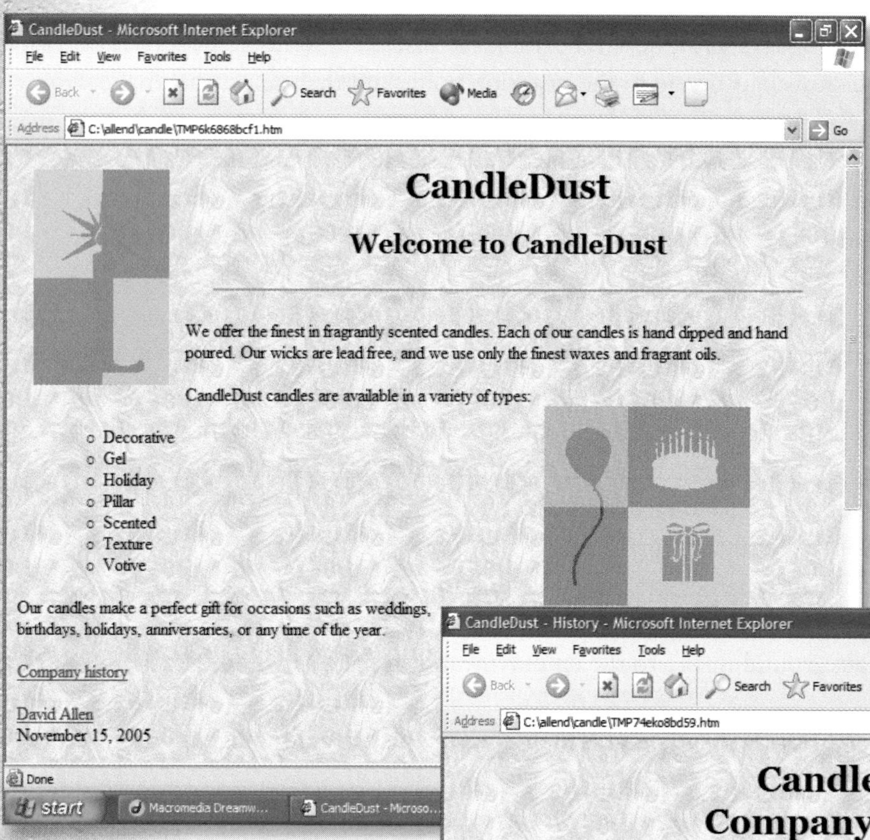

(a) CandleDust Index (Home) Page

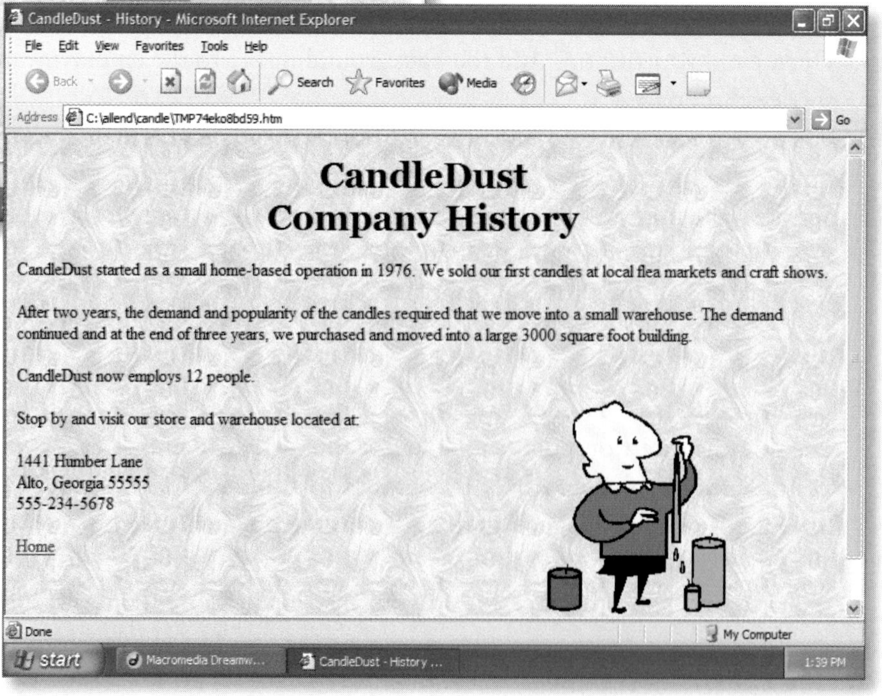

(b) CandleDust - History Web Page

FIGURE 2-91

In the Lab

Table 2-5 Image Property Settings for the CandleDust Web Site

IMAGE NAME	W	H	V SPACE	H SPACE	ALIGN	ALT
candle1.gif	126	192	6	15	Left	Logo
candle2.gif	192	178	None	75	Right	Candles
candle_dip.gif	164	191	10	100	Right	Candle dipping

Instructions: Perform the following tasks:

1. Use the Windows My Computer option to copy the data files and images to your candle folder.
2. Start Dreamweaver. Display the panel groups. Select CandleDust on the Files pop-up menu in the Files panel. Double-click the index.htm file in the Files panel. If necessary, click the expander arrow to expand the Property inspector. If necessary, display the Standard toolbar.
3. Click index.htm in the Files panel to select it. Right-click index.htm and then click Set as Home Page on the context menu.
4. Position the insertion point to the left of the heading and then drag the candle1.gif image to the insertion point. Select the image. Apply the settings in Table 2-5 to align the image and enter the Alt text.
5. Position the insertion point to the right of the text, CandleDust candles are available in a variety of types:, and then drag the candle2.gif image to the insertion point. Select the image and then apply the settings in Table 2-5.
6. Position the insertion point to the right of the text, Our candles make a perfect gift for occasions such as weddings, birthdays, holidays, anniversaries, or any time of the year, and then press the ENTER key. Type `Company history`. Select the Company history text and use the drag-and-drop method to create a link to the history.htm page. Select your name. Use the Insert menu to create an e-mail link using your e-mail address. Save the index page (Figure 2-91a on the previous page).
7. Open history.htm. Apply the background image to the history.htm page. Click Modify on the menu bar and then click Page Properties. Click the Browse button in the Page Properties dialog box, click the images folder, and then select the candlebg.gif image. Click the OK button in the Select Image Source dialog box and in the Page Properties dialog box.
8. Position the insertion point at the end of the sentence – CandleDust now employs 12 people – and then drag the candle_dip.gif image to the insertion point. Select the image and then apply the settings in Table 2-5. Title the page CandleDust - History.
9. Select Home and then create a relative link to the index page. Save the History page (Figure 2-91b on the previous page).
10. View your pages in your browser and verify that your links work. Print a copy of each page if required and hand the copies in to your instructor. Close your browser. Quit Dreamweaver.

2 Modifying the Credit Protection Web Site

Problem: Marcy Cantu has received favorable comments about the Web page and site you created about credit information. Her law firm wants to utilize the Web site to provide additional information to its clients. Marcy

(continued)

In the Lab

Modifying the Credit Protection Web Site *(continued)*

has asked you if you would be willing to work with her and another intern at the firm to create two more Web pages to add to the site. They want one of the pages to discuss credit protection and the other page to contain information about identity theft. The revised Web site is shown in Figures 2-92a, 2-92b, and 2-92c (on the next page). Table 2-6 includes the settings and Alt text for the images. Software and hardware settings determine how a Web page displays in a browser. Your Web pages may display differently in your browser than those in the figures do.

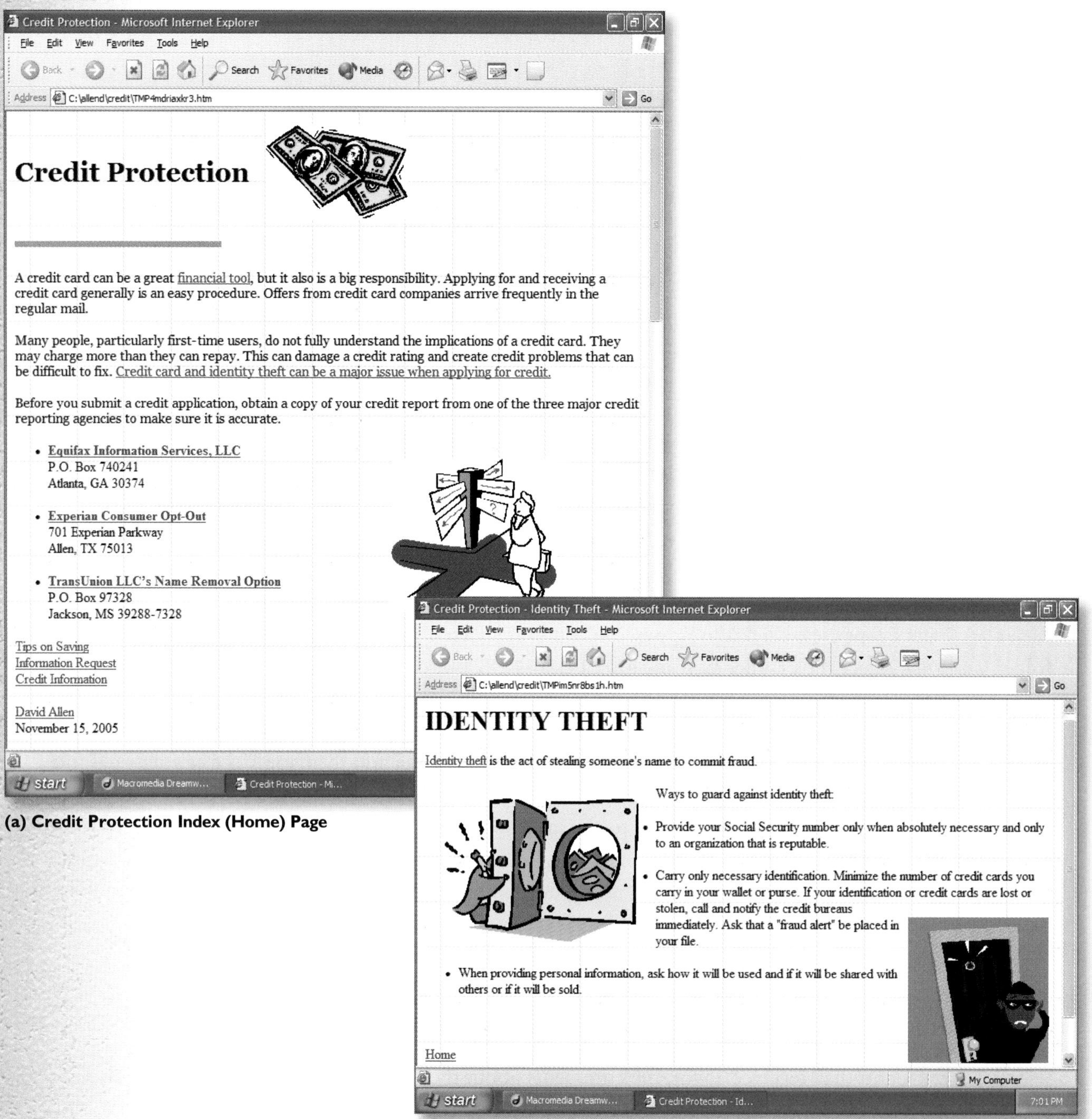

(a) Credit Protection Index (Home) Page

(b) Credit Protection - Identity Theft Web Page

FIGURE 2-92

In the Lab

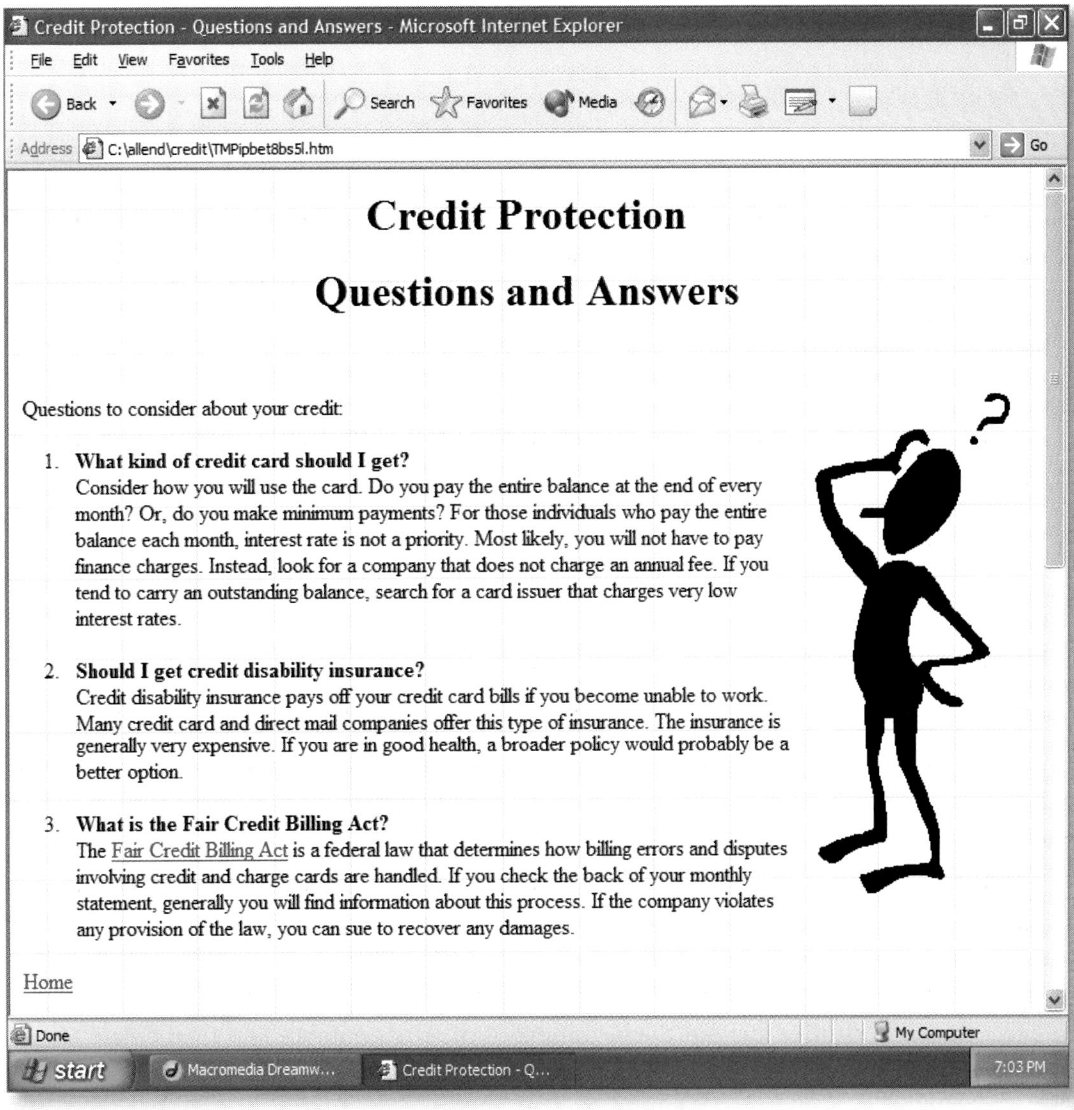

(c) Credit Protection - Questions and Answers Web Page

FIGURE 2-92 (*continued*)

Table 2-6 Image Property Settings for the Credit Protection Web Site

IMAGE NAME	W	H	V SPACE	H SPACE	ALIGN	ALT
money1.gif	174	110	None	20	Absolute Middle	Money
answer.gif	202	176	None	100	Right	Reporting options
protection.gif	240	170	14	20	Left	Identity theft
theft.gif	172	169	20	None	Right	Protect personal information
question.gif	148	366	None	15	Right	Questions?

(continued)

In the Lab

Modifying the Credit Protection Web Site *(continued)*

Instructions: Perform the following tasks:

1. Use the Windows My Computer option to copy the data files to your credit folder. The data files consist of five image files and two data files, questions.htm and theft.htm.
2. Start Dreamweaver. Display the panel groups. Select Credit Protection on the Files pop-up menu in the Files panel. Open index.htm.
3. If necessary, display the Property inspector and the Standard toolbar. Expand the Property inspector.
4. Right-click the index.htm file and set the page as the home page.
5. Position the insertion point to the right of the heading and then drag the money1.gif image to the insertion point. Select the image and then apply the settings in Table 2-6 on the previous page. Position the insertion point to the right of the text, Equifax Information Services, LLC. Drag the answer.gif image to the insertion point and then select the image. Apply the settings in Table 2-6.
6. Select the text, financial tool, located in the first sentence of the first paragraph. Create a relative link from the selected text to questions.htm. Select the name of the company in the first bulleted list item (Equifax Information Services, LLC) and create an absolute link using http://www.equifax.com. Create a link from the other two company names, using http://www.experian.com and http://www.transunion.com.
7. Position the insertion point at the end of the second paragraph. Press the SPACEBAR. Type `Credit card and identity theft can be a major issue when applying for credit.` Select the text you just typed and then create a relative link to the theft.htm file. Add an e-mail link to your name. Save the index page (Figure 2-92a on page DW 190).
8. Open theft.htm and apply the background image (creditbg.htm) to the theft.htm page.
9. Position the insertion point to the left of the second line and then drag the protection.gif image to the insertion point. Select the image. Apply the settings in Table 2-6 on the previous page. Position the insertion point after the first sentence in the second bulleted point and then drag the theft.gif image to the insertion point. Select the image. Apply the settings in Table 2-6.
10. Drag to select the text, Identity theft, at the beginning of the first sentence and then create an absolute link using http://www.consumer.gov/idtheft/ as the URL. Create an absolute link from the protection.gif image using the same URL. Select the image and then type the URL in the Link box. Select Home and then create a relative link to the index.htm page. Title the page Credit Protection - Identity Theft. Save the Theft page (Figure 2-92b on page DW 190).
11. Open questions.htm. Apply the background image that you added to the theft.htm page in Step 8. Create a relative link to the index page.
12. Position the insertion point to the right of the first line of text (Questions to consider about your credit:) and then drag the question.gif image to the insertion point. Select the image. Apply the settings in Table 2-6.
13. Create an absolute link from the Fair Credit Billing Act text in question 3. Use http://www.ftc.gov/bcp/conline/pubs/credit/fcb.htm as the URL. Title the page Credit Protection - Questions and Answers. Save the Questions page (Figure 2-92c on the previous page).
14. View the site in the Site Map. Then view the Web site in your browser and verify that your external and relative links work. ***Hint:*** Click the image on the theft.htm page. Print a copy of each page if required and hand the copies in to your instructor. Close your browser and quit Dreamweaver.

In the Lab

3 Modifying the Plant City Web Page

Problem: Juan Benito recently became a member of a marketing group promoting Plant City's strawberry history. He wants to expand the Web site you created for him by adding two new Web pages that will highlight other features of Plant City, Florida. You inform Juan that you can create the new pages. The revised Web site is displayed in Figures 2-93a, 2-93b, and 2-93c (on pages DW 193–194). Table 2-7 on the next page includes the settings and Alt text for the images. Software and hardware settings determine how a Web page displays in a browser. Your Web pages may display differently in your browser than those in the figures do.

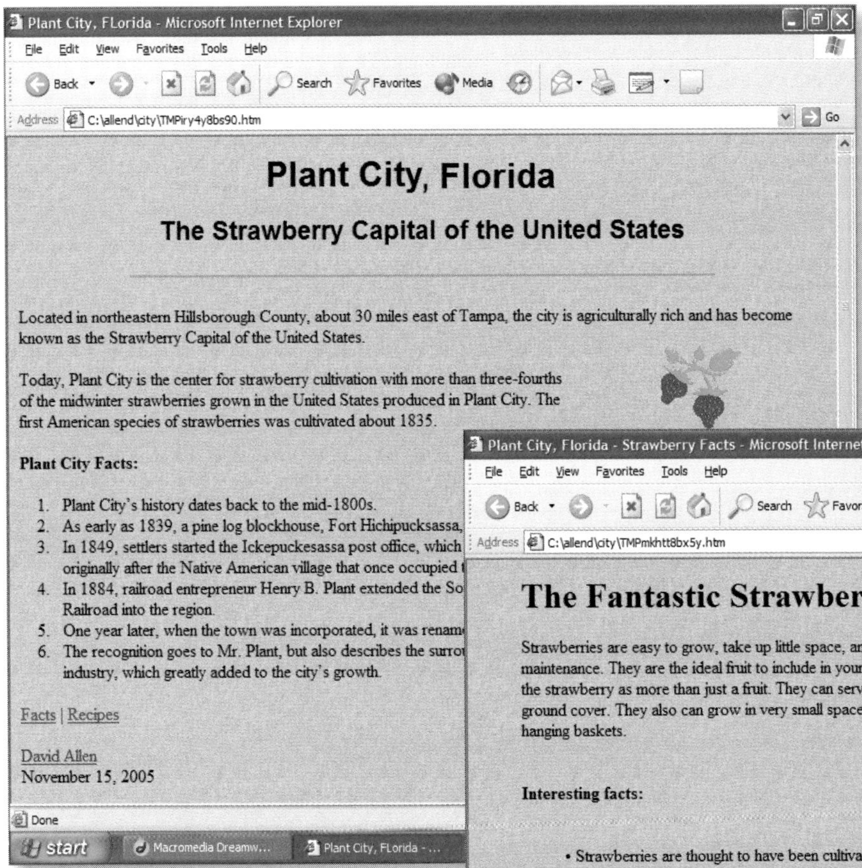

Plant City, FLorida - Microsoft Internet Explorer
File Edit View Favorites Tools Help
Back Search Favorites Media
Address C:\allend\city\TMPiry4y8bs90.htm Go
Plant City, Florida
The Strawberry Capital of the United States
Located in northeastern Hillsborough County, about 30 miles east of Tampa, the city is agriculturally rich and has become known as the Strawberry Capital of the United States.
Today, Plant City is the center for strawberry cultivation with more than three-fourths of the midwinter strawberries grown in the United States produced in Plant City. The first American species of strawberries was cultivated about 1835.
Plant City Facts:
1. Plant City's history dates back to the mid-1800s.
2. As early as 1839, a pine log blockhouse, Fort Hichipucksassa,
3. In 1849, settlers started the Ickepuckesassa post office, which
originally after the Native American village that once occupied
4. In 1884, railroad entrepreneur Henry B. Plant extended the So
Railroad into the region.
5. One year later, when the town was incorporated, it was renam
6. The recognition goes to Mr. Plant, but also describes the surro
industry, which greatly added to the city's growth.
Facts | Recipes
David Allen
November 15, 2005
Done
start Macromedia Dreamw... Plant City, FLorida - ...

(a) Plant City, Florida Index (Home) Page

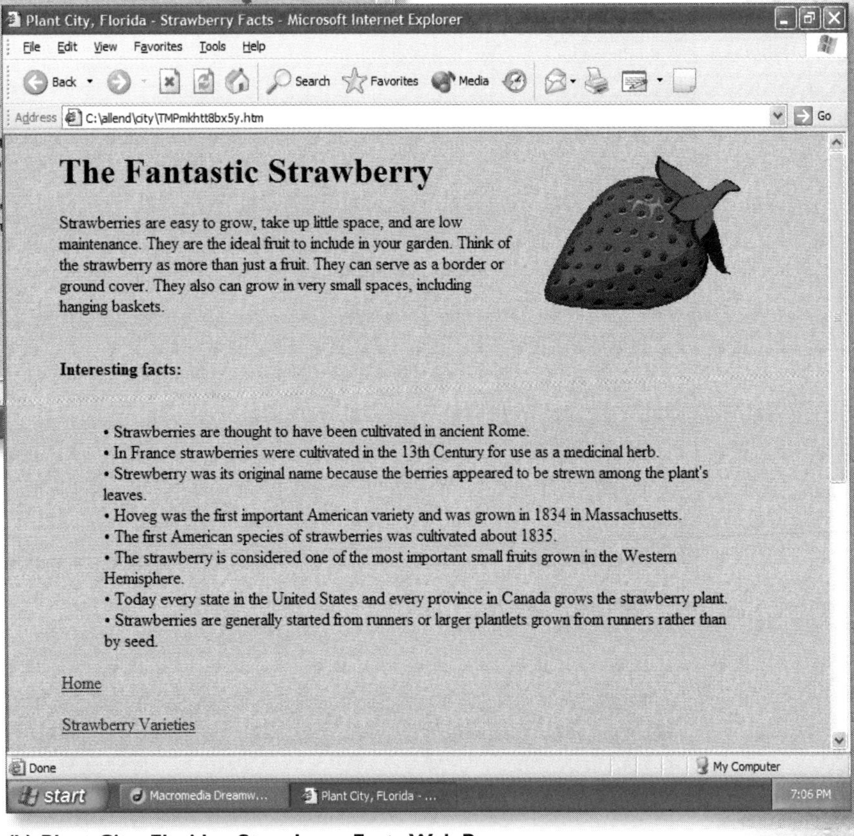

(b) Plant City, Florida - Strawberry Facts Web Page

FIGURE 2-93 (*continued*)

(continued)

In the Lab

Modifying the Plant City Web Page *(continued)*

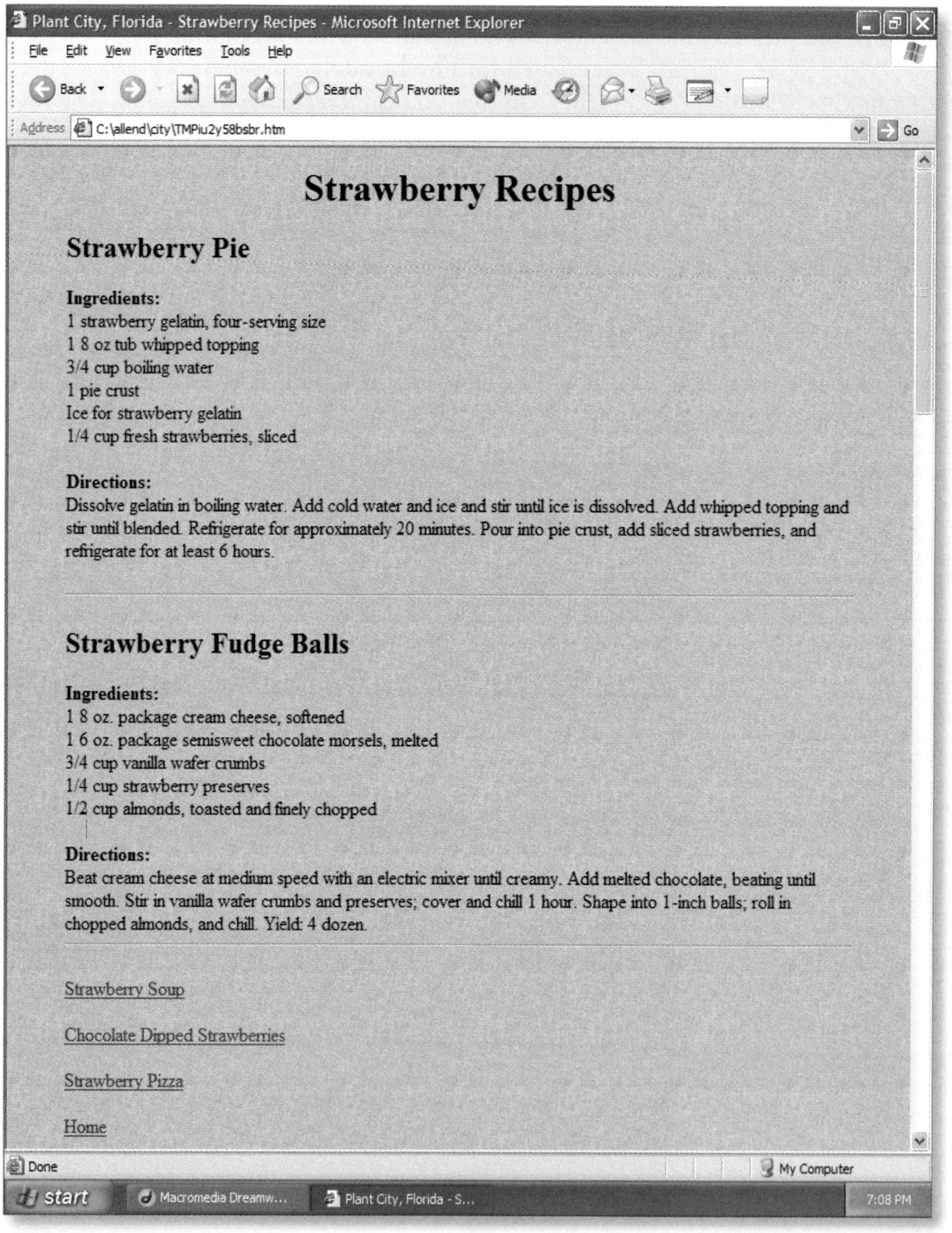

(c) Plant City, Florida - Strawberry Recipes Web Page

FIGURE 2-93 (*continued*)

Table 2-7 Image Property Settings for the Plant City Web Site

IMAGE NAME	W	H	V SPACE	H SPACE	ALIGN	ALT
strawberry01.gif	77	75	None	80	Right	Strawberry
train.gif	225	140	6	8	Right	Train
strawberry02.gif	200	145	None	25	Right	Strawberry

In the Lab

Instructions: Perform the following tasks:

1. Use the Windows My Computer option to copy the data files. The data files consist of three images and two Web pages, facts.htm and recipes.htm.
2. Start Dreamweaver. Display the panel groups. Select Plant City on the Files pop-up menu.
3. Open index.htm. If necessary, display the Property inspector and the Standard toolbar. Expand the Property inspector.
4. Select the index.htm file and set the index.htm page as the home page.
5. Position the insertion point after the last numbered item (6) on the page and then press the ENTER key. Click the Ordered List button to deselect the numbered list. Type `Facts | Recipes` as the link text.
6. Create a relative link from the text, Facts, to the facts.htm page and then create a relative link from the text, Recipes, to the recipes.htm page.
7. Position the insertion point to the right of the first line of the first paragraph and then drag the strawberry01.gif image to the insertion point. Select the image. Apply the settings in Table 2-7 on the previous page.
8. Insert the train.gif image to the right of the first numbered item. Apply the settings in Table 2-7. Insert an e-mail link. Save the index page (Figure 2-93a on page DW 193).
9. Open facts.htm and apply the citybg.gif image to the background.
10. Position the insertion point to the left of the heading and then drag the strawberry02.gif image to the insertion point. Select the image. Apply the settings in Table 2-7.
11. Scroll to the bottom of the page and then select Home. Create a relative link to the index.htm page. Click to the right of Home. Press the ENTER key and then type `Strawberry Varieties`. Select the text and create an absolute link to http://www.extension.umn.edu/extensionnews/2002/New StrawberryVarieties.html. Title the page Plant City, Florida - Strawberry Facts. Save the Facts page (Figure 2-93b on page DW 193).
12. Open recipes.htm. Apply the citybg.gif image to the background.
13. Position the insertion point at the end of the second horizontal rule and then press the ENTER key. Type the following text. Press the ENTER key after typing each line of text:
    `Strawberry Soup`
    `Chocolate Dipped Strawberries`
    `Strawberry Pizza`
    Add absolute links to these three items as follows:
    For Strawberry Soup, type `http://www.sweettechnology.com/straw1.htm` as the URL; for Chocolate Dipped Strawberries, type `http://momo.essortment.com/recipestrawberr_pwh.htm` as the URL; and for Strawberry Pizza, type `http://www.recipesource.com/main-dishes/pizza/strawberry01.html` as the URL.
14. Use a search engine and find another Web site with strawberry recipes. Select a recipe you like and make a note of the URL. Position the insertion point at the end of the text, Strawberry Pizza, and then press the ENTER key. Type the name of the recipe you selected and then create an absolute link to the Web site.
15. Create a relative link to the index page. Title the page Plant City, Florida - Strawberry Recipes. Save the Recipes page (Figure 2-93c on the previous page).
16. View the Web site in your browser and verify the links. Print a copy of each page if required and hand in the copies to your instructor. Close your browser and quit Dreamweaver.

Cases and Places

The difficulty of these case studies varies:
■ are the least difficult and ■■ are the most difficult. The last exercise is a group exercise.

1 ■ In Project 1, you created a Web site and a Web page listing your favorite sport. Now, you want to add another page to the site. Create and format the page. The page should include general information about your selected sport. Create a relative link from the home page to the new page and from the new page to the home page. Add a background image to the new page and insert an image on one of the pages. Include an appropriate title for the page. Save the page in the sports subfolder. For a selection of images and backgrounds, visit the Dreamweaver MX 2004 Media Web page (scsite.com/dreamweavermx04/media) and then click Media below Project 2.

2 ■ Several friends of yours were impressed with the Web page and Web site you created about your favorite hobby in Project 1. They have given you some topics they think you should include on the site. You decide to create an additional page that will consist of details about your hobby and the topics. Format the page. Add an absolute link to a related Web site and a relative link from the home page to the new page and from the new page to the home page. Add a background image to the new page. Create an e-mail link on the index page. Title the page the name of the selected hobby. Save the page in the hobby subfolder. For a selection of images and backgrounds, visit the Dreamweaver MX 2004 Media Web page (scsite.com/dreamweavermx04/media) and then click Media below Project 2.

3 ■■ Modify the favorite type of music Web site you created in Project 1 by creating a new page. Format the page. Discuss your favorite artist or band on the new page. Add a background image to the new page. On the index page, align the image to the right, and on the new page, align the image to the left. Position each image appropriately on the page by adding H Space and V Space. Add appropriate Alt text for each image. Add an e-mail link on the index page, and add text and a relative link from the new page to the index page. View your Web pages in your browser. Give the page a meaningful title and then save the page in your music subfolder. For a selection of images and backgrounds, visit the Dreamweaver MX 2004 Media Web page (scsite.com/dreamweavermx04/media) and then click Media below Project 2.

Cases and Places

4 ■■ In Project 1, you created a Web site and a Web page to publicize your running for office campaign. Develop two additional pages to add to the site. Apply a background image to the new pages. Apply appropriate formatting to the two new pages. Scan a picture of yourself or make a picture with a digital camera and include the picture on the index page. Add a second image illustrating one of your campaign promises. Include at least two images on one of the new pages and one image on the other new page. Add appropriate H Space and V Space to position the images, and add Alt text for all images. Create e-mail links on all three pages and create relative links from the home page to both pages and from each of the pages to the home page. Create an absolute link to a related site on one of the pages. Set the index page as the home page. Give each page a meaningful title and then save the pages in the office subfolder. For a selection of images and backgrounds, visit the Dreamweaver MX 2004 Media Web page (scsite.com/dreamweavermx04/media) and then click Media below Project 2.

5 ■■ **Working Together** The student trips Web site you and your classmates created in Project 1 is a success. Everyone loves it. The dean is so impressed that she asks the group to continue with the project. Your team creates and formats three additional Web pages, one for each of three possible locations for the trip. Add a background image to all new pages. Add two images to each of the pages, including the index page, and set the index page as the home page. Resize one of the images. Add appropriate H Space and V Space to position each image, and then add Alt text for each image. Create a link from the index page to each of the three new pages and a link from each page to the index page. Create an absolute link to a related informational Web site on each of the three new pages. Add an appropriate title to each page. Preview in a browser to verify the links. Save the pages in your trips subfolder. For a selection of images and backgrounds, visit the Dreamweaver MX 2004 Media Web page (scsite.com/ dreamweavermx04/media) and then click Media below Project 2.

MACROMEDIA
Dreamweaver MX 2004

Tables and Page Layout

PROJECT 3

CASE PERSPECTIVE

The Florida Parks Web site has been very successful thus far. David has received several e-mail messages asking for additional information about the three national parks. Joan suggests that a separate page on each park would be a good addition to the Web site. Both David and you agree this is a good idea. The two of you volunteer to research various sources and to create the content for the three new pages.

Joan further suggests that, in addition to adding the same background to these pages as that on the rest of the site, the three new pages also should have some consistency in the displayed information. The team decides that each page should include a header with the name of the park, that the information contained in the body content should describe the location and contain some interesting facts, and that each page should list the park's address, including an e-mail link. The footer will contain links to the home page and to the other two national parks pages. You all are eager to get started on this new addition to the Florida Parks Web site.

As you read through this project, you will learn how to plan and design Web pages and how to create pages using tables. You also will learn how to modify and delete tables.

MACROMEDIA
Dreamweaver MX 2004

Tables and Page Layout

PROJECT 3

Objectives

You will have mastered the material in this project when you can:

- Understand and plan page layout
- Describe Standard mode and Layout mode
- Design a Web page using tables in Standard mode
- Design a Web page using tables in Layout mode
- Describe visual guides
- Modify a table structure
- Describe HTML table tags
- Add content to a table
- Format table content
- Format a table
- Create head content

Introduction

Project 3 introduces the use of tables for page layout and the addition of head content elements. Page layout is an important part of Web design. Page layout refers to the way your page will display in the browser, which is one of the major challenges for any Web designer.

Dreamweaver's table feature is a great tool for designing a Web page. The table feature is very similar to the table feature in word processing programs such as Microsoft Word. A table allows you to add vertical and horizontal structure to a Web page. Using a table, you can put just about anything on your page and have it display in a specific location. You can lay out tabular data. You can create columns of text or navigation bars. You can delete, split, and merge rows and columns; modify table, row, or cell properties to add color and alignment; and copy and paste cells.

Dreamweaver provides two views, or ways, to use the table feature: Standard mode and Layout mode. Standard mode uses the Insert Table dialog box, and Layout mode is a free-form process in which you draw the table and the individual cells. This project discusses both views and the advantages and disadvantages of each.

The second part of the project discusses the addition and value of head content. When you create a Web page, the underlying HTML code is made up of two main sections: the head section and the body section. The body section contains the page content that displays in the browser. In Projects 1 and 2, you created your Web pages in the body section. The head section contains a variety of information. With the exception of the page title, all head content is invisible when viewed in the

Dreamweaver Document window or in a browser. Some head content is accessed by other programs, such as search engines, and some content is accessed by the browser. This project discusses the head content options and the importance of this content.

Project Three Florida Parks Page Layout —

In this project, you continue with the creation of the Florida Parks Web site. You use tables to create three new Web pages focusing on Florida's three national parks. You then add these new pages to the parks Web site and link to them from the national.htm Web page (Figures 3-1a, 3-1b, and 3-1c on pages DW 202 through 203). When you complete your Web page additions, you will add keywords and a description as the head content.

(a) Everglades National Park Page

FIGURE 3-1 (*continued*)

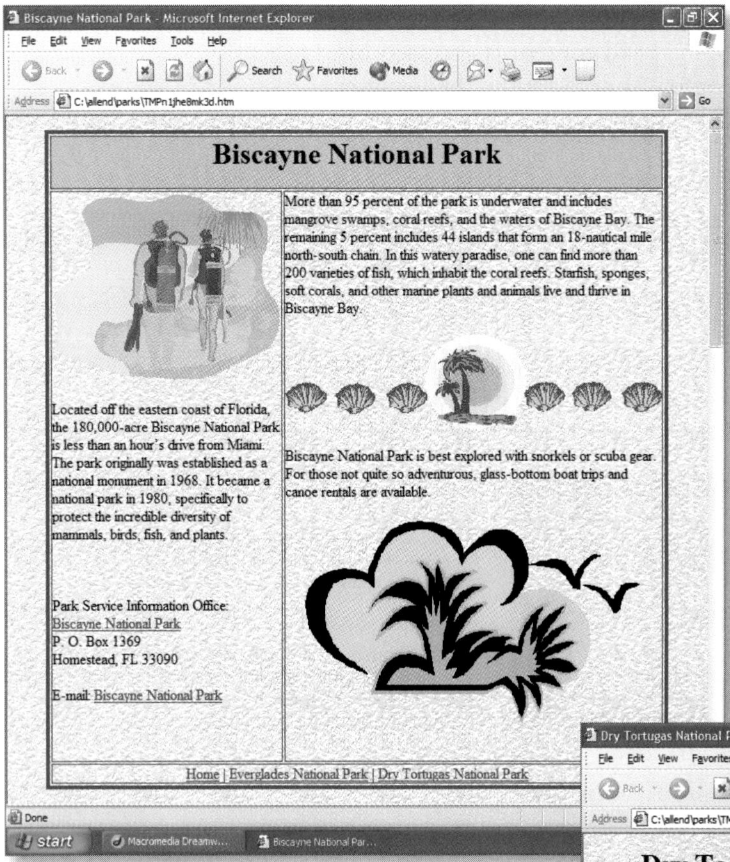
Biscayne National Park - Microsoft Internet Explorer
File Edit View Favorites Tools Help
Back Search Favorites Media
Address C:\allend\parks\TMPn1jhe8mk3d.htm
Go
Biscayne National Park
More than 95 percent of the park is underwater and includes mangrove swamps, coral reefs, and the waters of Biscayne Bay. The remaining 5 percent includes 44 islands that form an 18-nautical mile north-south chain. In this watery paradise, one can find more than 200 varieties of fish, which inhabit the coral reefs. Starfish, sponges, soft corals, and other marine plants and animals live and thrive in Biscayne Bay.
Located off the eastern coast of Florida, the 180,000-acre Biscayne National Park is less than an hour's drive from Miami. The park originally was established as a national monument in 1968. It became a national park in 1980, specifically to protect the incredible diversity of mammals, birds, fish, and plants.
Biscayne National Park is best explored with snorkels or scuba gear. For those not quite so adventurous, glass-bottom boat trips and canoe rentals are available.
Park Service Information Office:
Biscayne National Park
P. O. Box 1369
Homestead, FL 33090
E-mail: Biscayne National Park
Home | Everglades National Park | Dry Tortugas National Park
Done
start
Macromedia Dreamw...
Biscayne National Par...

(b) Biscayne National Park Page

Dry Tortugas National Park - Microsoft Internet Explorer
File Edit View Favorites Tools Help
Back Search Favorites Media
Address C:\allend\parks\TMPp1vpj8sk2h.htm
Go
Dry Tortugas National Park
The Dry Tortugas National Park is located about 70 nautical miles west of Key West, Florida. This cluster of seven coral reefs and sand islands, along with surrounding shoals and waters, make up the Dry Tortugas National Park. Ponce de Leon discovered these islands in 1513. He named them Dry Tortugas for their absence of fresh water and abundance of tortoises.
Dominating the Garden Key Island is Fort Jefferson. This fort is the largest of the nineteenth-century American coastal forts. Fort Jefferson's construction began on Garden Key in 1846 and continued for 30 years, but was never finished.
In 1935, President Franklin D. Roosevelt declared Fort Jefferson and the surrounding waters a national monument. In 1992, the area was designated as the Dry Tortugas National Park to protect the natural and historical qualities. Dry Tortugas is one of the country's more inaccessible national parks. Of the park's 64,657 acres, 99 percent is water and submerged islands.
Park Service Information Office
Dry Tortugas National Park
P. O. Box 6208
Key West, FL 33041
E-mail: Dry Tortugas National Park
Home | Everglades National Park | Biscayne National Park
Done
My Computer
start
Macromedia Dreamw...
Dry Tortugas Nationa...
8:31 PM

(c) Dry Tortugas National Park Page

FIGURE 3-1

This project uses a hierarchical structure. The structure now is expanded to include the three new pages (Figure 3-2).

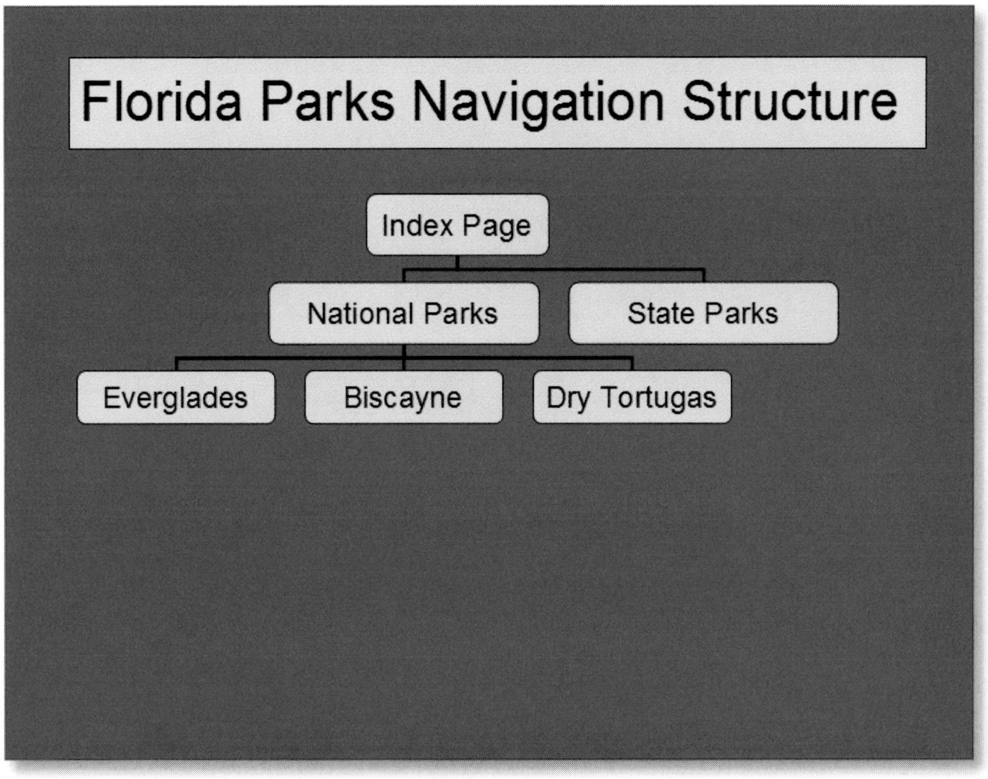

FIGURE 3-2

Understanding and Planning Page Layout

Page layout is the process of arranging the text, images, and other elements on the page. The basic rules of page layout are that your site should be easy to navigate, easy to read, and quick to download. Studies indicate that visitors will lose interest quickly in your Web site if the majority of a page does not download within 15 seconds. One popular design element that downloads quickly is tables.

Tables download very fast because they are created with HTML code. They can be used anywhere — for the home page, menus, images, navigation bars, frames, and so on. Tables originally were intended for use in presenting data arranged by rows and columns, such as tabular data within a spreadsheet. Web designers, however, quickly seized upon the use of tables to produce specific layout effects. You can produce good designs by using tables creatively. Tables provide the ability to position elements on a Web page with much greater accuracy. Using tables for layout provides the Web page author with endless design possibilities.

A typical Web page is composed of three sections: the header, the body, and the footer (Figure 3-3). The **header**, generally located at the top of the page, can contain logos, images, or text that identifies the Web site. The header also may contain hyperlinks to other pages within the Web site.

The **body** of the Web page contains informational content about your site. This content may be in the form of text, graphics, animation, video, and audio.

The **footer** provides hyperlinks for contact information. Many Web designers also include navigational controls in the footer. This may be in addition to the navigation controls in the header. Other common items contained within a footer are the name and e-mail address of the author or of the Webmaster. Sometimes, hyperlinks to other resources or to Help information are part of the footer. A typical Web page structure is displayed in Figure 3-3.

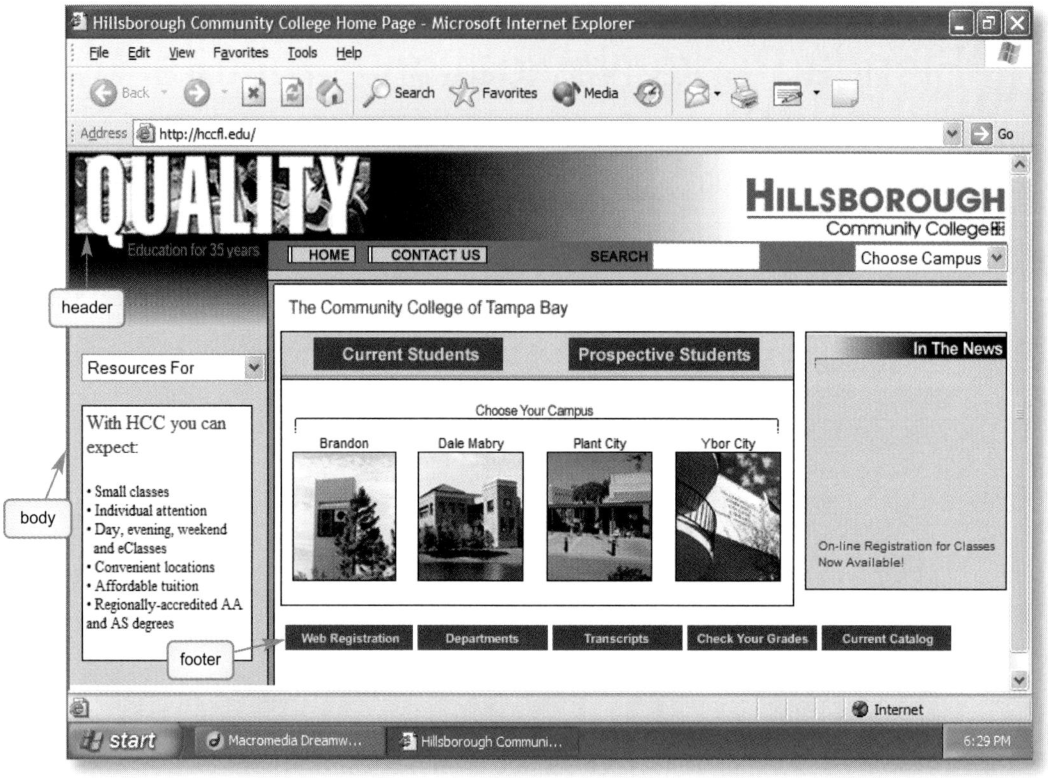

FIGURE 3-3

It is easy to create this header/body/footer structure with tables or to create any other layout structure applicable to your specific Web page needs. The entire structure can be contained within one table or a combination of multiple and nested tables. You will use a structure similar to that in Figure 3-3 to create the three new pages for the Florida Parks Web site.

Standard Mode and Layout Mode

Dreamweaver provides two options for creating tables: Standard mode and Layout mode. In **Standard mode**, a table is presented as a grid of rows and columns. This view is similar to a Microsoft Excel spreadsheet or a table created in a word processing program such as Microsoft Word. In **Layout mode**, you can draw, resize, and move boxes on the page while Dreamweaver still uses tables for the underlying structure. If you have used a desktop publishing program such as Microsoft Publisher or Adobe PageMaker, then you are familiar with the format in which layout tables are created. Using Layout mode, you can place content at any location in the Document window.

Copying Data Files to the Local Web Site

Your Data Disk contains images for Project 3. These images are in an images folder. You use the Windows My Computer option to copy the Project 3 images to your parks images folder. See the inside back cover for instructions for downloading the Data Disk or see your instructor for information about accessing the files required for this book.

The DataFiles folder for this project is stored on Local Disk (C:). The location on your computer may be different. If necessary, verify with your instructor the location of the DataFiles folder. The following steps illustrate how to copy the files to the parks local root folder.

To Copy Data Files to the Parks Web Site

1. **Click the Start button on the Windows taskbar and then click My Computer.**
2. **Double-click Local Disk (C:) and then navigate to the location of the data files for Project 3.**
3. **Double-click the DataFiles folder and then double-click the Proj03 folder.**
4. **Double-click the parks folder and then double-click the images folder.**
5. **Click the birds.gif image file or the first file name in the list.**
6. **Hold down the SHIFT key and then click the turtle.jpg image file (or the last file name in the list) to select the ten image files.**
7. **Right-click the selected files to display the context menu.**
8. **Click the Copy command and then click the My Computer Back button the number of times necessary to navigate to the your name folder.**
9. **Double-click the your name folder, double-click the parks folder, and then double-click the images folder.**
10. **Right-click anywhere in the open window to display the context menu, and then click Paste (Figure 3-4).**
11. **Click the images window Close button.**

The 10 new image files are pasted into the Florida Parks Web site images folder (Figure 3-4).

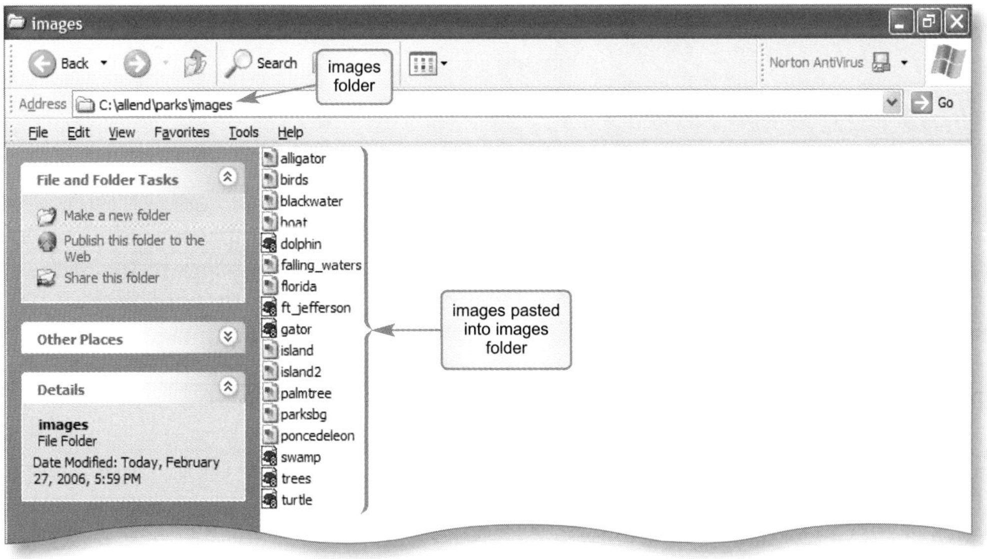

FIGURE 3-4

Starting Dreamweaver and Opening a Web Site

Each time you start Dreamweaver, it opens to the last site displayed when you closed the program. It, therefore, may be necessary for you to open the parks Web site. The **Files pop-up menu** in the Files panel lists sites you have defined. When you open the site, a list of pages and subfolders within the site displays. The following steps show how to start Dreamweaver and open the Florida Parks Web site.

To Start Dreamweaver and Open the Florida Parks Web Site

1. **Click the Start button on the Windows taskbar.**
2. **Point to All Programs on the Start menu, point to Macromedia on the All Programs submenu, and then click Macromedia Dreamweaver MX 2004 on the Macromedia submenu.**
3. **Click the Files panel box arrow and point to Florida Parks on the Files panel pop-up menu.**
4. **Click Florida Parks.**

The Florida Parks Web site hierarchy displays in the Files panel (Figure 3-5).

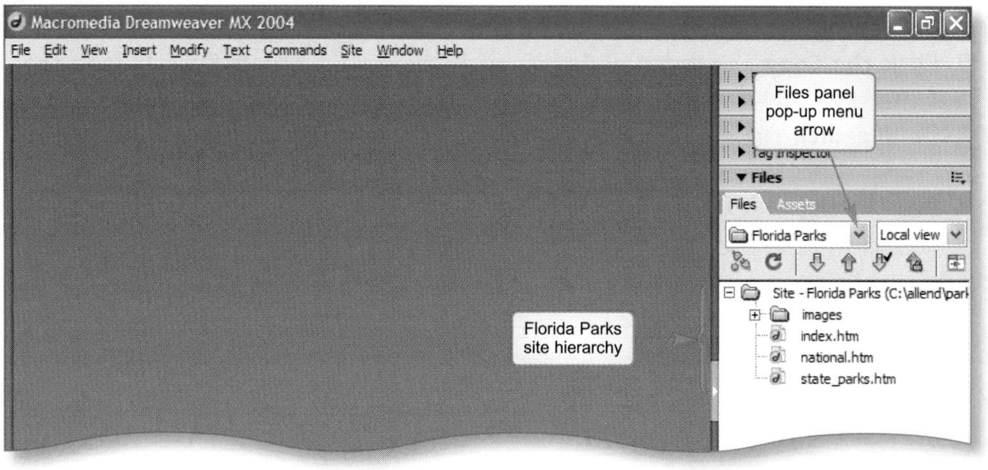

FIGURE 3-5

Adding Pages to a Web Site

You copied the images necessary to begin creating your new Web pages to the parks local root folder in the Files panel. You will add three additional pages to the Web site: Everglades, Biscayne, and Dry Tortugas national parks. You first create the Everglades National Park Web page. You then add the background image and a heading to the new page. Next, you use Dreamweaver's Standard mode to insert tables and add text, images, and links into the cells within the table.

Opening a New Document Window

The next step is to open a new Document window. This will become the Everglades National Park page. The following steps illustrate how into open a new Document window and save the page as everglades.

To Open a New Document Window

1. **Click File on the menu bar and then point to New.**
2. **Click New. If necessary, click the General tab and then click Basic page in the Category list.**
3. **If necessary, click HTML in the Basic page list.**
4. **Click the Create button.**
5. **Click the Save button on the Standard toolbar.**
6. **Type** `everglades` **as the file name. If necessary, select the parks folder, and then click the Save button.**

The everglades.htm page is saved in the parks local folder and displays in Dreamweaver's Files panel. The path and file name (parks/everglades.htm) appear on the Dreamweaver title bar (Figure 3-6).

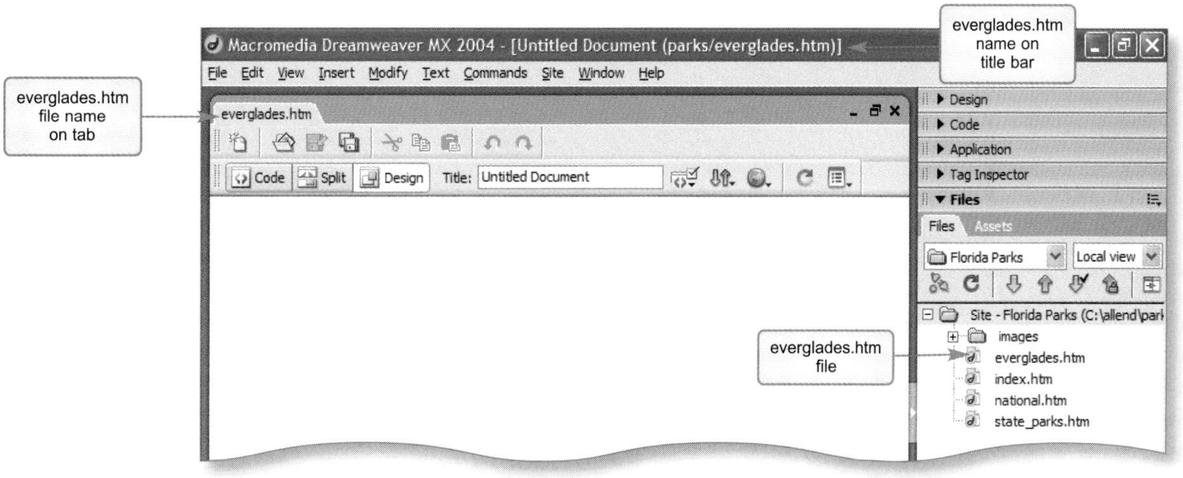

FIGURE 3-6

Creating the Everglades National Park Web Page

You start creating the Everglades National Park page by applying a background image. This is the same background image you used for the Florida Parks Web site pages in Projects 1 and 2. To provide additional space in the Document window, you hide the panel groups. You expand the Property inspector to display the additional table options. The following steps illustrate how to apply the background image.

To Add a Background Image to the Everglades National Park Web Page

1. **Click the panel groups expand/collapse arrow to hide the panel groups.**
2. **If necessary, click the Property inspector expander arrow to display both the top and lower sections.**
3. **Click Modify on the menu bar and then click Page Properties.**
4. **Click the Browse button to the right of the Background image box.**
5. **If necessary, navigate to the parks\images folder.**

6 Click parksbg.gif and then click the OK button in the Select Image Source dialog box.

7 Click the OK button in the Page Properties dialog box.

The background image is applied to the Everglades National Park page. The panel groups is hidden, and the Property inspector is expanded. The insertion point is aligned at the left (Figure 3-7).

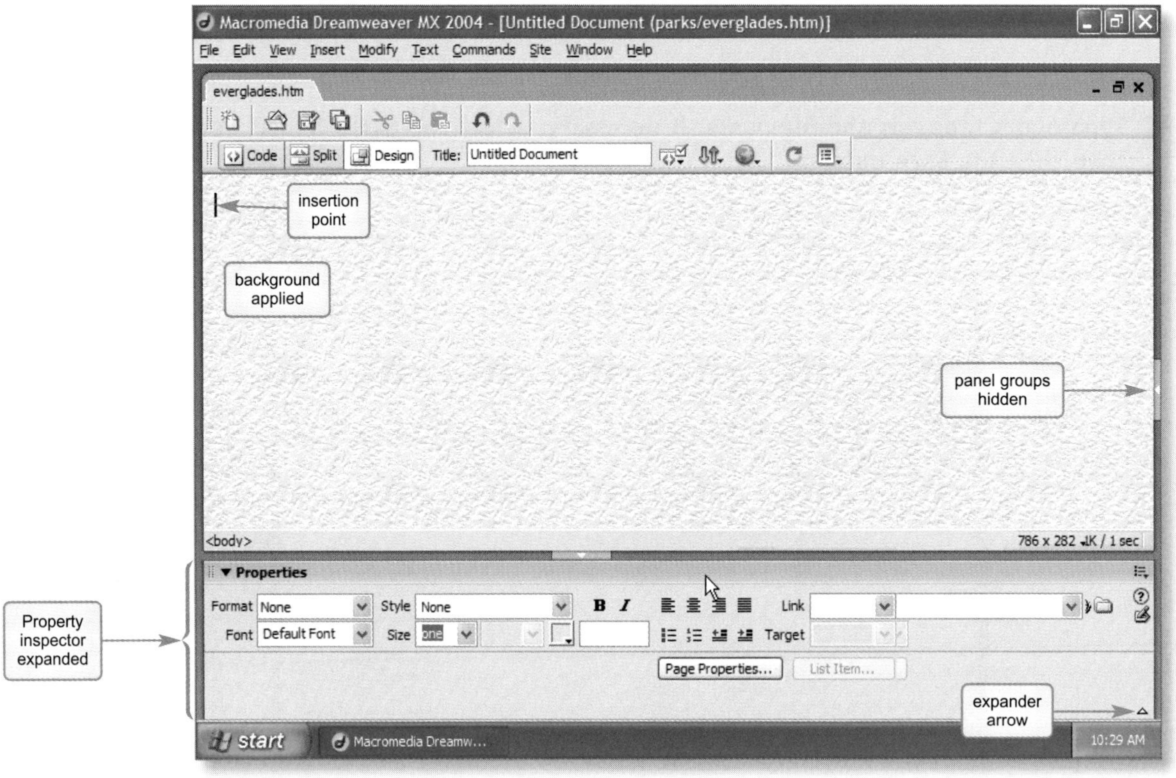

FIGURE 3-7

Next, you add and format the heading. The following steps show how to add the heading and apply the Heading 1 format.

To Insert and Format the Heading

1 Click the Document window. Type `Everglades National Park` **as the heading.**

2 Apply Heading 1, click the Align Center button in the Property inspector, and then press the ENTER key.

3 Click the Align Left button.

4 Title the page Everglades National Park.

5 Click the Save button on the Standard toolbar.

The heading is centered and formatted, and the title is added (Figure 3-8).

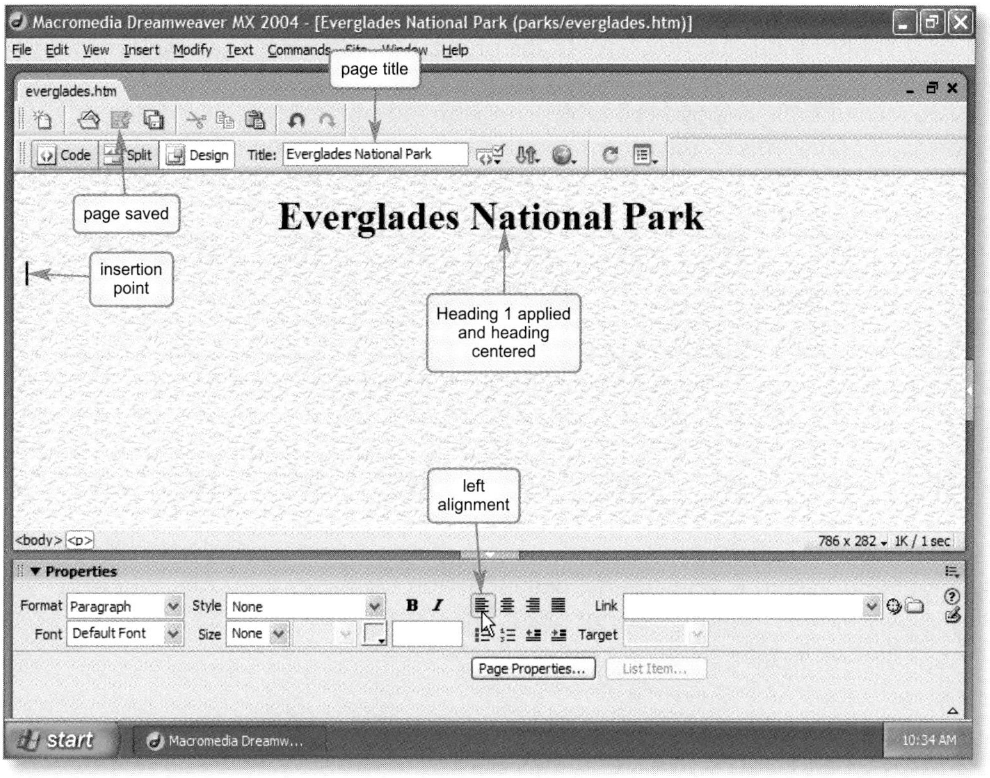

FIGURE 3-8

Understanding Tables

Tables have many uses in HTML design. The most obvious is a table of data, but, as already mentioned, tables also are used for page layout, such as to place text and graphics on a page at just the right location. Tables provide Web designers with a method to add vertical and horizontal structure to a page. A **table** consists of three basic components: rows, columns, and cells. A **row** is a horizontal collection of cells, and a **column** is a vertical collection of cells. A **cell** is the container created when the row and column intersect. Each cell within the table can contain any standard element you use on a Web page. This includes text, images, and other objects.

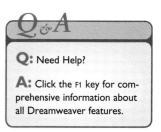

> *Q&A*
>
> **Q:** Need Help?
>
> **A:** Click the F1 key for comprehensive information about all Dreamweaver features.

Inserting a Table into the Everglades National Park Page

You will add two tables to the Everglades National Park page and then add text and images to the cells within the tables. The first table will consist of three rows and two columns with a cell padding of 2 and cell spacing of 20. The border is set to 0. When the table displays in Dreamweaver, a border outline is displayed around the table. When the table's border is set to 0 and the table is viewed in a browser, however, this outline does not display.

The table width is 90 percent. When specifying the width, you can select percent or pixels. A table with the width specified as a **percent** expands with the width of the window and monitor size in which it is being viewed. A table with the width specified as **pixels** will remain the same size regardless of the window and monitor size. If you select percent and an image is larger than the selected percent, the cell and table will expand to accommodate the image. Likewise, if the **No Wrap** property is enabled and the text will not fit within the cell, the cell and table will expand to accommodate the text. It is not necessary to declare a table width. When no value is specified, the table is displayed as small as possible and then expands as content is added. If modifications are necessary to the original specified table values, these values can be changed in the Property inspector.

The second table is a one-cell table, consisting of one row and one column. This table will contain links to the Home page and to the other two national parks pages. You use the Insert bar with the Layout category and the Property inspector to control and format the tables.

The Insert Bar

The Insert bar is considered to be a panel, but is quite different from other Dreamweaver panels. It displays at the top of the window below the menu bar. This panel group contains buttons for creating and inserting objects such as tables, layers, and images. The Insert bar contains eight separate categories, and is fully customizable through the Favorites category. When the current document contains server-side code, additional categories display.

Some categories have buttons with pop-up menus. When you select an option from a pop-up menu, it becomes the default action for the button. Any time you select a new option from the pop-up menu, the default action for the button changes. You can hide or display the Insert bar as necessary.

Category Types

The default Insert bar contains the following categories:

COMMON CATEGORY The **Common category** contains buttons for the most frequently used Web publishing tasks.

LAYOUT CATEGORY The **Layout category** contains buttons pertaining to the design modes for Web publishing and enables you to insert tables, div tags, layers, and frames. You also can choose from among three table modes: Standard (default), Expanded Tables, and Layout. When you select Layout mode, you can use the Dreamweaver layout tools: Draw Layout Cell and Layout Table.

FORMS CATEGORY The **Forms category** contains buttons for creating forms and inserting form elements.

TEXT CATEGORY The **Text category** contains buttons for text formatting.

HTML CATEGORY The **HTML category** contains buttons related to HTML code for head content, horizontal rules, tables, scripts, and frames.

SERVER-CODE CATEGORIES **Server-code categories** display only for pages that use a particular server language, including ASP, ASP.NET, CFML Basic, CFML Flow, CFML Advanced, JSP, and PHP. Each of these categories provides server-code objects that you can insert in Code view.

APPLICATION CATEGORY The **Application category** contains buttons relating to records, dynamic data, and other database elements.

FLASH ELEMENTS CATEGORY The **Flash elements** category contains a button allowing you to insert Flash elements.

FAVORITES CATEGORY The **Favorites category** enables you to group and organize the Insert bar buttons you use the most in one common place.

You use the Layout category to assist with the page design and insert tables. The following steps illustrate how to display the Insert bar and select the Layout category.

To Display the Insert Bar and Select the Layout Category

1

- **If necessary, click Window on the menu bar and then point to Insert.**

The Window menu is displayed, and the Insert command is highlighted (Figure 3-9).

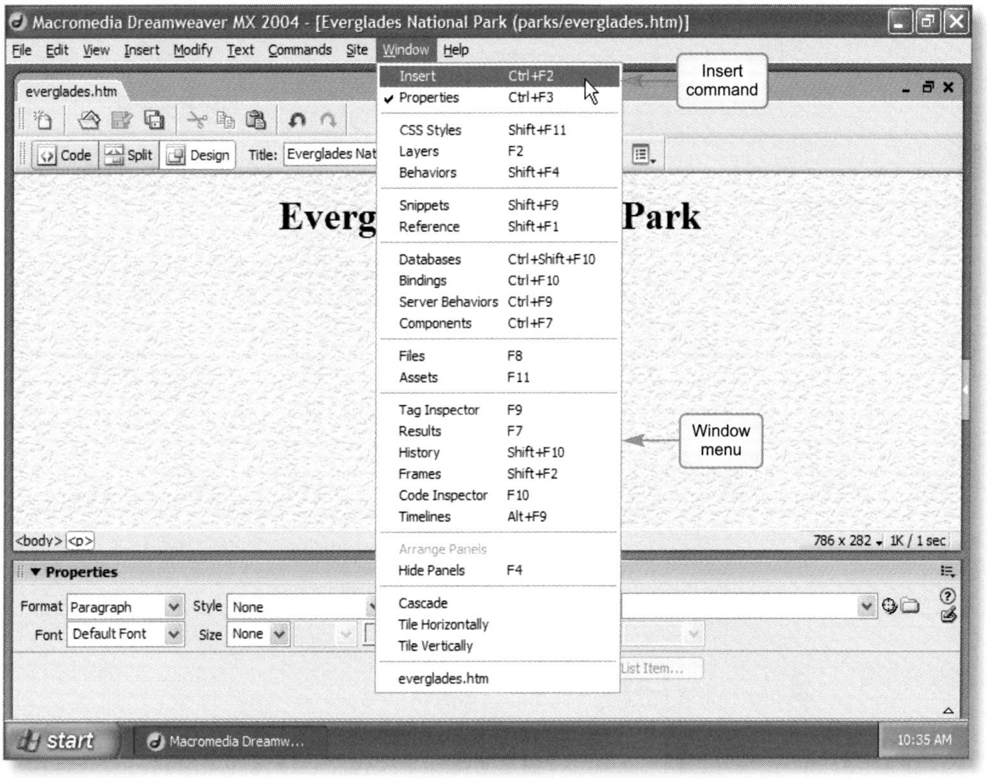

FIGURE 3-9

2

- **Click the Insert command.**

The Insert bar is displayed at the top of the screen below the menu bar and the Common category also is displayed (Figure 3-10). The category last displayed becomes the default category, so your screen may display a different category.

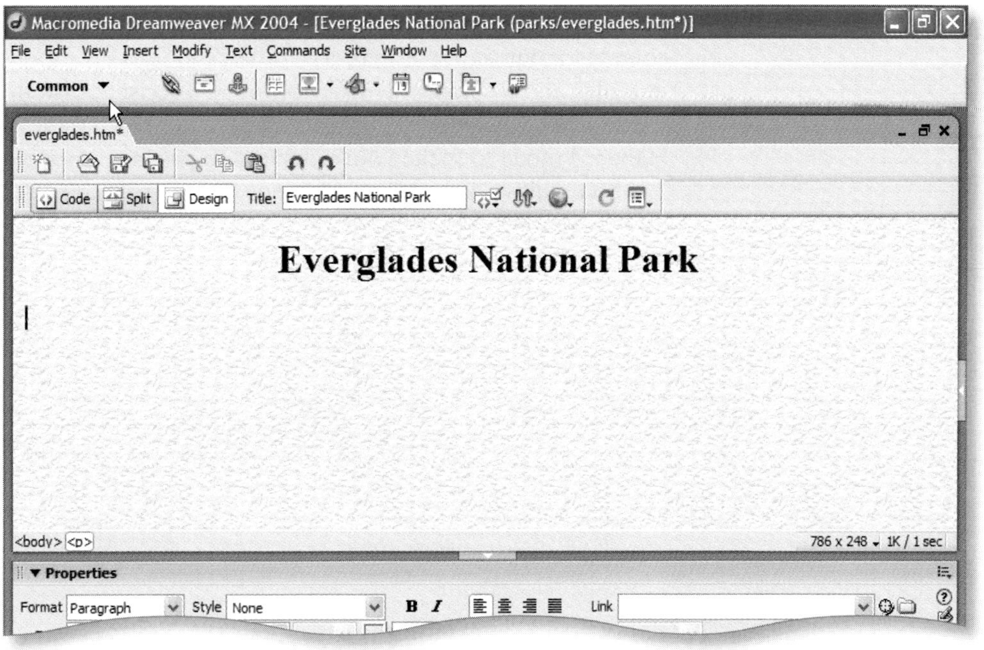

FIGURE 3-10

3

• **Click the arrow to the right of the Common category, and then point to Layout on the Common category pop-up menu.**

The Common category pop-up menu is displayed (Figure 3-11).

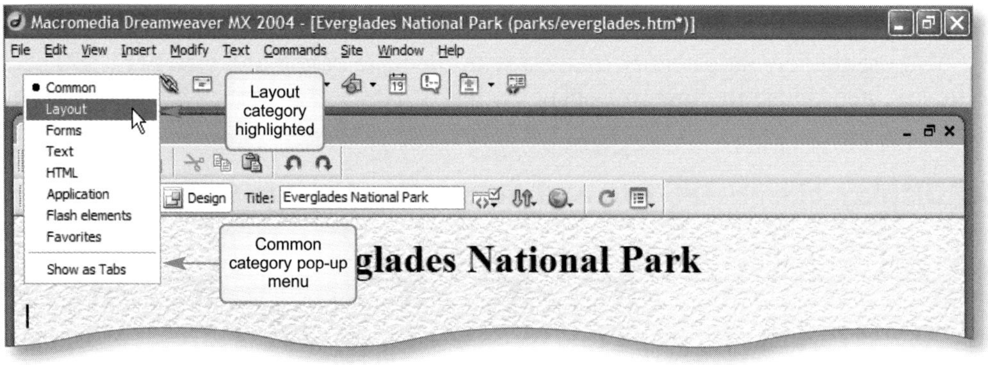

FIGURE 3-11

4

• **Click the Layout command.**

The Layout category is displayed (Figure 3-12).

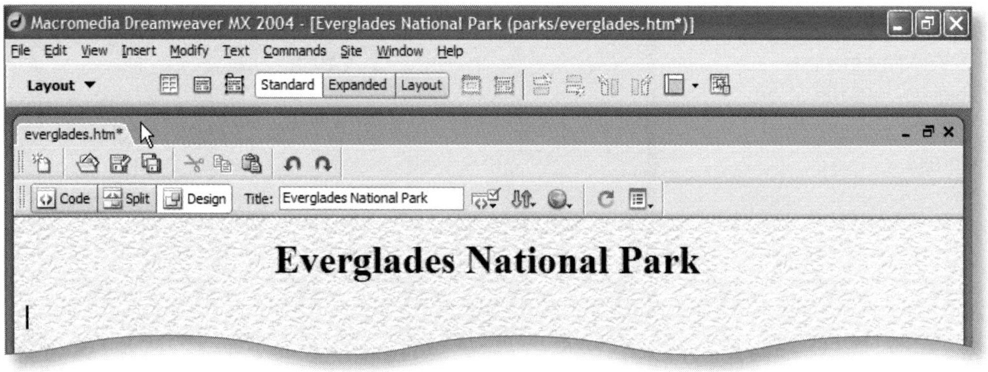

FIGURE 3-12

Layout Category

The Layout category (Figure 3-13) enables you to work with tables and layers. Dreamweaver provides two ways to create tables — Standard mode and Layout mode. In Standard mode, a table displays as a grid and expands as you add text and images. You define the structure of the table using the Insert Table dialog box. In Layout mode, you create tables and cells by drawing them. The Layout category also contains a button for Expanded Tables mode. This mode enables you to select items in tables and to place the insertion point precisely. Use this mode as a temporary visual aid for insertion point placement. After placing the insertion point, return to Standard mode to make your edits and to provide a better visualization of your changes.

You will work with Layout mode later in this project. Table 3-1 on the next page lists the button names and descriptions available in the Insert bar Layout category.

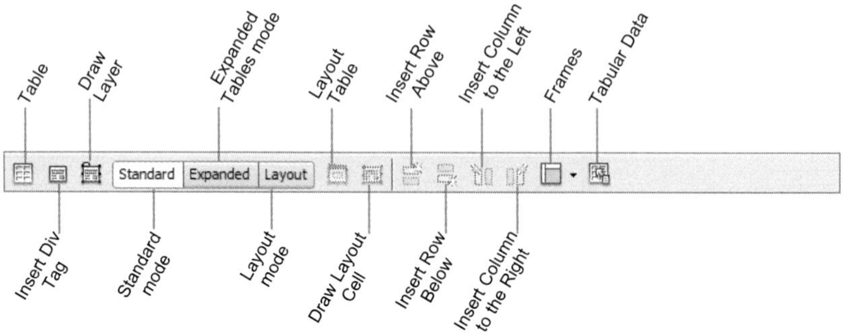

FIGURE 3-13

Table 3-1 Buttons on the Layout Insert Bar

BUTTON NAME	DESCRIPTION
Table	Places a table at the insertion point
Insert Div Tag	Inserts a <div> tag
Draw Layer	Creates a layer
Standard mode	Displays a table as a grid of lines
Expanded Tables mode	Temporarily adds cell padding and spacing
Layout mode	Displays a table as boxes that can be drawn, dragged, and resized
Layout Table	Used to draw a layout table in the Design view of the Document window
Draw Layout Cell	Used to draw individual table cells in the Design view of the Document window
Insert Row Above	Used to insert a row above the selected row
Insert Row Below	Used to insert a row below the selected row
Insert Column to the Left	Used to insert a column to the left of the selected column
Insert Column to the Right	Used to insert a column to the right of the selected column
Frames	Displays Frames pop-up menu
Tabular Data	Import tabular data

More About

Dreamweaver Table Views

For more information about Dreamweaver MX 2004 table views, visit the Dreamweaver MX 2004 More About Web page (scsite.com/dreamweavermx04/more.htm) and then click Dreamweaver MX 2004 Tables.

Table Defaults and Accessibility

When you insert a table, the Table dialog box displays and contains default settings for each of the table attributes. The Table dialog box in Figure 3-14 contains the values shown in Table 3-2 on the next page. After you have created a table, however, and made changes to these defaults, the settings displayed are the settings from the last table created.

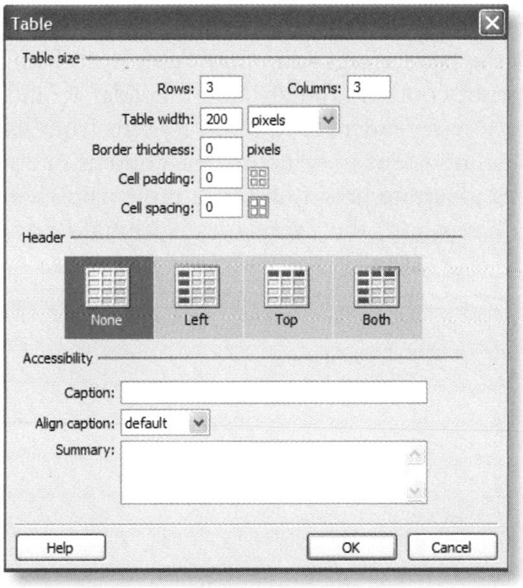

FIGURE 3-14

Table 3-2 Table Dialog Box Default Values

ATTRIBUTE	DEFAULT	DESCRIPTION
Rows	3	Determines the number of rows in the table
Columns	3	Determines the number of columns in the table
Table width	200 pixels	Specifies the width of the table as a percentage of the browser window's width or in pixels
Border	0 pixels	Specifies the border width in pixels or percent
Cell padding	0	Specifies the number of pixels between a cell's border and its contents
Cell spacing	0	Specifies the number of pixels between adjacent table cells
Header	None	Specifies if the top row and/or column is designated as a header cell
Caption	None	Provides a brief description of the table
Align caption	default	Specifies where the table caption appears in relation to the table
Summary	None	Provides a table description; used by screen readers

Q&A

Q: What is the Web site address for Macromedia online support?

A: You can find Macromedia online support at www. macromedia. com/support/ dreamweaver/.

It is advisable to use headers for tables when the table presents tabular information. Screen readers read table headings and help screen-reader users keep track of table information. Additionally, the Caption option provides a table title that displays outside of the table, the Align caption option specifies where the table caption appears in relation to the table, and the Summary option provides a table description. Screen readers read the summary text, but the text does not appear in the user's browser. Summary text is similar to the Alt text you added for images in Project 2.

Standard Mode

When using a table for layout, however, other options apply. Structurally and graphically, the elements in a table used for layout should be invisible in the browser. For instance, when using a table for layout, use the None option for headers. The None option prevents the header tags <th> and <\th> from being added to the table. Because the table does not contain tabular data, a header would be of no benefit to the screen-reader user. Screen readers read table content from left to right and top to bottom. It, therefore, is important to structure the content in a linear arrangement.

The following steps illustrate how to insert a table using Standard mode with three rows and two columns into the Everglades National Park Web page.

To Insert a Table Using Standard Mode

1

- **Click the Standard button on the Insert bar and then click the Table button.**

The Table dialog box is displayed (Figure 3-15). The settings displayed are the default settings from the last table created, so your dialog box may contain different values.

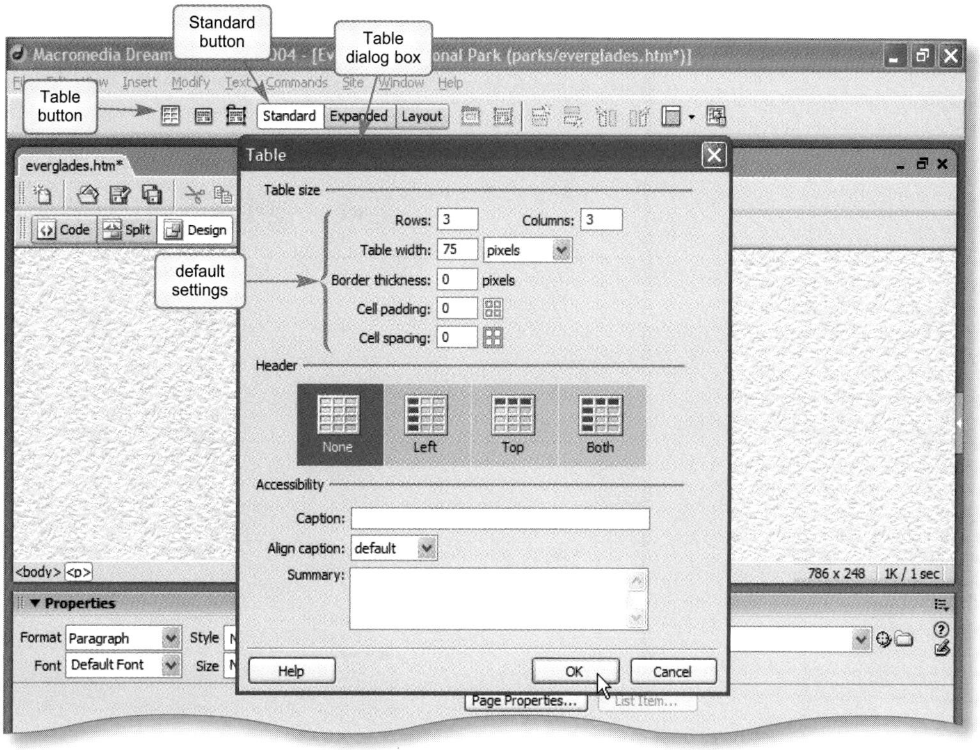

FIGURE 3-15

2

- **If necessary, type** 3 **and then press the** TAB **key to move to the Columns box.**
- **Type** 2 **as the new value in the Columns box and then press the** TAB **key.**
- **Type** 90 **as the new value in the Table width box and then click the Table width arrow.**
- **Select percent and then press the** TAB **key.**
- **Type** 0 **in the Border thickness box and then press the** TAB **key.**
- **Type** 2 **in the Cell padding box and then press the** TAB **key.**
- **Type** 20 **in the Cell spacing box and then press the** TAB **key.**
- **If necessary, select None for the Header.**
- **Click the Summary text box and type** `Table layout for Everglades National Park Web page. The table contains three rows and two columns with images and text in the table cells.`

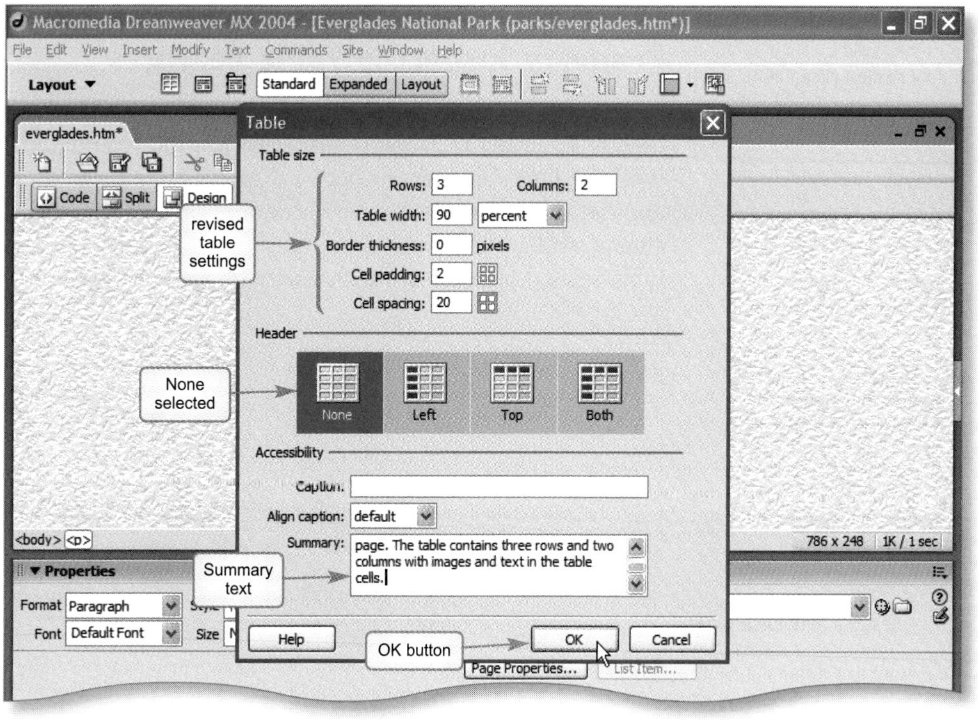

FIGURE 3-16

The Table dialog box displays with the new settings, as shown in Figure 3-16.

3

• **Click the OK button.**

The table is inserted into the Document window (Figure 3-17). The dark border around the table and the three handles on the lower and right borders indicate the table is selected. The <table> tag displays as highlighted in the tag selector, also indicating the table is selected. The cell spacing between each cell is 20 pixels. The default alignment for the table is left. The border is set to 0 and displays as an outline when the table is viewed in Dreamweaver. When the table is viewed in a browser, however, no border is displayed.

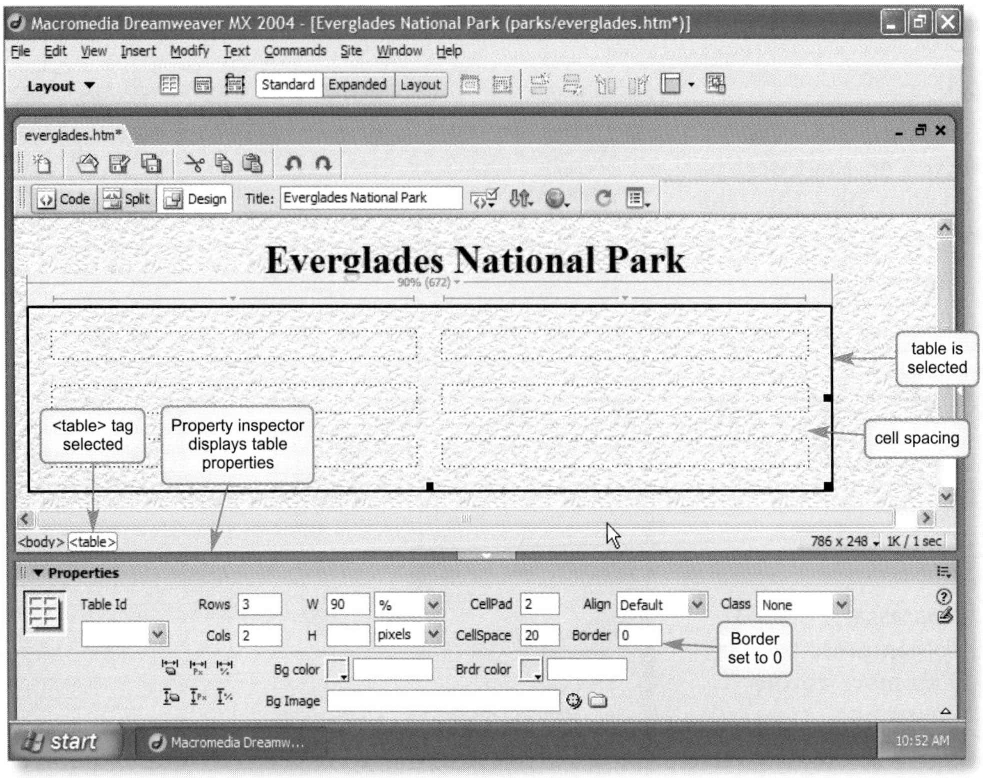

FIGURE 3-17

Other Ways

1. On Insert menu click Table, select table properties, click OK button
2. Press CTRL+ALT+T

Property Inspector Table Features

As you have seen, the Property inspector options change depending on the selected object. You use the Property inspector to modify and add table attributes. When a table is selected, the Property inspector displays table properties in both panels. When another table element — a row, column, or cell — is selected, the displayed properties change and are determined by the selected element. The following section describes the table-related features of the Property inspector shown in Figure 3-18.

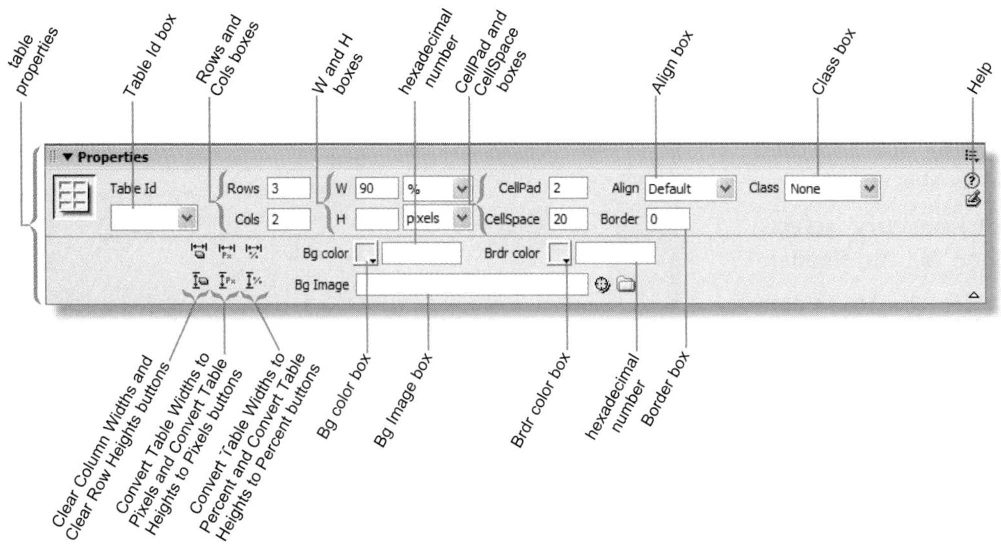

FIGURE 3-18

TABLE ID An identifier used for Cascading Style Sheets, scripting, and accessibility. A table ID does not need to be assigned.

ROWS AND COLS The number of rows and columns in the table.

W Used to specify the minimum width of the table in either pixels or percent. If a size is not specified, the size can vary depending on the monitor and browser settings. A table width specified in pixels is displayed at the same size in all browsers. A table width specified in percent is altered in appearance based on the user's monitor resolution and browser window size.

H Used to specify the height of the table in either pixels or percent. Generally, the height of a table consists of the height of the collective rows and is not specified.

CELLPAD The number of pixels between the cell border and the cell content.

CELLSPACE The number of pixels between adjacent table cells.

ALIGN Determines where the table appears, relative to other elements in the same paragraph, such as text or images. The default alignment is to the left.

BORDER Specifies the border width in pixels.

CLEAR COLUMN WIDTHS AND CLEAR ROW HEIGHTS Deletes all specified row height or column width values from the table.

CONVERT TABLE WIDTHS TO PIXELS AND CONVERT TABLE HEIGHTS TO PIXELS Sets the width or height of each column in the table to its current width expressed as pixels.

CONVERT TABLE WIDTHS TO PERCENT AND CONVERT TABLE HEIGHTS TO PERCENT Sets the width or height of each column in the table to its current width expressed as a percentage of the Document window's width and also sets the width of the whole table to its current width as a percentage of the Document window's width.

BG COLOR The table background color.

BRDR COLOR The table border color.

BG IMAGE The table background image.

CLASS An attribute used with Cascading Style Sheets.

Cell, Row, and Column Properties

When a cell, row, or column is selected, the properties in the upper pane of the Property inspector are the same as the standard ones for text. You can use these properties to incorporate standard HTML formatting tags within a cell, row, or column. The part of the table selected determines which properties display in the lower pane of the Property inspector. The properties for all three features (cell, row, and column) are the same, except for one element—the icon displayed in the lower-left pane of the Property inspector. The section beginning on the next page describes the row-related features (Figure 3-19), cell-related features (Figure 3-20), and column-related features (Figure 3-21) of the Property inspector.

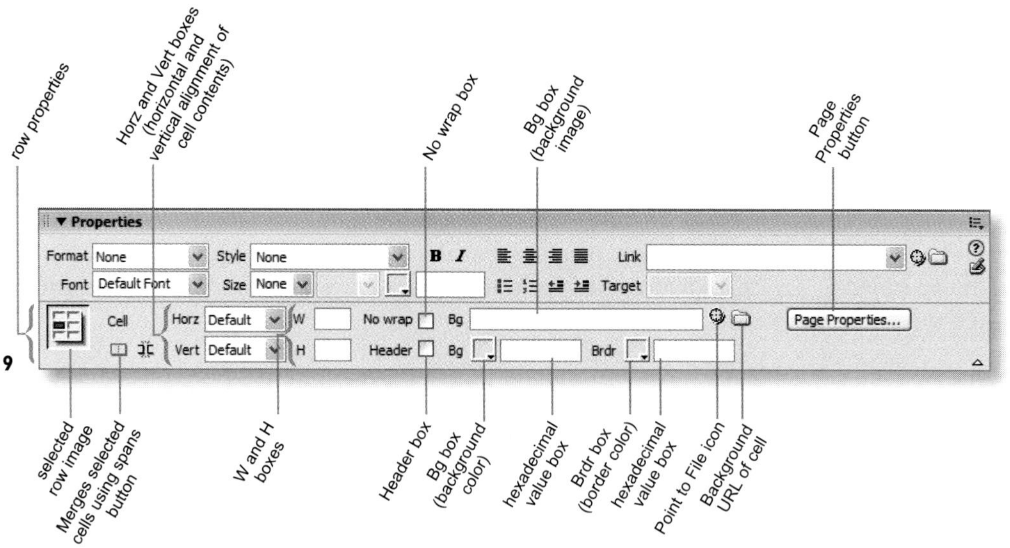

FIGURE 3-19

FIGURE 3-20

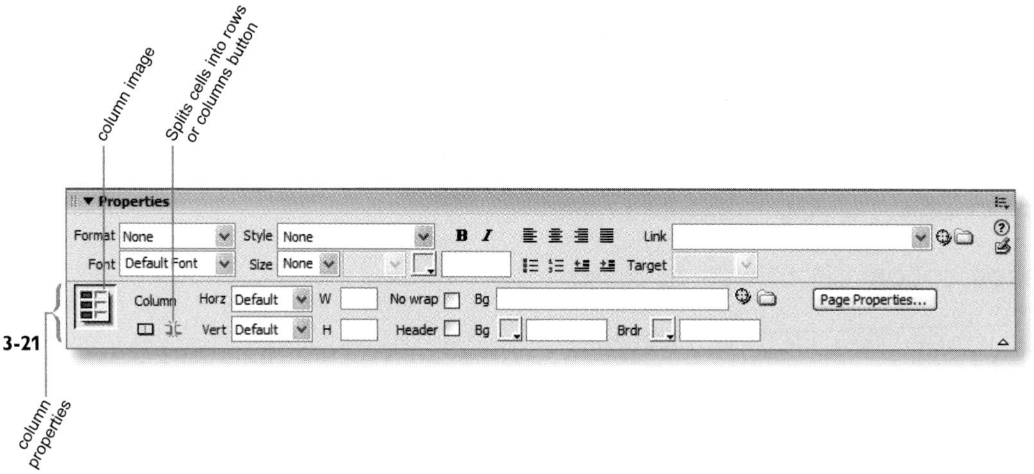

FIGURE 3-21

HORZ Specifies the horizontal alignment of the contents of a cell, row, or column. The contents can be aligned to the left, right, or center of the cells.

VERT Specifies the vertical alignment of the contents of a cell, row, or column. The contents can be aligned to the top, middle, bottom, or baseline of the cells.

W AND H Specifies the width and height of selected cells in pixels or as a percentage of the entire table's width or height.

BG (UPPER TEXT FIELD) The file name of the background image for a cell, column, or row.

BG (LOWER COLOR BOX AND TEXT FIELD) The background color of a cell, column, or row, using the color picker.

BRDR The border color for the cells.

NO WRAP Prevents line wrapping, keeping all text in a given cell on a single line. If No Wrap is enabled, cells widen to accommodate all data as it is typed or pasted into a cell.

HEADER Formats the selected cells as table header cells. The contents of table header cells are bold and centered by default.

MERGE CELLS Combines selected cells, rows, or columns into one cell (available when rows or columns are selected).

SPLIT CELLS Divides a cell, creating two or more cells (available when a single cell is selected).

Table Formatting Conflicts

When formatting tables in Standard mode, you can set properties for the entire table or for selected rows, columns, or cells in the table. When you are applying these properties, however, a potential for conflict exists. To resolve this potential conflict, HTML assigns levels of precedence. The order of precedence for table formatting is cells, rows, and table. When a property, such as background color or alignment, is set to one value for the whole table and another value for individual cells, cell formatting takes precedence over row formatting, which in turn takes precedence over table formatting.

If you set the background color for a single cell to green, and then set the background color of the entire table to red, for example, the green cell does not change to red, because cell formatting takes precedence over table formatting. Dreamweaver, however, does not always follow the precedence. The program will override the settings for a cell if you change the settings for the row that contains the cell. To eliminate this problem, you should change the cell settings last.

More About

Table Formatting Conflicts

For more information about Dreamweaver MX 2004 table formatting conflicts, visit the Dreamweaver MX More About Web page (scsite.com/dreamweavermx04/more.htm) and then click Dreamweaver MX 2004 Tables.

Understanding HTML Structure within a Table

As you work with and become more familiar with tables, it is helpful to have an understanding of the HTML structure within a table. Suppose, for example, you have a table with two rows and two columns, displaying a total of four cells, such as the following:

First cell	Second cell
Third cell	Fourth cell

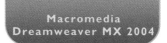

The general syntax of the table is:

```
<table>
<tr>
    <td> First cell </td>
    <td> Second cell </td>
</tr>
<tr>
    <td> Third cell </td>
    <td> Fourth cell </td>
</tr>
</table>
```

When you view your table in Dreamweaver, the tag selector displays the <table>, <td>, and <tr> tags. The <table> tag indicates the whole table. Clicking the <table> tag in the tag selector selects the whole table. The <td> indicates table data. Clicking the <td> tag in the tag selector selects the cell containing the insertion point. The <tr> tag indicates table row. Clicking the <tr> tag in the tag selector selects the row containing the insertion point.

Selecting the Table and Selecting Cells

The Property inspector displays table attributes only if the entire table is selected. To select the entire table, click the upper-left corner of the table, anywhere on the top or bottom edge of the table, or on a row or column's border. When you move the pointer over the border, the pointer changes to a table grid icon, indicating that when the mouse button is clicked, the table is selected (Figure 3-22).

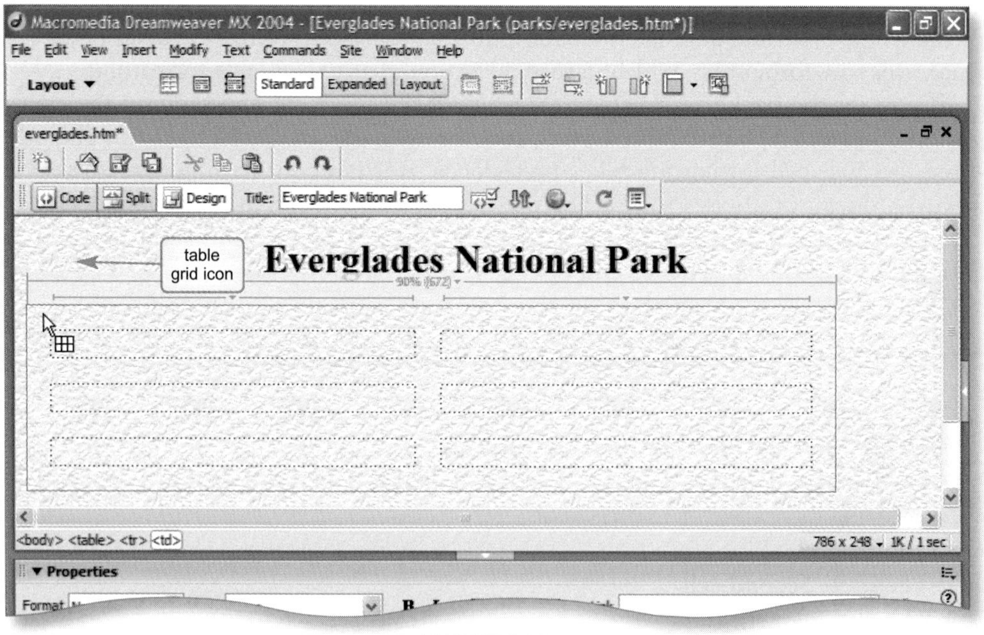

FIGURE 3-22

As discussed previously, another method for selecting a table is to click anywhere in the table and then click the <table> tag in the tag selector. When selected, the table will display with a dark border and selection handles on the table's lower and right edges (Figure 3-23 on the next page).

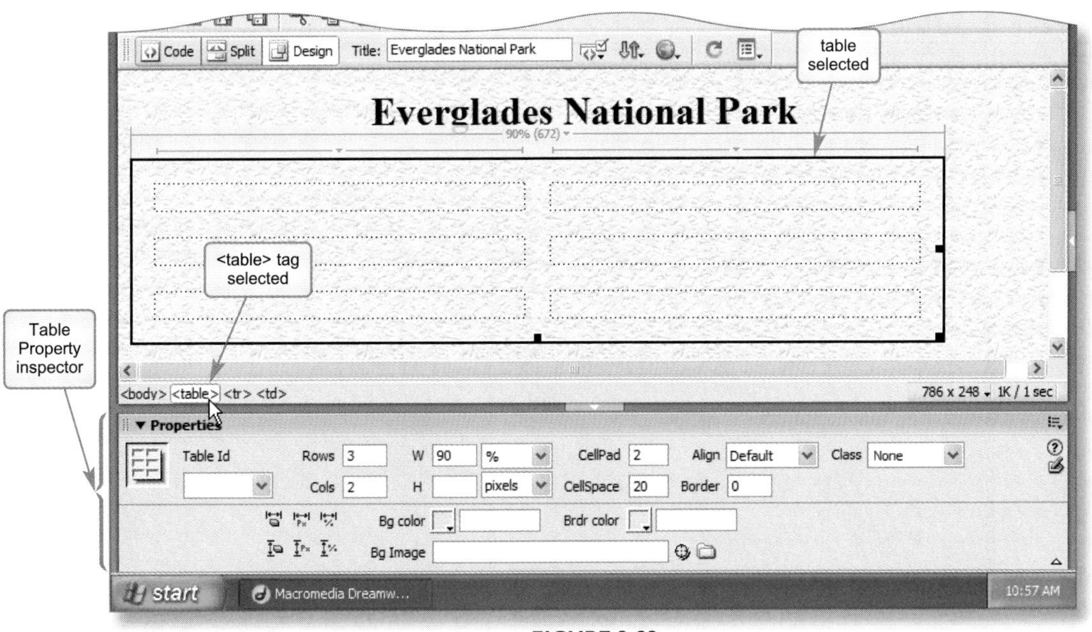

FIGURE 3-23

Selecting a row, column, or cell is easier than selecting the entire table. When a cell, row, or column is selected, the selected item has a dark border. To select a cell, click inside the cell. To select a row or column, click inside one of the cells in the row or column and drag to select the other cells. A second method for selecting a row or column is to point to the left edge of a row or the top edge of a column. When the pointer changes to a selection arrow, click to select the row or column. In Figure 3-24, the selection arrow is pointing to a row and the row is selected.

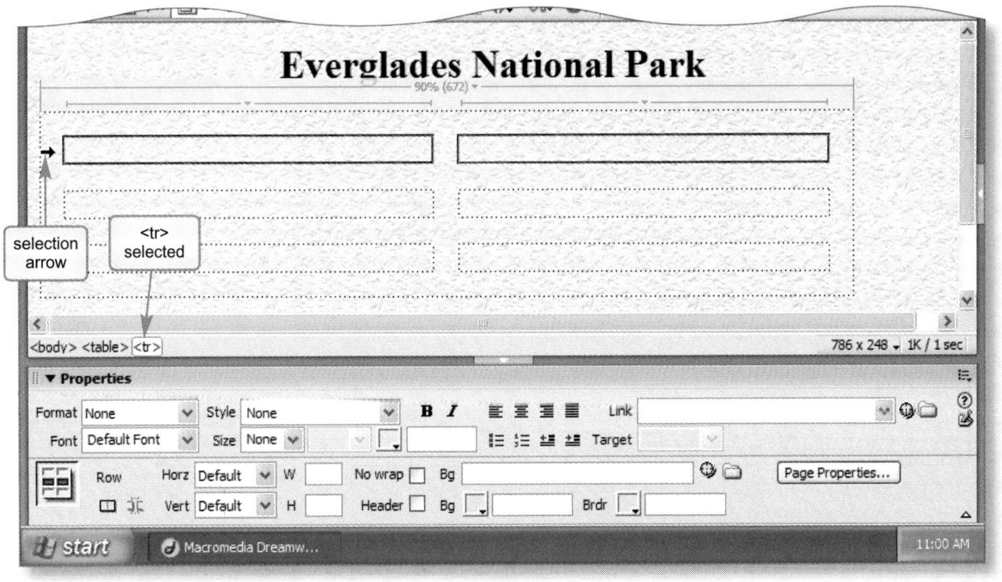

FIGURE 3-24

Centering a Table

When a table is inserted into the Document window with a specified width, it defaults to the left. Using the Property inspector, you can center the table by selecting it and then applying the Center command. The following steps illustrate how to select and center the table.

More About

Formatting a Table

Dreamweaver MX 2004 includes a number of preset table designs. To view these table designs, select the table, click Commands on the menu bar, and then click Format Table. Make your selections in the Format Table dialog box.

To Select and Center a Table

1

- **Click row 1, column 1.**

The insertion point is in the first cell of the first row and the first column (Figure 3-25).

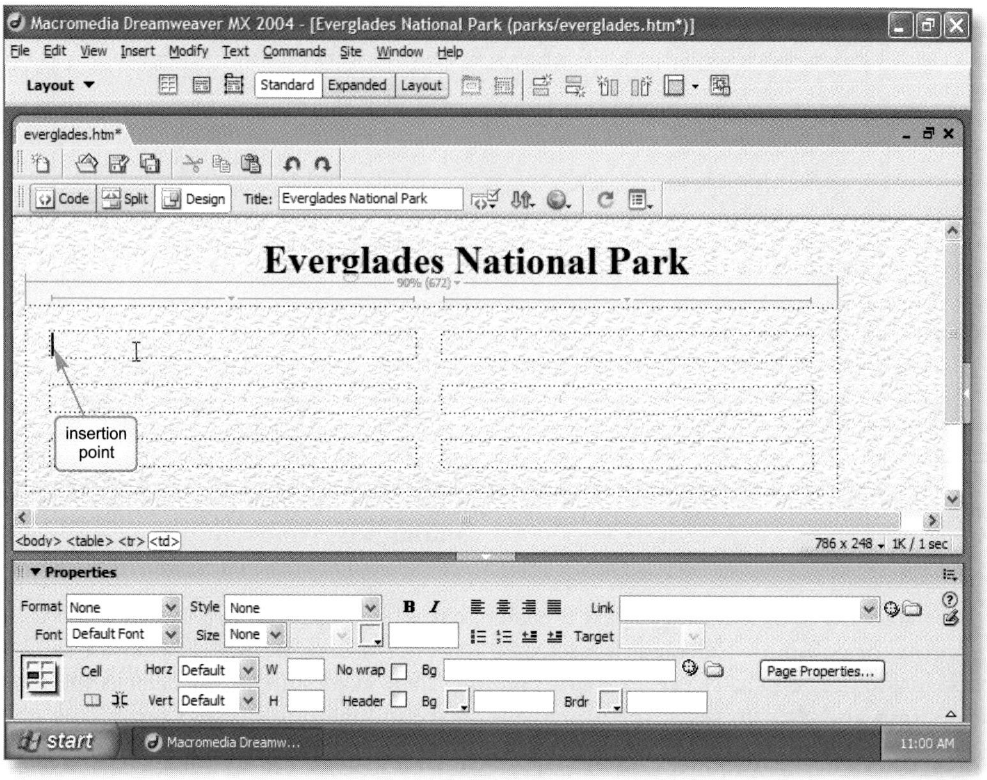

FIGURE 3-25

2

- **Click <table> in the tag selector.**
- **Click the Align box arrow in the Property inspector and then point to Center.**

The table is selected, and handles are displayed on the lower and right borders of the table. The <table> tag is bold, indicating it is selected. Center is highlighted in the Align pop-up menu (Figure 3-26).

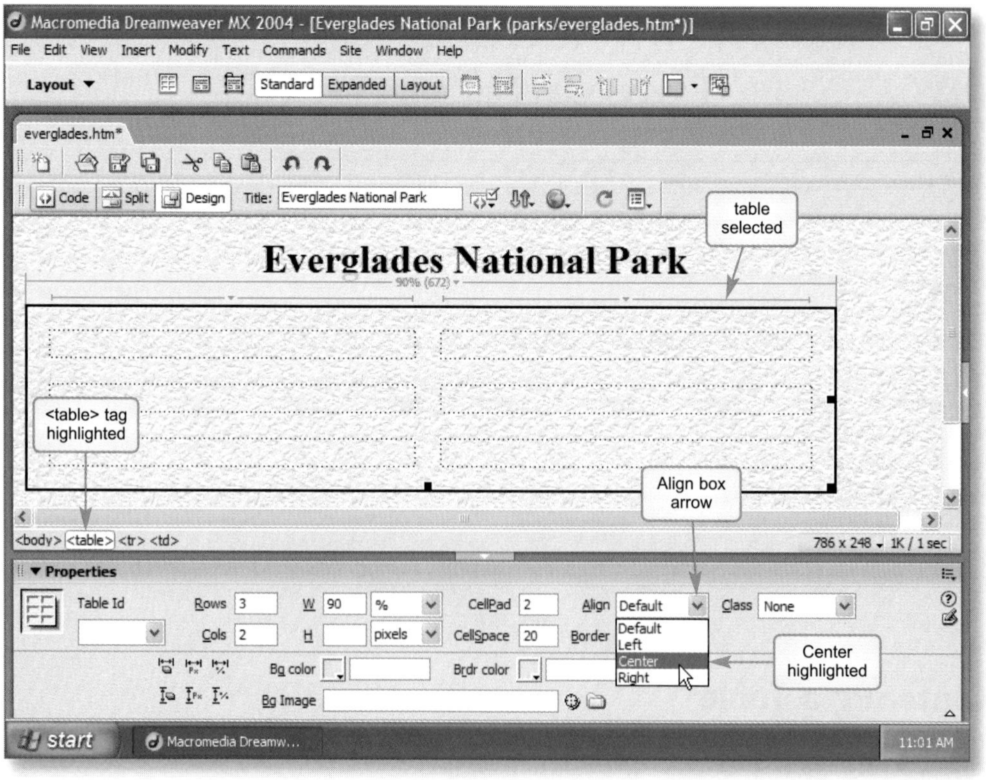

FIGURE 3-26

3

• **Click Center.**

The table is centered in the Document window (Figure 3-27).

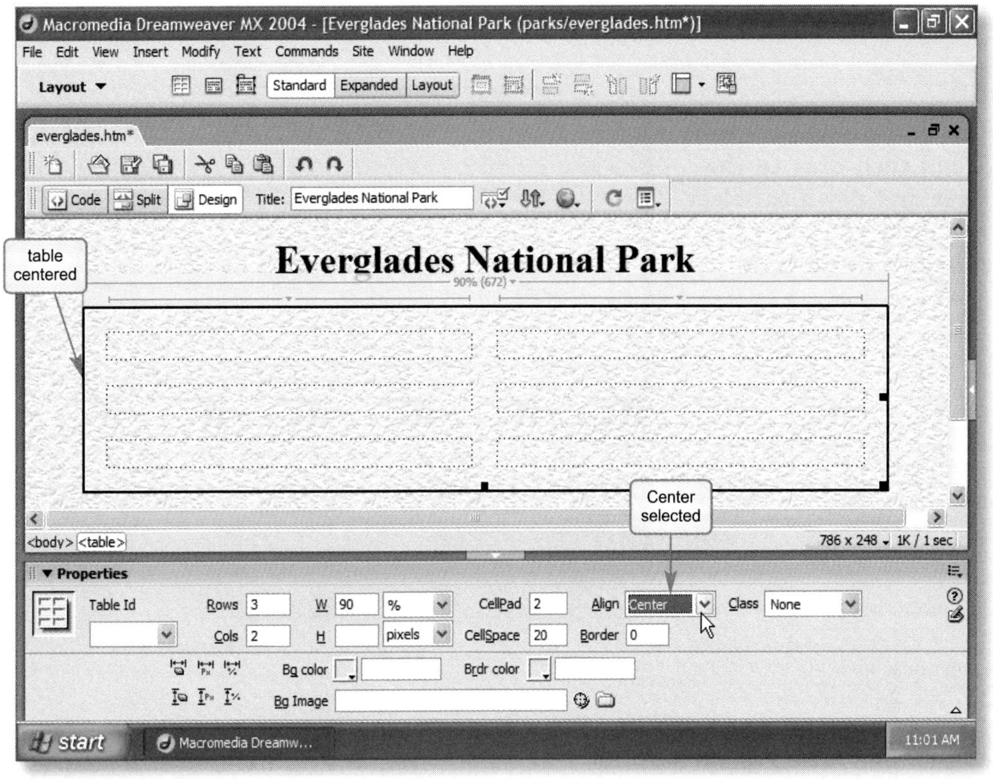

FIGURE 3-27

> ***Other Ways***
>
> 1. Right-click lower or right edge of table border, point to Align on context menu, click Center on Align submenu

Changing the Default Cell Alignment

The default horizontal cell alignment is left. When you enter text or add an image to a cell, it defaults to the left margin of the cell. You can change the left alignment through the Property inspector by clicking the cell and then changing the default to center or right. The default vertical cell alignment is middle, which aligns the cell content in the middle of the cell. Other vertical alignment options include the following:

Top — aligns the cell content at the top of the cell.
Bottom — aligns the cell content at the bottom of the cell.
Baseline — aligns the cell content at the bottom of the cell (same as Bottom).

You can change the vertical alignment through the Property inspector by clicking the cell and then selecting another vertical alignment option.

The following steps show how to select the cells and change the default vertical alignment from middle to top.

To Change Vertical Alignment from Middle to Top

1

- **Click in row 1, column 1 and then drag to the right and down to select the three rows and two columns in the table.**
- **Click the Vert box arrow and then point to Top in the Vert pop-up menu.**

The three rows in the table are selected. The Property inspector changes to reflect the properties for a row. The Vert pop-up menu is displayed, and Top is highlighted (Figure 3-28).

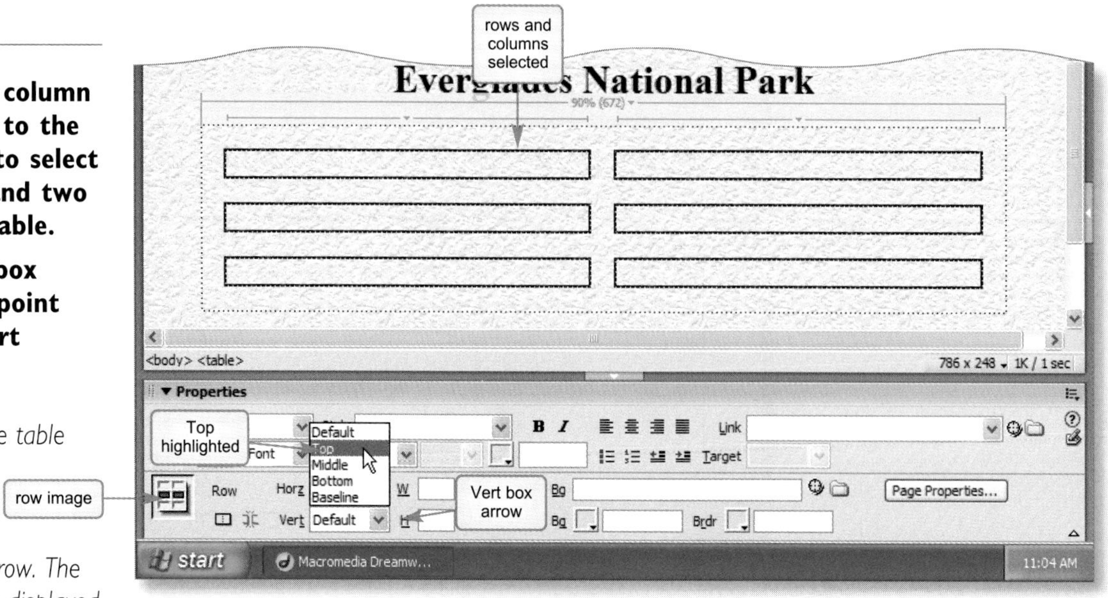

FIGURE 3-28

2

- **Click Top.**

The vertical alignment is changed to top (Figure 3-29). This change does not display in the Document window.

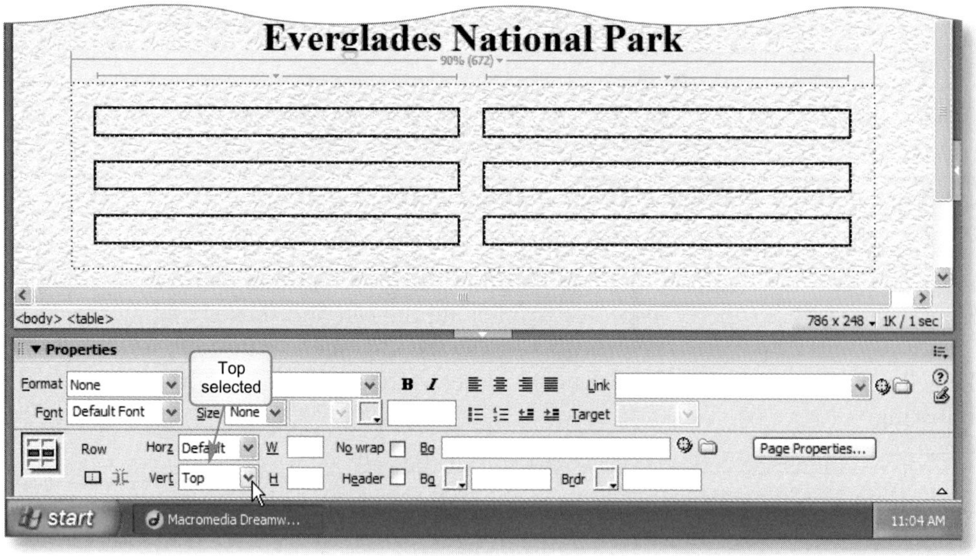

FIGURE 3-29

Specifying Column Width

When a table width is specified as a percentage, each column's width expands to accommodate the text or image. When you add content to the table, this expansion can distort the table appearance and make it difficult to visualize how the final page will display. You can control this expansion by setting the column width. The objective for the Everglades National Park page is to display the page in two columns of equal width of 50 percent. The following step shows how to specify column width.

To Specify Column Width

1

- **Click the cell in row 1, column 1 and then drag to select all cells in column 1.**
- **Click the W box in the Property inspector. Type** `50%` **and then press the ENTER key.**
- **Click the cell in row 1, column 2 and then drag to select all cells in column 2.**
- **Click the W box in the Property inspector. Type** `50%` **and then press the ENTER key.**

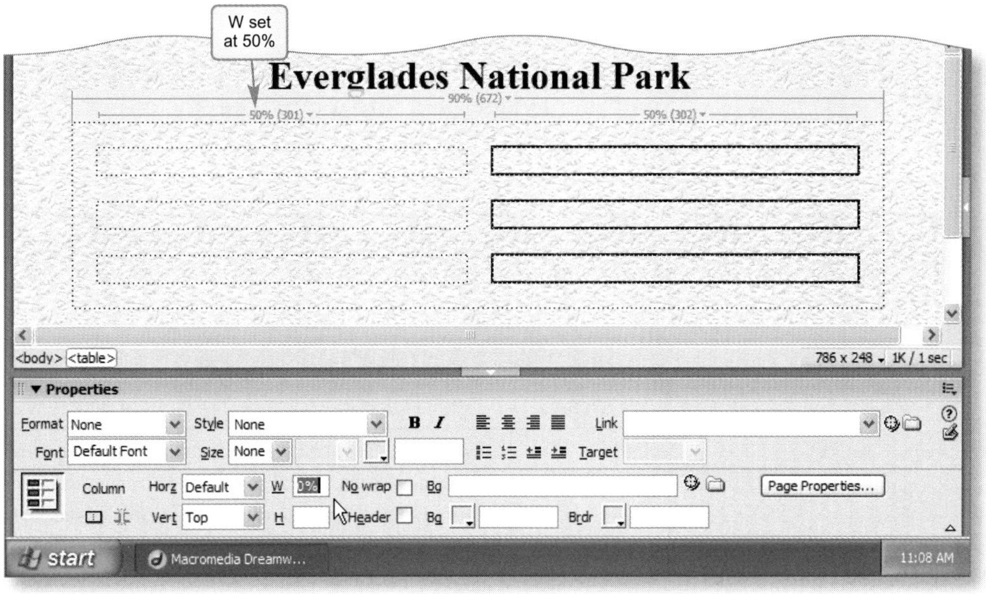

FIGURE 3-30

The width for column 1 and column 2 is specified as 50% at the top of the table (Figure 3-30). The W box in the Property inspector shows only a portion of the 50% value.

Table ID and Accessibility

Earlier in this project, the accessibility options available through the Table dialog box were discussed. The Property inspector for tables contains another accessibility option — table ID. For accessibility purposes, it is recommended that you add a table ID. This provides a name for the table within the HTML code. The table ID is similar to the alternate text for an image, identifying the object to devices that read browser screens. You must select the table to display the Table Id text box. The following step illustrates how to add a table ID to the Everglades National Park feature table.

To Add a Table ID to the Everglades National Park Feature Table

1

- **Click <table> in the status bar to select the table.**
- **Click the Table Id text box and then type** `Everglades National Park feature page` **as the table ID text.**
- **Press the ENTER key.**

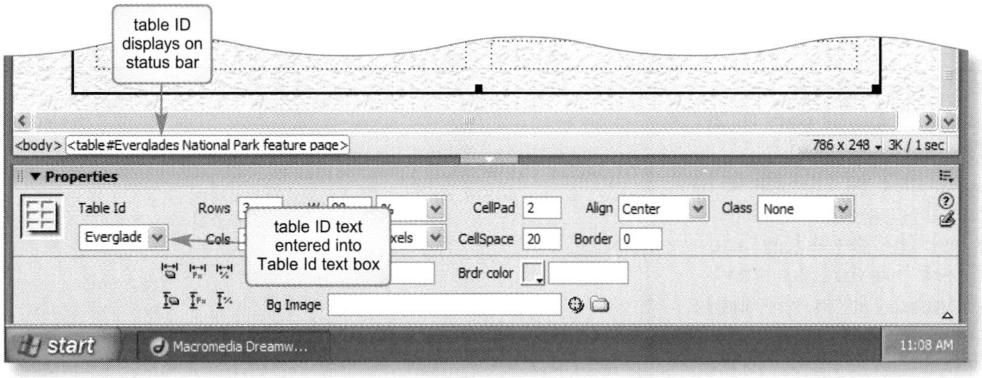

FIGURE 3-31

The table ID is added to the Table Id text box and appears on the status bar (Figure 3-31).

Adding Text to the Everglades National Park Web Page

Next, you will enter and format the text for the Everglades National Park Web page. Table 3-3 on the next page includes the text for the first table. The text is entered into the table cells. If you have not set the width and height of a cell, when you begin to enter text into a table cell, the cell expands to accommodate the text. The other cells may appear to shrink, but they also will expand when you type in the cells or add an image to the cells.

The steps on the next page show how to add text to the Everglades National Park page. Press the ENTER key or insert a line break, <br>, as indicated in the table. Press SHIFT+ENTER to insert a line break. Press the TAB key to move from cell to cell.

Table 3-3 Everglades National Park Web Page Text

SECTION	TEXT FOR EVERGLADES NATIONAL PARK WEB PAGE
Part 1	Everglades National Park, located at the southern tip of Florida, is the largest remaining subtropical wilderness in the United States. It is the only ecosystem of its kind on the planet and the only place in the world where alligators and crocodiles coexist.<ENTER> A freshwater river, 50 miles wide and six-inches deep, flows from Lake Okeechobee through marshy grassland into Florida Bay. The Everglades National Park was created in 1947 by President Harry S. Truman to preserve the wetlands and this slow-moving "River of Grass."<ENTER> The 1.5 million acres of Everglades National Park provide habitats for more than 1,600 varieties of plants and innumerable animals, including more than 350 species of tropical and temperate birds, 40 species of mammals, 50 species of reptiles, and 18 species of amphibians. The sea and wetland wilderness invites exploration by canoe or boat. Walking and tram tours are excellent ways to observe the extensive wildlife.
Part 2	The park is open year round.<ENTER> Park Service Information Office Everglades National Park 40001 State Road 9336 Homestead, FL 33034<ENTER> E-mail: Everglades National Park

More About

Table Data

If you have a table that contains data that requires sorting, you can perform a simple table sort based on the contents of a single column, or you can perform a more complicated sort based on the contents of two columns. Click Commands on the menu bar and then click Sort Table.

To Add Everglades National Park Text

1

- **Type the three paragraphs of Part 1 in Table 3-3 in row 1, column 2 of the table in the Document window. Press the ENTER key and insert line breaks <br> as indicated in the table.**

The three paragraphs are entered into row 1, column 2. Figure 3-32 shows the third of the three paragraphs.

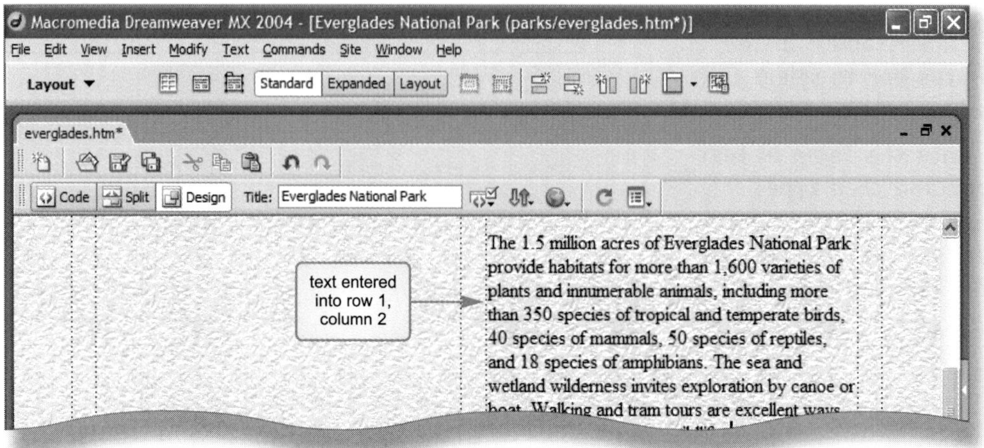
Macromedia Dreamweaver MX 2004 - [Everglades National Park (parks/everglades.htm*)]
File Edit View Insert Modify Text Commands Site Window Help
Layout
Standard Expanded Layout
everglades.htm*
Code Split Design Title: Everglades National Park
text entered into row 1, column 2
The 1.5 million acres of Everglades National Park provide habitats for more than 1,600 varieties of plants and innumerable animals, including more than 350 species of tropical and temperate birds, 40 species of mammals, 50 species of reptiles, and 18 species of amphibians. The sea and wetland wilderness invites exploration by canoe or

FIGURE 3-32

2

- **If necessary, scroll down to display the rest of the table. Type the text of Part 2, as shown in Table 3-3, into row 3, column 1 of the Document window. Use SHIFT+ENTER to insert the line breaks.**

The text is entered (Figure 3-33). The insertion point still is within the cell and may not display because a line break was added. A line break moves the insertion point to the next line, but does not always create a blank space within a table cell such as when the ENTER key is pressed.

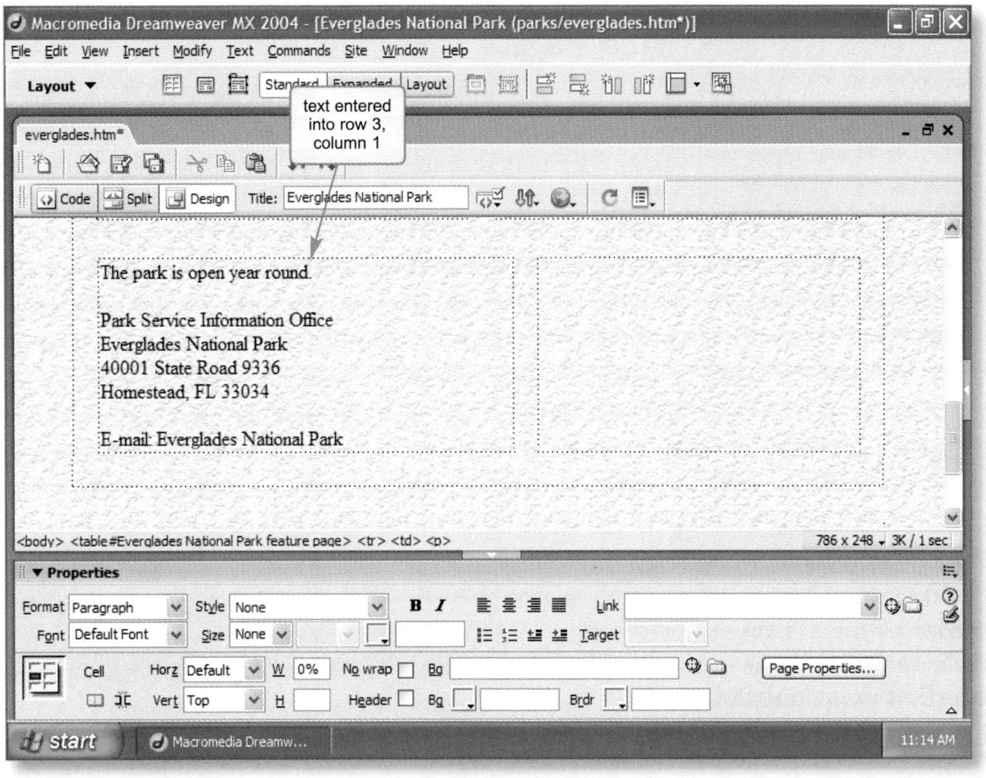

FIGURE 3-33

3

- **Select the text in row 3, column 1.**
- **Click the Align Right button in the Property inspector.**

The text is aligned to the right in the cell (Figure 3-34).

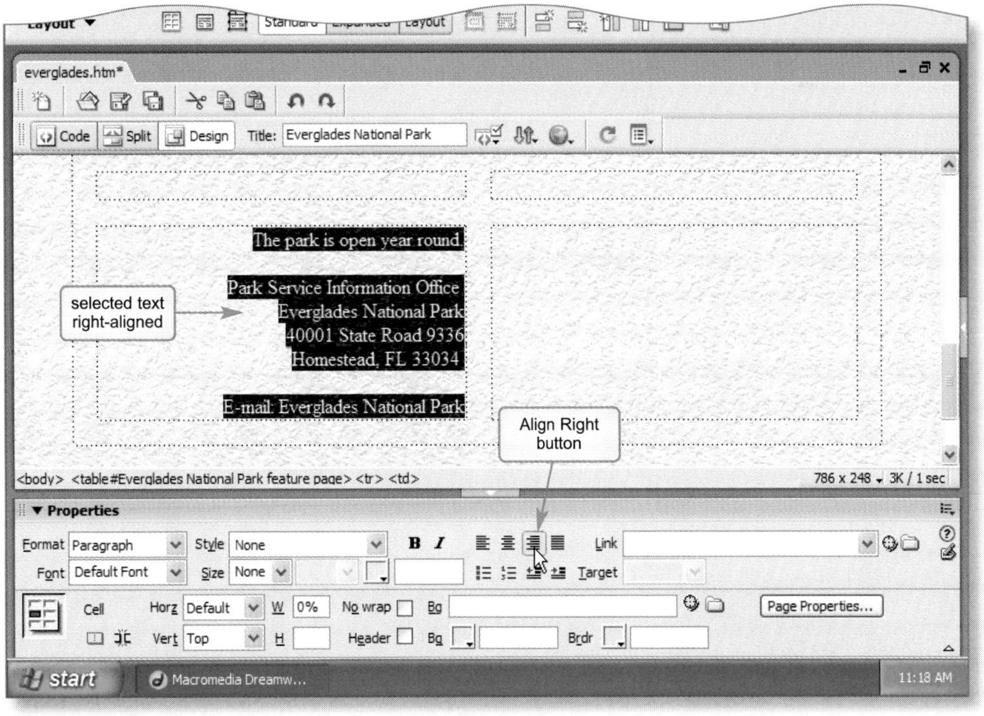

FIGURE 3-34

Other Ways

1. Right-click selected text, point to Align on context menu, click Right on Align submenu

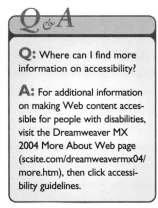

> **Q&A**
>
> **Q:** Where can I find more information on accessibility?
>
> **A:** For additional information on making Web content accessible for people with disabilities, visit the Dreamweaver MX 2004 More About Web page (scsite.com/dreamweavermx04/more.htm), then click accessibility guidelines.

Adding a Second Table to the Everglades National Park Web Page

Next, you add a second table to the Everglades National Park Web page. This table will contain one row and one column and will serve as the footer for your Web page. The text is centered in the cell and will contain links to the home page and to the other two national parks Web pages. The following steps show how to add the second table and text.

To Add a Second Table to the Everglades National Park Web Page

1

- **Click outside the right border of the existing table to position the insertion point outside the table.**

The insertion point is located and blinking to the right of the table border (Figure 3-35).

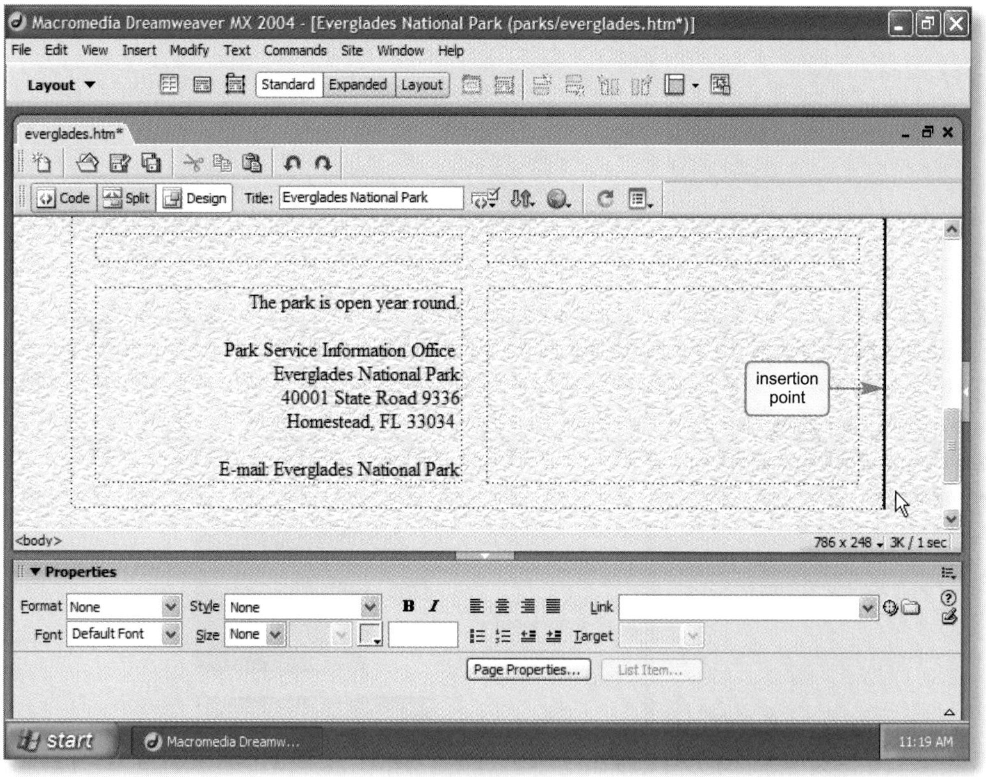

FIGURE 3-35

2

- **Press the ENTER key.**
- **Click the Table button on the Layout Insert bar.**

The Table dialog box is displayed (Figure 3-36). The dialog box retains the settings from the first table. The dialog box on your computer may show different settings.

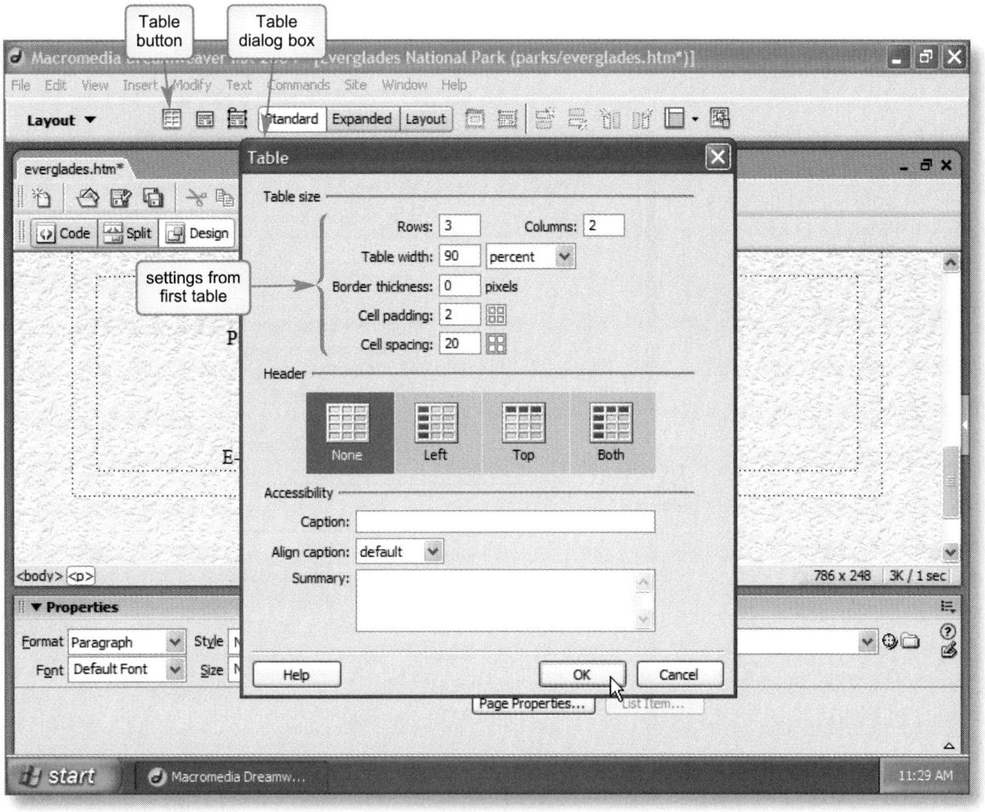

FIGURE 3-36

3

- **Change the number of rows to 1, the number of columns to 1, the width to 75, the cell padding to 0, and the cell spacing to 10.**
- **Type** `Links table` **in the Summary text box.**
- **If necessary, change other settings to match the settings shown in Figure 3-37.**

The Table dialog box displays the new table settings, as shown in Figure 3-37.

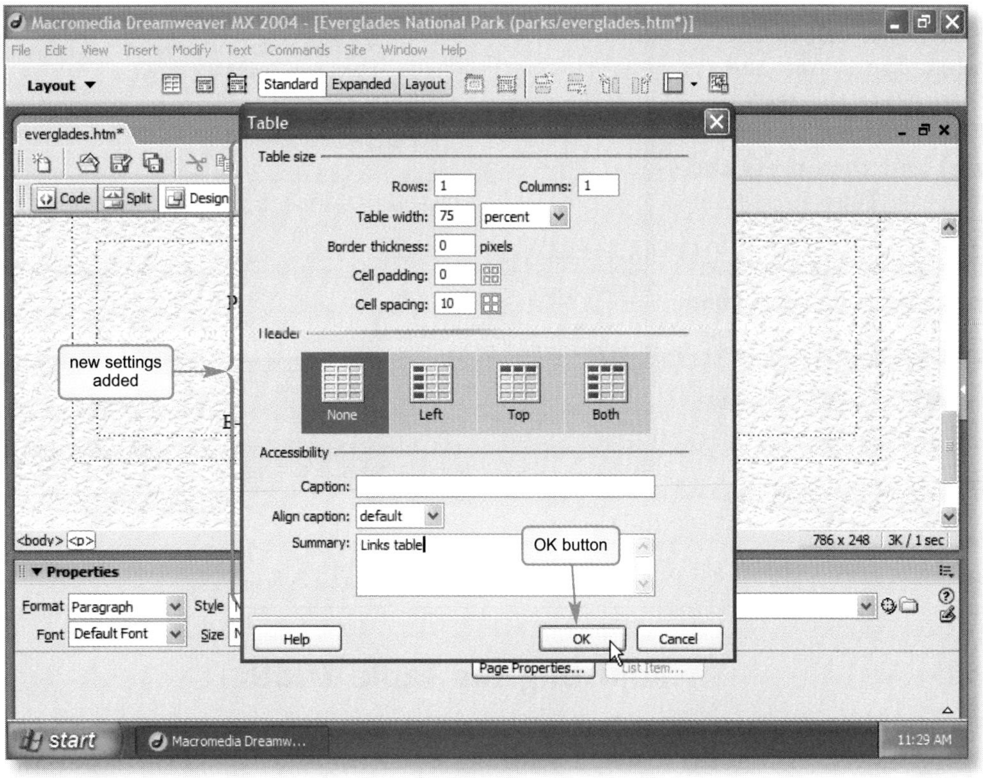

FIGURE 3-37

4

• **Click the OK button.**

The table is inserted into the Document window (Figure 3-38). The dark border and handles indicate the table is selected. The table contains one cell and is centered. If, however, the table defaults to the left, click the Align box arrow and then click Center.

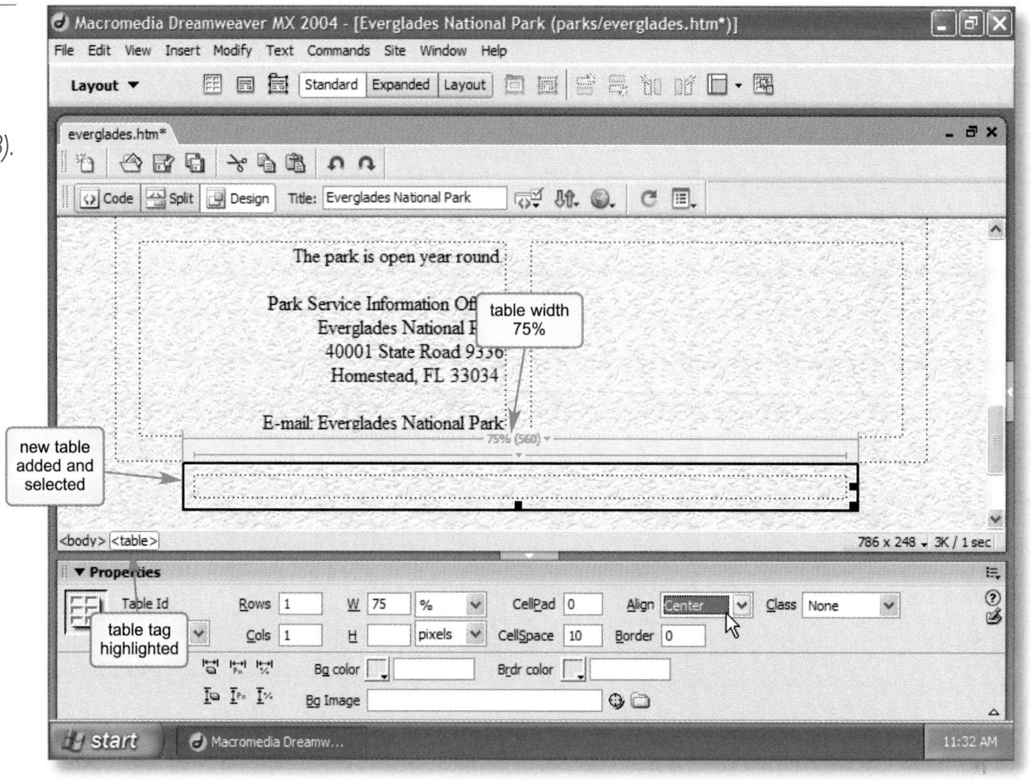

FIGURE 3-38

5

• **Click the cell in the table. Type** `Home` **and then press the SPACEBAR. Press SHIFT + | (vertical bar) and then press the SPACEBAR. Type** `Biscayne National Park` **and then press the SPACEBAR. Press SHIFT + | and then press the SPACEBAR. Type** `Dry Tortugas National Park` **as the last link text.**

The text is entered into the table (Figure 3-39).

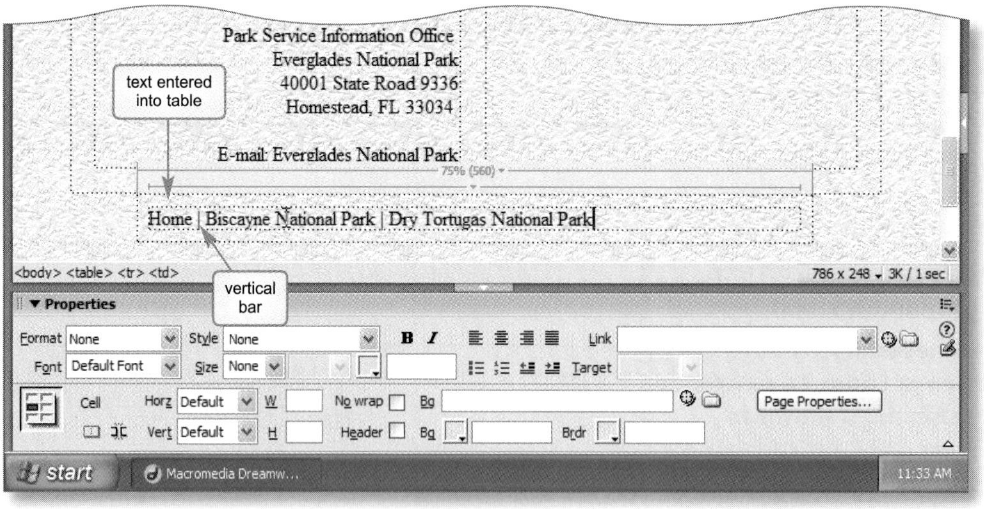

FIGURE 3-39

Adjusting the Table Width

Determining table width is a matter of judgment. You may overestimate or underestimate the table width when first inserting it into the Document window. When this happens, it is easy to make adjustments to the table width through the Property inspector. The table with the names that will contain links is too wide for the text it contains and needs to be adjusted. You adjust the table width by selecting the table and then changing the width in the Property inspector. The following steps illustrate how to adjust the width and add the table ID.

To Adjust the Table Width, Center the Text, and Add the Table ID

1

- **Click the cell in table 2. Click <table> in the tag selector to select the table.**
- **Double-click the W box in the Property inspector.**
- **Type `60` and then press the ENTER key.**

The dark border around the table indicates the table is selected. The Property inspector displays table properties. The table width is decreased (Figure 3-40).

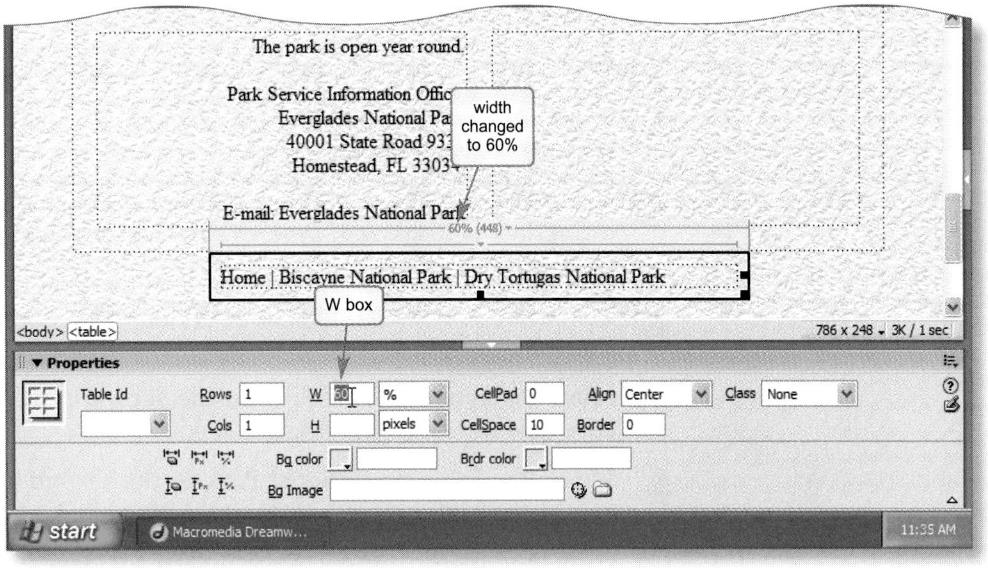

FIGURE 3-40

2

- **If necessary, click <table> in the tag selector to select the table.**
- **Click the cell in the table.**
- **Click the Align Center button in the Property inspector.**
- **Click the Table Id text box, type `Everglades links table`, and then press the ENTER key.**
- **Click anywhere in the Document window to de-select the table.**

The text is centered in the cell, and the table is named (Figure 3-41). This is a one-cell table, so the text also is centered in the table.

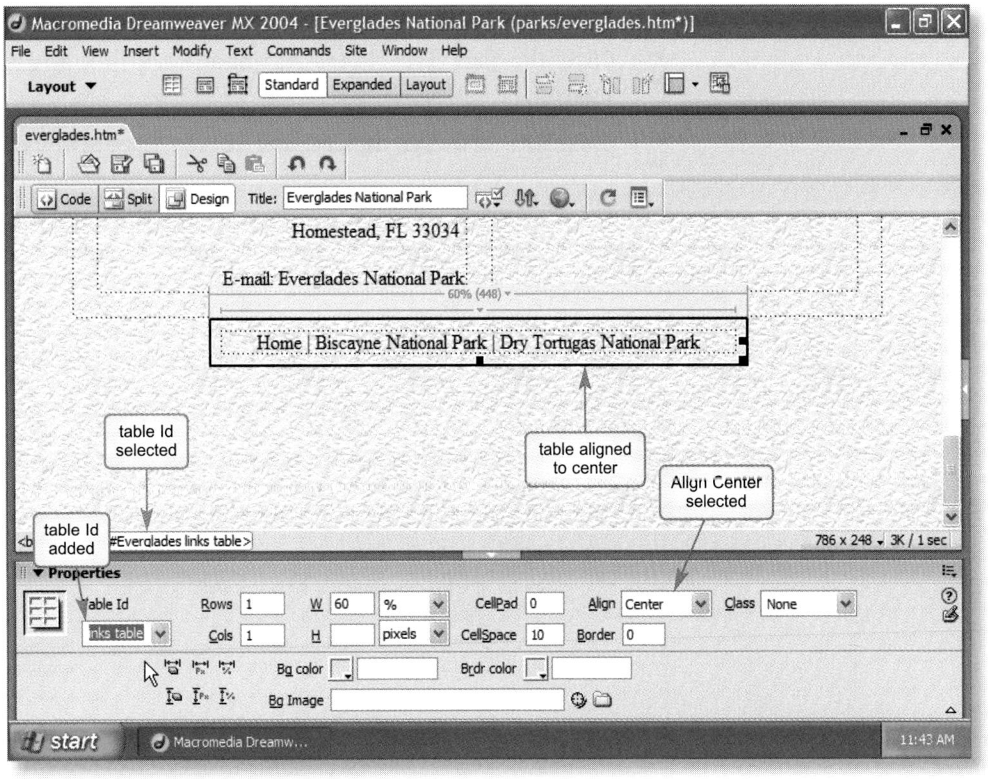

FIGURE 3-41

Next, you add relative, absolute, and e-mail links to the Everglades National Park page. The following steps show how to add the links.

To Add Links to the Everglades National Park Page

1. **Select the first instance of Everglades National Park located in the first table in row 3, column 1.**
2. **Type** `http://www.nps.gov/ever/` **in the Link box to create an absolute link.**
3. **Select the second instance of Everglades National Park located in the first table in row 3, column 1.**
4. **Click Insert on the menu bar and then click Email Link. When the Email Link dialog box is displayed, type** `everglades@parks.gov` **as the e-mail address. Click the OK button.**
5. **Select Home in the second table. Type** `index.htm` **in the Link box to create the relative link.**
6. **Select Biscayne National Park in the second table. Type** `biscayne.htm` **in the Link box to create the relative link.**
7. **Select Dry Tortugas National Park in the second table. Type** `dry_tortugas.htm` **in the Link box to create the relative link.**
8. **Click the SAVE button on the Standard toolbar.**
9. **Press the F12 key to view the Web page. Scroll down to view the links, as shown in Figure 3-42.**
10. **Click the first Everglades National Park link and then click the Browser back button.**
11. **Close the browser and return to the Dreamweaver window.**

The links are added to the Web page (Figure 3-42). The links for Biscayne National Park and Dry Tortugas National Park are not active at this point. You will add these two pages later in this project.

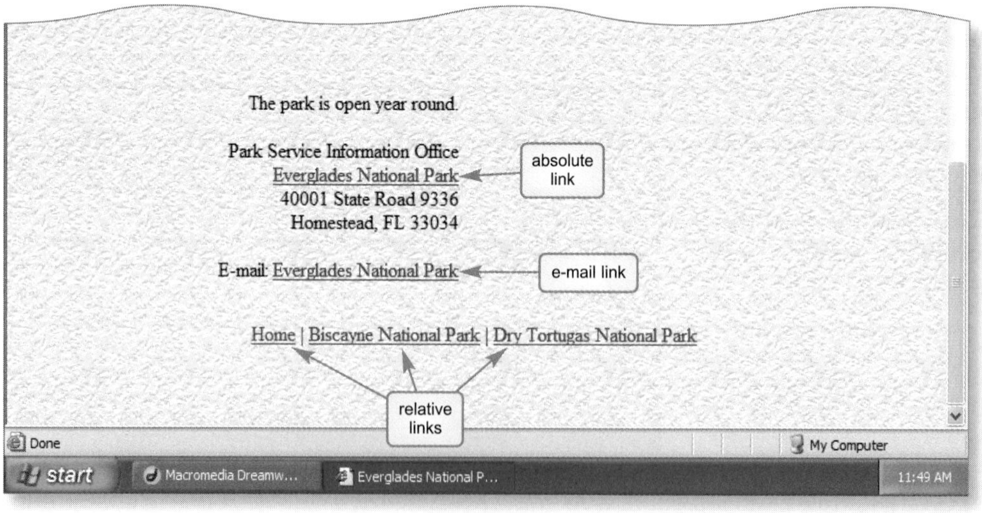

FIGURE 3-42

Editing and Modifying Table Structure

Thus far, you have created two tables and made adjustments in Dreamweaver for the Everglades National Park Web page. For various reasons, as you create and develop Web sites, you will need to edit and modify a table, change the dimensions of a table, add rows and columns, or delete the table and start over. The following section on the next page describes how to accomplish editing, modifying, and deleting table elements within the structure.

> *More About*
>
> **Resizing a Table**
>
> Before resizing a table, first clear any set cell widths or heights. Select the table and click the Clear Row Heights button or the Clear Column Widths button in the Property inspector.

DELETE A ROW OR COLUMN Select a row or column and then press the DELETE key. You also can delete a row or column by clicking a cell within the row or column, right-clicking to display the context menu, pointing to Table, and then clicking Delete Row or Delete Column on the Table submenu.

INSERT A ROW OR COLUMN To insert a row or column, click in a cell. Right-click to display the context menu, point to Table, and then click Insert Row or Insert Column on the Table submenu. To insert more than one row or column and to control the row or column insertion point, click in a cell, right-click to display the context menu, point to Table, and then click Insert Rows or Columns on the Table submenu to display the Insert Rows or Columns dialog box (Figure 3-43). Make your selections and then click the OK button. To add a row automatically, press the TAB key in the last cell of a table.

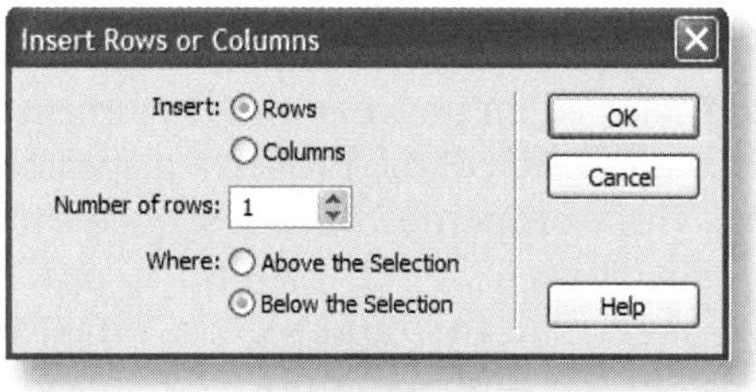

FIGURE 3-43

MERGE AND SPLIT CELLS By merging and splitting cells, you can set alignments more complex than straight rows and columns. To merge two or more cells, select the cells and then click Merge Cells in the Property inspector. The selected cells must be contiguous and in the shape of a line or a rectangle. You can merge any number of adjacent cells as long as the entire selection is a line or a rectangle. To split a cell, click the cell and then click Split Cells in the Property inspector to display the Split Cell dialog box (Figure 3-44). In the Split Cell dialog box, specify how to split the cell and then click the OK button. You can split a cell into any number of rows or columns, regardless of whether it was merged previously. When you split a cell into two rows, the other cells in the same row as the split cell are not split. The same is true if a cell is split into two or more columns — the other cells in the same column are not split. To select a cell quickly, click the cell and then click the <td> tag on the tag selector.

> *More About*
>
> **Deleting Cells**
>
> If you delete a cell, the content also is deleted. Dreamweaver does not caution you that this will occur. If you accidentally remove content, click the Undo button on the Standard toolbar or, on the Edit menu, click the Undo command.

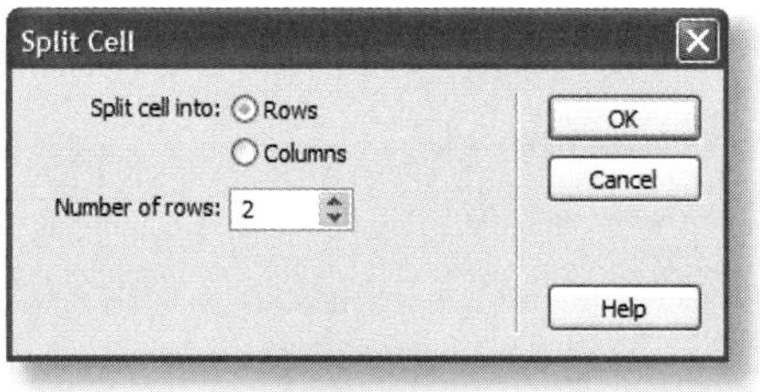

FIGURE 3-44

RESIZE A TABLE, COLUMNS, AND ROWS You can resize an entire table or resize individual rows and columns. To resize the table, select the table and change the W (width) in the Property inspector. A second method is to select the table and then drag one of the table selection handles. When you resize an entire table, all of the cells in the table change size proportionately. If you have assigned explicit widths or heights to a cell or cells within the table, resizing the table changes the visual size of the cells in the Document window but does not change the specified widths and heights of the cells. To resize a column or row, select the column or row and change the properties in the Property inspector. A second method to resize a column is to select the column and then drag the right border of the column. To resize a row, select the row and then drag the lower border of the row.

DELETE A TABLE You easily can delete a table. Select the table tag in the tag selector and then press the DELETE key. All table content is deleted along with the table.

More About

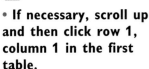

Splitting and Merging Cells

An alternative approach to merging and splitting cells is to increase or decrease the number of rows or columns spanned by a cell.

Merging Cells and Adding Images

The concept of merging cells probably is familiar to you if you have worked with spreadsheets or word processing tables. In HTML, however, merging cells is a complicated process. Dreamweaver makes this easy by hiding some complex HTML table restructuring code behind an easy-to-use interface in the Property inspector. Dreamweaver also makes it easy to add images to a table. When you add and then select an image in a table cell, the Property inspector displays the same properties as were displayed when you added and selected an image in the Document window in Project 2. When the image in the cell is not selected, the Property inspector displays the same properties as it does for any cell. These properties were described earlier in this project.

You will merge two cells (rows 1 and 2, column 1) and add three images to the Everglades National Park page. The first and second images go into the merged cells, and the third image goes in row 3, column 2. The following steps show how to merge two cells.

To Merge Two Cells

1

- **If necessary, scroll up and then click row 1, column 1 in the first table.**
- **Drag to select the cells in rows 1 and 2 in column 1.**

The two cells are selected (Figure 3-45).

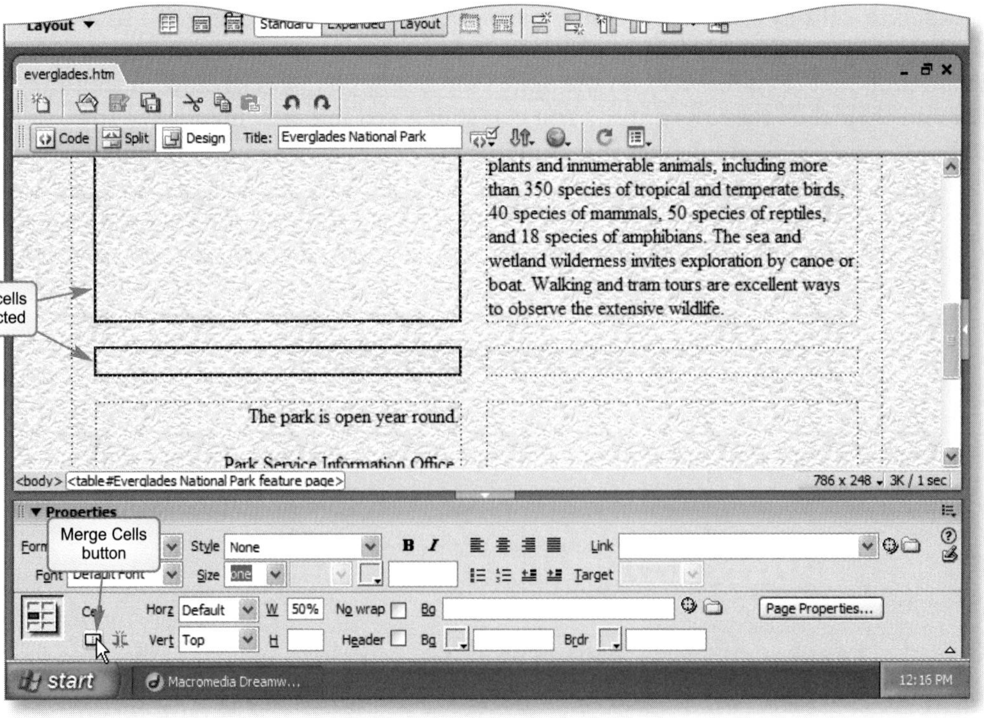

FIGURE 3-45

2

- **Click the Merge Cells button.**

The two cells are merged (Figure 3-46).

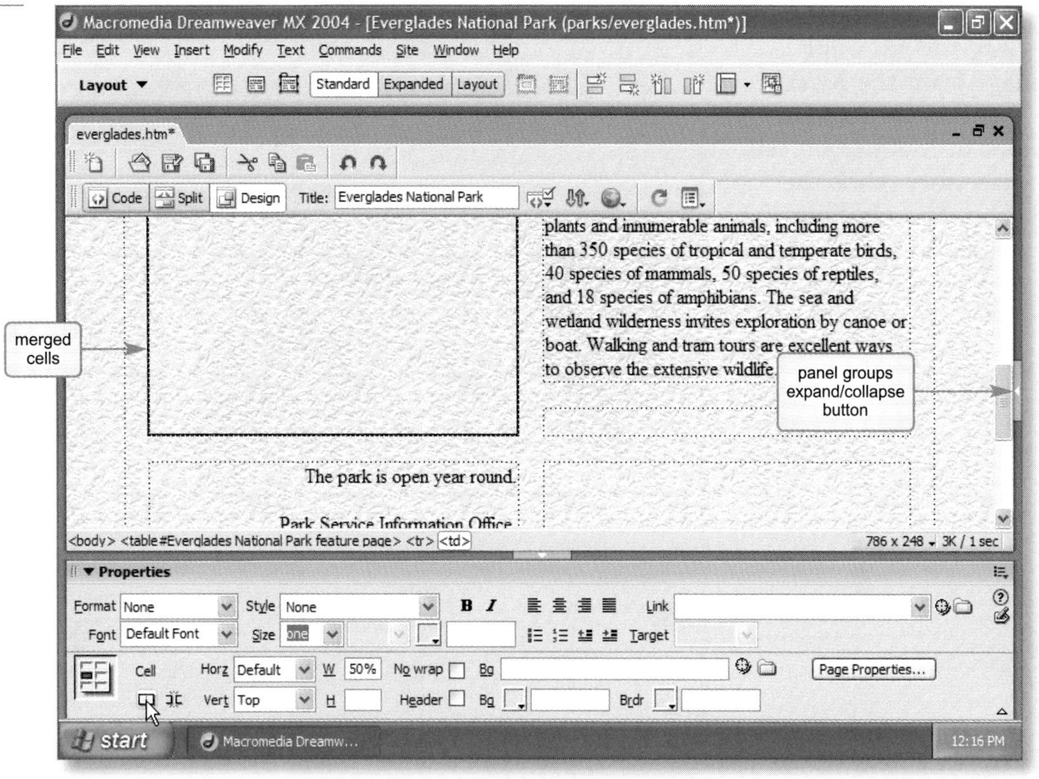

FIGURE 3-46

Next, you add three images to the table. You then align and modify the size of the images. The following steps illustrate how to display the images in the Assets panel and then add, align, and modify images in a table displayed in Standard mode.

To Add Images to a Standard Mode Table

1

- **Click the panel groups expand/collapse button and then click the Assets tab in the panel groups.**
- **Scroll to the top of the table and then click the cell in row 1, column 1.**
- **Press the ENTER key.**

The insertion point is positioned in the merged cell (Figure 3-47). The gator.jpg image will be inserted at the location of the insertion point.

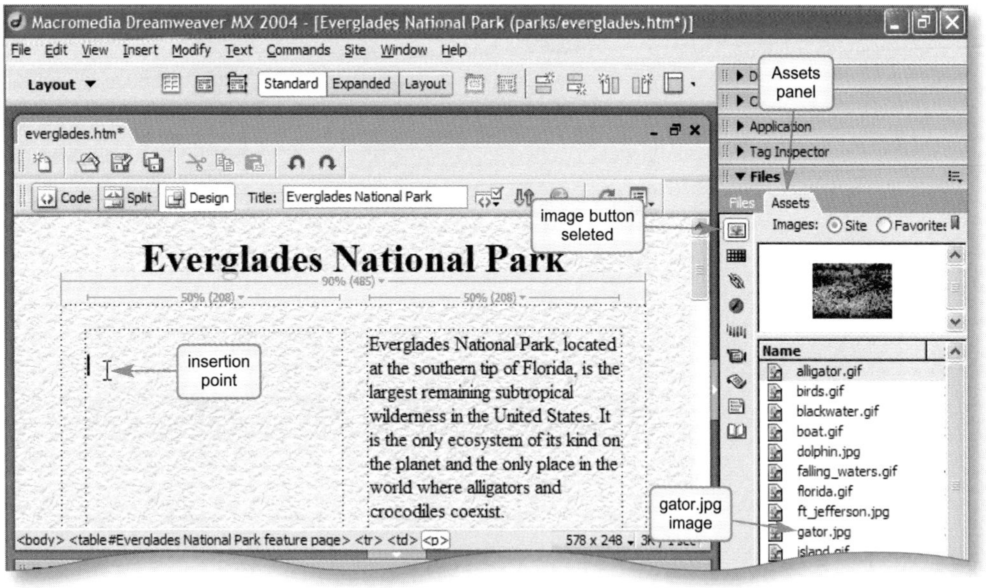

FIGURE 3-47

2

• Drag the gator.jpg image from the Assets panel to the insertion point in the merged cell. If necessary, click the Refresh Site List button to view the images.

The gator.jpg image is inserted in the cell and selected (Figure 3-48). The Property inspector for images displays.

FIGURE 3-48

3

• Click below the gator.jpg image.

The insertion point displays below the gator.jpg image (Figure 3-49). The swamp.jpg image will be inserted at the location of the insertion point.

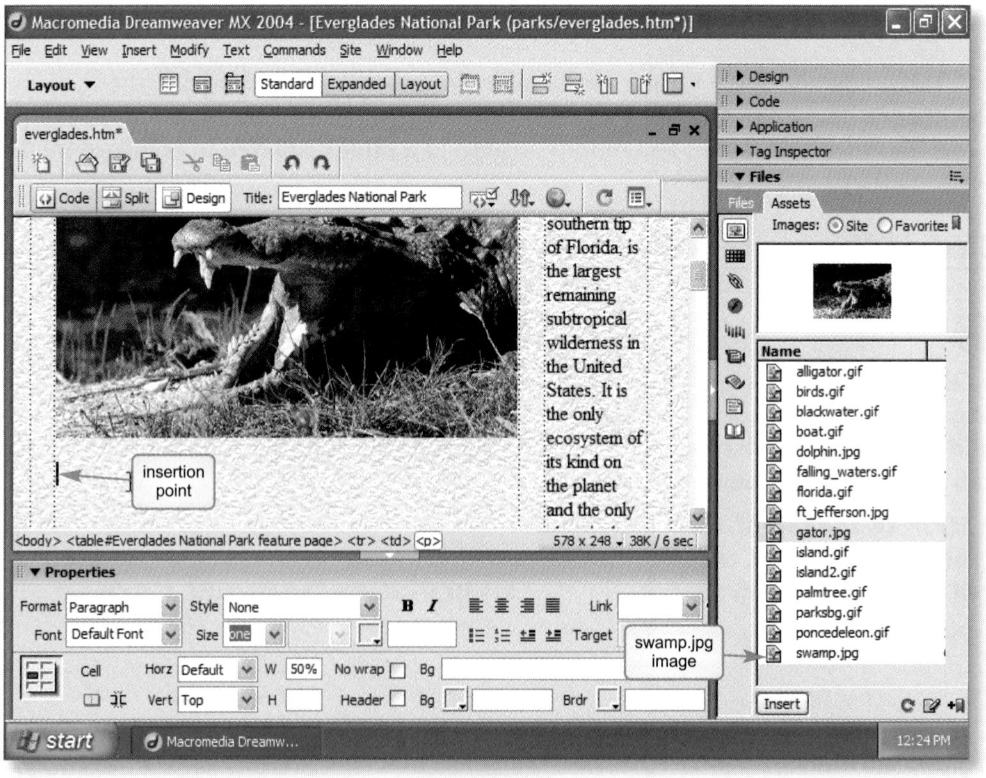

FIGURE 3-49

4

• **Drag the swamp.jpg image to the insertion point.**

The swamp.jpg image is displayed below the gator.jpg image and is selected (Figure 3-50). The image is larger than the cell, and the cell expands to accommodate the image.

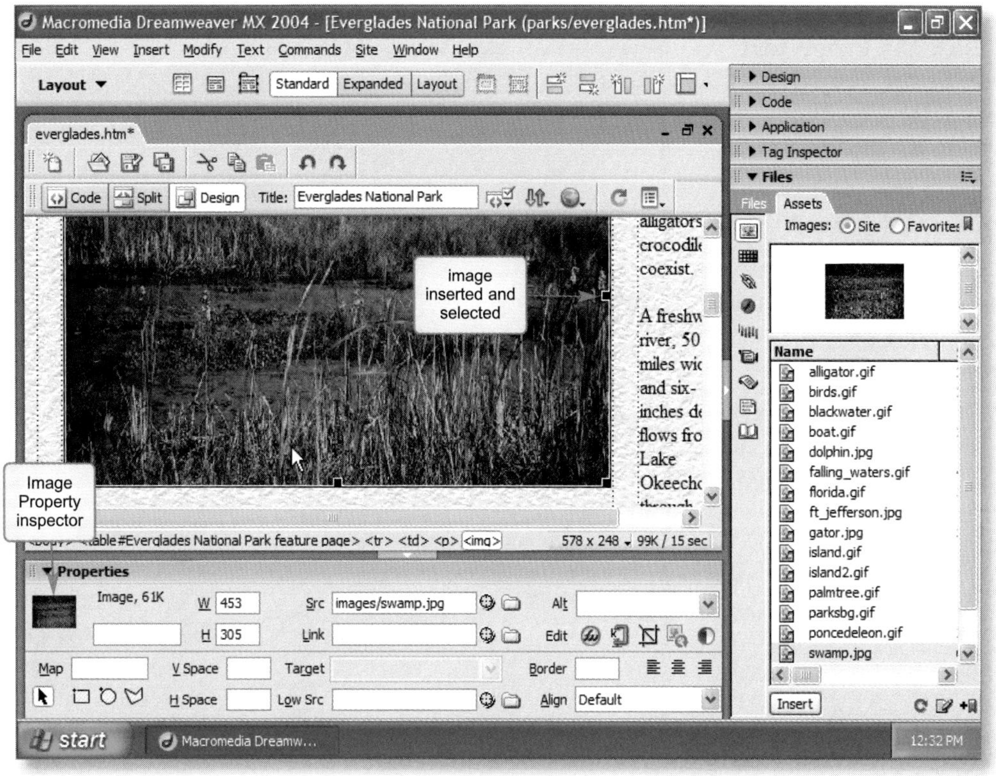

FIGURE 3-50

5

• **Scroll up and click the gator.jpg image to select it.**

The gator.jpg image is selected (Figure 3-51). The Property inspector displays image properties.

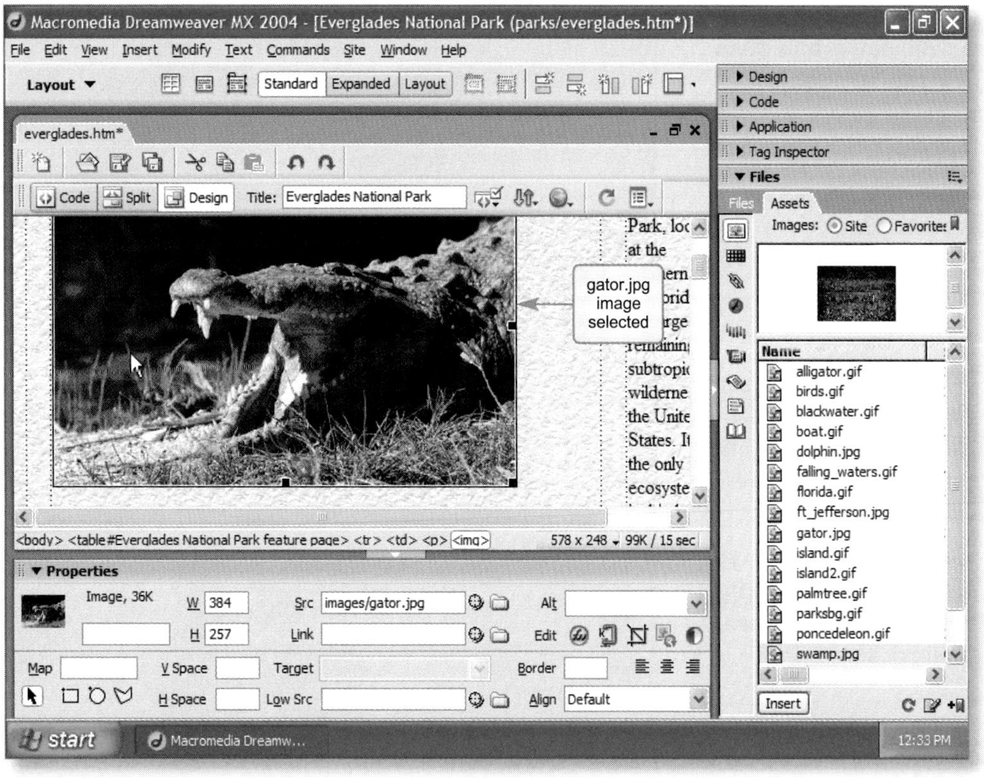

FIGURE 3-51

6

- **Click the Image text box in the Property inspector and type** `Gator` **as the image ID.**
- **Press the TAB key and type** `340` **in the W box.**
- **Press the TAB key to move to the H box and then type** `260` **as the new value.**
- **Click the Alt box, type** `Florida alligator` **as the Alt text, and then press the ENTER key.**

The specified properties are applied to the gator.jpg image (Figure 3-52).

FIGURE 3-52

7

- **Scroll down and then click the swamp.jpg image to select it.**
- **Click the Image text box in the Property inspector and then type** `Swamp` **as the image ID.**
- **Press the TAB key and then type** `330` **in the W box.**
- **Press the TAB key to move to the H box and then type** `220` **as the new value.**
- **Click the Alt box, type** `Florida swamp` **as the Alt text, and then press the ENTER key.**

The specified properties are applied to the swamp.jpg image (Figure 3-53).

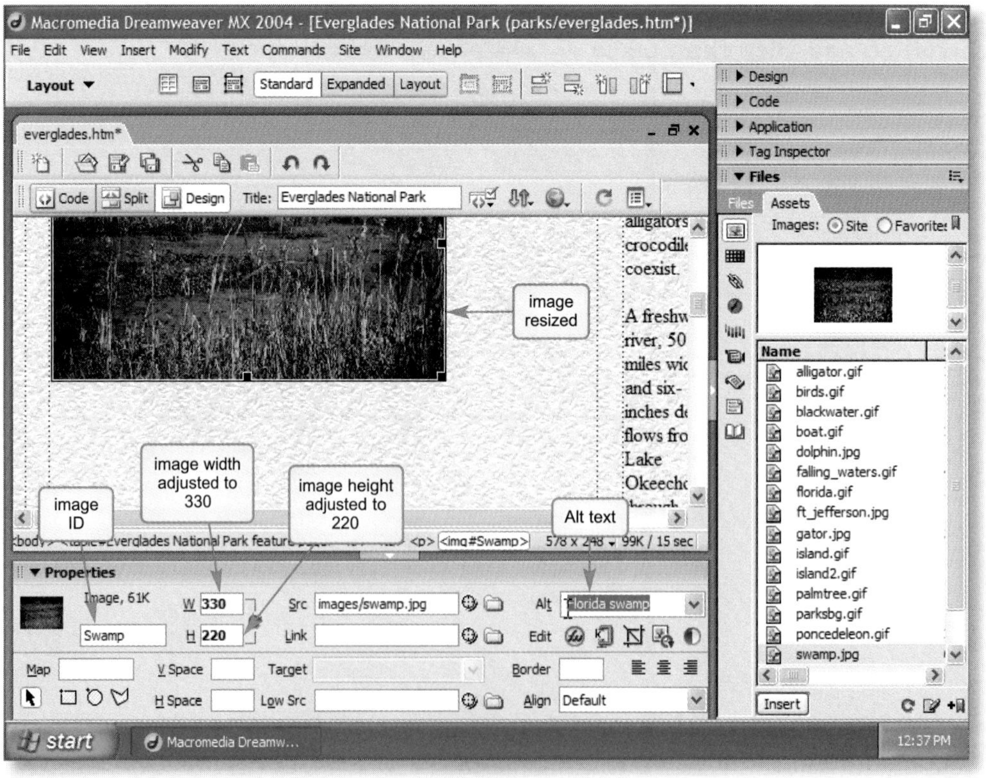

FIGURE 3-53

8

- **Scroll down and to the right. Click row 3, column 2.**

The insertion point is displayed in the cell (Figure 3-54). The birds.gif image will be inserted at the location of the insertion point.

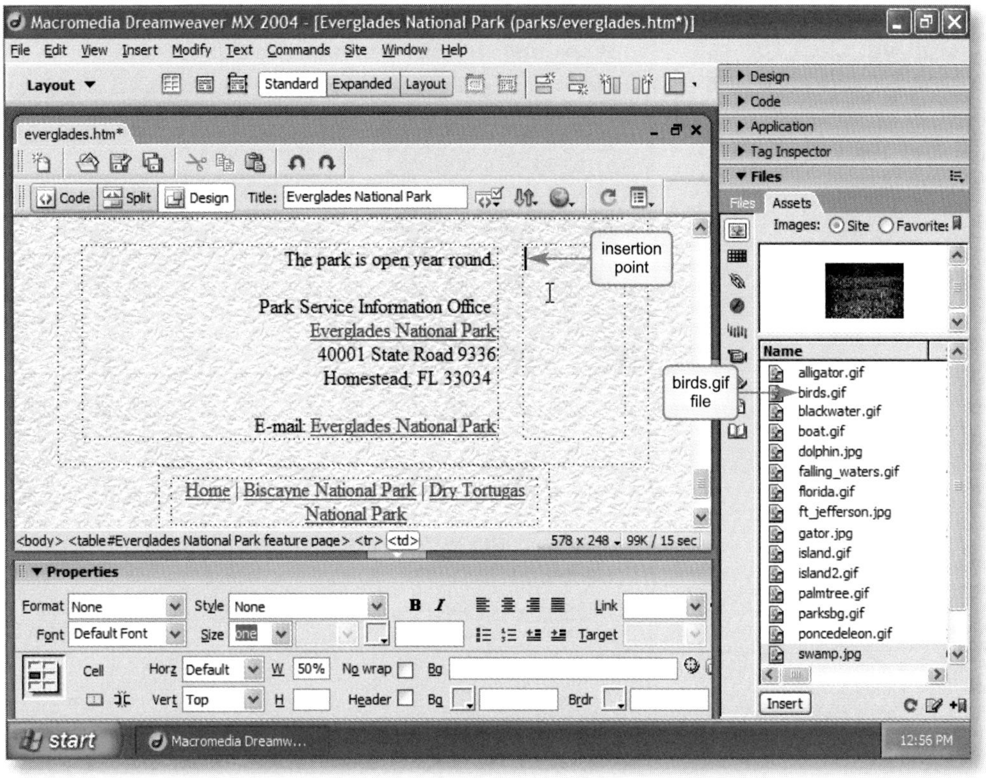

FIGURE 3-54

9

- **Drag the birds.gif image from the Assets panel to the insertion point in row 3, column 2.**
- **Verify that the birds.gif image is selected, click the Image text box, and type** `florida_birds`**. Click the Alt box, type** `Florida birds` **as the Alt text, and then press the ENTER key.**

The birds.gif image is displayed in the cell and is selected (Figure 3-55). The Alt text is entered. The cell expands to accommodate the image.

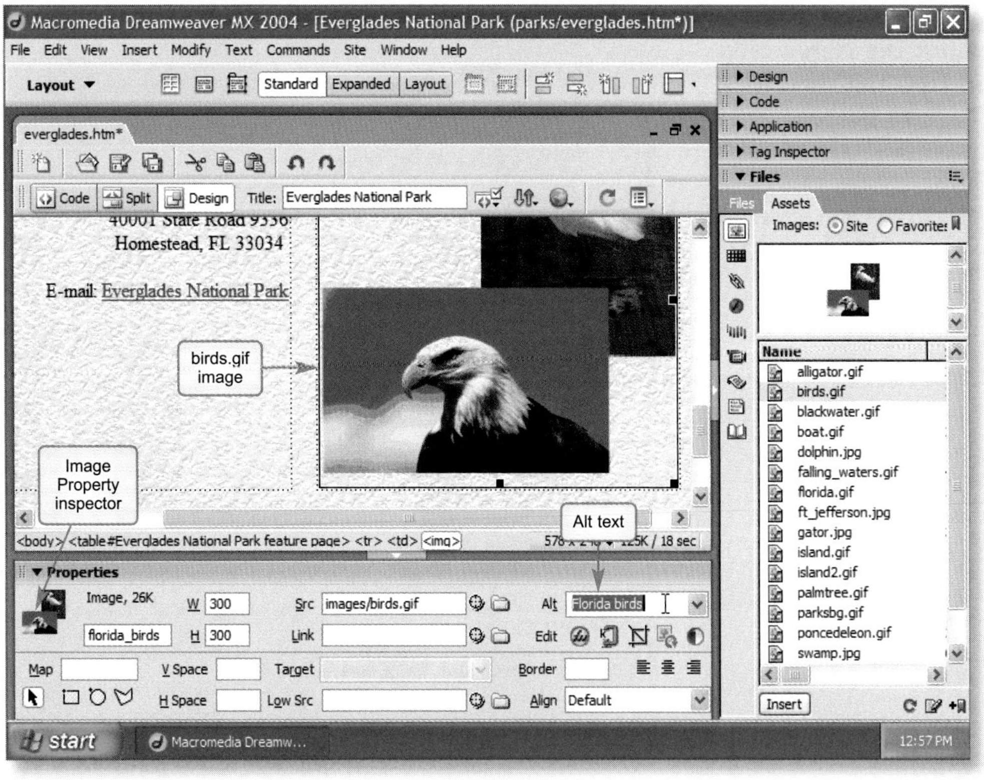

FIGURE 3-55

10

• **Scroll up. Click the cell in row 2, column 2 and then drag to select this cell and the cell in row 3, column 2.**

The two cells are selected (Figure 3-56).

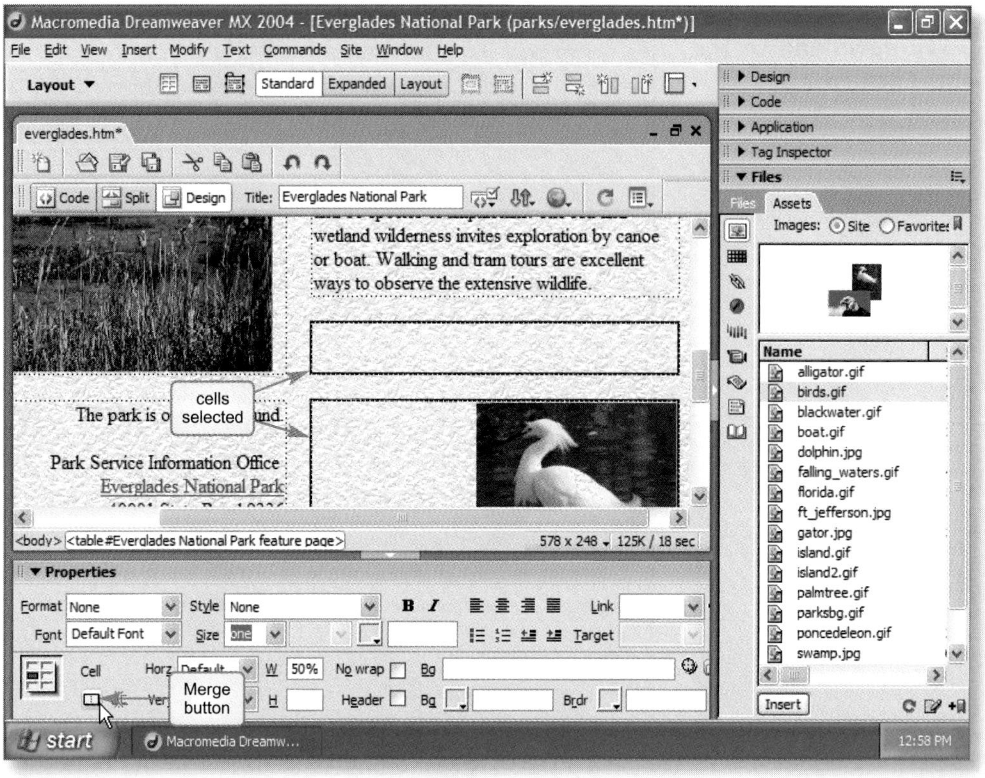

FIGURE 3-56

11

• **Click the Merge cells button, and then click the Save button.**

The two cells are merged, and the birds.gif image moves to the top of the cell. The page is saved (Figure 3-57).

FIGURE 3-57

12

- **Press the F12 key to view the page in your browser.**
- **The Everglades National Park page displays in the browser (Figure 3-58).**

13

- **Close the browser window.**

Dreamweaver displays.

FIGURE 3-58

Creating the Biscayne National Park Web Page

To create the Biscayne National Park Web page, you open a new Document window. You start by applying the background image. This is the same background image you used for the Florida Parks Web site in Projects 1 and 2. The following steps illustrate how to open a new Document window and apply a background image.

To Open a New Document Window and Add a Background Image to the Biscayne National Park Web Page

1. **Click File on the menu bar and then click New. If necessary, click the General tab and then click Basic page in the Category list. If necessary, click HTML in the Basic page list.**
2. **Click the Create button.**
3. **Click Modify on the menu bar and then click Page Properties.**
4. **Click the Browse button to the right of the Background image box.**
5. **If necessary, navigate to the parks\images folder.**
6. **Click parksbg.gif and then click the OK button in the Select Image Source dialog box.**
7. **Click the OK button in the Page Properties dialog box. If a warning dialog box displays, click OK.**
8. **Click the Save button on the Standard toolbar and then type** `biscayne` **as the file name. Save the Web page in the parks folder.**

The biscayne.htm page is saved in the parks local folder. The path and file name (parks/biscayne.htm) appear on the Dreamweaver title bar (Figure 3-59).

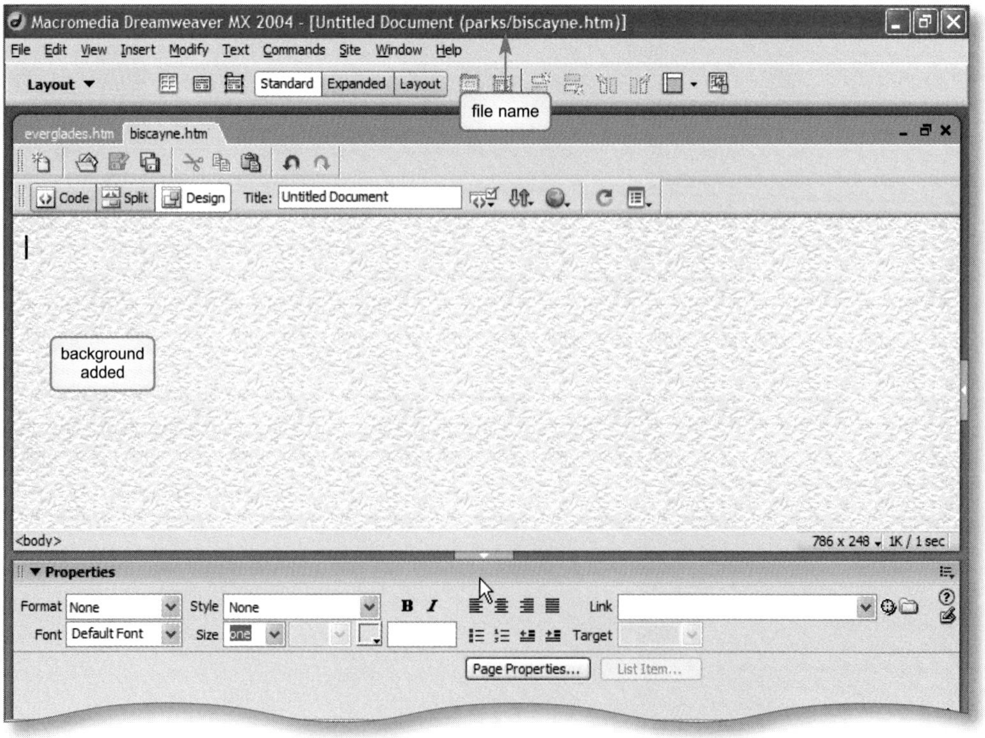

FIGURE 3-59

Next, you insert and center a three-row, two-column table. Then you add the page title to the Biscayne National Park page. You also add three images to the table. One of the images is centered within a cell. The DIV, or page division, element is a tag that defines logical divisions within the content of a page. Primarily you apply this tag when using Cascading Style Sheets (which are discussed in Project 5). In Dreamweaver Code Format preferences, however, the centering default is to add the DIV tag. If this option is selected within Preferences, and you center a single image within the table, then all elements within the table, including text and other images, are centered. The following steps show how to turn off the DIV tag centering option.

To Turn Off the DIV Tag Centering Option

1

- **Click Edit on the menu bar and then click Preferences.**
- **Click the Code Format category and then click the Use CENTER tag option button.**

The Use CENTER tag option button is selected (Figure 3-60).

2

- **Click the OK button.**
- **Collapse the panel groups.**

The settings are applied, but no visible difference is noticeable in the Document window.

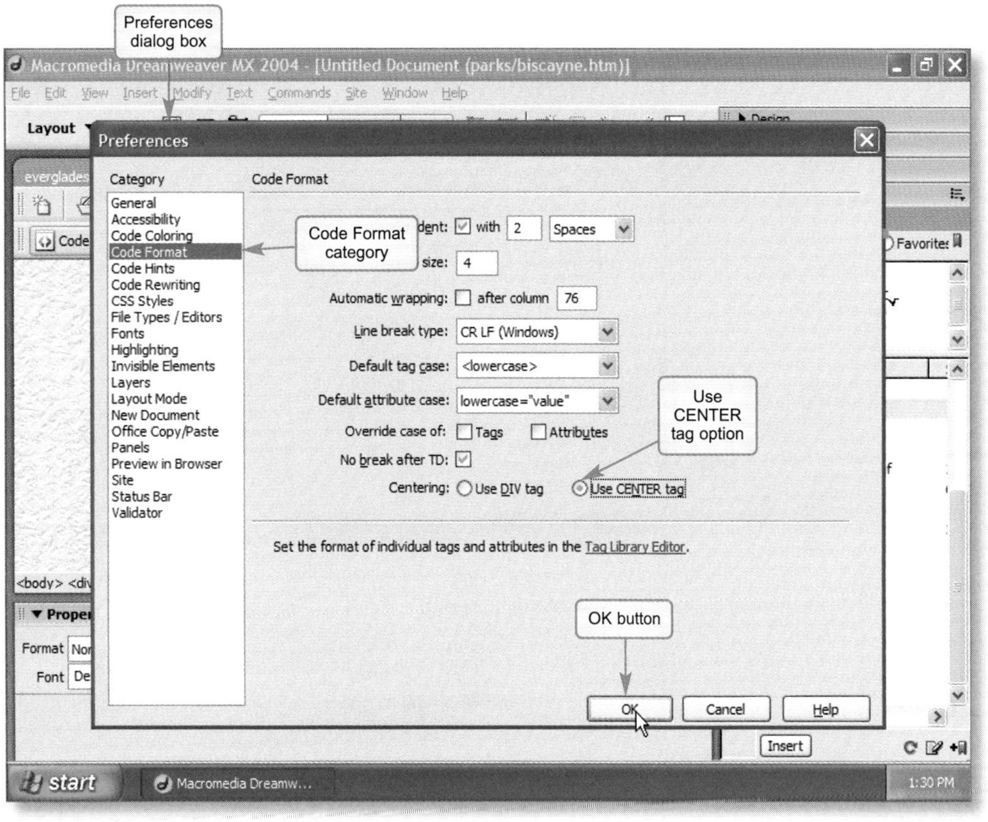

FIGURE 3-60

The next step is to insert and center a table and to add a title to the table, as shown in the following steps.

To Insert and Center a Table

1 **Click the Table button.**

2 **In the Table dialog box, change the settings as follows: Rows** 3**, Columns** 2**, W** 90 **Percent, Border** 4**, Cell padding** 0**, and Cell spacing** 2**.**

3 **Click the Summary text box and then type** `Biscayne National Parks feature page` **as the summary text.**

4 **Press the OK button to insert the table.**

5 **Title the page Biscayne National Park.**

6 **Click the Table Id text box in the Property inspector and then type** `Biscayne National Park feature page` **as the table ID. Click the Align box arrow and then click Center.**

7 **Click the Save button on the Standard toolbar.**

The centered table is added to the Web page (Figure 3-61). The Web page is saved in the parks folder. The <center> tag may not be displayed on your tag selector.

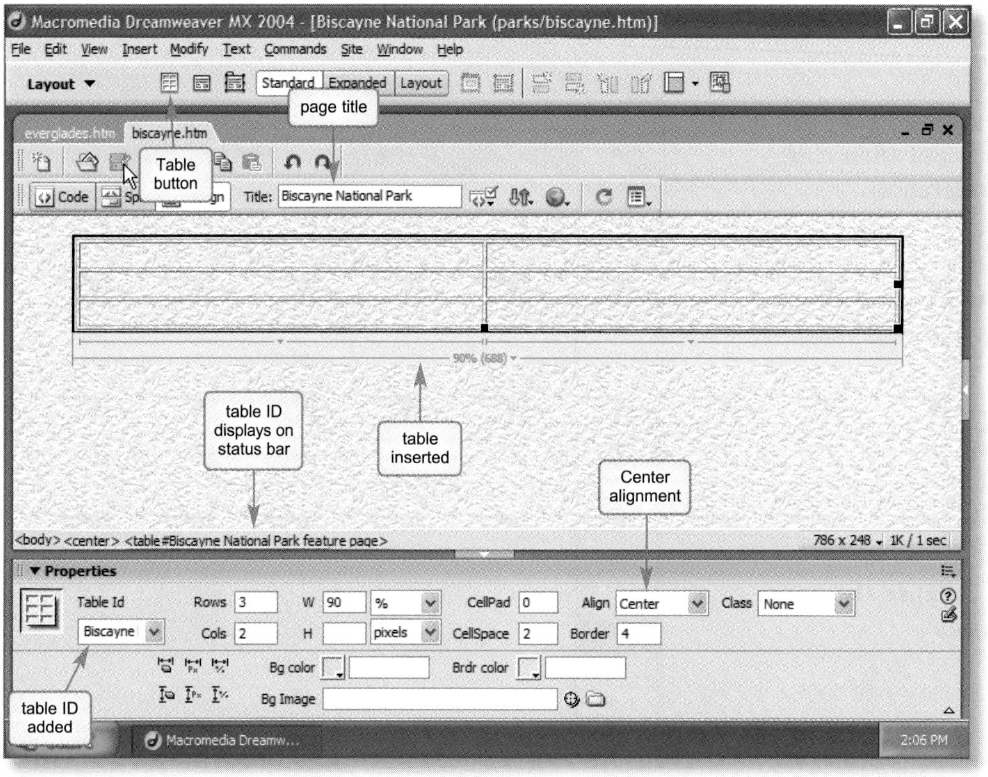

FIGURE 3-61

An understanding of HTML and how it relates to a table and to parts of a table provides you with the ability to select a table and table components and to modify a table through the code. Merging and varying the span of columns (as you did in the Everglades National Park page) and merging and varying the span of rows is helpful for grouping information, adding emphasis, or deleting empty cells. When you merge two cells in a row, you are spanning a column. Continuing with the <table> example on pages DW 195 and 196 and spanning the two cells in row 1, the HTML tags would be <td colspan="2">First cellSecond cell</td>. When you merge two cells in a column, you are spanning a row. The attribute ROWSPAN would replace COLSPAN in the above example. Understanding COLSPAN and ROWSPAN will help you determine when and if two columns or two rows have been merged.

For the Everglades National Park page, you entered a heading outside the table and links to the other pages in a second table. For the Biscayne National Park page, you merge the cells in row 1 and then merge the cells in row 3. You enter a heading in row 1 and then enter text for the links to the home page and other national parks pages in row 3. The steps on the next page illustrate how to merge the cells in row 1 and merge the cells in row 3.

To Merge Cells in Row 1 and in Row 3

1. **Click row 1, column 1 and then drag to select all of row 1.**
2. **Click the Merge Cells button in the Property inspector.**
3. **Click row 3, column 1 and then drag to select all of row 3.**
4. **Click the Merge Cells button in the Property inspector.**

The cells in row 1 are merged into one column, and the cells in row 3 also are merged into one column (Figure 3-62).

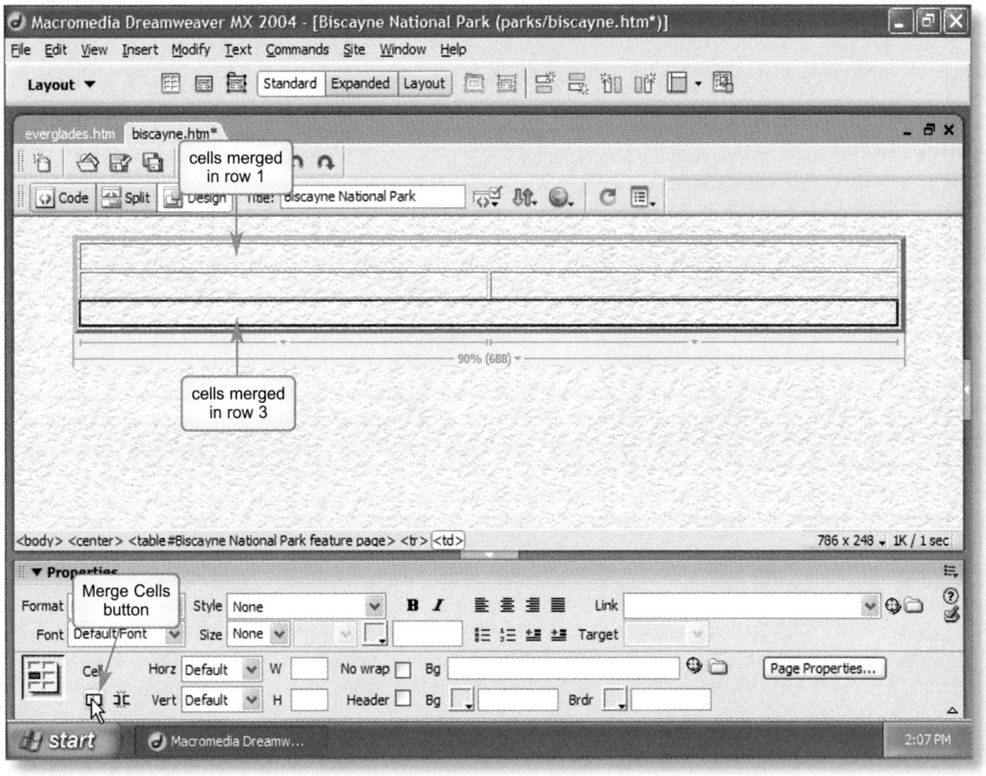

FIGURE 3-62

Next, you add and center a heading in row 1 of the table. The following steps show how to add and center the heading in row 1.

To Add a Heading to Row 1

1

- **Click row 1 and then click the Align Center button in the Property inspector.**

The insertion point is aligned in the middle of the row (Figure 3-63).

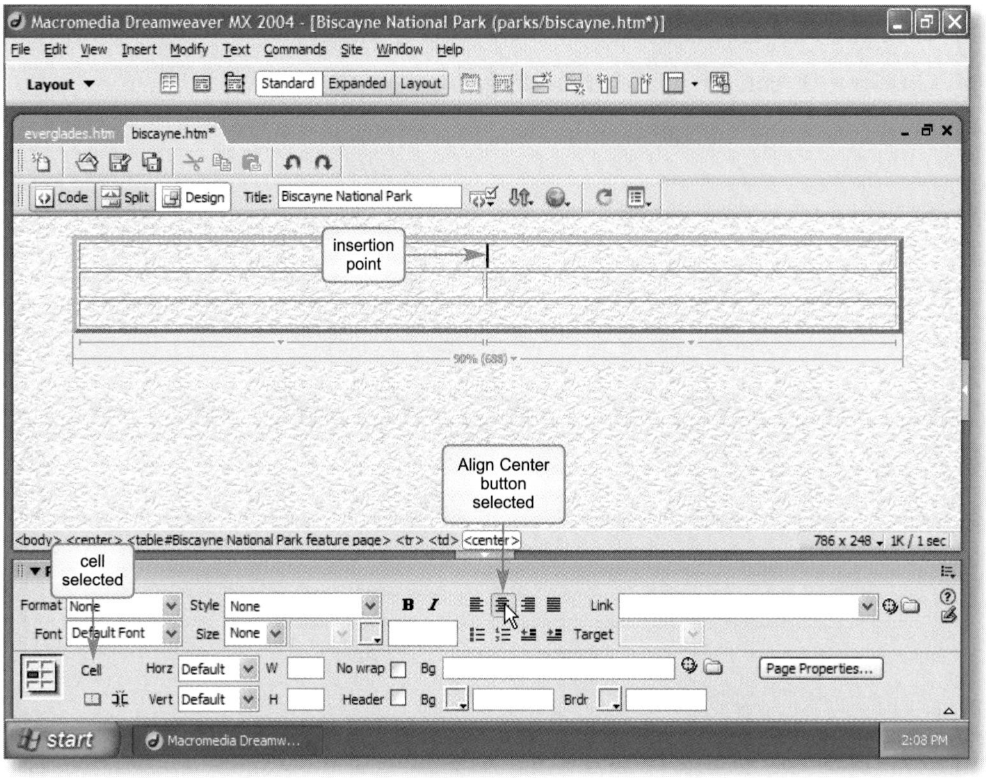

FIGURE 3-63

2

- **Type** `Biscayne National Park` **and then use the Format pop-up menu to apply Heading 1.**

The heading is centered in row 1, and Heading 1 is applied to the text (Figure 3-64).

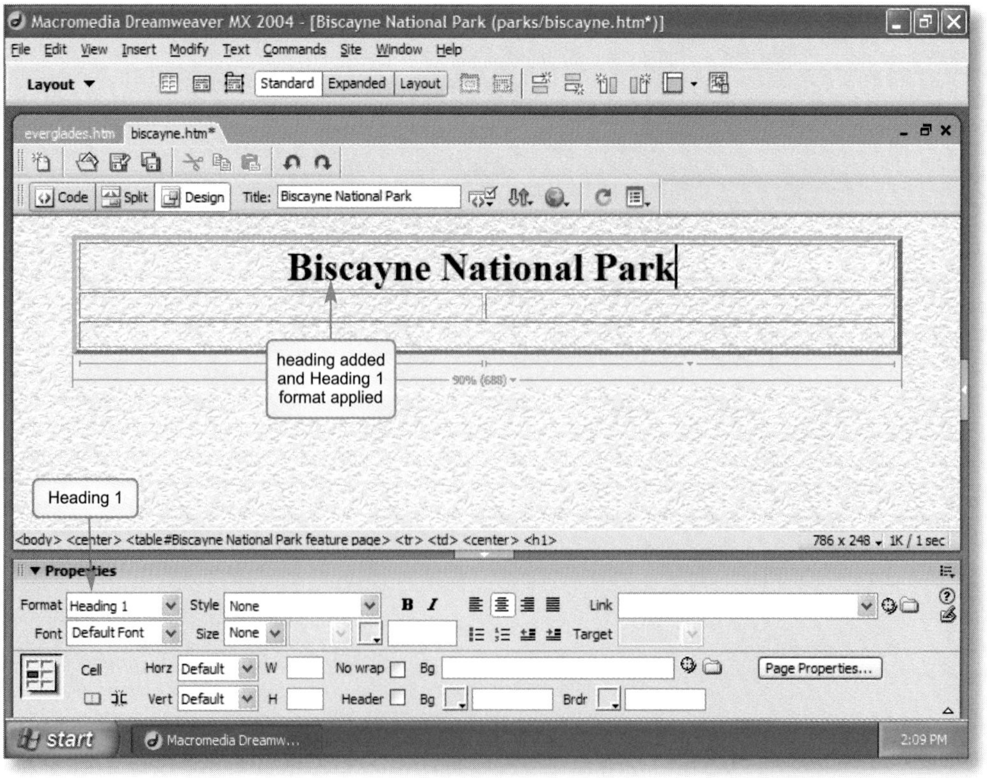

FIGURE 3-64

3

- **Click row 3 and then click the Align Center button in the Property inspector.**

The insertion point is centered in row 3 (Figure 3-65).

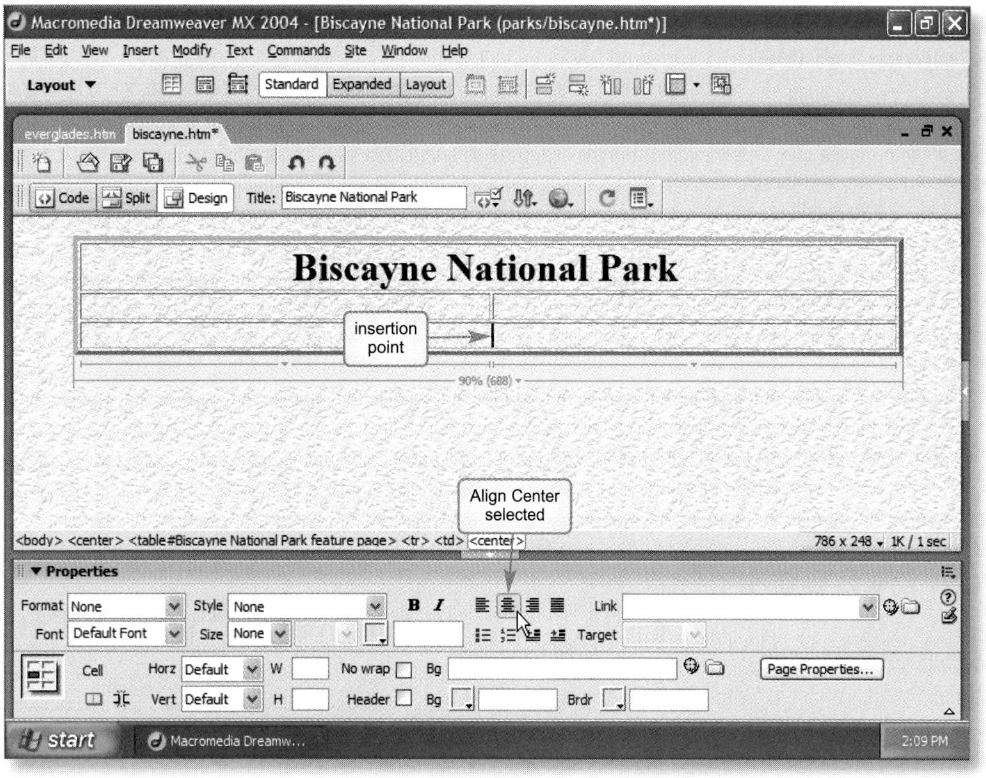

FIGURE 3-65

4

- **Type** `Home` **and then press the SPACEBAR.**
- **Press SHIFT + | (vertical bar) and then press the SPACEBAR.**
- **Type** `Everglades National Park` **and then press the SPACEBAR.**
- **Press SHIFT + | and then press the SPACEBAR.**
- **Type** `Dry Tortugas National Park` **as the last link text.**

The text for the links is centered in the row (Figure 3-66).

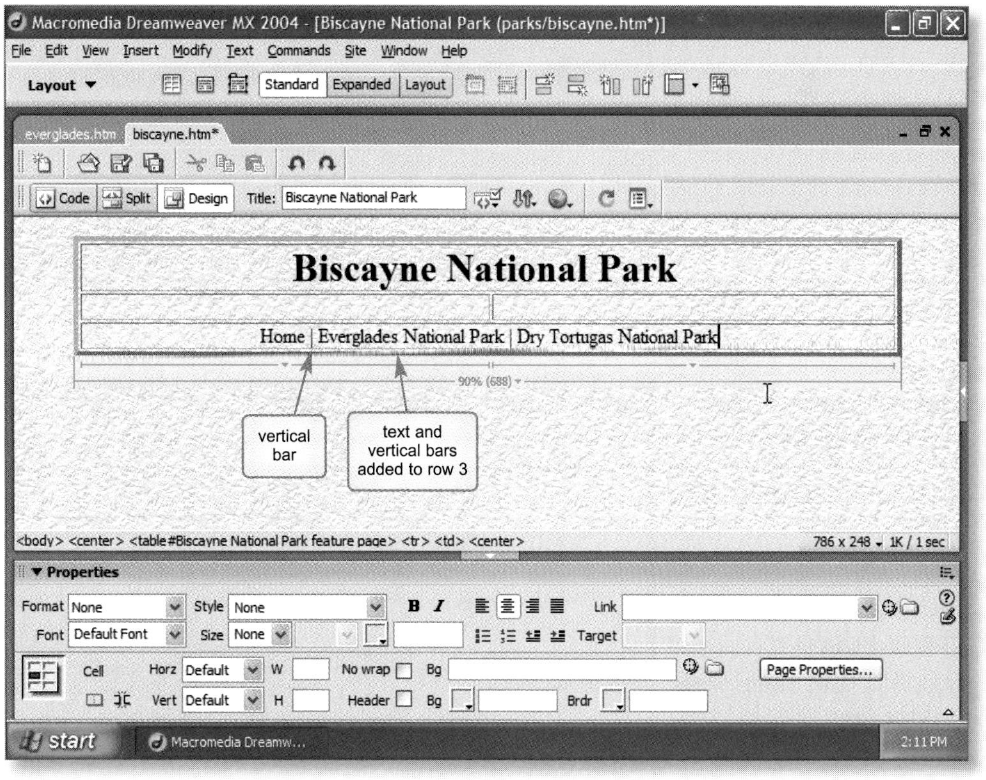

FIGURE 3-66

More About

Column Width

In addition to using the Property inspector to change the width or height of a column, you also can change cell widths and heights directly in the HTML code.

Splitting and Merging Cells

Tables in a traditional sense generally are thought of as having an internal **symmetry**; that is, cells of the same size form neatly arranged columns and rows. On a Web page, however, by varying the size of a cell, you can use tables to create an asymmetrical arrangement. This design option allows for more visual variation on a Web page. In a three-column table, for example, you could specify the width of the first column as 20 percent and that of the second and third columns as 40 percent each. Depending on the number of columns, hundreds of percentage variations can be applied. In the Biscayne National Park page, you adjust the width for columns 1 and 2 and then change the vertical alignment to Top within both columns. The following steps show how to adjust the width and change the vertical spacing.

To Adjust the Column Width

1

- **Click row 2, column 1.**

The insertion point is located in row 2, column 1 (Figure 3-67).

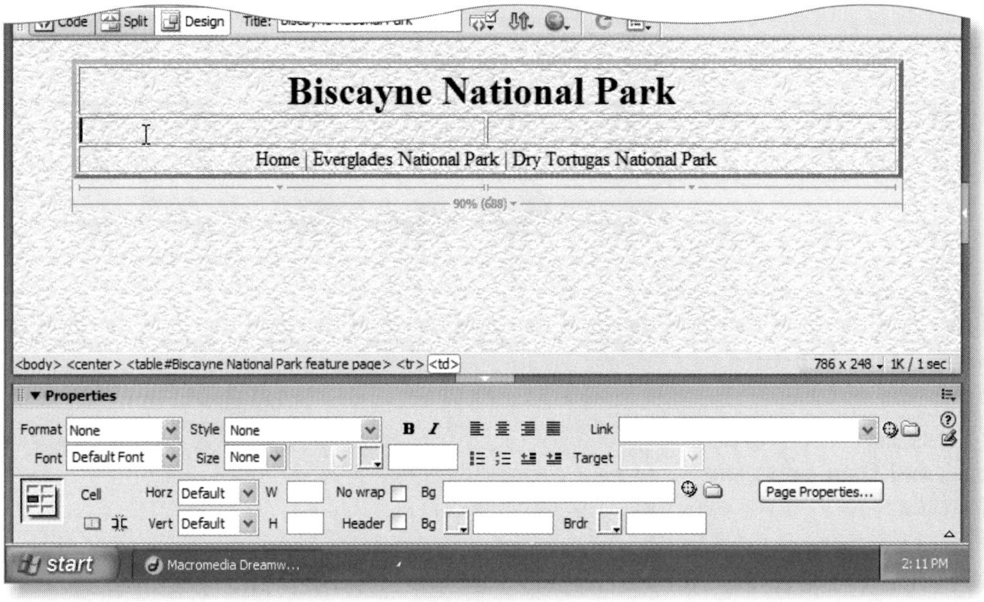

FIGURE 3-67

2

- **Click the W box in the Property inspector.**
- **Type** 40% **and then press the ENTER key.**
- **Click row 2, column 2.**
- **Click the W box in the Property inspector.**
- **Type** 60% **and then press the ENTER key.**

Column 1 is decreased in size to reflect the new percentage. and column 2 is increased in size to reflect the new percentage (Figure 3-68).

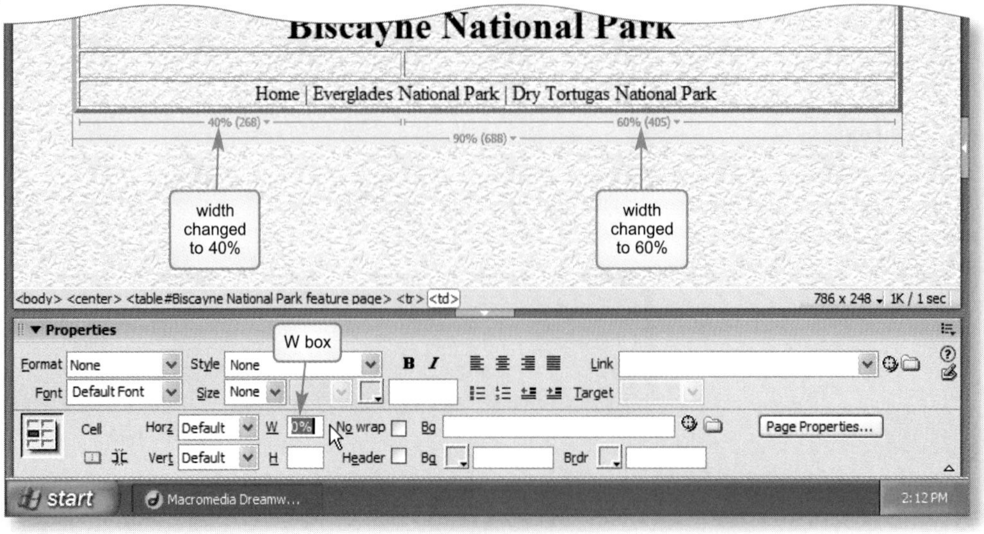

FIGURE 3-68

3

- **Select row 2, columns 1 and 2.**
- **Click the Vert box arrow in the Property inspector and then select Top from the Vert pop-up menu.**

Top is selected in the Vert box (Figure 3-69). No noticeable differences display in the table. Any image or text in these cells, however, will align to the top.

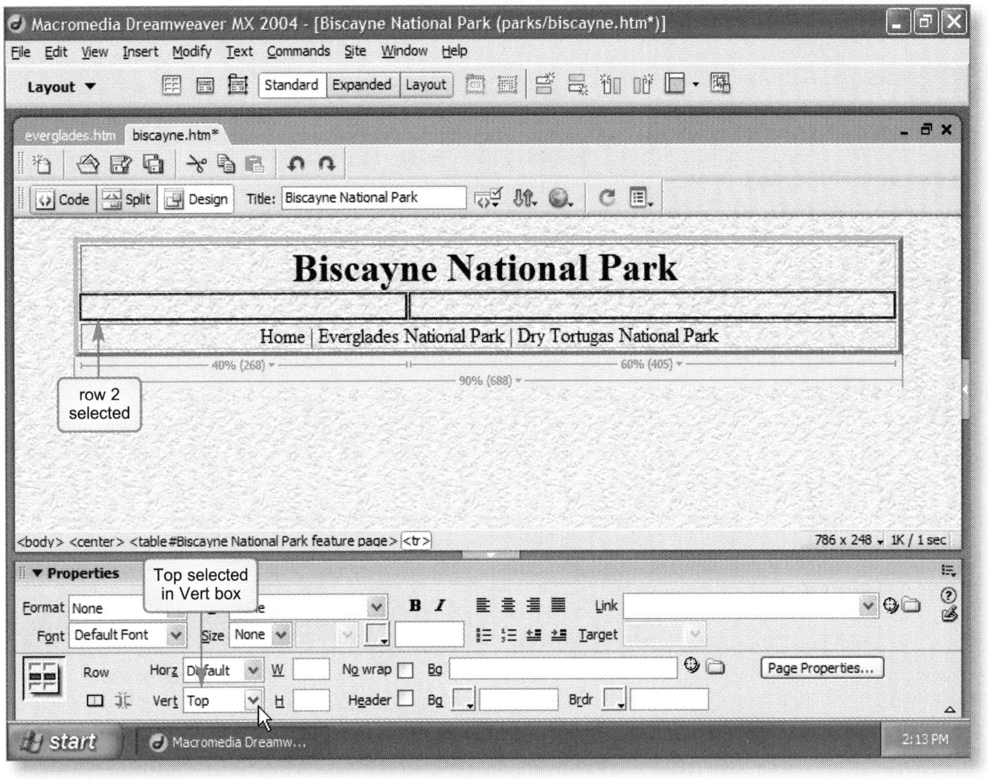

FIGURE 3-69

Now you add the text and images to row 2, columns 1 and 2. Table 3-4 contains the text for the Biscayne National Park Web page.

Table 3-4 Biscayne National Park Web Page Text

SECTION	TEXT FOR BISCAYNE NATIONAL PARK WEB PAGE
Part 1	Located off the eastern coast of Florida, the 180,000-acre Biscayne National Park is less than an hour's drive from Miami. The park originally was established as a national monument in 1968. It became a national park in 1980, specifically to protect the incredible diversity of mammals, birds, fish, and plants.<ENTER><ENTER>
Part 2	Park Service Information Office: Biscayne National Park P. O. Box 1369 Homestead, FL 33090<ENTER> E-mail: Biscayne National Park
Part 3	More than 95 percent of the park is underwater and includes mangrove swamps, coral reefs, and the waters of Biscayne Bay. The remaining 5 percent includes 44 islands that form an 18-nautical mile north-south chain. In this watery paradise, one can find more than 200 varieties of fish, which inhabit the coral reefs. Starfish, sponges, soft corals, and other marine plants and animals live and thrive in Biscayne Bay.<ENTER><ENTER>
Part 4	Biscayne National Park is best explored with snorkels or scuba gear. For those not quite so adventurous, glass-bottom boat trips and canoe rentals are available.<ENTER>

More About

Inserting Images into a Table

In Macromedia Dreamweaver MX 2004, you can work in Design view or Code view to insert images in a document.

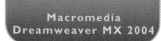

To Add Text and Images to the Biscayne National Park Web Page

1

- **Click row 2, column 1.**
- **Press the ENTER key and then type the text of Part 1 as shown in Table 3-4.**
- **When typing the text, press the ENTER key as indicated in Part 1, Table 3-4.**

The text is entered as shown in Figure 3-70.

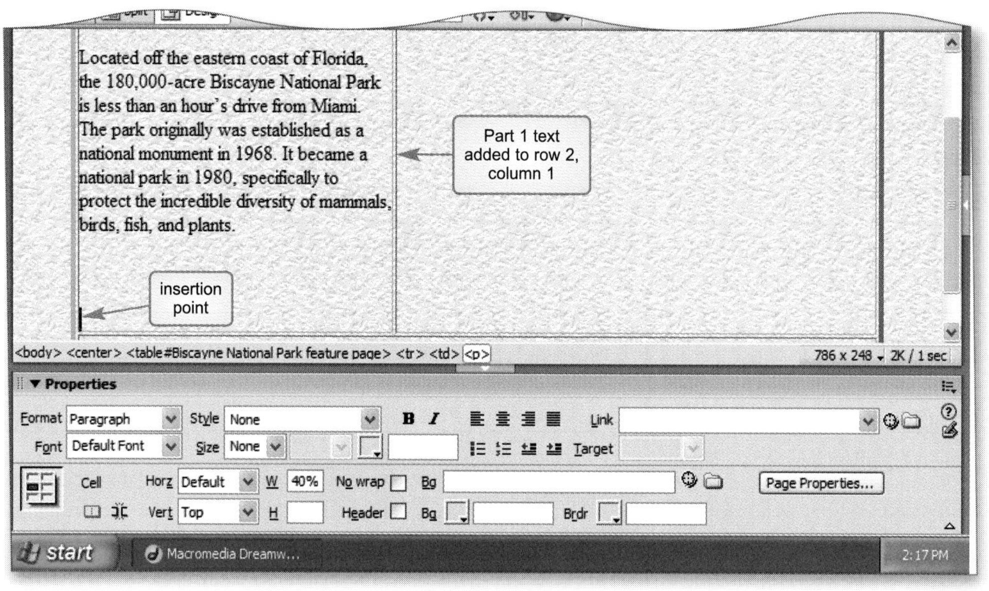

FIGURE 3-70

2

- **Type the text of Part 2 as shown in Table 3-4 on the previous page.**
- **Insert line breaks and then press the ENTER key as indicated in Table 3-4.**

The text is entered as shown in Figure 3-71.

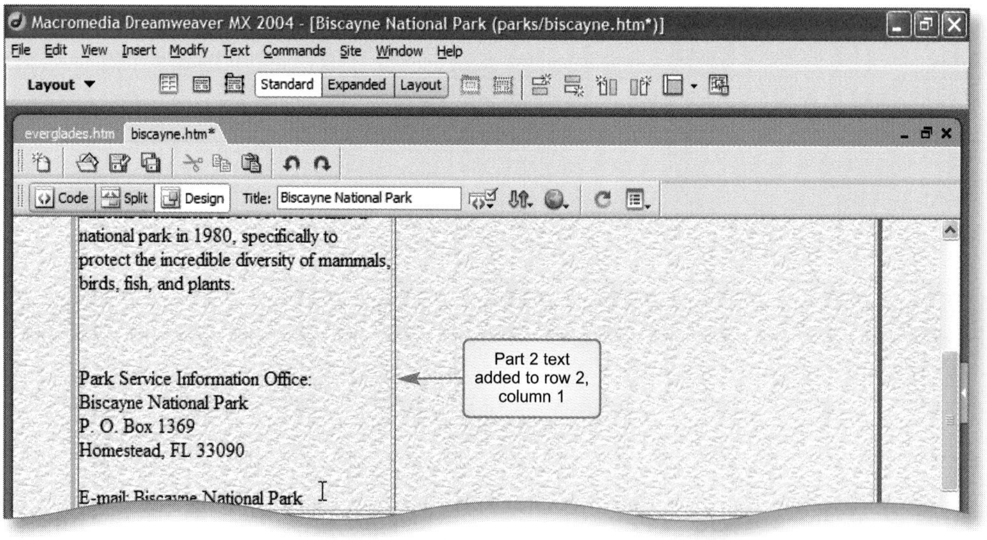

FIGURE 3-71

3

- **Scroll up and click row 2, column 2.**

The insertion point is positioned in row 2, column 2 (Figure 3-72).

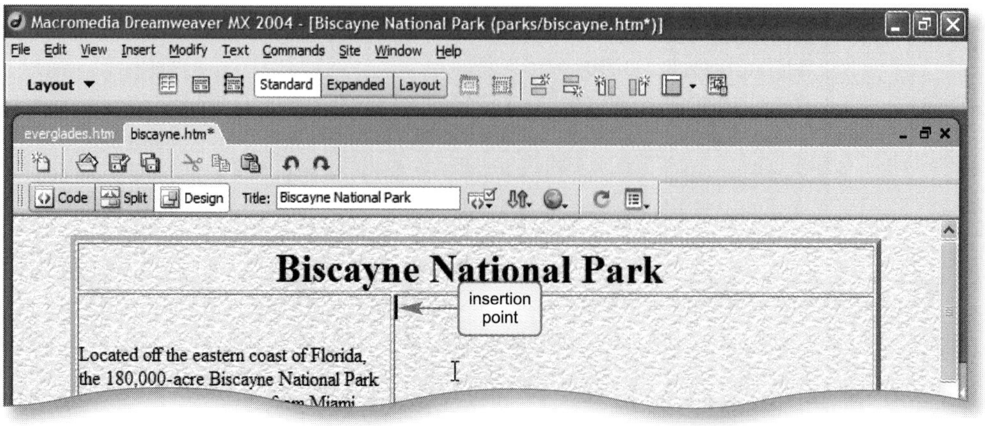

FIGURE 3-72

4

- **Type the text of Part 3 as shown in Table 3-4.**
- **Press the ENTER key as indicated in Table 3-4.**

The text is entered as shown in Figure 3-73.

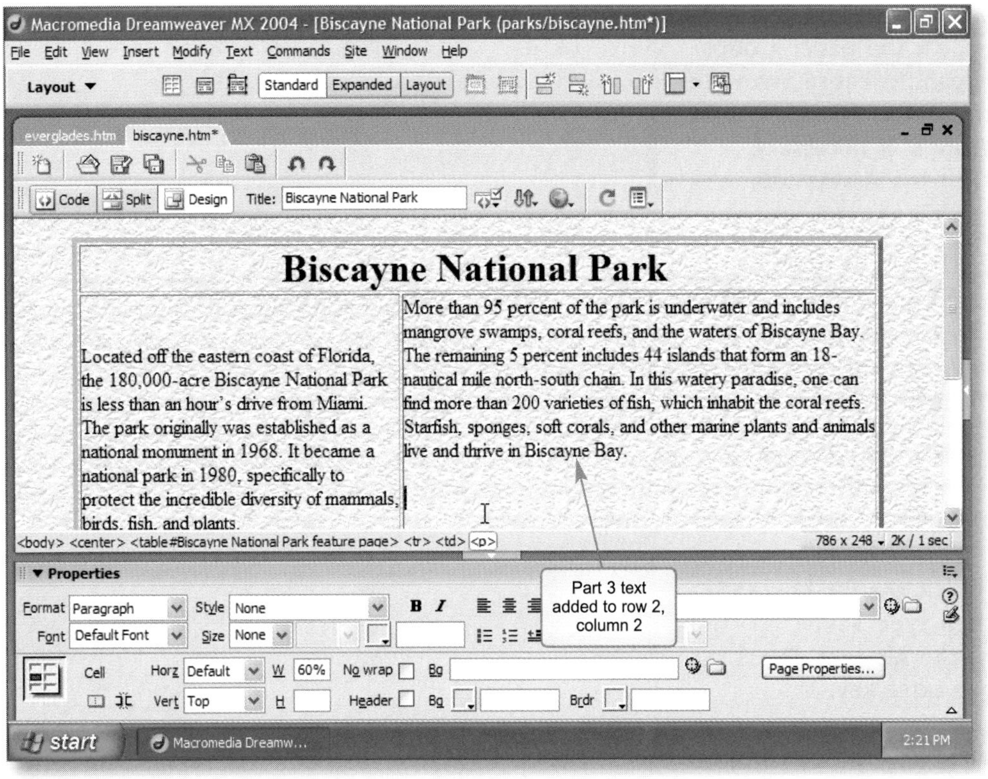

FIGURE 3-73

5

- **Type the text of Part 4 as shown in Table 3-4.**
- **Press the ENTER key as indicated in Table 3-4.**

The text is entered as shown in Figure 3-74.

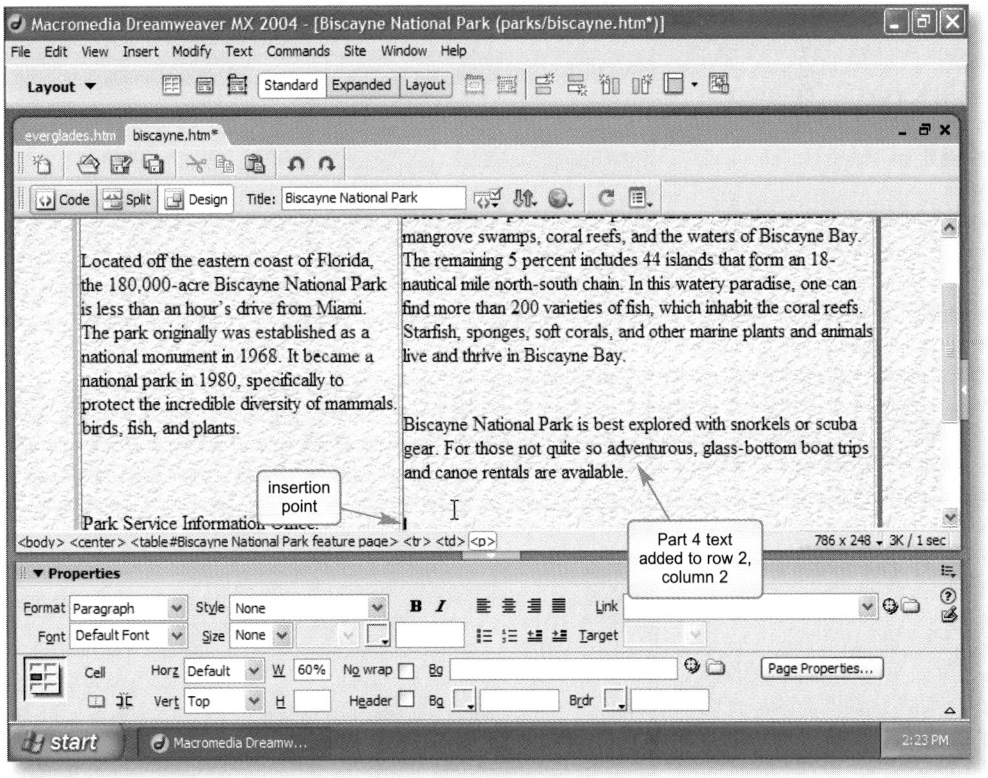

FIGURE 3-74

6

- **Click the panel groups expand/collapse arrow to display the panel groups. If necessary, click the Assets tab.**
- **Click row 2, column 1 above the text you typed in Part 1.**
- **Drag the island.gif image to the insertion point in row 2, column 1.**
- **Click the Image text box and then type** `scubadiving` **as the image ID.**
- **Click the Alt box and then type** `Scuba diving` **as the Alt text. Press the ENTER key.**

The island.gif image displays in row 2, column 1, and the image is selected (Figure 3-75).

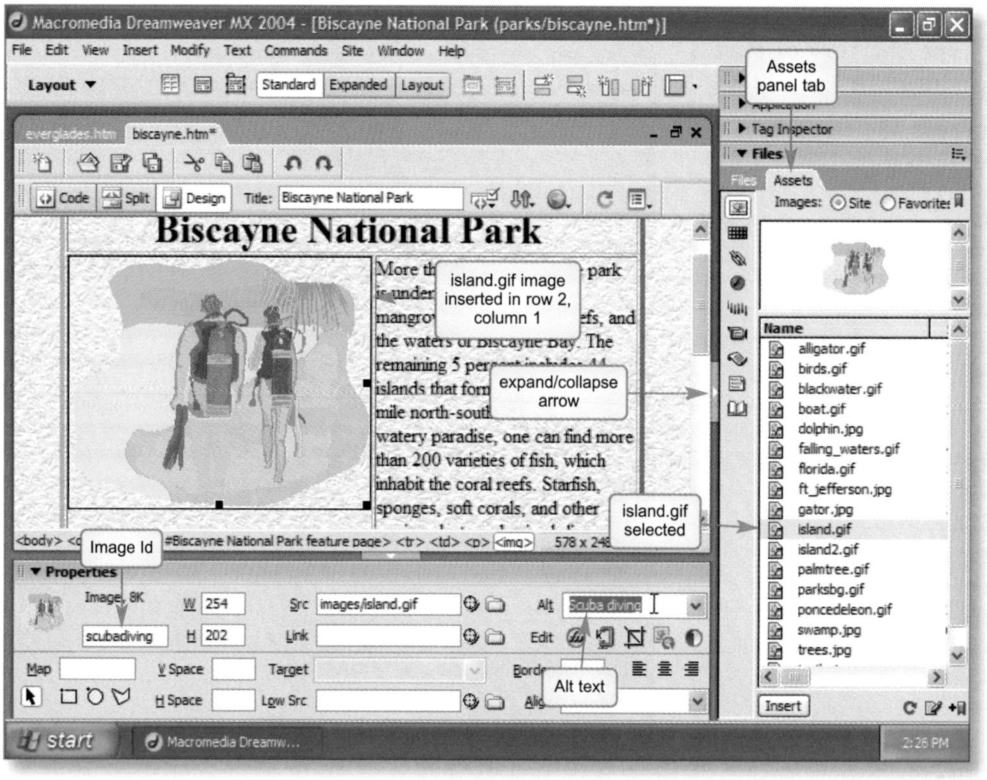

FIGURE 3-75

7

- **Click row 2, column 2 below the text you typed in Part 3.**
- **Drag the palmtree.gif image to the insertion point.**
- **Click the Image text box and then type** `palmtree` **as the image ID.**
- **Click the Alt text box and then type** `Palm tree` **as the Alt text.**
- **Press the ENTER key.**

The palmtree.gif image displays in row 2, column 2. The image is selected (Figure 3-76).

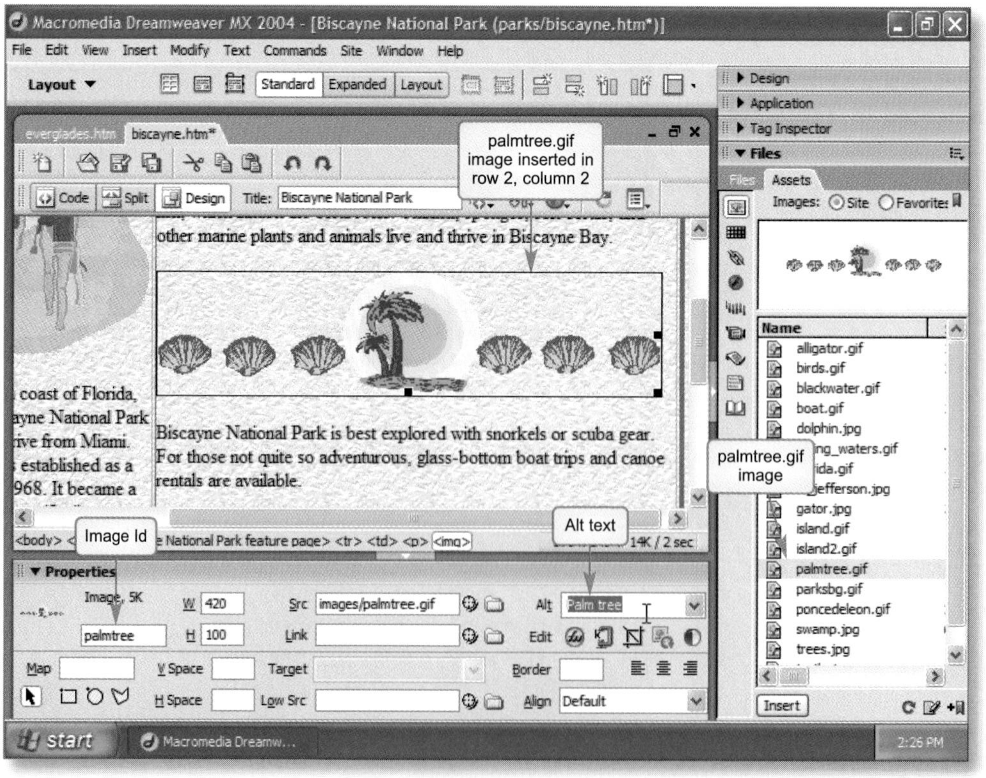

FIGURE 3-76

8

- **Click row 2, column 2 below the text you typed in Part 4.**
- **Drag the island2.gif image to the insertion point.**
- **Double-click the W box in the Property inspector and then type** 375 **as the new value.**
- **Press the TAB key and type** 220 **as the new value in the H box.**
- **Click the Align Center button.**
- **Click the Image text box and then type** island **as the image ID.**
- **Type** Island **as the Alt text and then press the ENTER key.**

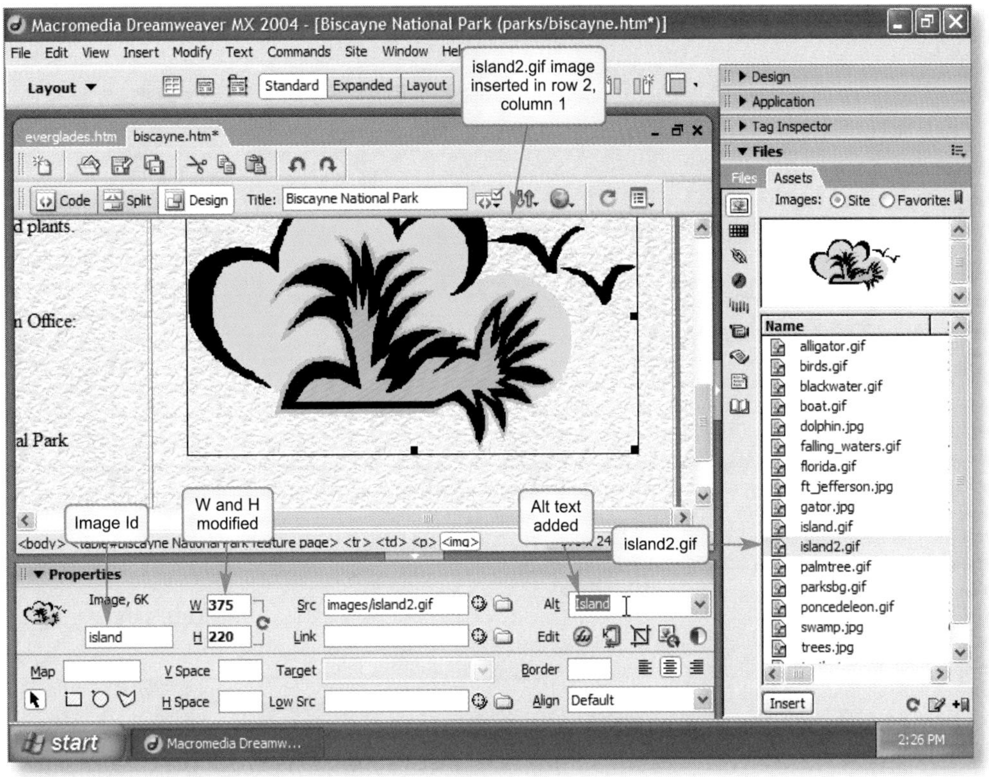

FIGURE 3-77

The image is inserted into the cell, resized, and centered (Figure 3-77).

Adding a Border and a Border Color

A **border** is the width, in pixels, of the table border. The purpose of most tables in a Web page is to provide a structure for the positioning of text and images. When a table is created within Dreamweaver, therefore, the default border is 0 (zero), or no border. Adding a border to a Web page, however, transforms the table into a graphical element itself. Depending on the content, a border can become a visual cue for the reader by separating content. For the Biscayne National Park page, a border is applied to the full table. You cannot apply a border to an individual cell unless the table consists of only one cell.

When you created the table for the Biscayne National Park Web page, you specified a border size of 4. By default, borders are gray, but the border color can be changed. Using the color picker, you can apply a color of your choice. You can apply a border color to a single cell or to a range of cells.

Background images and background color work the same for a table as they do for a Web page. The image or color, however, is contained within the table and does not affect the rest of the page. Background color and images can be applied to a single cell or to a range of cells. The steps on the next page illustrate how to add a border color to the table and a background color to a merged cell.

More About

Borders

A border can help separate content within a table. Borders are especially useful if the table includes information that contains data that must be read across a row or down a column.

To Add Border Color and Cell Background Color

1

- **Click <table#Biscayne National Park feature page> in the tag selector and then click the Brdr Color box arrow in the Property inspector. Point to row 9, column 2.**

The table is selected, and the Continuous Tone color palette is displayed (Figure 3-78).

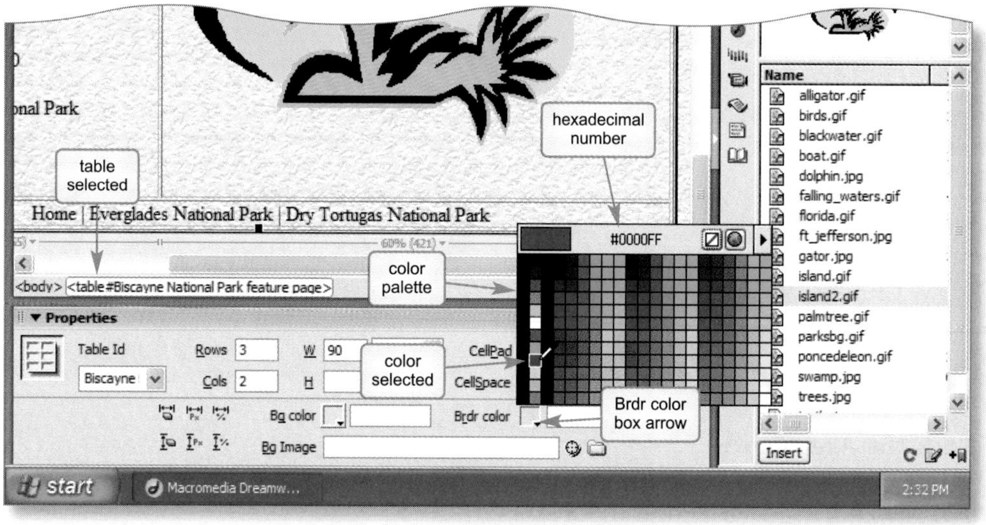

FIGURE 3-78

2

- **Click row 9, column 2 to select the blue color, hexadecimal #0000FF. Press the TAB key.**

A shade of blue is applied to the border (Figure 3-79).

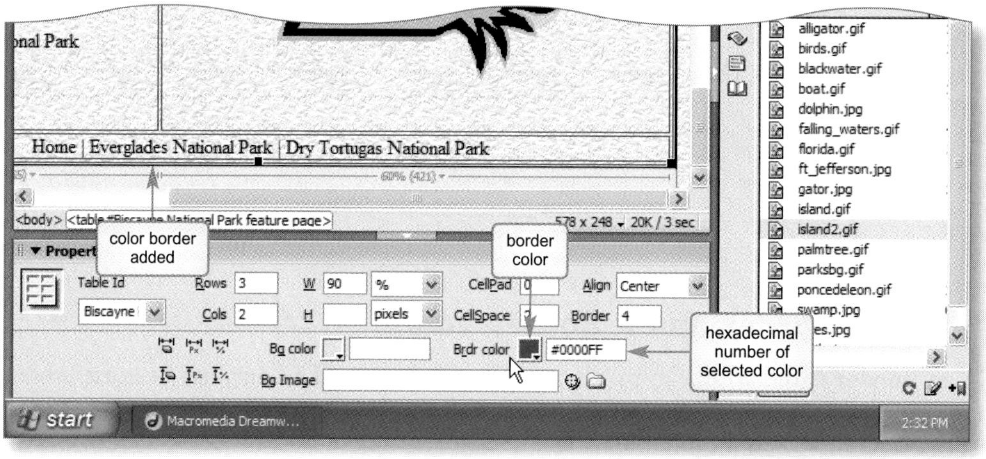

FIGURE 3-79

3

- **If necessary, scroll up and left. Click anywhere in row 1.**
- **Click the Bg Color box arrow. If necessary, select the Color Cubes palette and then point to the second column from the right and fourth row from the bottom — hexadecimal color #FFCC66.**

The color palette displays the selected background color (Figure 3-80).

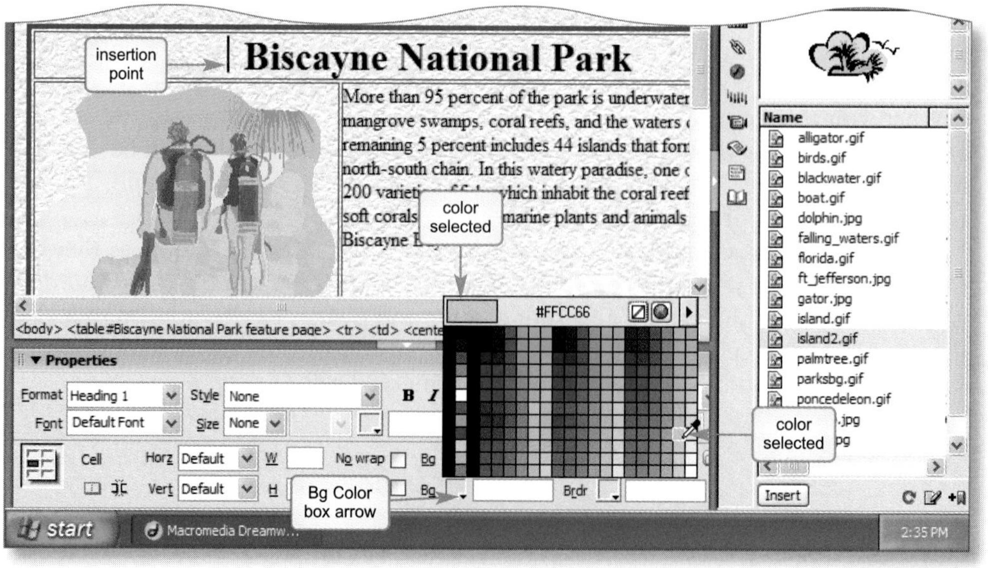

FIGURE 3-80

4

• **Click the mouse pointer.**

The palette is closed, and the background color is applied to the row (Figure 3-81).

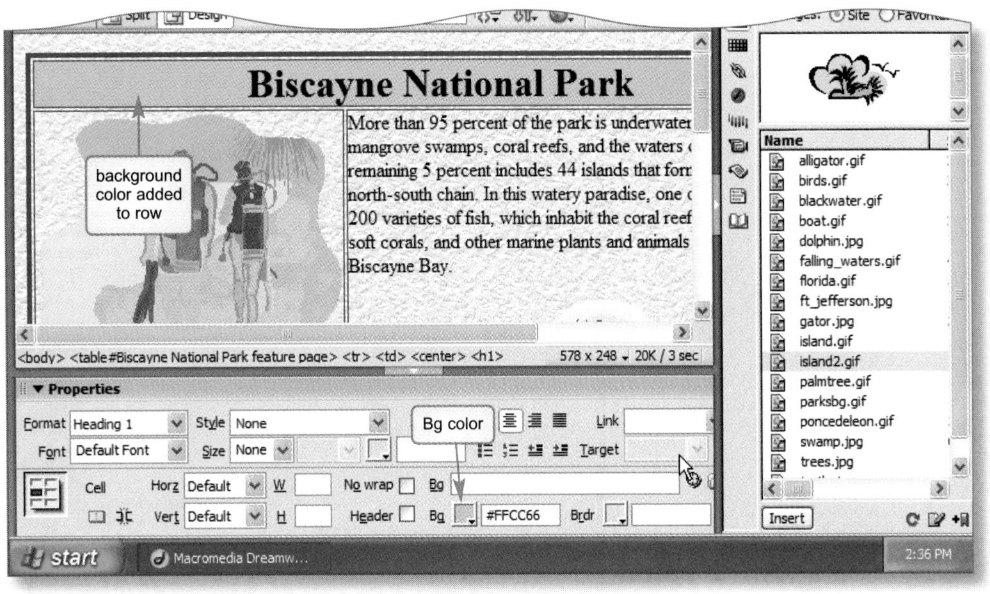

FIGURE 3-81

Your last tasks for the Biscayne National Park page are to add links, spell check, and save the page. The following steps illustrate how to spell check; add the absolute, relative, and e-mail links to the Biscayne National Park page; and then save the Web page.

To Add Links To and Spell Check the Biscayne National Park Page

1. **Click the panel groups expand/collapse button to hide the panel groups.**
2. **Scroll down and select the first instance of Biscayne National Park in the address in row 2, column 1. Type** `http://www.nps.gov/bisc/` **in the Link box and then press the ENTER key.**
3. **Select the second instance of Biscayne National Park. Click Insert on the menu bar and then click Email Link. Type** `biscayne@parks.gov` **in the E-Mail text box. Click the OK button in the Email Link dialog box.**
4. **Select the text, Home, in row 3, type** `index.htm` **in the Link box, and then press the ENTER key.**
5. **Select the text, Everglades National Park, type** `everglades.htm` **in the Link box, and then press the ENTER key.**
6. **Select the text, Dry Tortugas National Park, type** `dry_tortugas.htm` **in the Link box, and then press the ENTER key.**
7. **Click Text on the menu bar and then select the Check Spelling command. Check the spelling.**
8. **Click the Save button on the Document toolbar.**
9. **Press the F12 key to view the Web page in your browser, as shown in Figure 3-82. If necessary, save any changes. Close the browser and then close the Web page.**

In the browser, the Biscayne National Park page is displayed (Figure 3-82).

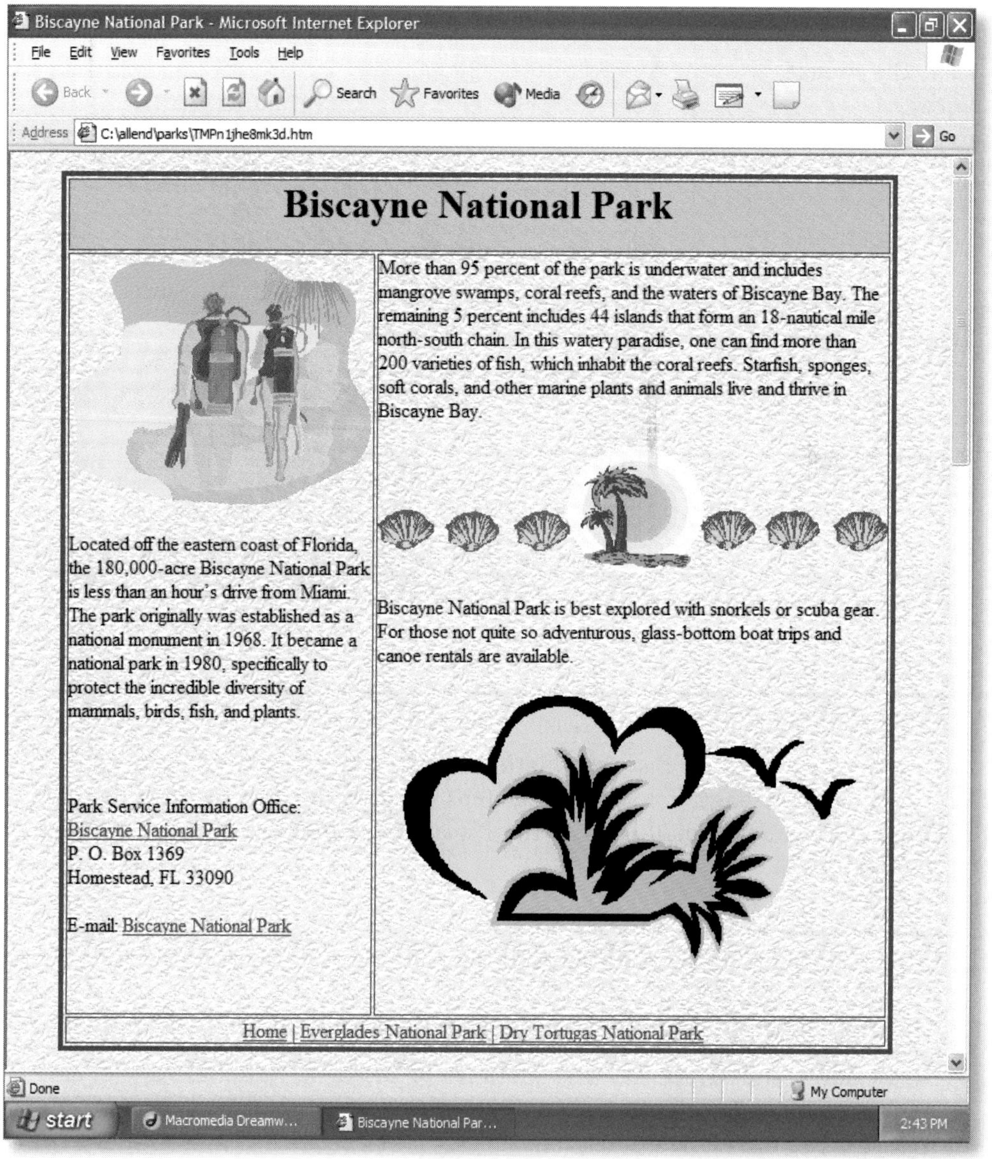

FIGURE 3-82

Layout Mode

Tables created in Standard mode are useful for creating Web pages that are simple in format or contain tabular data. A second option for creating tables in Dreamweaver is the Layout mode. Layout mode provides more flexibility than Standard mode. In Layout mode, you draw your own table and cells. When using Layout mode, you are creating the framework for the entire table. The layout can be as simple or as complex as you want.

Layout mode is a tool unique to Dreamweaver. Terms such as Layout mode and layout cell do not exist in HTML. When you draw a **layout table**, Dreamweaver creates an HTML table. When you draw a **layout cell**, Dreamweaver creates a tag (<td>) in the table. The <td> tag is a container for the content rendered inside one cell of a table element. When a cell is drawn in a layout table, it stays within the row-and-column grid as it does in Standard mode. Cells cannot overlap, but they can span rows and columns. When you draw cells of different widths and different heights, Dreamweaver creates additional cells in the HTML table to fill in the empty spots. These cells display with a gray background.

You can use Layout mode to modify the structure of an existing page created in Standard mode. Layout mode, however, provides the greatest advantage when you are designing the page from the start. As you draw the table and/or cells in Layout mode, Dreamweaver creates the code. If you draw a layout cell first, a layout table is inserted automatically to serve as a container for the layout cell. A layout cell cannot exist outside of a layout table. You can create your page using one layout table with several layout cells contained within the table or you can have multiple layout tables. For uncomplicated pages, use one layout table. For a more complicated layout, use multiple tables. Using multiple layout tables isolates parts of your layout so one section does not affect another. For example, the cell size within a table can affect the other cells in the same row and column. Multiple tables eliminate this problem, especially for pages with numerous elements.

> **Q&A**
>
> **Q:** Does Dreamweaver support nested layout tables?
>
> **A:** Yes — you can draw a layout table inside another layout table.

When you draw a table in Layout mode, Dreamweaver outlines the table in green. A tab labeled Layout Table displays at the top of each table. Clicking the tab selects the table. When you complete your page design for the Dry Tortugas National Park, it will look similar to the page shown in Figure 3-83 on the next page.

The steps on the next page show how to add a new page, add a background image, and prepare the work area of the page. This page contains one layout table and 10 layout cells.

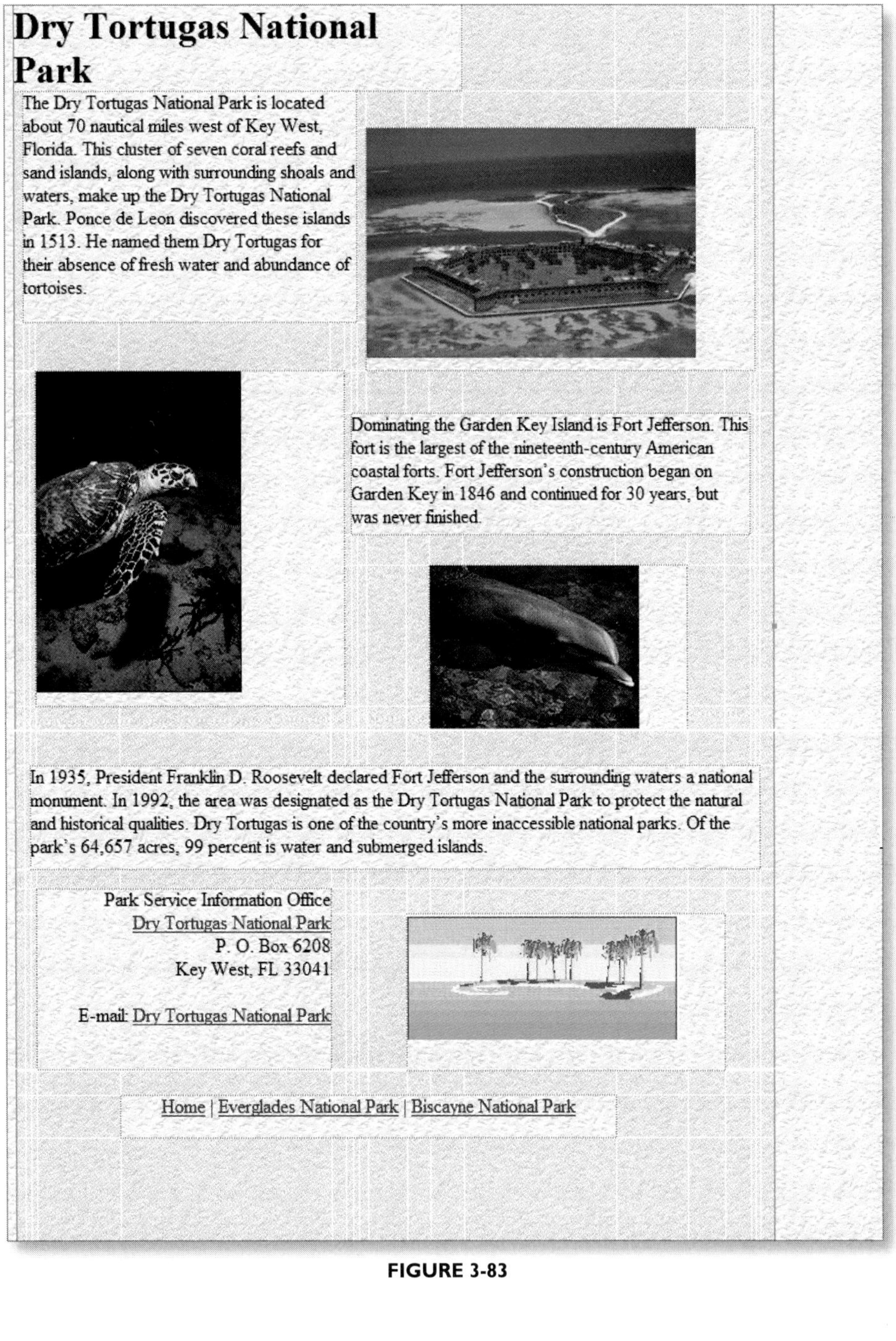
Dry Tortugas National Park
The Dry Tortugas National Park is located about 70 nautical miles west of Key West, Florida. This cluster of seven coral reefs and sand islands, along with surrounding shoals and waters, make up the Dry Tortugas National Park. Ponce de Leon discovered these islands in 1513. He named them Dry Tortugas for their absence of fresh water and abundance of tortoises.
Dominating the Garden Key Island is Fort Jefferson. This fort is the largest of the nineteenth-century American coastal forts. Fort Jefferson's construction began on Garden Key in 1846 and continued for 30 years, but was never finished.
In 1935, President Franklin D. Roosevelt declared Fort Jefferson and the surrounding waters a national monument. In 1992, the area was designated as the Dry Tortugas National Park to protect the natural and historical qualities. Dry Tortugas is one of the country's more inaccessible national parks. Of the park's 64,657 acres, 99 percent is water and submerged islands.
Park Service Information Office
Dry Tortugas National Park
P. O. Box 6208
Key West, FL 33041
E-mail: Dry Tortugas National Park
Home | Everglades National Park | Biscayne National Park

FIGURE 3-83

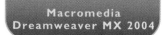

To Add a New Page and Add a Background Image to the Dry Tortugas National Park Web Page

1. **Click File on the menu bar and then click New. If necessary, click the General tab and then click Basic page in the Category list. If necessary, click HTML in the Basic page list.**
2. **Click the Create button.**
3. **Click Modify on the menu bar and then click Page Properties.**
4. **Click the Browse button to the right of the Background image box.**
5. **If necessary, navigate to the parks\images folder.**
6. **Click parksbg.gif and then click the OK button in the Select Image Source dialog box.**
7. **Click the OK button in the Page Properties dialog box. If a Macromedia alert dialog box appears, click OK.**
8. **Type** `Dry Tortugas National Park` **as the title.**
9. **Click the expand/collapse button in the panel groups to hide the panels.**
10. **Click the Save button on the Standard toolbar and save the Web page in the parks folder. Type** `dry_tortugas` **as the file name.**

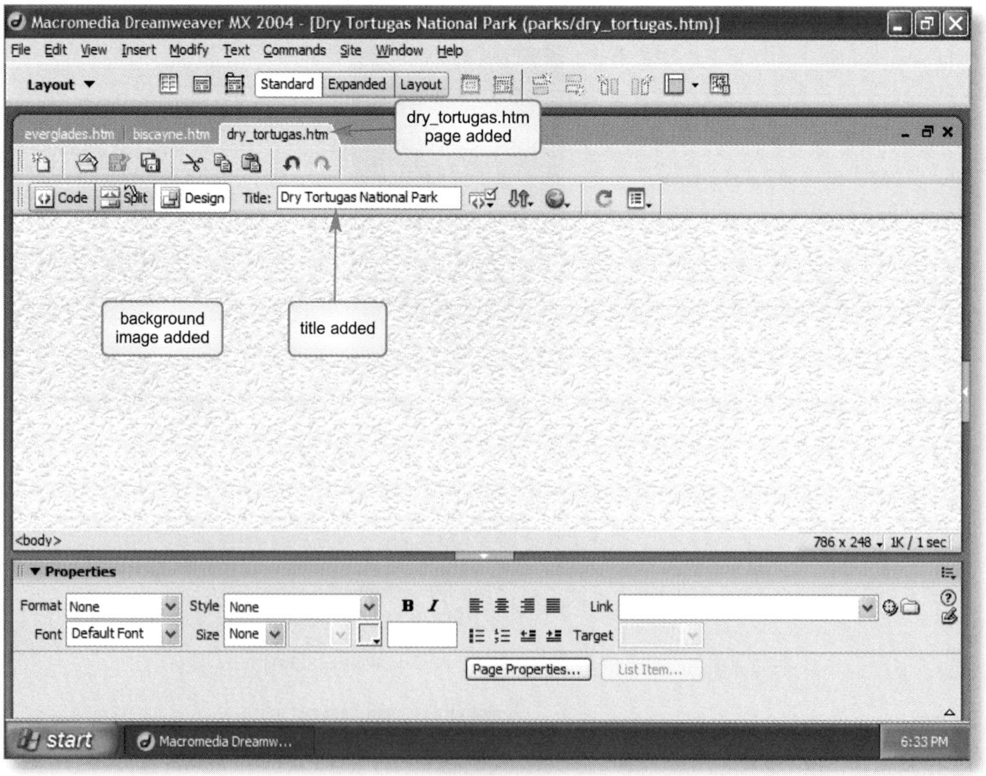

FIGURE 3-84

Using Visual Guides

Dreamweaver provides three types of visual guides to help you design documents and project how the page will appear in a browser: rulers, tracing image, and grid.

RULERS Provide a visual cue for positioning and resizing layers or tables.

TRACING IMAGE Used as the page background to duplicate a design.

GRID Provides precise positioning and resizing of layers.

You can use the rulers to help approximate cell width and height and cell location within a table or you can use the pixel measurements that display in the right corner of the status bar. Then, if necessary, you can make final adjustments to the cells and table using the settings in the Property inspector. The steps on the next page illustrate how to display the rulers in the Document window.

More About

The Grid Feature

Dreamweaver's grid feature is a visual guide that allows for precise positioning. Options include changing the grid square size and specifying that table and cell edges snap to the grid edges. To turn on the grid, click View on the menu bar, point to Grid, and then click Show Grid on the Grid submenu.

To Display the Rulers

1

- **Click View on the menu bar, point to Rulers, and then point to Show on the Rulers submenu.**

Dreamweaver displays the View menu and the Rulers submenu (Figure 3-85).

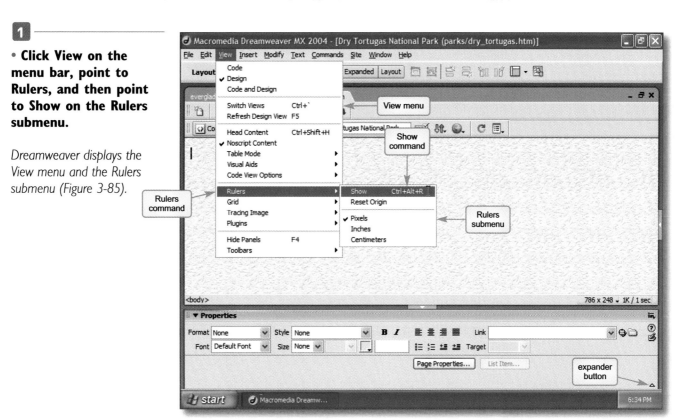

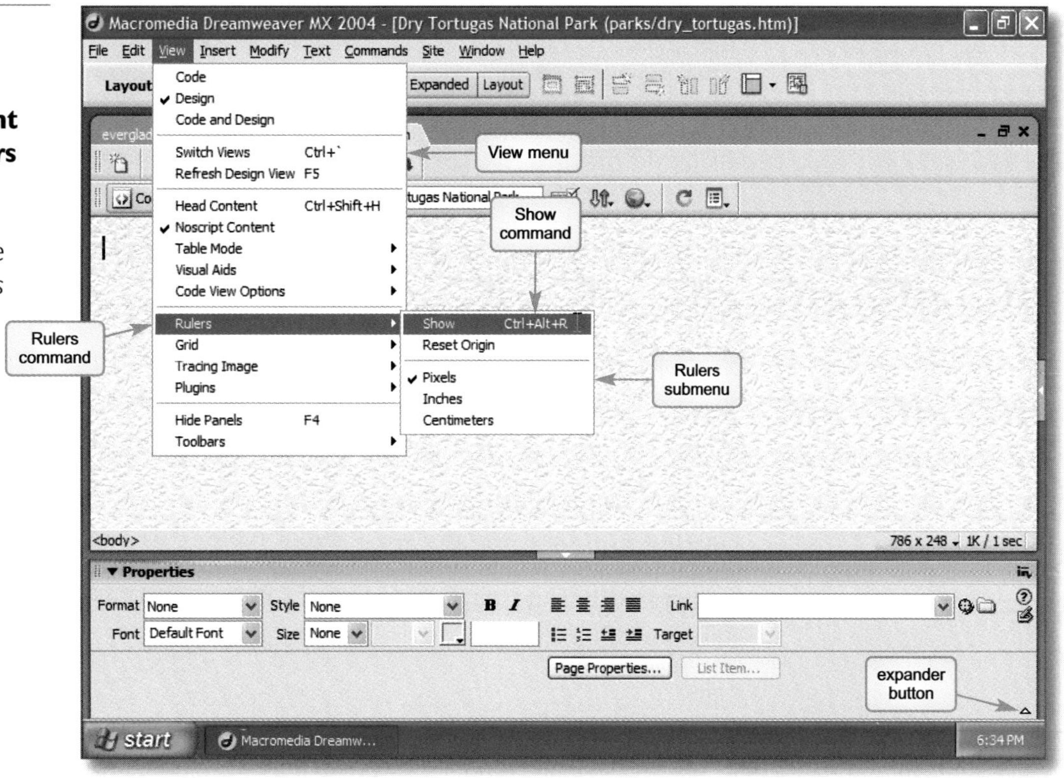

FIGURE 3-85

2

- **Click Show.**
- **If necessary, select the Layout category in the Insert bar.**
- **Click the Property inspector expander button.**

The Layout category is selected, and the rulers are displayed at the top and left margins of the Document window (Figure 3-86). The rulers' measurements are in pixels. The lower pane of the Property inspector collapses.

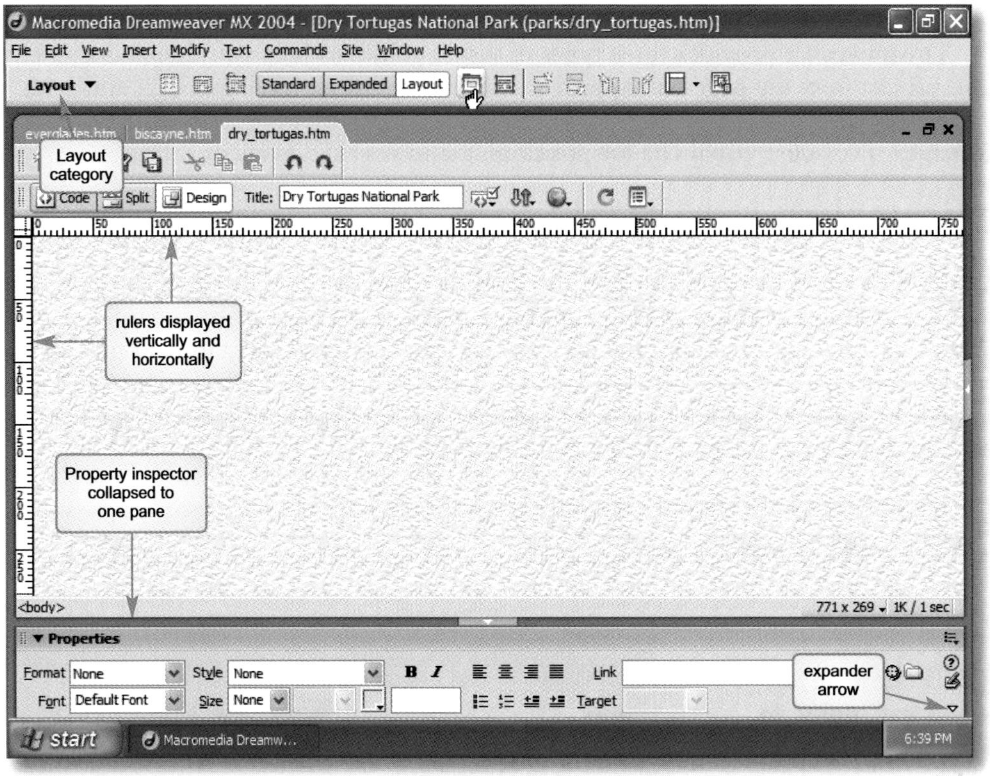

FIGURE 3-86

Creating a Layout Table for the Dry Tortugas National Park Web Page

You begin creating the Dry Tortugas National Park page by drawing a table. In the table, you create ten cells: one cell to hold the heading, four cells to hold text content, four cells to hold images, and one cell to contain links to the home page and the other two national park pages.

Your next task is to draw the layout table. This table has an approximate width of 650 pixels and an approximate height of 925 pixels. The following steps illustrate how to create the layout table. Figure 3-83 on page DW 257 provides a good visual guide for cell locations.

To Create the Layout Table

1

- **Click the Layout Mode button.**

Layout mode, with an exit option, displays at the top of the screen (Figure 3-87). If a Getting Started in Layout Mode dialog box displays, read the information and click OK. The dialog box may not display if the Don't show me this message again check box was checked previously.

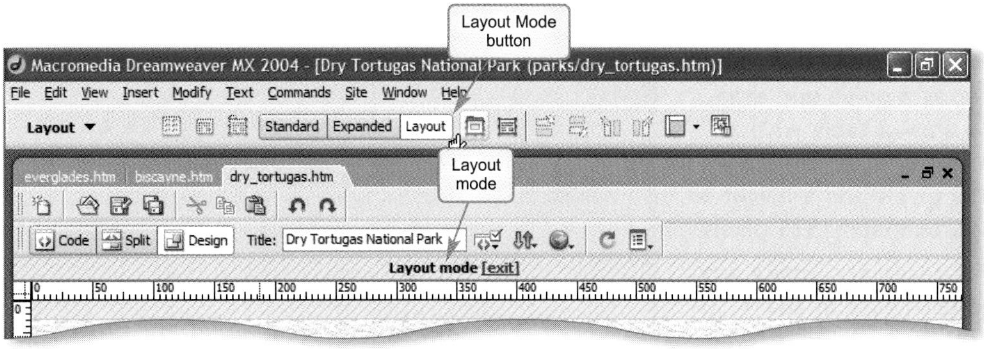

FIGURE 3-87

2

- **Click the Layout Table button.**
- **Position the mouse pointer at the insertion point in the upper-left corner of the Document window.**

The mouse pointer changes to a plus sign, which indicates you can draw a table (Figure 3-88).

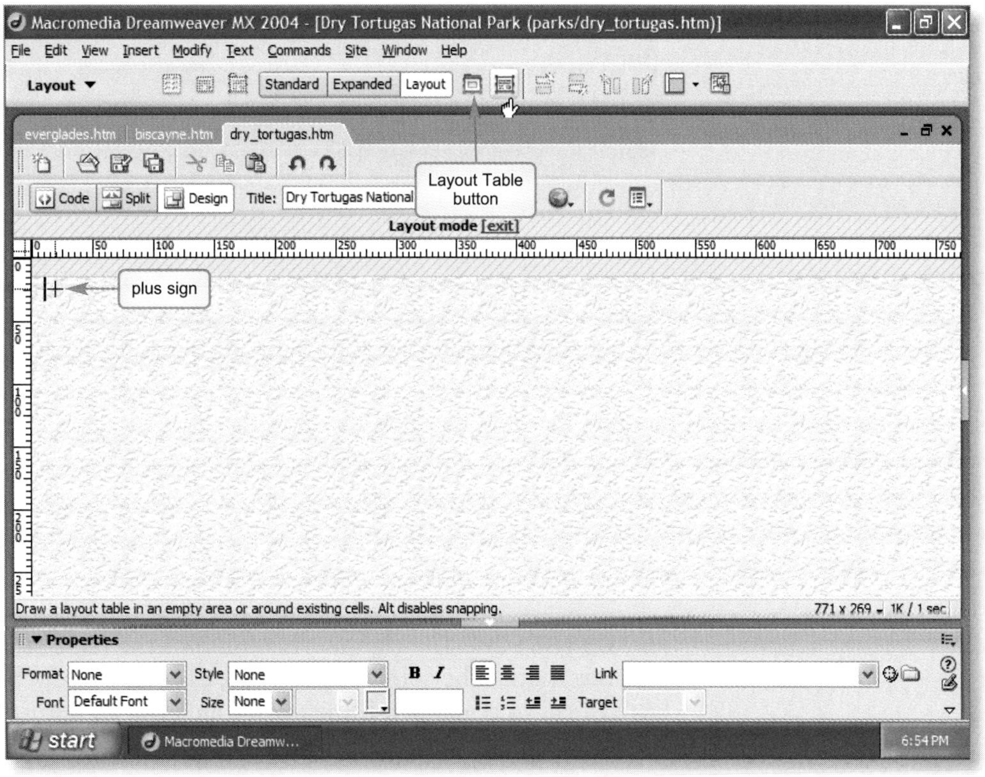

FIGURE 3-88

3

- **Use the rulers and pixel measurements in the right corner of the status bar as a guide and drag to draw a table with a width of approximately 650 pixels and a height of approximately 925 pixels.**
- **If necessary, make any adjustments in the Property inspector Width and Height boxes.**

The table is added to the Document window and is outlined in green. The Property inspector changes to reflect the table in Layout mode (Figure 3-89). The Layout Table tab is displayed at the top of the table, and the table displays with a gray background.

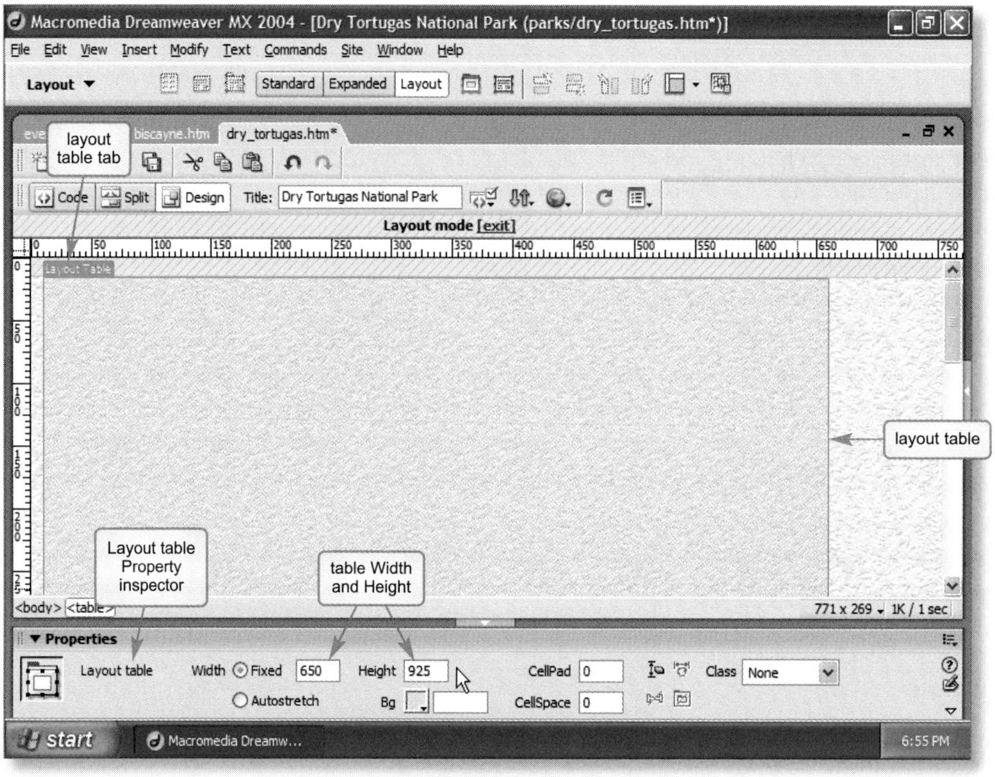

FIGURE 3-89

Layout Table and Layout Cell Properties

When a layout table is selected, the Property inspector displays properties related to the layout table. Some properties, such as width and height, background color, cell padding, and cell spacing, are the same as those for a table in Standard mode. The following describes the properties unique to the table in Layout mode (Figure 3-90).

FIXED Sets the table to a fixed width.

AUTOSTRETCH The rightmost column of the table stretches to fill the browser window width. The column header area for an autostretch column displays a wavy line instead of a number. If the layout includes an autostretch column, the layout always fills the entire width of the browser window.

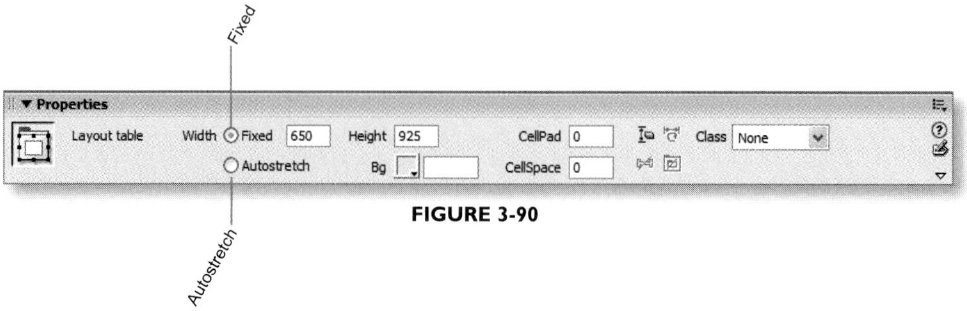

FIGURE 3-90

If the table is not the correct width or height or needs other modifications, adjustments can be made through the Width, Height, and other properties of the Property inspector.

For maximum flexibility, you should draw each cell as you are ready to add content to the cell. This method leaves blank space in the table, making it easier to move or resize cells. The next step is to add a cell that will contain the table heading. Once the cell is added, you type and format the heading within the layout cell. The heading is aligned to the left at the top of the table. The following steps illustrate how to add a layout cell and to enter and format a left-aligned heading.

To Add a Layout Cell and Heading

1

- **Click the Draw Layout Cell button on the Layout tab.**

The status bar indicates the function of the button (Figure 3-91).

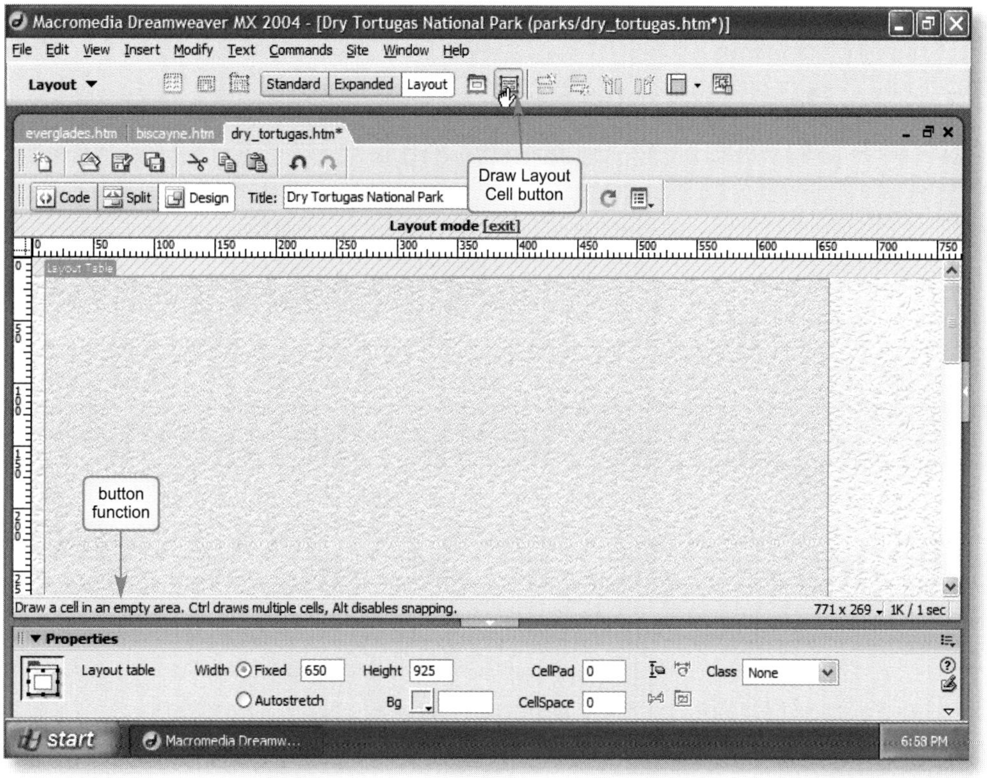

FIGURE 3-91

2

- **Click the upper-left corner of the layout table and drag to draw a cell with an approximate width of 425 and an approximate height of 50.**
- **Click the cell outline or the <td> in the tag selector to select the cell and make any necessary width and height adjustments in the Property inspector Width and Height boxes.**

A layout cell is created in the upper-left corner of the layout table. The cell displays in the table with a blue outline (Figure 3-92). The handles on the borders indicate the cell is selected.

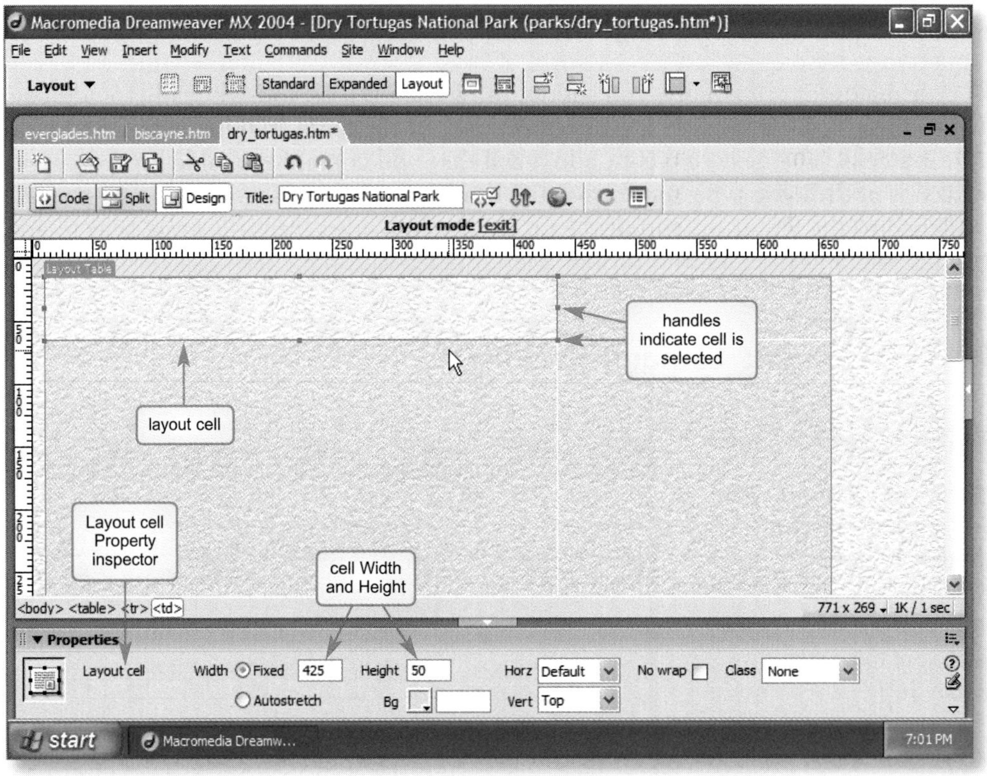

FIGURE 3-92

3

- **Click the cell and type** `Dry Tortugas National Park` **as the heading.**
- **Apply Heading 1 to the text.**

The heading is inserted into the cell, and Heading 1 is applied to the text (Figure 3-93). Text properties are displayed in the Property inspector.

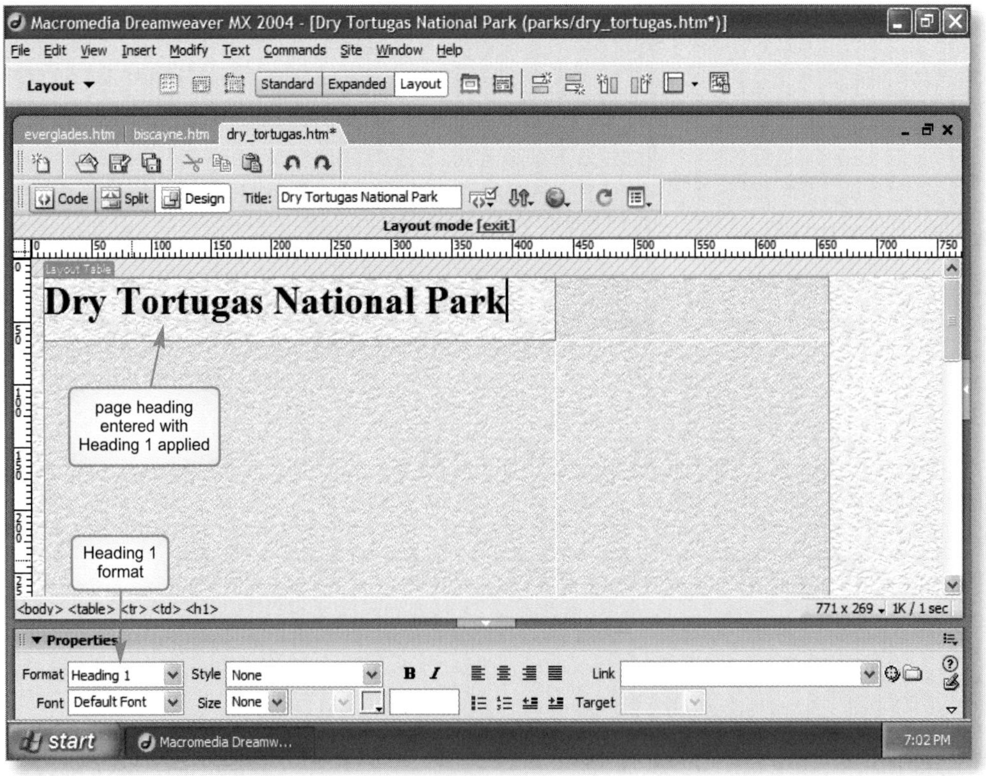

FIGURE 3-93

Adding Content and Images to the Cells

In the previous steps, you added content to a layout cell. Adding text content and images to layout cells is similar to adding content and images to cells in a Standard mode table. The only place content can be inserted in a layout table is in a layout cell. When Dreamweaver creates a layout cell, it automatically assigns a vertical alignment of Top. You have the same options as you did in Standard mode to change the alignment to Middle, Bottom, or Baseline. When you insert an image into a layout cell, all the properties in the Property inspector that were available for images in Standard mode also are available in Layout mode. If you need to move a layout cell, click the outline of the cell to select it. Hold down the mouse button and drag the cell to a new location. To move the cell in small increments, select the cell and then press the Up, Down, Left, or Right Arrow keys.

Next, you draw a layout cell directly below the heading cell. This cell will hold text. You enter the text into the layout cells just as you entered it in the cells in the Standard mode table. Table 3-5 contains the text for the Dry Tortugas National Park Web page. If necessary, refer to Figure 3-83 on page DW 257 for a visual guide on the layout cell's placement.

Table 3-5 Dry Tortugas National Park Web Page Text

SECTION	TEXT FOR DRY TORTUGAS NATIONAL PARK WEB PAGE
Part 1	The Dry Tortugas National Park is located about 70 nautical miles west of Key West, Florida. This cluster of seven coral reefs and sand islands, along with surrounding shoals and waters, make up the Dry Tortugas National Park. Ponce de Leon discovered these islands in 1513. He named them Dry Tortugas for their absence of fresh water and abundance of tortoises.
Part 2	Dominating the Garden Key Island is Fort Jefferson. This fort is the largest of the nineteenth-century American coastal forts. Fort Jefferson's construction began on Garden Key in 1846 and continued for 30 years, but was never finished.
Part 3	In 1935, President Franklin D. Roosevelt declared Fort Jefferson and the surrounding waters a national monument. In 1992, the area was designated as the Dry Tortugas National Park to protect the natural and historical qualities. Dry Tortugas is one of the country's more inaccessible national parks. Of the park's 64,657 acres, 99 percent is water and submerged islands.
Part 4	Park Service Information Office: Dry Tortugas National Park P. O. Box 6208 Key West, FL 33041<ENTER> E-mail: Dry Tortugas National Park<ENTER>
Part 5	Home | Everglades National Park | Biscayne National Park

To Add Text to a Layout Cell for the Dry Tortugas National Park Web Page

1

- **Click the Draw Layout Cell button.**
- **Click about 50 pixels to the right of and below the first cell, and then draw a cell with an approximate width of 250 and an approximate height of 190, as shown in Figure 3-94.**
- **Click the cell to select it and make any necessary width and height adjustments in the Property inspector Width and Height boxes.**
- **If necessary, select and drag the cell or use the keyboard arrow keys for placement.**

The second cell is added to the table and is selected (Figure 3-94). This cell will contain text.

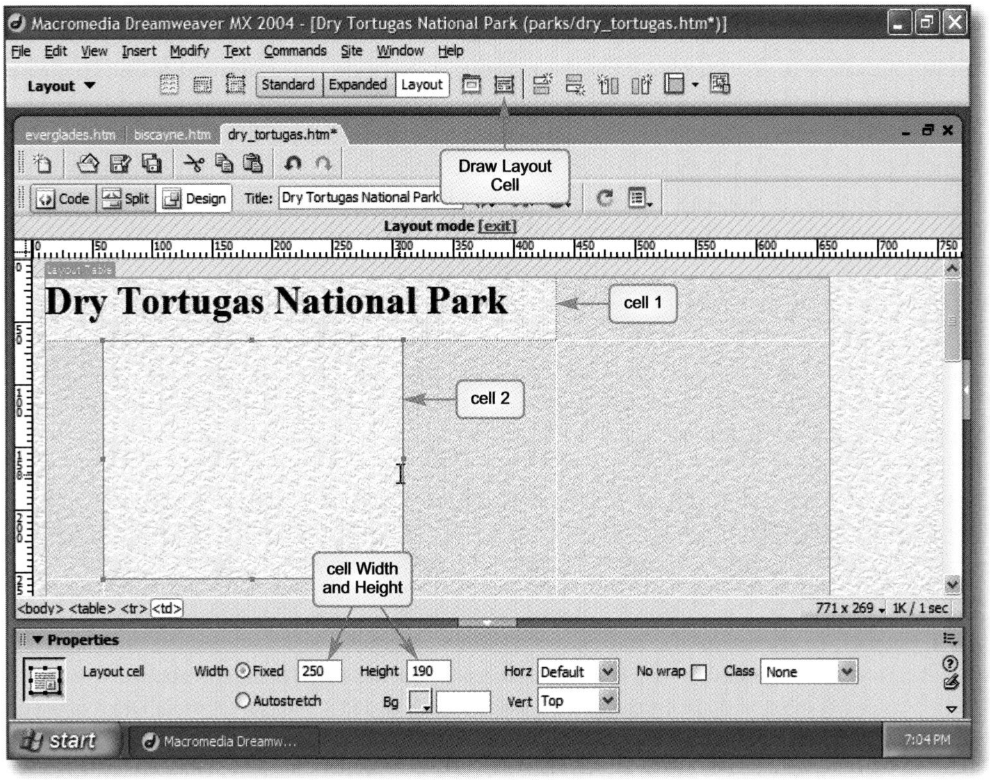

FIGURE 3-94

2

- **Click in the cell and type the text of Part 1 as shown in Table 3-5 on page DW 265.**

The text is entered into the second cell (Figure 3-95).

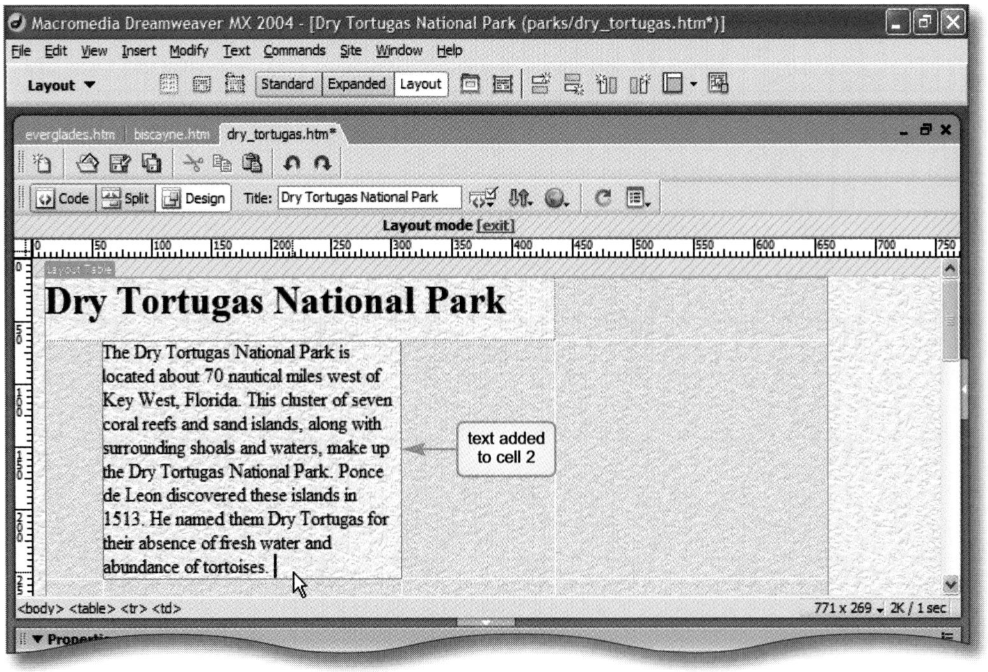

FIGURE 3-95

The third cell you draw will contain an image. You draw this cell to the right of the second cell. You add images to the layout cells just as you added images to the cells in the Standard mode table — by dragging the image from the Assets panel to the cell. The steps on the next page show how to draw the third cell and insert an image into the cell.

To Add an Image to a Layout Cell

1

- **Click the Draw Layout Cell button and then draw a cell to the right of and about 25 pixels below the second cell, with an approximate width of 290 and an approximate height of 200, as shown in Figure 3-96.**
- **Click the cell outline to select it and make any necessary width and height adjustments in the Property inspector Width and Height boxes.**
- **Click the panel groups expand/collapse button and then, if necessary, click the Assets tab.**
- **If necessary, scroll to view the entire cell.**

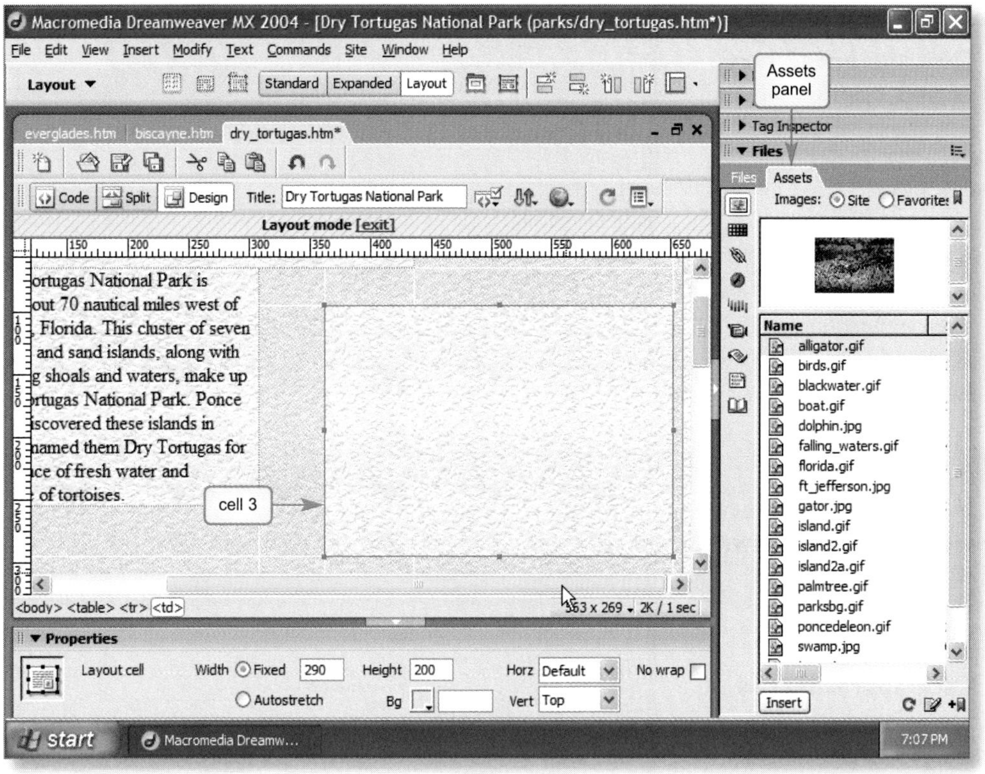

FIGURE 3-96

The third cell is added to the table and is selected, and the Assets panel displays (Figure 3-96). This third cell will contain an image.

More About

Positioning Images

The Property inspector contains two different sets of tools for positioning images. The top panel of the Property inspector lets you change the alignment of the image itself. The bottom panel of the Property inspector contains tools that change the cell's alignment settings.

2

- **Drag the ft_jefferson.jpg file from the Assets panel to the insertion point.**
- **Click the Alt text box in the Property inspector and then type** `Ft. Jefferson` **as the Alt text.**
- **Click the Image text box and type** `ftjefferson` **as the image ID. Press the ENTER key.**

The image is selected and displays in the third cell, and the Alt text and image ID display in the Property inspector (Figure 3-97).

FIGURE 3-97

3

- **If necessary, deselect the image, scroll down and to the left, and then click the Draw Layout Cell button.**
- **Click approximately 20 pixels below the second cell and about 20 pixels to the right of the table border.**
- **Draw a cell with a width of approximately 180 and a height of approximately 275, as shown in Figure 3-98.**
- **Click the outline of the cell to select it and make any necessary width and height adjustments in the Property inspector Width and Height boxes.**

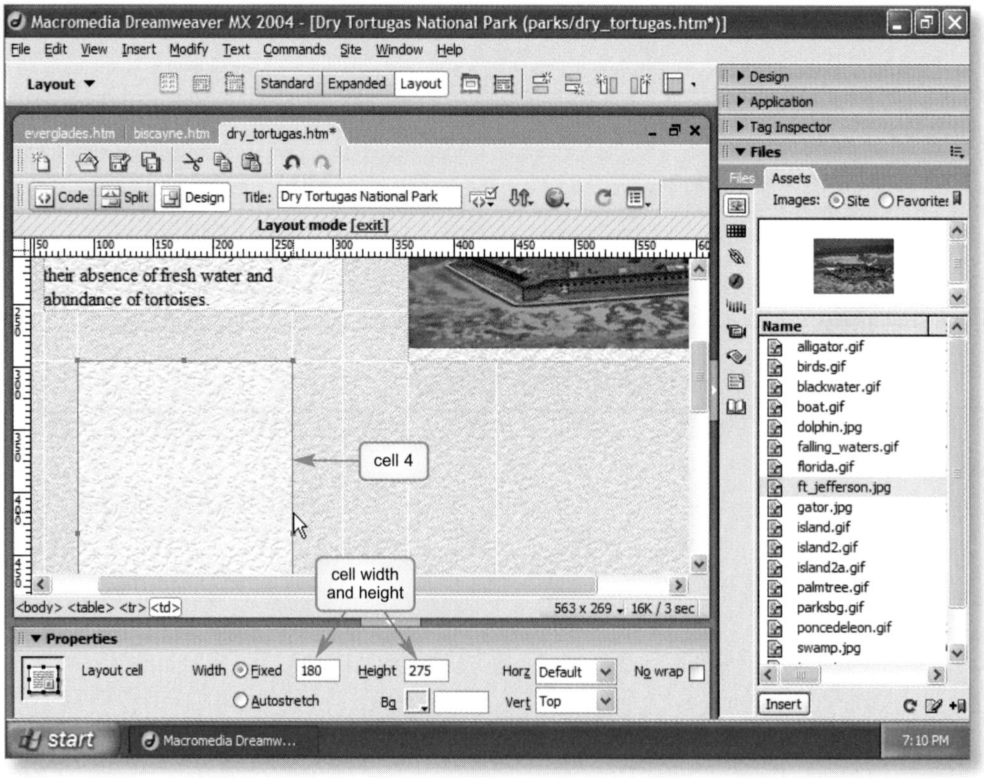

FIGURE 3-98

The fourth cell is added to the table and is selected (Figure 3-98). The cell will contain an image.

4

- **Drag the turtle.jpg image from the Assets panel to the cell.**
- **Click the Alt text box in the Property inspector and type** `Florida Turtle` **as the Alt text.**
- **Click the Image text box and type** `turtle` **as the image ID. Press the ENTER key.**

The image is selected and displays in the fourth cell, and the Alt text and image ID display in the Property inspector (Figure 3-99).

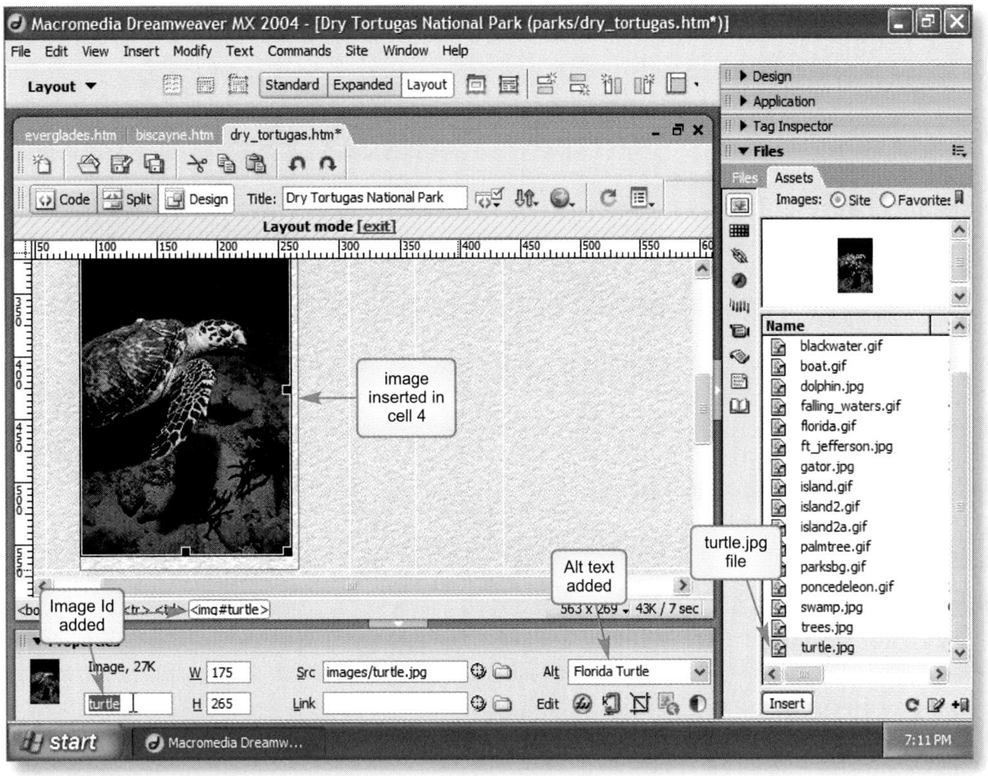

FIGURE 3-99

5

- **Click anywhere on the page to deselect the image.**

So far, you have added four cells to the layout table — one containing the heading, one containing text, and two containing images. Now you add five more cells. Two of the cells will contain images and three will contain text. The following steps show how to add the additional five cells.

> *More About*
>
> **Layout Cells**
>
> To delete a layout cell, click the edge of the cell to select it, and then press the DELETE key. The space is replaced with non-editable cells.

To Add Five Additional Cells to the Dry Tortugas National Park Web Page

1

- **Click the panel groups expand/collapse button to hide the panel groups.**
- **Click the Draw Layout Cell button.**
- **Click 20 pixels below and 50 pixels to the left of the third cell, and draw a cell with a width of approximately 325 and a height of approximately 100.**
- **Click the outline of the cell to select it and make any necessary width and height adjustments in the Property inspector Width and Height boxes.**
- **Click in the cell and type the text of Part 2 as shown in Table 3-5 on page DW 265.**

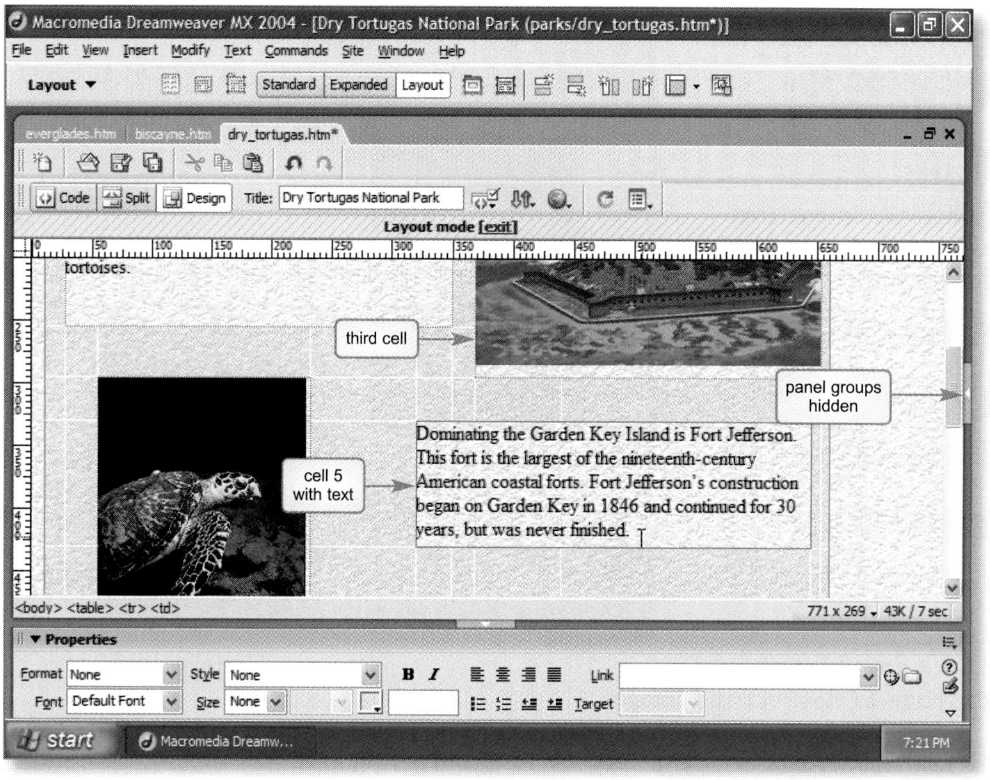
Macromedia Dreamweaver MX 2004 - [Dry Tortugas National Park (parks/dry_tortugas.htm*)]
third cell
panel groups hidden
cell 5 with text
Dominating the Garden Key Island is Fort Jefferson. This fort is the largest of the nineteenth-century American coastal forts. Fort Jefferson's construction began on Garden Key in 1846 and continued for 30 years, but was never finished.
Layout mode [exit]
Properties

FIGURE 3-100

The fifth cell is added to the table. The cell contains text (Figure 3-100).

2

- **Click the Draw Layout Cell button.**
- **Click about 20 pixels below and about 50 pixels to the right of the fifth cell, and draw a cell with a width of approximately 185 and a height of approximately 135, as shown in Figure 3-101.**
- **Click the cell outline to select it and then make any necessary width and height adjustments in the Property inspector Width and Height boxes.**
- **Click the panel groups expand/collapse button. If necessary, scroll to view the cell.**
- **Click in the sixth cell and then drag the dolphin.jpg image to the cell.**
- **Click the Alt text box in the Property inspector and then type** `Florida dolphin` **as the Alt text.**
- **Click the Image text box and type** `dolphin` **as the image ID.**
- **Click the Save button on the Standard toolbar.**

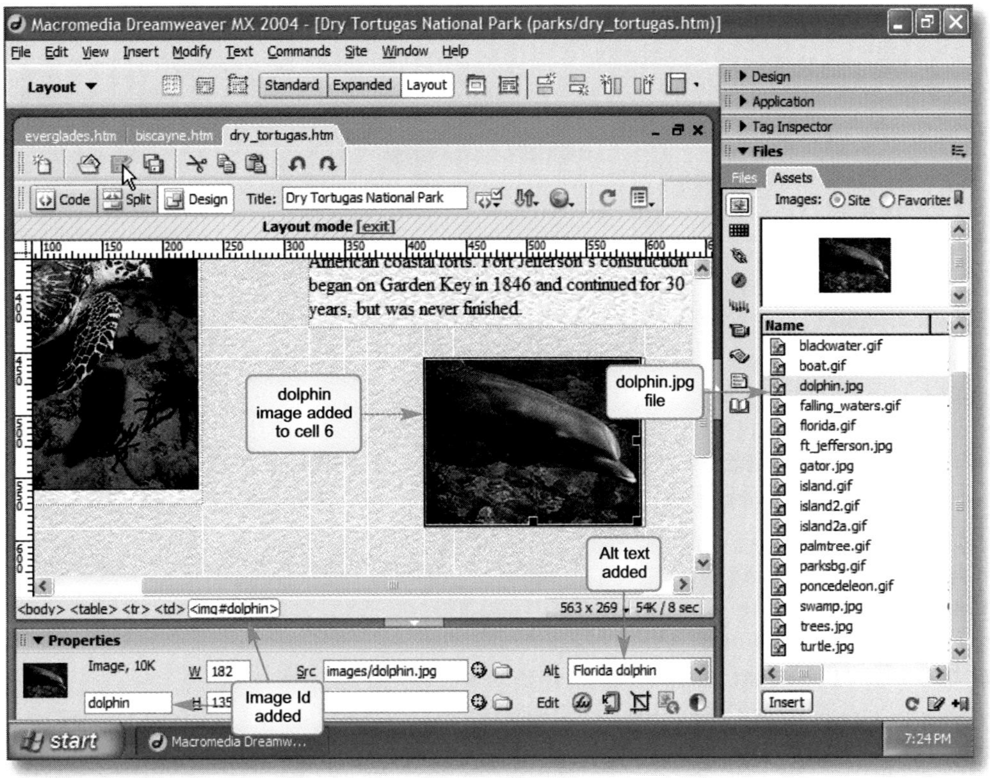

FIGURE 3-101

The sixth cell is added to the table and contains the dolphin.jpg image (Figure 3-101).

3

- **Click the panel groups expand/collapse button to hide the panels.**
- **Click the Draw Layout Cell button.**
- **Click at the left margin about 20 pixels below the sixth cell.**
- **Drag to the left to create a table with an approximate width of 620 and an approximate height of 85, as shown in Figure 3-102.**
- **Click the cell outline to select it and make any necessary width and height adjustments in the Property inspector Width and Height boxes.**
- **Click in the cell and then type the text of Part 3 as shown in Table 3-5 on page DW 265.**

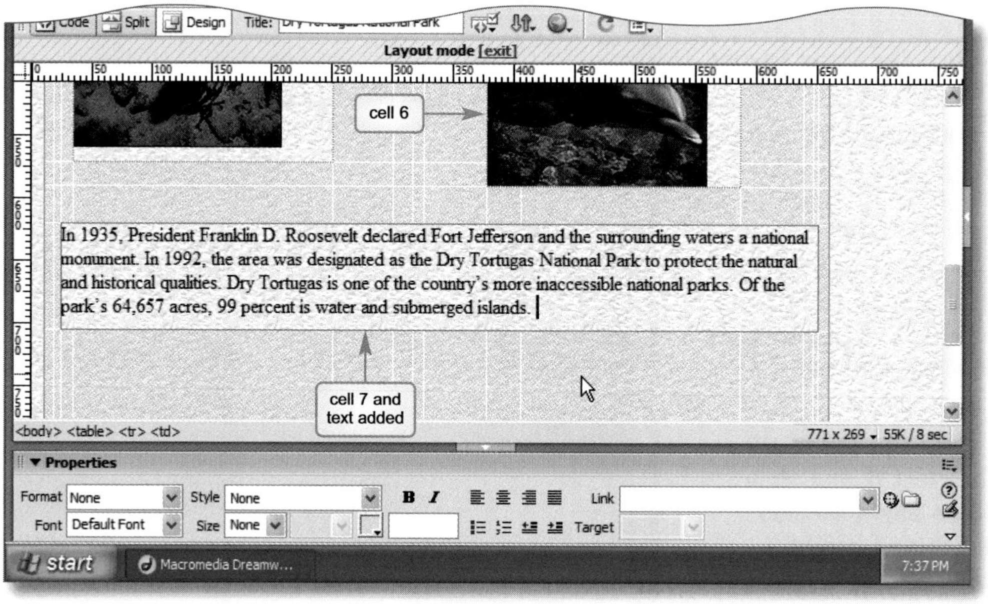

FIGURE 3-102

The seventh cell is inserted, and the text displays (Figure 3-102).

4

- **Click the Draw Layout Cell button and draw an eighth cell about 5 to 10 pixels below the seventh cell, with an approximate width of 250 and an approximate height of 150.**
- **Select the cell and make any necessary adjustments to the width and height in the Property inspector.**
- **Click in cell 8 and type the text of Part 4 as shown in Table 3-5 into the cell.**
- **Align the text to the right.**

The eighth cell is inserted, and the text displays centered in the cell (Figure 3-103).

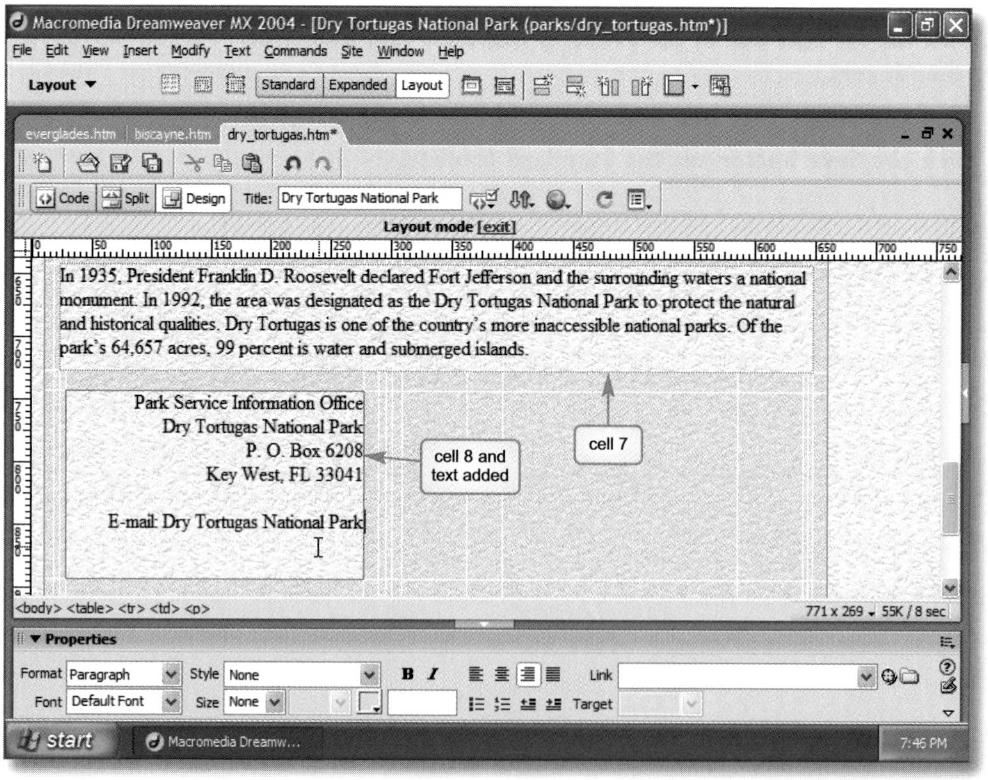

FIGURE 3-103

5

- **Click the Draw Layout Cell button and draw the ninth cell to the right of the eighth cell and about 5 to 10 pixels below cell 8, with an approximate width of 275 and an approximate height of 130.**
- **Select the cell and make any necessary adjustments to the width and height in the Property inspector.**
- **Display the Assets panel and then drag the trees.jpg image to the ninth cell.**
- **Type** `Palm trees` **as the Alt text and** `palmtrees` **as the image ID.**

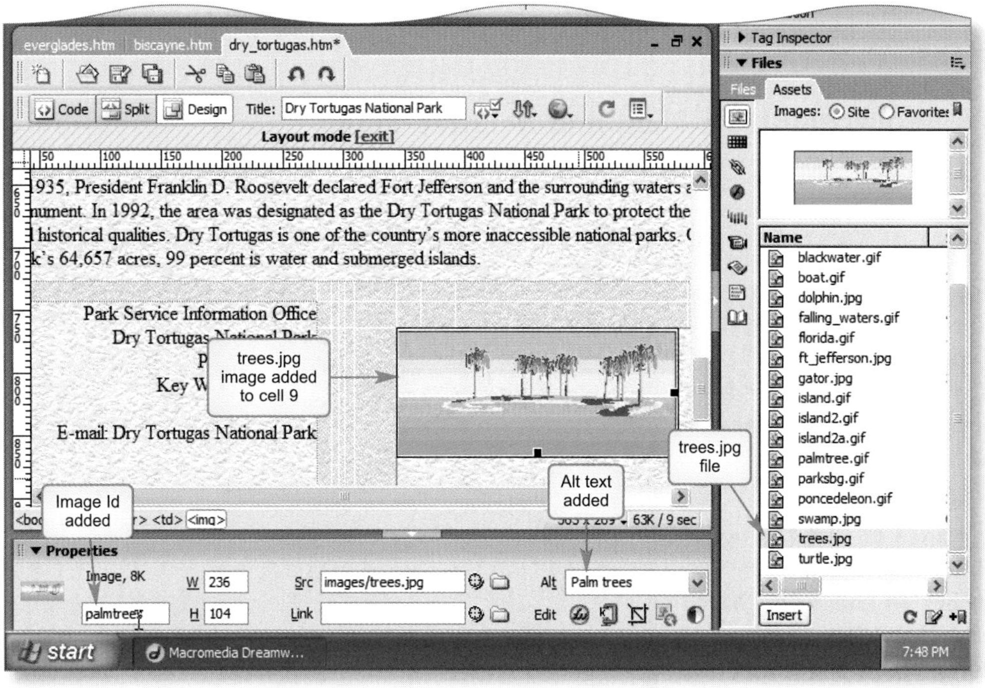

FIGURE 3-104

The ninth cell is inserted, and the trees.jpg image displays (Figure 3-104).

6

- **Hide the panel groups.**
- **Scroll down and then click the Draw Layout Cell button.**
- **Draw the tenth cell about 10 pixels below cells 8 and 9 and about 100 pixels from the left border, with an approximate width of 425 and an approximate height of 35.**
- **Select the cell and make any necessary adjustments to the width and height in the Property inspector.**

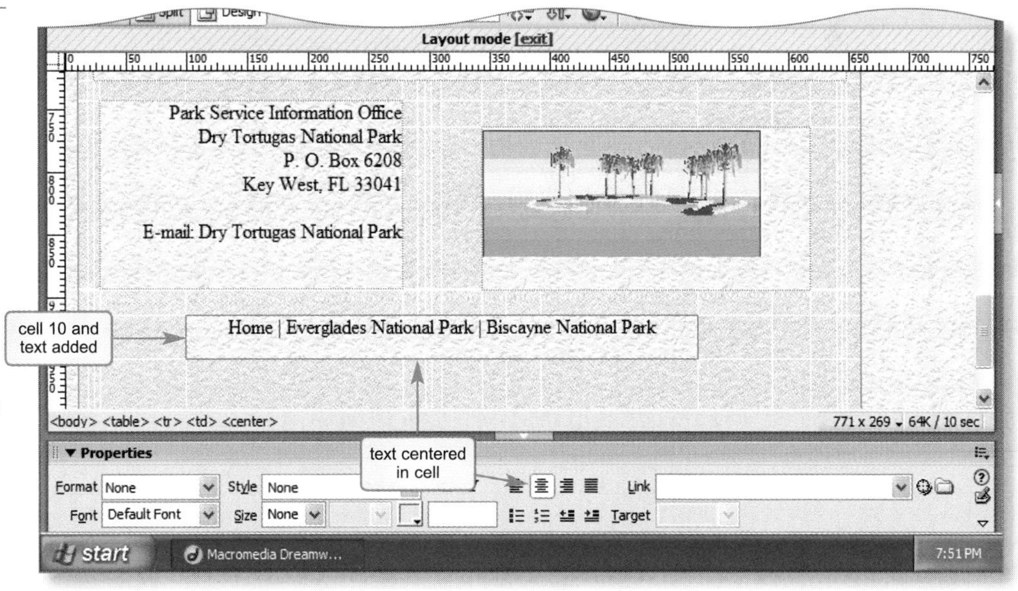

FIGURE 3-105

- **Click in cell 10 and then type the text of Part 5 as shown in Table 3-5 into the cell.**
- **Click the Align Center button in the Property inspector.**
- **Click the Save button.**

The text for the links displays centered in cell 10, and the page is saved (Figure 3-105).

Next, you add absolute, e-mail, and relative links to the Dry Tortugas National Park page. The following steps show how to add the links.

To Add Absolute, E-Mail, and Relative Links

1

- **Select the first instance of Dry Tortugas National Park in cell 8. Type** `http://www.nps.gov/dry_tort/` **in the Link box to create an absolute link.**
- **Select the second instance of Dry Tortugas National Park. Click Insert on the menu bar and then click Email Link. When the Email Link dialog box is displayed, type** `dry_tortugas@parks.gov` **as the e-mail address. Click the OK button.**
- **Select Home in cell 10 (the last cell in the table). Type** `index.htm` **in the Link box to create the relative link.**
- **Select Everglades National Park in cell 10. Type** `everglades.htm` **in the Link box to create the relative link.**
- **Select Biscayne National Park in cell 10. Type** `biscayne.htm` **in the Link box to create the relative link.**
- **Click the Save button on the Standard toolbar.**

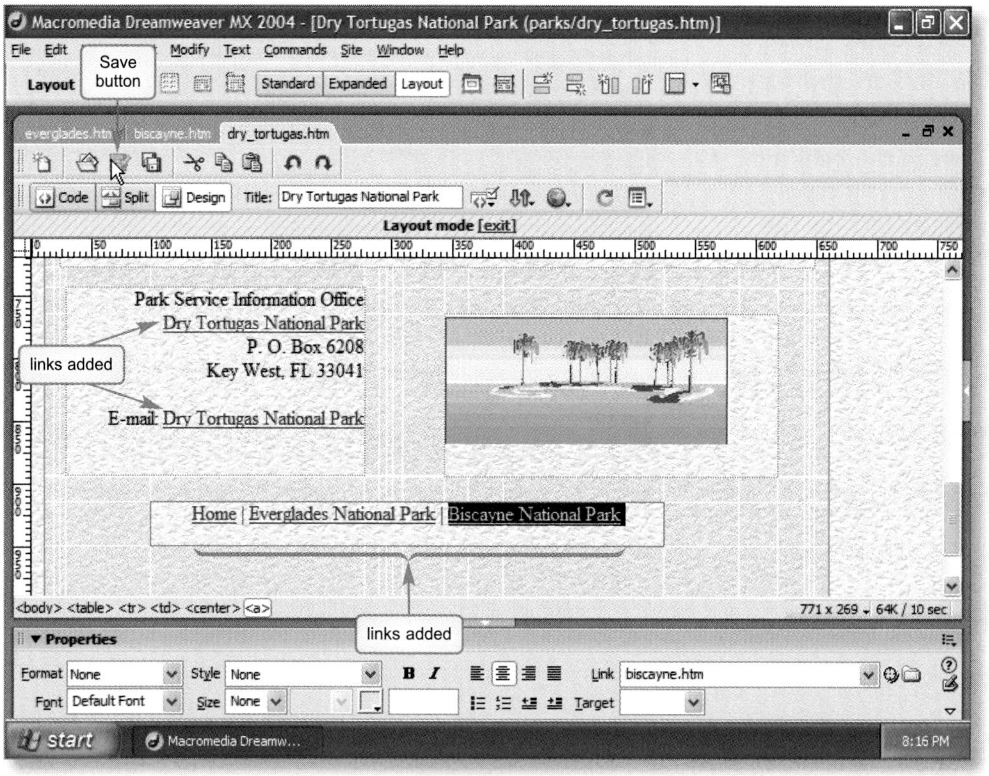

FIGURE 3-106

The page is saved, and the links are added, as shown in Figure 3-106.

Centering the Table in Standard Mode

Layout mode does not provide all the features that are provided for a table in Standard mode. For example, you cannot select a number of rows or select a number of columns when creating Web pages in Layout mode, and you cannot center a table when in Layout mode. To access these features requires that the table be displayed in Standard mode. Your next task is to center the table. The following steps illustrate how to display the Web page in Standard mode, to center the table, and to turn off the rulers.

To Center a Table Created in Layout Mode

1

- **Click the Standard Mode button on the Layout tab. Click any cell in the table and then click the <table> tag in the tag selector.**

The table displays in Standard mode and is selected (Figure 3-107).

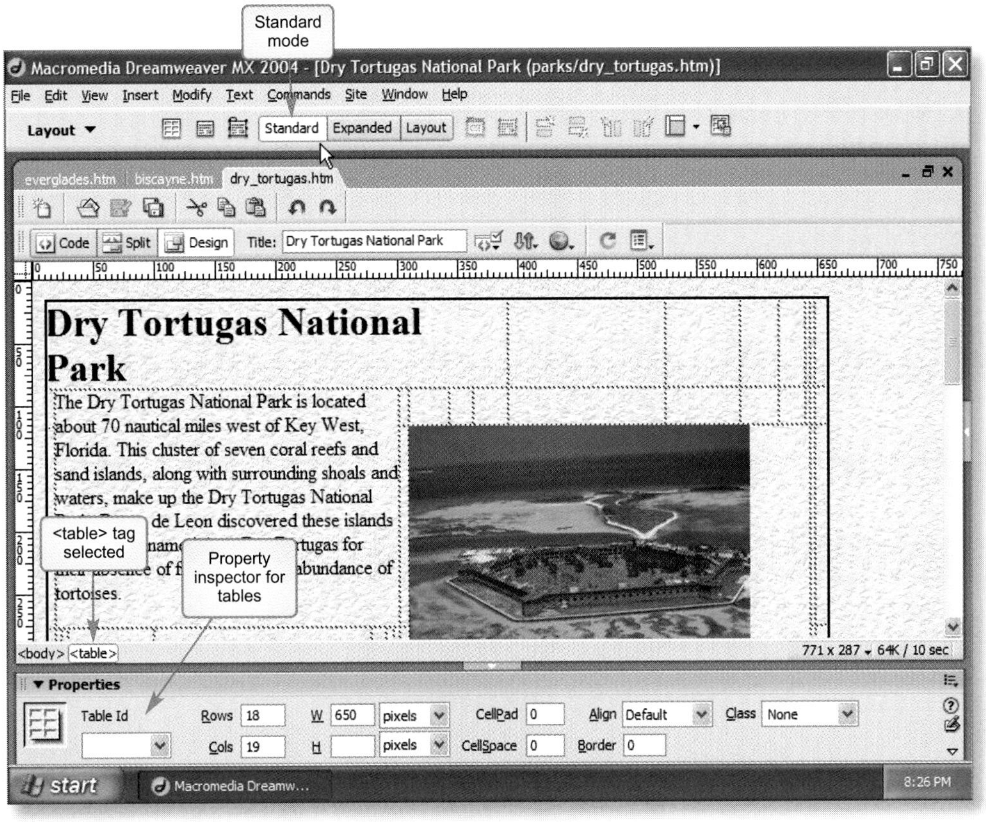

FIGURE 3-107

2

- **Click the Align box arrow in the Property inspector, press the ENTER key, and then click Center.**

The table is selected and centered in the Document window (Figure 3-108).

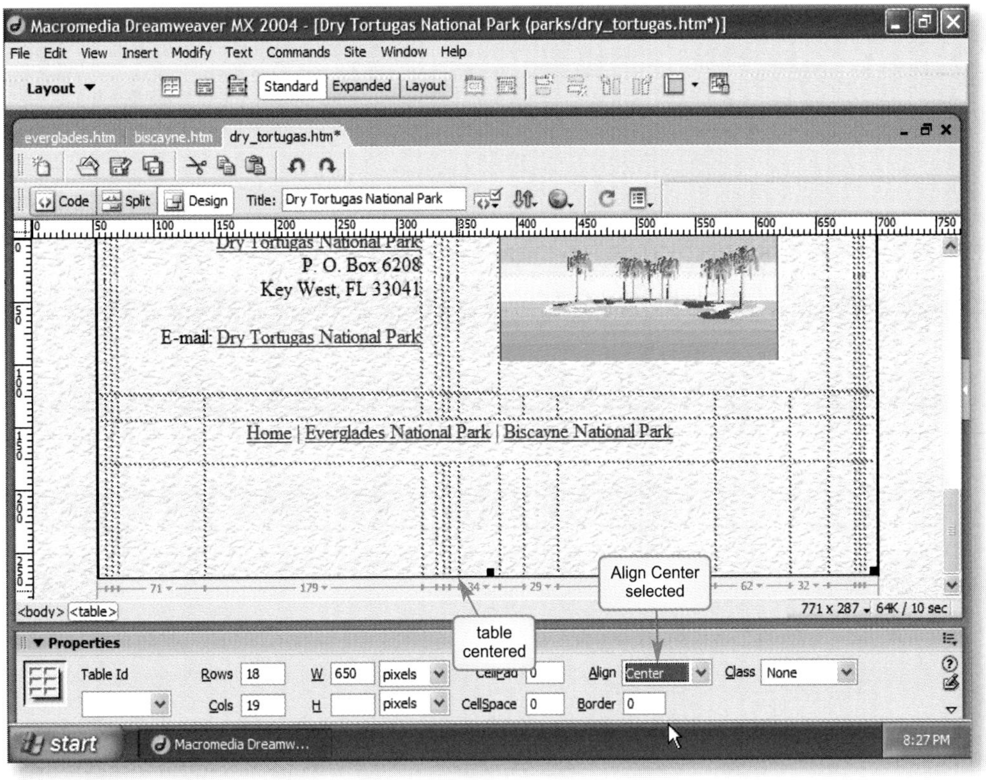

FIGURE 3-108

3

- **Click the Save button on the Standard toolbar and then press the F12 key to view the page in your browser.**

The Web page displays centered in the browser (Figure 3-109).

4

- **Close the browser.**

5

- **Click View on the menu bar, click Rulers, and then click the Show command to deselect it.**

More About

Layout Tables

For more information about Dreamweaver MX 2004 layout tables, visit the Dreamweaver MX 2004 More About Web page (scsite.com/dreamweavermx04/more.htm) and then click Dreamweaver MX 2004 Layout Tables.

Dry Tortugas National Park - Microsoft Internet Explorer
File Edit View Favorites Tools Help
Back Search Favorites Media
Address C:\allend\parks\TMPp1vpj8sk2h.htm
Go
Dry Tortugas National Park
The Dry Tortugas National Park is located about 70 nautical miles west of Key West, Florida. This cluster of seven coral reefs and sand islands, along with surrounding shoals and waters, make up the Dry Tortugas National Park. Ponce de Leon discovered these islands in 1513. He named them Dry Tortugas for their absence of fresh water and abundance of tortoises.
Dominating the Garden Key Island is Fort Jefferson. This fort is the largest of the nineteenth-century American coastal forts. Fort Jefferson's construction began on Garden Key in 1846 and continued for 30 years, but was never finished.
In 1935, President Franklin D. Roosevelt declared Fort Jefferson and the surrounding waters a national monument. In 1992, the area was designated as the Dry Tortugas National Park to protect the natural and historical qualities. Dry Tortugas is one of the country's more inaccessible national parks. Of the park's 64,657 acres, 99 percent is water and submerged islands.
Park Service Information Office
Dry Tortugas National Park
P. O. Box 6208
Key West, FL 33041
E-mail: Dry Tortugas National Park
Home | Everglades National Park | Biscayne National Park
Done
My Computer
start
Macromedia Dreamw...
Dry Tortugas Nationa...
8:31 PM

FIGURE 3-109

The Web site has expanded to include pages on the three national parks located in Florida. To integrate the page within the Web site, you add links from the national.htm page. The following steps show how to add the links.

To Add Links to the National Parks Web Page

1

- **Click File on the menu bar, select Open, and then open the national.htm page in the parks folder.**

The national.htm page displays (Figure 3-110).

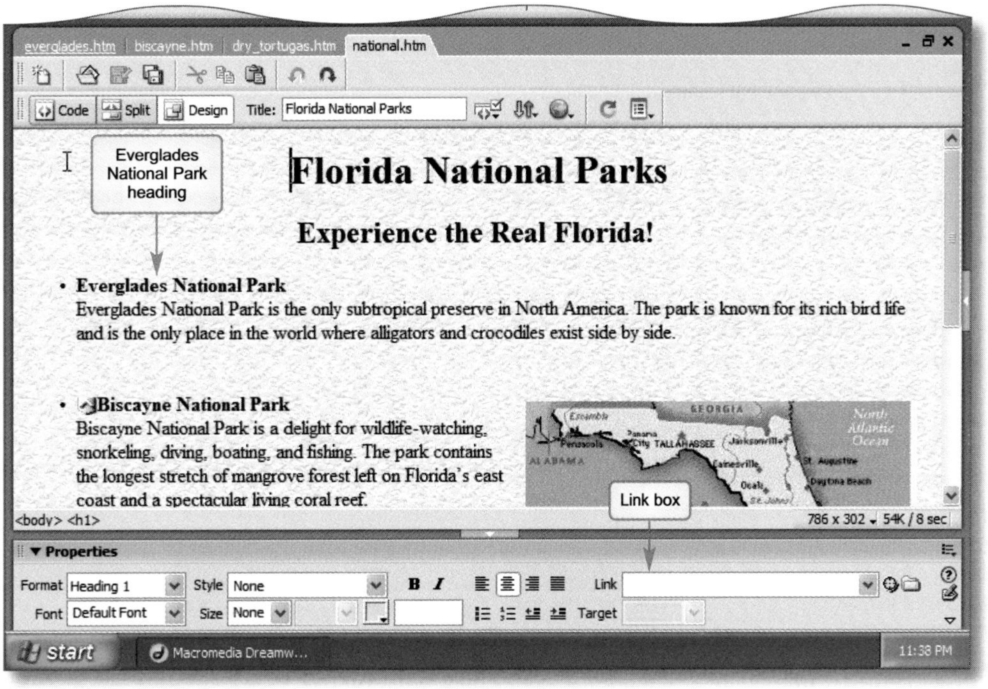

FIGURE 3-110

2

- **Select the Everglades National Park heading and then type** `everglades.htm` **in the Link box.**
- **Select the Biscayne National Park heading and then type** `biscayne.htm` **in the Link box.**
- **Select the Dry Tortugas National Park heading and then type** `dry_tortugas.htm` **in the Link box.**

The links are added to the three parks (Figure 3-111).

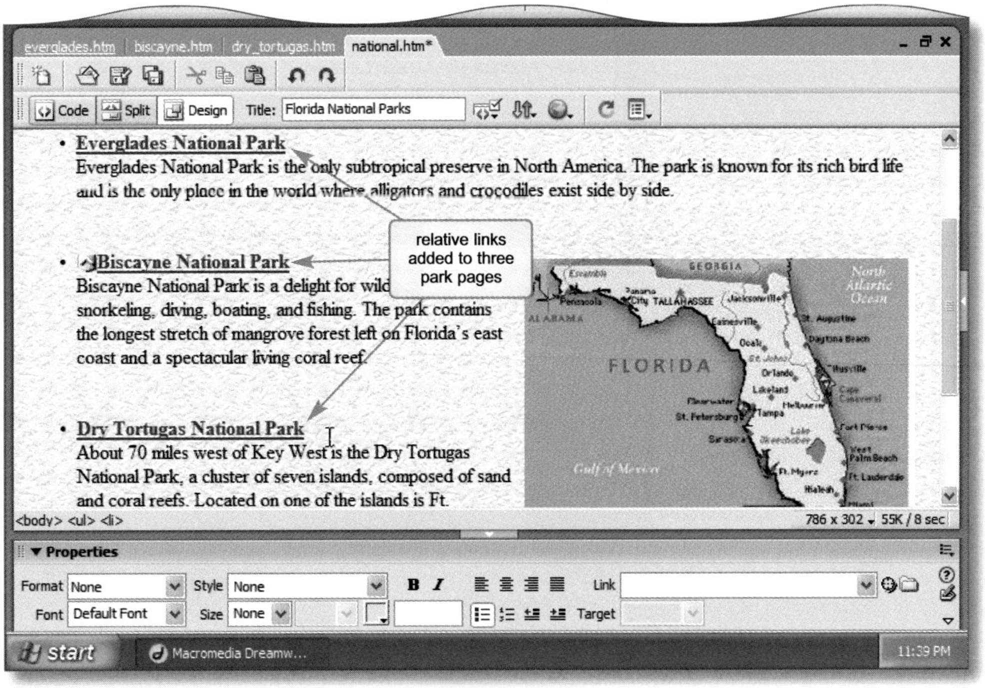

FIGURE 3-111

3

- **Press the F12 key to view the page in your browser. Test each link and then close the browser.**
- **Save the national.htm page and then close the page.**
- **Close the other three pages — everglades.htm, biscayne.htm, and dry_tortugas.htm.**

Q&A

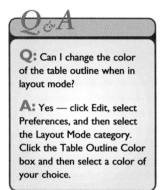

Q: Can I change the color of the table outline when in layout mode?

A: Yes — click Edit, select Preferences, and then select the Layout Mode category. Click the Table Outline Color box and then select a color of your choice.

Head Content

HTML files consist of two main sections: the head section and the body section. The head section is one of the more important sections of a Web page. A standard HTML page contains a <head> tag and a <body> tag. Contained within the head section is site and page information. With the exception of the title, the information contained in the head does not display in the browser. Some of the information contained in the head is accessed by the browser, and other information is accessed by other programs such as search engines and server software. In Figure 3-112, the head content of the index page is displayed. The title and the default meta tag are the only pieces of information currently contained between the start <head> and end </head> tags.

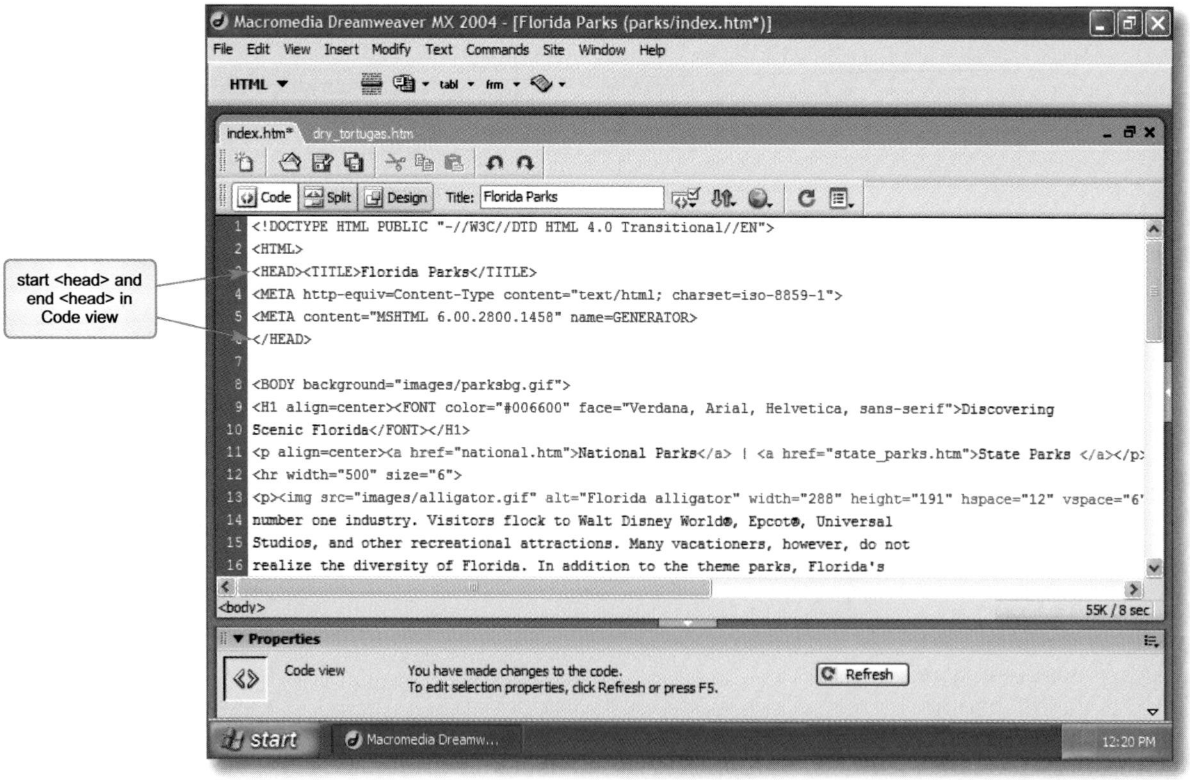

FIGURE 3-112

Head Content Elements

Dreamweaver makes it easy to add content to the head section by providing a pop-up menu in the Insert bar HTML category. The Head pop-up menu contains the following elements that can be added to your Web page.

META A <meta> tag contains information about the current document. This information is used by servers, browsers, and search engines. HTML documents can have as many <meta> tags as needed, but each item uses a different set of tags.

KEYWORDS Keywords are a list of words that someone would type into a search engine search field.

DESCRIPTION The description contains a sentence or two that can be used in a search engine's results page.

REFRESH The <refresh> tag is processed by the browser to reload the page or load a new page after a specified amount of time has elapsed.

BASE The base tag sets the base URL to provide an absolute link and/or a link target that the browser can use to resolve link conflicts.

LINK The link element defines a relationship between the current document and another file. This is not the same as a link in the Document window.

Keywords, descriptions, and refresh settings are special-use cases of the meta tag. The following steps show how to add keywords and a description to the index.htm page.

> *More About*
>
> **Head Content**
>
> Meta tags are information inserted into the head content area of Web pages. The meta description tag allows you to influence the description of a page in the search engines that support the tag. For more information about meta tags, visit the Dreamweaver MX 2004 More About Web page (scsite.com/dreamweavermx04/more.htm) and then click Dreamweaver MX 2004 Meta Tags.

To Add Keywords and a Description

1

- **Open the index.htm file.**
- **Click the Insert box arrow and then select HTML from the pop-up menu. Point to the Head button (Figure 3-113).**

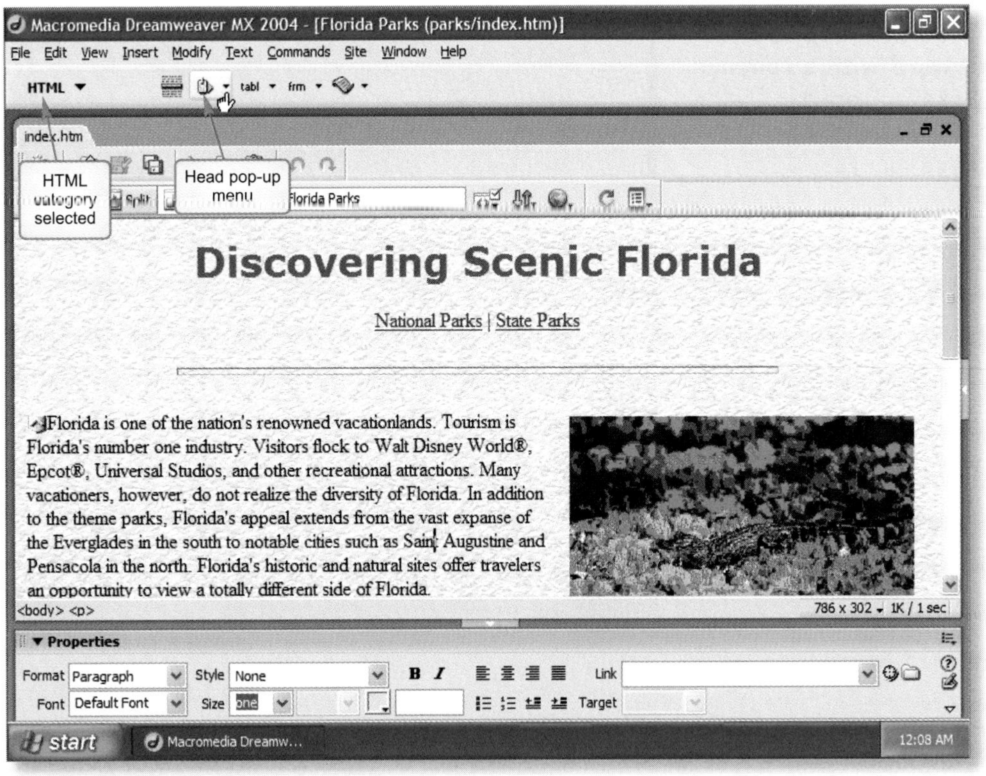

FIGURE 3-113

2

• Click the Head button and then point to Keywords on the pop-up menu.

The pop-up menu displays, and Keywords is highlighted (Figure 3-114).

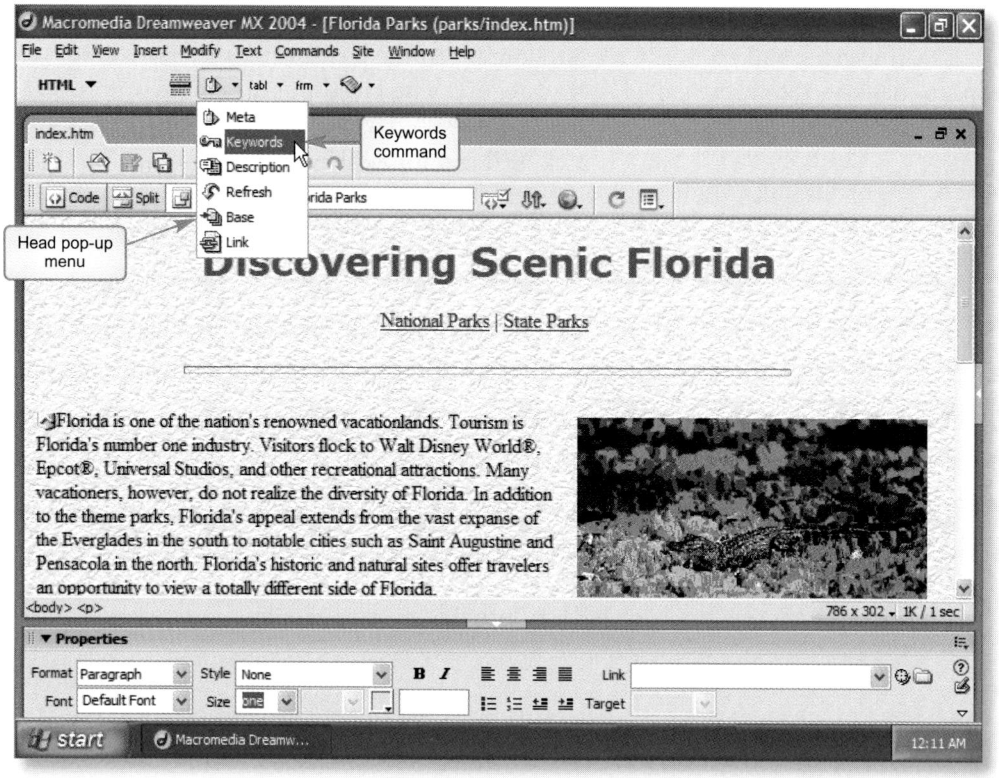

FIGURE 3-114

3

• Click Keywords on the Head pop-up menu. Type the following keywords in the Keywords text box, separating each keyword with a comma: `parks, Florida, national parks, state parks`.

Keywords are added to the Keywords dialog box (Figure 3-115). When a search is done with a search engine for any of the keywords, the Web site address will be displayed in the browser search results.

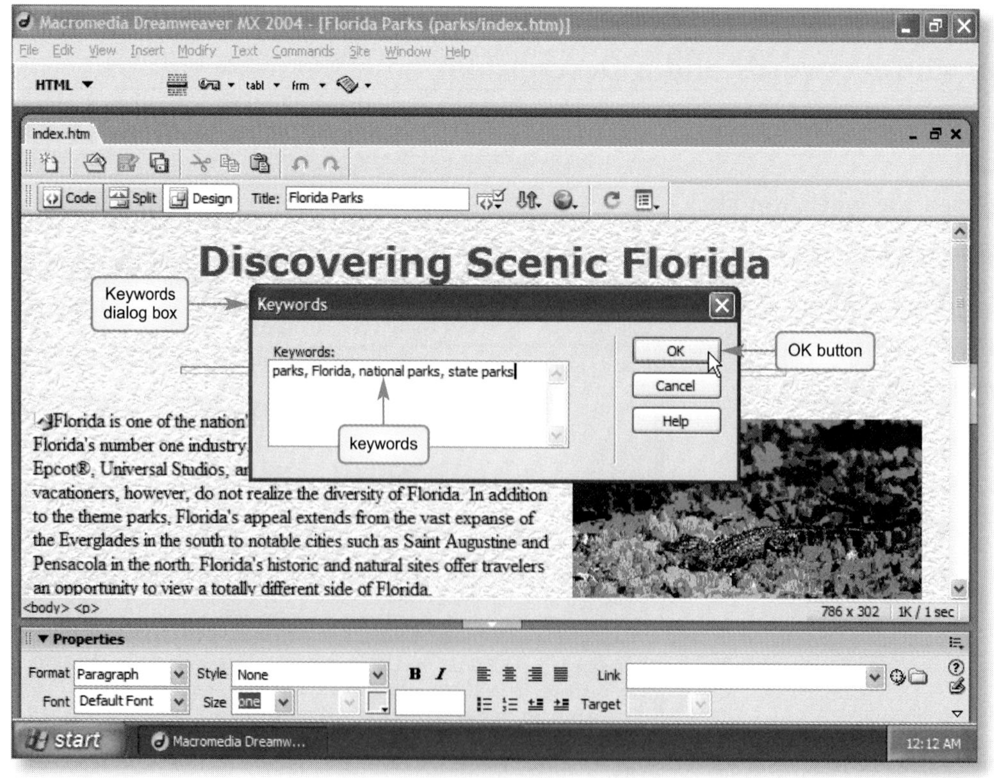

FIGURE 3-115

4

• Click the OK button, click the Head pop-up menu, and then click Description. Type `A Web site featuring Florida state and national parks` **in the Description text box.**

The Description dialog box is displayed as shown in Figure 3-116.

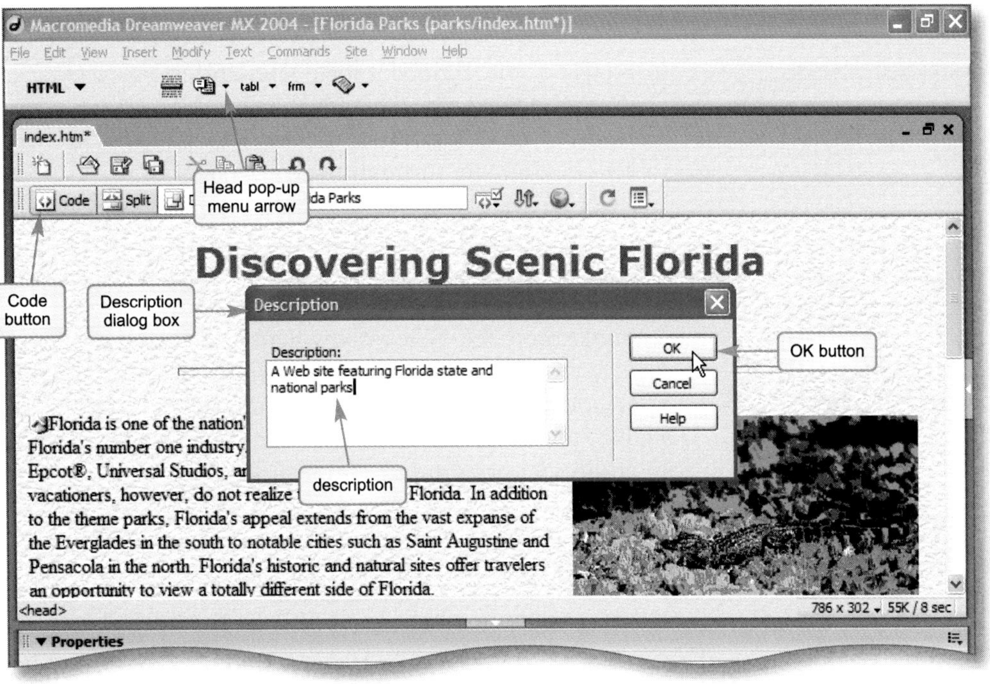

FIGURE 3-116

5

• Click the OK button and then click the Code button on the Document toolbar.

The keywords and description that you entered are displayed in Code view (Figure 3-117).

6

• Click the Design button on the Document toolbar and then click the Save button on the Standard toolbar.

The Web page is saved.

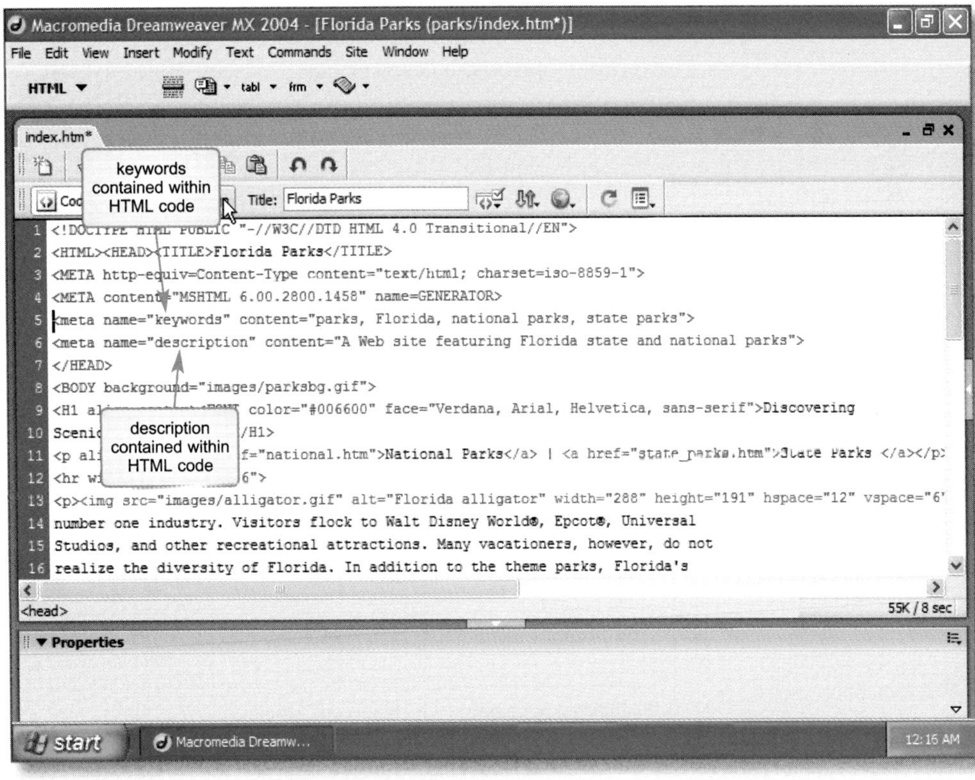

FIGURE 3-117

Other Ways

1. Click Code button on Document toolbar, type keywords code in code window

Publishing a Web Site

In Project 1 you defined a local site, and in Projects 1, 2, and 3, you added Web pages to the local site. This local site resides on your computer's hard disk, a network drive, or possibly a Zip disk. You can view the organization of all files and folders in your site through the Files panel.

To prepare a Web site and make it available for others to view requires that you **publish** your site by putting it on a Web server for public access. A **Web server** is an Internet- or intranet-connected computer that delivers, or *serves up*, Web pages. You **upload** files to a folder on a server and **download** files to a folder in the Files panel on your computer. Generally, when Web site designers publish to a folder on a Web site, they do so by using a file transfer (FTP) program such as WS_FTP or Cute FTP, or Windows XP Web Folders. Dreamweaver, however, includes built-in support that enables you to connect and transfer your local site to a Web server without requiring an additional program. To publish to a Web server requires that you have access to a Web server.

Publishing and maintaining your site using Dreamweaver involves the following steps:

1. Use the Site Definition Wizard to enter the FTP information.
2. Specify the Web server to which you want to publish your Web site.
3. Connect to the Web server and upload the files.
4. Synchronize the local and remote sites.

Your school or company may have a server that you can use to upload your Web site. Free Web hosting services such as those provided by Angelfire, Tripod, or GeoCities are other options. These services, as well as many other hosting services, also offer low-cost Web hosting from approximately $3.95 to $9.95 a month. The FreeSite.com contains a list of free and inexpensive hosting services, and FreeWebspace.net provides a PowerSearch form for free and low-cost hosting.

Table 3-6 contains a list of Web hosting services. Appendix C contains step-by-step instructions on publishing a Web site to a remote folder.

Table 3-6 Web Site Hosting Services

NAME	WEB SITE	COST
Angelfire®	angelfire.lycos.com	Free (ad-supported); starting at $4.95 monthly ad-free
Yahoo! GeoCities	geocities.yahoo.com	Free (ad-supported); starting at $4.95 monthly ad-free
Tripod®	tripod.lycos.com/	Free (ad-supported); starting at $4.95 monthly ad-free
The FreeSite.com	thefreesite.com/Free_Web_Space	A list of free and inexpensive hosting sites
FreeWebspace.net	freewebspace.net	A searchable guide for free Web space

For an updated list of Web site hosting services, visit the Macromedia Dreamweaver MX 2004 Web page (scsite.com/dreamweavermx04) and then click Web Hosting. If required by your instructor, publish the Florida Parks Web site to a remote server by following the steps in Appendix C.

With your work completed, you are ready to quit Dreamweaver.

More About

Publishing Your Florida Parks Web Site

Appendix C contains step-by-step instructions on publishing the Florida Parks Web site.

Quitting Dreamweaver

After you add pages to your Web site and add the head content, Project 3 is complete. The following step illustrates how to close the Web site, quit Dreamweaver MX 2004, and return control to Windows.

To Close the Web Site and Quit Dreamweaver

1 Click the Close button on the right corner of the Dreamweaver title bar.

The Dreamweaver window, the Document window, and the Florida Parks Web site all close. If you have unsaved changes, Dreamweaver will prompt you to save the changes. Clicking the Yes button in the Dreamweaver MX 2004 dialog box saves the changes.

Project Summary

Project 3 introduced you to tables and to Web page design using tables. You created three Web pages, using the Standard mode for two pages and the Layout mode for the third page. You merged and split cells and learned how to add text and images to the tables. Next, you added a border color and cell background color. Finally, you added head content to one of the Web pages.

What You Should Know

Having completed this project, you should be able to perform the tasks below. The tasks are listed in the same order they were presented in the project. For a list of the buttons, menus, toolbars, and commands introduced in this project, see the Quick Reference Summary at the back of this book and refer to the Page Number column.

Learn It Online

Instructions: To complete the Learn It Online exercises, start your browser, click the Address bar, and then enter the Web address `scsite.com/dreamweavermx2004/learn`. When the Dreamweaver MX 2004 Learn It Online page is displayed, follow the instructions in the exercises below. Each exercise has instructions for printing your results, either for your own records or for submission to your instructor.

1 Project Reinforcement TF, MC, and SA

Below Dreamweaver Project 3, click the Project Reinforcement link. Print the quiz by clicking Print on the File menu for each page. Answer each question.

2 Flash Cards

Below Dreamweaver Project 3, click the Flash Cards link and read the instructions. Type 20 (or a number specified by your instructor) in the Number of playing cards text box, type your name in the Enter your Name text box, and then click the Flip Card button. When the flash card is displayed, read the question and then click the ANSWER box arrow to select an answer. Flip through Flash Cards. If your score is 15 (75%) correct or greater, click Print on the File menu to print your results. If your score is less than 15 (75%) correct, then redo this exercise by clicking the Replay button.

3 Practice Test

Below Dreamweaver Project 3, click the Practice Test link. Answer each question, enter your first and last name at the bottom of the page, and then click the Grade Test button. When the graded practice test is displayed on your screen, click Print on the File menu to print a hard copy. Continue to take practice tests until you score 80% or better.

4 Who Wants To Be a Computer Genius?

Below Dreamweaver Project 3, click the Computer Genius link. Read the instructions, enter your first and last name at the bottom of the page, and then click the PLAY button. When your score is displayed, click the PRINT RESULTS link to print a hard copy.

5 Wheel of Terms

Below Dreamweaver Project 3, click the Wheel of Terms link. Read the instructions, and then enter your first and last name and your school name. Click the PLAY button. When your score is displayed, right-click the score and then click Print on the shortcut menu to print a hard copy.

6 Crossword Puzzle Challenge

Below Dreamweaver Project 3, click the Crossword Puzzle Challenge link. Read the instructions, and then enter your first and last name. Click the SUBMIT button. Work the crossword puzzle. When you are finished, click the Submit button. When the crossword puzzle is redisplayed, click the Print Puzzle button to print a hard copy.

7 Tips and Tricks

Below Dreamweaver Project 3, click the Tips and Tricks link. Click a topic that pertains to Project 3. Right-click the information and then click Print on the shortcut menu. Construct a brief example of what the information relates to in Dreamweaver to confirm you understand how to use the tip or trick.

8 Newsgroups

Below Dreamweaver Project 3, click the Newsgroups link. Click a topic that pertains to Project 3. Print three comments.

9 Expanding Your Horizons

Below Dreamweaver Project 3, click the Expanding Your Horizons link. Click a topic that pertains to Project 3. Print the information. Construct a brief example of what the information relates to in Dreamweaver to confirm you understand the contents of the article.

10 Search Sleuth

Below Dreamweaver Project 3, click the Search Sleuth link. To search for a term that pertains to this project, select a term below the Project 3 title and then use the Google search engine at google.com (or any major search engine) to display and print two Web pages that present information on the term.

Apply Your Knowledge

1 Modifying the B & B Lawn Service Web

Instructions: Start Dreamweaver. See the inside back cover of this book for instructions for downloading the Data Disk or see your instructor for information on accessing the files in this book.

The B & B Lawn Service Web site currently contains four pages. You will add a fifth page with a table created using Standard mode. The new Web page will include a seven-row, three-column centered table with a list of services, how often the services are scheduled, and the price of each service. You merge one of the rows and then add and center an image in the row. A border color is applied to the entire table, and the first row has a background color applied. Keywords and a description are added. You then add a link to the home page, save the page, and upload the Web site to a Web server. The new page added to the Web site is shown in Figure 3-118. Software and hardware settings determine how a Web page is displayed in a browser. Your Web page may display differently than the one shown in Figure 3-118.

Appendix C contains instructions for uploading your local site to a remote site.

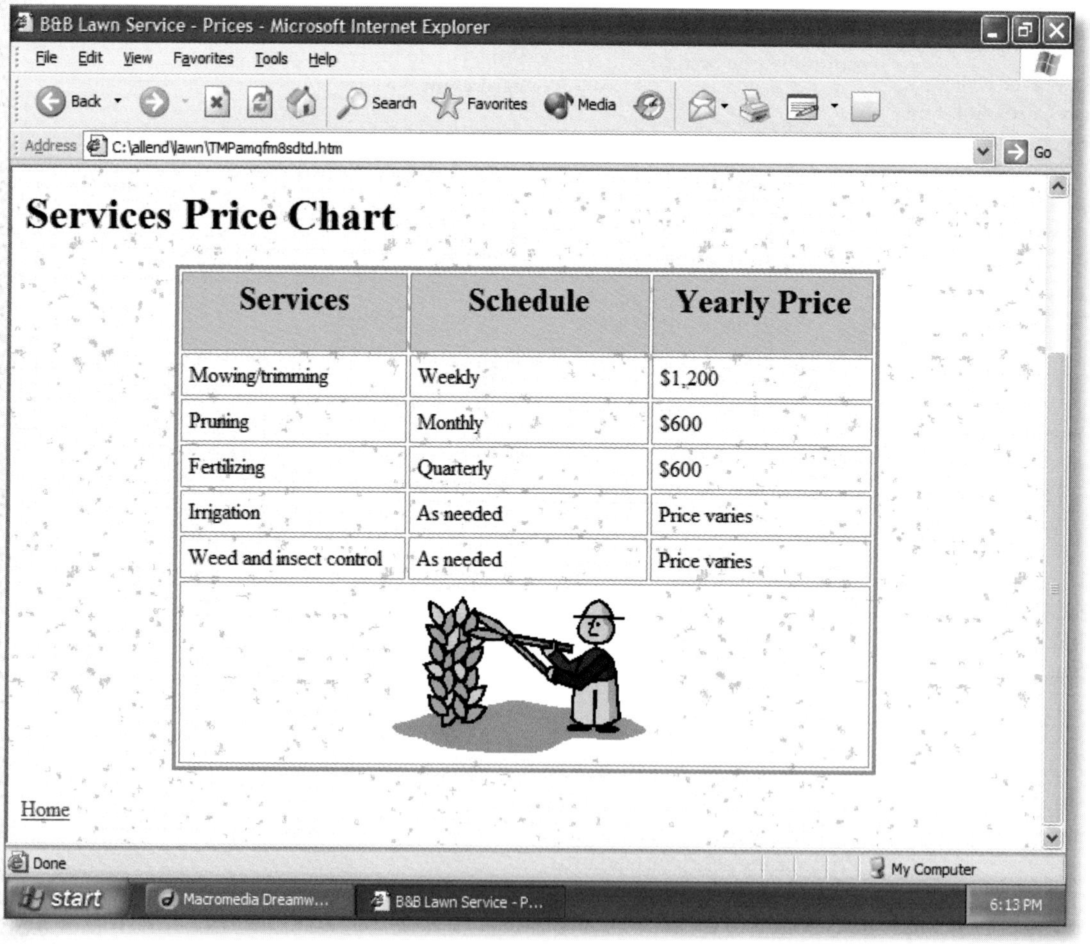

FIGURE 3-118

Apply Your Knowledge

1. Use the Windows My Computer option to copy the triming.gif image from the DataFiles folder to your /lawn/images folder.
2. Select Lawn Service from the Site pop-up menu in the Files panel. Click File on the menu bar and then click New. If necessary, click the General tab and then click Basic page in the Category list. Click the Create button. Save the page as prices.
3. Use the Page Properties dialog box to apply the lawnbg.gif image to the new page.
4. If necessary, display the Insert bar. Click the upper-left corner of the Document window. Type `Services Price Chart` and then apply Heading 1 to the text. Press the ENTER key and then click the Layout category on the Insert bar. If necessary, click the Standard Mode button and then click the Table button in the Layout category. Type the following data in the Table dialog box: `7` for Rows, `5` for Cell padding, `3` for Columns, `2` for Cell spacing, `70` for Width, and `3` for Border.
5. Type the text as shown in Table 3-7. Press the TAB key to move from cell to cell.

Table 3-7 Lawn Services Price Chart

Services	Schedule	Yearly Price
Mowing/trimming	Weekly	$1,200
Pruning	Monthly	$600
Fertilizing	Quarterly	$600
Irrigation	As needed	Price varies
Weed and insect control	As needed	Price varies

6. Click anywhere in row 1 and then click the <tr> tag in the tag selector to select row 1. Apply Heading 2 and center the heading. Click the Bg box in the Property inspector and apply background color #FFCC99 (Color Cubes palette, row 3 from the bottom and column 2 from the right).
7. Click anywhere in row 7 in the table and then click the <tr> tag in the tag selector to select row 7. Click the Merge Cells button and then click the Align Center button in the Property inspector. If necessary, display the Assets panel. With the insertion point in the middle of the merged row 7, drag the triming.gif image to the insertion point. Select the image and then type `Tree trimming` as the Alt text.
8. Click the <table> tag in the tag selector and then apply border color #FF9900 (Color Cubes palette, row 7 from the top and column 3 from the right). Center the table.
9. Position the insertion point outside the table by clicking to the right of the table. Press the ENTER key and then click the Text Indent button two times. Type `Home` and then create a relative link to the index.htm file.
10. Click the HTML category on the Insert bar, click the Head pop-up menu, and then click the Keywords command. When the Keywords dialog box is displayed, type `lawn service, price schedule, your name` in the Keywords text box and then click the OK button. Click the Head pop-up menu and select click the Description command. When the Description dialog box is displayed, type `B & B Lawn Service price schedule` in the Description text box and then click the OK button.
11. Title the page B & B Lawn Service - Prices. Check spelling. Save the Web page.
12. Open the index.htm page and then scroll to the end of the page. Click above your name and then press the ENTER key. Type `Check our Prices` and then create a link from the word, Prices, to the prices.htm page.
13. Print a copy of the page if required by your instructor. If required by your instructor, publish the Lawn Service Web site to a remote server by following the steps in Appendix C. Close the Lawn Service Web site. Close Dreamweaver.

In the Lab

1 Adding a Page with a Table to the CandleDust Web Site

Problem: Publicity from the Web site has generated several requests for examples of Mary Stewart's candles. Mary has asked you to add a page to the site that shows some of her creations and the price of each candle. The Web page will have a link to the home page and will be named products. The new page is shown in Figure 3-119. Appendix C contains instructions for uploading your local site to a remote site.

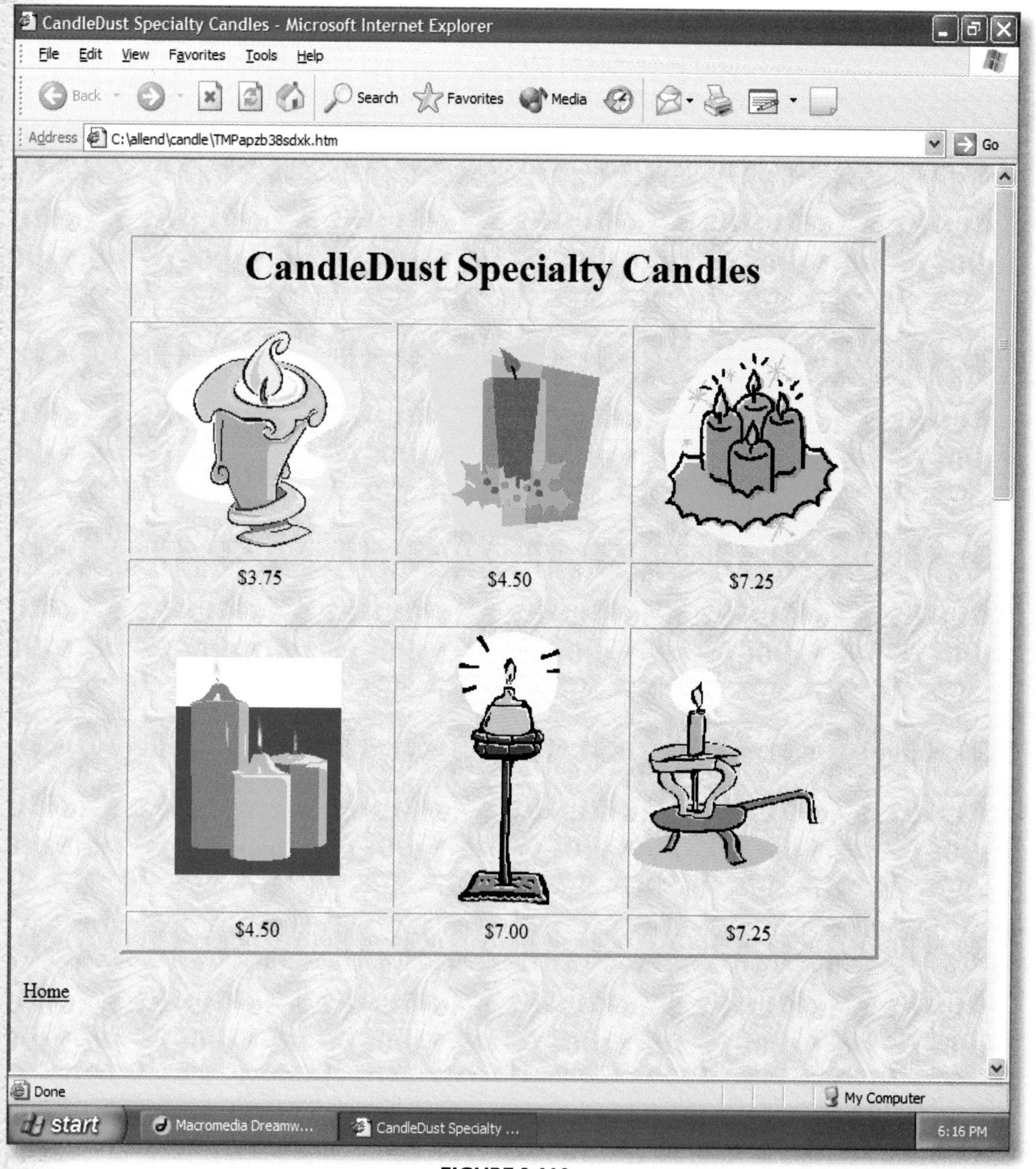

FIGURE 3-119

In the Lab

Instructions: Perform the following tasks:

1. Use the Windows My Computer option to copy the six images (candle3.gif through candle8.gif) from the DataFiles folder to your /candle/images folder.
2. Start Dreamweaver. Select CandleDust from the Files pop-up menu in the Files panel. Click File on the menu bar and then click New. If necessary, click the General tab and then click Basic page in the Category list. Click the Create button. Save the page as products.
3. Use the Page Properties dialog box to add the background.gif image. Title the page CandleDust Specialty Candles.
4. Click the upper-left corner of the page and then press the ENTER key.
5. If necessary, click the Insert bar's Layout category, the Standard Mode button, and then the Table button. Enter the following data in the Table dialog box: `6` for Rows, `3` for Cell padding, `3` for Columns, `3` for Cell spacing, `80` for Width, and `3` for Border. Center the table.
6. Merge the three cells in row 1 into one cell. Click the Align Center button in the Property inspector and then type `CandleDust Specialty Candles` as the heading. Apply Heading 1 to the text heading.
7. Click column 1, row 2 and then drag to select all cells in rows 2 through 6. Click the Align Center button, click the Vert box arrow, and then select Middle. Select column 1, rows 2 through 6. Click the Width box and type `33%` as the new width. Repeat this step for column 2, rows 2 through 6, and column 3, rows 2 through 6.
8. Display the Assets panel. Click column 1, row 2 and drag candle3.gif to the insertion point. Repeat this step, dragging candle4.gif to column 2, row 2, and candle5.gif to column 3, row 2.
9. Type the following information in row 3: `$3.75` in column 1, `$4.50` in column 2, and `$7.25` in column 3.
10. Merge the three cells in row 4.
11. Click column 1, row 5 and drag candle6.gif to the insertion point. Repeat this step, dragging candle7.gif to column 2, row 5, and candle8.gif to column 3, row 5.
12. Type the following information in row 6: `$4.50` in column 1, `$7.00` in column 2, and `$7.25` in column 3.
13. Click outside of the table to the right and then press the ENTER key. Type `Home` and create a link from the products.htm page to the index.htm page.
14. Open the index.htm page and click below the Company History link. Type `Products` and then create a link to the products.htm page. Save the index.htm page.
15. Save the products.htm page and then view your page in your browser. Verify that your link works. Print a copy of the Web page if required and hand it in to your instructor. If required by your instructor, publish the CandleDust Web site to a remote server by following the steps in Appendix C. Close your browser. Close Dreamweaver.

2 Adding a Table Page to the Credit Web Site

Problem: The Credit Protection Web site has become very popular. Marcy receives numerous e-mail messages requesting that the Web site be expanded. Several messages have included a request to provide some hints and tips about how to save money. Marcy asks you to create a new page for the Web site so she can share some of this information. Figure 3-120a on the next page shows the table layout, and Figure 3-120b on page DW 271 shows the Web page. Appendix C contains instructions for uploading your local site to a remote site.

(continued)

In the Lab

Adding a Table Page to the Credit Web Site *(continued)*

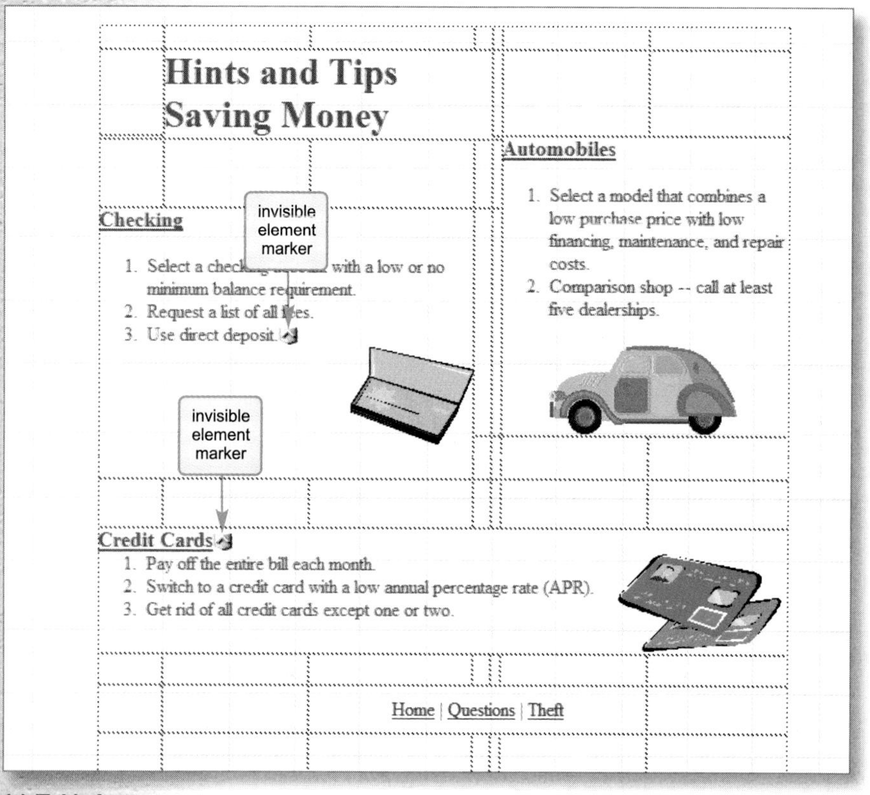

(a) Table Layout

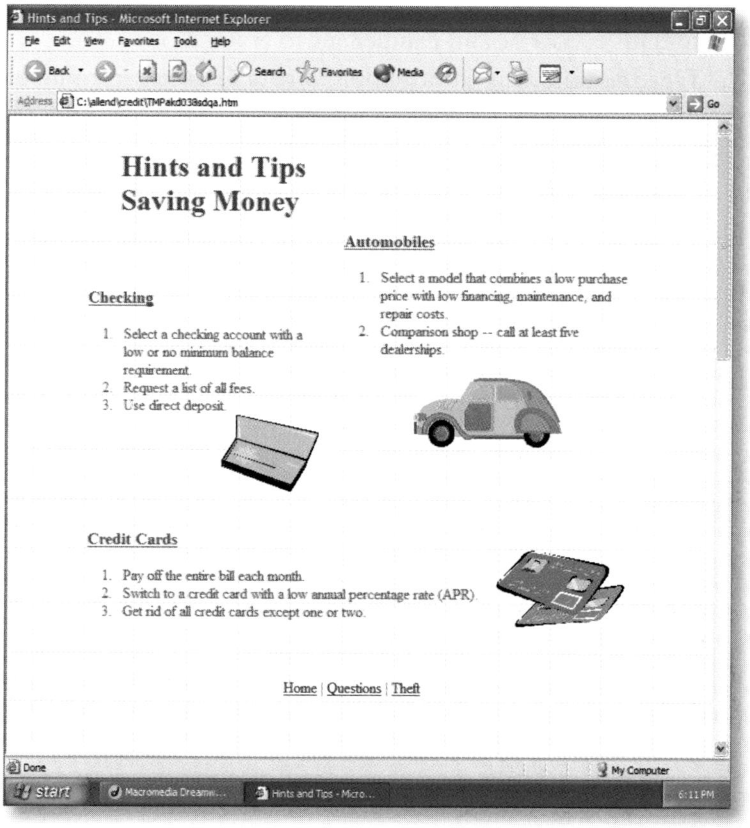

(b) Web Page

FIGURE 3-120

In the Lab

Instructions: Perform the following tasks:

1. Use the Windows My Computer option to copy the three images (car.gif, check.gif, and credit_card.gif) from the DataFiles folder to your /credit/images folder. Start Dreamweaver. Select Credit Protection from the Site pop-up menu in the Files panel.
2. Add a new Web page and name it saving. Add the creditbg.gif image. Title the page Tips and Hints.
3. Display the rulers. Click the Insert bar's Layout category and then click the Layout button.
4. Click the Draw Layout Table button on the Layout tab and then create a table with a fixed width of approximately 600 pixels and a height of approximately 615 pixels.
5. Use Figure 3-120a on page DW 295 as a guide and draw the five layout cells. Use the information in Table 3-8 for the widths and heights.

Table 3-8 Credit Protection Cell Layout Guide

NUMBER	CELL NAME	W	H	IMAGE ALT TEXT	IMAGE NAME
1	Heading	285	75	None	None
2	Checking	325	210	Checking Account	check.gif
3	Automobiles	250	235	Car	car.gif
4	Credit Cards	600	105	Credit Cards	credit_card.gif
5	Links	295	40	None	None

6. Use Figure 3-120b on the previous page as a reference and type the text into each of the layout cells. Apply Heading 1 to the text in the first cell. Apply Heading 3 to the headings in cells 2 through 4 and then underline the headings.
7. Insert the images into the cells. Refer to the invisible element marker in Figure 3-120b as the insertion point for the images in cells 2 and 4. For cell 3, press the ENTER key after item 2 and then click the Align Center button in the Property inspector. Drag the car.gif to the insertion point.
8. Add relative links to the three text items in cell 5.
9. Click the Standard mode button on the Layout tab, select the table, and then center the table.
10. Click the Head button in the HTML category of the Insert bar. Click the Keywords button in the pop-up menu and then type `credit, money, tips, checking, saving, [your name]` in the Keywords dialog box. Click the Description button and then type `Tips and hints on how to save money` in the Description dialog box. Save the Web page.
11. Open the index.htm page and click below the last bulleted item. Type `Tips on Saving` and create a link from this text to the saving.htm page. Save the index.htm page.
12. View the Web site in your browser and verify that your links work. Close the browser. If required, print a copy for your instructor. If required by your instructor, publish the Credit Protection Web site to a remote server by following the steps in Appendix C.

In the Lab

3 Adding a Table Page to the Plant City Web Site

Problem: In his job as a member of the Plant City marketing group, Juan Benito has been exploring the city's history. On a recent tour, Juan discovered that the city contains many well-preserved historic homes. He would like to feature some of these homes on the Web site and has requested that you add a new page to the Plant City Web site. You elect to use a layout table to create this page. The Web page is displayed in Figure 3-121. Appendix C contains instructions for uploading your local site to a remote site.

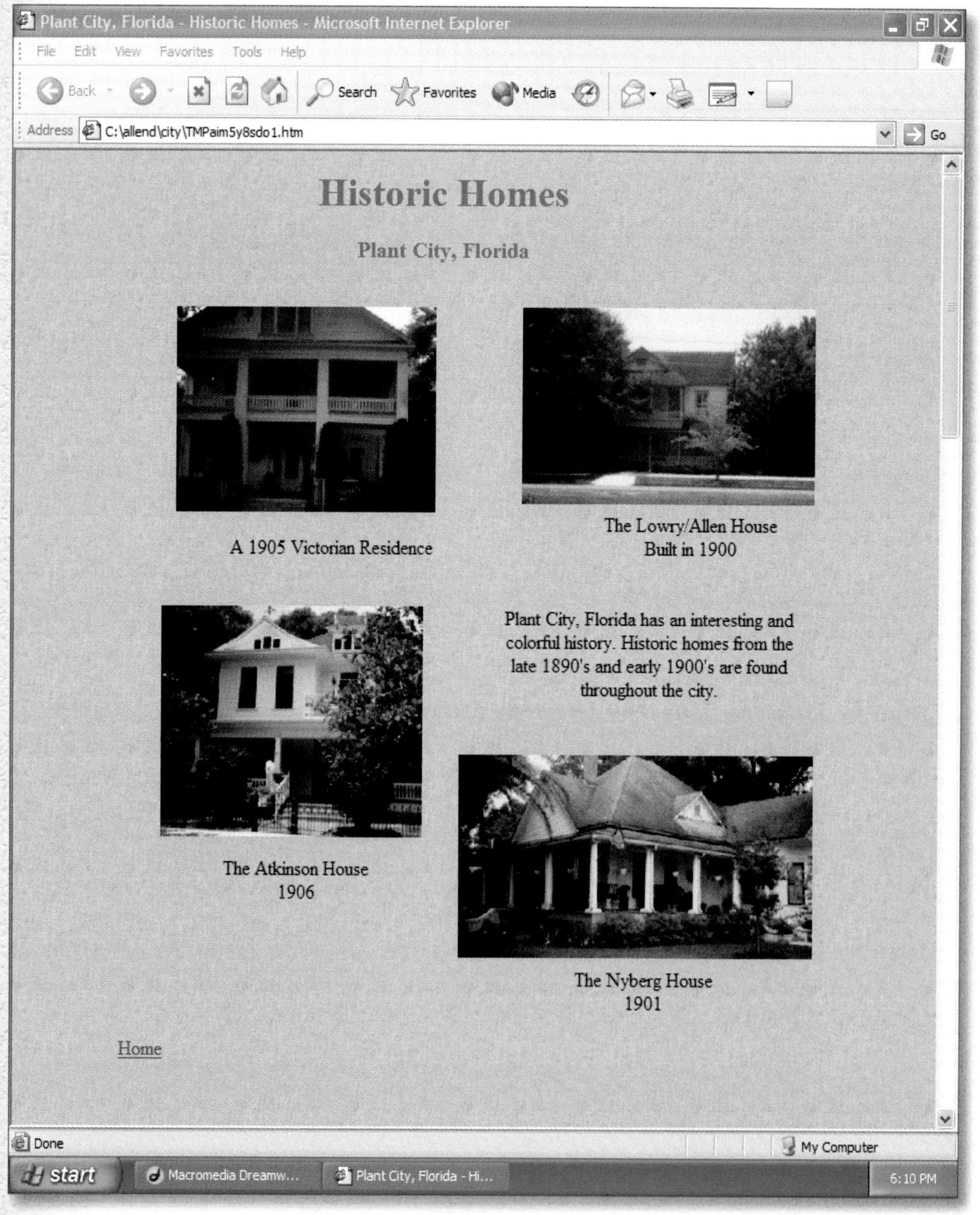

FIGURE 3-121

In the Lab

Instructions: Perform the following tasks:

1. Use the Windows My Computer option to copy the four images (house01.gif through house04.gif) from the DataFiles folder to your /city/images folder. Start Dreamweaver. Select Plant City from the Site pop-up menu in the Files panel.
2. Add a new page and then add the background image you added in Project 1. Title the page `Plant City, Florida - Historic Homes` and then save the page with the file name `homes`.
3. Display the rulers. Click the Insert bar's Layout category and then click the Layout button.
4. Create a layout table with a fixed width of approximately 650 pixels and a height of approximately 675 pixels.
5. Use Figure 3-121 on the previous page as a guide and draw the 10 layout cells. Use the information in Table 3-9 for the widths, heights, and file names.

Table 3-9 Plant City Cell Layout Guide

NUMBER	CELL NAME	W	H	IMAGE ALT TEXT	FILE NAME
1	Heading	390	85	None	None
2	Victorian House	220	160	Victorian House	house01.gif
3	Text	220	50	None	None
4	Atkinson House	225	190	Atkinson House	house02.gif
5	Text	160	70	None	None
6	Lowry/Allen House	245	160	Lowry/Allen House	house03.gif
7	Text	245	50	None	None
8	Text	245	90	None	None
9	Nyberg House	300	170	Nyberg House	house04.gif
10	Text	300	40	None	None

6. Type the text into each of the layout cells as indicated. Apply Heading 1 to the first line of text in the first cell and Heading 3 to the second line of text.
7. Insert the images into the cells. Refer to Table 3-9 for the image file names.
8. Click the Standard mode button on the Layout category, select the table, and then center the table. Add a link at the bottom of the page to the Home page.
9. Click the Keywords button, and then type `Plant City, Florida, homes, history, your name` in the Keywords dialog box. Click the Description button and then type `A tour of Plant City, Florida historic homes` in the Description dialog box.
10. Open the index.htm page. Click to the right of the Recipes link. Add a vertical line and then type `Historic Homes`. Create a link from the `Historic Homes` text to the homes.htm page.
11. View the Web site in your browser. Close the browser. If required by your instructor, publish the Plant City Web site to a remote server by following the steps in Appendix C. If required, print a copy for your instructor.

Cases and Places

The difficulty of these case studies varies:
■ are the least difficult and ■■ are the most difficult. The last exercise is a group exercise.

1 ■ The sports Web site has become very popular. Several of your friends have suggested that you add a statistics page. You agree that this is a good idea. Create the new page. Using the Internet or other resources, find statistics about your selected sport. Add a background image to the page and use Standard mode to insert a table that contains your statistical information. Add an appropriate heading to the table and an appropriate title for the page. Create a link to the home page. Save the page in your sports Web site. For a selection of images and backgrounds, visit the Dreamweaver MX 2004 Media Web page (scsite.com/dreamweavermx04/media) and then click Media below Project 3.

2 ■ Modify your hobby Web site. Expand the topic and add an additional page with a table created in Standard mode. The table should contain a minimum of three rows and three columns, and a 2-pixel border. Include information in the table about your hobby. Include a minimum of two images in the table. Merge one of the rows or one of the columns and add a border color. Add a background image to the page and give your page a title. Create a link to the home page. Save the page in your hobby Web site. For a selection of images and backgrounds, visit the Dreamweaver MX 2004 Media Web page (scsite.com/dreamweavermx04/media) and then click Media below Project 3.

3 ■■ Modify your favorite type of music Web site by adding a new page. The new page should contain a table with three columns and four rows created in Standard mode. Merge one of the rows and add a background color to the row. Add at least two images to your table. Center the images in the cell. View your Web pages in your browser. Give your page a title and save the page in your music subfolder. Appendix C contains instructions for uploading your local site to a remote site. For a selection of images and backgrounds, visit the Dreamweaver MX 2004 Media Web page (scsite.com/dreamweavermx04/media) and then click Media below Project 3.

Cases and Places

4 ■■ Your running for office campaign is going well. You want to add a new page to the Web site to include pictures and text listing some of your outstanding achievements. Apply a color scheme and a background image to the page. Draw a layout table with a minimum of four layout cells. Include your picture in one of the cells. Add an appropriate title, keywords, and a description to the page. Center the table. Save the page in the office subfolder and then view the page in your browser. Appendix C contains instructions for uploading your local site to a remote site. For a selection of images and backgrounds, visit the Dreamweaver MX 2004 Media Web page (scsite.com/dreamweavermx04/media) and then click Media below Project 3.

5 ■■ **Working Together** The students at your school are requesting more information about the student trips. To accommodate the request, the members of your team decide to add another page to the Web site. Each team member is responsible for researching possible destinations and developing content for the selected destination. Add a heading to the new page and format it appropriately. Draw a layout table with a minimum of six layout cells. Each member adds at least one image and text content to a cell. One member formats the page — including the text and images. Add a title, keywords, meta tags, and a description. Save the page and view it in your browser. Appendix C contains instructions for uploading your local site to a remote site. For a selection of images and backgrounds, visit the Dreamweaver MX 2004 Media Web page (scsite.com/dreamweavermx04/media) and then click Media below Project 3.

Appendix A

Dreamweaver Help

Dreamweaver Help

This appendix shows you how to use the many components of Dreamweaver Help. At any time while you are using Dreamweaver, you can interact with its Help system and display information on any Dreamweaver topic. It is a complete reference manual at your fingertips.

The Using Dreamweaver Help system is viewed through your browser. The Using Dreamweaver MX Help system contains comprehensive HTML-based information about all Dreamweaver features, including the following:

- A table of contents in which the information is organized by subject.
- An alphabetical index that points to important terms and links to related topics.
- A search tool that allows you to find any character string in all topic text.
- A Favorites folder to which you can add frequently accessed topics.

Other Help features include tutorial lessons, context-sensitive help, information on Dreamweaver extensions, help on using Cold Fusion, and 11 online reference manuals, including an HTML reference manual. For additional tutorials and online movies, you can access the Macromedia Dreamweaver Web site at http://www.macromedia.com/software/dreamweaver/productinfo/features/brz_tour/.

The Dreamweaver Help Menu

One of the more commonly used methods to access Dreamweaver's Help features is through the **Help menu** and function keys. Dreamweaver's Help menu provides an easy system to access the available Help options (Figure A-1 on the next page). Table A-1 on the next page summarizes the commands available through the Help menu.

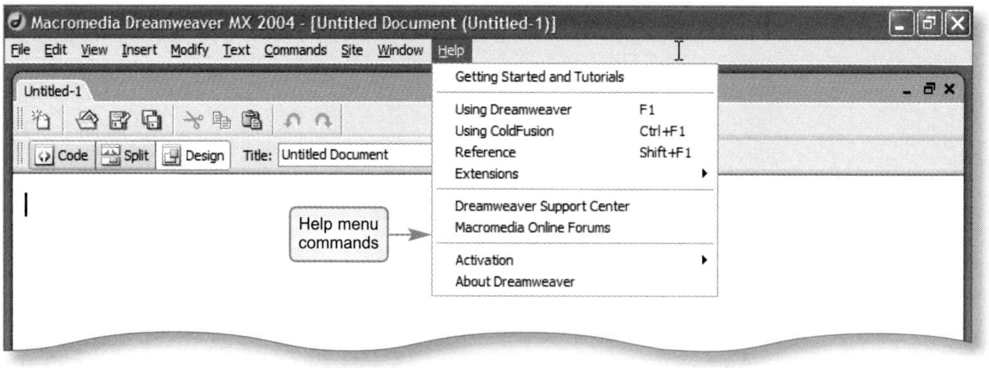

FIGURE A-1

Table A-1 Summary of Help Commands on the Help Menu

COMMAND ON HELP MENU	FUNCTION
Getting Started and Tutorials	The Getting Started and Tutorials command accesses the Getting Started window. This window provides access to several links and tutorials. Each tutorial takes 30 to 45 minutes to complete.
Using Dreamweaver	The Using Dreamweaver command displays the Using Dreamweaver window. This feature is commonly used for locating information. Using Dreamweaver is covered in more detail later in this appendix.
Using ColdFusion	The Using ColdFusion command displays the Using ColdFusion window. ColdFusion MX is a Web application server that lets you create applications that interact with databases.
Reference	When you click the Reference command, the Reference panel displays in the Dreamweaver panel groups. The Reference panel contains the complete text from several reference manuals, including references on HTML, Cascading Style Sheets, JavaScript, and other Web-related features.
Extensions	An **extension** is an add-on piece of software or a plug-in that enhances Dreamweaver's capabilities. Extensions provide the Dreamweaver developer with the capability to customize how Dreamweaver looks and works. Clicking the Extensions command displays a submenu with the following commands: Extending Dreamweaver, API Reference, and Creating and Submitting. Each of these commands opens a related Help window.
Dreamweaver Support Center	The Dreamweaver Support Center command provides access to the online Macromedia Dreamweaver Support Center. This Web site offers a search option, support solutions, support topics, and other support resources.
Macromedia Online Forums	The Macromedia Online Forums command provides access to the Macromedia Online Forums Web page. The forums provide a place for developers of all experience levels to share ideas and techniques.
Activation	The Activation command provides access to product activation, license transfer, online registration, and printing the registration.
About Dreamweaver	The About Dreamweaver command opens a window that provides copyright information and the product license number.

Navigating the Dreamweaver MX 2004 Help System

The Using Dreamweaver command accesses Dreamweaver's primary Help system and provides comprehensive information about all Dreamweaver features. Four options are available: Contents, Index, Search, and Favorites.

Using the Contents Sheet

The **Contents** sheet is useful for displaying Help when you know the general category of the topic in question, but not the specifics. Each topic in the Contents list is preceded by a book icon or question mark icon. A **book icon** indicates subtopics are available. Clicking the book icon (or associated link) displays the list of subtopics below that particular book. A **question mark icon** means information on the topic will display if you click the icon or the associated linked text. The next example shows how to use the Contents sheet to obtain information on how to spell check a Web page.

To Obtain Help Using the Contents Sheet

1

- **Click Help on the menu bar and then click Using Dreamweaver.**
- **Dreamweaver displays the Using Dreamweaver window.**
- **If necessary, double-click the title bar to maximize the window and click the Contents tab.**
- **To display a better view of the text, you can adjust the width of the left pane by moving the mouse pointer over the border separating the two panes.**
- **When the mouse pointer changes to a double-headed arrow, drag to the right or left to adjust the width of the left pane.**

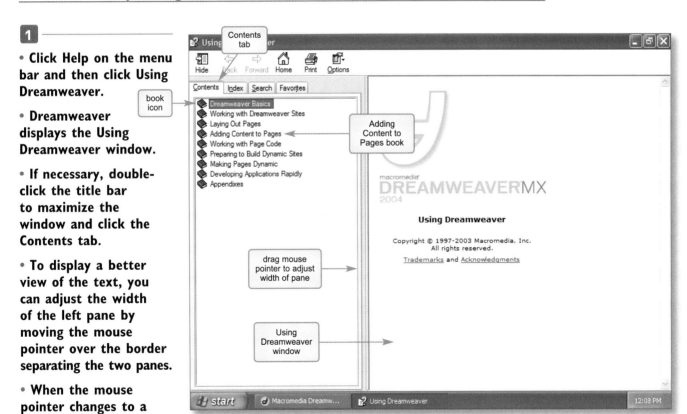

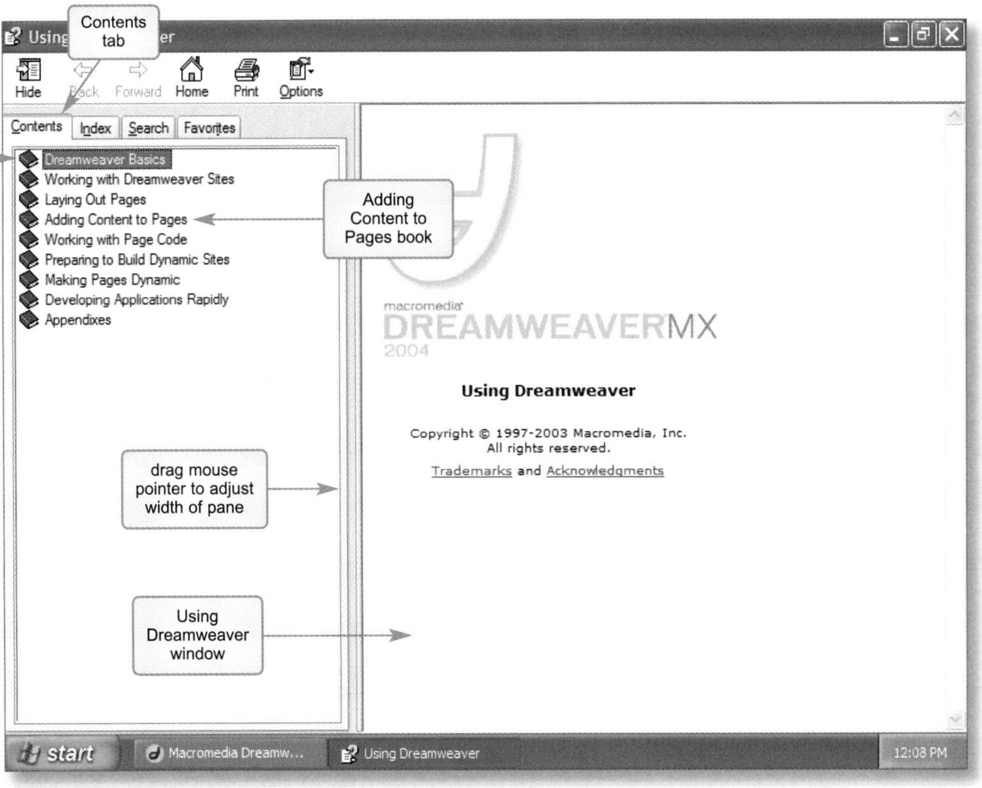

FIGURE A-2

The Using Dreamweaver window displays (Figure A-2). Four options are available: Contents, Index, Search, and Favorites.

2

• Click the Adding Content to Pages link.

The Adding Content to Pages book is opened, and the help information is displayed in the right pane (Figure A-3). Additional books are displayed below the chosen topic. Links to these books also are displayed in the right pane.

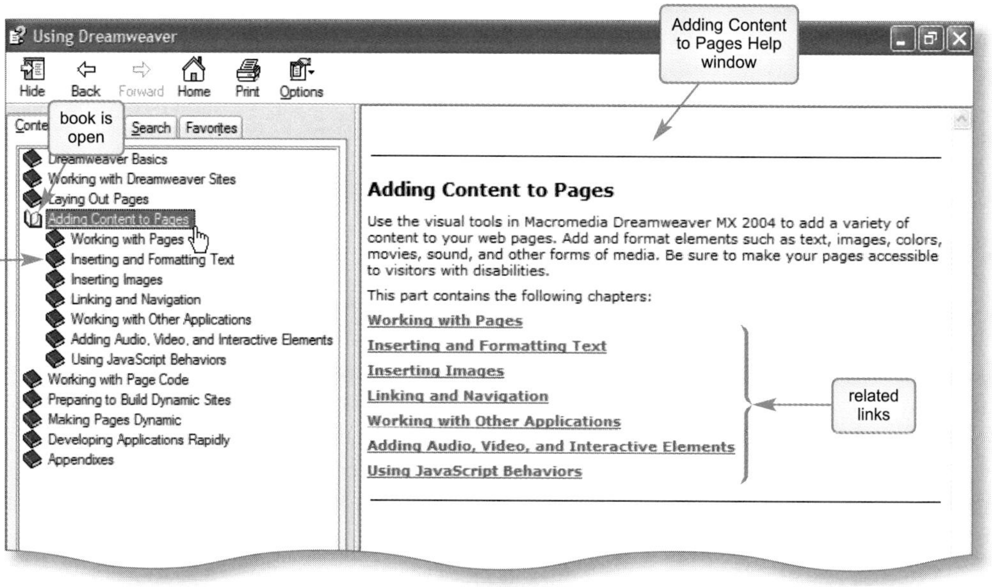

FIGURE A-3

3

• Click the Inserting and Formatting Text book and then click the Checking spelling link.

The information on the subtopic displays in the right pane (Figure A-4).

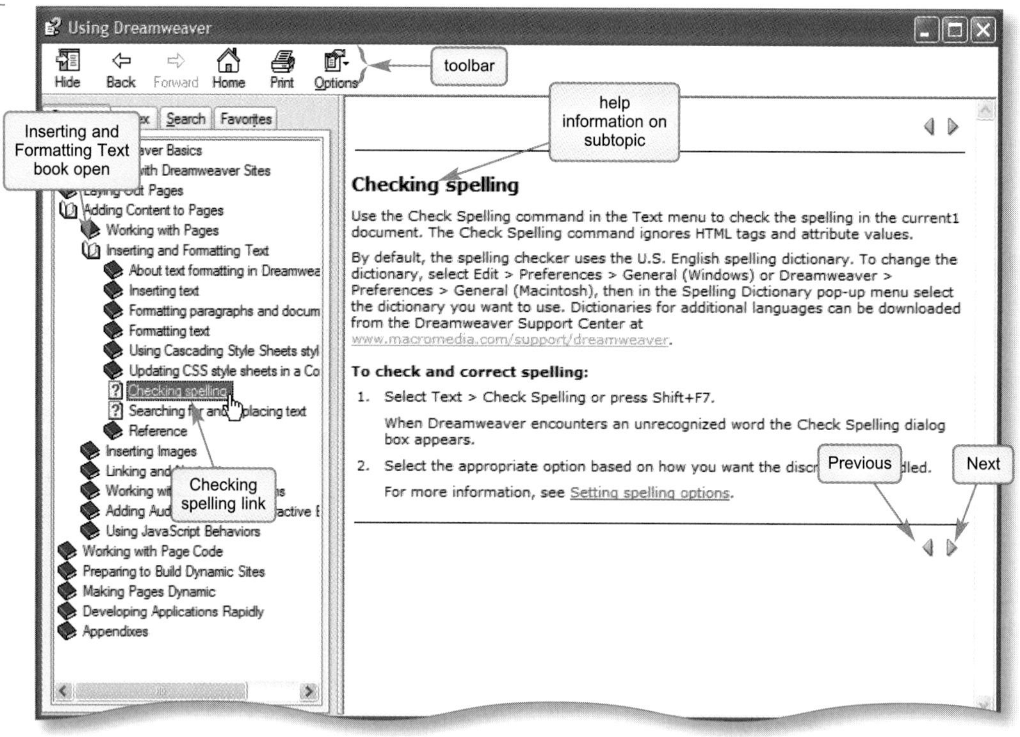

FIGURE A-4

Once the information on the subtopic displays, you can read it, you can click a link contained within the subtopic, or you can click the Print button on the toolbar to obtain a printed copy. Other buttons on the toolbar are Hide, Back, Forward, Home, and Options. The Home button returns you to your original location. The Back and Forward buttons move you back or move you forward to previously accessed screens. The Hide button hides the left pane, and the Options button displays a pop-up menu with all of the displayed buttons, plus Internet options. To view related topics, click the Previous or Next button in the displayed window.

Using the Index Sheet

The second sheet in the Using Dreamweaver window is the Index sheet. Use the **Index** sheet to display Help when you know the keyword or the first few letters of the keyword. The next steps show how to use the Index sheet to obtain help on inserting images.

To Use the Index Sheet

1

- **Click the Index tab.**

The Index sheet is displayed (Figure A-5). The insertion point is blinking in the Type in the keyword to find text box.

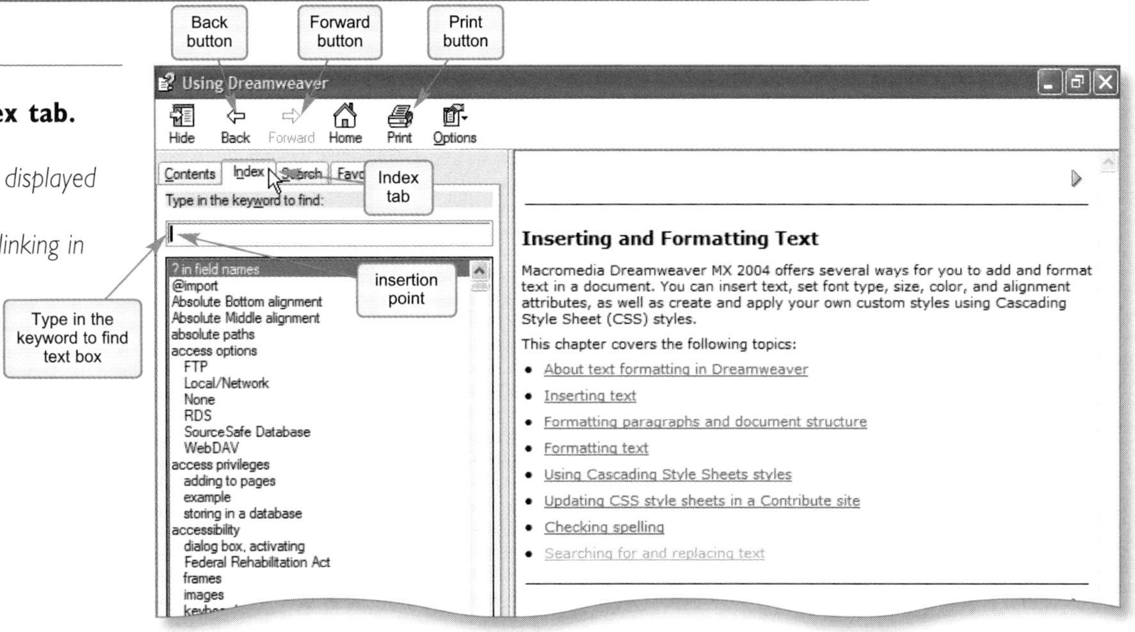

FIGURE A-5

2

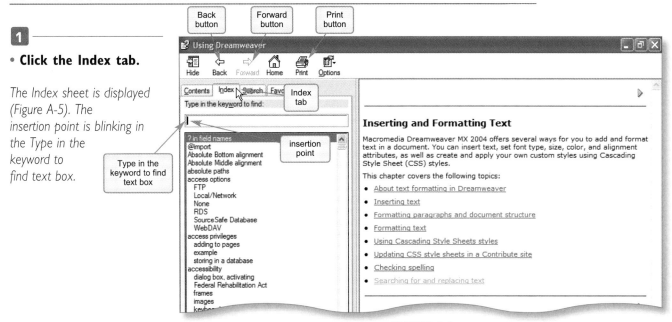

- **Type** `images` **in the text box. Point to the inserting subtopic.**

As you type, Dreamweaver scrolls through the list of topics. The topic, images, and subtopics below the images topic display in the left pane (Figure A-6).

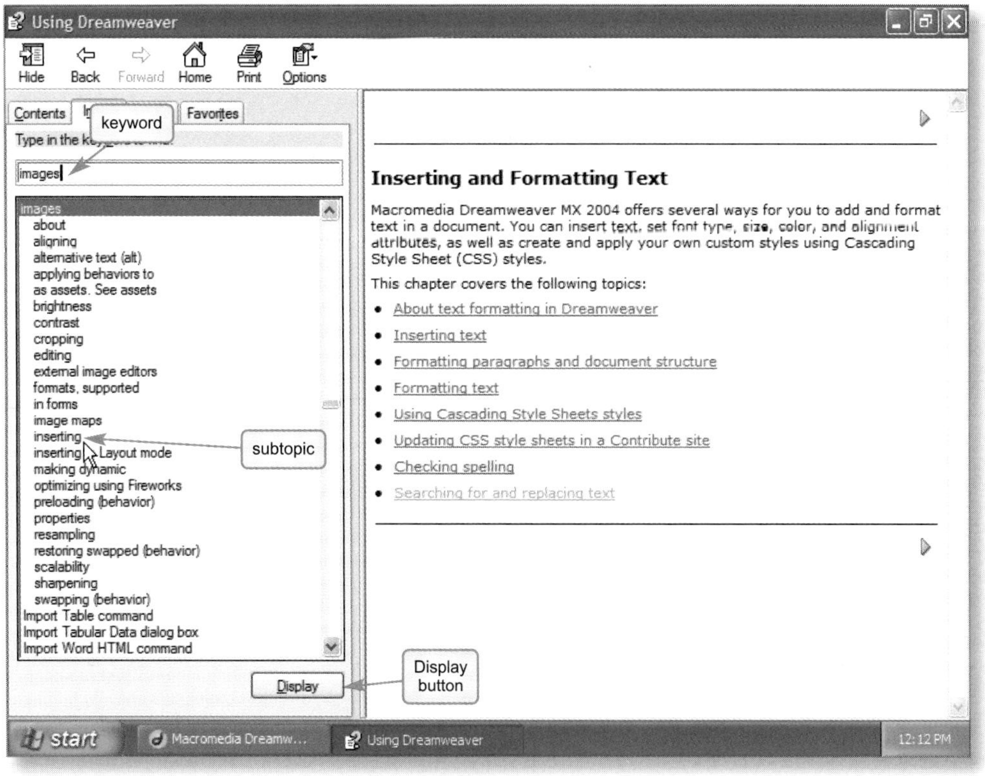

FIGURE A-6

3

• Click the inserting subtopic and then click the Display button.

Information about inserting an image displays in the right pane (Figure A-7).

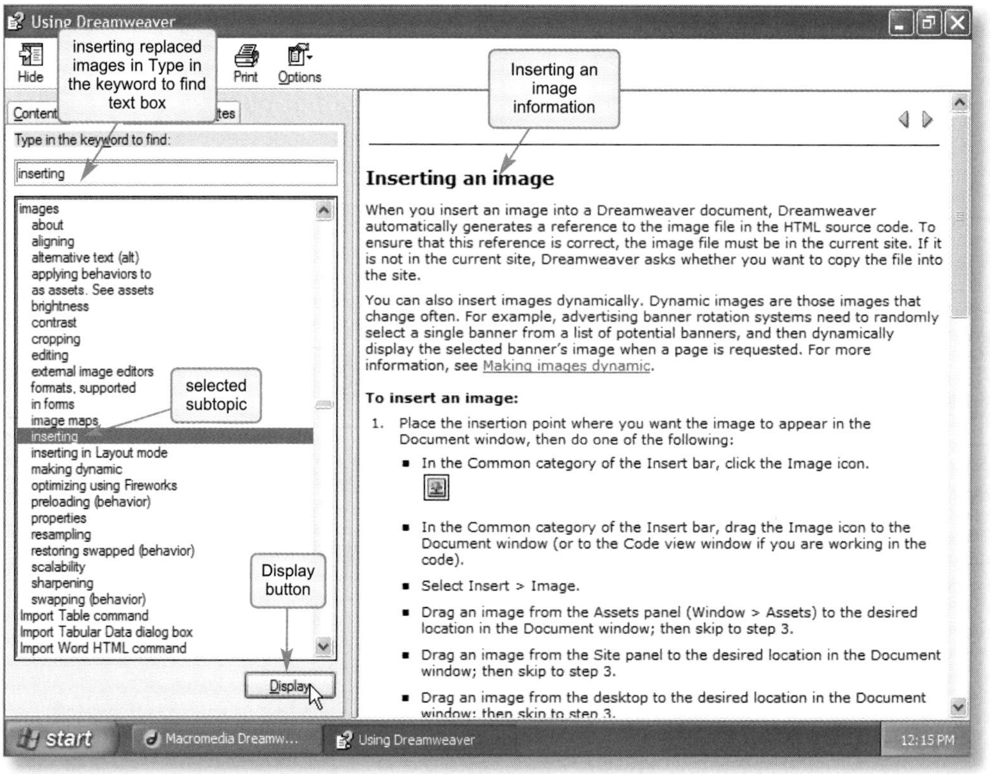

FIGURE A-7

Using the Search Sheet

Using the **Search** feature allows you to find any character string, anywhere in the text of the Help system. The next steps show how to use the Search sheet to obtain help about using bold text.

To Use the Search Sheet

1

- **Click the Search tab.**
- **Type** `Bold text` **in the Type in the keyword to find text box.**
- **Click the List Topics button.**
- **Click Setting text property options in the Select Topic to display box.**

The Search sheet displays a list of topics containing references to bold and text in the left pane (Figure A-8). All of these topics contain the words bold and text somewhere within the document.

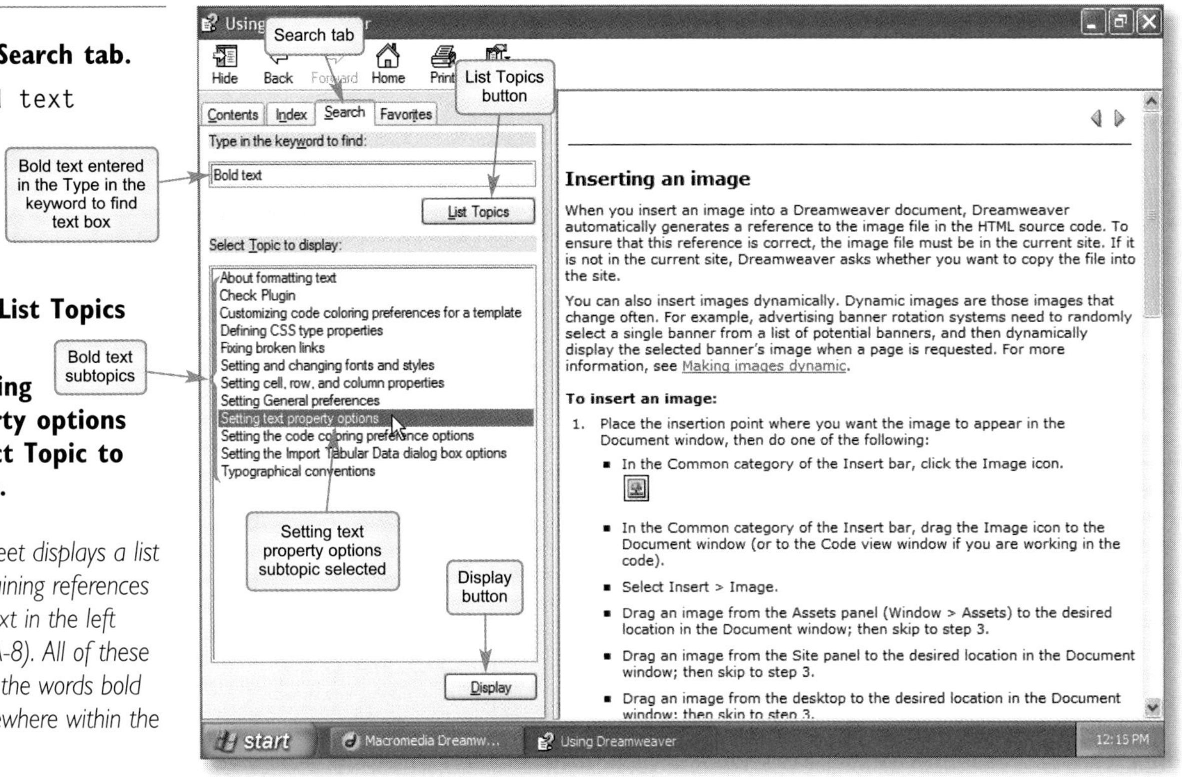

FIGURE A-8

2

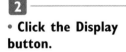

- **Click the Display button.**

The Help screen for Setting text property options displays in the right pane. All incidents of the words bold and text are highlighted in the document in the right pane (Figure A-9).

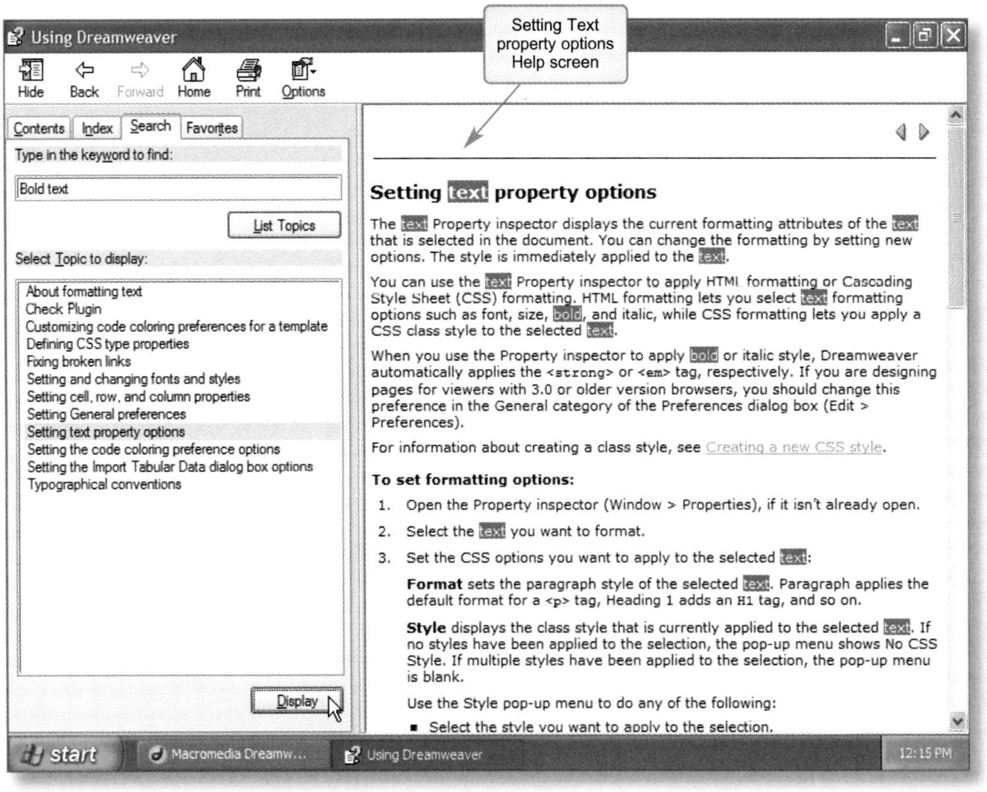

FIGURE A-9

Using the Favorites Sheet

If you find that you search or reference certain topics frequently, you can save these topics in the Favorites sheet. The following steps show how to add the information about the Setting text property options topic to the Favorites sheet.

To Add a Topic to the Favorites Sheet

1

- **Click the Favorites tab. Point to the Add button.**

The Favorites sheet displays in the left pane. The title of the information (Setting text property options) is displayed in the Current topic text box in the left pane. The information on bold text that displayed because of your previous search is displayed in the right pane (Figure A-10).

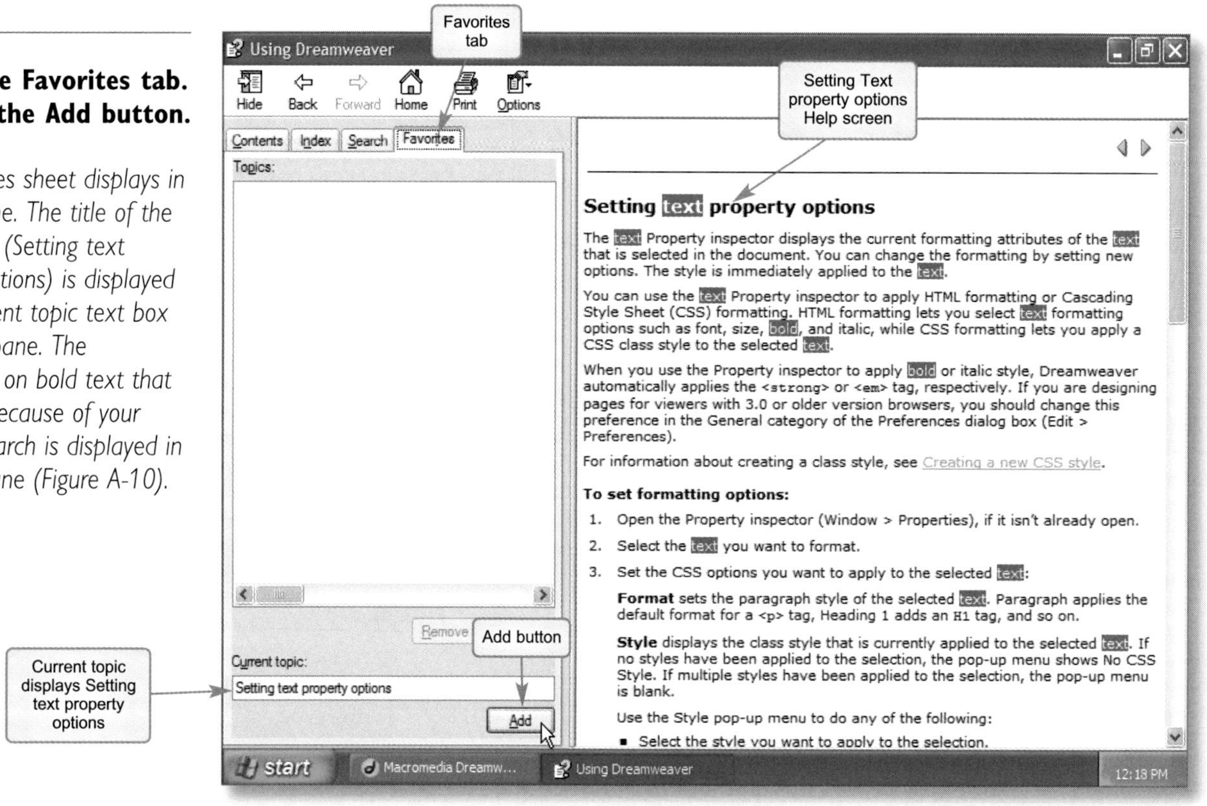

FIGURE A-10

2

• **Click the Add button.**

The Setting text property options topic is added to the Favorites sheet (Figure A-11).

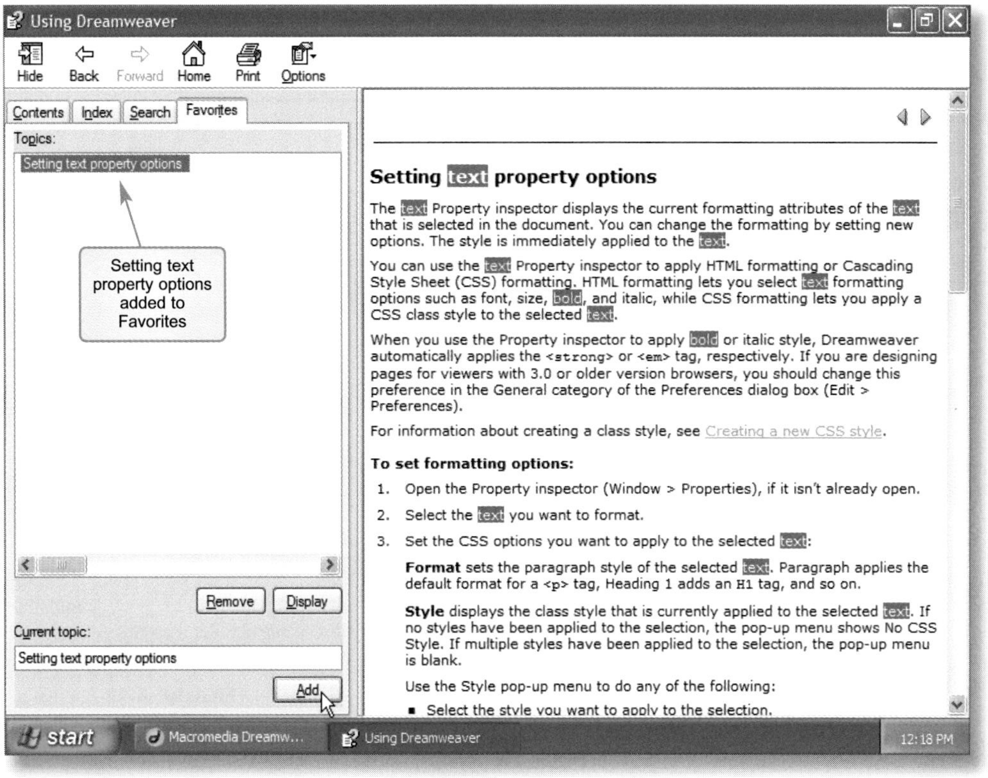

FIGURE A-11

3

• **Close the Using Dreamweaver Help window and return to Dreamweaver.**

Context-Sensitive Help

Using **context-sensitive help**, you can open a relevant Help topic in panel, inspectors, and most dialog boxes. To view these Help features, click a Help button in a dialog box, choose Help on the Options pop-up menu in a panel group, or click the question mark icon in an inspector.

Using the Question Mark Icon to Display Help

Many of the panels and inspectors within Dreamweaver contain a question mark icon. Clicking this icon displays context-sensitive help. Assume for the following example that you want to know about tables. The following steps show how to use the question mark icon to view context-sensitive help through the Property inspector. In this example, a table is displayed and selected in the Document window and the Property inspector displays table properties.

To Display Context-Sensitive Help on Tables

1

- **Point to the question mark icon in the Property inspector (Figure A-12).**

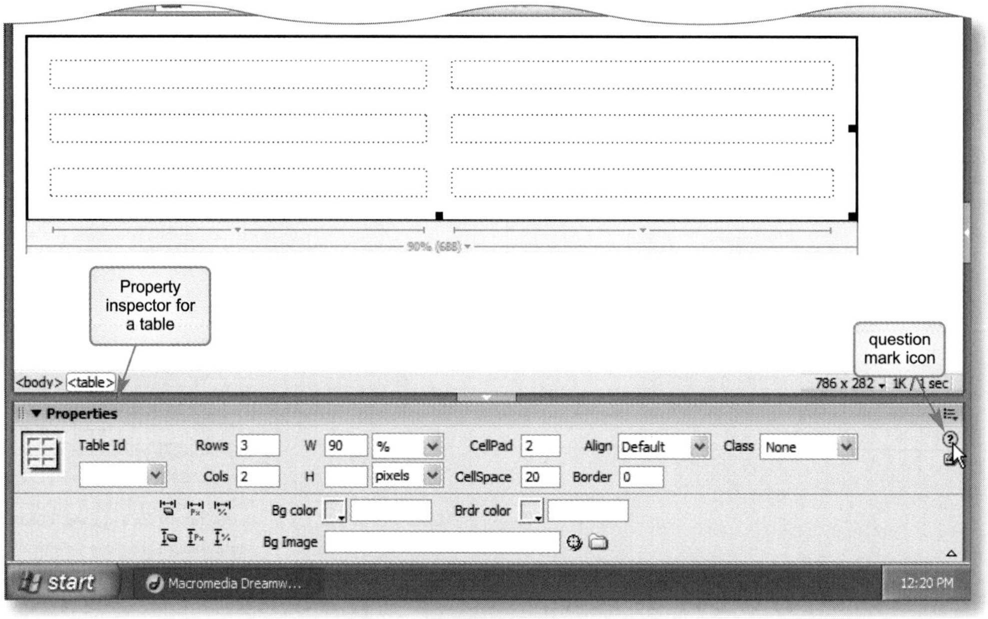

FIGURE A-12

2

- **Click the question mark icon.**

The Using Dreamweaver window displays and information pertaining to table properties displays in the right pane (Figure A-13). The Favorites tab is selected in the left pane because this was the last tab previously selected.

3

- **Close the Using Dreamweaver window and return to Dreamweaver.**

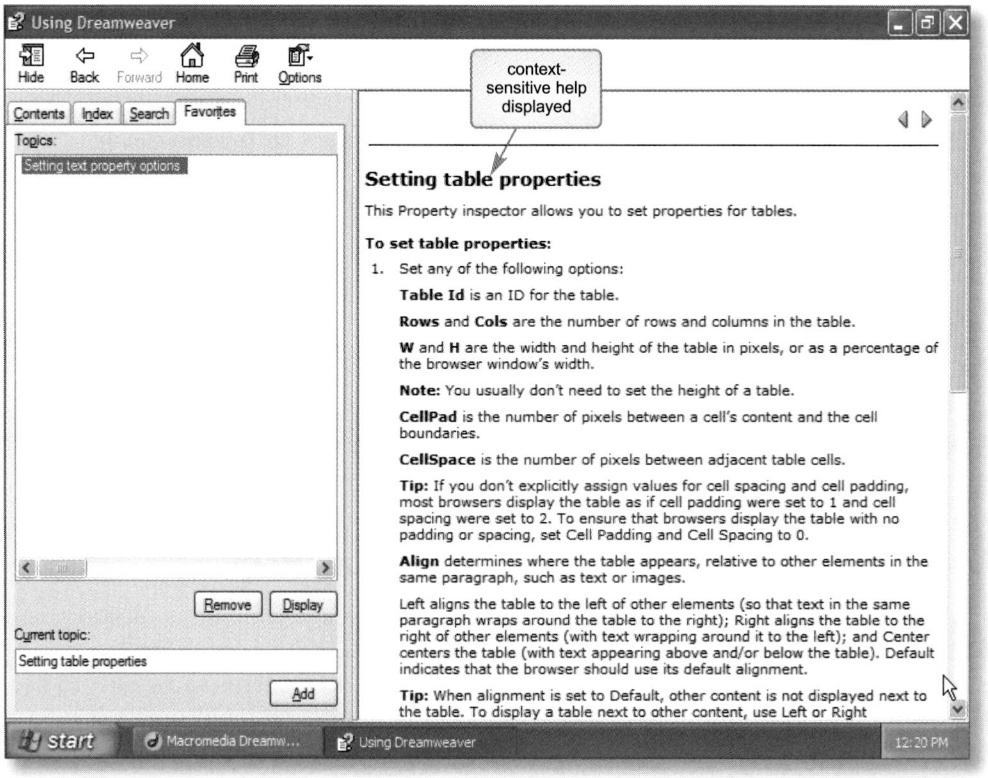

FIGURE A-13

Using the Options Menu to Display Help

Panels and dialog boxes also contain context-sensitive help. The following steps show how to display context-sensitive help for the Files panel. In this example, the Files panel is open and displayed within the Dreamweaver window.

To Use the Options Menu to Display Context-Sensitive Help for the Files Panel

1

- **Click the Options button on the Files title bar and then point to Help on the Options pop-up menu.**

The Options pop-up menu is displayed (Figure A-14).

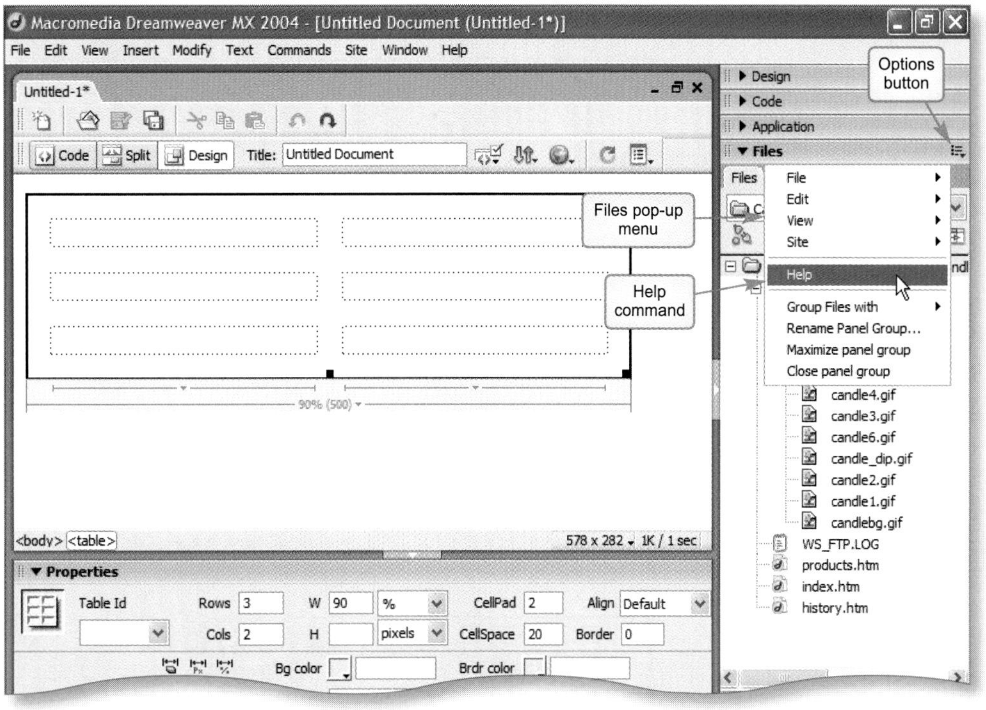

FIGURE A-14

2

- **Click the Help command.**

The Using Dreamweaver window displays, and information pertaining to using the Files panel is displayed in the right pane (Figure A-15). The Favorites tab is selected in the left pane because this was the last tab previously selected.

3

- **Close the Using Dreamweaver window and return to Dreamweaver.**

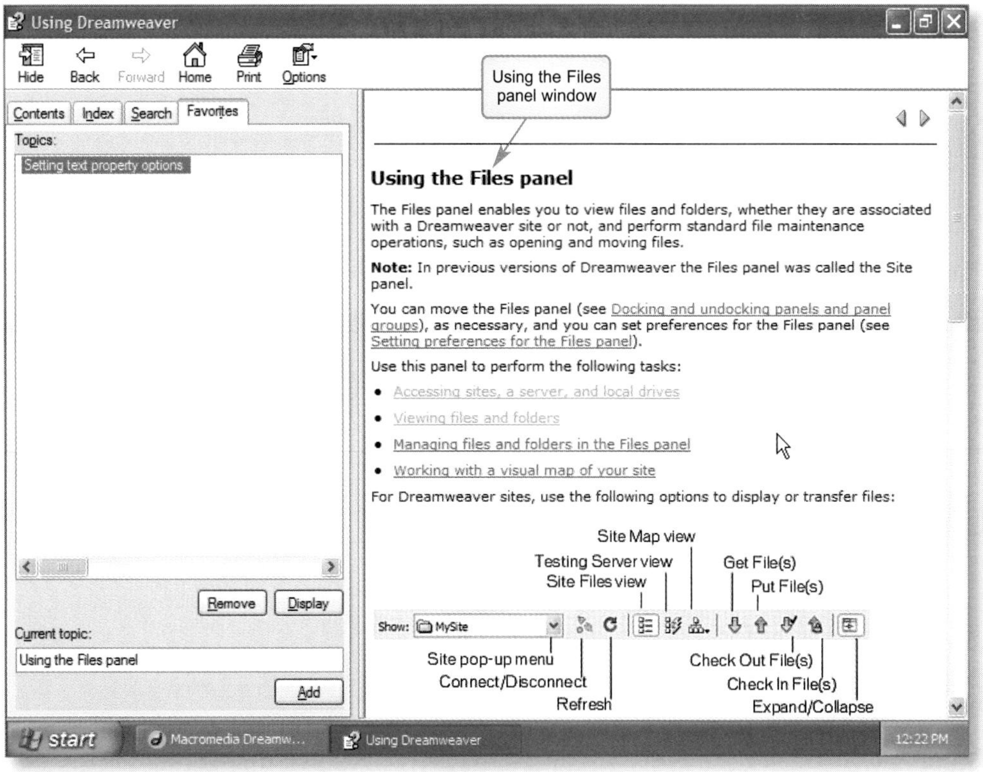

FIGURE A-15

Using the Reference Panel

The Reference panel in the panel groups is another valuable Dreamweaver resource. The Reference panel provides you with a quick reference tool for HTML tags, JavaScript objects, Cascading Style Sheets, and other Dreamweaver features. The next example shows how to access the Reference panel, review the various options, and select and display information on the <body> tag.

To Use the Reference Panel

1

• Click Window on the menu bar and then point to Reference (Figure A-16).

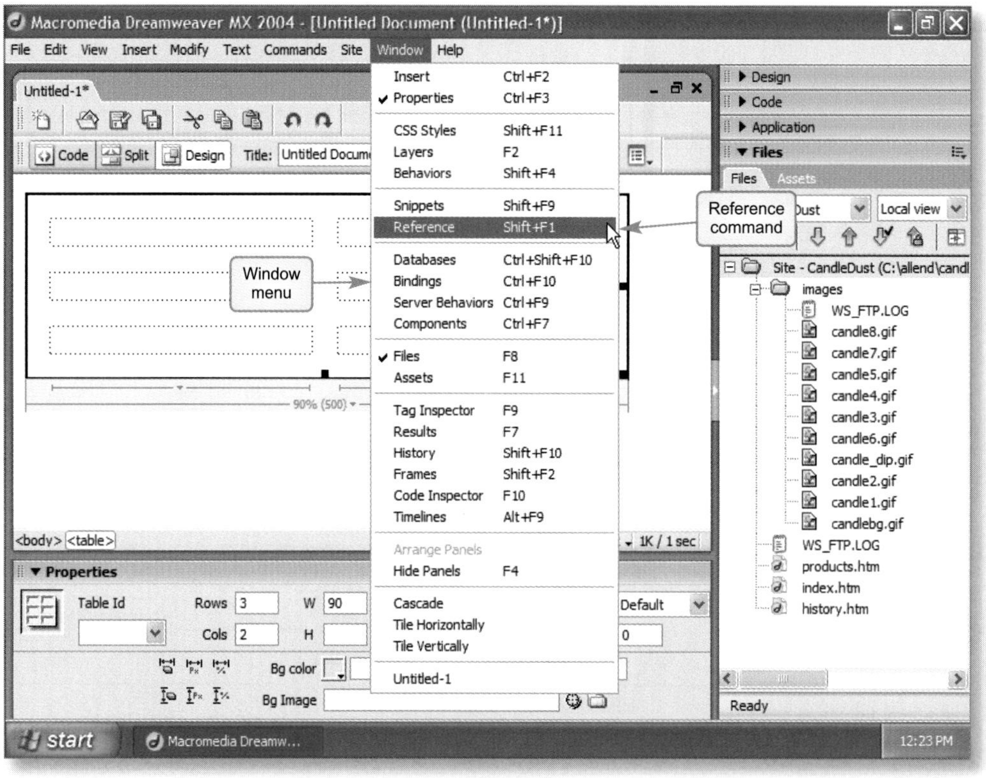

FIGURE A-16

2

• Click Reference, and then click O'REILLY HTML Reference in the Book pop-up menu.

The Reference panel in the Code panel group displays a welcome message (Figure A-17).

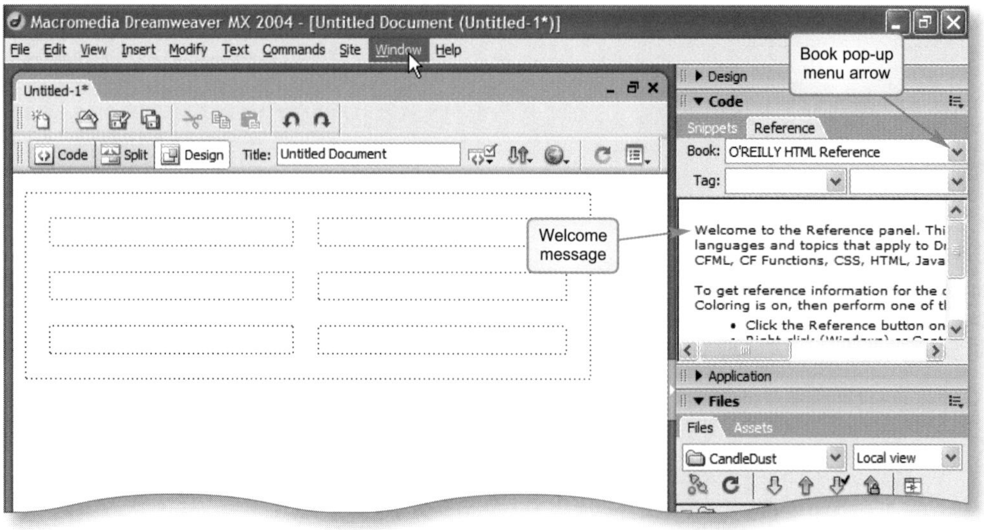

FIGURE A-17

3

- **Click the Tag box arrow and then point to BODY in the tag list.**

BODY is highlighted in the tag list (Figure A-18).

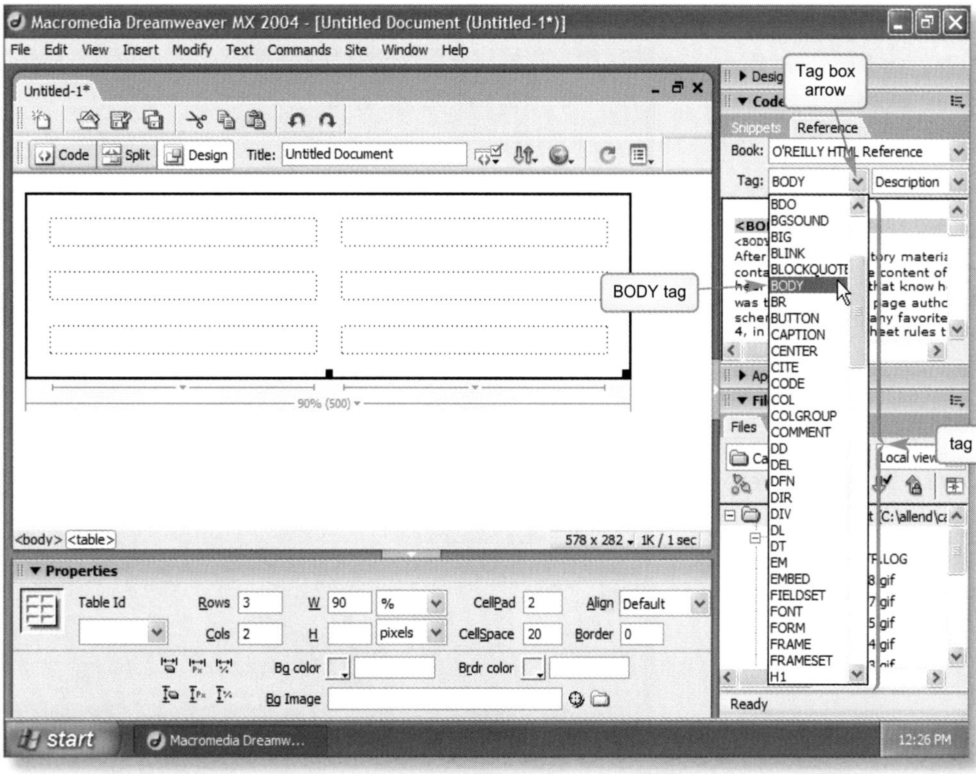

FIGURE A-18

4

- **Click BODY.**

Information on the <body> tag is displayed (Figure A-19).

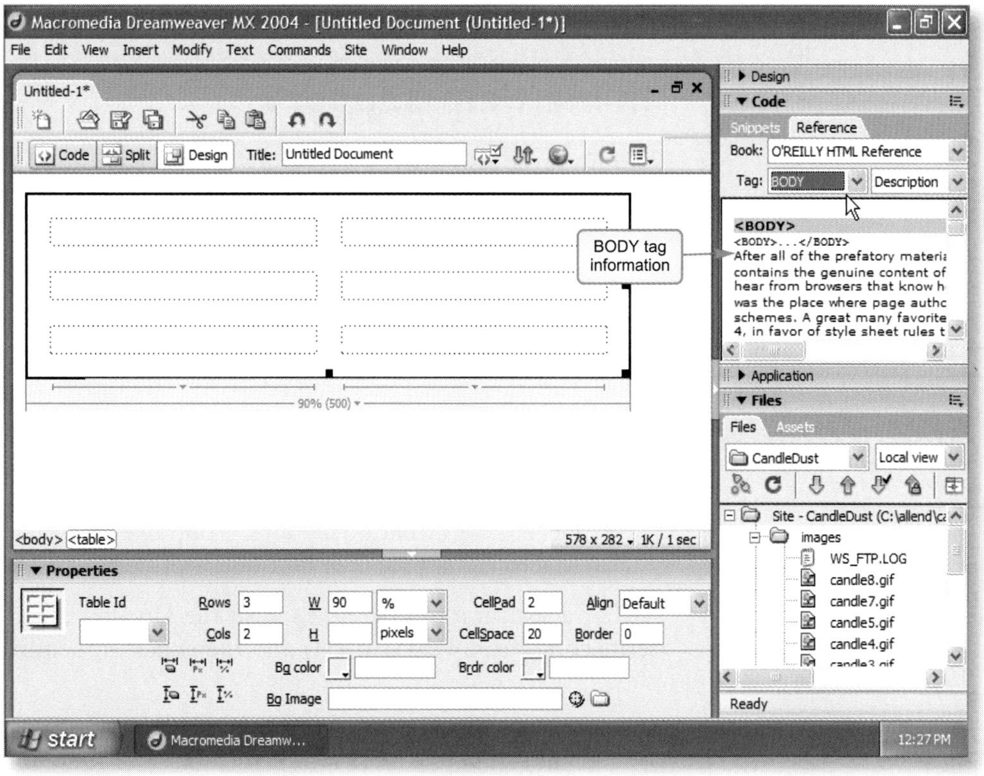

FIGURE A-19

5

• **Click the Book box arrow and review the list of available reference books.**

A list of 11 reference books displays (Figure A-20). These are complete books and can be accessed in the same way the HTML reference book was accessed.

6

• **Close Dreamweaver.**

• **If the Macromedia Dreamweaver dialog box to save changes is displayed, click the No button.**

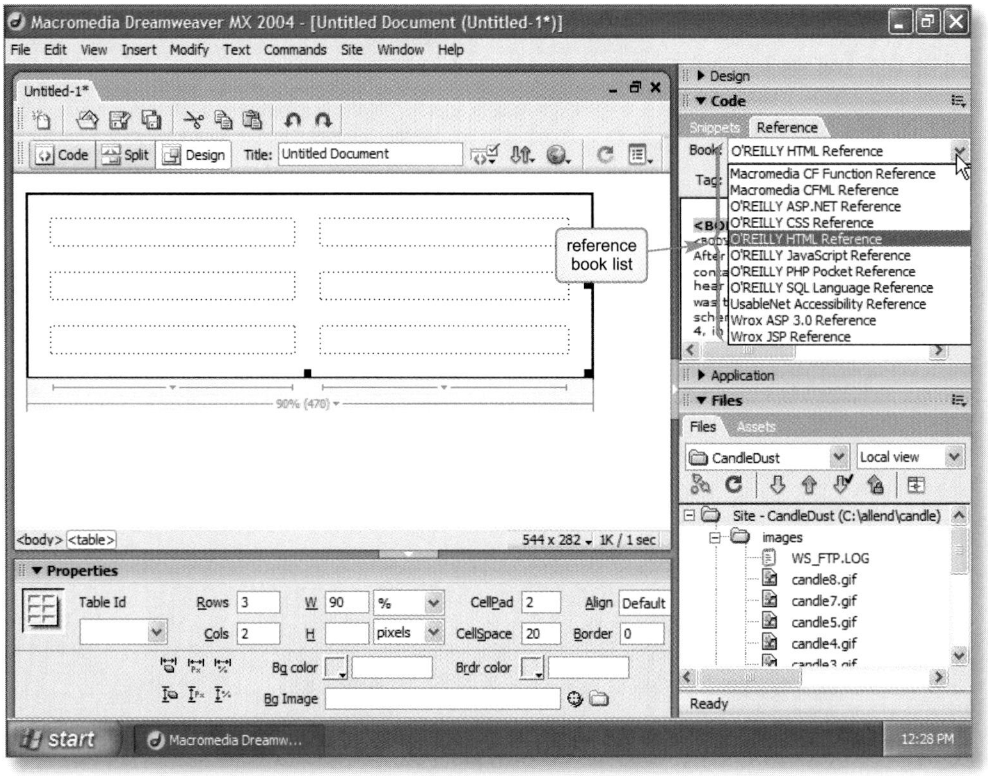

FIGURE A-20

Online Help Support

Dreamweaver also provides several support Web sites, including online forums and links to third-party online forums. Examples of these online forums and discussion groups are as follows:

- Dreamweaver — For Dreamweaver users developing Web sites.
- Dreamweaver Application Development — For Dreamweaver users creating dynamic Web sites.
- Dreamweaver Extensibility — For Dreamweaver users interested in extending the functionality of Dreamweaver.
- Dynamic HTML — This group discusses questions and issues regarding Dynamic HTML.
- General Information — This group discusses general information regarding Macromedia products that does not pertain to the other online forums.

For a selection of Help links, visit the Dreamweaver MX 2004 Web page (scsite.com/dreamweavermx04) and then click Appendix Help.

Apply Your Knowledge

1 Viewing the Dreamweaver What's New Features

Instructions: Start Dreamweaver. Perform the following tasks using the Dreamweaver What's New feature.

1. Click Help on the menu bar and then click Getting Started and Tutorials to open the Getting Started window.
2. Click Tutorial: Creating a Static Page and then click Open and Save a new page.
3. Read the information in the right pane.
4. Use a word processing program to write a short overview of what you learned.
5. Print a copy and submit or e-mail your overview to your instructor.

2 Using the Index Sheet

Instructions: Start Dreamweaver. Perform the following tasks using the Index sheet in the Using Dreamweaver Help system.

1. Press the F1 key to display the Using Dreamweaver window.
2. Click the Index tab and then type `links` in the Type in the keyword to find text box.
3. Click checking in the subtopic list and then click the Display button. Read the information in the right pane.
4. Use a word processing program to write a short overview of what you learned.
5. Print a copy and submit or e-mail your overview to your instructor.

3 Using Context-Sensitive Help

Instructions: Start Dreamweaver. Perform the following tasks using context-sensitive help in the Assets panel.

1. Click the Assets tab in the Files panel group.
2. Click the Options button and then click Help on the Options pop-up menu.
3. Read each of the topics about the Assets panel.
4. Use your word processing program to prepare a report on how to set up a favorite list of assets.
5. Print a copy and submit or e-mail your overview to your instructor.

Appendix B

Dreamweaver and Accessibility

Dreamweaver and Accessibility

Tim Berners-Lee, World Wide Web Consortium (W3C) founder, and inventor of the World Wide Web, indicates that the power of the Web is in its universality. He says that access by everyone regardless of disability is an essential aspect of the Web. In 1997, the W3C launched the **Web Accessibility Initiative** and made a commitment to lead the Web to its full potential. The initiative includes promoting a high degree of usability for people with disabilities. The United States government established a second initiative addressing accessibility and the Web through Section 508 of the Federal Rehabilitation Act.

Dreamweaver includes features that assist you in creating accessible content. To design accessible content requires that you understand accessibility requirements and make subjective decisions as you create a Web site. Dreamweaver supports three accessibility options: screen readers, keyboard navigation, and operating system accessibility features.

Using Screen Readers with Dreamweaver

Screen readers assist the blind and vision-impaired by reading text that is displayed on the screen through a speaker or headphones. The screen reader starts at the top-left corner of the page and reads the page content. If the Web site developer uses accessibility tags or attributes during the creation of the Web site, the screen reader also recites this information and reads non-textual information such as button labels and image descriptions. Dreamweaver makes it easy to add text equivalents for graphical elements and to add HTML tags to tables and forms through the accessibility dialog boxes. Dreamweaver supports two screen readers: JAWS and Window Eyes.

Activating the Accessibility Dialog Boxes

To create accessible pages in Dreamweaver, you associate information, such as labels and descriptions, with your page objects. After you have created this association, the screen reader can recite the label and description information.

You create the association by activating and attaching the accessibility dialog boxes to objects on your page. These dialog boxes appear when you insert an object for which you have activated the corresponding Accessibility dialog box. You activate the Accessibility dialog boxes through the Preferences dialog box. You can activate Accessibility dialog boxes for form objects, frames, images, and media. Accessibility for tables is accomplished by adding Summary text to the Table dialog box and adding image Ids and Alt text through the Property inspector. The steps on the next page use the Florida Parks index page as an example to show how to display the Preferences dialog box and activate the Image Accessibility dialog box.

To Activate the Images Accessibility Dialog Box

1

- **Start Dreamweaver and close all open panels. Click Edit on the menu bar and then point to Preferences (Figure B-1).**

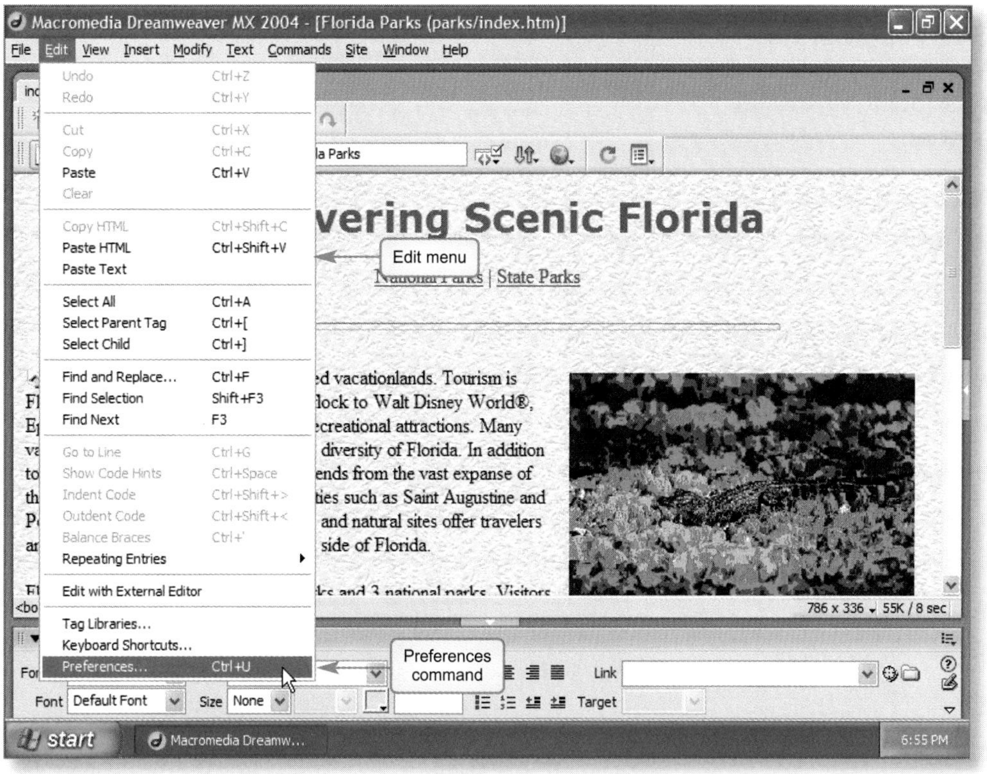

FIGURE B-1

2

- **Click Preferences.**

The Preferences dialog box is displayed (Figure B-2).

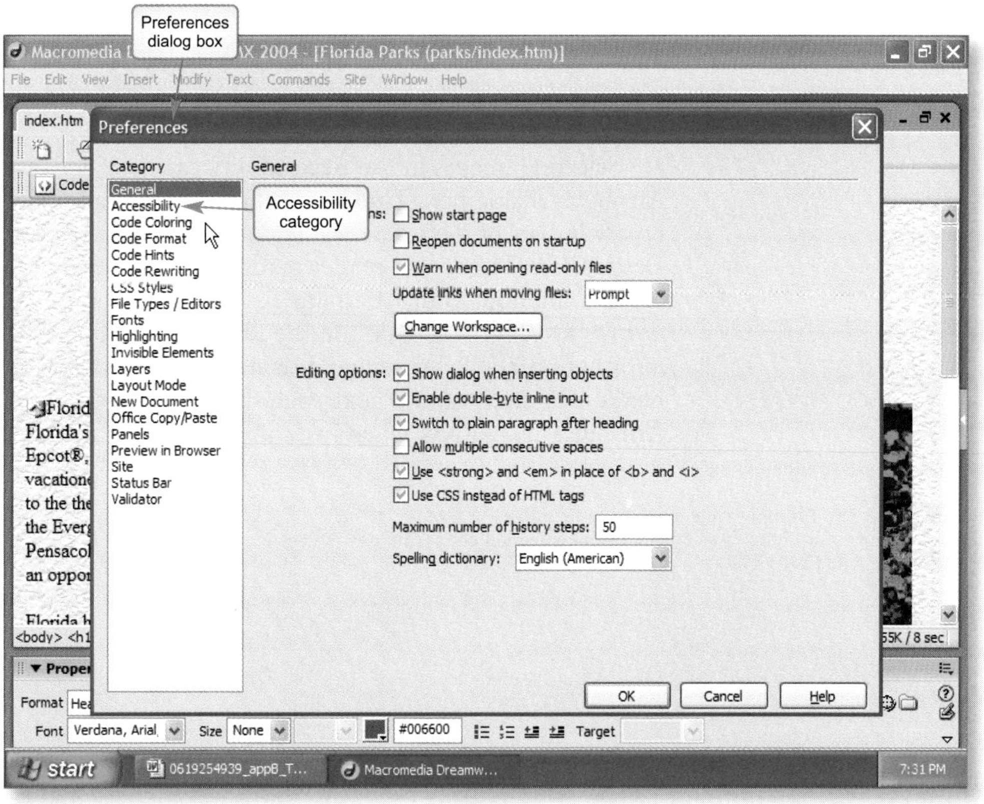

FIGURE B-2

3

• **Click Accessibility in the Category list, click Images in the Accessibility area, and then point to the OK button.**

The Accessibility category is highlighted, and the Images check box is selected (Figure B-3). The Accessibility area includes five different options for which you can activate Accessibility dialog boxes: Form objects, Frames, Media, and Images.

4

• **Click the OK button.**

The Preferences dialog box closes, and the Dreamweaver Document window is displayed. No change is apparent in the Document window, but the Image Tag Accessibility Attributes dialog box is activated.

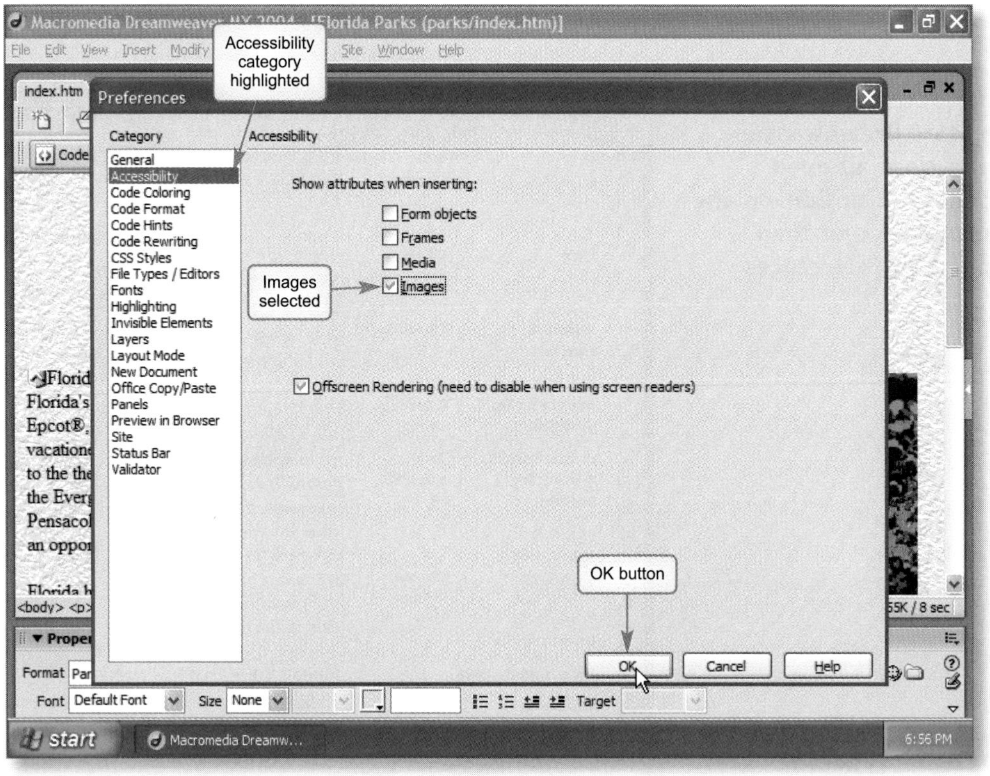

FIGURE B-3

Inserting Accessible Images

Selecting Images in the Accessibility category activates the Image Tag Accessibility Attributes dialog box. Thus, any time you insert an image into a Web page, this dialog box will display. This dialog box contains two text boxes: Alternate Text and Long Description. The screen reader reads the information you enter in both text boxes. You should limit your Alternate Text entry to about 50 characters. For longer descriptions, provide a link in the Long Description text box to a file that gives more information about the image. It is not required that you enter data into both text boxes. The steps on the next page show how to use the Image Tag Accessibility Attributes dialog box when inserting an image.

To Insert Accessible Images

1

• **Click Insert on the menu bar and then point to Image (Figure B-4).**

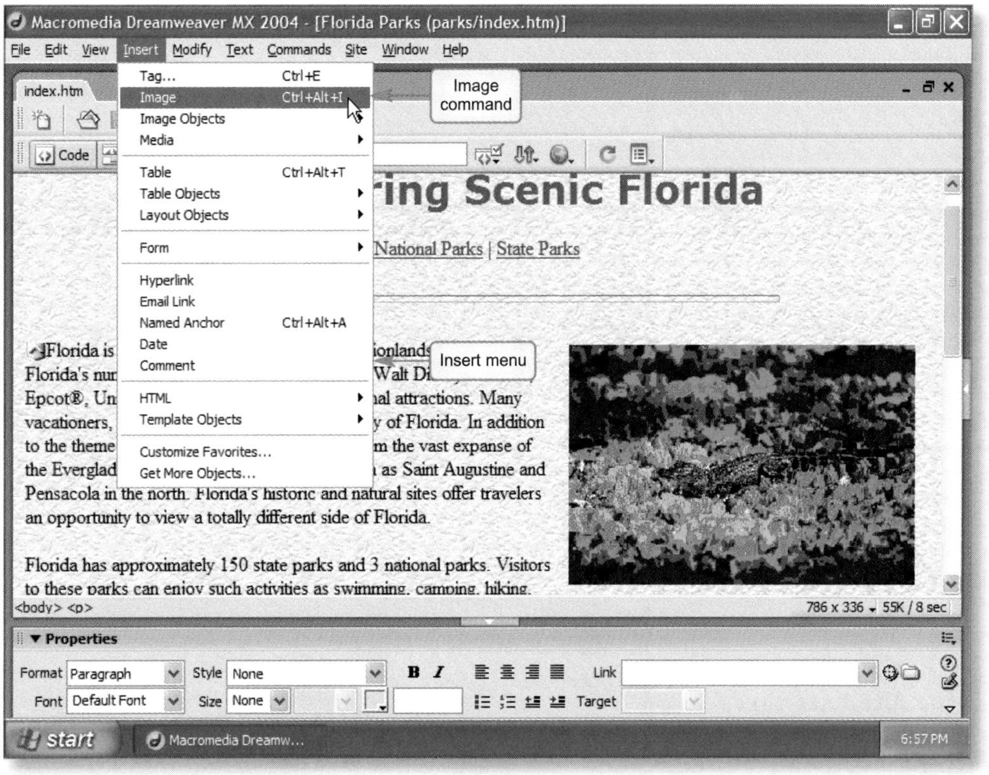

FIGURE B-4

2

• **Click Image. If necessary, open the images folder and then click a file name. Point to the OK button.**

The Select Image Source dialog box is displayed (Figure B-5).

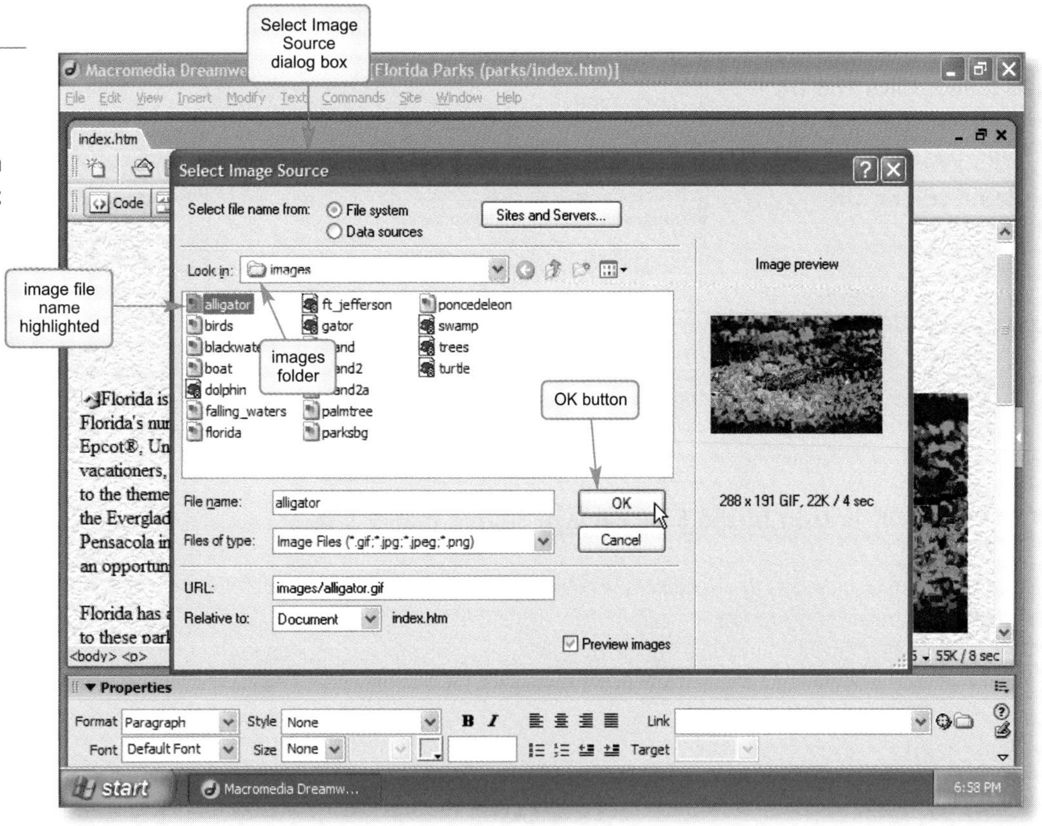

FIGURE B-5

3

- **Click the OK button.**

The Image Tag Accessibility Attributes dialog box is displayed. The insertion point is blinking in the Alternate text text box (Figure B-6). To display the Image Tag Accessibility Attributes dialog box, you must insert the image by using the Insert menu or by clicking the Image button on the Common tab of the Insert bar. Dragging an image from the Assets or Files panel to the Document window does not activate the Image Tag Accessibility Attributes dialog box.

FIGURE B-6

4

- **Type a brief description of the image in the Alternate text text box.**
- **Click the folder icon to display the Select File dialog box. Locate and then click the description file name. Click the OK button in the Select File dialog box.**
- **Point to the OK button.**

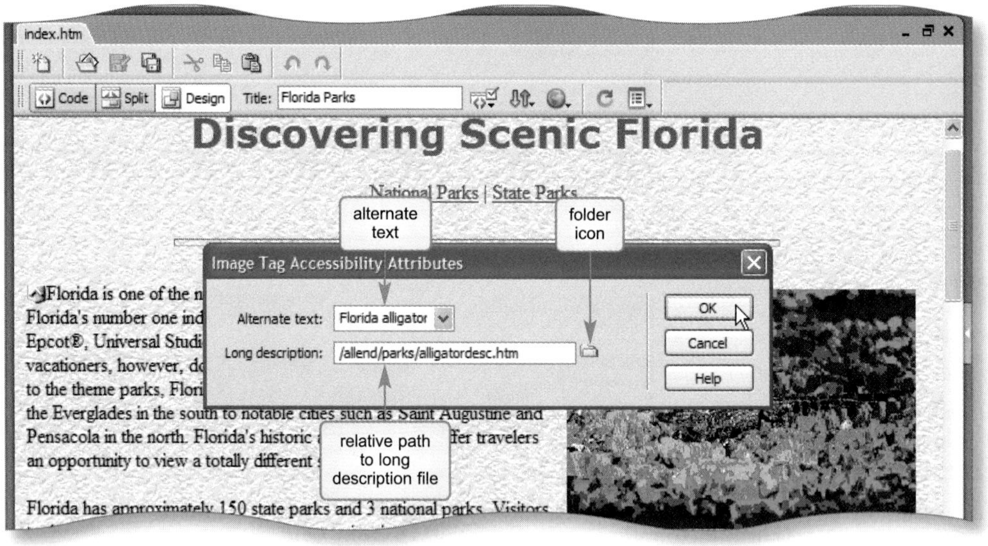

FIGURE B-7

The image description is displayed in the Alternate text text box, and the long description file location is displayed in the Long description text box (Figure B-7).

5

- **Click the OK button in the Select Image Source dialog box.**

No changes are displayed in the Document window. When the page is displayed in the browser, however, the screen reader recites the information you entered in the Image Tag Accessibility Attributes Alternate text text box. If you included a link to a file with additional information in the Long description text box, the screen reader accesses the file and recites the text contained within the file.

6

- **Close Dreamweaver. Do not save the changes to the Web page.**

Navigating Dreamweaver with the Keyboard

Keyboard navigation is a core aspect of accessibility. This feature also is of particular importance to users who have repetitive strain injuries (RSIs) or other disabilities, and to those users who would prefer to use the keyboard instead of a mouse. You can use the keyboard to navigate the following elements in Dreamweaver: floating panels, the Property inspector, dialog boxes, frames, and tables.

Using the Keyboard to Navigate Panels

When you are working in Dreamweaver, several panels may be open at one time. To move from panel to panel, press CTRL+ALT+TAB. A dotted outline around the panel title bar indicates the panel is selected (Figure B-9). Press CTRL+ALT+SHIFT+TAB to move to the previous panel. If necessary, expand the selected panel by pressing the SPACEBAR. Pressing the SPACEBAR again collapses the panel. Use the arrow keys to scroll the panel choices. Press the SPACEBAR to make a selection.

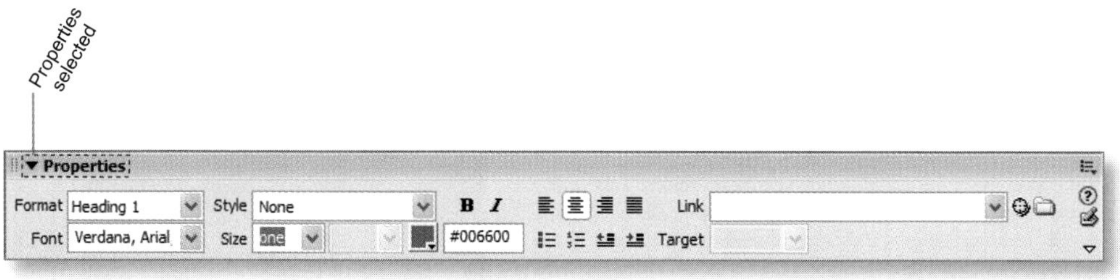

FIGURE B-8

Using the Keyboard to Navigate the Property Inspector

The following steps use the Florida Parks index page to show how to use the keyboard to navigate the Property inspector.

To Use the Keyboard to Navigate the Property Inspector

1

- **Start Dreamweaver and close all panels. Open a Web page. If necessary, press CTRL+F3 to display the Property inspector and then press CTRL+ALT+TAB until the Property inspector is selected.**

The dotted black outline around the word, Properties, indicates that the focus is on the Property inspector (Figure B-10).

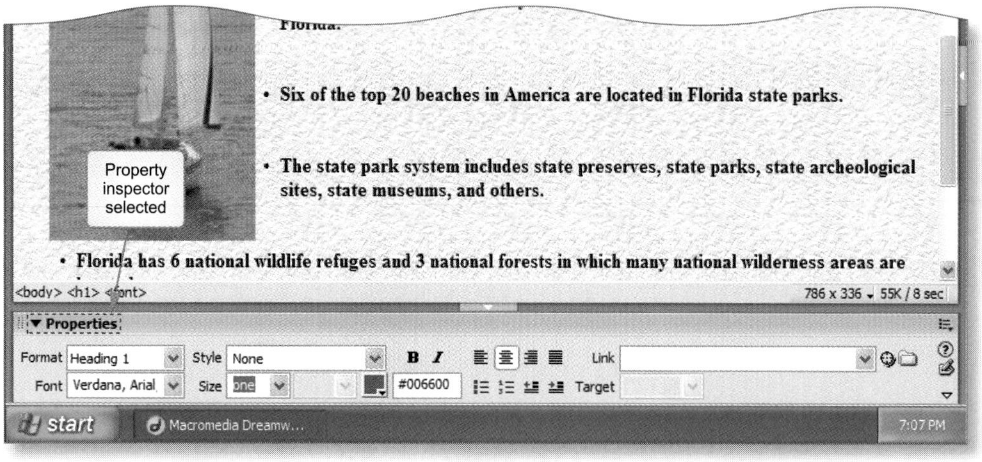

FIGURE B-9

2

• **Press the TAB key to move to the Format box.**

Heading 1 is highlighted in the Format box (Figure B-11).

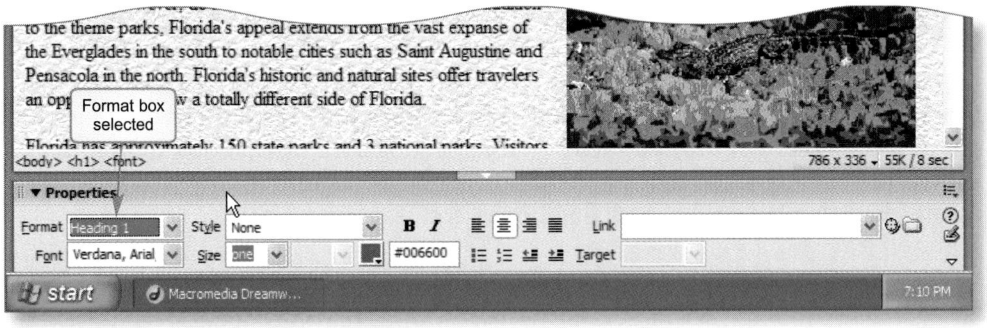

FIGURE B-10

3

• **Use the keyboard Down Arrow key to select Heading 3 and then press the ENTER key.**

A dotted outline is displayed around the Heading 3 selection (Figure B-12). Heading 3 is applied to the text.

4

• **Close Dreamweaver. Do not save any of the changes.**

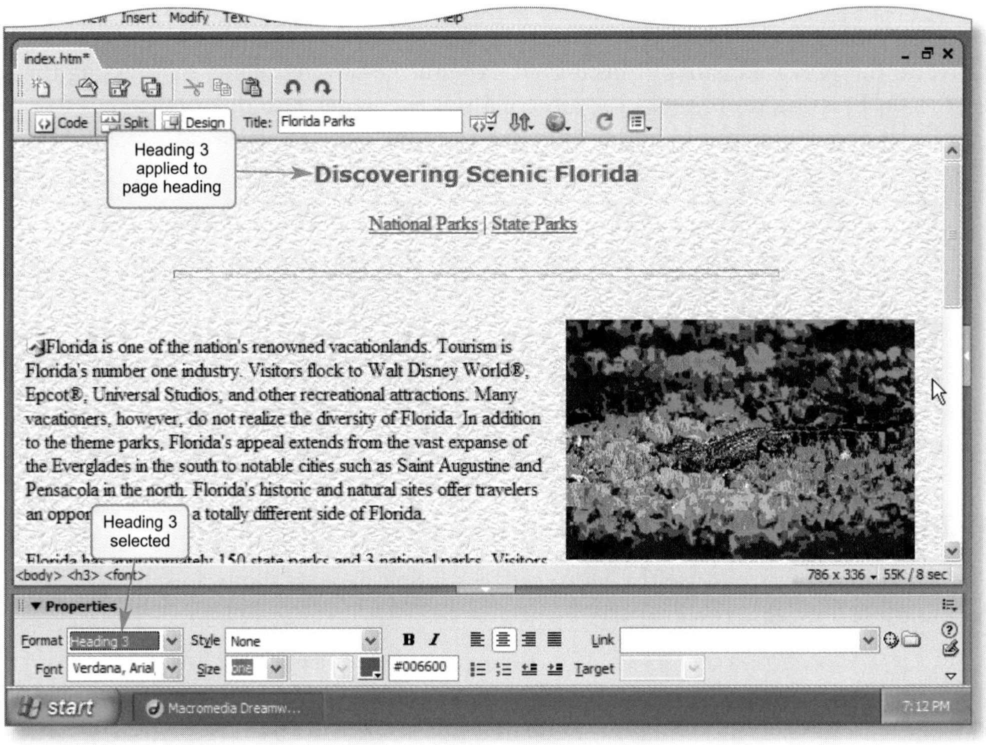

FIGURE B-11

Operating System Accessibility Features

The third method of accessibility support in Dreamweaver is through the Windows operating system high contrast setting. **High contrast** changes the desktop color themes for individuals who have vision impairment. The color schemes make the screen easier to view by heightening screen contrast with alternative color combinations. Some of the schemes also change font sizes.

You activate this option through the Windows Control Panel. The high contrast setting affects Dreamweaver in two ways:

- The dialog boxes and panels use system color settings.
- Code view syntax color is turned off.

Design view, however, continues to use the background and text colors you set in the Page Properties dialog box. The pages you design, therefore, continue to render colors as they will display in a browser. The steps on the next page show how to turn on high contrast and how to change the current high contrast settings.

To Turn On High Contrast

1

- **In Windows XP, click the Start button on the taskbar and then click Control Panel on the Start menu. If necessary, switch to Classic View and then double-click the Accessibility Options icon.**

The Accessibility Options dialog box is displayed (Figure B-13).

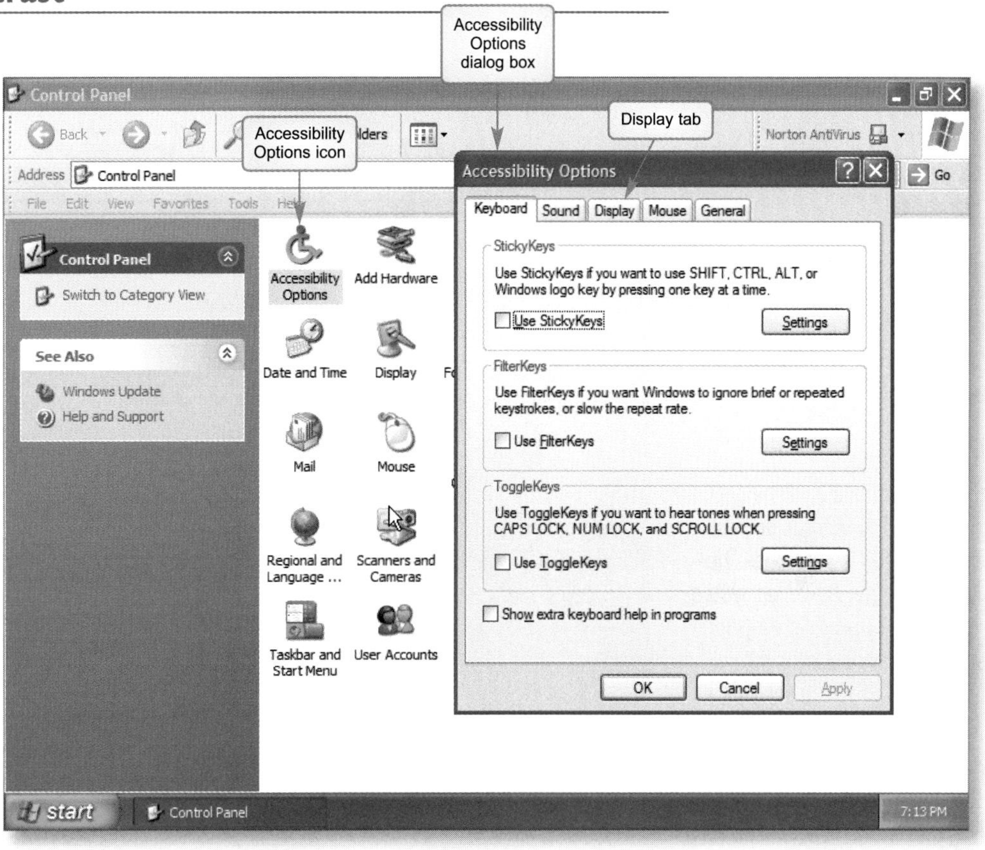

FIGURE B-12

2

- **Click the Display tab and then click Use High Contrast.**

The Display sheet is displayed. A checkmark appears in the Use High Contrast check box (Figure B-14).

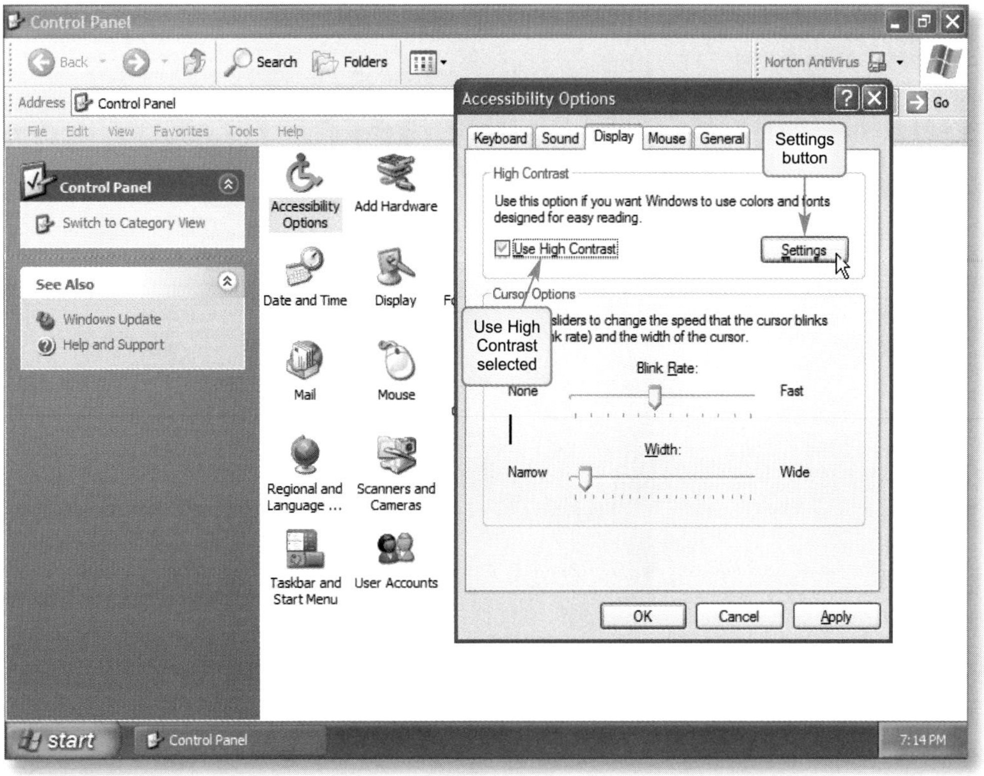

FIGURE B-13

3

• **Click the Settings button.**

The Settings for High Contrast dialog box is displayed (Figure B-15).

4

• **Click the Your current high contrast scheme is box arrow.**

A list of available high contrast options is displayed (Figure B-16). High Contrast Black (large) is selected. The Web designer, however, would select the appropriate option to meet the needs of the project for which he or she is designing.

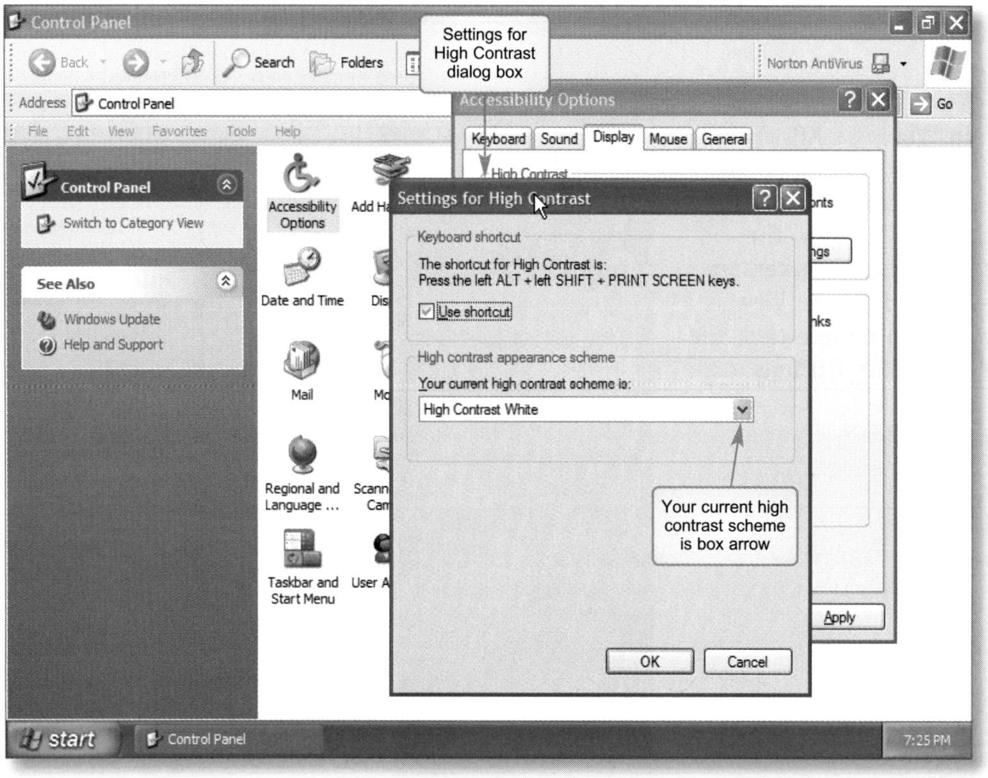

FIGURE B-14

5

• **Click the Cancel button.**

The settings return to their original values. To retain these settings on your computer would require that you click the OK button.

6

• **Click the Control Panel Close button.**

The Control Panel closes, and the Windows XP desktop displays.

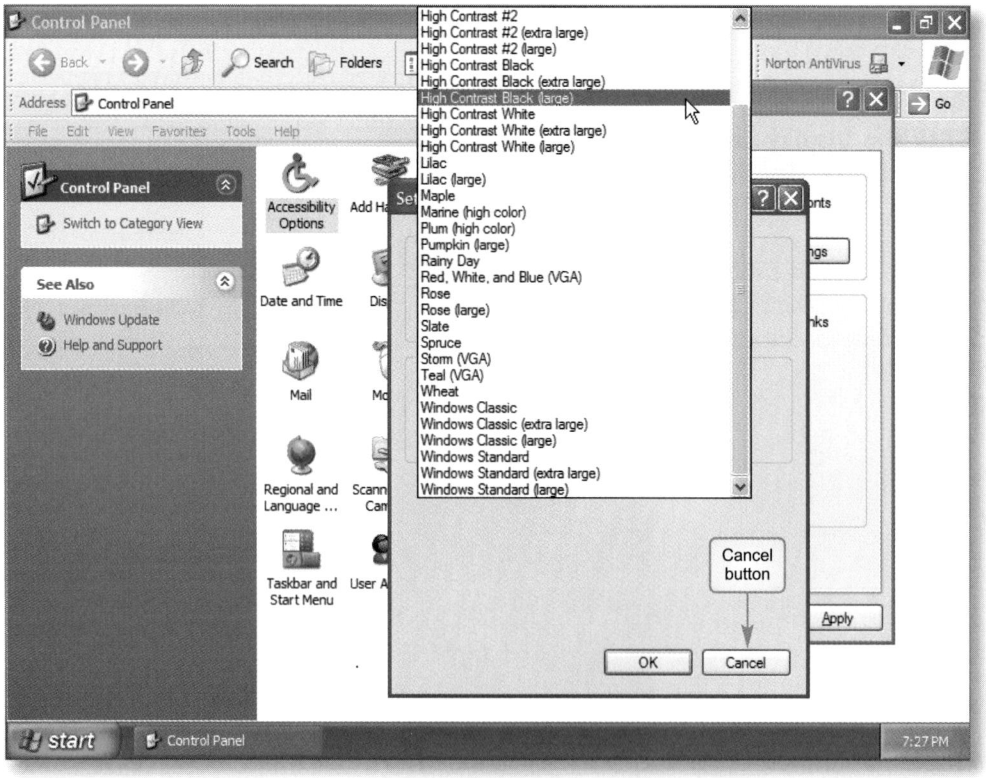

FIGURE B-15

Appendix C

Publishing to a Web Server

Publishing to a Remote Site

With Dreamweaver, Web designers usually define a local site and then do the majority of their site designing using the local site. In Project 1 you defined a local site. In creating the projects in this book, you have added Web pages to the local site, which resides on your computer's hard disk, a network drive, or possibly a Zip disk. To prepare a Web site and make it available for others to view requires that you publish your site by putting it on a Web server for public access. A Web server is an Internet- or intranet-connected computer that delivers the Web pages to visitors online. Dreamweaver includes built-in support that enables you to connect and transfer your local site to a Web server. To publish to a Web server requires that you have access to a Web server. Your instructor will provide you with the location, user name, and password information for the Web server on which you will publish your Web site.

After you establish access to a Web server, you will need a remote site folder. The remote folder is the folder that will reside on the Web server and will contain your Web site files. Generally, the remote folder is defined by the Web server administrator or your instructor. The name of your local root folder in this example is your last name and first initial. Most likely, the name of your remote folder also will be your last name and first initial. You upload your local site to the remote folder on the Web server. The remote site connection information must be defined in Dreamweaver through the Site Definition Wizard. You display the Site Definition Wizard and then enter the remote site information. Dreamweaver provides five different protocols for connecting to a remote site. These methods are as follows:

- **FTP** (File Transfer Protocol) This protocol is used on the Internet for sending and receiving files. It is the most widely used method for uploading and downloading pages to and from a Web server.
- **Local/Network** This option is used when the Web server is located on a local area network (LAN) or a company or school intranet. Files on LANs generally are available for internal viewing only.
- **SourceSafe Database, RDS (Remote Development Services), and WebDAV** These three protocols are systems that permit users to edit and manage files collaboratively on remote Web servers.

Most likely, you will use the FTP option to upload your Web site to a remote server.

Defining a Remote Site

You define the remote site by changing some of the settings in the Site Definition dialog box. To allow you to create a remote site using FTP, your instructor will supply you with the following information:

- **FTP host** is the Web address for the remote host of your Web server.
- **Host directory** is the directory name and path on the server where your remote site will be located.
- **Login** is your user name.
- **Password** is the FTP password to authenticate and access your account.

Assume for the following example that you are defining a remote site for the Florida Parks Web site.

To Define a Remote Site

1

- **Click Site on the menu bar and then click Manage Sites.**
- **Click Florida Parks in the Manage Sites dialog box.**

The Manage Sites dialog box displays, and Florida Parks is selected (Figure C-1).

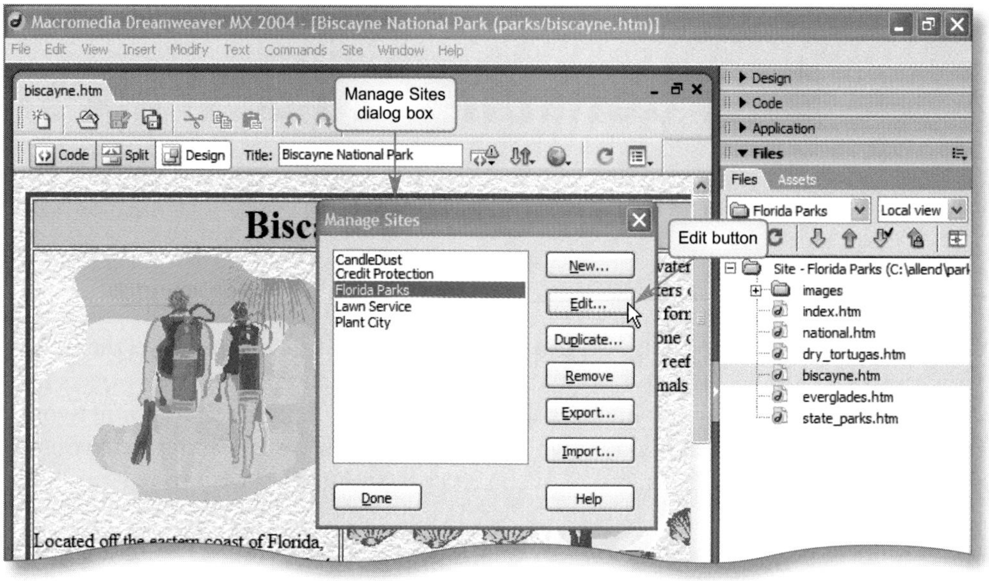

FIGURE C-1

2

- **Click the Edit button. Click the Advanced tab.**

The Site Definition dialog box displays, and Local Info is selected in the Category column (Figure C-2).

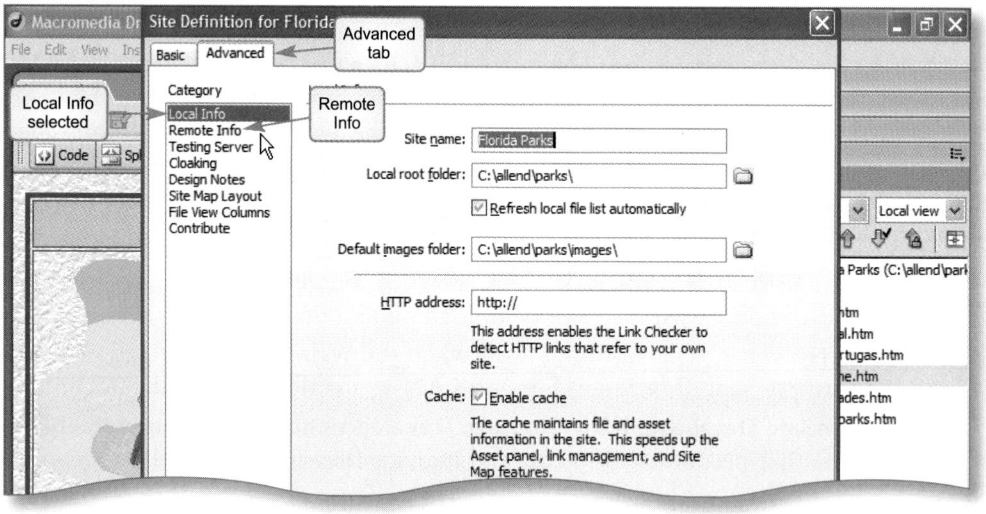

FIGURE C-2

3

- **Click the Remote Info category.**
- **Click the Access box arrow in the Remote Info pane and point to FTP.**

Remote Info is selected, and FTP is highlighted (Figure C-3).

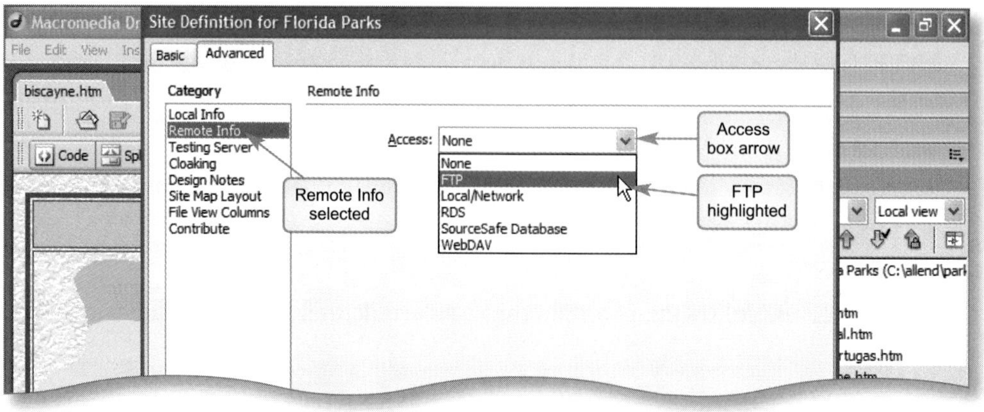

FIGURE C-3

4

- **Click FTP.**
- **Click each of the following boxes and fill in the information as provided by your instructor: FTP host, Host directory, Login, and Password.**

Information for David Allen displays in Figure C-4. Your screen will contain the information provided by your instructor.

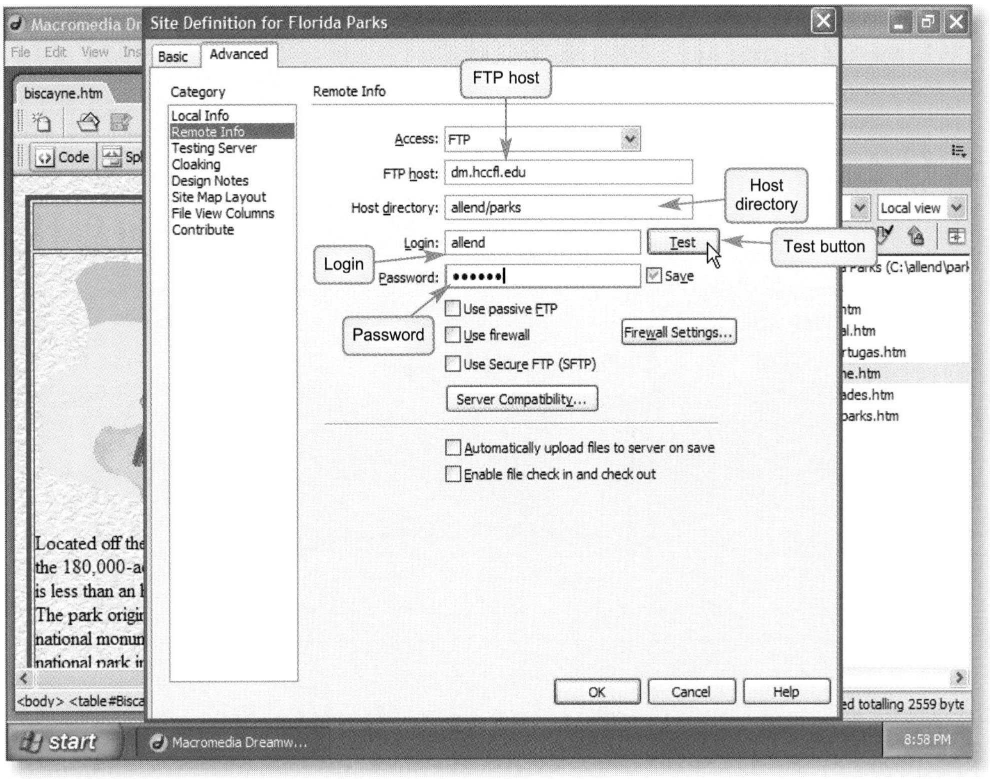

FIGURE C-4

5

- **Click the Test button to test the connection.**
- **If your connection is not successful, review your text box entries and make any necessary corrections. If all entries are correct, check with your instructor.**

Dreamweaver tests the connection and responds with a Macromedia Dreamweaver MX 2004 dialog box (Figure C-5).

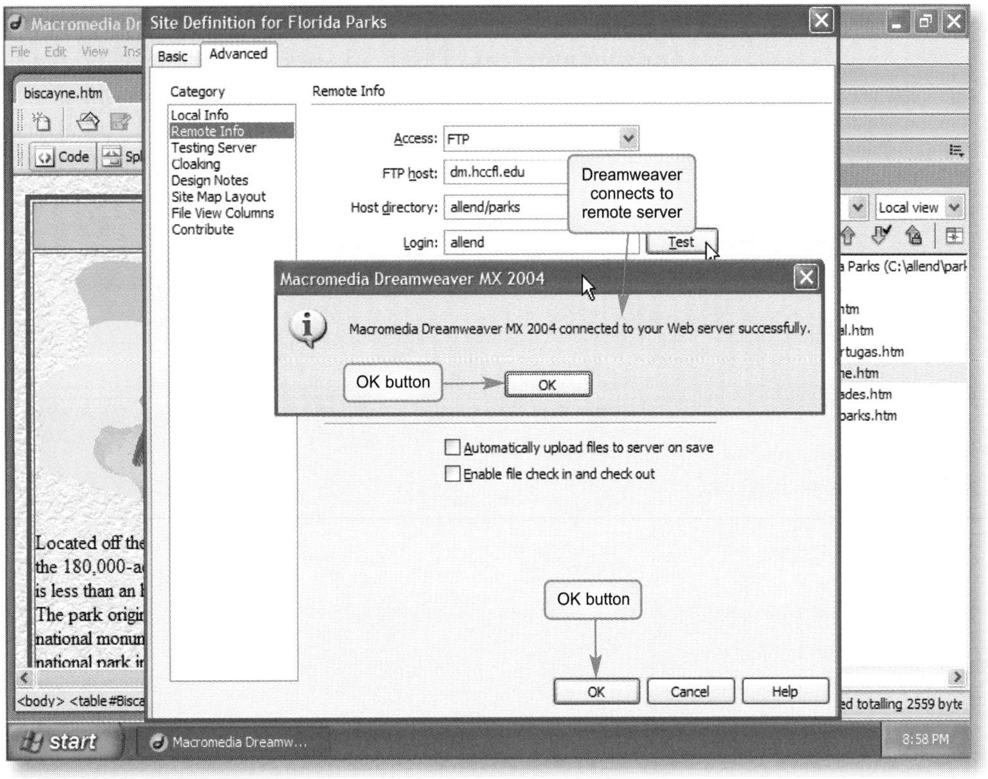

FIGURE C-5

6

• Click the OK button in the Macromedia Dreamweaver MX 2004 dialog box and then click the OK button in the Site Definition dialog box to return to the Dreamweaver workspace. Close the Manage Sites dialog box.

The Biscayne National Park page displays (Figure C-6).

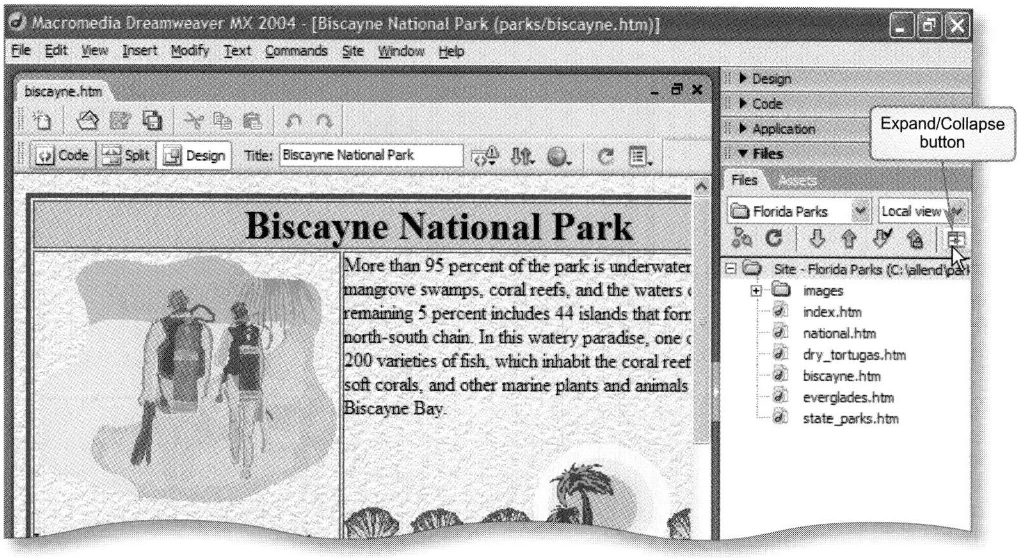

FIGURE C-6

Connecting to a Remote Site

Now that you have completed the remote site information and tested your connection, you can interact with the remote server. The remote site folder on the Web server for your Web site must be established before a connection can be made. This folder, called the **remote site root**, generally is created by the Web server administrator or your instructor. This book uses the last name and the first initial (allend) for the name of the remote site folder. Naming conventions other than your last name and first initial may be used on the Web server to which you are connecting. Your instructor will supply you with this information. If all information is correct, connecting to the remote site is done easily through the Files panel. The following steps illustrate how to connect to the remote site and display your remote site folder.

To Connect to a Remote Site

1

• Click the Files panel Expand/Collapse button.

The Site panel expands to show both a right and left pane (Figure C-7). The right pane contains the local site. The left pane contains information for accessing your remote files by clicking the Connects to remote host button.

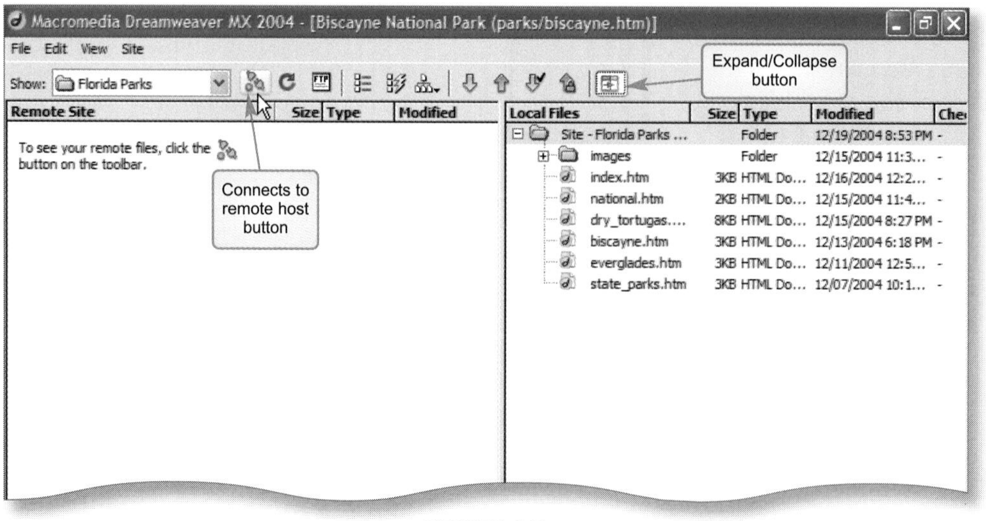

FIGURE C-7

2

• **Verify that the root folder is selected. Click the Connects to remote host button.**

The connection is made, and the parks root folder displays (Figure C-8). The Connects to remote host/Disconnects from remote host button is a toggle button and changes to indicate that the connection has been made. The root folder on the remote site must be created by your instructor or Web server administrator before a connection can be made.

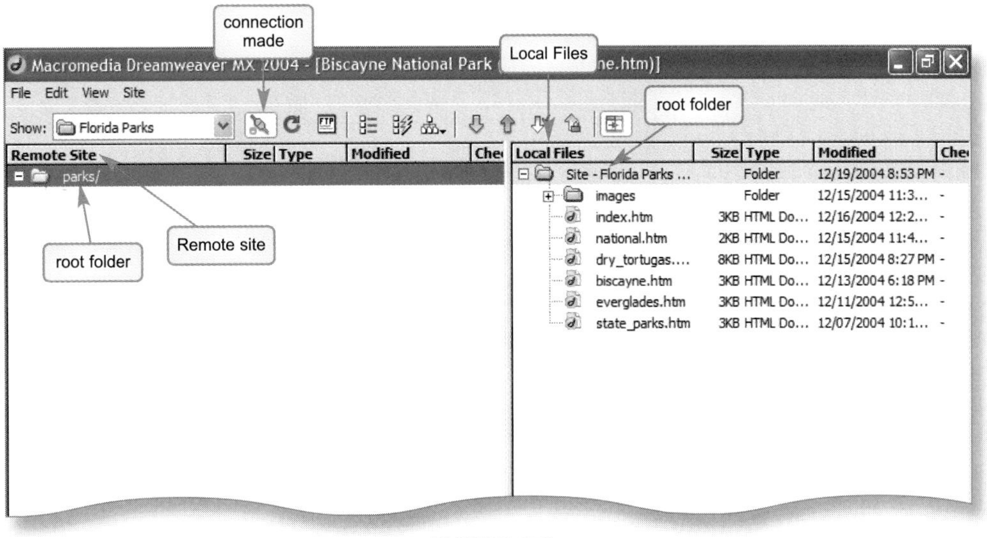

FIGURE C-8

Uploading Files to a Remote Server

Your next step will be to upload your files to the remote server. **Uploading** is the process of transferring your files from your computer to the remote server. **Downloading** is the process of transferring files from the remote server to your computer. Dreamweaver uses the term **put** for uploading and **get** for downloading.

To Upload Files to a Remote Server

1

• **Click the Put File(s) button. Point to the OK button.**

The Macromedia Dreamweaver MX 2004 dialog box is displayed to verify that you want to upload the entire site (Figure C-9).

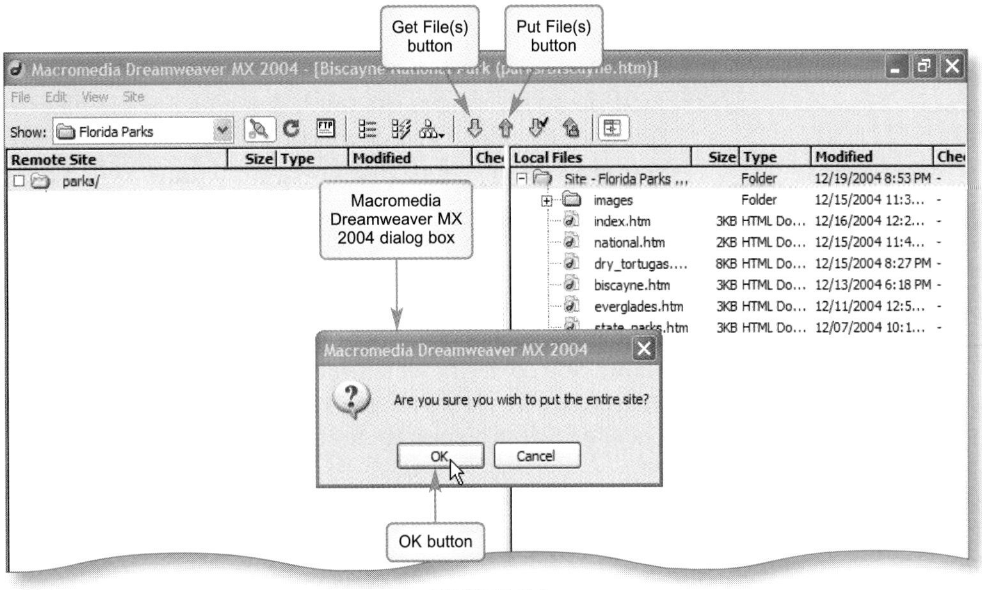

FIGURE C-9

2

- **Click the OK button.**

As the files begin to upload, a Status dialog box displays the progress information. The files are uploaded to the server (Figure C-10). The files may display in a different order from that on the local site. The display order on the server is determined by the settings on that computer.

3

- **Close Dreamweaver.**

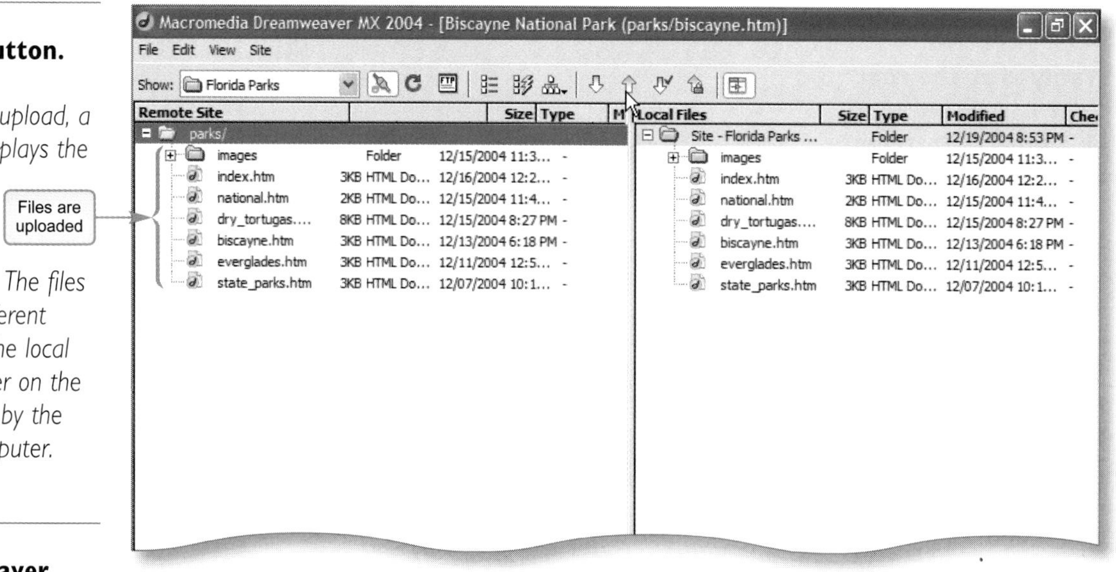

FIGURE C-10

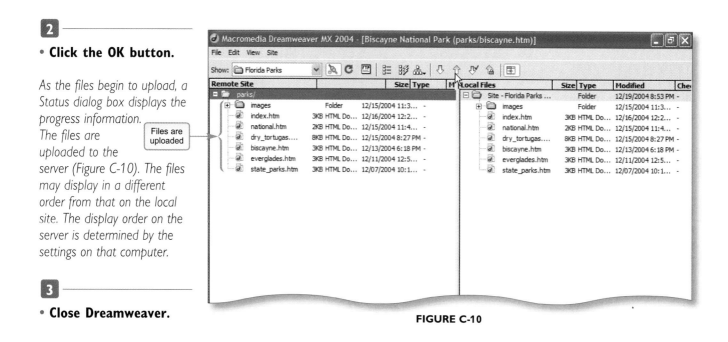

Remote Site Maintenance and Site Synchronization

Now that your Web site is on a Web server, you will want to continue to maintain the site. When you are connected to the remote site, you can apply many of the same commands to a folder or file on the remote site as you do to a folder or file on the local site. You can create and delete folders; cut, copy, delete, duplicate, paste, and rename files; and so on. These commands are available through the context menu.

To mirror the local site on the remote site, Dreamweaver provides a synchronization feature. **Synchronizing** is the process of transferring files between the local and remote sites so both sites have an identical set of the most recent files. You can select to synchronize the entire Web site or select only specific files. You also can specify Direction. Within **Direction**, you have three options: upload the newer files from the local site to the remote site (put); download newer files from the remote site to the local site (get); or upload and download files to and from the remote and local sites. Once you specify a direction, Dreamweaver automatically synchronizes files. If the files are already in sync, Dreamweaver lets you know you that no synchronization is necessary. To access the Synchronize command, you first connect to the remote server and then select Synchronize on the Site menu (Figure C-11).

To save the verification information to a local file, click the Save Log button at the completion of the synchronization process. Another feature within Dreamweaver allows you to verify which files are newer on the local site or the remote site. These options are available through the Files panel Edit menu by selecting Select Newer Local or Select Newer Remote.

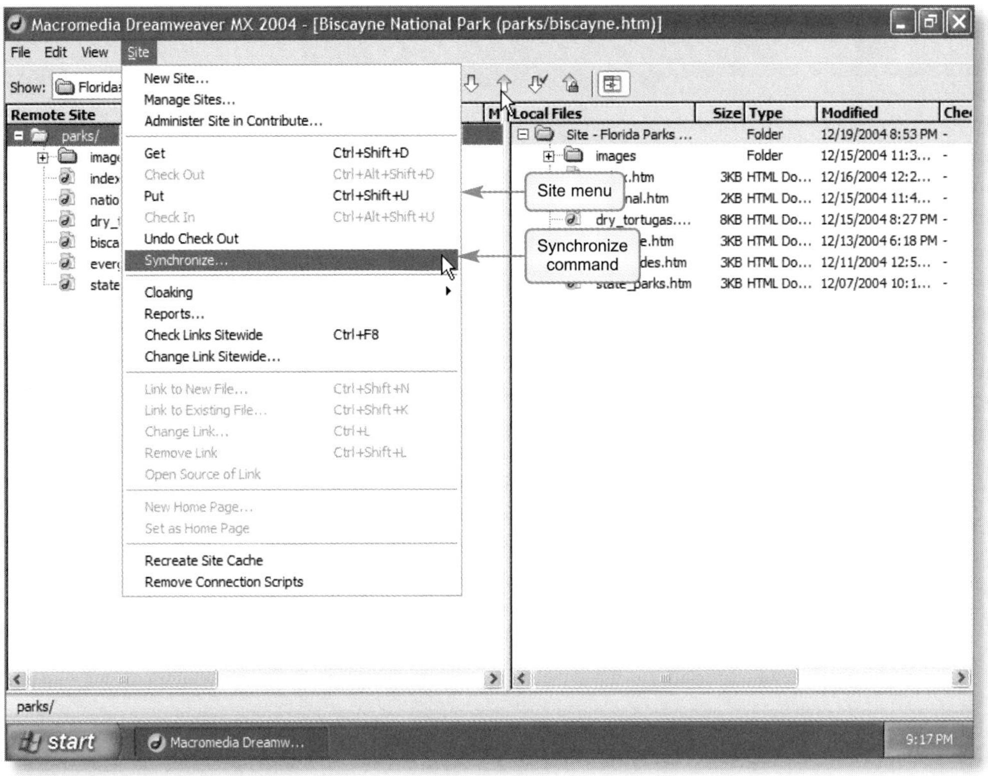

FIGURE C-11

Apply Your Knowledge

1 Defining and Uploading the B & B Lawn Service Web to a Remote Server

Instructions: Perform the following steps to define and upload the B & B Lawn Service Web site to a remote server.

1. Click Site on the menu bar, click Manage Sites, and then click Lawn Service. Click the Edit button. When the Site Definition dialog box displays, click the Advanced tab and then click Remote Info. Fill in the information as provided by your instructor, and then test the connection. Click the OK button.
2. Click the Expand/Collapse button on the Files panel toolbar and then click the Connects to remote host button. Click the local file root folder and then click the Put File(s) button on the Site panel toolbar to upload your Web site. Click the OK button in response to the Are you sure you wish to put the entire site? dialog box. Review your files to verify that they were uploaded. The files on the remote server may be displayed in a different order from that on the local site.
3. Click the Disconnects from remote host button on the Files panel toolbar. Click the Expand/Collapse button on the Files panel toolbar to display the local site and the Document window.
4. Close Dreamweaver.

Apply Your Knowledge

2 Defining and Uploading the CandleDust Web Site to a Remote Server

Instructions: Perform the following steps to define and upload the CandleDust Web site to a remote server.

1. Click Site on the menu bar, click Manage Sites, and then click CandleDust. Click the Edit button to display the Site Definition dialog box. Click the Advanced tab and then click Remote Info. Fill in the information as provided by your instructor, and then test the connection. Click the OK button.
2. Click the Expand/Collapse button on the Files panel toolbar and then click the Connects to remote host button. Click the local file root folder and then click the Put File(s) button on the Files panel toolbar to upload your Web site. Click the OK button in response to the Are you sure you wish to put the entire site? dialog box. Review your files to verify that they were uploaded. The files on the remote server may display in a different order from that on the local site.
3. Click the Disconnects from remote host button. Click the Expand/Collapse button on the Files panel toolbar to display the local site and the Document window. Close Dreamweaver.

3 Defining and Uploading the Credit Protection Web Site to a Remote Server

Instructions: Perform the following steps to define and upload the Credit Protection Web site to a remote server.

1. Click Site on the menu bar, click Manage Sites, and then click Credit Protection. Click the Edit button. Click the Advanced tab and then click Remote Info. Fill in the information as provided by your instructor, and then test the connection. Click the OK button.
2. Click the Expand/Collapse button on the Files panel toolbar and then click the Connects to remote host button. Click the local file root folder and then click the Put File(s) button on the Files panel toolbar to upload your Web site. Click the OK button in response to the Are you sure you wish to put the entire site? dialog box. Upload your files to the remote site. Review your files to verify that they were uploaded. The files on the remote server may display in a different order from that on the local site.
3. Disconnect from the site. Click the Expand/Collapse button on the Files panel toolbar to display the local site and the Document window. Close Dreamweaver.

4 Defining and Uploading the Plant City Web Site to a Remote Server

Instructions: Perform the following steps to define and upload the Plant City Web site to a remote server.

1. Click Site on the menu bar, click Manage Sites, and then click Plant City. Click the Edit button. Click the Advanced tab and then click Remote Info. Fill in the information as provided by your instructor, and then test the connection. Click the OK button.
2. Connect to the remote site and then click the local file root folder. Upload your files to the remote site. Disconnect from the site. Click the Expand/Collapse button on the Files panel toolbar to display the local site and the Document window. Close Dreamweaver.

macromedia DREAMWEAVER MX 2004

Quick Reference for Windows

FILE MENU

Action	Shortcut
New Document	Control+N
Open an HTML file	Control+O, or drag the file from the Explorer or Files panel to the Document window
Open in frame	Control+Shift+O
Close	Control+W
Close all	Control+Shift+W
Save	Control+S
Save as	Control+Shift+S
Exit/Quit	Control+Q or Alt+F4

EDIT MENU

Action	Shortcut
Undo	Control+Z or Alt+Backspace
Redo	Control+Y or Control+Shift+Z
Cut	Control+X or Shift+Delete
Copy	Control+C or Control+Insert
Paste	Control+V or Shift+Insert
Clear	Delete
Select all	Control+A
Select parent tag	Control+[
Select child	Control+]
Find and replace	Control+F
Find next	F3
Show code hints	Control+Spacebar
Go to line	Control+G
Indent code	Control+Shift+>
Outdent code	Control+Shift+<
Balance braces	Control+'
Copy HTML (in Design view)	Control+Shift+C
Paste HTML (in Design view)	Control+Shift+V
Preferences	Control+U

PAGE VIEWS

Action	Shortcut
Layout mode	Control+F6
Expanded Tables mode	F6
Live Data mode	Control+R
Live Data	Control+Shift+R
Switch to next document	Control+Tab
Switch to previous document	Control+Shift+Tab
Switch between Design and Code views	Control+`
Server debug	Control+Shift+G
Refresh Design view	F5

VIEWING PAGE ELEMENTS

Action	Shortcut
Visual aids	Control+Shift+I
Show rulers	Control+Alt+R
Show grid	Control+Alt+G
Snap to grid	Control+Alt+Shift+G
Page properties	Control+J

CODE EDITING

Action	Shortcut
Switch to Design view	Control+`
Print code	Control+P
Validate markup	Shift+F6
Edit tag	Control+F5
Open Quick Tag Editor	Control+T
Open Snippets panel	Shift+F9
Show code hints	Control+Spacebar
Insert tag	Control+E
Balance braces	Control+'
Select all	Control+A
Bold	Control+B
Italic	Control+I
Copy	Control+C
Find and replace	Control+F
Find next	F3
Paste	Control+V
Cut	Control+X
Redo	Control+Y
Undo	Control+Z
Toggle breakpoint	Control+Alt+B
Delete word left	Control+Backspace
Delete word right	Control+Delete
Go to line	Control+G
Select line up	Shift+Up
Select line down	Shift+Down
Character select left	Shift+Left
Character select right	Shift+Right
Move to page up	Page Up
Move to page down	Page Down
Select to page up	Shift+Page Up
Select to page down	Shift+Page Down
Move word left	Control+Left
Move word right	Control+Shift+Right
Move to start of line	Home
Move to end of line	End
Select to start of line	Shift+Home
Select to end of line	Shift+End
Move to top of code	Control+Home
Move to end of code	Control+End
Select to top of code	Control+Shift+Home
Select to end of code	Control+Shift+End

EDITING TEXT

Action	Shortcut
Create a new paragraph	Enter
Insert a line break 	Shift+Enter
Insert a nonbreaking space	Control+Shift+Spacebar
Move text or object to another place in the page	Drag selected item to new location
Copy text or object to another place in the page	Control-drag selected item to new location
Select a word	Double-click
Go to next word	Control+Right
Go to previous word	Control+Left
Go to previous paragraph	Control+Up
Open and close the Property inspector	Control+F3
Close window	Control+F4
Check spelling	Shift+F7

FORMATTING TEXT

Action	Shortcut
Indent	Control+Alt+]
Outdent	Control+Alt+[
Format > None	Control+0 (zero)
Paragraph Format	Control+Shift+P
Apply Headings 1 through 6 to a paragraph	Control+1 through 6
Align > Left	Control+Alt+Shift+L
Align > Center	Control+Alt+Shift+C
Align > Right	Control+Alt+Shift+R
Align > Justify	Control+Alt+Shift+J
Make selected text bold	Control+B
Make selected text italic	Control+I
Edit style sheet	Control+Shift+E

FINDING AND REPLACING TEXT

Action	Shortcut
Find	Control+F
Find next/Find again	F3
Replace	Control+H

WORKING IN TABLES

Action	Shortcut
Select table (with insertion point inside the table)	Control+A
Move to the next cell	Tab
Move to the previous cell	Shift+Tab
Insert a row (before current)	Control+M
Add a row at end of table	Tab in the last cell
Delete the current row	Control+Shift+M
Insert a column	Control+Shift+A
Delete a column	Control+Shift+- (hyphen)
Merge selected table cells	Control+Alt+M
Split table cell	Control+Alt+S
Increase column span	Control+Shift+]
Decrease column span	Control+Shift+[

WORKING WITH TEMPLATES

Action	Shortcut
Create new editable region	Control+Alt+V

WORKING IN FRAMES

Action	Shortcut
Select a frame	Alt+click in frame
Select next frame or frameset	Alt+Right Arrow
Select previous frame or frameset	Alt+Left Arrow
Select parent frameset	Alt+Up Arrow
Select first child frame or frameset	Alt+Down Arrow
Add a new frame to frameset	Alt+drag frame border
Add a new frame to to frameset using push method	Alt+Control-drag frame border

WORKING WITH LAYERS

Action	Shortcut
Select a layer	Control+Shift-click
Select and move layer	Shift+Control-drag
Add or remove layer from select	Shift-click layer border
Move select layer by pixels	Arrow keys
Move selected layer by snapping increment	Shift+Arrow keys
Resize selected layer by pixels	Control+Arrow keys
Resize selected layer by snapping increment	Control+Shift+Arrow keys
Toggle the display of the grid	Control+Alt+G
Align layers left	Control+Shift+1
Align layers right	Control+Shift+3
Align layers top	Control+Shift+4
Align layers bottom	Control+Shift+6
Make same width	Control+Shift+7
Make same height	Control+Shift+9

WORKING WITH IMAGES

Action	Shortcut
Change image source attribute	Double-click image
Edit image in external editor	Control-double-click image

GETTING HELP

Action	Shortcut
Using Dreamweaver Help topics	F1
Using ColdFusion Help topics	Control+F1
Reference	Shift+F1

MANAGING HYPERLINKS

Action	Shortcut
Create links	Shift+F8
Create hyperlink (select text)	Control+L
Remove hyperlink	Control+Shift+L
Drag and drop to create a hyperlink from a document	Select the text, image, or object, then Shift-drag the selection to a file in the Files panel
Drag and drop to change a hyperlink using the Property inspector	Select the text, image, or object, then drag the point-to-file icon in the Property inspector to a file in the Files panel
Open the linked to document in Dreamweaver	Control-double-click link
Check links selected	Shift+F8
Check links in the entire site	Control+F8

TARGETING AND PREVIEWING IN BROWSERS

Action	Shortcut
Preview in primary browser	F12
Preview in secondary browser	Shift+F12 or Control+F12

DEBUGGING IN BROWSERS

Action	Shortcut
Debug in primary browser	Alt+F12
Debug in secondary browser	Control+Alt+F12

SITE MANAGEMENT AND FTP

Action	Shortcut
Connect/Disconnect	Control+Alt+Shift+F5
Refresh	F5
Create new file	Control+Shift+N
Create new folder	Control+Alt+Shift+N
Delete file	Control+X
Copy file	Control+C
Paste file	Control+V
Duplicate file	Control+D
Rename file	F2
Get selected files or folders from remote FTP site	Control+Shift+D or drag files from Remote to Local pane in Files panel
Put selected files or folders on remote FTP site	Control+Shift+U or drag files from Local to Remote pane in Files panel
Check out	Control+Alt+Shift+D
Check in	Control+Alt+Shift+U
View site map	Alt+F8
Refresh Local pane	Shift+F5
Refresh remote site	Alt+F5
Cancel FTP	Escape

HISTORY PANEL

Action	Shortcut
Open the History panel	Shift+F10
Start/stop recording command	Control+Shift+X

SITE MAP

Action	Shortcut
View site files	F8
Refresh Local pane	Shift+F5
View as root	Control+Shift+R
Link to new file	Control+Shift+N
Link to existing file	Control+Shift+K
Change link	Control+L
Remove link	Control+Shift+L
Show/Hide link	Control+Shift+Y
Show page titles	Control+Shift+T
Zoom in site map	Control++ (plus)
Zoom out site map	Control+- (hyphen)

RECORDING COMMANDS

Action	Shortcut
Start recording	Control+Shift+X

PLAYING PLUGINS

Action	Shortcut
Play plugin	Control+Alt+P
Stop plugin	Control+Alt+X
Play all plugins	Control+Alt+Shift+P
Stop all plugins	Control+Alt+Shift+X

INSERTING OBJECTS

Action	Shortcut
Any object (image, shockwave movie, and so on)	Drag file from the Explorer or Files panel to the Document window
Image	Control+Alt+I
Table	Control+Alt+T
Flash	Control+Alt+F
Shockwave	Control+Alt+D
Named anchor	Control+Alt+A

OPENING AND CLOSING PANELS

Action	Shortcut
Insert bar	Control+F2
Properties	Control+F3
CSS Styles	Shift+F11
Behaviors	Shift+F3
Tag inspector	F9
Snippets	Shift+F9
Reference	Shift+F1
Databases	Control+Shift+F10
Bindings	Control+F9
Components	Control+F7
Assets	F11
Results	F7
Code inspector	F10
Frames	Shift+F2
History	Shift+F10
Layers	F2
Show/Hide panels	F4

Index